Handbook of Aging
and the Family

Handbook of Aging and the Family

Edited by
ROSEMARY BLIESZNER and
VICTORIA HILKEVITCH BEDFORD

Foreword by LILLIAN E. TROLL

Greenwood Press
WESTPORT, CONNECTICUT · LONDON

Library of Congress Cataloging-in-Publication Data

Handbook of aging and the family / edited by Rosemary Blieszner and
   Victoria Hilkevitch Bedford ; foreword by Lillian E. Troll.
       p.   cm.
    Includes bibliographical references and index.
    ISBN 0-313-28395-8 (alk. paper)
       1. Aging.   2. Aged—Family relationships.   I. Blieszner,
   Rosemary.   II. Bedford, Victoria Hilkevitch.
   HQ1061.H3353   1995
   305.26—dc20   94-17988

British Library Cataloguing in Publication Data is available.

Library of Congress Catalog Card Number: 94-17988
ISBN: 0-313-28395-8

First published in 1995

Greenwood Press, 88 Post Road West, Westport, CT 06881
An imprint of Greenwood Publishing Group, Inc.

Printed in the United States of America

∞™

The paper used in this book complies with the
Permanent Paper Standard issued by the National
Information Standard Organization (Z39.48–1984).

10 9 8 7 6 5 4 3 2

Contents

Figures and Tables

TABLES

Foreword

Lillian E. Troll

This handbook heralds the coming-of-age of our field of families and aging. Although we remain rooted in our parent fields of gerontology, on one hand, and family studies, on the other, we are now declaring our maturity. The flourishing of both parent fields is evident in their respective massive handbooks and proliferating journals, and with this lineage, we ourselves can expect to continue to flourish. I want to congratulate the editors, Rosemary Blieszner and Victoria Bedford, for their foresight and efforts in producing this volume.

Whether or not families that have aging members are qualitatively different from those with only young and middle-aged members, the act of focusing on such families definitely opens new issues and points to new aspects of old issues. (Of course, most families are families of late life, but it seems necessary to adopt our perspective or focus to see this.) Just the evidence that family life continues after children are reared expands the scope of questions to be asked. If nothing else, our shift in focus challenges old definitions of structure and function. When the focus of family research is restricted to couple formation and child rearing, the classic definition of a family as people related by blood or marriage living together under one roof might still be useful (even if only marginally so in today's changing world). When the focus broadens to a life span view, we have to expand the structure to include people with past ties of blood or marriage whether or not they are living together now. We have to deal with more than two generations and turn to definitions like Eugene Litwak's construct of a modified-extended family in which several households are linked by past and present ties.

We also have to expand the functions. For the child-rearing, nuclear family, the primary function could be the care and rearing of "good" children (as defined by the culture and family value systems) and the maintenance of marital ties so that "good" children can be produced. For the late-life family, primary functions would also have to include the care of aging members and the maintenance of harmonious relationships both within and across generations. Even the function of rearing "good" children has to look to the contributions of more than parents—at least to those of grandparents.

My comments here are not intended to be a systematic review or critique of the chapters in this volume. Such comments are provided by the editors' introduction that follows. Instead, I touch down more or less randomly on a number of issues that interest me.

ISSUES

The 23 chapters in the present handbook address several generic issues and many more specific ones. They vary in perspective, in definition of constructs, and in breadth, reflecting the current facets of the literature on families with old members. Among the more generic issues are the construction of theoretical models, the historical changes in structure and function resulting from changes in demography and economics, and variations by gender and ethnicity. There is much more interest in family functions than family structure, although, in line with current policy preoccupations with caregiving of needy elders, many discussions view with alarm the combined effects of increased numbers of very old people and decreased numbers of kin available to care for them. The assumption in this gerontological literature is that the presence of more old people means the presence of more sick and helpless people. The possibility that ability to live longer could mean extended years of health and vigor is only recently being considered (e.g., Suzman, Harris, Hadley, Kovar, & Weindruch, 1992). There are also empirical findings that caretaking is not by multiple caretakers. Even if there are many children in a family, usually only one person does the major work so that a shift to smaller families would not necessarily leave the older members stranded.

The specific issues attended to in this handbook reflect the current overwhelmingly practical emphasis in the field of family gerontology: caregiving, social policy, social support, laws, therapy. Unfortunately, this emphasis is frequently accompanied by a perception of older family members as somehow being outside family boundaries, as essentially nonmembers. They are too often seen as problems for families to solve or bear rather than as participants in family decision making, as kinkeepers, or as equals in family relationships. Old people's contributions to their families and mutuality and reciprocity of interactions are too often ignored, as is the probability that their care involves a long history of interrelationships between the old members and the other members who are candidates for becoming their caretakers or decision makers. Lest it seem that the field of family and aging is completely biased against the aging, however, we should recognize that old people are also examined in the following chapters as people (individuals) who work, retire, and have leisure occupations, who are wives or husbands, parents (sometimes even children), siblings, and grandparents, and whose deaths are mourned. While it would be nice if the unit of analysis could widen from individuals and dyads to family systems, it is good that old members are seen not only as *objects* of family research but sometimes as *subjects,* in the phenomenological sense.

One of the topics that emerges from an opening of the boundaries of concern from nuclear child-rearing families to families with older members is the examination of long-lasting relationships: husbands and wives, parents and children, and siblings. Contacts and feelings do not end when an individual moves from a family of orientation to a family of procreation, and they continue through many transitions in the family of procreation. In fact, as Margaret Huyck notes in her chapter on marital relations, continuity of relationships over half a century or more has been tied to continuity in individual personalities. Swings in satisfaction and harmony or conflict have been traced to such intervening events as departure of children and retirement, as have changes in relationship styles. Relationships between parents and children, as reviewed in the chapter by Jill Suitor and her colleagues, also exhibit continuity as well as change. Whereas less is known about sibling relationships, Victoria Bedford's chapter seems to show the same kind of mixture of continuity and event-linked change.

Interest in family relationships in general, as I noted earlier, takes second place in the literature to dyadic relationships. There are some references to multidirectional influencing among family members throughout life, reminding us of the research of Gunhild Hagestad (1984) and others a decade or so earlier. A little is even said about the quality of relationships as people live longer and interact with each other longer. Beth Hess and Joan Waring (1978) cautioned that mother-daughter feelings could be strained by failing health and capacities. Sometimes, though, they may become more harmonious over time.

Salient events in the family relationships of later life are the emptying of the nest, retirement, deaths (even births), and increasing disability. Clearly, a few of these events are also important in family studies in earlier life, notably births and deaths. Another commonality is the importance of work, even though retirement gets stressed here.

There is interest in gender differences in light of the frequent finding that women are most often the linkers and doers in families, in modified-extended families as much as in nuclear family units. In fact, the chapter by Toni Antonucci and Hiroko Akiyama in this volume introduces the theme of possible overburdening of women as a result of their greater family service. As Colleen Johnson points out, ethnic or cultural variability must be considered to keep us from coming to ethnocentric or biased conclusions. Families differ markedly, and what is considered "good" family behavior in one culture is not so considered in others. Even when cultures agree on what is "good" behavior, economic and historic circumstances can make such behavior impossible to achieve or maintain. Hyman Rodman (1971) pointed long ago to the gap between what families want to do and what they can do.

Study of the role of the family or, commonly, specific family members in taking care of their needy elders has focused primarily on "instrumental" care such as nursing, housekeeping, and transportation instead of what is termed "expressive" care. Contributions to maintenance of daily living seem more concrete, immediate, and arduous than contributions to good feelings and morale; they are also easier to measure. Fortunately, both kinds of care are represented in the present volume.

MEASUREMENT

As David Mangen points out in his chapter on methodology, the way one goes about answering any research question depends primarily upon the question asked. If one wants to know how prevalent a particular family form or practice is, survey research is appropriate. If one wants to know whether mother-daughter relations have changed over time, longitudinal research is needed, at a minimum. Cross-sequential research would be better. If one wants to know whether there are feelings or behaviors among family members that are unpredictable or unobvious, qualitative analysis is useful. The unit of analysis in almost all our studies has been the individual, and the data are largely self-report, whether we are using survey research, longitudinal research, qualitative research, or combinations thereof. Experimental methods are almost nonexistent, although family therapeutic efforts may sometimes be classified this way. Mangen feels that survey research has been overused, although its use reflects our prevailing interest in finding out what is going on out there. The constructionist attitude among investigators of family structure and function assumes that there is a universe of existing, even "right" data that must be revealed.

I am particularly interested in three measurement issues that Mangen mentions: the choice of unit analysis, whether individual, dyad, triad, or family system; the variables studied, whether contact frequency, helping behavior, or feelings of closeness; and the problem of combining data from several individuals to yield "family" measures. Up to now, most of our information is about individuals, and we have to put together individual responses and perspectives in some more or less arbitrary way in order to get a more "family" picture of what is going on. We are also more interested in contact frequency than in feelings, believing it to be a "truer" measure. Will we ever achieve a method of analyzing whole family systems without piecing together individual and dyadic data?

PERSPECTIVES

A focus on caregiving often induces in the researcher or policymaker a perspective from outside the family. The goal is to find rules and procedures for efficient provision of care to the oldest people in the family regardless of the unique feelings and situations of the other family members involved. This vision of the family is narrowed primarily to the old and needy and secondarily to their most responsible kin. Both care needer and care provider tend to be perceived as objects, not subjects. But even when the perspective is inside the family, it is often not from the viewpoint of the old or of multiple family members or the family system as a whole. It is possible to have a perspective from the inside even if one is not a member of a family, but, too often, thinking of the family as an entity to be saved, even from itself, makes it hard to take the perspective of the family as a complex system of complex individuals in complex relationships.

Families, by definition, are composed of more than one person. In the case of families of the old, there are at least an old husband and wife or an old parent and his or her child or children, not to mention grandchildren and great-grandchildren or a pair of old siblings. In focusing on the viewpoint or condition of only one of these family members, it is easy for service providers and researchers of service provision to assume that no one in the family is important unless that person has needs to be provided for. I first came across this tendency to limit perspective when I was a child psychologist in a school system looking at the lack of consideration that most of my colleagues gave to people they were trying to help, whether these were parents or teachers or sometimes even the children whom they were trying to rescue, let alone other people who might have been in the picture, such as siblings or grandparents. Many of my younger colleagues (I had gone back to work after my children were old enough to be in school and, as a somewhat older mother, I was not in the same place as most of my colleagues just out of college) at that time seemed to feel that they were champions battling to save the children from the evil influences of parents or teachers.

I found the same tendency at the other end of the age scale when I became a gerontologist—a gerontologist who was herself growing old. Again, many of my colleagues seemed to feel that they were champions battling to save vulnerable old people from the depredations of their children or other possible evil influences. Many, in fact, also seemed to feel they were saving the vulnerable old people from themselves. Maybe this kind of champion perspective helps to fire interest and enthusiasm for saving particular others. Unfortunately, it also tends to ignore potential strengths in clients and their families that would help solve many problems that exist. It is even possible that ignoring these family strengths can turn potential allies into adversaries and vitiate efforts to help. Destroying a family system in the provision of care is always a danger.

Part of the problem of perspectives derives from problems of definition. What is a family? Who should be included? As noted earlier, when we are considering old people, we certainly cannot use a definition such as a nuclear family, people living together in a common household. Not in Western society, anyway. An old husband and wife may live together, but old parents and their children often do not; they may live nearby and visit frequently and help when necessary, but many old people today prefer to live alone or at least in their own homes, and many are able to do so (Shanas, Townsend, Wedderburn, Friis, Milhøj, & Stehouwer, 1968). When we are considering the families of old people in our society today, we are necessarily considering the modified-extended family (Litwak, 1960a, 1960b).

Although the old definition of family is no longer heuristic, no new definition has achieved common acceptance in a society where variety of lifestyles and family styles is getting to be the rule. What is notable in the contents of this handbook, in fact, is the use of a variety of definitions of family. These are not always stated overtly. Many definitions seem primarily dyadic: an old couple, an old parent and his or her caregiving child. I suppose this is more inclusive than focusing on individual family roles like spouse or parent or grandparent, but it sidesteps the existence of the family as more than a backdrop or stage on which individuals play their parts. Isn't it time to start considering the system as a whole? When an old mother is being taken care of by a daughter, there are often other daughters and sons who have an input on decisions and who praise or blame the caretaker's acts to complicate the picture. A few years ago, there was a lot of interest in the "sandwich generation," although by the time caretakers are involved with feeble parents, their children tend to be grown. We need to be more inclusive, to consider in-laws as well as spouses, grown children, and grandchildren. I would also like to consider past family members who are no longer alive but whose impact on the current scene was, and probably still is, substantial. In working with Colleen Johnson in her research on the oldest-old, I have repeatedly been impressed with the continuing significance of relatives who are no longer living (Johnson & Troll, 1992). The respondents show their pictures on tables and walls, they talk about them, and sometimes they even talk to them. Maybe the next edition of the handbook will be able to find literature on family systems involving old members who have died.

PERSONAL REMARKS

My own professional history over the past three decades reflects the general development of interest in families of the aging, just as that development has been influenced by historical changes in Western life expectancy. I first became interested in the study of families beyond the study of individuals when I worked as a school psychologist in Newton, Massachusetts, in the 1950s. I found on that job that the children I was supposed to diagnose and treat were not independent entities, as I had been taught in graduate school, but were parts of families and that their parents were much more than the causes of their learning and behavior problems—or gifts, as the case might be. These parents were essential parts of the scene, interacting with their children overtly or covertly at every turn. It was clear to me that the only way I could help the children, as I had been hired to do, was to widen my scope to include the families of which they were a part. Working with these families turned me from my original limited focus on young children to one on adult parents and then beyond that to grand-parents and cousins and aunts. As my scope broadened, so did the questions I was led to ask. Because it was time to finish a doctoral dissertation, I turned from an original dissertation on music ability tests to this new passion, family relationships. Specifically, I examined personality and value similarities between college-age men and women and their middle-aged parents. The age range of my interest continued to move up thereafter, and with it the scope of my inquiries broadened. Where in the beginning I had been concerned with the families of school-age children, from kindergarten to adulthood, I am now concerned with the families of people over 85, from birth to death. Where in the beginning I was concerned with person-ality similarities—with transmission of personality—I am now concerned with extended family structure and functioning. It is rewarding to see in this volume that so many other behavioral scientists are now involved in this area of research. If feels good to have company.

My first published overview of family literature, "The Family of Later Life: A Decade Review," which appeared in 1971, is, to my delight and somewhat to my embarrassment, still being cited. After all, I have updated it at least three times (Troll, Miller, & Atchley, 1979; Troll, 1982; Troll, 1986). Bernice Neugarten had originally been asked to write that first-decade review for the *Journal of Marriage and the Family,* but I became the lucky inheritor of the project when she found herself too busy to do more than serve as my adviser.

The decade of the 1960s had witnessed a burst of family and aging re-search, so that my bibliography for that review included 161 items, which I discussed in 28 pages. I can't count the number of books and articles reviewed for the current handbook, but the number of pages is definitely more like 30 times 28. On rereading the first few paragraphs of that 1971 essay, I am amused at some of the ways my thinking has changed, just as I am impressed with the amount of similarity in issues and even content between research of the 1960s and the research of the 1980s and 1990s, almost a quarter-century later.

One example of my own changed perspective is right in my first sentence in that article, where I refer to the "family life cycle," a term I have since eschewed because it implies that old people are equivalent to children. Unfortunately, that term is still in frequent use, and many people still think old people are to be treated as infants or toddlers by their own children. Another thing I said in 1971 was that we know less about marital satisfaction in middle and old age than in the early years of marriage. "Marital satisfaction" is no longer a construct I would use because it is contingent and therefore treacherous. It is contingent on expectations. People who expect less are more easily satisfied. There are still studies of marital satisfaction, but fortunately no chapter in this handbook is devoted to it. There certainly would have been one if the handbook had been written 25 years ago. I can still see that life span curve of marital satisfaction that goes down from the honeymoon to the empty nest and up again thereafter. I don't know how many times I drew it on the blackboard, inserted it into a textbook, or asked questions about it in an exam.

Third, I said in that first review of the family of later life that the literature on the family is far more abundant with regard to the first half of life than to the second half. This is still true. Most of the general family literature today still seems to be concentrated on the formation of couples or variations on coupleness. This topic is perhaps rivaled only by studies of abuse—child abuse, spouse abuse, and parent abuse. There has been some move away, however, from assuming that the only right families are the traditional ones.

Fourth, in 1971, I noted that gerontologists were concerned primarily with patterns of social adaptation and accordingly with the role of the family in promoting good adjustment on the part of aging men and women. There is still some concern with this issue, but primarily the interest now seems to be more on the effect of aging family members on the adjustment of their kin caretakers rather than on their own well-being. The move toward looking at the contribution of the oldest generation to the rest of the family is still a feeble one, confined primarily to the grandparenting of needy young children.

PIONEERS

Many of the pioneers in research on the aging family are still involved in the field today. I mentioned Bernice Neugarten, whose paper with Karol Weinstein (Neugarten & Weinstein, 1964) was probably the first to look at grandparenting as a family role and is still cited widely. Grandparenting is still high on the list of family research topics, and there is a chapter on grandparenting in this volume. Joan Robertson notes the shift in focus from the experience or types of grandparenting to their practical function of caring for young children. Both foci, of course, deal essentially with middle-aged or younger grandparents than with old ones. Robertson also notes that Neugarten and Weinstein's study shifted the focus from an earlier anthropological/structural one to a functional one. The original broader

range of interest in grandparents, which included varieties of grandparenting, meaning of grandparenting to grandparents and grandchildren, relationships between grandparents—of all ages—and their children and
grandchildren, has, as Robertson notes, given way to a narrower, applied,
and practical range of interest.

Ethel Shanas produced substantive research on family demographics of
later life that is still relevant. Shanas and her colleagues' (1968) cross-
national study of *Old People in Three Industrial Societies* contains a chapter on the family that lays out the issues and is a model to this day. Gordon
Streib's volume with Ethel Shanas (1965), *Social Structure and the Family:
Generational Relations,* was perhaps the first review of literature on aging
and the family.

Eugene Litwak (1960a, 1960b) published two related studies on family
consequences of occupational and geographic mobility that countered the
prevailing myths of family fragmentation (still prevailing) and pointed to
the existing Western modified-extended family structure. There was one
other notable pioneer in the field, Reuben Hill. I did not review the im-
pressive volume by him and others on three generations of adults, *Family
Development in Three Generations,* in 1971 because it was not published
until 1970, but I did read and refer to some of his preliminary papers (Hill,
Foote, Aldous, Carlson, & Macdonald, 1970).

Finally, I congratulate the editors and authors. I know that their product
will be widely and happily used, for this handbook should be invaluable
to anyone interested in research in families and aging. It will also be useful
and interesting to scholars in the parent areas of aging and family studies.

REFERENCES

Hagestad, G. (1984). The continuous bond: A dynamic, multigenerational perspective on parent-child relations between adults. In M. Perlmutter (Ed.), *Minnesota Symposium on Child Psychology* (pp. 129–158). Hillsdale, NJ:
Erlbaum.

Hess, B., & Waring, J. M. (1978). Parent and child in later life: Rethinking the
relationship. In R. M. Lerner & G. B. Spanier (Eds), *Child influences on
marital and family interaction* (pp. 241–273). New York: Academic Press.

Hill, R., Foote, N., Aldous, J., Carlson, R., & Macdonald, R. (1970). *Family development in three generations.* Cambridge, MA: Schenkman.

Johnson, C. L., & Troll, L. E. (1992). Family functioning in late life. *Journal of
Gerontology: Social Sciences, 47,* S66–S72.

Litwak, E. (1960a). Geographic mobility and extended family cohesion. *American
Sociological Review, 25,* 385–394.

Litwak, E. (1960b). Occupational mobility and extended family cohesion. *American
Sociological Review, 25,* 9–21.

Neugarten, B. L., & Weinstein, K. K. (1964). The changing American grandparent.
Journal of Marriage and the Family, 26, 299–304.

Rodman, H. (1971). *Lower-class families: The culture of poverty in Negro Trinidad*. New York: Oxford University.

Shanas, E., & Streib, G. (Eds.). (1965). *Social structure and the family: Generational relations*. Englewood Cliffs, NJ: Prentice-Hall.

Shanas, E., Townsend, P., Wedderburn, D., Friis, H., Milhøj, P., & Stehouwer, J. (1968). *Old people in three industrial societies*. New York: Atherton.

Suzman, R. M., Harris, T., Hadley, E. C., Kovar, M. G., & Weindruch, R. (1992). The robust oldest old: Optimistic perspectives for increasing healthy life expectancy. In R. M. Suzman, D. P. Willis, & K. A. Manton (Eds.), *The oldest-old* (pp. 341–358). New York: Oxford University.

Troll, L. E. (1971). The family of later life: A decade review. *Journal of Marriage and the Family, 33*, 263–290.

Troll, L. E. (1982). *Continuations: Adult development and aging*, Chapters 18–22. Monterey, CA: Brooks/Cole.

Troll, L.E. (Ed.). (1986). *Family issues in current gerontology*. New York: Springer Publishing Co.

Troll, L. E., Miller, S. J., & Atchley, R. C. (1979). *Families in later life*. Belmont, CA: Wadsworth.

Preface

Gerontology and family studies are multidisciplinary fields with fairly long histories of research and scholarship rooted in psychology, sociology, anthropology, and biology and encompassing, more recently, a wide array of supporting areas such as public policy analysis, history, the humanities, medicine, social work, communications, and other fields. As research progressed in these fields, it was natural that family studies and aging eventually would be joined. After all, gerontologists came to recognize the importance of family relationships to older adults, and family scholars saw in demographic trends the greater prominence of old people in family life. Thus the decade reviews of research sponsored by the National Council on Family Relations and published in the *Journal of Marriage and the Family* in 1971, 1980, and 1990 included articles on family and aging. With the emergence of "family gerontology" as a recognized subdiscipline among gerontologists and family scholars comes the need for a major reference book that includes a review, synthesis, and critique of the existing body of literature and suggestions for research to advance knowledge about families and aging.

This handbook offers a comprehensive analysis of family and aging, including both traditional topics such as reviews of the findings related to particular kinds of relationships (marriage, parent-child, siblings) and newer topics of study such as feminist analysis of family relationships, non-marital partnerships, and the interface between the family and long-term care institutions. In the chapters, the authors show how various theoretical frameworks and research designs can be applied to both long-standing and emergent topics in the study of families and aging, in addition to illuminating significant gaps in the literature. The book should thus serve as a stimulus for new research.

The existing resources on family and aging issues are somewhat limited.

The decade review pieces are journal-article length. They tend to highlight a series of studies with little depth of analysis because they cover so many topics within the page limits. The few textbooks on family relationships in later life are brief, and the edited works tend to be compilations of individual research studies rather than comprehensive overviews of topics. The existing handbooks on gerontology contain only one or two chapters on family and aging issues, not a thorough set of reviews. This new handbook on aging and the family thus fills an important niche.

The handbook was designed as a research and reference tool for researchers in family gerontology, gerontologists, and family scholars who have other specialties but need a good resource on family and aging issues for teaching and research support, graduate students in both family studies and adult development and aging, and undergraduate students working on course assignments. It should also be useful to practitioners who deliver services to older adults and their families, persons who work in state and federal government agencies or staff the Senate and House committees on aging, journalists, health care specialists, and others who need to know the latest information on family gerontology issues.

The five sections of the book provide background material, useful theoretical frameworks and discussions of research methods and data analysis, information on specific family relationships, examination of the context of family life, and review of major turning points and relevant interventions in the family of the later years. The volume is integrated insofar as all the chapters address aspects of family gerontology, but in accordance with the purposes of a handbook, each chapter has a distinct focus.

Although one of us (RB) originally received the invitation from Greenwood Press to develop the handbook, she immediately asked the other (VHB) to become involved. We wish to emphasize that we have contributed equally to this project, strengthening our mutual respect for each other's scholarship and our appreciation of our friendship along the way.

We are pleased to acknowledge the foresight of George F. Butler, acquisitions editor at Greenwood Press, who initiated the handbook, and the help of Mildred Vasan, senior editor at Greenwood Press, who assisted with its completion. The contributors to this volume also deserve special mention. These hardworking scholars accepted suggestions graciously, if not gratefully. They complied with deadlines and our many demands in a spirit of cooperation. We are deeply grateful to them.

We appreciate the support of Jay A. Mancini, head of the Department of Family and Child Development at Virginia Polytechnic Institute and State University. We gratefully acknowledge the careful reading of much of the manuscript by University of Indianapolis students Dianna G. Cooper, Adrianne Croyle, Jennifer DeWester, Patricia Harris, Erika Sullivan, Theresa Thomas, and Keri Wooldridge, who would not let us forget their perspectives and insights. We hope, then, that this volume is more accessible to undergraduate students than it might have been without their comments and editorial suggestions. For careful word processing, we thank Nadean D. Jarels, secretary senior, and Phyllis A. Greenberg and Leigh A. Faulconer, graduate students, all in the Department of Family and Child Development at Virginia Polytechnic Institute and State University. Leigh also provided invaluable assistance with constructing the book index.

Most of all, we thank our "innermost circle" of social support, immediate family members and very closest friends who sustained us on a daily basis—our husbands, Steve Gerus and Eric Bedford; our children, Suzanne, Mark, Sibyl, and Iris; and our friends, Rebecca G. Adams, Paula S. Avioli, Margaret D. Cohn, Linda B. Smith, S. Holly Stocking, and Catherine A. Surra. Also, we must credit those who have inspired us in our interest in aging and the family—our intellectual forebears, Gunhild O. Hagestad, Bernice L. Neugarten, and Lillian E. Troll, and also the Midwest Council for Social Research in Aging family. Finally, we acknowledge our extended families of grandparents, parents, in-laws, aunts and uncles, siblings, cousins, and nieces and nephews, some of whom have provided models for growing old in a family context and others of whom will accompany us on our own journey.

—Rosemary Blieszner
Blacksburg, Virginia

—Victoria Hilkevitch Bedford
Indianapolis, Indiana

Part I
BACKGROUND

1

The Family Context of Aging: Trends and Challenges

*Rosemary Blieszner and
Victoria Hilkevitch Bedford*

Publication of the *Handbook of Aging and the Family* reflects the maturation of the field of family gerontology. A sufficient amount of research has been reported to warrant compiling review chapters on diverse topics. At the same time, this wealth of accumulated studies suggests the timeliness of taking stock of the field by offering constructive critiques and suggestions for new research directions. Thus we challenged the chapter authors (1) to provide overviews of the major thrusts of research on their topics, including discussion of both theoretical and substantive concerns; (2) to use a multicultural framework from which to evaluate the literature reviewed in terms of the family forms and functions studied, the subpopulations sampled, and the methods employed; and (3) to offer ideas about theoretical directions, substantive topics, and empirical approaches in future family gerontology research.

In this introductory chapter, we first summarize the contents of each section of the *Handbook*, building upon the comments offered by Lillian Troll in her Foreword. Then we provide recommendations for future research directions, building upon the suggestions of the chapter authors.

THE CURRENT STATE OF FAMILY GERONTOLOGY SCHOLARSHIP

Historical and Demographic Trends

The first part of the book includes some background material designed to provide a perspective from which readers can consider the contents of all the other chapters. In the chapter giving a historical overview, Hareven points out that family relations in old age are shaped by the intersecting influences of individual life experiences, historical events, and social and economic conditions. For example, the status accorded older family members or values as expressed in caregiving practices fluctuates across eras. The nature and timing of life transitions (e.g., marriage, retirement), which, in turn, affect relationships within and between generations in the family, also vary across time. Similarly, Kinsella shows how demographic and epidemiologic trends affect family structure and functioning. Extending the vantage point beyond the United States, Kinsella describes the situation of aged individuals and their families both in other developed regions of the world besides the United States and in developing regions of the world. He focuses on issues surrounding fertility, mortality, and causes of death, and he points out trends over time related to marital status, household size, and living arrangements. He discusses the implications of these trends for the support available to older family members now and in the future. Kinsella reiterates Hareven's point that personal choices and external circumstances occurring earlier in life have implications for old age well-being. We hope readers will keep the issues and concepts introduced by Hareven and Kinsella in mind as they examine the many dimensions of family gerontology presented in the rest of the volume.

Theoretical Frameworks and Research Methods

Although all of the authors address theory and methods, chapters in the second section of the book are dedicated exclusively to theoretical perspectives and research methods that are especially useful and important in family gerontology scholarship. Cohler and Altergott begin by noting that traditional family studies theories typically do not acknowledge families of later life. These authors advocate better integration of research on aging and research on families, suggesting family development theory, family stress theory, and critical theory as fruitful approaches for such work. In turn, Ryff and Seltzer note that traditional developmental theories typically do not acknowledge the family setting of most people's lives. They examine personal development in the middle and later years from the vantage point of the family context in which such development takes place. According to their perspective, application of individual-level theories such as social comparison and attribution would yield greater understanding of family-level dynamics such as support exchanges and caregiving. Together, the chapters by Cohler and Altergott and by Ryff and Seltzer spell out significant theoretical insights for family gerontologists by blending conventional family and developmental principles with the study of aging.

Next, Lopata addresses the value of taking a feminist stance when engaging in family gerontology inquiry. The gendered nature of American institutions, gender stratification in society, and the two-sphere ideology that has dominated work and family life all have significant implications for the experience of aging yet have been disregarded in much family gerontology research. Lopata also demonstrates the propensity of quantitative methods to reduce the complexity of women's and men's lives to single variables, thus masking experiences of family and aging. Further, she discusses the limitations of drawing conclusions about future cohorts of older adults from studies of contemporary aged persons.

In the following chapter, Mancini and Sandifer examine the theoretical contributions to family gerontology of an often-overlooked discipline, leisure studies. They provide an overview of four conceptual perspectives that can be applied to the study of older adults and their kin. The leisure lifestyles framework focuses specifically on customary pursuits during unrestricted time, whereas theories of relationship functions, symbolic interaction, and family development can be implemented in new ways by asking questions about family leisure pursuits. All these approaches have potential for enlarging the scope of information available about the influences of social interaction on personal and family well-being

In the final chapter of Part II, Mangen reminds readers of the importance of linking methods to theory and using methods appropriately in relation to the research questions at hand. He describes the use of theory to develop and refine measures of family interaction as well as to develop and refine hypotheses. Increasingly sophisticated statistical procedures are available for assessing complex relationships among variables, but they, too, must be employed within the proper theoretical context. In addition, he provides a refreshing perspective on the "qualitative-quantitative" debate.

Family Relationships

The four chapters in the third part of the *Handbook* focus on specific family relationships of older adults. The first two concern peer ties, with Huyck assessing couple relationships and Bedford analyzing sibling associations in middle and old age. The other two chapters focus on intergenerational relationships, between aged parents and adult children in the case of Suitor, Pillemer, Keeton, and Robison and between grandparents and grandchildren as reviewed by Robertson.

In describing marital and other couple relationships in old age, Huyck points out the dearth of information about nontraditional couple types and members of racial ethnic minority groups. The information that is available, primarily on married Caucasian couples, reveals the great variety of romantic relationship styles that exist as well as the propensity toward stability of interaction patterns over the course of adulthood. Huyck concludes with a review of strategies for enhancing close relationships of older adults.

In Bedford's chapter, the theme of life course continuity is echoed with respect to sibling relationships. She reviews the literature in terms of whether the costs (negative feelings and interactions) and benefits (positive affect, companionship, caregiving, and personal welfare) of the relationship remain stable, wane, or increase across adulthood. Sources of individual differences in the direction and intensity of sibling relationship continuity lead to consideration of the early relationship and to diversity in family forms. An added complication is differentiating whether findings refer to the sibling group (the two or more who constitute a siblingship) or to personal sibling relationships between members of dyads.

Turning to parent-child dyads, Suitor and her colleagues focus on influences on relationship quality and the most effective means of assessing them. Like so many of the other contributors to this volume, they find the life course framework a suitable canvas on which to paint the detailed effects of historical trends, conflict and consensus, and normative versus nonnormative transitions on adjacent generations and their interactions. Robertson then takes up the task of updating readers on new issues that affect grandparents in relation to their grandchildren. Following an overview of the connection between societal changes and changes in grandparental roles and functions, she centers on the recent trend toward an increasing number of grandparents' serving as primary care providers for their grandchildren. This situation illustrates the changing nature of individual and family development over time. It has profound implications for personal well-being and family relationships in the later years and thus warrants increased research attention.

The Context of Family Life

Part IV of the volume highlights several significant contexts in which older adults and their families exist. The first chapter, by Harrington Meyer and Bellas, focuses on social and economic policies that affect later-life families. They describe the Social Security, Supplemental Security Income, Medicare, and Medicaid programs in detail. Limitations of existing programs and policies include their basis in traditional conceptions of the family and their tendency to perpetuate inequities associated with gender, class, and race in old age. The second chapter, by Wacker, addresses the legal context in which aged persons and their relatives live. Whether involved at a primary or secondary level, family members have a stake in the laws that govern intergenerational interaction. Examples of such laws concern grandparental visitation rights, power of attorney, admission agreements for long-term care facilities, and government benefits.

Many authors mention similarities and differences in experiences of aging according to racial ethnic group membership and other social statuses, but Johnson's chapter specifically addresses the contextual issue of cultural diversity. She analyzes the extent to which families meet the needs of older members in terms of three family types: traditional, nuclear, and opportune/postmodern. Differential endorsement of filial responsibility and other norms across family types and ethnic groups differentially affects the well-being of elderly members. McCulloch extends the discussion of contexts of aging to the implications of growing older in rural areas. Differences in the status of older adults in the family, resources, and environmental factors occur within rural regions as well as between rural and urban localities. Readers are reminded in both chapters of the necessity of developing studies that capture, rather than conceal, heterogeneity in family gerontology.

The final context mentioned in this section is social networks as conceptualized by Antonucci and Akiyama in their life course model of social convoys. Family members (and friends) play many important roles in the lives of older adults, including provision of assistance, social support, and emotional sustenance. Because of these multifaceted and complex functions, social relations can have significant impact on physical health and psychological well-being in old age.

Turning Points and Interventions in Family Life

The domain of Part V is life transitions and mediations designed to assist those who experience them. The first transition is retirement, as examined by Szinovacz and Ekerdt. Contrary to traditional approaches, they illustrate the importance of considering retirement to be a family transition, not an individual one. That is, resignation from the world of work and attendant changes in finances influence household roles, marital quality and power, and extended kin relationships. Next, Dwyer looks at the implications for family life of old age chronic illnesses within the context of social structural changes that affect family caregiving. He records restrictions on activities and psychological problems associated with those restrictions that not only affect the aged person but also come to dominate interactions with spouses, children, and other family members. Dwyer admonishes policymakers to remember that policies affecting Americans have serious consequences for the caregiving they are able to provide their older family members who are ill. Thus, the economic well-being and health of Americans underlie their caregiving capacities.

In the third chapter on turning points, Moss and Moss discuss death and bereavement within the family, both when an older member dies and when an older member suffers loss of a loved one. Regardless of whether one is old or young, a person's reaction to bereavement often hinges on the quality of the previous relationship. A unique feature of the death or bereavement of elderly family members, however, is disfranchisement: both the passing of an old person and the grief of an old person are deemed less important than death of a young person or losses experienced by younger family members. In the fourth chapter, O'Bryant and Hansson focus specifically on death of a spouse in later life. Like others, this transition affects the entire family system as all members cope with loss, and the bereaved spouse establishes a new identity and new roles in the family. Patterns of interaction and support shift, emphasizing the intersection of individual and family lives, and the effects of the shifts differ for widows and widowers.

The last two chapters of the book concern intervention issues associated with transitions and other aspects of family life in the later years. Travis examines the intersection of informal care provided by family members with formal care provided by professionals using attachment, exchange, and symbolic interaction theories as bases. She covers numerous aspects of research on use of long-term care services but maintains that advancement in this investigative arena depends upon conceptualizing the transition from informal to formal care as complex, not linear, and acknowledging potential conflicts between family members and formal care providers. Qualls then links the fields of family development and family therapy, providing suggestions based on clinical models for enhanced research on family functioning in the later years. Application of systems, behavioral, and psychoanalytic models of individual and family coping provides new concepts and hypotheses about adaptive versus maladaptive functioning in the later years.

Supplementary Materials

The authors identified the five most important references from their chapters, which we compiled into a Bibliography. This reference list features the current set of the most important sources related to family gerontology. In addition, an index is available to aid in readers' investigations of particular topics. Finally, biographical sketches provide some background information on the authors and editors to aid readers in interpreting the theoretical and experiential perspectives that influenced development of the *Handbook* chapters. We hope readers find these sections useful.

CHALLENGES FOR THE FUTURE IN FAMILY GERONTOLOGY SCHOLARSHIP

Collective Themes in the Chapters

Each chapter of this *Handbook* targets a specialized aspect of family gerontology, yet several themes, having implications for future research directions, emerge when looking across all of them. Besides these commonly held themes, each chapter includes numerous specific suggestions for new studies associated with the focal topics.

One of the fundamental issues acknowledged by the *Handbook* authors is the influence on the experiences of individuals and families of interactions among personal development, social transactions, culture and society, and historical events. Cohorts differ as a result of these dynamic effects, leading to generational differences as well; both kinds of differences merit additional study. These powerful influences also lead to differences among subgroups of the population, necessitating research that examines aging and family experiences according to characteristics such as gender, race, ethnicity, socioeconomic status and class, sexual preference, family structure, and geographic locality. Moreover, several authors admonish scholars to adopt a perspective that places emphasis on older adults as contributors to family well-being, rather than merely as sources of family problems and stress, regardless of the substantive topic of research.

Another motif heard across the chapters is the call for better integration of theory in family gerontology research. Quite a few authors spell out the merits of taking life span development and life course perspectives when planning new research to analyze the aging/family interface. In addition, many suggestions are offered for creative applications of existing theories found in history, demography, economics, family studies, feminist studies, psychology, sociology, anthropology, leisure studies, public policy, law, and family therapy. Of course, the authors also recognize that new theory can emerge from more careful descriptive work in family gerontology research. They emphasize the advantageous possibility of discovering causal mechanisms within family systems that can result from grounding research in theory. Several authors also lament the tendency to conceptualize family processes as simple linear progressions, rather than as complex patterns of interaction.

The chapter writers urge utilization of more diverse research designs and methods than have been employed to date. They mention incorporation of prospective and cross-sequential strategies and judicious use of multivariate statistics, where appropriate, in family gerontology investigations. The authors also indicate many places where qualitative studies permit identification of the full range of personal and family experiences, meanings associated with situations and events, processes by which families create and sustain their own realities, the influence of older members on the rest of the family, and the influences of the rest of the family on their older members. Many note that sampling must be more intentional, both to capture diversity among individuals and families and to achieve greater representativeness and generalizability of results. Careful use of existing data sets can aid in accomplishing this goal. Advancement of *family* gerontology research requires extension of the focal unit of analysis from the individual to dyads and family systems.

Finally, authors of numerous chapters emphasize the importance of using sound family gerontology research results to evaluate existing policies and interventions geared toward elders and their families. Because cohorts change in the context of changing social structure, previously developed intervention strategies do not necessarily retain their effectiveness. Thus, family gerontology research findings should also be applied as a basis for

developing new policies and programs. Returning to a refrain mentioned
earlier, authors note that policies should reflect the contributions of older
adults to their families and society and that policies should utilize the
unique resources of elderly citizens. In general, all of the issues mentioned
in this section are familiar to scholars of aging; the *Handbook* authors
reiterate their importance in studying family-related topics in gerontology.

Additional New Directions

We offer four conceptual distinctions for scholars to consider, then propose new research topics that were not emphasized by the chapter authors.

*Subject and object distinctions in the study of aging
and the family*

Family gerontology at the most general level can be conceptualized from
two inseparable perspectives. One side of the coin highlights the experiences
(or lack of experiences) of family by people who are growing older. The
other side of the coin reflects the families' experiences with their older members (or lack of such experiences). Both perspectives can focus on positive
and negative aspects of the aging/family interface for older adults and for
the other family members.

We offer this distinction to reinforce a point implicit in other *Handbook*
chapters. Conceptual clarity and precision demand that researchers are
aware of which side of the coin is guiding their investigations. More important, the goal of comprehensiveness within family gerontology requires
researchers to capture both sides of the coin, if not in a particular study,
at least within their ongoing program of scholarship. An interesting and
revealing exercise would be to catalog all the research cited in this *Handbook* according to this dual perspective of family gerontology. To what
extent does the literature capture both sides of the coin? We suspect that
many substantive areas are deficient in addressing this dual vantage point
because researchers have employed only a unidirectional focus on either
older people or families dealing with older members. Thus, flipping the
coin—looking up and down the generational lines—would greatly
strengthen the family gerontology literature.

This approach mandates two other distinctions: level of variables and
sources of data. Researchers can focus on individual-level variables (in any
generation of the family) and gather information about them from either
one person or multiple informants. But researchers can also focus on re-
lationship-level variables (for any combination of generations in the family)
and gather information about them from either one person or multiple
informants. In both cases, the informants can be either family members
self-reporting or outsiders reporting on a family of their acquaintance. This
approach seems particularly important given demographic projections of

an increasing number of extant generations within families, implying increased complexity of family life. Playing out the full array of study possibilities based on this distinction would further add to the comprehensiveness of the family gerontology literature.

A final distinction in family gerontology focuses on families with older members as institutions and examines them in relation to other institutions in society. Again, an array of informants exists, including older adults, their family members, those who have professional contact with families that include elderly members, or those who might be more remote from family gerontology issues and yet have a stake in them, such as legislators, product developers, market analysts, media producers, and the like. Ascertaining the impressions of these sources about the societal roles and responsibilities of older adults and their families would provide revealing information for development of policies, advocacy programs, volunteer and employment opportunities, services, and other applied projects emerging from family gerontology research.

New research topics

A book on family gerontology is grounded on the assumption that people grow old in a family context. Indeed, most people do. But scholars know that families are increasingly diverse in form and function, that definitions of *family* differ widely across subcultural groups, and that some people have no relatives or are estranged from them. All these contemporary conditions suggest the need to ask study participants explicitly about their definition of family instead of assuming what the shared definition of family is or assuming that members who fit certain criteria, such as most frequently contacted, are automatically the most important ones. Such contemporary conditions also highlight the importance of investigating fictive kin relationships. Incorporation of friends, neighbors, and service providers into topics of research typically found in family gerontology studies would probably reveal different and more extensive networks of close significant others in the lives of older adults than current findings would suggest. Also, this approach is essential when studying marginalized members of society, such as older people who are ever-single, gay/lesbian, socially isolated, homeless, or mentally ill—those whose "family" members might not be traditional or immediately apparent. For all kinds of people, deceased relatives can still exert powerful influences, requiring documentation via new, creative methodologies.

Much family gerontology literature has focused on older adults' typical events and experiences of family life. It is time to rectify this rather skewed view by investigating elderly members' participation in, and reactions to, other family events, such as milestones accomplished by children, teens, and younger adults as well as the pitfalls the younger relatives experience.

Along the same lines, it would be fruitful to focus on perceptions of family relationships per se, rather than on events, transitions, and problems.

The *Handbook* does not include chapters on the implications of older adults' paid or volunteer work for family life, on the implications of family rituals transmitted by older members for the lives of other members, or on spirituality in relation to aging and the family. These topics reflect significant domains in people's lives and thus merit investigation. Also, review of international aspects of family gerontology should not be limited to a few specialized chapters. Rather, a global perspective should be sought for all of the topics mentioned in this and other chapters. Such a strategy would go a long way toward reducing the ethnocentricity common in Americans' views of aging/family issues.

The *Handbook* includes a chapter on the intersection between family and individual development, which provides an organizing principle within which several neglected topics can be developed. For instance, how do older persons' political and community involvements affect their family relationships and the development of their family members? Further, from the older family members' points of view, are their goals, aspirations, and developmental needs facilitated or frustrated by their families? If so, how? In other words, what are the growth-enhancing and growth-debilitating aspects of these families, for all members?

These many suggestions should have conveyed by now that the development of this *Handbook* has been guided by a desire to launch the next era in the study of aging in families. The authors have carefully laid foundations in many areas from which new studies can be developed. We have attempted to cull their recommendations for future research and to generate additional suggestions in other domains not yet initiated. We are excited about the prospects that lie ahead, for there is much work to be done to prepare for a world increasingly populated by old people and where biomedical advancements are sometimes divorced from issues of quality of life. The study of family and aging is about the quality of life for old people and for their relatives. Advancements in the field of family gerontology should benefit all of us. We hope this *Handbook* marks an important milestone in its development.

2

Historical Perspectives on the Family and Aging

Tamara K. Hareven

INTRODUCTION

An understanding of the family arrangements and supports for older people in American society has been clouded by myths about the past, on one hand, and by a narrow treatment of contemporary problems at one time, on the other hand. A historical perspective increases understanding of changes that have occurred over time and illuminates the ways in which historical events and circumstances have affected the life history of different age groups (Fischer, 1977). A life course perspective illuminates the impact of historical conditions on the life history of different cohorts and their consequences for these groups' adaptation in the later years of life (Elder, 1974; Riley, 1978; Hareven, 1991b).

The emergence of old age as a social problem can be best understood in the context of the entire life course and of the historical changes affecting people in various stages of life. An understanding of the current problems older people and their families are experiencing depends on a knowledge of the larger processes of change that have affected the timing of life course transitions, family patterns, and generational relations. Family relations in old age are molded by individual members' cumulative life histories and by the specific historical circumstances that have affected them over their lives. The adaptation of individuals and their families to the social and economic conditions they face in the later years of life is thus contingent on the pathways by which they reach old age (Hareven, 1978a, 1981; Elder, 1982). Relations of mutual support are formed over life and are reshaped by historical circumstances, such as migration, wars, and the decline or collapse of local economies. Hence, patterns of support and expectations for receiving and providing assistance in old age are part of a continuing process of interaction among parents, children, and other kin over their life course, as they move through historical time.

A life course perspective sheds light on the ways in which the earlier life experiences of older adults, as shaped by historical events, and their cultural heritage have affected their values governing family relations, their expectations of kin supports, and their ability to interact with welfare agencies and institutions (Clark & Anderson, 1976). Rather than viewing older people simply as a homogeneous group, a life course perspective views them as age cohorts moving through history—each cohort with its distinct life experiences, which were shaped by the circumstances its members encountered earlier in life (Hareven, 1978a; Elder, 1978). The life course enables us to interpret individual and family life transitions as part of a continuous process of historical change.

Following a historical and life course perspective, this chapter examines changes in demographic behavior, in family and household organization, in the timing of life course transitions, and in kin assistance of men and women in American society since the settlement in the seventeenth century and their impact on individuals' adaptation in old age.

THE LIFE COURSE PERSPECTIVE

A life course perspective helps focus attention on the interaction of demographic, social structural, and cultural factors in shaping family patterns and generational relations in the later years of life. Underlying the life course approach are three major dimensions: the timing of life transitions in relation to external historical events; the synchronization of individual life transitions with collective familial ones as they affect generational relations; and the impact of earlier life events, as shaped by previously encountered historical circumstances, on subsequent events (Hareven, 1978b).

The timing of transitions (Hareven, 1978a) involves the balancing of individuals' entry into, and exit from, different work and family roles (education, family, work, and community) over their life course. For example, how did individuals time and sequence their work life and educational transitions in the context of changing historical conditions? In all these areas, the pace and definition of "timing" hinge upon the social and cultural contexts in which transitions occurred.

A second dimension of the life course approach involves the synchronization of individual life transitions with collective family transitions, most notably, the juggling of a multiplicity of family- and work-related roles over their lives. Individuals engage in a variety of familial configurations that change over the life course and vary under different historical conditions. Although age is an important determinant of the timing of transitions, it is not the only significant variable; changes in family status and in accompanying roles are often as important as age, if not more so (Hareven,

1991b; Hareven & Masaoka, 1988). The synchronization of individual transitions with familial ones is a crucial aspect of the life course, especially when individual goals are in conflict with the needs and dictates of the family as a collective unit. For example, in the nineteenth century, the timing of individual transitions was often in conflict with the demands and needs of aging parents. Along these lines, Hareven and Adams (in press) found that parents discouraged the younger daughter from leaving home and marrying, so that she would continue to support them. Daughters succumbed to these dictates, despite their preference to leave and start a life of their own. Hogan, Eggebeen, and Snaith (in press) documented the interlocking of generational transitions in the later years of life: the death of an aging parent enabled caretaking children who were themselves old to turn to providing for their own old age and for their adult children or their grandchildren.

The third feature of the life course approach is the cumulative impact of earlier life events on subsequent ones. The "early" or "delayed" timing of certain transitions affects the pace of later ones. Events experienced earlier in life might continue to influence an individual's or a family's life path in different forms throughout their lives. For example, Elder (1974) documented the negative impact that the Great Depression had on the cohort of young men and women who encountered it in their transition to adulthood. Delayed timing in education or early commencement of employment also affected subsequent delays and disorderliness in the careers of the depression cohort. Historical forces thus play a crucial role in this complex, cumulative pattern of individual and familial life trajectories. They not only have a direct impact on the life course of individuals and families at the time when they encounter them but also continue to have an indirect impact. This means that the social experiences of each cohort are shaped both by the historical events and conditions encountered at a certain point in life and by the historical processes that shaped their earlier life transitions.

The impact of historical forces on the life course can continue over several generations. One generation transmits to the next the ripple effects of the historical circumstances that shaped its life history. Elder and Hareven (1992) found that in the same age cohorts in two different communities, delays or irregularities in the parents' timing of their work and family careers as a result of the Great Depression affected their children's timing of life transitions. The children thus experienced the impact of historical events on two levels—directly, through their encounter with these events, and indirectly, in the ripple effects of these events across the generations.

A life course perspective provides a framework for understanding variability in the patterns of support in the later years of life, as well as differences in the expectations of the recipients and the caregivers, who are influenced by their respective social and cultural milieus. Patterns of generational assistance are shaped by values and experiences that evolve or are modified over the entire life course. For example, in the United States, ethnic values formed in premigration cultures call for a more exclusive dependence on filial and kin assistance than the more contemporary attitudes, which advocate reliance on supports available from government programs and community agencies (Hareven & Adams, in press). Such differences in values are expressed in the caregiving practices and attitudes of successive cohorts. The earlier life course experiences of each cohort, as shaped by historical events, also have an impact on the availability of resources for their members and on their modes of assistance and coping abilities in the later years of life.

The life course perspective also helps clarify the distinction between generation and cohort and provides insight into the interrelationship of these two concepts, which have been frequently confused in the gerontological literature. A generation designates a kin relationship (e.g., parents and children or grandparents and grandchildren); it encompasses an age span often as wide as 30 years or more. A cohort consists of a more specific age group that has shared a common historical experience. Most important, a cohort is defined by its interaction with the historical events that affect the subsequent life course development of that group (Riley, 1978). A generation might consist of several cohorts, each of which has encountered different historical experiences that have affected its life course. In Hareven and Adams's (in press) comparison of patterns of assistance of two cohorts of adult children to aging parents in a New England community, the difference between cohort and generation emerged with particular clarity: in families with large numbers of children, siblings in the same family belonged to two different cohorts, with different historical experiences and attitudes toward generational assistance.

MYTHS ABOUT THE PAST

Historical research has dispelled the myths about the existence of ideal, three-generational families in the American past, according to which the elderly coresided with their adult children and were supported by the younger generations after they reached dependent old age. In reality, in the American colonies and in preindustrial Europe, there never was an era when coresidence of three generations in the same household was the dominant familial arrangement. The "great extended families" that became part of the folklore of modern society rarely existed. As in the present, families in the past tended to reside in nuclear units. Early American households and families were nuclear in their structure. The older generation resided in a separate household from their children but often resided nearby. Given the high mortality rate, most grandparents could not have expected to overlap with their grandchildren over a significant period of their lives (Greven, 1970; Demos, 1970; Laslett & Wall, 1971). It would thus be futile to argue that industrialization destroyed the great extended households of the past and led to the isolation of the elderly. In reality, such a household type rarely existed (Hareven, 1971). Although aging parents in the seventeenth and eighteenth centuries did not coreside with their adult children in the same household, they lived nearby, often on the same land but in separate households. Thus, opportunities for contact and cooperation among the generations abounded in what was characterized as a "modified extended family system" (Greven, 1970). But these types of voluntary, reciprocal relations were different from an institutionalized stem family system, which characterized the coresidence of generations in Central Europe and in Ireland, for example.

Nor was there a "golden age" in the family relations of older people in the American or European past. Even in the colonial period, elderly people were insecure in their familial supports, though they were revered and accorded higher social status than they are today. Aging parents had to enter into contracts with their inheriting sons in order to secure supports in old age in exchange for land. The emphasis on detail in such contractual arrangements suggests the potential tensions and insecurities that parents anticipated concerning their care when they became too frail to support themselves (Demos, 1978; Smith, 1973).

Similarly, older people were not guaranteed supports from their children in urban, industrial society in the nineteenth and twentieth centuries. In American society, familial supports and care for older people, as well as more general patterns of kin assistance, have always been voluntary and based on reciprocal relations over the life course. The fact that the elderly did not hold land deprived them of the important bargaining power that they had held in rural society. In the absence of Social Security and institutions of social welfare, norms dictated that kin engage in more intensive reciprocal relations of assistance than today. Adult children were expected to be the main caregivers for their aging parents (Demos, 1970; Hareven, 1982). Still, these patterns of care were voluntary, rather than enforced by law.

CORESIDENCE

The fact that aging parents and adult children rarely coresided in multigenerational households does not mean that elderly couples or widows lived in isolation. Even in urban, industrial society, solitary residence was most uncommon throughout the nineteenth century for all age groups. In the characteristic form of residence, the older generations maintained separate households from those of their married children. Autonomy in old age—partly expressed in the opportunity for older people to head their own households—hinged, however, on some form of support from an adult child living at home or on the presence of unrelated individuals in the household. The ideal was proximity in residence on the same land in rural areas or in the same building or the same neighborhood in urban areas. "Intimacy from a distance," the preferred mode of generational interaction in contemporary American society, has been persistent since the early settlement and reaches back into the European past (Laslett & Wall, 1971).

Despite an overall commitment to residence in nuclear households practiced by members of various ethnic groups and native-born Americans, nuclear households included extended kin in times of need or at the later stages of the life course (Hareven, 1991a). Household space was an important resource to be shared and exchanged over the life course. Older people, whose own children had left home, shared household space with boarders and lodgers in exchange for services or rent or with their own children who had already left home and married but who returned with their spouses to reside in their parents' household, due to economic crises, housing shortages, or frailty of aged parents. Because household space was considered, to a large extent, an economic resource, its membership changed in relation to the family's economic needs over the life course or in response to other needs and opportunities (Hareven, 1990).

Aging parents who were unable to live alone were joined by an adult child who returned to live with them, or they moved into a child's household (Smith, 1979; Ruggles, 1987). Elderly couples who had no children or whose children had moved far away took in boarders and lodgers in exchange for money or assistance. Boarding provided an important means of mutual exchanges between the generations even if they were not related. About one-third of the men and women in their 20s and 30s in late nineteenth-century American urban communities boarded with other families. For young men and women in a transitional stage between leaving their parents' homes and establishing their own families, boarding in older people's households offered surrogate familial settings. For older people, particularly for widows, it provided the extra income needed to maintain their own residence. It also helped avert isolation after their own children had left home (Modell & Hareven, 1973). In some cases the function was reversed, and older people who could not live alone but who had no children or relatives moved in as boarders into other people's households. Solitary residence, a practice that has become increasingly prominent among older people today, was rarely experienced in the nineteenth century (Kobrin, 1976).

In the later years of life, boarding and lodging served as the "social equalization of the family," a strategy by which young men and women who left their parents' home communities moved into the households of people whose own children had left home (Modell & Hareven, 1973). Sharing household space with boarders and lodgers thus made it easier for families to adhere to their traditional values without slipping below the margin of poverty. The practice of taking boarders into the household was more widespread than admitting extended kin. Despite preferences for un-related individuals, families also took kin into the household, though usu-ally for limited periods during times of need or at specific stages in the life course. Sharing one's household space with kin was an important life course strategy for aged people. Only about 12% to 18% of all urban households in the late nineteenth and early twentieth centuries contained relatives other than members of the nuclear family (Hareven, 1977). In urban industrial communities, which attracted large numbers of migrants from the countryside or immigrants from abroad, coresidence with ex-tended kin increased greatly over the nineteenth century (Anderson, 1971; Hareven, 1982). The proportion of households taking in kin increased to 25%, then declined to 7% by 1950 (Ruggles, 1987). Coresidence with extended kin was most common in the later years of life, when aging par-ents shared their coveted household space with their newly wed children, who delayed establishment of an independent household because of hous-ing shortages.

The powerful commitment to the continued autonomy of the household was clearly in conflict with the needs of people as they were aging. In the absence of adequate public and institutional supports, older people striving to maintain independent households were caught in the double bind of living separately from their children yet having to rely on their children's assistance in order to do so (Chudacoff & Hareven, 1979). Holding on to the space and headship of their household in exchange for future assistance in old age was an important survival strategy for older people in urban society, a strategy reminiscent of the contracts between rural older people and inheriting sons in preindustrial Europe and colonial New England, discussed earlier (Hareven, 1991a). These types of accommodations in the past reflect greater flexibility in household arrangements than those in con-temporary society.

Aging parents or widowed mothers strove to maintain their autonomy by retaining the headship of their own households, rather than move in with their children, relatives, or strangers. To achieve this, they had at least one adult child remain at home. Even older widows continued to head their own households for as long as they were able to. If no children were avail-able or able to help, widows took in boarders and lodgers. Once they were unable to continue to live independently, widows, more frequently than widowers, eventually had to move in with relatives or strangers (Chudacoff & Hareven, 1978, 1979; Hareven & Uhlenberg, 1994). As I explain later, the unwritten rules about separate residence of the generations in American society were modified when aging parents became frail, chronically ill, or demented and, therefore, unable to live independently. Under such circum-stances frail elderly usually coresided with a child or with other kin if no children were available.

An examination of generational patterns of coresidence raises several questions related to household headship and to the nature of the supports. When a household record in a census listed a parent as being the head of the household and an adult child as residing in the household, who in reality headed the household, and what are the dynamics of flow of assets and assistance within such a household? It is difficult to answer these questions from cross-sectional data, nor can such data provide an explanation as to what the dynamics were in this pattern of coresidence. Did the son become the head of the household after his father retired or became too old or frail to support himself and manage the family's affairs, or did the parents move into the son's household? Under what circumstances did the older generation coreside with adult children or other kin, and under what circumstances did they reside separately and interact with adult children and other kin in various forms of assistance outside the household?

Rates of coresidence recorded in cross-sectional data might reflect a life course pattern in which elderly parents who did not coreside with their children at the time a census or survey is taken might do so later when they become more dependent. In the National Survey of Families and Households, Hogan and associates (in press) found that cross-sectional data can obscure considerable variation in patterns of coresidence over the life course: only 7% of Americans aged 55 years and older with a surviving parent had the parent living with them at the time of the survey, but by their late 50s, one-quarter of persons had an aging parent living with them at some point in their lives.

HISTORICAL CHANGES IN THE TIMING OF
LIFE TRANSITIONS

Demographic changes in American society since the late nineteenth century have significantly affected age configurations within the family and the timing of life course transitions. These changes have had a major impact on the later years of life (Hareven, 1976; Uhlenberg, 1974). The decline in mortality since the late nineteenth century has resulted in greater uniformity in the life course of American families and has dramatically increased the opportunities for intact survival of the family unit over the lifetime of its members. Thus, an increasing portion of the population has lived out its life in family units, except when disrupted by divorce (Uhlenberg, 1978). The culturally established life course sequence for women—marriage, motherhood, survival with a husband through the parenting years, the launching of children, and finally, a protracted period of widowhood—was experienced in the nineteenth century by only 44% of females born in 1870 who survived beyond age 15. The remaining 56% never achieved this typical life course pattern, either because they died young, never married, were childless, or became widowed prematurely. The chances for children to survive to adulthood and to grow up with their siblings and both parents alive have also increased over time. Similarly, the opportunities for women to fulfill the societal script of their family lives have increased dramatically (Uhlenberg, 1978).

Impact of Changes in Timing of Life Transitions on Generational Relations

Under the impact of demographic, economic, and cultural change, the timing of the major transitions to adulthood, such as leaving home, entry into and exit from the labor force, marriage, parenthood, the "empty nest," and widowhood, has changed considerably over the past century (Chudacoff & Hareven, 1978). Age uniformity in the timing of life transitions has become increasingly more marked. In the twentieth century, transitions to adulthood have become more uniform for the age cohorts undergoing them, more orderly in sequence, and more rapidly timed. The timing of life transitions has become more regulated according to specific age norms, rather than in relation to the needs of the family. Individual life transitions have become less closely synchronized with collective family ones, thus causing a further separation between the generations (Modell, Furstenberg, & Hershberg, 1976).

By contrast, in the nineteenth century these transitions occurred more gradually and were less rigidly timed. The time range necessary for a cohort to accomplish the transitions to adulthood (leaving school, starting work, getting married, and establishing a separate household) was wider, and the sequence in which transitions followed one another was not rigidly established. The nineteenth-century pattern of transitions allowed for a wider age spread within the family and for greater opportunity for interaction among parents and adult children. Demographic changes, combined with the increasing rapidity in the timing of the transitions to adulthood, the separation of an individual's family of origin from its family of procreation, and the introduction of publicly regulated transitions such as mandatory retirement, converged to isolate and segregate age groups in the larger society.

Since early and later life transitions are interrelated, these changes have affected the status of older people in the family and their sources of support, generating new kinds of stresses on familial needs and obligations (Hareven, 1981). The later life transitions, such as to the empty nest, to widowhood, and to other people's households, followed no ordered sequence and extended over a relatively longer time period. Older women experienced more marked transitions than men did because of widowhood, although the continuing presence of at least one adult child in the household meant that widowhood did not necessarily represent a dramatic transition into the empty nest (Chudacoff & Hareven, 1979; Hareven, 1981; Smith, 1979).

   The most marked discontinuity in the adult life course over this century, especially since World War II, has been the empty nest stage during a couple's middle age. As a result of the decline in mortality, the combination of earlier marriage and the bearing of fewer children overall, with segregation of childbearing to the early stages of the family cycle and a more uniform pattern in children's leaving home earlier in their parents' lives, has resulted in a more widespread emergence of the empty nest as a characteristic of the middle and later years of life (Glick, 1977). This has meant a more extended period of life without children in a couple's or a widow's middle years. At the same time, women's tendency to live longer than men has resulted in a protracted period of widowhood in the later years of life. The empty nest has contributed to a separation between the generations when parents are still in middle age and to a longer period for aged couples or widowed mothers without children in the household. By contrast, in the nineteenth century, later age at marriage, higher fertility, and shorter life expectancy rendered family configurations different from those characterizing contemporary society. The parenting period, with children remaining in the household, extended over a longer time period, sometimes over the parents' entire life. Most important, the nest was rarely empty, because usually one adult child was expected to remain at home while the parents were aging (Hareven, 1976, 1982; Smith, 1981).
   Demographic factors account only in part for the occurrence or nonoccurrence of the empty nest. Children did not remain in their aging parents' household simply because they were too young to move out. Even where sons and daughters were in their late teens and early 20s and therefore old enough to leave home, at least one child remained at home to care for aging parents if no other assistance was available (Chudacoff & Hareven, 1979; Hareven, 1982). Nineteenth-century families did not pass through clearly marked stages. Leaving home did not so uniformly precede marriage, and the launching of children did not necessarily leave the nest empty. Frequently, a married child would return to the parental home, or the parents would take in boarders or lodgers. Familial obligations, dictated by the insecurity of the times and by cultural norms of familial assistance, took precedence over strict age norms (Modell et al., 1976; Hareven, 1982).
   In the nineteenth century, the timing of life transitions was erratic because it followed family needs and obligations rather than specific age norms. Over the twentieth century, on the other hand, age norms have emerged as more important determinants of timing than familial obligations. As Modell and associates (1976, p. 30) concluded: " 'Timely' action to 19th century families consisted of helpful response in times of trouble; in the 20th century, timeliness connotes adherence to a socially-sanctioned schedule." A rigid, age-related timing of family transitions in accordance with age norms is mainly a twentieth-century phenomenon.

As greater differentiation in stages of life began to develop and as social and economic functions became more closely related to age, a greater segregation between age groups emerged. Since the turn of the century, this segregation occurred first in the middle class and only later extended to the working class. It also varied considerably among ethnic groups.

Since the 1980s, however, more erratic and flexible patterns of timing of life course transitions have emerged again. These new patterns, departing from the earlier age-related rigidities along the life course, reflect changes in family arrangements and values and new policies governing work life. The movement of young adult children in and out of the parental home has become more erratic: young adults stay in the parental home or return after they have left home. This pattern differs, however, from the one in the past in a fundamental way. In the late nineteenth century, children continued to stay in the parental home or moved back and forth, in order to meet the needs of their family of orientation—taking care of aging parents or, in some cases, young siblings and others. In contemporary society, young adult children return home in order to meet their own needs, because of their inability to develop an independent work career or to find affordable housing. Another contemporary variant of the filling of the nest is the return of divorced or unmarried daughters with their own young children to the parental household. In this instance, again, the main purpose is generally not for the daughter to assist an aging mother but rather to receive help in housing and child care.

Prior to the beginning of this century, the family was the most critical agent in initiating and managing life transitions. Control over the timing of individual members' life transitions was a crucial factor in the family's efforts to manage its resources, especially by balancing different members' contributions to the family economy. In contemporary American society, one is accustomed to thinking of most transitions to family roles and work careers as individual moves, except for certain ethnic and cultural groups. But in the past, individual members' transitions had to be synchronized with familial ones. Early life transitions were bound up with later ones in a continuum of one's family's needs and obligations. The life transitions of the younger generation were intertwined with those of the older generation. The timing of leaving home, getting married, and setting up a separate household was contingent on the timing of the older generation's transitions into retirement or on inheritance (Hareven, 1982). This interdependence dictated parental control over the timing of their children's life transitions, especially of leaving home and getting married. How did parents control their children's timing of leaving home and marriage? The strategies that parents and children followed in determining exchanges and transfers in their interactions over the timing of life transitions represent, therefore, an important theoretical and empirical theme.

INTERDEPENDENCE AMONG KIN

Even though the nuclear family resided separately from extended kin, its members were engaged in various patterns of mutual assistance with kin outside the household. Whether they resided separately or in the same household, interdependence with extended kin was the basis of survival for members of the nuclear family. Kin served as the most essential resource for economic assistance and security and carried the major burden of welfare functions for individual family members. Contrary to prevailing myths, urbanization and industrialization did not break down traditional ties and patterns of mutual assistance. Various historical studies have documented the survival of viable functions of kin in the nineteenth century, especially their critical role in facilitating migration, in finding jobs and housing, and in assistance in critical life situations (Anderson, 1971; Hareven, 1982). Kin assistance was pervasive in the neighborhood and extended back to the communities of origin of immigrants and migrants, maintaining various exchanges. Immigrants in the United States often sent back remittances for their aging parents and other relatives in their communities of origin (Hareven, 1982).

Under the historical conditions in which familial assistance was the almost exclusive source of security, the multiplicity of obligations that individuals incurred over life toward their relatives was more complex than in contemporary society. In addition to the ties they retained with their family of origin, individuals carried obligations toward their family of procreation and toward their spouses' family of origin. Such obligations cast individuals into various overlapping and, at times, conflicting roles over the course of their lives. The absence of institutional supports, in the form of welfare agencies, unemployment compensation, and Social Security, added to the pressures imposed on family members.

Kin were crucial in coping with critical life situations, such as unemployment, illness, or death, as well as with regular life course transitions (Anderson, 1971; Hareven, 1982). The absence of a narrow, age-related timing of transitions to adult life allowed for a more intensive interaction among different age groups within family and community, thus providing a greater sense of continuity and interdependence among people at various points in the life course. Under these conditions, individual choices had to be subordinated to collective family needs. Individuals' sense of obligation to their kin was dictated by their family culture. It expressed a commitment to the survival, well-being, and self-reliance of the family, which took priority over individual needs and personal happiness. Autonomy of the family, essential for self-respect and good standing in the neighborhood and community, was one of the most deeply ingrained values (Hareven, 1982).

Mutual assistance among kin, although involving extensive exchanges, was not strictly calculative. Rather, it expressed an overall principle of reciprocity over the life course and across generations. Individuals who subordinated their own careers and needs to those of the family as a collective unit did so out of a sense of responsibility, affection, and familial obligation, rather than with the expectation of immediate gain. Such sacrifices were not made, however, without protest and, at times, involved competition and conflict among siblings as to who should carry the main responsibility for support for aging parents (Hareven, 1982).

GENERATIONAL SUPPORTS OVER THE LIFE COURSE

Close contact and mutual exchanges among parents, their adult children, and other kin persisted throughout the nineteenth century and survived into the twentieth century in various forms in the lives of working-class and ethnic families. Parents expected their grown children to support them in their old age in exchange for supports they themselves had rendered their children earlier in life. Societal values rooted in their respective ethnic cultures provided ideological reinforcements for these reciprocal obligations (Hareven, 1982).

Adult children's involvement with the care of their aging parents was closely related to their earlier life course experiences, to their ethnic and cultural traditions, and to the historical context affecting their lives. Routine assistance from children to aging parents set the stage for the children's coping with parents' later life crises, such as widowhood and dependence in old age. Despite the strong tradition of kin assistance, children carried the main responsibilities of care for aging parents. Other kin provided sociability and occasional help, but the major responsibilities fell on the children, usually on one child. Regardless of how many children a couple had, one child usually emerged in the role of caregiver (Chudacoff & Hareven, 1979; Hareven & Adams, in press; Smith, 1979).

Children, most commonly daughters, took a parent into their own household under circumstances of extreme duress—when parents were too frail to live alone or when they needed extensive help with their daily activities and regular care. There was no prescribed rule as to which child would become a "parent keeper." If the child was not already residing with the parent, the selection of the parent keeper was governed by that particular child's ability and willingness to take the parent in, by the consent or support of the parent keeper's spouse, and by the readiness of the parent to accept the plan (Hareven & Adams, in press).

Most parent keepers evolved into that role over their life course; some were pushed into it through a sudden family crisis. Earlier life course experience was, however, an overwhelming factor in the designation of a parent keeper. Children who had been involved in a closer day-to-day interaction with their parents during their own child-rearing years were also more likely than their siblings to take on responsibilities for caring for their parents. Parent keepers fulfilled their responsibilities at a high price to themselves and to their spouses and other family members. Caregiving disrupted the daughter's work career, led to crowding in her household, often caused tension and strain in her marriage, and made her vulnerable in preparing for her own and her spouse's retirement and old age (Brody, 1990; Cantor, 1983; Hareven & Adams, in press; Dwyer & Seccombe, 1991).

Most commonly, the parent keeper was the child who continued to reside with a parent after the other siblings had left home. Even when both parents were alive, as previously noted, the youngest daughter was expected to remain at home and postpone or give up marriage in order to ensure support for the parents in their old age. This pattern was pervasive among various ethnic groups until World War II. As an immigrant woman from Quebec in a New England industrial community described it:

Father was always saying "we have this French saying that someone stays home to be the support of the elderly parents." Most of the time it seemed to be the youngest of the family, or the youngest girl. The oldest grew up and got married, and the parents were getting on in age. By the time the youngest grew up, the parents were getting old enough. . . . So, instead of settling down, that one was almost like naturally left to take care of the family (Hareven & Adams, in press).

A caretaking daughter's decision to marry caused a great deal of tension with her elderly parents or widowed mother. Under these circumstances, couples waited sometimes for decades until their parents died before they could marry (Hareven, 1982).

HISTORICAL IMPLICATIONS

An increasing separation between the family of origin and the family of procreation over the past century, combined with a privatization of family life and the erosion of mutual assistance among kin, has tended to increase insecurity and isolation as people age, most markedly in areas of need that are not met by public welfare programs.

Although some of the intensive historical patterns of kin interaction have survived among first-generation immigrant, black, and working-class families, a gradual weakening of mutual assistance among kin over time has occurred. Gerontological studies insisting that kin assistance for older people has persisted in contemporary society have not documented the intensity, quality, and consistency of kin support that older people are receiving from their relatives (Litwak, 1965; Shanas, 1979; Sussman, 1959). Until more systematic evidence is available, it would be a mistake to assume that kin are carrying, or should be carrying, the major responsibility for assistance to older people.

Determining how consistent and continuous the support from nonresident children or other kin to aging parents has been in the United States is still open to future research. Earlier studies have documented visiting patterns and telephone communication rather than regular caretaking (Shanas, 1979). More recent research has emphasized the presence of various supports from adult children to aging parents in contemporary society, even if they are not residing in the same household. The contact that aged people have with kin, as Shanas (1979) and others have found, might represent a form of behavior characteristic of specific cohorts rather than a continuing pattern. The cohorts that are currently aged, especially the oldest-old, have carried over the historical attitudes and traditions of a strong reliance on kin prevalent in their youth (Hareven, 1978a). Future cohorts, as they reach old age, might not have the same strong sense of familial interdependence, nor might they have sufficient numbers of kin available on whom to rely. It would be a mistake, therefore, to leave kin to take care of their own at a time when the chances for people to do so effectively have considerably diminished.

Nor should the historical evidence about the continuity in kin relations be misused in support of proposals to the public sector to return welfare responsibilities from the public sector to the family without providing basic additional supports. Historical precedents reveal the high price that kin had to pay in order to assist each other without the appropriate societal supports. Past experience thus offers a warning against romanticizing kin relations, particularly against the attempt to transfer responsibility for the support of the elderly back to the family without adequate governmental assistance for caregiving relatives.

The major changes that have led to the isolation of older people in society today were rooted not so much in changes in family structure or residential arrangements, as has generally been argued, but in the transformation and redefinition of family functions. Changes in functions and values—especially the replacement of an instrumental view of family relations with sentimentality and intimacy as the major cohesive forces in the family—have led to the weakening of the role of kin assistance in middle-class families in particular. The decline in instrumental relations among kin and their replacement by an individualistic and sentimental orientation toward family relations have led to an increasing isolation of the elderly in American society (Hareven, 1986).

Over the nineteenth century, the family surrendered many of the functions previously concentrated within it to other social institutions. The retreat from public life and a growing commitment to the privacy of the modern, middle-class family have drawn sharper boundaries between family and community and intensified the segregation of different age groups within and outside the family. The transfer of social welfare functions from the family to public institutions further exacerbated the likelihood that the needs of older people might not be met. The family has ceased to be the only available source of support for its dependent members. The community has ceased to rely on the family as the major agency of welfare and social control (Demos, 1970). No adequate substitute agencies for the care of elderly dependent people have been developed, however.

This shift of responsibility has generated considerable ambiguity, particularly in the expectations for support and assistance for aging relatives from their own kin. On one hand, people assume that the welfare state has relieved children of the obligation of supporting their parents in old age; on the other hand, these public measures are not sufficient in the economic area, nor do they provide the kind of supports and sociability in areas that had been traditionally provided by the family. It is precisely this ambiguity and the failure of American society to consummate the historical process of the transfer of functions from the family to the public sector and to strengthen the family in carrying out these functions that have become one of the major sources of the problems currently confronting older people.

FUTURE DIRECTIONS AND RESEARCH NEEDS

Over the past two decades, the history of aging and the history of the family have each received continuing attention as separate entities. The interrelationship between the family and aging in a historical context has not been subjected to a consistent research effort. The historical study of aging has focused primarily on changing attitudes and images of aging and on changing policies of retirement and the emergence of Social Security. From a demographic perspective, historical studies have emphasized changing population patterns and changes in the timing of life transitions and in coresidence in the later years of life. Little systematic research has been carried out on the internal dynamics in the households of older people, especially their relations with their children or other kin, if they coresided with them. Nor have there been systematic studies of the interaction of older people with nonresident kin in the past and the ways in which this interaction has changed over time.

The area of generational relations, especially the development of reciprocal relation over the life course, and their impact on supports in the later years of life also require further investigations (Rossi & Rossi, 1990). Although the contemporary gerontological literature has placed a great deal of emphasis on "women in the middle" as caretakers, this theme has not been investigated systematically in a historical context (Brody, 1990). Finally, differences among various ethnic groups in terms of family patterns in the later years of life and the care of aged relatives require systematic investigation. This theme is particularly important given the persistence of certain historic patterns of family and generational relations among various ethnic groups and of reciprocal supports among kin.

REFERENCES

Anderson, M. S. (1971). *Family structure in nineteenth century Lancashire.* Cambridge, England: Cambridge University Press.

Brody, E. M. (1990). *Women in the middle: Their parent-care years.* New York: Springer Publishing Co.

Cantor, M. H. (1983). Strain among caregivers: A study of experience in the U.S. *Gerontologist, 12,* 597–624.

Chudacoff, H., & Hareven, T. K. (1978). Family transitions to old age. In T. K. Hareven (Ed.), *Transitions: The family and the life course in historical perspective* (pp. 217–243). New York: Academic Press.

Chudacoff, H., & Hareven, T. K. (1979). From the empty nest to family dissolution. *Journal of Family History, 4,* 69–84.

Clark, M., & Anderson, B. B. (1976). *Culture and aging: An anthropological study of older Americans.* Springfield, IL: Charles C. Thomas.

Demos, J. (1970). *A little commonwealth: Family life in Plymouth Colony.* New York: Oxford University Press.

Demos, J. (1978). Old age in early New England. In J. Demos and S. Boocock (Eds.), *Turning Points: American Journal of Sociology Supplement 84,* S248–S287.

Dwyer, J. W., & Seccombe, K. (1991). Elder care as family labor: The influence of gender and family position. *Journal of Family Issues, 12,* 229–247.

Elder, G. H. (1974). *Children of the Great Depression.* Chicago: University of Chicago Press.

Elder, G. H. (1978). Family history and the life course. In T. K. Hareven (Ed.), *Transitions: The family and the life course in historical perspective* (pp. 17–64). New York: Academic Press.

Elder, G. H. (1982). Historical experiences in the later years. In T. K. Hareven & K. Adams (Eds.), *Aging and life course transitions: An interdisciplinary perspective* (pp. 75–107). New York: Guilford Press.

Elder, G. H., & Hareven, T. K. (1992). Rising above life's disadvantages: From the Great Depression to global war. In J. Modell, G. H. Elder, Jr., & R. Parke (Eds.), *Children in time and place* (pp. 47–72). New York: Cambridge University Press.

Fischer, D. H. (1977). *Growing old in America.* New York: Oxford University Press.

Glick, P. C. (1977). Updating the life cycle of the family. *Journal of Marriage and the Family, 31,* 5–13.

Greven, P. (1970). *Four generations: Population, land and family in colonial Andover, Massachusetts.* Ithaca, NY: Cornell University Press.

Hareven, T. K. (1971). The history of the family as an interdisciplinary field. *Journal of Interdisciplinary History, 2,* 339–494.

Hareven, T. K. (1976). The last stage: Historical adulthood and old age. *Daedalus: American Civilization: New Perspectives, 105,* 13–27.

Hareven, T. K. (1977). The historical study of the family in urban society. In T. K. Hareven (Ed.), *Family and kin in urban communities, 1700–1930* (pp. 1–15). New York: Franklin & Watts.

Hareven, T. K. (1978a). Historical changes in the life course and the family. In J. M. Yinger & S. J. Cutler (Eds.), *Major social issues: Multidisciplinary view* (pp. 338–345). New York: Free Press.

Hareven, T. K. (1978b). Introduction: The historical study of the life course. In T. K. Hareven (Ed.), *Transitions: The family and the life course in historical perspective* (pp. 1–16). New York: Academic Press.

Hareven, T. K. (1981). Historical changes in the timing of family transitions: Their impact on generational relations. In J. G. March, R. W. Fogel, E. Hatfield, S. B. Kiesler, & E. Shanas (Eds.), *Aging: Stability and change in the family* (pp. 143–165). New York: Academic Press.

Hareven, T. K. (1982). *Family time and industrial time*. Cambridge, England: Cambridge University Press. [Reprinted 1993, Lanham, New York, London: University Press of America.]

Hareven, T. K. (1986). Historical changes in the social construction of the life course. *Human Development, 29,* 171–180.

Hareven, T. K. (1990). A complex relationship: Family strategies and the processes of economic and social change. In R. Friedland & A. F. Robertson (Eds.), *Beyond the marketplace* (pp. 215–244). New York: Aldine de Gruyter.

Hareven, T. K. (1991a). The history of the family and the complexity of social change. *American Historical Review, 96,* 95–124.

Hareven, T. K. (1991b). Synchronizing individual time, family time and historical time. In J. Bender & D. E. Wellbery (Eds.), *Chronotypes: The construction of time* (pp. 167–182). Stanford, CA: Stanford University Press.

Hareven, T. K., & Adams, K. (in press). The generation in the middle: Cohort comparisons in assistance to aging parents in an American community. In T. K. Hareven (Ed.), *Aging and generational relations over the life course: A historical and cross-cultural perspective*. Berlin: Walter de Gruyter.

Hareven, T. K., & Masaoka, K. (1988). Turning points and transitions: Perceptions of the life course. *Journal of Family History, 13,* 271–289.

Hareven, T. K., & Uhlenberg, P. (1994). *Aging in the past: Demography, society and old age*. Berkeley: University of California Press.

Hogan, D. P., Eggebeen, D. J., & Snaith, S. M. (in press). The well-being of aging Americans with very old parents. In T. K. Hareven (Ed.), *Aging and generational relations over the life course: A historical and cross-cultural perspective*. Berlin: Walter de Gruyter.

Kobrin, F. E. (1976). The fall of household size and the rise of the primary individual in the United States. *Demography, 13,* 127–138.

Laslett, P., & Wall, R. (Eds.). (1971). *Household and family in past time*. Cambridge: Cambridge University Press.

Litwak, E. (1965). Extended kin relations in an industrial democratic society. In E. Shanas & G. F. Streib (Eds.), *Social structure and the family: Generational relations* (pp. 290–323). Englewood Cliffs, NJ: Prentice-Hall.

Modell, J., Furstenberg, F., & Hershberg, T. (1976). Social change and transitions to adulthood in historical perspective. *Journal of Family History, 1,* 7–32.

Modell, J., & Hareven, T. K. (1973). Urbanization and the malleable household: Boarding and lodging in American families. *Journal of Marriage and the Family, 35,* 467–479.

Riley, M. W. (1978). Aging, social change and the power of ideas. *Daedalus: Generations, 107,* 39–53.

Rossi, A. S., & Rossi, P. H. (1990). *Of human bonding: Parent-child relations across the life course.* Hawthorne, NY: Aldyne de Gruyter.

Ruggles, S. (1987). *Prolonged connections: The rise of the extended family in nineteenth-century England and America.* Madison: University of Wisconsin Press.

Shanas, E. (1979). Social myth as hypothesis: The case of the family relations of old people. *Gerontologist, 19,* 3–9.

Smith, D. S. (1973). Parental power and marriage patterns: Analysis of historical trends in Hingham, Massachusetts. *Journal of Marriage and the Family, 35,* 419–428.

Smith, D. S. (1979). Life course, norms, and the family system of older Americans in 1900. *Journal of Family History, 4,* 285–299.

Smith, D. S. (1981). Historical change in the household structure of the elderly in economically developed societies. In J. G. March, R. W. Fogel, E. Hatfield, S. B. Kiesler, & E. Shanas (Eds.), *Aging: Stability and change in the family* (pp. 91–114). New York: Academic Press.

Sussman, M. B. (1959). The isolated nuclear family: Fact or fiction? *Social Problems, 6,* 333–347.

Uhlenberg, P. (1974). Cohort variations in family life cycle experiences of U.S. females. *Journal of Marriage and the Family, 34,* 284–292.

Uhlenberg, P. (1978). Changing configurations of the life course. In T. K. Hareven (Ed.), *Transitions: The family and the life course in historical perspective* (pp. 65–97). New York: Academic Press.

3

Aging and the Family: Present and Future Demographic Issues

Kevin Kinsella

In the early 1980s, Myers and Nathanson (1982) framed three paramount issues regarding population aging and the family. These concerns involve (1) the extent to which changing concepts of social duties and responsibilities alter traditional ways of providing care for aged people within the family context; (2) the potential social support burden arising from reduced economic self-sufficiency of aged people, longer life expectancy that might involve prolonged episodes of chronic disease morbidity and functional impairment, and increased complexity of social life resulting from urbanization and modernization; and (3) the processes by which countries determine funding priorities for national care systems given competing demands for scarce resources.

The salience of these issues intensified during the 1980s and early 1990s. Governments are concerned not only about the need to provide care and services to growing numbers of aged individuals but about the mix of resources among generations. Short of a revolution in cultural norms, the broad growth of elderly populations ensures that an increased proportion of Social Security resources and expenditures will be allocated to maintaining an adequate income for the elderly. Such a fiscal increase might compete with finances available for traditional family support. A central political tension in developed countries arises from the tendency to withdraw resources from the direct support of families, while promoting an implicit expectation for families to increase support for an elderly generation (ILO, 1989; see also Dwyer, this volume).

The purpose of this chapter is to outline several interrelated demographic trends that affect both the structure and functioning of the family institution worldwide. These trends do not presage a mechanistic determination of the future, but they will significantly shape the decisions that families and governments make with regard to care of, and services for, older constituents. The plethora of family types among and within societies precludes any detailed analysis of global familial evolution.[1] Rather, I seek to highlight distinctions between developed and developing regions of the world. Although these overarching categories[2] mask many differences among nations, they do serve as useful foci for identifying general phenomena that affect specific nations to a greater or lesser degree.

DEMOGRAPHIC FACTORS AFFECTING FAMILY STRUCTURE

Evolving Population Age Structure

Underlying many of the changes in family relationships are shifts in population age structure. Population aging refers most simply to an increasing proportion of elderly[3] persons within an overall population. In most countries today, the aging process is determined primarily by fertility rates and secondarily by mortality rates, so that populations with high fertility tend to have low proportions of older persons and vice versa. Demographers use the term *demographic transition* to refer to a gradual process wherein a society moves from a situation of high rates of fertility and mortality to one of low rates of fertility and mortality. The initial stage of this transition is characterized by declines in infant and childhood mortality as infectious and parasitic diseases are eradicated. The resulting improvement in life expectancy at birth occurs while fertility tends to remain high, thereby producing large birth cohorts and an expanding proportion of children relative to adults.

Whole populations begin to age when fertility rates decline and mortality rates at all ages improve. Successive birth cohorts might eventually become smaller and smaller, although many countries experience a "baby boom echo" as women from prior large birth cohorts reach childbearing age. International migration usually does not play a major role in the population aging process but can be important in small nations. Certain island nations, for example, have experienced a combination of emigration of working-age adults, immigration of elderly retirees from other countries, and return migration of former emigrants who are above the average population age; all three factors contribute to population aging.

Figure 3.1 illustrates the historical and projected aggregate population age-structure transition in developed versus developing countries. At one time, most countries had a youthful age structure similar to that of developing countries as a whole in 1950, with a large percentage of the entire population under the age of 15. Given the relatively high rates of fertility that prevailed in most developing countries from 1950 through the early 1970s, the overall pyramid shape had changed very little by 1990. The effects of fertility decline can be seen in the projected[4] pyramid for 2025,

Figure 3.1
Population, by Age and Sex: 1950, 1990, and 2025

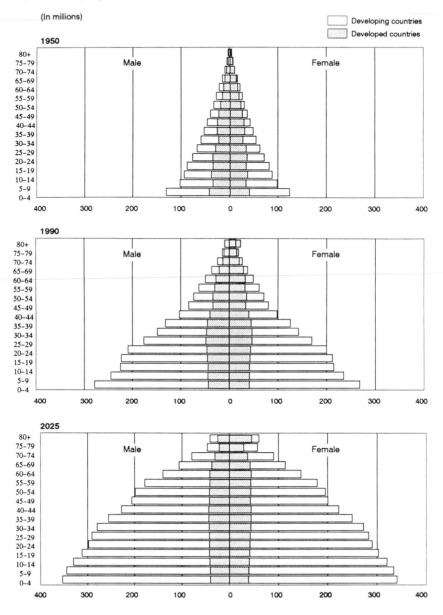

however, in which the strictly triangular shape changes as the elderly portion of the total population increases.

The picture in developed countries has been, and will be, quite different. In 1950, relatively little variation existed in the size of 5-year groups between the ages of 5 and 24. The beginnings of the post–World War II high-fertility baby boom can be seen in the 0-to-4-year age group. By 1990, the baby boom cohorts were 25 to 44 years old, and the cohorts under age 25 were becoming successively smaller. Several developed countries (e.g., Italy, Germany, Hungary, Sweden) have had total fertility rates below the natural replacement level of 2.1 children per woman for some time. Successive small birth cohorts have contributed to the large proportions of elderly people in these societies. If fertility rates remain relatively low through 2025, the aggregate developed-country pyramid will start to invert, with more weight on the top than on the bottom.

Within aging populations, older age groups tend to grow at different rates. The average age of a nation's elderly population often increases because the oldest-old (persons aged 80 years and over) are the fastest growing portion of many elderly populations worldwide. This oldest group constituted 16% of the world's elderly in 1992: 22% in developed countries and 12% in developing countries. As seen in Figure 3.1, the prominence of the oldest-old—especially women—will increase over time.

Lengthening Life Expectancy

Developed countries have made enormous strides in extending life expectancy since the beginning of this century. From 1900 to 1950, many Western nations were able to add 20 years or more to their average life expectancy at birth. In some countries, life expectancy more than doubled from 1900 to 1990 (Table 3.1). In the eighteenth and nineteenth centuries, low life expectancy meant that persons spent a relatively short amount of time in a multigenerational family (UNDIESA, 1990). Although most persons lived their older years with family members, time spent in extended families was limited because the average individual died shortly after becoming a grandparent (Hareven, this volume; Ruggles, 1987).

Declining fertility and increased longevity have enhanced the joint survival of different generations. In developed countries, this has led to the emergence of the *beanpole family* (Bengtson, Rosenthal, & Burton, 1990). This vertical extension of family structure is characterized by an increase in the number of living generations within a lineage and a decrease in the number of members within each generation. If fertility rates continue to decline or remain at low levels, four-generation families may soon become the norm in developed countries. The post–World War II baby boom generation could become the great-grandparent boom of the 2020s (Taeuber, 1992).

Table 3.1
Life Expectancy at Birth for Selected Developed Countries: 1900–1990

Region/Country	Circa 1900		Circa 1950		1990	
	Male	Female	Male	Female	Male	Female
WESTERN EUROPE						
Austria	37.8	39.9	62.0	67.0	73.5	80.4
Belgium	45.4	48.9	62.1	67.4	73.4	80.4
Denmark	51.6	54.8	68.9	71.5	72.6	78.8
England/Wales	46.4	50.1	66.2	71.1	73.3	79.2
France	45.3	48.7	63.7	69.4	73.4	81.9
Germany	43.8	46.6	64.6	68.5	73.4	80.6
Italy	42.9	43.2	63.7	67.2	74.5	81.4
Norway	52.3	55.8	70.3	73.8	73.3	80.8
Sweden	52.8	55.3	69.9	72.6	74.7	80.7
SOUTHERN and EASTERN EUROPE						
Czechoslovakia	38.9	41.7	60.9	65.5	68.7	76.5
Greece	38.1	39.7	63.4	66.7	75.0	80.2
Hungary	36.6	38.2	59.3	63.4	67.2	75.4
Poland	n/a	n/a	57.2	62.8	68.2	76.7
Spain	33.9	35.7	59.8	64.3	74.8	81.6
OTHER						
Australia	53.2	56.8	66.7	71.8	73.5	79.8
Canada	n/a	n/a	66.4	70.9	74.0	80.7
Japan	42.8	44.3	59.6	63.1	76.4	82.1
New Zealand	n/a	n/a	67.2	71.3	72.2	78.4
United States	48.3	51.1	66.0	71.7	72.1	79.0

Sources: UNDIESA, 1988; Siampos, 1990; U.S. Bureau of the Census, unpublished estimates/
   projections; and various national sources.
Note: Figures for Germany refer to what was West Germany.

The widening gender differential in life expectancy has been a central
feature of mortality trends in the twentieth century. In 1900, the gender
gap in life expectancy was typically 2 to 3 years in Europe and North
America. Today, women in most developed countries outlive men by 5 to
9 years, reflecting the fact that females have lower mortality than males in
every age group and for most causes of death. Average female life expec-

tancy now exceeds 80 years in at least 15 countries and is approaching this threshold in many other nations. The gender differential is usually smaller in developing countries and is even reversed in some South Asian and Middle East societies where cultural factors (low female social status, preference for male rather than female offspring) are thought to contribute to higher male than female life expectancy at birth.

Although the effect of fertility decline is usually the driving force behind changing population age structure, current and future changes in mortality (mostly at older ages) assume greater weight in countries that already have high proportions of elderly citizens. Caselli, Vallin, Vaupel, and Yashin (1987) demonstrated the growing impact of mortality change in population projections for France and Italy. Even if Italian fertility is held to a very low level of 1.4 children per woman through the year 2040, more than half the increase in the proportion of population aged 60 and over will be due to mortality change and less than half to fertility change.

The Epidemiologic Transition

The term *epidemiologic transition,* coined by Omran (1971) and now in its third decade of use, refers to a long-term change in leading causes of death from infectious and acute to chronic and degenerative diseases. In general, the epidemiologic transition is related to, but lags behind, the demographic transition. The initial mortality declines that characterize the demographic transition result largely from reductions in infectious diseases at young ages. As children survive and age, they are increasingly exposed to risk factors linked to chronic disease and accidents. As fertility declines begin to induce population aging, growing numbers of older persons shift national morbidity profiles toward a greater incidence of continuous and degenerative ailments (Frenk, Frejka, Bobadilla, Stern, Sepulveda, & Jose, 1989). Such conditions exact a toll not only on those who suffer from them but on family members who must respond to long-term care needs.

Although comparable cross-national morbidity data are scarce, the implications of epidemiologic change for individual and family care can be ascertained from mortality statistics. Obstructive heart disease has been, and remains, the leading cause of adult mortality in developed (and some developing) countries, though cancers now rank a very close second. In North America, death rates from heart disease peaked in the 1960s and have fallen by almost 50% since that time. Many Western European nations have recorded more modest declines of 10% to 20%, whereas mortality rates from heart disease have increased in several Eastern European nations. Overall age-standardized death rates for malignant neoplasms (cancer) in developed countries have risen 30% to 50% among men since 1950 and fallen by about 10% among women. Such broad trends, however, often are the net result of quite different changes in mortality for the leading sites of disease. In the United States and Western Europe, stomach cancer has been declining steadily since the 1930s, a decline clearly attributed to nutritional change (i.e., a reduction in the salt content of food, especially in preserved food) (Lopez, 1990). On the other hand, a dramatic rise in lung cancer has occurred since World War II, initially among men but now increasingly among women because of increased tobacco use.

The pace of epidemiologic transition varies throughout the developing world. The situation in much of Latin America and the Caribbean is similar to that of developed countries. Data from the Pan American Health Organization (1990) indicate that cardiovascular diseases are the principal cause of death in the populations of 27 of the 37 countries of the Americas for which recent mortality data are available. In 6 of the remaining 10 countries, either cancer or cerebrovascular disease (stroke) is the leading killer. The proportion of deaths attributable to cardiovascular diseases increased from 27% in 1975 to 33% in 1985; if North American data were excluded, the increase would be larger still. The proportion of mortality due to cancer also increased, although the percentage of deaths from strokes declined during the decade.

In several East and Southeast Asian nations the pace of epidemiologic change appears quite rapid. In Singapore, for example, life expectancy at birth rose 30 years in barely one generation, from 40 years in 1948 to 70 years in 1979. During the same period, deaths due to infectious diseases declined from 40% to 12% of all deaths, whereas the share of cardiovascular deaths rose from 5% to 32%. Recent data from China indicate that cardiovascular diseases are often the primary killers in both urban and rural locales; heart disease and cancer together account for 59% of reported deaths in cities and 46% in rural areas. Similar patterns have been reported for Turkey and Sri Lanka, but to date, comparable indicators for the majority of Southern and Western Asia and for Africa are not available.

Overall gains in life expectancy imply, other factors being equal, a greater potential for coresident multigenerational families and an enhanced opportunity to provide care for older family members (see Dwyer, this volume; Travis, this volume). The experience of many developed countries, however, has not substantiated the implication. Numerous researchers (e.g., Rice, 1984; Liu & Manton, 1985; Doty, 1988) documented the direct relationship between population age-sex structure, age-sex-specific rates of chronic disease and disability, and the need for long-term care. But the confluence of several macrotrends in developed countries—older population age structures, higher incidence of noncommunicable diseases, lowered fertility, increased geographical mobility, and rapid advances in medical technology—encouraged the formation of an institutionalized response to population aging. As families no longer could, nor desired, to provide direct care for needy elderly members, medical and nonmedical facilities adopted this role.

The highest rates of institutional use are found in many of the world's oldest countries (as measured by the percentage of the population aged 65 and over), and absolute numbers of users have tended to expand in spite of efforts to enhance community-based services and to avoid or greatly reduce levels of institutionalization. By the early 1990s, however, signs of change appeared. Rates of institutional use were declining in the United States and several other developed countries (see Dwyer, this volume; Harrington Meyer & Bellas, this volume). At the same time, age-specific disability rates seem to be decreasing, at least in the United States (Corder, 1992), such that some elderly populations might be spending a greater proportion of their remaining years in a healthy, rather than in a disabled, state (Robine, 1991). If real and sustained, this trend will have enormous import for the well-being of elderly families and younger relatives and for social costs associated with treatment and long-term care. It remains the task of researchers to determine the prevalence of such change and the extent to which it is due to cohort effects.

EFFECTS OF DEMOGRAPHIC CHANGE ON FAMILIES AND HOUSEHOLDS

Changing Marital Status

The marital status of older men is very different from that of older women throughout the world. Although widowhood rates rise with age for both sexes, a large majority of men aged 65 and over are married. Even at ages 75 and over, married men usually outnumber widowers. Quite the opposite is true for women; in many countries, the percentage of widows among elderly women exceeds 50%. Several reasons for the gender disparity in widowhood emerge in both developing and developed nations. The most obvious factor is simply that women live longer on average than do men. Also, the nearly universal tendency for women to marry men older than themselves compounds the likelihood of their outliving their spouses. Finally, widowers are much more likely than widows to remarry; in the United States, for example, elderly widowed men have remarriage rates over eight times higher than those of elderly women.

Recent trends for developed countries indicate that growing proportions of older populations are married, declining proportions are widowed, and the percentage of older people who are divorced or separated is small but steadily rising. One might expect that the wide difference in life expectancy that favors women would lead to the increased probability of widowhood. Myers (1990) suggested, however, that the increase in joint survival has meant that higher proportions of husband-wife families reach age 65 and continue intact for some time. Thus, in the United States, actuarial data show that a couple could anticipate 47 years of married life in the mid-

Figure 3.2
Percent Increase in Number of Widows Age 65 and Older in Selected Countries

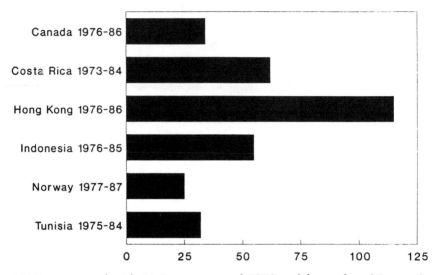

1980s, compared with 44.5 years around 1970 and fewer than 35 years in the early 1900s.

In one sense, then, concerns about growing proportions of elderly widows might be less onerous than previously thought. It is crucial, however, to consider absolute numbers as well as proportions. Numbers of older widows, especially in large developing countries, often are increasing rapidly (Figure 3.2). In Indonesia, for example, the number of elderly widows rose from 1.4 million in 1976 to 2.2 million in 1985. If the gender trend in life expectancy in developing countries follows the historical pattern in developed countries, an increasing share of their older populations will be women. The net result might be an overall improvement in status for women under the age of 65 or 70 due to spousal survival but a worsening of the situation for older women, who are at greater risk in terms of loss of spouse, lack of economic resources, and frail health.

In most countries, more women than men are divorced or separated, probably reflecting gender differences in remarriage rates. Increases in numbers of divorced and separated persons have been observed among the older populations of virtually all countries (Kinsella & Taeuber, 1993). About 5% of both elderly men and elderly women in the United States were divorced (and had not remarried) in 1990, compared with fewer than 2% in 1960. Projections of the U.S. Social Security Administration indicate a continuation of this trend, implying that 8% of elderly men and 14% of elderly women will be divorced by 2020 (Taeuber, 1992).

Proportions of persons never married are likely to become much more significant to the analysis of family structure. A study of 14 European countries (Gonnot & Vukovich, 1989) showed that proportions of never-married men and women increased during the 1980s in all five-year age groups between ages 20 and 40 (with two exceptions) in all countries. The highest such proportions ever recorded in Europe are in Sweden: as of 1985, 39% of all men and 30% of all women had never married.[5] Percentages of never-married Swedish elderly are much lower—roughly 12% for men and women—but still high by international standards. Double-digit percentages of never-married people also obtain among the elderly of both sexes in Norway and among elderly women in several other developed countries.

Rising divorce and nonmarriage rates raise important questions about the likelihood of changing family networks and future social support. Part of the decline in European nuptiality is related to the increasing prevalence of consensual unions, particularly among young adults. The duration of such unions and their implications for later life are as yet unclear. Also unclear is the extent to which sibling interaction and support are substitutes for spouse/child support among both never-married and divorced persons (see Bedford, this volume).

Declining Household Size and Altered Living Arrangements

The intersection of the demographic transition and other social forces—urbanization, economic growth, increased female education and labor force participation—produces changing household structures. The enormous worldwide variability in family and household structure makes it difficult to generalize about patterns of change. Nevertheless, it is fair to say that the latter half of the twentieth century has been characterized by declining household size and a trend toward the nuclear family.

Lowered fertility and increased migration have reduced average household size in both developed and developing countries and led to more dispersed family networks. At the same time, increasing proportions of persons are living alone in single-person households. This is partially due to normative changes—delayed marriage and changing gender roles—but is also related to higher rates of marital dissolution and growing numbers of elderly persons whose spouses have died (see Hareven, this volume). The end result is that the number of households in many countries is growing faster than the total population.

The most prominent change in household profiles in developed countries has been the trend toward single-person households. In Sweden, more than a third of all households consist of a single individual. In rapidly aging Japan, the percentage of single-person households rose from 5% in 1960 to 21% in 1985 (UNDIESA, 1990). In addition to having an effect on aggregate saving and spending patterns in a given society, the rise in single-person households shifts a society's caregiving equation as fewer and geographically dispersed children are available for traditional family support functions.

Table 3.2 presents proportions of persons aged 65 years and over (unless otherwise noted) who live alone in 57 countries. These figures refer to persons living in what typically are private, noninstitutional households. In developed countries, the proportions range from a low of 10% in Japan to more than 38% in Denmark, Sweden, and what was West Germany. Considerable variation exists within Europe, with the younger countries (in terms of percentage of total population aged 65 years and over)—Spain; Portugal; Ireland; and, to a lesser extent, Greece—exhibiting the lowest rates of single habitation.

Among older individuals, living alone is most often the result of having outlived a spouse and even children or siblings (Kasper, 1988). Consequently, the likelihood of living alone increases with age, although a decline might occur at the oldest ages, especially among women. The decline might be explained by the fact that some of the oldest-old obtain care within institutions, whereas others might seek additional income and/or assistance in maintaining a home by taking in a companion or boarder. Because women on average outlive men and tend to be younger than their spouses, it is not surprising to find that in all older age groups the percentage of women living alone is usually much higher than that of men. Cross-tabulations of marital status and living arrangements are not commonplace, but data from New Zealand and the United States reinforce the intuitive impression that most elderly women living alone are widows—roughly 80% in both countries. Hence, it has become a truism that in most developed countries, women should anticipate a period of living alone at some point during their older years.

Both numbers and proportions of elderly people living alone have risen sharply during the past three decades. Data from Canada illustrate the trend common to most developed countries that the increase in absolute numbers largely consists of women. The 1986 Canadian census recorded 526,000 elderly women living alone, or 200,000 more than a decade earlier. Put in different terms, the number of women living alone grew at an average annual rate of 6.3% from 1961 to 1986. The rate of growth for the entire Canadian population during this period was 1.3%.

In spite of the frequently high proportions of elderly who live alone in developed countries, the fact remains that a majority of those aged 65 years and over live with other persons. Comparable data for 12 Western and Southern European nations from the early 1980s showed that the proportion of elderly that lived with one other elderly person only (in most cases, a spouse) was higher than the proportion that lived singly. The share of elderly population residing with only one other elderly person varied widely, from just under 22% in Ireland to 41% in the United Kingdom. Between 10% and 15% of elderly adults in the 12 European nations lived

Table 3.2

Percent of Household Population Age 65 Years and Older (unless Noted) Living Alone: Latest Available Data, 1980–1990

EUROPE

Austria, 1980 (60+)	30.9
Belgium, 1981	31.9
Czechoslovakia, 1983 (60+)	32.4
Denmark, 1981	38.3
France, 1982	32.6
Germany (West), 1982	38.9
Greece, 1981	14.7
Hungary, 1984	24.8
Ireland, 1981	20.1
Italy, 1981	25.0
Luxembourg, 1981	22.6
Malta, 1980 (60+)	10.5
Netherlands, 1982	31.3
Poland, 1988 (60+)	36.2
Portugal, 1981	17.7
Spain, 1981	14.1
Sweden, 1982	40.0
United Kingdom, 1989	35.8

CARIBBEAN

Barbados, 1982	27.1
British Virgin Is., 1980	20.4
Cuba, 1981	10.0
Dominica, 1980	18.6
Grenada, 1981	21.0
Guadeloupe, 1982	32.4
Jamaica, 1984	23.0
Martinique, 1982	30.6
Montserrat, 1980	25.2
St. Lucia, 1980	19.7
St. Vincent, 1980	16.5
Trinidad/Tobago, 1985 (60+)	13.6
Turks and Caicos, 1980	17.9

OTHER DEVELOPED

Australia, 1981	26.2
Canada, 1986	27.7
Japan, 1985	9.7
New Zealand, 1981	26.4
United States, 1990	31.0

ASIA

China (PRC), 1987 (60+)	3.4
Indonesia, 1986 (60+)	8.0
Israel, 1985	26.1
Korea, Rep. 1984 (60+)	2.2
Malaysia, 1986 (60+)	6.4
Philippines, 1984 (60+)	3.0
Singapore, 1986 (60+)	2.3
Sri Lanka, 1987 (60+)	7.6
Taiwan, 1989	8.9
Thailand, 1986	6.4

CENTRAL/SOUTH AMERICA

Argentina, 1980	12.0
Brazil, 1908	9.8
Chile, 1984-85 (60+)	7.0
Costa Rica, 1985-86	6.9
French Guiana, 1982	40.0
Mexico, 1981 (60+)	6.4
Uruguay, 1985	16.2

OTHER

Cote d'Ivoire, 1986	2.8
Fiji, 1984 (60+)	2.0
Kenya, 1983 (50+)	16.1
Reunion, 1982	23.3

Source: Compiled at the Center for International Research, U.S. Bureau of the Census from primary census and survey volumes, international compendia, and published research.

Notes: Chile and Czechoslovakia—refer to urban areas; rural Czech percentage is 24.5. *Hungary* refers to pensioners and persons of retirement age. *Sweden* refers to pensioners, with usual pension age being 65 years. *United Kingdom* refers to men 65 years and over, women 60 years and over. *Costa Rica* refers to two cantons only. *Mexico* refers to urban and suburban elderly in four states. *Jamaica* refers to a single urban community of Kingston. *Indonesia* refers to the island of Java. *Malaysia* refers to three Peninsular states. *Kenya* refers to three districts only (Nairobi, Kakamega, Machakos).

with one other person younger than 65 years of age; many of these elders were likely to be either men living with a younger spouse or widowed and divorced persons living with a child. The next most common household arrangement was a single elderly person residing with two or three other persons under age 65 years; this group ranged from only 3% or 4% in Denmark and the Netherlands to 14% in Greece. Small proportions of elderly people (under 3%) lived in three-person households where all members were aged 65 years or over.

Although many factors are related to the changing likelihood of elderly persons' living alone or with their spouse only, rising income appears to be the primary vehicle that affords older individuals the opportunity to maintain households apart from younger family members. The desire for intimacy at a distance is frequently cited in Western gerontological literature. One cross-national study of the propensity of older women to live alone confirms the importance of income and posits that economic factors (income per capita and housing stock per capita) are more pivotal than demographic forces in producing change in residence patterns over time (Wolf, 1990).

Japan is unique among developed countries insofar as a high proportion of older adults—65% in 1985—reside with one or more of their offspring. Three national sample surveys taken during the 1980s showed that roughly one-half of persons aged 60 and over lived with married children, another 20% lived with unmarried children, 22% resided with their spouse only, and the remaining 10% lived alone. The high prevalence of cohabitation with married children is an indication of Japan's traditional *stem family,* which in classic form consists of a married couple living with their unmarried children, the eldest son, his wife, and their grandchildren. In rural areas, such an arrangement is still typical (Kamo, 1988).

Most nonstatistical writing on living arrangements of the elderly in developing countries asserts that relatively few elderly individuals live alone. Although this assertion appears to be true on balance, regional differences are apparent from Table 3.2. In the Caribbean, which in toto is the oldest of the world's developing regions, between one-fifth and one-third of many elderly populations live alone. Asian countries have higher proportions of older women than men living alone, but in the Caribbean, older men are more likely than older women to live singly. This difference might be related to patterns of migration and marital status unique to parts of the Caribbean region.

In all other developing regions of the world, the paramount living arrangement for elderly persons is with children, with or without grandchildren. Available Latin American data from the 1970s and 1980s indicate that a majority of persons aged 60 years and over lived in *complex family* households consisting of members who belong to more than one conjugal unit (e.g., an older couple, a married child, and grandchildren). Roughly one-fourth to one-fifth of older persons lived in *simple family* households (a married couple or unmarried individual living with unmarried child(ren)), although in Uruguay and urban Chile this proportion was as high as for complex households. In several Latin American nations, time series data reveal declining proportions of elderly in complex (extended) households and greater shares of persons living alone or in nuclear families, reminiscent of the historic trend observed in developed countries.

Surveys in Asia and the Pacific show aggregate residence patterns similar to those observed in Latin America. According to findings from 1984 World Health Organization surveys, in Malaysia, the Philippines, Fiji, and the Republic of Korea, between 72% and 79% of older respondents (aged 60 and over) lived with children (Andrews, Esterman, Braunack-Mayer, & Rungie, 1986). The figures for Malaysia and the Philippines were reconfirmed in later surveys, and similar results have been observed in Indonesia and Singapore. The percentage living with spouse ranged from only 6% in the Philippines to 15% in Indonesia (ASEAN, 1988).

With regard to determinants of living arrangements, data from both Latin America and Asia suggest that marital status is the strongest demographic determinant of whether an older person lives in a complex family household. As might be expected, spouse survival reduces the likelihood of living with children. At the same time, availability of children reduces the likelihood of spouse-only arrangements. Of more interest are associations involving age, sex, education, and urban versus rural residence. The effects of these variables on living arrangements in Latin America appear ambiguous, with no clear trends evident among countries (De Vos, 1990; Christenson & Hermalin, 1989). In Asian nations, males and young-old adults were generally more likely to live with their children than were females or old-old persons (Martin, 1988). This is surprising in view of the commonly held notion that the latter two categories of the elderly population tend to be the most vulnerable in terms of spousal availability and economic resources and, therefore, most in need of support from offspring (unless other relatives provide support). Where urban residence influenced living arrangements, it did so by increasing coresidence with children. This has been observed in other studies (UNDIESA, 1985) and might be related to shortages and high costs of housing in urban areas of developing countries.

Such information hints at the diversity of living arrangements found throughout the developing world. A more detailed portrayal of differences emerges from a comparison of communities in seven countries, part of a United Nations University project (Social Support Systems in Transition) that assembles comparative data on living arrangements in disparate contexts. Although the data refer only to single communities in each nation, the sites are at different stages of urbanization and might reveal differences in patterns of adaptation to the urbanization process as a result of differing social and historical conditions (Hashimoto, 1991).

Several observations arise from a comparative view of the seven communities. The importance of coresidence with family members in both urban and rural settings is reaffirmed, but the proportion of elderly persons (aged 60 years and over) who live with family members of direct descent is highest in the four Asian countries (India, the Republic of Korea, Singapore, and Thailand), more so than in Egypt, Zimbabwe, and Brazil. The stem family predominates in the Asian communities, whereas in Zimbabwe the *skip-generation* arrangement (elderly without children but with grandchildren) is most common. Nuclear households predominate in urban Egyptian and Brazilian communities, and the relatively high share of single and conjugal (spouse-only) households in the Brazilian case indicates a pattern very different from that of the other samples. As might be expected, the likelihood of residing with a married child increases with age in all seven communities. Not as expectedly, the percentage of elderly living alone also increases with age.

The foregoing summary reflects the importance of cultural norms that define family types and the resulting effects on living arrangements. In Cote d'Ivoire, very few old men or women live alone, but for very different reasons. For men, it is difficult to become a widower because polygamy is increasingly common across age groups until late in life; nearly a third of men aged 65 to 74 years have more than one wife, and 13% of men aged 70 to 74 years have three or more wives (Deaton & Paxson, 1991). Hence, more than 80% of elderly men live in households with at least one spouse. In stark contrast, 71% of elderly women are widowed and live either with their children, with a brother's family, or with more distantly related relatives.

Data for the developing world generally are insufficient for documenting changes over time in living arrangements of the elderly. Existing information tends to support the assumption that the family (in its various cultural forms) provides direct support for the vast majority of older persons. A commonly voiced concern in developing nations, however, is that the twin processes of modernization and industrialization are shaking traditional family structures and threatening to create, as a by-product, a marginalized class of older citizens. We know that in many countries, rural areas have become disproportionately older as young adults migrate to urban centers in search of employment (Kinsella, 1988). Beyond anecdotal information, however, it is not yet clear what impact this migration of the young has an older rural residents.

Although the case of Japan does not appear immediately relevant to the situation of developing countries, the extended family structure common to developing countries historically has been a feature of Japanese society. Even after the rapid post–World War II period of economic development and subsequent fertility decline, the large numbers of elderly Japanese persons living with their married children challenge the contention that the nuclear family might be an inevitable product of industrialization. Nevertheless, time series data clearly show that the number and proportion of extended-family households are decreasing (Way, 1984; Wada, 1988), whereas the proportion of childless elderly couples is rising—from 7% in 1960 to 18% in 1985 to a projected level of 30% in the early twenty-first century (Sodei, 1991). These trends have led one author to suggest that the effects of industrialization are so strong that the indigenous culture of Japan vis-à-vis the status of elderly citizens is steadily being undermined in favor of nuclear families (Kamo, 1988). One result of this nuclearization process was identified by Burgess (1986), who reported that significant numbers of elderly people lead "destitute, solitary lives. More than 900,000 women aged 65 years and over live alone in Japan, many of them scraping by on meager pensions, doing menial work, dreaming of getting into shabby government nursing homes" (p. A21).

Changing Social Support Ratios

The notion of social support is at the heart of policy planning for aging populations. Changing modes of family support and care for older members might have considerable economic impact on the role of government. Much of the difficulty in planning for evolving social support burdens is related to the complex and shifting nature of the concept. A substantial number of researchers have addressed intergenerational solidarity, familial obligations, and kinship relations—all of which vary by cultural context—but the heterogeneity of results has precluded firm conclusions (Antonucci, 1990; Bengtson et al., 1990).

Demographic assessments of intergenerational support often have focused on social support ratios, also known as dependency ratios. Such ratios are seen as indicative of economic dependency within a society and of potential problems concerning provision of health and social services, pension benefits, adequate housing, and (indirectly) family relationships. One such measure, the *elderly support ratio,* relates in a crude fashion the number of persons aged 65 and over to the size of the working-age population aged 20 to 64 years. The combination of declining fertility and increasing longevity has produced rising elderly support ratios in most developed countries. Because the large baby boom cohorts are still of working age, however, the rise has been, and will continue to be, modest in most countries until after the turn of the century. In France, the United Kingdom, Australia, the United States, and several other developed nations, elderly support ratios of the 1990s will increase 10% to 15% by the year 2010. However, between 2010 and 2025 the rise will be 35% to 50% as the large working-age cohorts begin to retire (Figure 3.3). By 2025, Japan's elderly support ratio will be nearing 50, and many European countries are projected to be in the 40-to-46 range.

Figure 3.3
Elderly Support Ratios

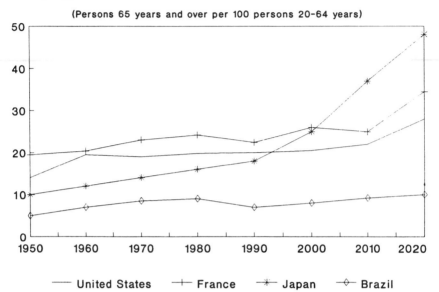

(Persons 65 years and over per 100 persons 20-64 years)

─── **United States**   ─┼─ **France**   ─✳─ **Japan**   ─◇─ **Brazil**

In contrast, the majority of developing countries will experience little, if any, change in their elderly support ratios during the next 20 years. This is because the high-fertility cohorts of the 1960s and 1970s will still be in the denominator of the ratio (i.e., under the age of 65). In countries as varied as Zimbabwe, Jamaica, Israel, and Pakistan, the elderly support ratio is expected to decline by 2010, even though the absolute numbers of elderly population are increasing. Eastern and Southeastern Asia and parts of Latin America, on the other hand, will see real change over the next three to four decades. The elderly support ratio is projected to double between now and 2025 in China, Indonesia, Thailand, Brazil, Colombia, and Costa Rica and to more than triple in South Korea and Singapore.

The major flaw in standard dependency ratios is the implicit assumption that age itself indicates need for support. Although this assumption essentially might be true at younger ages, concepts of the traditional needs of elderly adults are being challenged by prolonged health, enhanced financial security, and new forms of social organization. In countries with well-established pension and Social Security programs, many elderly adults are now providing increasing support—instrumental and emotional—to adult children who have run afoul of economic recession, broken marriages, and lack of affordable housing. In developing countries where elderly citizens' economic assets are minimal, aged adults contribute to family maintenance in ways ranging from socialization, housekeeping, and child care to some-times-exclusive responsibility for child rearing. Such activities free younger adult women for both modern-sector and agricultural production (Hashimoto, Kendig, & Coppard, 1992). Thus it is important to realize that many elderly people are not dependent on younger ones, and when dependency does occur, it may be episodic rather than permanent.

Caretaker Ratios

Given the affective nature of family relations and embedded conceptions of member support, demographic analyses have moved beyond the crude category of elderly support ratios. An alternative approach examines *caretaker* or *familial support ratios,* measures that relate one generation to another. Several such ratios can be constructed across an age spectrum, depending on the generations under study. For purposes of this chapter, the caretaker ratio is the ratio of the population aged 80 years and over—those most likely to be in need of long-term care and economic support—to the population aged 50 to 64 years, which, in a general sense, relates the oldest-old to their offspring who were born when most of the oldest-old were 20 to 35 years old.

Potential caretaker ratios evolve very differently both within and among world regions. In most developing countries, the ratio of persons aged 80 years and over to those aged 50 to 64 years was between 3% and 6% in 1950. In East and Southeast Asia, this ratio has risen slowly during the past 40 years but will increase significantly in the next 35 years; by 2025, Japan's ratio will be nearing 50. In South Asia, however, the rise has been, and will continue to be, slight. In Latin America, the historical and projected rise appears more constant across time, whereas in Africa, most countries will see little future change in the ratio, even though oldest-old populations are growing rapidly. The most dramatic changes have occurred in the industrialized world; in the Scandinavian and several other countries (including the United States), the ratio is now greater than 20. In some nations, especially in Eastern Europe, the ratio will continue to rise sharply through 2025, whereas other developed countries will see little change over the next three decades.

Women traditionally have been the primary care providers for elderly parents, and this remains true (UNDIESA, 1990; Sundstrom, 1986). Examining the ratio of persons aged 80 years and over to *women* aged 50 to 64 years reveals patterns similar to those just mentioned, but the ratios are, of course, much higher. Projections to the year 2025 suggest that Japan will have 91 persons aged 80 years and over per 100 women aged 50 to 64 years, with most other developed-country ratios in the 60-to-76 range.

Reduced Kin Availability

Living with other people reduces the likelihood of using formal medical care and increases the use of informal care, at least in the U.S. context

(Cafferata, 1988). Because most physical, emotional, and economic care to older individuals is provided by family members, the demography of population aging is increasingly concerned with understanding and modeling *kin availability* (the number of family members that will potentially be available to elderly individuals if and when various forms of care are needed).[6] Although smaller families obviously imply fewer potential caregivers, this is offset to some extent by increased population longevity and caregiver survival. Modeling is further complicated by the fact that whereas demographic forces impose constraints on family, household, and kin structures, these structures also are determined by social and cultural factors (Myers, 1992).

The consensus to date foresees a declining biological kinship support network for elderly persons in developed and some developing countries. In addition, future older cohorts are likely to live at greater distances from their children, perhaps resulting in decreased face-to-face interaction (Crimmins & Ingegneri, 1990). We know, however, that decreased coresidence has not necessarily led to less familial interaction; patterns of reciprocal support continue to characterize older people and their children (Mancini & Blieszner, 1989).

Research on prospective kin availability is now expanding in the context of developing countries. This is particularly true in East and Southeast Asian countries, driven in large part by the rapid declines in fertility that have greatly reduced the average family size of young-adult cohorts. The complex interplay of demographic and cultural factors is illustrated by the case of the Republic of (South) Korea, where two-thirds of the elderly are economically dependent on their adult children (Korea Institute for Health and Social Affairs, 1991) and where cultural norms dictate that sons provide economic support for elderly women who have lost their husbands.

Lee and Palloni (1992) showed that although declining fertility results in an increase in the proportion of South Korean women with no surviving son, increased male longevity means that the proportion of elderly widows also will decline (their husbands will live longer). Thus from the elderly woman's point of view, family status will not deteriorate significantly in the coming years. From society's perspective, however, the demand for support of elderly women will increase, because the momentum of rapid population aging means that the fraction of the overall population that is elderly women (especially sonless and childless widows) will increase among successive cohorts. Given the strong trend toward nuclearization of family structure in the Republic of Korea and the traditional absence of state involvement in socioeconomic support, the future standard of living for a growing number of elderly widows is tenuous. A similar prospect looms in Taiwan and Japan (Tu & Liang, 1988; Hermalin, Ofstedal, & Chang, 1992; Burgess, 1986) and, to a lesser extent, in numerous developing nations worldwide.

In spite of gloomy predictions regarding family support in developing countries, most nations will have favorable demographic support ratios for the next several decades. High-fertility population cohorts of the recent past will swell the ranks of working-age populations in many countries at, or shortly after, the turn of the century, thereby providing a large potential tax base for social support at both ends of the age spectrum. In theory, rising family incomes will allow adult children to fulfill obligations to aged parents even if extended family structures become less prevalent and economies modernize.

DIRECTIONS FOR FUTURE RESEARCH

As populations age, the economic dimensions of social support take on added importance. At the heart of many current debates is the issue of the proper mix of public versus private economic support for older citizens. Researchers of aging and the family should seek to inform the policy debate via an integration of demographic and economic perspectives. For example, studies show that patterns of reciprocity and support exist among family members in all societies. More information is needed, however, about the economic sufficiency of such patterns (for all parties involved), as well as their variability within a given society. One overarching research goal should be the identification of patterns of economic vulnerability in old age and the social aspects (e.g., class, gender, economic status, parental status) that correlate with individual and familial vulnerability.

In addition to identifying vulnerable family types, research needs to anticipate the changing profile of future families. Wider application of family-status life tables (e.g., Yi, 1988) and microsimulation methodologies (e.g., Yang, 1992; UNDIESA, 1990) could give policy planners concrete scenarios of expected kinship structures and living arrangements. Another, even more promising methodology is the cohort approach to population-based forecasts (e.g., Stone & Ng, 1992), wherein inter- and intracohort heterogeneity can be measured, analyzed, and accounted for when projecting variables such as joint kin survival and health service use requirements.

In addition, it is important to link demographic trends in population aging with an analysis of housing options, housing availability, and the housing needs and desires of end users. Housing is an important variable in the income support and care of older persons in the community, yet housing outcomes in old age are largely dictated by economic and planning decisions not directed toward older people (Kendig, 1990).

Finally, policy options and outcomes that already exist must be used in the preparation for demographic change. Although new programs will surely evolve, they should emerge from assessments and evaluations of extant efforts (e.g., tax incentives, home assistance schemes, self-help programs) to assist families vis-à-vis support and care of elderly members. As has been noted in a variety of cultural contexts, current evaluations of outcomes are based more on expectations and hopes of policymakers than on objective, scientific evidence (Hashimoto et al., 1992). This is especially true in many developing countries where official pronouncements routinely refer to the need to strengthen traditional family structures but ignore the indisputable social forces that have altered such structures throughout the world.

NOTES

The views expressed in this chapter are those of the author and do not necessarily represent the views of the U.S. Census Bureau.

1. For a discussion of difficulties involved in cross-national comparisons of the family, see Myers (1992). For an excellent summary of diversity in family structure within a single nation—the United States—see Bengtson, Rosenthal, and Burton (1990).

2. The "developed" and "developing" country categories used in this chapter correspond directly to the "more developed" and "less developed" classification employed by the United Nations. Developed countries comprise all nations in Europe (including the former Soviet Union) and North America, plus Australia, Japan, and New Zealand. The remaining nations of the world are considered to be developing countries.

3. To facilitate comparisons among countries, the admittedly heterogeneous term *elderly* refers to all persons aged 65 years or over.

4. Unless otherwise noted, projected population figures in this chapter are those of the Center for International Research, U.S. Bureau of the Census, as of midyear 1992.

5. Overall figures in the United States are much lower, although among black women aged 35 to 39, 25% had never married as of 1990.

6. Numerous analytic and simulation models of kinship structure have been generated since the mid-1970s. See Wolf (1988) for an overview of such models and a microsimulation methodology applied to developed countries and Yang (1992) for a developing country example (rural China).

REFERENCES

In addition to the following sources, primary census and survey publications of individual nations were used to calculate many of the statistics in this chapter. The majority of these data are contained in an International Data Base on Aging; see Kinsella & Taeuber (1993) for further information.

Andrews, G., Esterman, A. J., Braunack-Mayer, A. J., & Rungie, C. M. (1986). *Aging in the Western Pacific; A four country study* (Western Pacific Reports and Studies No. 1). Manila: World Health Organization Regional Office for the Western Pacific.
Antonucci, T. C. (1990). Social supports and social relationships. In R. H. Binstock

& L. K. George (Eds.), *Handbook of aging and the social sciences* (3rd ed., pp. 205–226). San Diego: Academic Press.

Association of South East Asian Nations (ASEAN). (1988). *Socioeconomic consequences of the ageing of the population* (Phase III Population Project, Inter-Country Final Report.) Jakarta: ASEAN.

Bengtson, V., Rosenthal, C., & Burton, L. (1990). Families and aging: diversity and heterogeneity. In R. H. Binstock & L. K. George (Eds.), *Handbook of aging and the social sciences* (3rd ed., pp. 263–287). San Diego: Academic Press.

Burgess, J. (1986, October 12). Japan faces "graying" of population. *Washington Post*, A21.

Cafferata, G. (1988). Marital status, living arrangements, and the use of health services by elderly persons. *Journal of Gerontology: Social Sciences, 42,* S613–618.

Caselli, G., Vallin, J., Vaupel, J. W., & Yashin, A. (1987). Age-specific mortality trends in France and Italy since 1900: Period and cohort effects. *European Journal of Population, 3,* 33–60.

Christenson, B., & Hermalin, A. (1989, November). *A demographic decomposition of elderly living arrangements: A Mexican example.* Paper presented at the 42nd Annual Scientific Meeting of the Gerontological Society of America, Minneapolis.

Corder, L. (1992, June). *National long term care survey.* Paper presented to the Inter-Agency Forum on Aging Related Statistics, U.S. National Institute on Aging, Bethesda, MD.

Crimmins, E. M., & Ingegneri, D. G. (1990). Interaction and living arrangements of older parents and their children. *Research on Aging, 12,* 3–35.

Deaton, A., & Paxson, C. (1991). *Patterns of aging in Thailand and Cote d'Ivoire* (Living Standards Measurement Study Working Paper No. 81). Washington, DC: World Bank.

De Vos, S. (1990). Extended family living among older people in six Latin American countries. *Journal of Gerontology: Social Sciences, 45,* S87–94.

Doty, P. (1988). Long-term care in international perspective. *Health Care Financing Review* (Annual Supplement), 145–155.

Frenk, J., Frejka, T., Bobadilla, J. L, Stern, C., Sepulveda, J., & Jose, M. (1989). The epidemiologic transition in Latin America. In *International Population Conference, New Delhi* (Vol. 1, pp. 419–431). Liege, Belgium: International Union for the Scientific Study of Population.

Gonnot, J.-P., & Vukovich, G. (1989). *Recent trends in living arrangements in fourteen industrialized countries* (Working paper 89–34). Laxenburg, Austria: International Institute for Applied Systems Analysis.

Hashimoto, A. (1991). Urbanization and changes in living arrangements of the elderly. In *Ageing and urbanization* (pp. 307–328). New York: United Nations. (ST/ESA/SER.R/109)

Hashimoto, A., Kendig, H. L., & Coppard, L. (1992). Family support to the elderly in international perspective. In H. L. Kendig, A. Hashimoto, & L. Coppard (Eds.), *Family support for the elderly: The international experience* (pp. 293–308). Oxford: Oxford University Press.

Hermalin, A., Ofstedal, M. B., & Chang, M.-C. (1992). Types of supports for the aged and their providers in Taiwan. *Comparative study of the elderly in Asia*

(Research Report 92-14). Ann Arbor: University of Michigan Population Studies Center.

International Labour Office (ILO). (1989). *From pyramid to pillar. Population change and social security in Europe.* Geneva: International Labour Organization.

Kamo, Y. (1988). A note on elderly living arrangements in Japan and the United States. *Research on Aging, 10,* 297–305.

Kasper, J. D. (1988). *Aging alone. Profiles and projections.* Baltimore: Commonwealth Fund Commission on Elderly People Living Alone.

Kendig, H. L. (1990). Comparative perspectives on housing, aging, and social structure. In R. H. Binstock & L. K. George (Eds.), *Handbook of aging and the social sciences* (3rd ed., pp. 288–306). San Diego: Academic Press.

Kinsella, K. (1988). *Aging in the third world* (U.S. Bureau of the Census International Population Report No. 79). Washington, DC: U.S. Government Printing Office.

Kinsella, K., & Taeuber, C. (1993). *An aging world II* (U.S. Bureau of the Census International Population Report No. P95/92–3). Washington, DC: U.S. Government Printing Office.

Korea Institute for Health and Social Affairs. (1991). *KIHASA Bulletin,* Number 21. Seoul: Institute for Health and Social Affairs.

Lee, Y.-J., & Palloni, A. (1992). Changes in the family status of elderly women in Korea. *Demography, 29,* 69–92.

Liu, K., & Manton, K. (1985, June). *Disability and long-term care.* Paper presented at the workshop on Methodologies of Forecasting Life and Active Life Expectancy, U.S. National Institute on Aging, Bethesda, MD.

Lopez, A. (1990, July). Mortality trends in the ECE region: Prospects and implications. *Seminar on Demographic and Economic Consequences and Implications of Changing Population Age Structures.* Ottawa: United Nations Economic Commission for Europe.

Mancini, J. A., & Blieszner, R. (1989). Aging parents and adult children: Research themes in intergenerational relations. *Journal of Marriage and the Family, 51,* 275–290.

Martin, L. (1988). *Living arrangements of the elderly in Fiji, Korea, Malaysia, and the Philippines.* Honolulu: East-West Population Institute.

Myers, G. (1990). Cross-national patterns and trends in marital status among the elderly. In *Populations agees et revolution grise* (pp. 469–481). Louvain-La-Neuve: Université Catholique de Louvain.

Myers, G. (1992). Demographic aging and family support for older persons. In H. L. Kendig, A. Hashimoto, & L. Coppard (Eds.), *Family support for the elderly: The international experience* (pp. 31–68). Oxford: Oxford University Press.

Myers, G., & Nathanson, C. (1982). Aging and the family. *World Health Statistics Quarterly, 35,* 225–238.

Omran, A. R. (1971). The epidemiologic transition: A theory of the epidemiology of population change. *Milbank Memorial Fund Quarterly, 49,* 509–538.

Pan American Health Organization (PAHO). (1990). *Health conditions in the*

Americas (1990 ed., Vol. 1). Washington, DC: Pan American Health Organization.

Rice, D. (1984). Long-term care of the elderly and the disabled. *Long-term care and social security* (Studies and Research No. 21). Geneva: International Social Security Association.

Robine, J.-M. (1991, June). *Changes in health conditions over time.* Fourth workgroup meeting of the International Research Network on Healthy Life Expectancy, Noordwijkerhout, the Netherlands.

Ruggles, S. (1987). *Prolonged connections: The rise of the extended family in nineteenth-century England and America.* Madison: University of Wisconsin Press.

Siampos, G. (1990). Trends and future prospects of the female overlife by regions in Europe. *Statistical Journal of the United Nations Economic Commission for Europe, 7,* 13–25.

Sodei, T. (1991). *Elderly people living alone in Japan.* New York: International Leadership Center on Longevity and Society.

Stone, L., & Ng, E. (1992). *New approaches to decomposition of population aging.* Ottawa: Analytical Studies Branch, Statistics Canada.

Sundstrom, G. (1986). Family and state: Recent trends in the care of the aged in Sweden. *Ageing and Society, 6,* 169–196.

Taeuber, C. (1992). *Sixty-five plus in America* (U.S. Bureau of the Census Current Population Reports, Series P-23, No. 178). Washington, DC: U.S. Government Printing Office.

Tu, E.J.C., & Liang, J. (1988, April). *Demographic transition, kinship structure and population aging in Taiwan.* Paper presented at the Annual Meeting of the Population Association of America, New Orleans.

United Nations Department of International Economic and Social Affairs (UN-DIESA). (1985). *The world aging situation: Strategies and policies.* New York: United Nations.

United Nations Department of International Economic and Social Affairs (UN-DIESA). (1988, September). *Economic and social implications of population aging.* Proceedings of the International Symposium on Population Structure and Development, Tokyo. New York: United Nations. (ST/ESA/SER.R/85)

United Nations Department of International Economic and Social Affairs (UN-DIESA). (1990, October). *Overview of recent research findings on population aging and the family.* United Nations International Conference on Aging Populations in the Context of the Family, Kitakyushu. New York: United Nations. (IESA/P/AC.33/6)

Wada, S. (1988). Daily life in later life in the changing Japanese context. In K. Altergott (Ed.), *Daily life in later life: Comparative perspectives* (pp. 205–228). Newbury Park, CA: Sage.

Way, P. (1984). *Issues and implications of the aging Japanese population* (Center for International Research Staff Paper No. 6). Washington, DC: U.S. Bureau of the Census.

Wolf, D. (1990). Household patterns of older women: Some international comparisons. *Research on Aging, 12,* 463–486.

Wolf, D. A. (1988). Kinship and family support in aging societies. *Economic and social implications of population aging* (pp. 305–330). New York: United Nations (ST/ESA/SER.R/85).

Yang, H. (1992). Population dynamics and kinship of the Chinese rural elderly: A microsimulation study. *Journal of Cross-Cultural Gerontology, 7,* 135–150.

Yi, Z. (1988). Changing demographic characteristics and the family status of Chinese women. *Population Studies, 42,* 183–203.

Part II

THEORETICAL FRAMEWORKS AND RESEARCH METHODS

4

The Family of the Second Half of Life: Connecting Theories and Findings

Bertram J. Cohler and Karen Altergott

Much has been written about the dramatic changes that have taken place in the constellation of the American family since the end of World War II (Bane, 1976; Glick, 1988; Masnick & Bane, 1980; Popenoe, 1988). Social changes across the past three decades have highlighted the importance of better understanding such pressing issues as the rise in single-parent households, the significance for personal and social life of families of choice, the reality of reconstituted families, the delay in marriage and family formation, and increased consideration of voluntary childlessness among married couples (Veevers, 1979). At the same time, most adults still choose to marry, and most married couples elect to have children (Blumstein & Schwartz, 1983; Whyte, 1990). Parenthood and grandparenthood continue as cardinal roles in the lives of most adults (Bengtson & Robertson, 1985; Bengtson & Treas, 1980; Cherlin & Furstenberg, 1986; Cohler & Grunebaum, 1981; LaRossa & LaRossa, 1981). Families continue to provide both reciprocal socialization between generations and multiple forms of support and assistance across and within generations in spite of substantial changes in family structure (Glass, Bengtson, & Dunham, 1986; Hagestad, 1982; Rossi & Rossi, 1991).

With the aging of the population and large numbers of much older men and women living independently, study of the family of later life has increased. This research has added to understanding of both continuity and change in lives over time and also the impact of family life upon morale among generations within the family (Brody, 1990; Shanas, 1979a). In this chapter we consider the significance of aging within family and society for the construction of theories about family life. This discussion points to the need to understand the place of family within the social order in a manner that more adequately reflects the importance of relations among adult generations in the study of personal development and family process across the life course.

CONNECTED REALITIES: AGING IN A FAMILY CONTEXT

In large part as a consequence of the significance of the family for the socialization of young children, much of both family study and family theory across the past half-century has focused on family formation and relations within the family of the first half of life (Bengtson & Allen, 1993; Troll & Bengtson, 1979). With the aging of society following World War II, however, interest in research on the family of the adult years has increased. For the first time, families might include five generations, showing the significance of studying relations across multiple adult generations (Bengtson, Rosenthal, & Burton, 1990; Hill, Foote, Aldous, Carlson, & MacDonald, 1970; Troll, Miller, & Atchley, 1979). Nevertheless, systematic study of relations across the generations has had little impact on theories of family and society; to date, much of family theory continues to focus on such issues as mate selection, transition to parenthood, and dual-career family life among young adults, while paying much less attention to such issues as the role of grandparents or the significance of continuing contact and support among younger, middle-aged, and older adults within the family (Berger & Berger, 1983).

For example, many young adults lived with their parents during the 1980s rather than leaving home to form independent households. Other adults returned home due to changes in economic or family status. In either case, both parents and adult offspring renegotiated roles, faced mixed sentiments, and experienced problems, as well as benefits, from living in a shared household. If the return home were due to such misfortune as alcoholism, mental illness, or unemployment, the costs to the older generation might be high indeed (Greenberg & Becker, 1988). From the birth of a grandchild and other expectable life changes to those unexpected and generally adverse events such as illness or death of a family member, life changes affect all generations (Pruchno, Blow, & Smyer, 1984).

Family events, positive and negative, have transformed the aging experience of adults in the twentieth century. At the same time, the aging of society has transformed relations within the family. The impact of increases in longevity has been noted by historians and demographers (see Dwyer, this volume; Kinsella, this volume). Now larger numbers of persons are surviving through childhood and adulthood and into very late life than in previous times (Bould, Sanborn, & Reif, 1989; Uhlenberg, 1980). Concomitant changes in both family structure and life course experiences have been recognized widely and repeatedly by gerontologists over the last 30 years of analysis of aging and the family (Rosenmayr & Kockeis, 1963). Yet, challenges posed for the family of the second half of life have been neglected in family scholarship. To the extent that intergenerational relations are considered, focus has been largely on the burdens posed for middle-aged women caring simultaneously for still-dependent offspring and newly dependent parents (e.g., Brody, 1985, 1990). The aging of society has too often been associated with problem rather than promise. Discussions of policy in aging industrial societies also often assume aging is an inevitable decline, with accompanying burden on social services and health resources.

This portrayal of aging and decline is contradicted by many realities. For example, even among those over age 85, about half live independently in their own homes, and less than a quarter of even frail elderly adults must be relocated to long-term care facilities (Bould et al., 1989). The reality of contemporary family life includes older family members as continuing sources of socialization, caregiving, and financial support for younger generations. Older family members might provide the assistance that makes it possible for some parents of young children to pursue employment, while ensuring continuity of care and a source of both emotional and financial assistance during times of family emergency (Hill et al., 1970; Kamerman, 1980). The idea that older adults pose only burdens for other family members or are socially isolated from contacts with other family members appears to be more myth than reality (Shanas, 1979a, 1979b).

Changes in family forms and the extension of the life span make it necessary to integrate family and gerontological scholarship in new ways. Creating a theoretical framework that encompasses both family theory and research on individual aging would be useful for promoting understanding, for informing policy discussions, and for generating new scholarship regarding families across the second half of life. This theoretical framework would be especially useful as service providers, policy analysts, and scholars address family issues into the twenty-first century. In fact, without adequately conceptualizing the family during the second half of life, understanding of the family and its relation to society is incomplete. Within such realms as labor force, law, health care, and social services, decisions at local and national levels based on a misunderstanding of families could make it more difficult for families to meet the needs of members of all generations (see Harrington Meyer & Bellas, this volume).

The limits of existing theories are particularly evident in practice whenever the impact of divorce on children is studied without recognition of the role of grandparents (see Robertson, this volume), whenever family care to elderly members is analyzed without attention to productive family roles of elders, whenever stratification and status attainment are studied without reference to family systems or intergenerational transfers, and whenever poverty is studied without acknowledging the interdependence of multiple generations of impoverished adults. Systematic study has shown important overlaps between aging and family studies in each of these areas (Bould et al., 1989; Cherlin & Furstenberg, 1986; Cicirelli, 1983; Johnson, 1988;

Stack, 1974), but existing theoretical formulations fall short of integrating empirical work on adult development and aging into family scholarship.

STUDY OF THE FAMILY OF THE SECOND HALF OF LIFE

Our goal in this chapter is to review and integrate family scholarship and gerontological scholarship on families in the second half of life within the context of contemporary family theory. Review of existing knowledge of aging and of families suggests that connections between these two domains are difficult to make for at least four reasons. In the first place, the theoretical efforts in family studies and the empirical tradition in gerontology are incompatible. On one hand, philosophy of family social science has emphasized general theory, limiting the areas of study of family life viewed as relevant and significant. On the other hand, gerontological research on aging and the family is often without any clear theoretical direction. It is important to move toward a postpositivist philosophy of social science in order to bridge the gap between theory and findings.

In the second place, family theory has not been related to the complex, multigenerational family of contemporary urban society. Theories developed on the basis of intact nuclear units might be less relevant in understanding contemporary families. Contemporary societies have one- to five-generational family systems, with various members present and absent, with current and past linkages among members, and with complex relationships within and between generations. This diversity among families is greater during the second half of life. It is necessary to expand family theories to encompass the multigenerational family and the diversity of experience across the life course in order to understand families across the second half of life.

In the third place, it is difficult to integrate individual aging and family developmental studies and theories. The need to conceptualize multiple levels of social reality and the challenges associated with analyzing process (Hernes, 1976) are problematic. Overspecialization in the social science disciplines adds to this difficulty, but integrating two literatures might help overcome this dilemma. Research on family relationships in the aging literature compensates for the neglect of this area in the family studies field. Similarly, a family systems perspective on the aging individual compensates for the overly atomistic treatment of the person in the literature on aging.

Finally, social research on aging focuses on family problems, whereas family theory often deals with "normal" family processes. The social problem focus has narrowed the range of questions asked about the family in the second half of life. Often, theory is not brought to bear on the social problems facing families, although theory might be very useful to finding solutions. Study of family life of middle and later adulthood must be considered both in terms of such social issues as intergenerational relations or caregiving and within the context of theories of family structure and process (Antonucci, 1990; Kahn & Antonucci, 1980; Pruchno et al., 1984).

Connecting to New Philosophies of Social Science

Limitations imposed by present family theories for more effective inclusion of the study of the family of adulthood can be shown by discussion of two exemplary theories that offer promise for more effective integration of family gerontology research and family theory. The goal of this inquiry is to create a next generation of family scholarship guided both by recent advances in the philosophy of the social sciences and by advances in the study of the family of adulthood.

The family theory construction movement reflected the positivist philosophy of social science of the past several decades (Suppe, 1977; Toulmin, 1990). Theory construction represents an effort to move from empirical observation to testable hypotheses to be examined in subsequent study. This positivist approach to theory construction is represented in such collections as Christensen's (1964) text, Nye and Bernardo's (1966) effort at formulation of conceptual frameworks for family study, Burr's (1973) integrative effort at family theory construction, and the two-volume inventory edited by Burr, Hill, Nye, and Reiss (1979a, 1979b). These volumes all reflect essentially the same assumptions: (1) it is possible to construct general laws applicable to the family as a social group; and (2) these general laws need not be limited to families at a particular time, in particular circumstances, sharing particular value systems. The activity of family theory construction can be understood from a sociology of science perspective. Starting from the assumption that generality is preferred over the specific in science and that deduction from general laws represents more valued intellectual activity than observational inquiry, concern with a propositionally based family theory represents yet one more effort to legitimize family study.

The family theory project, encompassing much of the effort in family study across the 1970s (Burr, 1973; Burr et al., 1979a, 1979b; Nye & Bernardo, 1966), attempted systematization of a tradition in family study that had its antecedents in the social psychology of the period following World War I (Thomas & Wilcox, 1987). Concerned with broadening social science study from its focus on social problems to a more general view of social process, initial efforts by Goode (1959) and by Hill and his colleagues (Hill & Hansen, 1960; Hill & Rodgers, 1964) shaped a tradition of theory construction continuing until the present time.

Family theory construction represents a general approach to understanding structure and process that is separate from family life within a particular society. Burr et al. (1979a), in their inductive volume, organized findings from studies of family life in terms of empirically supportable propositions.

A deductive approach in a second volume of this project described how exchange theory, symbolic interactionism, systems theory, conflict theory, and phenomenology are applied to the study of family processes (Burr et al., 1979b). Whether deductive or inductive, theory construction efforts of the past two decades have generally not been successful in facilitating enhanced understanding of family life or in the manner in which the family responds to changes taking place over time as family members grow to adulthood. Nor have theory construction efforts been successful in responding to challenges imposed by historical and social change within the larger community (Hill, 1949, in Thomas & Wilcox, 1987).

Across the past two decades, an alternative perspective has emerged in the study of social life. Indeed, contemporary advances in the philosophy of science have led to a richness and vitality of inquiry that are without parallel across the past century. Current emphasis on the complex nature of social science inquiry has been inspired by the work of Wittgenstein and his students (e.g., Putnam, 1978; Toulmin, 1990), the powerful critiques of positivist social science (e.g., Rorty, 1980), developments in anthropology (e.g., Geertz, 1966) and sociology (e.g., Giddens, 1987), the challenge of phenomenology (e.g., Gadamer, 1960/1975; Heidegger, 1962), and critical theory (e.g., Horkheimer, 1972; Poster, 1978).

Within family studies, the new postpositivist philosophy of social science inquiry has been reflected most clearly within the feminist perspective (Klein & Jurich, 1993; Osmond & Thorne, 1993). Many scholars attempted to construct a gendered social theory of the family after Bernard (1972) critically assessed knowledge on marriage and Oakley (1974) published an analysis of housework. In recent years, the combination of feminist conceptualizations and interpretive methods has been common. Whereas some feminist scholars have defended reliance upon traditional survey and quantitative approaches, many feminists and postpositivist social scientists criticize a scientific method adopted from nineteenth-century mechanistic methods of inquiry (Kaufman, 1986; Klein & Jurich, 1993; Polkinghorne, 1983; Smith, 1987). Their philosophy reflects the centrality of subjective experience and the inclusion of women's voices, omitted in the past. Qualitative family scholars, such as LaRossa and LaRossa (1981), and those who take a biographical approach to lives, such as Bertaux and Kohli (1984), are adding to the breadth of family experience that both feminist and postpositivist trends legitimize.

Postpositivist perspectives within the social sciences recognize the complex interplay between the context of study and the evidence reported by the social scientist (Mishler, 1986, 1990; Rosenwald & Ochberg, 1992), emphasizing questions regarding the meaning of findings and the relationship between the social observer and data. Alexander (1982) maintains that postpositivist inquiry should be characterized by theory and empirical observation treated as inseparable; knowledge based on evidence in addition to empirical or experimental data; theory development proceeding through comparison and evaluation of alternative theories, which is as important as empirical falsification of specific theories; and both empirical proof and alternative theoretical perspectives deemed necessary to provide a shift in understanding social life.

Similarly, Polkinghorne's (1983) perspective is optimistic and inclusive, suggesting that knowledge about human life can be gained in many ways. His recommendations include using new criteria for knowledge, such as reasonableness and significance of concepts, methods, and findings for those whose lives are studied; respecting the subject as knower; using a wider range of methods to develop knowledge; and relying on different procedures to form theory. This focus on temporary and conditional aspects of knowledge is especially important in the study of adulthood and aging, because reasonable explanations of one cohort's aging experience might not provide the best explanation for that of another cohort. Respect for the subject as knower encourages the family scholar to explore issues that family members in the second half of life consider central. Building knowledge that is persuasive and believable to various audiences regarding the family in the second half of life would reflect a successful postpositivist approach. Expanding to new philosophies of science, in summary, would benefit study of the intergenerational family by contributing to a postpositivist family theory.

The Multigenerational Family of Later Life and Family Theory

Study of the family of the second half of life should be advanced through enlarging the view of what constitutes the relevant family system and incorporating knowledge regarding normative aging. Further, important changes in family life have been realized across the past two decades; few of these changes have been incorporated into either research on the family of later adulthood or family theory. For example, particularly in the study of older women, confidants or families of nonkin ("family of choice") might be as significant for maintenance of morale as contact with offspring and siblings (Lee, 1979). Increased consideration of multiple generations within family theory and the study of life changes among older adults would enhance family scholarship.

Theory about the family has often failed to include concepts of an extended kinship system. Because Parsons (1949) based his assumptions about the nuclear family on the unique circumstances characterizing American society following World War II, when large numbers of young families moved to the suburbs, where housing was more affordable than in the cities, contemporary theorists portray the American family as nuclear, in the sense that the immediate family of husband, wife, and children tends not to live with other relatives and has relatively few obligations to kin outside the household. This emphasis has led to the interpretation that the nuclear family has little connection to relatives and leaves multigenerational and nonnuclear structures outside existing theory. Litwak (1965), Adams (1970), and Rossi and Rossi (1991), among others, have suggested that this portrayal of family life is flawed both conceptually and empirically. For example, consider the reality of the reconstituted family of the present time (Masnick & Bane, 1980). As Johnson (1985, 1988) reported in a study of grandparents' relationships with the children of their divorced offspring, reconstituted families affect relationships among a large group of kindred across lineages within the modified extended family of contemporary society (see Robertson, this volume).

Family theory has not sufficiently incorporated the modified extended family (Cohler & Grunebaum, 1981; Cohler & Stott, 1987; Litwak, 1965; Pruchno et al., 1984). This family form consists in theory of husband, wife, and still-dependent children, all of whom exchange significant resources and services with each other and with financially independent adult offspring, as well as with older parents. Family research has sometimes failed to study the full range of relations within the family of adulthood, including shared activities and sources of mutual support and assistance reciprocally across generations, focusing instead on problems from a child-rearing perspective. Broadening understanding of families requires both adopting a multigenerational perspective and recognizing the reality that most adults maintain their health and vitality well into the ninth decade of life. For instance, reporting on her experiences on an elderhostel trip to Alaska, one 85-year-old woman observed that she could do everything she had done at age 40, but one-third as rapidly as earlier in life.

Too often, even when discussion of family process is extended to include the family of the second half of life, scholars assume that members of the oldest generation within the family are ill and infirm and that intergenerational relations are characterized principally by caregiving chores, financial assistance, and emotional support. In fact, as the Harris (1975) survey showed, nearly half of all adults over age 80 continue to make financial contributions to their middle-aged and older offspring. Only a small minority of older adults require relocation to long-term care. It is important that this changing perspective on the competence and vitality of older adults (Baltes & Baltes, 1990) be represented in family theory that focuses on the impact of continuing shared experiences and continuing reciprocal socialization, even among older adult offspring and their much older parents.

The tendency for each successive generation to live longer than ever before, remain healthy longer, and spend up to a third of the life span after retirement can lead to important theoretical advances in understanding of kinship and the effects of personal resources on the morale of all generations in the family. To date, family theory has paid little attention to such issues as social networks and personal and social resources in the study of the older family and the community. It is important to consider the changing nature of multigenerational roles within the aging family; elderly adults maintain commitments to work and community activities, visiting with friends and enjoying leisure. They continue to seek physical and psychological well-being and physical mobility well into very old age (Altergott, 1988; Bould et al., 1989). The family of later life remains a context and a resource for most older individuals.

Few concepts and propositions in theories of aging are available to guide research on the multigenerational family of the second half of life. Concerned with this problem, Rosenmayr and Kockeis (1963) attempted to delineate descriptive propositions and construct theory. Core issues in the effort at theory formation within the family of later life included intergenerational assistance with the activities of daily life, maintenance of intimacy across geographical distance, desocialization and attachments within the family, continuity of family emotional relations and the benefits of these relations for the older family member, limitations of role and function concepts, women's extensive presence in familial care, and the stages of family life as linked to age. These topics remain relevant to contemporary theorizing about the family of the second half of life.

Passuth and Bengtson's (1988) review connected major theories of sociology to emergent theories of aging. Disengagement, modernization, age stratification, and life course perspectives are special theories of aging present in structural functionalism. Further, activity theory, social breakdown, and subculture theories developed from the theory of symbolic interactionism.

Disengagement theory assumed that adjustment to aging led older adults to remove themselves from public roles and to withdraw into personal, often familial ones (Cumming & Henry, 1961). This focus upon personal experience at the cost of continuing responsibilities and obligations to others was assumed to enhance life satisfaction of older adults and enable them to settle life accounts and prepare for a good death. Critiques suggested that disengagement theory confused increased concern with self and place in the life course with the reality of continued participation in expectable adult roles (Hochschild, 1975; Neugarten, 1976). *Activity theorists* implicitly criticized community and society for the lack of active roles for older people. Substituting lost or diminished roles for new or expanded ones constituted adaptation within their framework. Persons remaining active and engaged in expectable roles were assumed to be successfully aging. Family roles were not specified as unique in any way; in fact, involvement in social activities outside, or in addition to, domestic and family life would lead to adaptation. This leaves family events and roles somewhat irrelevant to activity theory, except insofar as they are lost.

Modernization theory assumed that, in the past, older people enjoyed greater status and played more vital roles within family and society than at the present time (Cowgill, 1986; Fisher, 1978). The process of social change penalized older adults, leaving them disadvantaged and disfranchised. Modernization theory assumed that skills necessary to cope with technological change must be learned early in life in order to foster attitudes and competencies necessary to cope with a changing world. Based on the study of earlier, poorly educated European immigrant cohorts who were unable to keep up with the pace of social change as they grew older, modernization theorists mistakenly assumed that older adults must inevitably be unable to comprehend and respond to a changing world and must inevitably yearn for the presumed simplicity of the remembered world of their youth.

This "world we have lost" perspective has been critiqued in gerontology (e.g., Cherry & Magnuson-Martinson, 1981) and family studies (e.g., Laslett, 1965). In the first place, as Schaie (1984) showed, the very assumption that older adults lack competencies is flawed because it is based on cross-sectional, rather than cross-sequential, study of cognition and personality across the second half of life. Further, *life course theorists* have linked demography and role theory in the study of expectable events across the middle and later years of life. Thus, recent life course theory has provided a comprehensive framework for understanding reciprocal relationships between generations and both forward and reverse socialization processes across generations within contemporary society. This framework provides a means for understanding such aspects of aging as induction into the role of retiree of newly retired late-middle-aged offspring by one's own much older father or the significance of instruction in the use of computers provided for a school-age grandchild by a recently retired grandparent. From Cain's (1964) integration of sociological theory and age status to Riley, Foner, and Waring's (1968, 1972) construction of a social structural perspective on aging, age stratification has provided a macrosocial context for life course theories.

Elements of the *age stratification model* include a population structure consisting of people of different ages, an age-graded role structure such as various family roles; processes for socializing individuals into, and out of, roles; and processes of social change that transform both the role and population structures (Riley et al., 1972). The life course is patterned by ongoing role changes and by social-historical processes. Age stratification and life course approaches have important potential for understanding later-life families. Family events are common markers in any life course analysis. Too often, however, the events chosen for study concern changes such as marriage or transition to parenthood more characteristic of the first half of life than of middle age or aging (Glick, 1988; Hogan, 1981).

These special theories of aging provide examples of untapped potential for understanding family and society across the second half of life. Similarly, social breakdown, subculture, exchange, political economy, and social phenomenology are concepts that could be used as elements of a family theory of later life. The major contribution of gerontology to the analysis of families in later life lies in the empirical research that it could inspire. Having presented an overview of such theories, we next examine the reviews of knowledge about aging and the family that have been published over the past 30 years. These reviews illustrate the extensive knowledge base that research on aging has provided for the study of family theory across the second half of life.

In 1971, as now, "literature on the family is far more abundant with regard to the first half than to the second half of the cycle" (Troll, 1971, p. 263). Topics of concern during the 1960s included relations within the extended family and the role of family in individual adaptation (Troll, 1971). Troll predicted greater discourse between scholars of the family and gerontologists in the 1970s, suggesting that emerging family development theory might be "most suited to the study of the contracting family, which should ideally be viewed along a dimension of time" (p. 264). In this review, Troll faulted the lack of attention to roles, later-life family connections with extended kin, and the family transitions of later life. A decade later, Streib and Beck (1980) reviewed research on functions of the family and aging (nurturance, economic, residential, legal, and cultural functions), attending to intergenerational and other social relations. They focused on research on family links to bureaucratic and other organizations, as well as connections to kin. Emerging interest in cultural diversity was reflected in both ethnic and historical variation in family ties.

The third editions of the *Handbook of the Psychology of Aging* (Birren & Schaie, 1990) and the *Handbook of Aging and the Social Sciences* (Binstock & George, 1990) also contained summaries of the rapidly expanding and diversified literature on family in the later decades. Two of the six chapters on aging and the family published in the various editions of these *Handbooks* exemplified common themes. Demography was important in both the review of the psychological literature (Aizenberg & Treas, 1985) and the review of the social sciences (Bengtson, et al., 1990), with the latter chapter highlighting such changing demographic forces as increased divorce, reduced infant mortality, and the lengthening life span. Both sets of authors particularly emphasized that changes due to longevity lead to continuing relations across generations, fostering ongoing intergenerational support and assistance into the later life of both offspring and parents. Commonly considered aspects of this relationship across generations include contact, affection, and help. Bengtson and colleagues (1990) also examined normative solidarity (agreement about expectations and sanctions exchanged when expectations are violated) and consensual solidarity (agreement about beliefs and values). Both chapters contained sections on extended kin, diversity of family forms, and a variety of marital histories in later life. Aizenberg and Treas (1985) and Mancini and Blieszner (1989) both emphasized the importance of studying kin and friends of older adults within a larger theoretical context. Mancini and Blieszner (1989) further suggested an approach such as that provided by Bengtson and Schrader's (1982) typology of solidarity in kin relationships.

Reviewing the literature from the 1980s, Brubaker (1990) acknowledged the utility of the family development perspective. Family structure, family interaction, and family strategies to accommodate change were useful concepts for organizing the "burgeoning research" on families in later life (Brubaker, 1990, p. 959). He summarized developmental processes within marriage as well as within generational units, outlined complexities and challenges for researchers, and called for theory development and research guided by theory. These calls for theory to address family issues in the second half of life suggest that it might be time to move formulation of family theories beyond the family formation stage. Theories of aging, research on families in later life and on family events in the lives of older people, and theories of family life can be connected in order to enhance understanding.

Expanding Family Theories: Study of Life Course and Life Changes

The *Handbook of Marriage and the Family* contained a chapter on theory that highlighted symbolic interactionism, systems theory, and exchange theory (Thomas & Wilcox, 1987). Any one of these general theories could clearly guide the study of the family in the second half of life. Treas and Bengtson (1987) reviewed both the research literature and the social problems facing families in later life. The most complete link between aging theory and family theory, however, appears in the chapter on family development and the life course perspectives (Mattessich & Hill, 1987). Aldous (1990) subsequently articulated the differences between the individual-centered life course approach and the family-centered development theories, whereas White (1991) emphasized the similarities.

The *Sourcebook of Family Theories and Methods: A Contextual Approach* (Boss, Doherty, LaRossa, Schumm, & Steinmetz, 1993) contains comprehensive reviews of family theories. The editors showed the impact of sociocultural context on family research and theory, fostered comparison of theories, assessed multiple research methods and ways of knowing, and gave greater weight to theoretical frameworks than to empirical proof. This compendium integrates multiple levels of reality and includes child development and psychological theories as well as family systems theories. Further, this *Sourcebook* emphasizes the necessary relationship between theory and social action by adding commentary on the application of each theoretical perspective to a social issue confronting families, practitioners, or social policy. For example, Boss (1993) used symbolic interactionism and the concept of ambiguous loss to illustrate the case of Alzheimer's disease and family stress.

Connecting to new philosophies of science, integrating multiple levels of reality, and applying family theories to family social problems, the *Sourcebook* addresses several of the problems posing difficulty in the construction of family theory for the family of the second half of life. Yet chapters that could have incorporated findings regarding the family of the second half of life often included only early family life issues. For example, the chapter on contributions from developmental psychology simply reviewed infant attachment research (Bretherton, 1993), although developmental psychology has made substantial contributions to the understanding of adult development and aging relevant to family life. Aging as a biological reality in the second half of life received no analysis in the chapter on biosocial theories (Troost & Filsinger, 1993). Only one chapter, by Bengtson and Allen (1993), fully addressed issues of age and generation. The chapter on life course, race, and ethnicity (Dilworth-Anderson, Burton, & Johnson, 1993) did draw attention to the multigenerational family system. Whereas the chapter on family development provided a multigenerational framework, the family of the second half of life was included only in discussion of young adult offspring who were departing from home (Rodgers & White, 1993). In earlier formulations of family development (e.g., Aldous, 1978), retirement was viewed as leading to a distinct family structure, but other later life events were rarely discussed. Similarly, the most recent compendium of family theory contains little discussion of life changes such as retirement, grandparenthood, marital role transitions, disability, illness, or widowhood.

Connecting Family Theory and Family Social Problems

Finally, misplaced emphasis on positivism and scientism has resulted from the desire to improve the status of family study within the social sciences. Emerging after World War I as a systematic means for guiding home economics, family studies began as a problem-focused discipline concerned both with intervention and with study of the regularities of social relationships. The problem perspective has too often been viewed as nonintellectual, however, with enhancement of intervention, policy, and practice considered as separate from discovery of generalized, lawful regularities of family life.

Research on family dynamics over the second half of life has been inspired largely by such social problems as widowhood (Lopata, 1979); the status of older adults without families, including family of choice (Gubrium, 1975; Unruh, 1983); families struggling to provide humane care for older relatives afflicted with Alzheimer's disease (Boss, 1993); or elder abuse (Pillemer & Wolf, 1986; Steinmetz & Amsden, 1983; Strauss, 1990).

To the extent that family theory has maintained a life course perspective, including discussion of the oldest generations within the family, little mention is made of the manner in which generations manage both such expectable life changes as retirement or such adverse, unexpected changes as sudden illness or early death of a parent or grandparent. A problem-focused approach in social gerontology and a focus on development of formal propositions in family theory have separated research from the theory development movement. This trend has been disadvantageous to both social action and social knowledge. The connection between problematic events and family in later life can provide insight into family process; family theory that incorporates study of later life can be useful in solving family and societal challenges, inspired by new philosophies of social science.

RECENT DEVELOPMENTS IN FAMILY THEORY AND STUDY OF THE FAMILY OF LATER ADULTHOOD

The application of the principles developed in this chapter can be illustrated by showing how two exemplary theories could be used to account for relations across the generations within the family of adulthood. Family development theory and family stress theory were chosen as exemplars for three reasons: they are theories of process and change, they incorporate multiple levels of reality (minimally, the individual, the family, and the social context), and they are theoretically open systems. That is, scholarship within other theoretical traditions, such as structural theory, role theory, symbolic interactionism, contemporary psychoanalytic theory of self and other, feminist theory, conflict theory, and phenomenological theory, can be incorporated within the perspective provided by these two theories, as Mattesich and Hill (1987) showed. In addition, they meet many other post-positivist criteria of social science theories, such as richness, potential to inform application, acknowledgment of sociocultural context, ability to integrate personal experience, consistency, and clarity. As a conceptual framework, family development provides the more general theory for this section. Family stress theory is somewhat less abstract and would be labeled a middle-range theory (Boss et al., 1993). A third theoretical perspective discussed here, critical theory, does not incorporate later-life families.

Family Development Theory and Study of the Second Half of Life

Family development theory emphasizes three fundamental concepts. First, the family has a role structure and consists of interdependent and active individuals. Second, these individuals have a shared, complex, and mutually constructed history that impinges on current interactions and interpretations. Third, as a family moves through time, a number of events can trigger changes: development of the individual, changed roles of one or more individuals, changed participation in an external system or relationship, new expectations placed on the family from the community, or changed definitions of the situation. Hill and Mattessich's (1979) definition of family development is stated as "the process of progressive structural differentiation and transformation over the family's history,. . . the active acquisition and selective discarding of roles by incumbents of family positions as they seek to meet the changing functional requisites for survival and as they adapt to recurring life stresses as a family system" (p. 174).

Family career constitutes the "timing and scheduling of these changes" (Hill & Mattessich, 1979, p. 175). In contrast to many critics of the family development approach (Hudson & Murphy, 1980; Spanier, Sauer, & Larzelere, 1979), core concepts should be understood as focus on process and timing rather than as stages akin to those purporting to portray individual development. Family development theory accommodates multidirectional development and open potential for change. Yet, family development theory has some of the same problems facing individual developmental theories. It is difficult to differentiate change and development; also, the diversity of forces operating on individuals and families makes it difficult to form causal theories. Further, focusing on various levels of analysis from the biopsychosocial reality of individual development (Rossi & Rossi, 1991) up to the macrosocial environment (Riley, 1988) requires construction of theories better able than present efforts to include the interplay of social life, biology, and life circumstances (Hernes, 1976).

The family developmental approach has too often been limited to a focus principally upon the first half of life (e.g., White, 1991), but inclusion of the life course perspective linking individuals to their historical contexts (Elder, 1987, 1992; Hareven, 1984) would enrich this framework. The situation of older husbands and wives illustrates the utility of the family development model. Not only are recent cohorts of young-old people (aged 65 to 74 years) as healthy as their younger counterparts, but also many adults who remain married continue with the same work and community commitments as had characterized their contributions earlier in life (Clausen, 1993). With offspring now grown and financially independent, many of the tensions that had characterized earlier marital relationships might disappear. Even within working-class families, increased financial independence of offspring, pension income, a paid-off mortgage, relief from some real estate taxes, Medicare, and other assistance plans can provide a greater share of disposable income than earlier in the lives of husbands and wives. However, the impact of both expectable changes in later life, such as retirement or widowhood, and unexpected events, such as loss of the family home due to fire or storm, has not been well portrayed within existing family development models.

Part of the problem with family development theory is the difficulty of dealing with events at multiple levels of analysis (i.e., individual, dyadic, and family). Burgess's (1926) definition of the family as a unity of interacting personalities could be interpreted in either of two ways: that such family-level processes as interdependence or experienced level of stress represent the aggregate of individual family experiences, calculated by summing across individual scores or estimating transition probabilities for individuals; or that phenomena taking place at the level of the family as a whole differ from those taking place for individual family members. For example, remarriage of a previously widowed mother has implications for the intergenerational family unit that go well beyond those for the mother. Resources, role structures, and interdependencies shift. Thus, it is essential that family study focus on these family-level phenomena in addition to the experiences of individual family members.

An equally important issue in family study concerns the presumed invariance of stages viewed as akin to individual life cycle developmental tasks or stages. Family scholars have moved from the study of the individual to the study of the person, understood as a social construction, and from developmental task to predictable role change or transition. Stages of the family must be understood as normatively defined, reflecting the same socially constructed timetable as is relevant for the study of persons. White (1991) emphasized events rather than stages and probabilities of events' occurring rather than typologies. This parallels such theoretical innovations as the branching model of family development, charting alternative paths through family career, and conceptual clarifications such as the critical role transition (multiple co-occurring role changes in the family that result in movement to a new interactional structure) (Mederer & Hill, 1983). The accommodation of diverse trajectories, such as single parents and never-married adults (Hill, 1986; Murphy & Staples, 1979), is clearly possible within family development theory and adds refreshing realism to the earlier, reified perspective that characterized this theoretical approach.

Persons experience transitions *on time,* in the sense that they take place at a time socially defined as expectable, or *off time,* defined as early or late. Following Sorokin and Merton's (1937) discussion of social time, Roth (1963) and Neugarten (1976) suggested that persons are aware of the timetable for expectable life attainments such as grandparenthood, retirement, or widowhood. In general, transitions that take place early off time are more inherently a challenge to morale and adjustment than transitions taking place late off time. Early off-time changes are generally eruptive and adverse, posing problems both because little preparation or anticipatory socialization is possible (e.g., having watched others deal with the change) and also because social support is missing (e.g., from others who have already experienced this change) (Antonucci, 1990; Kahn & Antonucci, 1980). For example, widowhood for a woman in her 30s has quite different consequences from those experienced by a woman in her mid-to-late 70s, the age when widowhood is expected. Issues of social timing must also be considered in terms of gender. Once a spouse dies, men and women face different probabilities of remarriage. Using family development theory, it is possible to examine social expectations, larger family goals, and individual roles and definitions of the situation as predictors of remarriage. Both remarriage and remaining widowed would have consequences for the individual, the larger family, and the society.

An improved developmental perspective must include continuing social change as an intrinsic element. Indeed, maintaining a perspective based on the concept of socially defined expectations governing role transitions provides a means for including social change. Once family scholars move away from a concept of family development stage based on analogy with individual developmental tasks and recognize that lives are socially defined and organized, then the concept of life course, which has been so important in understanding particular lives over time, might be equally significant in the study of families. A formulation that includes social expectations, family definitions of reality, and the effect of earlier experiences on the current family patterns is very useful for studying the second half of life (Aldous, 1978; Bengtson & Allen, 1993; Rodgers, 1973).

Issues of social timing must also be considered in the context of changing social-historical realities. Linking the family development and life course frameworks, Aldous (1990) credited theories of the life course with bringing social change and historical time into family scholarship. For example, women's rate of employment represents a rapidly changing social reality transforming the process of family development. Within the present cohort of older women, there is great variation in prior labor force experiences as determined by World War II, periods of economic growth and decline in the postwar years, and social changes regarding marriage and divorce. Applied to the study of the family in the second half of life, integration of the family development and life course models requires close examination of the timing of events in individual lives (such as work), the timing of events and sources of change in the social context (such as war), and the impact of events and change on family patterns, roles, and relationships as they unfold over time.

Intrinsically related to the concept of social definition of lives are the dual concepts of cohort and generation. Much of family theory that includes discussion of the second half of life is founded on conceptions of aging as necessarily leading to personal and cognitive rigidity. This stereotyping of older family members has been based on a confusion of the concepts of aging, generation or place in the life course, and cohort. According to Troll (1971), *generation* refers to three separate phenomena: (1) age groups within the family (e.g., grandparents, parents, children), (2) developmental stage or age stratum within the life cycle (toddler, preschooler, schoolchild, adolescent, young adult, middle-aged adult, and older adult), and (3) historically defined cohorts understood in the context of particular sociohistorical changes (e.g., the generation of the Great Depression). Family scholars need to carefully assess the manner in which stereotypes such as the inability of older persons to learn new technology, adjust to social change, or maintain active participation within family and community might influence research on the family of later life. Findings might reflect not aging but, rather, particular experiences common to particular generations or cohorts of older adults. Moreover, generation defined as place in the life course sometimes becomes entangled with generation defined as historical cohort (Marshall, 1981). Research on individual development suggests that being older, as such, is not associated with any particular cognitive style or set. Rather, cohort differences might explain variations in behavior. The cohort containing large numbers of European immigrants who were not well educated might have contributed to stereotypes of old age because they appeared to be ethnocentric and they affirmed old-world traditions (Cohler & Grunebaum, 1981; Wallace, 1956). This cohort-specific finding is an example of limits to generalizing that must be addressed by family scholars.

Rosow (1978) noted the difficulty of determining what constitutes a cohort. No clear criterion related to sociohistorical events exists to mark cohort boundaries across groups. Furthermore, a demographic cohort can contain two or more distinct social groups, such as immigrants and native-born older people (Mannheim, 1936). Consideration of both cohort and historical context is necessary in the study of lives over time. For example, Elder (1974, 1979, 1984, 1987) studied children who were either pre-schoolers or adolescents at the time of the Great Depression and whose families either did or did not experience at least a one-third drop in income over a short period of time. Following these people and some of their parents provided additional insight into the enduring impact of historical conditions on the life course. Taking advantage of protocols from two cohorts included in three studies of families in the San Francisco Bay area followed for more than half a century, Elder showed variation in the impact of a seemingly singular event. He found that formerly hard-pressed middle-class children, particularly females, were more resilient and better able to recover from hardship than adults whose families had not earlier sustained adversity. The cohort of former preschool boys earlier had shown some adverse impact of this family crisis upon adjustment. At midlife, however, both children of adversity and children of fortune at the time of the Great Depression appeared quite similar on measures of personal and economic well-being. Elder (1992) suggested that the later effects of military service during World War II, opportunity for higher education following return to civilian life, and marriage to a supportive spouse all combined to offset the otherwise noxious impact of early life adversity. Elder's research showed the significance of early experiences within the family for the child's own adjustment and also the impact of subsequent life experience as a source of change in adult lives. Clausen (1993) added further to the demonstration of varying impact of this adversity in his discussion of the life histories of members of this study panel.

Among the most serious critiques of the initial family developmental approach was that it was built around the so-called traditional family with the husband at work and the wife tending to home and young children. This family of the postwar years is hardly characteristic of the family in contemporary society. Persons who were middle-aged in the late 1970s had a very different experience of family process than those coming into midlife a decade or two earlier. With the increasing reality of the reconstituted family in American society, quite different social ties and resources might be available for the next generation of older adults.

A cohort approach to study of family management of expectable life changes and unanticipated events, which incorporates the concept of historical period, permits comparison of family process over time. This approach fosters enhanced understanding of the family as a social institution affecting the lives of interdependent members. The impact of continuing social-historical change in the study of families in the second half of life requires attention to expectable transitions over the course of life and to the effects of such unexpected events and structural changes as the Great Depression, the two world wars, the advent of Medicare, the Vietnam and Persian Gulf wars, and the politics of the federal deficit.

A small number of social scientists have provided models for portraying personal development within a larger social and historical context (Demos, 1986; Elder, 1979; Hareven, 1980; Hogan, 1981; Hogan & Astone, 1986; Modell, 1989). Developmental models of family have emerged without sufficient consideration of the role of larger social-historical events as determinants of family process and of the family's relationship with the larger social order. Elder (1984) outlined the particular challenges imposed by the larger social order on generations within the modified extended family over the course of the twentieth century. The study of families in the second half of life provides a valuable corrective for family development theory because it is so difficult to ignore the impact of cohort history in understanding later life.

Encompassing individual, family, and societal time, the concept of *daily life* is a common metric and unifying construct underlying the study of lives, families, and social change (Altergott, 1988). Daily life serves as the domain for the activities and interactions that accrue to constitute a life. Observing daily life before and after transitions, at different historical moments, or at different times during the family career extends understanding of social change, aging, and family development.

Family Stress Theory and the Second Half of Life

Another theory that offers potential for understanding families in the second half of life, the stress-coping model, has developed over the postwar years. This stress-coping model, later termed the ABC-X model and most recently the double ABC-X model of family response to stressful events, provides an exemplar for the integration of family theory and family social problem research. Applications of the theory to normative and nonnormative family transitions (see McCubbin & Figley, 1983) illustrates the potential of this model for building theory and integrating basic and applied family studies.

Hill and his associates (Hill, 1949; Hansen & Hill, 1964; Klein & Hill, 1979) initially formulated the so-called ABC-X model of stress in which some event (A), generally adverse and unexpected, interacts with the family's ability to cope with that event, including available resources and sources of social support (B), and the family's particular understanding of that life change, including both objectively and subjectively defined elements (C), resulting in the creation of what at least some family members view as a crisis, role strain, overload, or conflict (X). This model evolved from Hill's (1949) research on the stress evoked by the experience of separation and reunion of husbands and fathers during World War II. Later work by Parsons and Fox (1952) on the social significance of illness for the family further revealed the complex problems posed by study of family response to adversity.

Although Hill documented a number of alternative means for resolving the crisis resulting from separation and reunion of servicemen and their families, McCubbin and Patterson (1983) maintained that Hill's initial model was too static and did not allow for study of change and response to life changes over time. McCubbin and his associates proposed the double ABC-X model, which more explicitly allows for study of change. The double A in this model consists of the initial adverse life change event, other changes within the family, either associated with the initial event or independent of this event, and significant additional changes resulting from this process. The double B includes available family resources, encompassing both initial social support and family coping resources as well as the newly mobilized support and resources of available community supports. The double C includes the family's definition of the initial change event, together with interpretations of other associated and independent events that the family defines as stressful. Coping can lead to role reorganization or role disintegration, depending on the A, B, and C factors.

For example, double C could be investigated in studies of caretaker burden among relatives of Alzheimer patients, older adults caring for a retarded or persistently psychiatrically ill middle-aged offspring (Cohler, Pickett, & Cook, 1990), or parents of divorced offspring caring for each divorced parent and the grandchildren (Johnson, 1988). Note that it is important to study both objective burden, such as the amount of nighttime supervision the older ill parent requires or the types of care grandchildren require, and subjective burden, such as the feeling of being housebound with little time for oneself. Gilhooly (1984) showed that negative aspects of the caregiver's definition of the situation might be more critical as determinants of outcome or strain than such positive aspects as the caretaker's beliefs regarding support for caretaking activities. As Hirschfeld (1983) observed, however, caretaking based on long-standing intimacy, such as between husband and wife, and provided out of a desire to make the patient's life more comfortable leads to a construction of meaning that is essentially positive and provides a buffer against feelings of strain and overload. Burden, or definition of the situation, is not independent of life changes associated with adversity. Also, as a result of the definition of the situation, family members might experience additional problems that become part of a set of intertwined, family-based life changes, such as premature departure of a young adult or job loss by the primary caretaker.

Finally, the double X in the double ABC-X model refers not just to sense of strain at one time, but, rather, as viewed over some period of time. McCubbin and Patterson (1983) suggested replacing the concept of crisis with that of relative adaptation, allowing for specification of both positive and negative outcomes, as well as the relative success realized by the family in response to the initial set of life changes. The experience of being able to manage affliction over a period of several years, such as having a family member with Alzheimer's disease, might foster enhanced caring and sharing within the larger modified extended family. Further, family members gain enhanced morale derived from the sense of living up to their expectations for themselves in caring for their relatives (Kohut, 1977). Caregiving makes demands but also provides rewards, often unexpected.

The pileup of negative life events (A) interacts with available social support systems, such as community resources, help from other relatives and friends, and coping mechanisms (B), and with the family's definition of the situation, including experience of burden (C), to influence family adaptation. As in so many situations of adversity, the more prolonged the illness, the more family members withdraw from potential sources of assistance available within the community (Grunebaum, Weiss, Cohler, Gallant, & Hartman, 1982). For example, findings from a survey of caregivers, including spouse, adult offspring, and other relatives, by George and Gwyther (1986) showed marked feelings of role strain, lowered levels of life satisfaction, and increased rates of physical illness among caregivers, as compared with noncaregiving counterparts.

To date, the work of the family stress research group has been important principally as a means of focusing thinking about the impact of adversity upon family functioning. Any life change could be studied using this model, however. This theory provides an important starting point for integrating family problems with family process theory if expanded to include study of expectable and eruptive changes within the family of the second half of life. Such research might lead to a modified interpretation of the model components. For example, the pileup of life events (A) might be quite different for the family of the first half of life, concerned with young dependent children, than for the family of the second half of life, for whom life events are likely to include those encountered by still financially dependent offspring as well as newly dependent parents and for whom a greater experiential history (shared and unshared) has accrued. Similarly, the nature of available resources and coping techniques (B) and the very definition of the events(s) regarded as stressful (C) shift across the course of life and as a consequence of particular social and historical events. Finally, the outcome of this effort at resolving tension within the family (X) is a function of all of these factors, understood over time and in the context of the family's place in the course of life. Uhlenhuth, Lipman, Balter, and Stern (1974) showed that older adults have fewer direct adverse life experiences than do young adults. To the extent that these older adults are committed to the modified extended family, however, they also experience a larger number of such adverse experiences indirectly as a consequence of the intertwined lives of older and young generations.

McCubbin and Figley (1983) provided support for this position when they observed that this model could bridge normative and catastrophic family events. Further, these two types of events could be integrated by transforming a typology into a continuum of extent of change, extent to which change is accepted by family members across generations, and extent of positive and negative impact of these changes. Moreover, this theory and family development theory could be integrated if the social problem/normal family process dichotomy could be overcome. The advantage of considering both the family development and the family stress theories is in their potential integration. This theoretical integration would benefit study of families across the second half of life by linking many events and transitions previously seen as separate.

Critical Theory: A Borrowed Theory and the Family of Later Adulthood

Critical theory approaches to the study of the family present many of the problems posed by virtually all other theoretical perspectives when applied to research on the family of adulthood. Within this theoretical perspective, inspired by the Frankfurt school of social inquiry and criticism, focus is nearly exclusively upon family formation and the role of parents in the socialization of young children (Poster, 1978), with little discussion of the larger family unit or the family throughout adulthood. Critical theory emerged as a critique of contemporary society (Frankfurt Institute for Social Research, 1956/1972). Social life had become anonymous; a mass society rendered persons and families helpless to respond. Emergence of mass society, in turn, could be traced to the family, and, yet, problems reflected within the family could be traced to mass society.

Following assumptions present in much of Marxist writing, Horkheimer (1959, 1972) maintained that many of the problems of mass society stemmed from the meaninglessness of work and the accompanying separation of the workplace and family life. Within the peasant family of premodern Europe in small villages, interpersonal ties were formed through a lifetime of working and living together. Relatively little division of labor based on gender occurred. Children learned the capacity for diffuse relationships with a wider community of others rather than the intense feelings that later were constrained within the bourgeois family. Accompanying industrialization and a dramatically changed relationship between the worker and the means of production (Marx, 1844/1978, 1845–46/1978), the bourgeois family form required delay of gratification as a part of adjustment to urban industrial life, including that within the sexual sphere, later portrayed by Freud as repression. Women were conceived of as asexual whereas men were conceived of as lustful and never satisfied. The work of husband and father moved outside the home, and his authority within the home was reduced.

Although bourgeois marriage was said to bind the couple together forever, sex and marriage became separate within the bourgeois family. Critical theory is particularly concerned with what is assumed to be the breakdown of the father's authority within the family, which was assumed critical for family stability and for the establishment of firm ideals within the younger generation. These changes in the emotional climate within the family were, in turn, attributed to changes in the worker's relationship to the means of production. The ideal of romantic love was compromised by tensions created as the increasing division of labor within the workplace was mirrored in the strict gender-role division of labor within the household. The result was that the husband's rational authority derived from participation in the workplace, and the wife's responsibility was at home with housework and children.

The hostile world of the workplace resulting from industrialization and the changing relationship of the worker and the means of production was contrasted with the home as a place of comfort and positive feeling. Home became a haven in a heartless land, buffering the strains accompanying modernization and rapid social change (Berger & Berger, 1983). Accompanying this new emphasis upon the psychosocial world of the family, the bourgeois family emphasized stability of conduct and the importance of the child as a unique individual (Berger & Berger, 1983), well socialized and with a clear sense of gender-appropriate tasks and within and without the family circle. This perspective led to the segregation of gender-based tasks and authority within the family portrayed by Parsons and Bales (1955). At the same time, the privacy of the home, free from state intervention, was contrasted with the public world outside the home.

Together, the meaninglessness of much of modern work, the reality that the worker's search for meaning becomes frustrated in a job experienced as not fulfilling, and the inability to maintain meaningful relationships at work combine to have a major adverse impact upon the family. From the perspective of critical theory, the burgeoning divorce rate is an inevitable outcome of mass society and the separation that is required by the industrial workplace. The employer demands that workers surrender autonomy and individuality and is reluctant to address family concerns of the worker as legitimate. The model of the bourgeois family became that of the working-class family as well. Focus on contract and commercial relationships becomes characteristic of all aspects of life, including relations within the family. Marriage, too, becomes another form of a contract easily broken.

A number of problems with this formulation are related both to the historical images of family life in premodern Europe and to the purported crisis of the present time. Assumptions regarding the normlessness and unfocused nature of contemporary society cannot easily be confirmed. Social change is assumed to be equivalent to social decay. Understood within the present context, the most significant problem with critical theory is that discussion is focused nearly exclusively on the family of the first half of life, with scant attention to study of the problems of older family members or to relations across the generations.

Concern with the impact of the Industrial Revolution upon family structure and process makes it somewhat difficult to focus upon adult family relations across the second half of life. It is only within the post–World War II period that issues of aging within the family became salient because of large-scale demographic changes. The aging of postindustrial society led to the emergence of larger numbers of older adults than ever before. Medical advances led both to reduction in infant, child, and adult mortality and, to a lesser extent, to increased health among older adults. The aging of society itself contributed to the dramatic increase in the number of families with four and even five generations.

The present time is the first in which those over 80 years of age constitute the most rapidly growing age group within society; the presence of this generation of very old adults spending a significant part of their lives post-retirement poses unique challenges for critical family theory. If relation to the means of production determines all manner of social relations (Marx, 1844/1978), particular problems are posed by the very concept of retirement. Retirement highlights all those problems of family and leisure that are neglected in earlier critical theory. Feelings of normlessness and lack of meaning in life were assumed implicit in work, but they would be highlighted by the concepts of leisure and retirement. The reality that most workers look forward to retirement and enjoy newfound opportunities must be attributed by critical theory to false consciousness.

The fact that for the first time men may have the opportunity to spend time with grandchildren and great-grandchildren is not discussed within critical theory. The impact of industrial capitalism upon the division of labor by gender within the family must be complemented by the division of labor according to generation. For example, the role of grandparents as providers of child care at a time when both parents are employed could be discussed by critical theorists. Although grandparents resent being relied upon as a primary source of child care (Cohler & Grunebaum, 1981), they recognize the importance of providing emergency services (see Robertson, this volume).

The postmodern family is characterized as never before by relations across four and even five generations within the family, by provision of both forward and reverse socialization across the course of life, and by the opportunity for adults to enjoy each other's company within the family, less circumscribed than in the past by issues of authority and provision of day-to-day necessities. Adult offspring are able to take advantage of the wisdom and support of their own older parents as they contemplate their own retirement or as they confront the adversity of widowhood. Older adults are able both to learn from and teach younger generations in the family and to conceive of their own lives in new ways. Few studies of positive relations within the family of later life and of opportunities for enhanced life satisfaction attendant upon such continuing close contact have been conducted (see Mancini & Sandifer, this volume, for such an attempt).

Even when intergenerational assistance might be available, emphasis upon autonomy and self-reliance, values important in industrial capitalism, makes it difficult for family members to feel comfortable relying upon each other for help (Cohler, 1983). Capitalist institutions, such as a profit-driven economy and a mobile labor force, make it difficult to enjoy the interdependence that is uniquely possible within a society in which two or more generations of adults are able to continue ties of long duration. Too often, when considering such extended ties, the research focus has been on assistance in time of need, rather than on dual consideration of both the problems and the satisfactions attendant on day-to-day family life.

Although some older family members do need assistance with various tasks, it is nevertheless important to move from a disease- and impairment-centered view of aging and family relations to one stressing the interdependence and satisfactions characteristic of family life on a day-to-day basis (Altergott, 1984; Cohler & Stott, 1987). Even among frail elderly persons, except for infrequent but disruptive and difficult periods of illness, everyday life consists of much more than the need for care. Models of aging and family relations have, for the most part, not been able to account for the reality of interdependent and, for the most part, enjoyable relations over time. Application of critical theory to the family of the second half of life would enrich our understanding of families. It would also force critical theorists to respond to important issues regarding work and retirement that they have overlooked in discussions to date. Issues of work, retirement, and intergenerational relations are central in considering problems related to work and leisure posed within the family of postindustrial society.

CONCLUSION: FUTURE DIRECTIONS IN THE STUDY OF THE FAMILY OF LATER ADULTHOOD

We have suggested new departures in both the philosophy of social science and areas of particular study that might further advance social theory applied to research on the family of the second half of life. Including new philosophies of social science will provide new possibilities for knowledge construction. Including families beyond child-rearing age in family scholarship will raise important questions regarding the entire life course, later decades of family experience, and multiple-generation structures. Including the full range of human experiences relevant to the family of the second half of life, including crisis, challenge, and social problems, will broaden understanding of life within the family of adulthood. Including the multiple levels, concepts, and methods of both aging and family scholarship will also enhance such understanding.

New theoretical approaches might be necessary in the study of the family of later life. Neither grand family theory nor the intensive effort to inductively discover a set of middle-range theories has lived up to initial promise. The failure of these efforts stems both from the narrow conception of science implicit in the program of family theory construction and from the abstraction of family theory from the experience of family life. Starting from the program of the received view of science (Kuhn, 1970; Rorty, 1980), family theorists attempted to generate propositions closely tied to theoretical perspectives. An effort was made to avoid deviant instances, social problems, or the specifics of the family as a psychosocial unit located at a particular intersect of both social order and historical time. The new perspective that we advocate admits of the social-historical context, as well as the prevailing cultural constructs, values, and practices regarding family and aging. Rather than viewing the goal of family research as leading to general, abstract theory construction, both family theory and family research might best be served by contextually and historically grounded knowledge regarding the family of adulthood and later life.

Families facing challenges in later life ought to be included within family theory. In fact, what is most interesting about family life is the effort to cope with issues of loss and change within the context of a web of relationships enduring over time. The complexity of providing both induction into new roles across the course of life for all generations within the family and also emotional support, assistance, and aid during times of distress requires theory development. Effort at founding a theory of family structure and process without regard for issues of expectable role transitions and without response to disruptive changes will fail to account for the reality of family life. It is important that family theory focus on the study of the modified extended family across the entire life course. The inclusion of concepts from the study of family stress and the study of family development is feasible and likely to produce important additional understanding of family, life course, and social processes.

Just as with the family development model, the stress-coping model has been most often applied in the study of family formation and care of young dependent children. Family theory clearly needs to include events, transitions, and structures of later life. Study of formation of the nuclear family unit without consideration for the intergenerational context in which family members lead their lives is too limited. The integration of research on multigenerational family roles, relationships, and realities of the second half of life might energize family theory. Recognition of the family as constructed around role transitions within the larger extended family is consistent with both findings from family study and narrative accounts provided by family members (Parker, 1972).

The development of family theory can advance through consideration of the total development trajectory of families. New philosophies of science could serve as a corrective to both overly concrete and "pure" approaches to knowledge. Recognition of the complexity of family problems as well as normal family process will make it possible for family theory to represent more closely the reality of family life and both enrich and benefit from family research, much of which is focused on social problems. Taking advantage of the inclusiveness represented by postpositivist human science, additional methods and concepts might be useful in knowledge-building efforts. These changes in family scholarship are requisite for understanding family life across the adult years. Natural histories of multigenerational families, creation of family stories out of the narratives of particular family members, use of case studies, and analysis of communication acts, as well as surveys, experiments, and observations, all will contribute to next steps in the construction of a theory of family relations across the second half of life.

REFERENCES

Adams, B. (1970). Isolation, function and beyond: American kinship in the 1960s. *Journal of Marriage and the Family, 32,* 575–597.

Aizenberg, R., & Treas, J. (1985). The family in late life: Psychosocial and demographic considerations. In J. Birren & K. W. Schaie (Eds.), *Handbook of the psychology of aging* (2nd ed., pp. 169–189). New York: Van-Nostrand Reinhold.

Aldous, J. (1978). *Family careers.* New York: Wiley.

Aldous, J. (1990). Family development and the life course: Two perspectives on family change. *Journal of Marriage and the Family, 52,* 571–583.

Alexander, J. (1982). *Theoretical knowledge in sociology* (Vol. 1). Berkeley: University of California Press.

Altergott, K. (1984). Managing interdependence: Family development, policy and the care system in an aging society. *Key Papers: Twentieth International CFR Seminar on Social Change and Family Policies.* Melbourne, Australia: Institute of Family Studies.

Altergott, K. (1988). Daily life in late life: Concepts and methods for inquiry. In K. Altergott (Ed.), *Daily life in later life: Comparative perspectives* (pp. 11–22). Newbury Park, CA: Sage.

Antonucci, T. (1990). Social supports and social relationships. In R. Binstock & L. K. George (Eds.), *Handbook of aging and the social sciences* (3rd ed., pp. 205–227). New York: Academic Press.

Baltes, P. B., & Baltes, M. (Eds.). (1990). *Successful aging: Perspectives from the behavioral sciences.* New York: Cambridge University Press.

Bane, M. J. (1976). *Here to stay: American families in the twentieth century.* New York: Basic Books.

Bengtson, V., & Allen, K. (1993). The life course perspective applied to families over time. In P. Boss, W. Doherty, R. LaRossa, W. Schumm, & S. Steinmetz (Eds.), *Sourcebook of family theories and methods: A contextual approach* (pp. 469–498). New York: Plenum Press.

Bengtson, V., & Robertson, J. (Eds.). (1985). *Grandparenthood.* Newbury Park, CA: Sage.

Bengtson, V., Rosenthal, C., & Burton, L. (1990). Families and aging: Diversity and heterogeneity. In R. H. Binstock & L. K. George (Eds.), *Handbook of aging and the social sciences* (3rd ed., pp. 263–287). New York: Academic Press.

Bengtson, V., & Schrader, S. (1982). Parent-child relations. In D. J. Mangen & W. A. Peterson (Eds.), *Research instruments in social gerontology* (Vol. 2, pp. 115–185). Minneapolis: University of Minnesota Press.

Bengtson, V., & Treas, E. (1980). Aging and family relations. *Marriage and Family Review, 3,* 51–76.

Berger, B., & Berger, P. (1983). *The war over the family.* New York: Anchor Press-Doubleday.

Bernard, J. (1975). *Women, wives and mothers.* Chicago: Aldine.

Bertaux, D., & Kohli, M. (1984). The life story approach: A continental view. *Annual Review of Sociology, 10,* 215–237.

Binstock, R., & George, L. K. (Eds.). (1990). *Handbook of aging and the social sciences* (3rd ed.). New York: Academic Press.

Birren, J., & Schaie, K. W. (Eds.). (1990). *Handbook of the psychology of aging* (3rd ed.). New York: Academic Press.

Blumstein, P., & Schwartz, P. (1983). *American couples.* New York: Morrow.

Boss, P. (1993). The reconstruction of family life with Alzheimer's disease: Generating theory to lower family stress from ambiguous loss. In P. Boss, W. Doherty, R. LaRossa, W. Schumm, & S. Steinmetz (Eds.), *Sourcebook of family theories and methods: A contextual approach* (pp. 163–166). New York: Plenum Press.

Boss, P., Doherty, W., LaRossa, R., Schumm, W., & Steinmetz, S. (Eds). (1993). *Sourcebook of family theories and methods: A contextual approach*. New York: Plenum Press.

Bould, S., Sanborn, B., & Reif, L. (1989). *Eighty-five plus: The oldest old*. Belmont, CA: Wadsworth.

Bretherton, I. (1993). Theoretical contributions from developmental psychology. In P. Boss, W. Doherty, R. LaRossa, W. Schumm, & S. Steinmetz (Eds.), *Sourcebook of family theories and methods: A contextual approach* (pp. 275–297). New York: Plenum Press.

Brody, E. (1985). Parent care as normative stress. *Gerontologist, 25,* 19–29.

Brody, E. (1990). *Women in the middle: Their parent care years*. New York: Springer.

Brubaker, T. (1990). Families in later life: A burgeoning research area. *Journal of Marriage and the Family, 52,* 959–982.

Burgess, E. (1926). The family as a unity of interacting personalities. *Family, 7,* 3–9.

Burr, W. (1973). *Theory construction and the sociology of the family*. New York: Wiley-Interscience.

Burr, W., Hill, R., Nye, F. I., & Reiss, I. L. (Eds). (1979a). *Contemporary theories about the family. Vol. 1: Research based theories*. New York: Free Press.

Burr, W., Hill, R., Nye, F. I., & Reiss, I. L. (Eds). (1979b). *Contemporary theories about the family Vol. 2: General theories/theoretical orientations*. New York: Free Press.

Cain, L. (1964). Life-course and social structure. In R. Faris (Ed.), *Handbook of modern sociology* (pp. 272–309). Chicago: Rand McNally.

Cherlin, A., & Furstenberg, F. (1986). *The new American grandparent*. New York: Basic Books.

Cherry, R., & Magnuson-Martinson, S. (1981). Modernization and the status of the aged in China: Decline or equalization? *Sociological Quarterly, 22,* 253–261.

Christensen, H. (1964). Development of the family field of study. In H. T. Christensen (Ed.), *Handbook of marriage and the family* (pp. 3–32). Chicago: Rand-McNally.

Cicirelli, V. (1983). Adult children and their elderly parents. In T. Brubaker (Ed.), *Family relationships in later life* (pp. 21–30). Beverly Hills, CA: Sage.

Clausen, J. (1993). *American lives: Looking back at the children of the Great Depression*. New York: Free Press.

Cohler, B. (1983). Autonomy and interdependence in the family of adulthood: A psychological perspective. *Gerontologist, 23,* 33–39.

Cohler, B., & Grunebaum, H. (1981). *Mothers, grandmothers, and daughters: Personality and childcare in three generation families*. New York: Wiley.

Cohler, B., Pickett, S., & Cook, J. (1990). The psychiatric patient grows older: Issues in family care. In E. Light & B. Lebowitz (Eds.), *The elderly with chronic mental illness* (pp. 82–110). New York: Springer Publishing Co.

Cohler, B., & Stott, F. (1987). Separation, independence, and social relations across the second half of life. In J. Feshbach-Moore & S. Feshbach-Moore (Eds.), *The psychology of separation and loss* (pp. 165–204). San Francisco: Jossey-Bass.

Cowgill, D. (1986). *Aging around the world*. Belmont, CA: Wadsworth.

Cumming, E., & Henry, W. (1961). *Growing old: The process of disengagement*. New York: Basic Books.

Demos, J. (1986). *Past and present: The family and life-course in American history*. New York: Oxford University Press.

Dilworth-Anderson, P., Burton, L., & Johnson, L. B. (1993). Reframing theories for understanding race, ethnicity, and families. In P. Boss, W. Doherty, R. LaRossa, W. Schumm, & S. Steinmetz (Eds.), *Sourcebook of family theories and methods: A contextual approach* (pp. 627–646). New York: Plenum Press.

Doherty, W., Boss, P., LaRossa, R., Schumm, W., & Steinmetz, S. (1993). Family theories and methods: A contextual approach. In P. Boss, W. Doherty, R. LaRossa, W. Schumm, & S. Steinmetz (Eds.), *Sourcebook of family theories and methods: A contextual approach* (pp. 3–30). New York: Plenum Press.

Elder, G. H. (1974). *Children of the Great Depression*. Chicago: University of Chicago Press.

Elder, G. H. (1979). Historical change in life patterns and personality. In P.B. Baltes & O. G. Brim, Jr. (Eds.), *Life span development and behavior* (Vol. 2, pp. 117–159). New York: Academic Press.

Elder, G. H. (1984). Families, kin, and the life course: A sociological perspective. In R. Parke (Ed.), *Review of child development research. Vol. 7: The family* (pp. 80–136). Chicago: University of Chicago Press.

Elder G. H. (1987). Families and lives: Some developments in life-course studies. *Journal of Family History, 12,* 179–199.

Elder, G. H. (1992). Life course. In E. Borgatta & M. Borgatta (Eds.), *Encyclopedia of sociology Vol. 3* (pp. 1120–1130). New York: Macmillan.

Fisher, D. H. (1978). *Growing old in America*. Oxford: Oxford University Press.

Frankfurt Institute for Social Research. (1956/1972). *Aspects of sociology* (J. Viertel, trans.). Boston: Beacon Press.

Gadamer, H. G. (1960/1975). *Truth and method*. (G. Barden & J. Cumming, Trans. & Ed.). New York: Continuum Books.

Geertz, C. (1966). Person, time and conduct in Bali. In C. Geertz (Ed.), *The interpretation of cultures* (pp. 360–412). New York: Basic Books.

George, L. K., & Gwyther, L. (1986). Caregiver well-being: A multidimensional examination of family caregivers of demented adults. *Gerontologist 26,* 253–259.

Giddens, A. (1987). *Social theory and modern sociology*. Stanford, CA: Stanford University Press.

Gilhooly, M. (1984). The impact of care-giving on care-givers: Factors associated with the psychological well-being of people supporting a demented relative in the community. *British Journal of Medical Psychology, 57,* 35–44.

Glass, J., Bengtson, V., & Dunham, C. (1986). Attitude similarity in three-generation families: Socialization, status inheritance, or reciprocal influence? *American Sociological Review, 51,* 85–698.

Glick, P. (1988). Fifty years of family demography: A record of social change. *Journal of Marriage and the Family, 50,* 861–873.

Goode, W. (1959). The sociology of the family. In R. K. Merton, L. Broom, & L. S. Cotrell, Jr. (Eds.), *Sociology today* (pp. 178–196). New York: Basic Books.

Greenberg, J., & Becker, M. (1988). Aging parents as family resources. *Gerontologist, 28,* 786–791.

Grunebaum, H., Weiss, J., Cohler, B., Gallant, D., & Hartman, C. (1982). *Mentally ill mothers and their children.* Chicago: University of Chicago Press.

Gubrium, J. (1975). *Living and dying at Murray Manor.* New York: St. Martin's Press.

Hagestad, G. (1982). Parent and child: Generations in the family. In T. Field, A. Huston, H. Quay, L. Troll, & G. Finley (Eds.), *Review of human development* (pp. 485–499). New York: Wiley.

Hansen, D., & Hill, R. (1964). Families under stress. In H. Christensen (Ed.), *Handbook of marriage and the family* (pp. 782–819). Chicago: Rand-McNally.

Hareven, T. (1980). The life-course and aging in historical perspective. In K. Back (Ed.), *Life-course: Integrative theories and exemplary populations* (pp. 9–26). Boulder, CO: Westview Press.

Hareven, T. (1984). Themes in the historical development of the family. In R. Parke (Ed.), *Review of child development research. Vol. 7: The Family* (pp. 137–178). Chicago: University of Chicago Press.

Harris, L., & Associates. (1975). *The myth and reality of aging in America.* Washington, DC: National Council on the Aging.

Heidegger, M. (1962). *Being and time* (J. Macquarrie & E. Robinson, Trans.). New York: Harper & Row.

Hernes, G. (1976). Structural change in social processes. *American Journal of Sociology, 82,* 513–546.

Hill, R. (1949). *Families under stress.* Westport, CT: Greenwood Press.

Hill, R. (1986). Life cycle stages for types of single parent families. *Family Relations, 35,* 19–29.

Hill, R., Foote, N., Aldous, J., Carlson, R., & MacDonald, R. (1970). *Family development in three generations.* Cambridge, MA: Schnekman.

Hill, R., & Hansen, D. (1960). The identification of conceptual frameworks utilized in family study. *Marriage and Family living, 22,* 299–311.

Hill, R., & Mattessich, P. (1979). Family development and life span development. In P. B. Baltes & O. G. Brim, Jr. (Eds.), *Life-span development and behavior* (Vol. 2, pp. 161–204). New York: Academic Press.

Hill, R., & Rodgers, R. (1964). The developmental approach. In H. Christensen (Ed.), *Handbook of marriage and the family* (pp. 171–211). Chicago: Rand-McNally.

Hirschfeld, M. (1983). Homecare versus institutionalization: Family caregiving and senile brain disease. *International Journal of Nursing Study, 20,* 23–31.

Hochschild, A. (1975). Disengagement theory: A critique and a proposal. *American Sociological Review, 40,* 553–569.

Hogan, D. (1981). *Transitions and social change: The lives of American men.* New York: Academic Press.

Hogan, D., & Astone, N. (1986). The transition to adulthood. *Annual Review of Sociology, 12,* 109–130.

Horkheimer, M. (1959). Authoritarianism and the family. In R. N. Anshen (Ed.), *The family: Its function and destiny* (rev. ed., pp. 381–398). New York: Harper.

Horkheimer, M. (1972). Authority and the family. In M. Horkheimer, *Critical theory: Selected essays* (M. O'Connell & others, Trans.). New York: Herder & Herder.

Hudson, W., & Murphy, W. (1980). The non-linear relationship between marital satisfaction and stages of the family life-cycle: An artifact of type I errors. *Journal of Marriage and the Family, 42,* 263–267.

Johnson, C. (1985). Grandparenting options in divorcing families: An anthropological perspective. In. V. L. Bengston & J. Robertson (Eds.), *Grandparenthood* (pp. 81–96). Newbury Park, CA: Sage.

Johnson, C. (1988). *Ex families: Grandparents, parents and children adjust to divorce.* New Brunswick, NJ: Rutgers University Press.

Kahn, R., & Antonucci, T. (1980). Convoys over the life course: Attachment, roles, and social support. In P. B. Baltes & O. G. Brim, Jr. (Eds.), *Life-span development and behavior.* (Vol. 3, pp. 253–286). New York: Academic Press.

Kamerman, S. (1980). *Parenting in an unresponsive society.* New York: Free Press.

Kaufman, S. R. (1986). *The ageless self: Sources of meaning in late life.* Madison: University of Wisconsin Press.

Klein, D., & Hill, R. (1979). Determinants of family problem-solving effectiveness. In W. Burr, R. Hill, F.I. Nye, & I. L. Reiss (Eds.), *Contemporary theories about the family* (pp. 493–548). New York: Free Press.

Klein, D., & Jurich, J. (1993). Metatheory and family studies. In P. Boss, W. Doherty, R. LaRossa, W. Schumm, & S. Steinmetz (Eds.), *Sourcebook of family theories and methods: A contextual approach* (pp. 31–70). New York: Plenum Press.

Kohut, H. (1977). *The restoration of the self.* New York: International Universities Press.

Kuhn, T. S. (1970). *The structure of scientific revolutions* (2nd ed.). Chicago: University of Chicago Press.

LaRossa, R., & LaRossa, M. M. (1981). *Transition to parenthood: How infants change families.* Beverly Hills, CA: Sage.

Laslett, P. (1965). *The world we have lost: England before the industrial age.* New York: Scribners.

Lee, G. (1979). Children and the elderly: Interaction and morale. *Research on Aging, 1,* 335–339.

Lezak, M. (1978). Living with the characterologically altered brain injured patient. *Journal of Clinical Psychiatry, 39,* 592–598.

Litwak, E. (1965). Extended kin relations in an industrial society. In E. Shanas & G. Streib (Eds.), *Social structure and the family: Generational relations* (pp. 290–323). Englewood Cliffs, NJ: Prentice-Hall.

Lopata, H. (1979). *Women as widows.* New York: Elsevier North Holland.

Mancini, J., & Blieszner, R. (1989). Aging parents and adult children: Research themes in intergenerational relations. *Journal of Marriage and the Family, 51,* 275–290.

Mannheim, K. (1936). *Ideology and utopia.* London: Routledge & Kegan Paul.

Mannheim, K. (1952). *Essays on the sociology of knowledge.* London: Routledge & Kegan Paul.

Marshall, V. (1981). *Last chapters: A sociology of death and dying.* Belmont, CA: Wadsworth.

Marx, K. (1844/1978). Economic and philosophic manuscripts of 1844. In R. Tucker (Ed.), *The Marx-Engels reader* (2nd ed., pp. 66–125). New York: Norton.

Marx, K. (1845–46/1978). The German ideology: Part I. In R. Tucker (Ed.), *The Marx-Engels reader* (2nd ed., pp. 147–200). New York: Norton.

Masnick, G., & Bane, M. J. (1980). *The nation's families, 1950–1990.* Dover, MA: Auburn House.

Mattessich, P., & Hill, R. (1987). Life-cycle and family development. In M. B. Sussman & S. Steinmetz (Eds.), *Handbook of marriage and the family* (pp. 437–469). New York: Plenum Press.

McCubbin, H., & Figley, C. (Eds.). (1983). *Stress and the family* (Vols. 1 & 2). New York: Brunner/Mazel.

McCubbin, H., & Patterson, J. (1983). The family-stress process: The double ABC-X model of adjustment and adaptation. *Marriage and Family Review, 6,* 7–38.

Mederer, H., & Hill, R. (1983). Critical transitions over the family life span: Theory and research. *Marriage and Family Review, 6,* 39–60.

Mishler, E. (1986). *Research interviewing: Context and narrative.* Cambridge, MA: Harvard University Press.

Mishler, E. (1990). Validation: The social construction of knowledge. *Harvard Educational Review, 60,* 415–442.

Modell, J. (1989). *Into one's own: From youth to adulthood in the United States, 1920–1975.* Berkeley: University of California Press.

Murphy, P., & Staples, W. (1979). A modernized family life cycle. *Journal of Consumer Research, 6,* 12–22.

Neugarten, B. L. (1976). Time, age, and the life-cycle. *American Journal of Psychiatry, 136,* 887–894.

Nye, F. I., & Bernardo, F. (1966). *Emerging conceptual frameworks in family analyses.* New York: Macmillan.

Oakley, A. (1974). *The sociology of housework.* New York: Pantheon.

Osmond, M., & Thorne, B. (1993). Feminist theories: The social construction of gender in family and society. In P. Boss, W. Doherty, R. LaRossa, W. Schumm, & S. Steinmetz (Eds.), *Sourcebook of family theories and methods: A contextual approach* (pp. 591–622). New York: Plenum Press.

Parker, B. (1972). *A mingled yarn: A chronicle of a troubled family.* New Haven, CT: Yale University Press.

Parsons, T. (1949). The social structure of the family. In R. Anshen (Ed.), *The family: Its function and destiny* (pp. 173–201). New York: Harper & Row.

Parsons, T., Bales F., & Associates. (1955). *Family, socialization and interaction processes.* New York: Free Press.

Parsons, T., & Fox, R. (1952). Illness, therapy, and the modern urban American family. *Journal of Social Issues, 8,* 32–44.

Passuth, P., & Bengtson, V. (1988). Sociological theories of aging: Current perspectives and future directions. In J. Birren & V. Bengtson (Eds.), *Emergent theories of aging* (pp. 333–355). New York: Springer Publishing Co.

Pillemer, K., & Wolf, R. (Eds.). (1986). *Elder abuse: Conflict in the family*. Dover, MA: Auburn.

Polkinghorne, D. (1983). *Methodology for the human sciences*. Albany: State University of New York Press.

Popenoe, D. (1988). *Disturbing the nest*. New York: Aldine de Gruyter.

Poster, M. (1978). *Critical theory of the family*. New York: Seabury Press.

Pruchno, R., Blow, F., & Smyer, M. (1984). Life-events and interdependent lives. *Gerontologist, 27*, 31–41.

Putnam, H. (1978). *Meaning and the moral sciences*. Boston: Routledge & Kegan Paul.

Riley, M. W. (Ed.). (1988). *Social structures and human lives*. Newbury Park, CA: Sage.

Riley, M. W., Foner, A., & Waring, J. (1968). *Aging and society. Vol. 1: An inventory of research findings*. New York: Russell Sage.

Riley, M. W., Foner, A., & Waring, J. (1972). *Aging and society. Vol. 3: A sociology of age stratification*. New York: Russell Sage.

Rodgers, R. (1973). *Family interaction and transaction: The developmental approach*. Englewood Cliffs, NJ: Prentice-Hall.

Rodgers, R., & White, J. (1993). Family development theory. In P. Boss, W. Doherty, R. LaRossa, W. Schumm, & S. Steinmetz (Eds.), *Sourcebook of family theories and methods: A contextual approach* (pp. 225–254). New York: Plenum Press.

Rorty, R. (1980). *Philosophy and the mirror of nature*. Princeton, NJ: Princeton University Press.

Rosenmayr, L., & Kockeis, E. (1963). Propositions for a sociological theory of action and the family. *International Social Science Journal, 15*, 410–426.

Rosenwald, G., & Ochberg, R. (1992). Introduction: Life-stories, cultural politics, and self-understanding. In G. Rosenwald & R. Ochberg (Eds.), *Storied lives: The cultural politics of self-understanding* (pp. 21–40). New Haven, CT: Yale University Press.

Rosow, I. (1978). What is a cohort and why? *Human Development, 21*, 65–75.

Rossi, A., & Rossi, P. (1991). *Of human bonding*. New York: Aldine de Gruyter.

Roth, J. (1963). *Timetables: Structuring the passage of time in hospital treatment and other careers*. Indianapolis, IN: Bobbs-Merrill.

Schaie, K. W. (1984). The Seattle longitudinal study: A 2-year exploration of the psychometric intelligence of adulthood. In K. W. Schaie (Ed.), *Longitudinal studies of personality* (pp. 64–135). New York: Guilford Press.

Shanas, E. (1979a). The family as a social support system in old age. *Gerontologist, 19*, 169–174.

Shanas, E. (1979b). Social myth as hypothesis: The case of the family relations of old people. *Gerontologist, 19*, 3–9.

Smith, D. E. (1987). *The everyday world as problematic*. Boston: Northeastern University Press.

Sorokin, P., & Merton, R. (1937). Social time: A methodological and functional analysis. *American Journal of Sociology, 42*, 615–629.

Spanier, G., Sauer, W., & Larzelere, R. (1979). An empirical evaluation of the family life-cycle. *Journal of Marriage and the Family, 41,* 27–38.

Stack, C. (1974). *All our kin.* New York: Harper & Row.

Steinmetz, S., & Amsden, D. (1983). Dependent elders, family stress, and abuse. In T. Brubaker (Ed.), *Family relationships in later life* (pp. 173–192). Beverly Hills, CA: Sage.

Strauss, A. (1990). *Never-ending care.* Newbury Park, CA: Sage.

Streib, G., & Beck, R. (1980). Older families: A decade review. *Journal of Marriage and the Family, 42,* 937–958.

Suppe, F. (1977). Afterward—1977. In F. Suppe (Ed.), *The search for philosophic understanding of scientific theories* (pp. 617–730). Urbana: University of Illinois Press.

Sussman, M. (1985). The family life of old people. In R. H. Binstock & E. Shanas (Eds.), *Handbook of aging and the social sciences* (2nd ed., pp. 415–449). New York: Van Nostrand-Reinhold.

Sussman, M., & Steinmetz, S. (Eds.). (1987). *Handbook of marriage and the family.* New York: Plenum Press.

Thomas, D., & Wilcox, J. (1987). The rise of family theory: A historical and critical analysis. In M. B. Sussman & S. K. Steinmetz (Eds.), *Handbook of marriage and the family* (pp. 81–102). New York: Plenum Press.

Toulmin, S. (1990). *Cosmopolis: The hidden agenda of modernity.* New York: Free Press.

Treas, J., & Bengtson, V. L. (1987). Family in later life. In M. Sussman & S. Steinmetz (Eds.), *Handbook of marriage and the family* (pp. 625–648). New York: Plenum Press.

Troll, L. (1970). Issues in the study of generations. *International Journal of Aging and Human Development, 9,* 199–218.

Troll, L. (1971). The family of later life: A decade review. *Journal of Marriage and the Family, 33,* 263–290.

Troll, L., & Bengtson, V. (1979). Generations in the family. In W. Burr, F. I. Nye, & I. L. Reiss (Eds.), *Contemporary theories about the family* (Vol. 1, pp. 127–161). New York: Free Press.

Troll, L., Miller, S., & Atchley, R. (1979). *Families in later life.* Belmont, CA: Wadsworth.

Troost, K. M., & Filsinger, E. (1993). Emerging biosocial perspectives on the family. In P. Boss, W. Doherty, R. LaRossa, W. Schumm, & S. Steinmetz (Eds.), *Sourcebook of family theories and methods: A contextual approach* (pp. 677–710). New York: Plenum Press.

Uhlenberg, P. (1980). Death and the family. *Journal of Family History, 5,* 313–320.

Uhlenhuth, E., Lipman, R., Balter, M., & Stern, M. (1974). Symptom intensity and life stress in the city. *Archives of General Psychiatry, 31,* 759–764.

Unruh, D. (1983). *Invisible lives: Social worlds of the aged.* Beverly Hills, CA: Sage.

Veevers, J. (1979). Voluntary childlessness: A review of issues and evidence. *Marriage and Family Review, 2,* 1–26.

Wallace, A. (1956). Revitalization movements. *American Anthropologist, 58,* 264–281.

White, J. M. (1991). *Dynamics of family development: A theoretical perspective.* New York: Guilford Press.

Whyte, M. K. (1990). *Dating, mating, and marriage.* New York: Aldine de Gruyter.

5

Family Relations and Individual Development in Adulthood and Aging

Carol D. Ryff and Marsha Mailick Seltzer

INTRODUCTION

The purpose of this chapter is to bring together two realms, family relations and individual development, that have typically been studied separately. Studies of individual development in adulthood and the later years show only oblique links with family life, even though the family is a central context in which individual development is embedded. Conversely, the extensive literature on family relations extends across different age groups and life periods, and yet, this body of research shows limited connection to theories of, and findings about, individual development. Although studies of family development (Mattessich & Hill, 1987) make use of individual developmental theory to characterize family stages, links between family and individual development are not explored.

Reasons for this division reflect, in part, the disciplinary training of the investigators. Family researchers typically have backgrounds in family sociology, family studies and development programs, or gerontology. Researchers of individual development are more typically located in fields of developmental, personality, or clinical psychology.

Another reason for the division is the assertion that the complexity of family research requires a shift in the unit of analysis from the individual family member to the family as a whole (Thompson & Walker, 1982). Thus, family-level data are called for to capture the patterns of interaction and exchange among all family members. We propose, alternatively, that assessment of individuals within the family unit, in addition to family-level assessment, is imperative if we are to track how family life both contributes to, and is influenced by, individual development.

In our conceptualization, family life is antecedent to individual development, and individual development is antecedent to change in family life, in a reciprocal pattern over time. While the role of an individual in a family changes dramatically from childhood to adulthood to old age, the context of the family remains a primary background against which individual development occurs. In a complementary fashion, family life is shaped by the characteristics and evolving challenges of the individuals who constitute the family unit.

We review two areas of literature in this chapter to illustrate the division between the family context and individual development. On the individual side, theories of personal development in adulthood and aging are examined to show that, for the most part, the development of adults has been studied without acknowledging their role as parents or children. Research on the psychological well-being of parents is noted, with the observation that this realm of inquiry is largely nondevelopmental.

On the family side, the literature on caregiving in middle and later adulthood is reviewed. We use past research to show that, for the most part, the literature on caregiving has not acknowledged how this role may have persistent consequences for the personal well-being and development of the caregiver outside this role.

We acknowledge that other research domains could be selected to illustrate linkages between family relationships and individual development. For example, the literatures on parent-child relations, intergenerational relations, and family solidarity (e.g., Bengtson, 1987; Bengtson & Mangen, 1988; Hagestad, 1987; Mancini & Blieszner, 1989) provide other forums for evaluating linkages of family relations and individual development. On the individual side, various theories of adult development provide insights into the challenges faced by individuals in the adult and later years of the life course (Buhler & Massarik, 1968; Erikson, 1959; Jung, 1933; Neugarten, 1973). Our decision to target caregiving vis-à-vis particular developmental theories reflects our own research agendas and, therefore, the findings with which we are most familiar.

In the final section, we discuss three issues critical to the linkage of research on individual development and studies of family relationships: reciprocal relationships between individuals and their families, nonnormative patterns of family life and individual development, and methodological issues relevant to the study of unfolding individuals in the context of unfolding families.

PERSPECTIVES ON INDIVIDUAL DEVELOPMENT

A leading theoretical perspective on the course of individual development across the life span is Erikson's (1950, 1959) psychosocial stage model, which postulated a series of eight stages or crises to be negotiated by the healthy personality. The theory is a leading exemplar of how individual development has been construed and therefore provides a useful context for assessing the links between family life and individual development.

Erikson (1959) presented "human growth from the point of view of the conflicts, inner and outer, which the healthy personality weathers, emerging and re-emerging with an increased sense of inner unity, with an increase of good judgment, and an increase in the capacity to do well, according to the standards of those who are significant to him" (p. 51). He argued that human growth has a ground plan, known as the epigenetic principle, which specifies that each aspect of development has its special time of ascendancy until all parts have arisen to form a functioning whole.

Review of Erikson's stages of development shows surprisingly few links between family life and individual development. Mother's caregiving is briefly described as critical to the development of a firm sense of trust (Stage 1), and parents are mentioned in one or two sentences regarding the crisis of autonomy versus shame and doubt (stage 2). As the child moves through subsequent stages of initiative versus guilt, industry versus inferiority, and identity versus diffusion, individuals outside the family, such as peers and schoolteacher, are briefly discussed.

Erikson's young adult transition, intimacy versus isolation, includes "work or study for a specified career, sociability with the other sex, and in time, marriage and a family of one's own" (p. 95) and thereby reinstates the significance of family life. However, generativity versus stagnation, Erikson's seventh stage, is most directly connected with family life, namely, parenthood. Nonetheless, parenthood is not seen as the only avenue for successful resolution of the crisis of generativity: "[T]here are people who, from misfortune or because of special and genuine gifts in other directions, do not apply this drive [generativity] to offspring but to other forms of altruistic concern and of creativity, which may absorb their kind of parental responsibility" (p. 97). Further, merely having children does not necessarily involve generativity, suggesting that many parents are unable to develop at this stage because of faulty identification with their own parents, excessive self-love, or a lack of faith in the human species.

The final stage, integrity versus despair, shows minimal connection with family life, with the exception of a brief statement about accepting one's parents as part of the task of integrity: "It [ego integrity] is the acceptance of one's own and only life cycle and of the people who have become significant to it as something that had to be and that, by necessity, permitted of no substitutions. It thus means a new different love of one's parents, free of the wish that they should have been different, and an acceptance of the fact that one's life is one's own responsibility" (p. 98).

These quotes convey the limited discussion of family life in the eight stages of development. Family members are intermittently present but are in the background, not a part of the central drama of individual development played out within the person. Even generativity, the most family-centered of Erikson's stages, is juxtaposed with other nonparental forms of generativity.

Empirical translations of Eriksonian theory have generally perpetuated this lack of connection between family life and individual development. The absence of family is evident on two levels. First, the actual operationalization of Eriksonian constructs—that is, items constructed to measure the developmental stages—are devoid of family content. Second, family roles, responsibilities, and relationships have limited presence in discussions of factors that might contribute to, or benefit from, individual development.

For example, studies of identity and intimacy development (Whitbourne & Tesch, 1985; Whitbourne, Zuschlag, Elliot, & Waterman, 1992) addressed the fundamental question of whether development and change actually occur in adulthood, or whether this period is primarily a stable plateau (e.g., as argued by Costa & McCrae, 1980; McCrae & Costa, 1990). Measures of the developmental stages in these inquiries did not include questions about family relationships, nor were marital or parental relationships considered in describing the sample or interpreting the findings. Similarly, work on self-perceived developmental changes (Ryff & Heincke, 1983; Ryff & Migdal, 1984), although guided by Eriksonian theory, also employed measurement items purged of family content (e.g., generativity items were written to apply to respondents of all ages, either sex, and all familial or nonfamilial statuses).

Recent work has expanded and refined Erikson's stage of generativity, building on the idea that generativity is by no means limited to the domain of parenthood: "One may be generative in a wide variety of life pursuits and in a vast array of life settings, as in work life and professional activities, volunteer endeavors, participation in religious and political organizations, neighborhood and community activism, friendships, and even one's leisure-time activities" (McAdams & St. Aubin, 1992, p. 1003).The authors noted, in fact, that some of Erikson's most compelling examples of generativity appear in his psychobiographies of Martin Luther and Mahatma Gandhi, both of whom were more generative in public action than in the private realm of family life.

The preceding research focused on the measurement of various aspects of generativity (e.g., self-report concerns, behavioral acts, narrative themes). The Loyola Generativity Scale (LGS), developed to measure generative concern, had all items referring to the caring for children *eliminated* in the scale construction process (because they were too highly correlated with social desirability). "Thus, the scale cannot be said to 'discriminate against' adults who do not have children, even though child rearing receives considerable attention in theoretical writing on generativity" (McAdams & St. Aubin, 1992, p. 1008). Thus, in this work, as in those prior, the construct of generativity was removed from the immediate sphere of family life.

Yet, parenthood remains an intriguing part of the research findings.

McAdams and St. Aubin (1992) found that men who were, or had been, fathers showed higher generativity scores compared with men without children. These differences could not be attributed to marital status, because marital status was unrelated to generativity scores for both sexes. "Rather, it is whether a man has ever been a father to a child that seems to make a difference in predicting his generativity on the LGS. The result is especially noteworthy in that no items on the LGS explicitly deal with being a father and raising children" (McAdams & St. Aubin, 1992, p. 1008). Because of the correlational nature of the data, it is unclear whether high generative concern among men is a predictor, consequence, or both, of parental status.

These studies could be augmented with other examples from Eriksonian research (e.g., Peterson & Stewart, 1990), as well as work emanating from other developmental perspectives (e.g., Gould, 1978; Jung, 1933; Levinson, 1986; Loevinger, 1976; Vaillant, 1977), to underscore the point that conceptions of growth and change in the adult years are typically remote from family life. Where family relationships are mentioned, it is frequently in the context of individual efforts to move beyond family ties to a new, higher level of functioning. Thus, Gould (1978) discussed the need to confront myths inherent in beliefs obtained from parents; Levinson, Darrow, Klein, Levinson, & McKee (1978) discussed the possible reorganization of the life structure in midlife, which may include changes in marital partners and family roles; and Jung (1933) discussed the possible tensions created in marital relationships when husbands discover their tenderness of heart at the same time wives discover their sharpness of mind.

Note that in the personality realm, efforts have been made to link personality development in adult women to changing family life statuses. Helson and Wink (1992), in a longitudinal sample of women, investigated associations between personality change on the California Psychological Inventory and menopausal status, empty nest status, or involvement in care for parents. No associations were found. Cooper and Gutmann (1987), however, using projective tests within psychoanalytic framework, found that post–empty nest women engaged in more active ego mastery style than pre–empty nest women. The former also indicated more masculine traits, consistent with Gutmann's claims that the parental imperative differentially channels the expression of psychological changes in adult men and women.

An extensive literature also exists on ways that parenthood influences the psychological well-being of adults, compared with those who do not become parents (McLanahan & Adams, 1987). Survey studies have pointed to primarily negative psychological consequences associated with parenthood (see, however, Umberson & Gove, 1989). This literature has addressed stages in the family life cycle, but issues of individual development generally have been neglected. Parental age, for example, is typically controlled for, rather than targeted as a key predictor variable, and no assessment is made of psychological development among parents (see Seltzer & Ryff, 1994, as an exception).

Mindful of these diverse literatures, we suggest that studies of development in adulthood and later life typically conceive of development as an individual phenomenon with limited connection to the contexts and roles of adult life, many of which ensue from the family. Despite hints that some aspects of development, particularly generativity, may contribute to, and benefit from, family experiences, the actual measurement of such constructs typically *excludes* family experiences. More compelling questions of adult development, such as *who changes, who does not, and why* (Block, 1981), necessitate closer attention to the family life experiences that provide contexts for fostering and enhancing, or impeding and diminishing, individual development.

PERSPECTIVES ON FAMILY CAREGIVING

In contrast to research on individual development in adulthood and old age, which has emphasized the individual without adequate consideration of the familial context, studies of family caregiving—our example of family relations research—have emphasized the family context but have obscured the impact of caregiving on individual development outside this context. In this section, we examine trends in past research on family caregiving and suggest new avenues of investigation that bring together the familial and individual contexts.

The caregiving literature has focused on three primary questions: (1) What social and demographic factors predict who becomes a caregiver? (2) How does the caregiver react to the demands of caregiving, primarily with respect to feelings of stress, burden, and depression? (3) What supports and interventions can be offered to caregivers to lessen these negative reactions?

In response to the first question, the literature has clarified that both gender and family relationship determine which family member becomes the caregiver. Women are more likely to become caregivers than are men, and a spouse is more likely to be a caregiver than is an adult child (Brody, 1985; Quayhagen & Quayhagen, 1988). Thus, this literature has pointed to structural and demographic factors, rather than individual personality characteristics, as indicators of who becomes a caregiver.

In response to the second question, the literature confirms that caregiving has negative effects, with caregivers showing more financial, physical, and emotional strains than noncaregivers (Cantor, 1983; Zarit, Reever, & Bach-Peterson, 1980). Further, caregiving is not a uniform experience but varies according to demographic and social status. Women, who provide more intensive personal care than men, tend to experience more burden and strain in the caregiving role (Barusch & Spaid, 1989); spouses are more negatively affected than are adult children (Rosenthal, Sulman, & Marshall,

1993; Quayhagen & Quayhagen, 1988); and coresident caregivers suffer more than those who live apart from the care recipient (Hoyert & Seltzer, 1992).

In response to the third question, interventions have been designed to provide support and relief for caregivers. Evaluations of the effectiveness of these interventions are inconclusive, however (Lawton, Brody, & Saperstein, 1989). Additional research is needed to clarify how or if services such as respite care reduce the stress and burden experienced by family caregivers. The question of whether such interventions have broader impacts on the caregiver (i.e, beyond the caregiver role) remains inadequately addressed.

The conceptual model that has most strongly influenced research on caregiving is the stress process model (Pearlin, Mullan, Semple, & Skaff, 1990), which conceptualizes caregiving as a primary stressor. External supports and personal resources mediate the caregiver's response to this source of stress. In general, the stress process model has resulted in an examination of the proximal, rather than the global, effects of caregiving. Put differently, this model emphasizes the responses of the individual to the situational stressors of the role of caregiver without explicit conceptualization of how caregiving might at the same time have an effect on the personal well-being of the caregiver *outside* this role.

An additional unresolved issue is whether the caregiving experience results in long-term changes in the caregiver's psychological well-being. Does this experience result in stress, burden, and lifestyle changes only during the period of time that the caregiver is actively providing care, or does being a caregiver alter the family member's well-being and psychological makeup in a more fundamental sense? Does this role affect the caregiver's views on aging, dependency, family, and self, or are the effects domain-specific? Does the caregiving experience result in more or less resiliency on the part of the caregiver, diminished or enhanced self-esteem, a sense of helplessness or of mastery, a clearer or more diffuse purpose in life, greater or lesser ego integrity? In light of the increased likelihood that women, in particular, will take on the role of caregiver at some point in their lifetimes, investigations of whether and how this role alters the well-being and life course of those who experience it are needed.

One approach to investigating the broader impacts of the caregiving experience is to examine how individuals change when they first have the responsibility of providing care to a relative, how they are affected during the course of caregiving, and how former caregivers react after caregiving ends. Most available studies of caregiving have been cross-sectional (e.g., George & Gwyther, 1984; Snyder & Keefe, 1985), averaging new and "experienced" caregivers together and omitting former caregivers (i.e., those who are bereaved and those who have placed the care recipient into a nursing home). This cross-sectional approach obscures the possibility that caregiving is a process that unfolds as the caregiver moves into, through, and out of this role. Whereas in the cross-section, caregivers appear to have poorer well-being than noncaregivers (Hoyert & Seltzer, 1992), the small body of longitudinal research on caregiving suggests that over time, a process of adaptation occurs. For example, Townsend, Noelker, Deimling, and Bass (1989) found that over a 14-month period, the majority of their noncoresiding sample of adult children caring for their elderly parents manifested improved caregiving effectiveness and no increase in depression. Similar results were reported by Zarit, Todd, and Zarit (1986), who found that caregivers for the elderly were able to improve their ability to cope with the problem behaviors manifested by the care recipient, even though these behaviors had become more extreme over time. Chiriboga, Yee, and Weiler (1992) studied the stress responses of adult children who provided care to a parent with Alzheimer's disease and found that the longer the time since the parent's diagnosis, the less the burden.

These studies suggest that caregiving is most stressful when it is a new role, but over time, it may provide an opportunity for the development of new coping strategies and psychological growth. It is possible, therefore, that the longer the duration of care, the greater the potential for adaptational processes to be manifested. It is also possible that curvilinear effects occur, with the early and end stages of caregiving most stressful, while adaptational processes may be more evident during the middle stage. Thus, longitudinal research might reveal that caregiving is a process, with a progression of stages from the beginning to the end of this responsibility. Additionally, these progressive responses to the caregiving challenge might interact with an individual's prior level of psychological resources, revealing individual differences in the commonly experienced stages of caregiving.

Another unanswered question is what happens to the family member *after* the caregiving role has ended. The caregiving literature has focused on the window of time between the point when the family member begins to provide care to the end of active caregiving. Virtually no study of the caregiver during the postcaregiving period has been conducted, reflecting the implicit assumption that the impacts of caregiving are restricted to the time when it is an active role, without attention to the possibility of persistent and diverse effects on the individual even after this responsibility has declined or ended. This omission points to the inattention of the available research to the individual and his or her development in the context of this family responsibility. More information exists on how caregiving affects the caregiver's time management, social life, employment status, and lifestyle (Brody, 1985) than on how this role affects the psychological characteristics of the person who performs it.

A related literature is research on bereavement. These studies report on family members' reactions to the death of a loved one (Lund, 1989). Unfortunately, most of these studies have begun their investigations at the point of bereavement, so connections from the prebreavement (in some cases, caregiving) stage to the bereavement (or postcaregiving) stage have not been drawn.

A few longitudinal studies have, however, provided the needed linkages from the caregiving to the bereavement stages by first measuring the reactions of caregivers while actively in this role and then continuing to track personal well-being after they become bereaved. For example, Mullan (1992) compared bereaved and continuing caregivers and found that a sense of mastery *increased* in those who were bereaved. In another report of the same study, Skaff (1991) found that, among caregivers whose family member had moved to a nursing home, a sense of competence increased, particularly for those who had provided a high level of personal care to the family member before placement. O'Bryant, Straw, and Meddaugh (1990) reported that widows who had provided care to their husbands had higher mastery scores than widows whose husbands had died suddenly. Together, these studies indicate that the caregiving experience may have long-term (i.e., postcaregiving) effects on at least one aspect of individual development, namely, mastery. The directional relationship is somewhat surprising, namely, that caregiving may *enhance* an individual's sense of mastery rather than diminish it.

Another omission in the caregiving literature concerns the experience of the *care recipient*. Although death is the most common cause for the end of caregiving, some recipients of family care recover, and others have a chronic condition that requires ongoing care and support from a family member. In these instances, it would be valuable to examine how being a care recipient affects one's psychological well-being. Little attention has been focused on how receiving care from a family member alters the individual in terms of self-esteem, aspirations, and other aspects of personality.

In sum, our review of the literature on family caregiving as an example of family relations calls for a new examination of the individual, both caregiver and care recipient. There is a need to learn how this alteration in previous family role relationships affects the older parents and their adult children, both during the period of care and after it has ended. Because it is now well accepted that caregiving is an increasingly common role in later life (Brody, 1985), the need to understand how this role contributes to later-life individual development is crucial.

FORGING LINKAGES AND AVENUES FOR FUTURE RESEARCH

Among the many issues that warrant attention in the conceptualization and design of future research on individual development and family relations, three stand out as particularly salient. These are the reciprocal influences of the individual and family and of parent and child across the life course, the similarities and differences of normative and nonnormative patterns of family life and individual development, and selected methodological issues pertinent to this research. Each of these is addressed in this final section.

Reciprocal Influences

The premise of this chapter is that individual development and family relations are reciprocal and that the influences unfold in tandem across the life course. An element of this premise is that parents influence their children at the same time that children influence their parents, although the nature of the bidirectional influence may shift over time. Rossi and Rossi (1990) demonstrated the predictable pattern of exchange of assistance and sentiment between parent and child, documenting the persistence of love and care given by parents to their children and reciprocally by adult children to their aging parents.

Nydegger (1991), in her exploration of Blenkner's concept of filial maturity, found evidence that fathers and their adult children have a strong influence on one another through "paced, parallel development" (p. 101). She extended the concept of *filial maturity,* a developmental challenge facing adult children, to include *parental maturity,* a developmental challenge facing older parents in their relationships with their adult children. Other researchers (e.g., Greenberg & Becker, 1988; Pillemer & Suitor, 1991) clarified that although these influences can have positive effects on both parents and their adult children, negative influences can occur as well. In particular, their work documents the negative influence of adult children's problems on the well-being of elderly parents.

Viewed in life span context, the vast majority of studies regarding directional influences between parents and children have been concerned with the effects parents have on the early development of their children (Goodnow & Collins, 1990; Sigel, McGillicuddy-DeLisi, & Goodnow, 1992; Seltzer & Ryff, 1994). Exceptions to this prevailing emphasis can be found in socialization research (Bell, 1968; Bell & Harper, 1977; Peterson & Rollins, 1987), where the prior unidirectional bias has been challenged. However, actual developmental studies of reciprocity between parent and child have been conducted primarily in infancy, with a focus on microanalytic episodes of interactive behavior.

An emerging literature has begun to address how children, as they grow older, influence their parents' well-being (Cook & Cohler, 1986; Hagestad, 1987; Ryff & Seltzer, in press). Children's developmental transitions provide a useful framework for investigating such influences. Silverberg (in press; Silverberg & Steinberg, 1990) has examined how children's adolescent transition is tied to parental well-being. Only modest direct relations were found between signs of adolescent development (i.e., pubertal maturation, heterosocial involvement, persuasive reasoning abilities) and parental well-being, although these relations were stronger when differences in parents' orientation toward the employment role were taken into consideration. Thus, parents' work experiences appeared to interact with their parental experiences to determine their well-being, illustrating the complex interplay among employment, family relations, and individual functioning.

Later, as children make the transition to adulthood, new issues emerge for parents, such as the general question of how their children have "turned out." These assessments may also contribute to parental well-being. Hagestad (1986) reported that mothers derived a sense of personal accomplishment from knowing that their adult children had mastered life tasks. Other investigators have found that multiple aspects of psychological well-being, such as parents' ratings of their purpose in life, environmental mastery, self-acceptance, personal growth, and positive relations with others, are significantly and positively predicted by their assessments of grown children, particularly the personal and social adjustment of these offspring (Ryff, Lee, Essex, & Schmutte, 1994; Ryff, Schmutte, & Lee, in press). Children's attainment (educational and occupational) also predict parental well-being, but with less pervasive effects.

These studies also clarify the mechanisms through which children's lives influence parental well-being. Social comparison processes constitute one such mechanism. Of interest has been how parents compare their children with other people's children (such as those of their siblings or friends) as well as with themselves. Comparisons with other people's children show limited effects on parental well-being. Parents' ratings of how their children compare with themselves, however, are significant predictors of multiple aspects of parental well-being, after controlling for the effects of how children had turned out (Ryff, Lee, Essex, & Schmutter, 1994; Ryff, Schmutte, & Lee, in press). The direction of these effects was largely negative, particularly in personal and social adjustments. Parents who felt their children were doing better in these areas than they themselves had in young adulthood had lower levels of well-being than did parents who felt their children compared less well with themselves.

Another mechanism by which children's lives may influence parental well-being is derived from attribution theory, which in the parental context addresses the extent to which parents feel responsible for how their children have turned out. Parents who view their children as less successful reported a lower sense of responsibility for children's lives than parents who viewed their children as more successful. Contrary to the hedonic bias in attribution research (i.e., tendency to see self as not responsible for negative outcomes), parents with lowest well-being perceived that their children had not turned out well *and* felt that they had little responsibility for the children's lives (Ryff & Schmutte, 1993; Ryff, Schmutte, & Lee, in press).

In sum, issues of reciprocal influences between individuals and their family lives point to the need to study these unfolding patterns across the life course, to attend to both positive and negative effects that may ensue between family members, and to address the mechanisms through which individuals influence, and are influenced by, their family relationships.

Nonnormative Patterns of Family Life and Individual Development

The literature we have reviewed indicates the salience of the relationship between older parents and their adult children during the long stretch of time after the child has left home and before the parents become frail and in need of care (i.e., when both are healthy and function independently). Cohler (1983), in his discussion of autonomy and interdependence in the family of adulthood, underscored the importance of the multigenerational family in understanding personality development in midlife. His generalizations focused primarily on the normative family—the family not marked by disability, tragic loss, or repeated disruptions.

There is a need to consider how these issues play out in the nonnormative family. Although the contemporary American family is marked by increasing diversity in structure and function (Marks, in press), some families experience events that alter family life in a fundamental sense (Cook & Cohler, 1986). Though rarely linked in research on individual development, nonnormative events often set off their own developmental processes (Bandura, 1982; Featherman, 1985; Parke, 1988).

A good example is the challenge of family caregiving. Whereas most literature on family caregiving in the context of the relationship between the adult child and aging parent focuses on the care provided by adult children to their aging parents, the reverse also occurs. Older parents whose adult children have significant dependency needs, such as mental retardation, mental illness, or acquired immunodeficiency syndrome (AIDS), often provide continuing care for their sons and daughters even as they confront the challenges of their own aging and need for support (Seltzer & Krauss, 1989).

Although the nonnormative role of parental caregiver to an adult child influences the well-being of such parents (Cook & Cohler, 1986), these influences emanate from the unique challenges posed by the child rather than from the role per se. To illustrate, Greenberg, Seltzer, and Greenley (1993), in their comparative study of older mothers of adults with mental illness and mental retardation, found that mothers of adults with mental illness were more negatively affected than their counterparts whose son or daughter had mental retardation. Seltzer, Krauss, Choi, and Hong (in press) further clarified that mothers of adults with mental retardation are at no greater risk of poor health, depression, or social isolation than other women their age. Thus, the particular problems posed by the adult child may affect the well-being of their parents more than the nonnormative role itself does. The challenge for future researchers with respect to the developmental outcomes of nonnormative events (such as having a child with a chronic illness or a disability) is to determine the mechanisms by which such events alter people's beliefs about themselves (Wortman & Silver, 1992), resulting in variations in individual adaptation and development.

Methodological Issues

We highlight three methodological issues of importance in understanding the linkages between family life and individual development. First, with regard to *research design,* we underscore the need for longitudinal studies to investigate the unfolding, bidirectional trajectories of individuals and their families. This admonition is fundamental to any developmental inquiry and, as such, verges on the obvious. The more interesting issue for research design is the task of deciding *when* to obtain these repeated measurements. What are, or should be, the critical assessment points? We argue that the timing of longitudinal assessments should be driven by substantive research issues, not merely the goal of obtaining multiple, cross-time assessments. Our perspective on family caregiving suggests, for example, that longitudinal measurements are critical during at least three phases of the caregiving process: the initial transition into caregiving, the actual period of caregiving, and the transition out of caregiving. Beyond the caregiving context, we have also argued that studies of how parents and children influence each other are usefully grounded in transition points, such as children's adolescent or young adult transitions. Other family transitions (marriages, births, divorces, retirements) in the lives of parents or children provide further guides for charting the timing of longitudinal assessments.

A second methodological issue pertains to the *outcome variables* that are included in research agendas on family relations and individual development. A wide array of indicators should be employed to assess individual functioning in the context of family life. Some measures follow directly from developmental theories, such as efforts to operationalize the Eriksonian construct of generativity (McAdams & St. Aubin, 1992; Peterson & Stewart, 1990; Ryff & Heincke, 1983). Other outcomes follow from a broadened conception of well-being that draws on not only developmental theory but also clinical conceptions of maturity and personal growth (e.g., Allport, 1961; Maslow, 1968; Rogers, 1961) and positive conceptions of mental health (Jahoda, 1958; see Ryff, 1989a, 1989b; Ryff & Essex, 1992). Still other outcomes are derived from stress paradigms (Cohler & Altergott, this volume; Pearlin et al., 1990), where indicators of physical and emotional strain are the relevant dependent variables. We endorse this diversity as a reflection of the complexity of measuring individual functioning in the family life context. Research agendas that include multiple components of development, well-being, and dysfunction are, in fact, best equipped to delineate what specific aspects of functioning are, and are not, influenced by family life experiences.

Finally, we raise the methodological issue of the choice of research respondents. The central question is, *From whom should researchers collect data,* when the goal is to understand the linkage between individual functioning and family life? We opened this chapter with the argument that assessment of individuals within the family is imperative for tracking how family life both contributes to, and is influenced by, individual development. Thus, data must be collected from those who are targets of research, whether they be parents, caregivers, care recipients, or other family members. That is, in linking individual well-being to particular family relationships, we view it as critical to have data representing such relationships from multiple points of view. This call to collect data from multiple family members is not new (Pruchno, Dempsey, & Burant, in press; Thompson & Walker, 1982). Inquiry involving multiple family respondents could, however, be employed for greater advantage than that of illuminating the quality of dyadic relationships or family climate. For example, even the assessment of individual functioning could benefit from evaluations of multiple respondents. How do adult children, for example, rate the well-being of their parents? How do these ratings square with parents' assessments of their own well-being? The magnitude of discrepancy between one's well-being, rated by self and by significant others, constitutes another relevant index, both of individual and of family functioning.

In summary, future research on family relations and individual development will benefit from greater attention to the ways in which individuals influence families and families influence individuals. This realm of inquiry must also be attentive to the distinctions between normative versus non-normative family life experiences and their effects on individual functioning. Methodologically, there is need for more longitudinal research with the timing of assessments substantively driven; for more diverse outcome measures that capture aspects of development and well-being as well as dimensions of dysfunction; and for data sets that represent individual functioning and family relationships from multiple family members and, thus, multiple points of view.

NOTE

The authors express their appreciation to Frank Floyd, Jan Greenberg, and Victor Marshall for their helpful comments on an earlier draft of this chapter.

REFERENCES

Allport, G. W. (1961). *Pattern and growth in personality.* New York: Holt, Rinehart & Winston.

Bandura, A. (1982). The psychology of chance encounters and life paths. *American Psychologist, 37,* 747–755.

Barusch, A. S., & Spaid, W. M. (1989). Gender differences in caregiving. *Gerontologist, 29,* 667–676.

Bell, R. Q. (1968). A reinterpretation of the direction of effects in studies of socialization. *Psychological Review, 75,* 81–95.

Bell, R. Q., & Harper, L. V. (1977). *Child effects on adults.* Hillsdale, NJ: Erlbaum.

Bengtson, V. L. (1987). Parenting, grandparenting, and intergenerational continuity. In J. B. Lancaster, J. Altmann, A. S. Rossi, & L. R. Sherrod (Eds.), *Parenting across the life span: Biosocial dimensions* (pp. 435–456). New York: Aldine de Gruyter.

Bengtson, V. L., & Mangen, D. J. (1988). Family intergenerational solidarity revisited. In D. J. Mangen, V. L. Bengtson, & P. H. Landry, Jr. (Eds.), *Measurement of intergenerational relations* (pp. 222–238). Newbury Park, CA: Sage.

Block, J. (1981). Some enduring and consequential structures of personality. In A. I. Rabin, J. Aronoff, A. M. Barclay, & R. A. Zucker (Eds.), *Further explorations in personality* (pp. 27–43). New York: Wiley.

Brody, E. M. (1985). Parent care as a normative family stress. *Gerontologist, 25,* 19–29.

Bühler, C., & Massarik, F. (Eds.). (1968). *The course of human life.* New York: Springer Publishing Co.

Cantor, M. H. (1983). Strain among caregivers. *Gerontologist, 23,* 597–604.

Chiriboga, D. A., Yee, B.W.K., & Weiler, P. G. (1992). Stress and coping in the context of caring. In L. Montada, S. Filipp, & M. J. Lerner (Eds.), *Life crises and experiences of loss in adulthood* (pp. 95–118). Hillsdale, NJ: Erlbaum.

Cohler, B. J. (1983). Autonomy and interdependence in the family of adulthood: A psychological perspective. *Gerontologist, 23,* 33–39.

Cook, J. A., & Cohler, B. J. (1986). Reciprocal socialization and the care of offspring with cancer and with schizophrenia. In N. Datan, A. L. Greene, & H. W. Reese (Eds.), *Life-span developmental psychology: Intergenerational relations* (pp. 223–243). Hillsdale, NJ: Erlbaum.

Cooper, K. L., & Gutmann, D. L. (1987). Gender identity and ego mastery style in middle-aged, pre- and post-empty nest women. *Gerontologist, 27,* 347–352.

Costa, P. T. Jr., & McCrae, R. R. (1980). Still stable after all these years: Personality as a key to some issues in aging. In P. B. Baltes & O. G. Brim, Jr. (Eds.), *Life-span development and behavior* (Vol. 3, pp. 66–102). New York: Academic Press.

Erikson, E. (1950). *Childhood and society.* New York: Norton.

Erikson, E. (1959). Growth and crises of the healthy personality. In Identity and the life cycle. *Psychological Issues, 1,* Monograph No. 1, 50–100.

Featherman, D. L. (1985). Individual development and aging as a population process. In J. Nesselroade & A. Von Eye (Eds.), *Individual development and social change: Explanatory analysis* (pp. 213–241). New York: Academic Press.

George, L. K., & Gwyther, L. P. (1984, November). *The dynamics of caregiver burden: Changes in caregiver well-being over time.* Paper presented to the Gerontological Society of America, San Antonio.

Goodnow, J. J., & Collins, W. A. (1990). *Development according to parents: The nature, sources, and consequences of parents' ideas.* Hillsdale, NJ: Erlbaum.

Gould, R. L. (1978). *Transformations: Growth and change in adult life.* New York: Simon & Schuster.

Greenberg, J., & Becker, M. (1988). Aging parents as family resources. *Gerontologist, 28,* 786–791.

Greenberg, J., Seltzer, M. M., & Greenley, J. (1993). Aging parents of adults with disabilities: The gratifications and frustrations of later-life caregiving. *Gerontologist, 33,* 542–550.

Hagestad, G. O. (1986). Dimensions of time and the family. *American Behavioral Scientist, 29,* 679–694.

Hagestad, G. O. (1987). Parent-child relations in later life: Trends and gaps in past research. In J. B. Lancaster, J. Altmann, A. S. Rossi, & L. R. Sherrod (Eds.), *Parenting across the life span: Biosocial dimensions* (pp. 405–433). New York: Aldine de Gruyter.

Helson, R., & Wink, P. (1992). Personality change in women from the early 40s to the early 50s. *Psychology and Aging, 7,* 46–55.

Hoyert, D. L., & Seltzer, M. M. (1992). Factors related to the well-being and life activities of family caregivers. *Family Relations, 41,* 74–81.

Jahoda, M. (1958). *Current concepts of positive mental health.* New York: Basic Books.

Jung, C. G. (1933). The stages of life. In C. J. Jung, *Modern man in search of a soul* (pp. 95–114). New York: Harcourt, Brace, & World.

Lawton, M. P., Brody, E. M., & Saperstein, A. R. (1989). A controlled study of respite service for caregivers of Alzheimer's patients. *Gerontologist, 29,* 8–15.

Levinson, D. J. (1986). A conception of adult development. *American Psychologist, 41,* 3–13.

Levinson, D. J., Darrow, C. N., Klein, E. B., Levinson, M. I., & McKee, B. (1978). *The season's of a man's life.* New York: Knopf.

Loevinger, J. (1976). *Ego development: Conceptions and theories.* San Francisco: Jossey-Bass.

Lund, D. A. (1989). *Older bereaved spouses: Research with practical applications.* New York: Hemisphere.

Mancini, J. A., & Blieszner, R. (1989). Aging parents and adult children: Research themes in intergenerational relations. *Journal of Marriage and the Family, 51,* 275–290.

Marks, N. (in press). Contemporary social demographics of American midlife parents. In C. D. Ryff, & M. M. Seltzer (Eds.), *The parental experience in midlife.* Chicago: University of Chicago Press.

Maslow, A. H. (1968). *Toward a psychology of being* (2nd ed.). New York: Van Nostrand.

Mattessich, P., & Hill, R. (1987). Life cycle and family development. In M. B. Sussman & S. K. Steinmetz (Eds.), *Handbook of marriage and the family* (pp. 437–468). New York: Plenum Press.

McAdams, D. P., & St. Aubin, E. (1992). A theory of generativity and its assessment through self-report, behavioral acts, and narrative themes in autobiography. *Journal of Personality and Social Psychology, 62,* 1003–1015.

McCrae, R. R., & Costa, P. T., Jr. (1990). *Personality in adulthood*. New York: Guilford Press.

McLanahan, S., & Adams, J. (1987). Parenthood and psychological well-being. *Annual Review of Sociology, 13,* 237–257.

Mullan, J. T. (1992). The bereaved caregiver: A prospective study of changes in well-being. *Gerontologist, 32,* 673–683.

Neugarten, B. L. (1973). Personality change in late life: A developmental perspective. In C. Eisdorfer & M. P. Lawton (Eds.), *The psychology of adult development and aging* (pp. 311–335). Washington, DC.: American Psychological Association.

Nydegger, C. N. (1991). The development of paternal and filial maturity. In K. Pillemer & K. McCartney (Eds.), *Parent-child relations throughout life* (pp. 93–112). Hillsdale, NJ: Erlbaum.

O'Bryant, S. L., Straw, L. B., & Edgar, E. D. (1991, November). *Comparisons of the well-being of widowed caregivers with that of widowed non-caregivers.* Paper presented at the Annual Scientific Meeting of the Gerontological Society of America, San Francisco.

O'Bryant, S. L., Straw, L. B., & Meddaugh, D. I. (1990). Contributions of the caregiving role to women's development. *Sex Roles, 23,* 645–658.

Parke, R. D. (1988). Families in life-span perspective. In E. M. Hetherington, R. M. Lerner, & M. Perlmutter (Eds.), *Child development in life-span perspective* (pp. 159–190). Hillsdale, NJ: Erlbaum.

Pearlin, L. I., Mullan, J. T., Semple, S. J., & Skaff, M. M. (1990). Caregiving and the stress process: An overview of concepts and their measures. *Gerontologist, 30,* 583–594.

Peterson, B. E., & Stewart, A. J. (1990). Using personal and fictional documents to assess psychosocial development: A case study of Vera Brittain's generativity. *Psychology and Aging, 5,* 400–411.

Peterson, G. W., & Rollins, B. C. (1987). Parent-child socialization. In M. B. Sussman & S. K. Steinmetz (Eds.), *Handbook of marriage and the family* (pp. 471–507). New York: Plenum Press.

Pillemer, K., & Suitor, S. (1991). "Will I ever escape my child's problems?" Effects of adult children's problems on elderly parents. *Journal of Marriage and the Family, 53,* 585–594.

Pruchno, R. A., Dempsey, N. P., & Burant, C. J. (in press). Teenage life events, parent-child disagreements, and parental well-being: Model development and testing. In C. D. Ryff & M. M. Seltzer (Eds.), *The parental experience in midlife*. Chicago: University of Chicago Press.

Quayhagen, M. P., & Quayhagen, M. (1988). Alzheimer's stress. *Gerontologist, 28,* 391–396.

Rogers, C. R. (1961). *On becoming a person*. Boston: Houghton Mifflin.

Rosenthal, C. J., Sulman, J., & Marshall, V. W. (1993). Depressive symptoms in family caregivers of long-stay patients. *Gerontologist, 33,* 249–257.

Rossi, A. S., & Rossi, P. H. (1990). *Of human bonding: Parent-child relations across the life course*. New York: Aldine de Gruyter.

Ryff, C. D. (1989a). Beyond Ponce de Leon and life satisfaction: New directions in quest of successful aging. *International Journal of Behavioral Development, 12,* 33–55.

Ryff, C. D. (1989b). Happiness is everything, or is it? Explorations on the meaning of psychological well-being. *Journal of Personality and Social Psychology, 57*, 1069–1081.

Ryff, C. D., & Essex, M. J. (1992). Psychological well-being in adulthood and old age: Descriptive markers and explanatory processes. In K. W. Schaie & M. P. Lawton (Eds.), *Annual Review of Gerontology and Geriatrics* (Vol. 11, pp. 144–171). New York: Springer Publishing Co.

Ryff, C. D., & Heincke, S. G. (1983). The subjective organization of personality in adulthood and aging. *Journal of Personality and Social Psychology, 44*, 807–816.

Ryff, C. D., Lee, Y. H., Essex, M. J., & Schmutte, P. S. (1994). My children and me: Mid-life evaluations of grown children and of self. *Psychology and Aging, 9*, 195–205.

Ryff, C. D., & Migdal, S. (1984). Intimacy and generativity: Self-perceived transitions. *Signs: Journal of Women in Culture and Society, 9*, 470–481.

Ryff, C. D., & Schmutte, P. S. (1993). *Parental responsibility for the lives of grown children.* Unpublished manuscript, University of Wisconsin, Institute on Aging and Adult Life, Madison.

Ryff, C. D., Schmutte, P. S., & Lee, Y. H. (in press). How children turn out: Implications for parental self-evaluation. In C. D. Ryff & M. M. Seltzer (Eds.), *The parental experience in midlife.* Chicago: University of Chicago Press.

Ryff, C. D., & Seltzer, M. M. (Eds.). (in press). *The parental experience in midlife.* Chicago: University of Chicago Press.

Seltzer, M. M., & Krauss, M. W. (1989). Aging parents with mentally retarded children: Family risk factors and sources of support. *American Journal on Mental Retardation, 94*, 303–312.

Seltzer, M. M., Krauss, M. W., Choi, S. C., & Hong, J. (in press). Midlife and later life parenting of adult children with mental retardation. In C. D. Ryff & M. M. Seltzer (Eds.). *The parental experience in midlife.* Chicago: University of Chicago Press.

Seltzer, M. M., & Ryff, C. D. (1994). Parenting across the life-span: The normative and nonnormative cases. In D. L. Featherman, R. M. Lerner, & M. Perlmutter (Eds.), *Life-span development and behavior* (Vol. 12, pp. 1–40). Hillsdale, NJ: Erlbaum.

Sigel, I. E., McGillicuddy-DeLisi, A. V., & Goodnow, J. J. (1992). *Parental belief systems: The psychological consequences for children* (2nd ed.). Hillsdale, NJ: Erlbaum.

Silverberg, S. B. (in press). Parental well-being at their children's transition to adolescence. In C. D. Ryff & M. M. Seltzer (Eds.), *The parental experience in midlife.* Chicago: University of Chicago Press.

Silverberg, S. B., & Steinberg, L. (1990). Psychological well-being of parents with early adolescent children. *Developmental Psychology, 26*, 658–666.

Skaff, M. M. (1991, November). *Caregiving: Changing conditions and changing self-concept.* Paper presented at the Annual Scientific Meeting of the Gerontological Society of America, San Francisco.

Snyder, B., & Keefe, K. (1985). The unmet needs of family caregivers for frail and disabled adults. *Social Work in Health Care, 10*, 1–14.

Thompson, L., & Walker, A. J. (1982). The dyad as the unit of analysis: Conceptual and methodological issues. *Journal of Marriage and the Family, 44,* 889–900.

Townsend, A., Noelker, L., Deimling, G., & Bass, D. (1989). Longitudinal impact of interhousehold caregiving stressors. *Psychology and Aging, 4,* 393–401.

Umberson, D., & Gove, W. R. (1989). Parenthood and psychological well-being: Theory, measurement, and stage in the family life course. *Journal of Family Issues, 10,* 440–462.

Vaillant, G. (1977). *Adaptation to life.* Boston: Little, Brown.

Whitbourne, S. K., & Tesch, S. A. (1985). A comparison of identity and intimacy statuses in college students and alumni. *Developmental Psychology, 21,* 1039–1044.

Whitbourne, S. K., Zuschlag, M. K., Elliot, S. B., & Waterman, A. S. (1992). Psychosocial development in adulthood: A 22-year sequential study. *Journal of Personality and Social Psychology, 63,* 260–271.

Wortman, C. B., & Silver, R. C. (1992). Reconsidering assumptions about coping with loss: An overview of current research. In L. Montada, S. H., Filipp, & M. J. Lerner (Eds.), *Life crises and experiences of loss in adulthood* (pp. 341–365). Hillsdale, NJ: Erlbaum.

Zarit, S. H., Reever, K. E., & Bach-Peterson, J. (1980). Relatives of the impaired elderly: Correlates of feelings of burden. *Gerontologist, 20,* 649–655.

Zarit, S. H., Todd, P. A., & Zarit, J. M. (1986). Subjective burden of husbands and wives as caregivers: A longitudinal study. *Gerontologist, 26,* 260–266.

6

Feminist Perspectives on Social Gerontology

Helena Znaniecka Lopata

The purpose of this chapter is to examine knowledge of aging and the family, as gained by social gerontology, from a general feminist perspective. Feminist contributions to any field include a critique and reevaluation of existing theories in order to discover new concepts, topics, and even new paradigms (Wallace, 1989). I proceed from a discussion of the feminist perspective on the concept of gender and on the methodologies by which social gerontologists have studied the elderly to an analysis of the historical changes in the lives of American women that need to be incorporated in these studies. The methods have tended to lump together all older people or all older women, neglecting their great heterogeneity of class, race, national origin, and religion, let alone society. In addition, much of social gerontology assumes that what is true of the present cohorts of older women is a consequence only of the processes of aging, neglecting the consequence of their living in a specific historical setting. This analysis is followed by examples of several areas in which knowledge has been influenced by the patriarchal structure and gender stratification of American society. This includes the gender-biased view of caregiving and of the influence of such life transitions as retirement and widowhood.

THE CONCEPT OF GENDER: MEANING AND USE IN SOCIAL SCIENCE

One of the major tasks of feminists in the social sciences and humanities has been to make women more visible. The absence of women artists, scientists, and writers in the histories of patriarchal societies is partly a consequence of neglect by male historians. In addition, this absence is due to the barriers these societies erected to opportunities for the development of female creators (Harding, 1986; Zuckerman, Cole, & Bruer, 1991). Early feminists shifted the study of women from the periphery of thought to the center. More recent feminists have changed the depth and breadth of analysis to a gendered understanding of all aspects of human culture and relationships (Acker, 1992; Stacey & Thorne, 1985). Now the emphasis of feminist scholars is on the ways gender influences, and is influenced by, social structure and situated (i.e., specifically located) relations among people. In order to proceed, we must deal with the question, What is gender? What follows is my personal interpretation of gender and its significance (see Lopata, 1993b; Lopata, 1994).

People at birth are identified, by those who have such classificatory power, by their biological characteristics, as falling into one of two sexual categories. Such an identification of the child immediately activates American society toward the girl or boy in many mutually exclusive ways with two consequences: structural and sociopsychological. American society divided its world into two spheres, the public sphere dominated by men and the private sphere assigned to women. The two spheres are seen as requiring very different types of persons. Girl children are imaged, and attempts are made to socialize them, to be dramatically different from boy children in abilities and potential for future involvements. Although the ideology claims that girls are by "nature" fitted for the private sphere, complex and lifelong socialization processes have been designed to ensure they know this. Biological sex is transformed into gender identity through the socialization process and self—as well as other—identification. Gender is a pervasive identity that people carry with them, influencing their role relations to varying degrees.

In the connection between gender identity and social role, much of research and theory relevant to aging becomes muddled. Several feminists and other social scientists seeking analytical tools by which to best understand human relationships developed the concept of *sex role*. Unfortunately, there is no such role. A *social role* is a set of negotiated, interdependent social relations between a social person and a social circle, involving obligations and rights on each side. A man and a woman relate to each other not in some general way as man and woman, but in social roles such as parent, colleague, or lover, in which their gender identity is involved to a greater or lesser degree (see Lopata & Thorne, 1978; Lopata, 1991a, 1994). *Social race,* a constructed set of categories in our society, is a similar pervasive identity. We do not take racial, or class, identity and try to make it into a social role (Stacey & Thorne, 1985). To restate the argument: gender is a pervasive identity that enters in varying degrees into the social relations that form the tie between the person and circle members in a social role.

Gender assignment carries other important consequences. A patriarchally based society such as America organizes itself along gender stratification lines, much as it does by class and social race lines. The private female sphere of the lived-in world is evaluated as inferior to the public male sphere. Placement into one or the other gender activates not only the socialization process leading to identity but also all forms of human ordering in all of American institutions—educational, political, religious, economic, even recreational, and certainly familial (Acker, 1992). Such a system provides historically developed resources for social domination, although age, class, race, and similar sources of power mediate male domination over women. Such influences vary the content and forms of social control, as do situational effects.

Methodological Problems in the Study of Aging

The patriarchal nature of American society is evident in its scientific world, in characteristics of researchers, and in its subject matter (Harding, 1986; see also Bleier, 1986). Feminists have brought to our attention the invisibility of the gendered world in past research and writing, as well as the lack of richness in attempts to understand it.

Although social gerontology's founders were of both genders, the study of aging was first developed in the biological and clinical sciences and later deeply influenced by psychology and psychiatry. Most of that work has emanated from very patriarchal, or male-biased, paradigms, as evidenced by personality tests that define characteristics most often assigned to women as less psychologically healthy than those claimed by men (Broverman, Broverman, Clarkson, Rosenkrantz, & Vogel, 1970). Much of behavioral science remains heavily influenced by biological assumptions as to gender differences in lifestyle and social relationships. Only recently have women been included in the medical longitudinal studies on the effects of aging on health and illness. Of equal prominence are psychiatric theories.

Another major problem of social gerontology has been its overdependence upon quantitative methods in attempts to reproduce the methods of the natural sciences. These methods can be helpful in demography but are often used indiscriminately and inappropriately. For example, the existence of gender identity as a category in the social structure has led social scientists to use it as a variable in quantitative analyses. Such a conversion of the multiplicity of variation into a single variable obfuscates the complexity of life. It flattens women (men also, of course) into a single dimension, ignoring their heterogeneity and seeing them as of significance only in contrast to the other gender. Survey research, of which such analysis is a major component, also removes people from the setting in which they are involved and objectifies them to the point of depersonalization and disembodiment, making many of the results meaningless (Smith, 1989). Even when other "variables," such as race, are held constant, the result makes understanding difficult, if not impossible. There are too many categorical generalizations in the social sciences (Fraser & Nicholson, 1990). An even worse problem exists when the researcher has reified variables to such an extent that these take on a life of their own. I recommend the work of Dorothy Smith (1987, 1989) for an in-depth analysis of the destructive effects of quantitative studies on human understanding.

HISTORICAL BACKGROUND

There is some historical justification for the stereotypical views of men and women developed by social gerontologists. Most of the persons we study have lived either in traditional settings or in transitional times bridging the traditional era and various forms of modernization or social development. One of the problems is that gender-specific results from the study of the current cohorts of the aged often push social gerontologists to an ethnocentric assumption that these are inevitable consequences of aging rather than consequences of the times. This assumption leads to misguided projections of the future and recommendations of social policies that will be decreasingly relevant for new cohorts.

Changes from Traditional to Transitional Times

The traditional domestic system typical of preindustrial agricultural economies with its mutually interdependent roles of men and women in the same setting gradually gave way to one that organized much of work into jobs in bureaucratized organizations. The process is usually attributed to industrialization of the nineteenth century and has accelerated at an increasing rate in the twentieth. Complexity of societal scale introduced many new jobs and systems into which they fit, requiring individuated involvement by those who left the home territory and earned incomes increasingly necessary to maintain themselves and those economically dependent upon them. The Protestant ethic focused the American value system on the economic institution. The separation of paid from unpaid labor and the expansion of economic and political life led to an ideology of two spheres, the public one being of greater importance. The private sphere became identified as mainly supportive of the public and reproductive of its future members. Women and children thus became personal dependents of fathers and husbands (Eichler, 1973). Men's involvement in the private sphere of home and family and women's commitment to jobs, careers, and other public roles were either made invisible or defined as deviant during the transitional period (Daniels, 1988; Lopata, 1993a, 1994).

We know most about the effects of the transitional times upon women from the studies of the American middle class. In spite of variations on the theme among many minority families, the nuclear family became relatively isolated from encompassing networks. The role of mother acquired tremendous importance. The burden of total physical and psychological care and responsibility for results fell upon her, with little support from anyone else—the extended family that became dispersed, the husband who was committed to his occupation, or the community that did not want to "invade the family's privacy," so defined by its laissez-faire value system. Many wives of that class, the largest in this society, became involved in a two-person career in which the husband was the title bearer and earner (Papanek, 1973). The women entered the public world as supports to the husband, as homemakers, and as mothers serving as connecting links for younger offspring. For this, they received vicarious rewards (Lipman-Blumen & Leavitt, 1976). They could not become committed to any other roles, volunteer or career, even that of friend, if these competed with the roles of mother and wife (Daniels, 1988). In other words, women's direct involvement in the public sphere was strongly and quite effectively discouraged during the transitional times. In the meantime, the obligation to be a good economic provider gave men justification for not providing the family personal, caring support and involvement. That was women's work.

Those women who entered on their own into volunteer work in the community or into broader political and economic arenas developed new skills and social relations. Such women tend to be lost in aggregated samples of American older people.

Modern Times

The ideology of a two-sphered world populated by mutually exclusive people has become increasingly dysfunctional in a society rapidly changing through modernization. The theory of modernization (see Inkeles, 1981; Inkeles & Smith, 1974), based upon studies of men, concluded that people gained freedom from the power of the patriarchal line due to education, mobility, and occupational opportunity. Commitment to the public sphere allegedly led to increased rationality, efficiency, complexity of life space, and individualization. Modernization is really so recent, as far as its influence on the lives of Americans, that only a relatively small proportion of elderly women have had enough experience throughout life to form autonomous, multidimensional social life spaces in cooperation with partners in various social roles who have also worked though dependency problems. However, the lives of increasing numbers of women of middle age, and certainly of those in younger cohorts, have introduced and experienced dramatic changes. They are obtaining more education in nontraditional fields, becoming committed to careers, entering demanding and identity-forming jobs, and sequencing life events in new ways. They are becoming less dependent upon men, marrying later or not at all, obtaining divorces or leading full lives as widows. The love relationships they maintain, according to Cancian (1987), involve two self-developed individuals, rather than two dependent and incomplete persons. They are avoiding or delaying parenthood, having fewer children, or not becoming restricted in social life space with these involvements. Their life span is longer, health is better, and, except for those caught in the vicious cycle of poverty, they can maintain themselves economically through a variety of ways. Above all, they are negating the construction of reality of the two-sphere world and the limiting features of the "feminine personality" imagery. These modern women are very different from those constrained by the transitional period of social development, and they certainly will be different older women.

THE INFLUENCE OF THE TWO-SPHERE IDEOLOGY ON THE STUDY OF AGING

I address four ways in which the two-sphere ideology growing out of the transition from the traditional to modern times has affected studies of aging and the family. In the first place, the two-sphere ideology has been carried into a gender-stereotypical, segregated view of women's and men's identities or personalities. Second, the ideology and the frequently used quantitative methodology have approached the aged as isolated individuals, ignoring the complexity of relations in their social worlds. Third, major areas of aging, such as caregiving, retirement, and widowhood, are portrayed in gender-biased ways. Finally, social gerontologists have, for the most part, ignored dramatic changes in women's lives, in their involvements, and in their self-concepts as they grow older within new contextual and constructed worlds.

Stereotypes of Women's and Men's Identities

Stereotypes are created categories that label behavior and generalize to a population defined as typically displaying this behavior. The stereotype organizes action toward the labeled population and often makes it virtually impossible for the respondents to enforce a more particularistic or at least less stereotypical construction of the interactional reality. The culture provides the stereotypes of the pervasive identities of societal members, which actually vary considerably in different places and times. Both Betty Friedan (1993) in her new book, *The Fountain of Age,* and Caroline Bird in the forthcoming *On Their Own: Secrets of Salty Old Women* devote long sections to the stereotype of the "little old woman," personality and variation wiped out in the aggregate.

Social scientists are not immune to these stereotypes, conveniently contained in the terminology of personality traits and translated into quantitative batteries of tests. The consequences of behavioral and attitudinal stereotyping can be illustrated in the concept of aggression. In American culture, this behavioral stance is defined in physical, masculine terms, ignoring many other forms of aggression. Femininity is still identified in nine-teenth-century Victorian terms most inappropriate to modern society.

Of course, there is a base to the stereotypes. Most older women and men whom social scientists study have lived in the transitional two-sphere world based on a strongly patriarchal system, the women focused on the family, the men on their occupations and other public involvements. They were socialized to be different types of people, and, not surprisingly, they have acted in many different ways. They and people with whom they interact are deeply influenced by prevailing personality stereotypes.

Social scientists have drawn several conclusions from the study of the current cohorts of older people. The most stereotypical, of course, is the view of all older people as being alike, different from active, involved, and so forth young adults. The next level of aggregation sees all old women as similar, contrasted not only to younger women but also to old men. As a symbolic interactionist, I have trouble with the stereotypical concept of personality as a set of traits, preferring to explain human behavior as a consequence of personal stances or approaches to specific relationships in specific contexts. The listing of personality traits tends to draw on transi-tional-era stereotypes, detrimental to the view of human beings as behaving in response to their own definitions of the situation. Behavioral continuity can be seen as at least partially a reflection of the continuity of the context of constructed reality. Restrictions upon the social roles entered by people and upon relations within these roles can operate throughout life. Those people who lead multidimensional lives as adults can be expected to con-tinue doing so as they age, while life space-restricted persons will remain so in old age.

The Older Woman and Her Social World

The next problem, in addition to the tendency to stereotype the elderly, lies in their methodological isolation. Human beings live in a social world, assisted by the symbolic construction of reality by all involved. This social world is organized in many ways, into social roles and systems of stratifi-cation. Within this social world, people age, changing roles and relations, modifying their stance and construction of reality. Some of our geronto-logical knowledge is based on the tendency, augmented by quantitative analysis, to pull the older person away from this world as if living in social isolation, within a personal bubble, unaffected by other people and what is happening in the society. We need to examine the social unit within which people interact, the ebb and flow of their relations over time. Aging, then, can be studied within a context. The greater the change in social roles or in the composition of the social circles of these roles, the more likely that new identities and behaviors emerge at each stage of the life course.

AGING AND MAJOR AREAS OF LIFE

The third influence of the two-sphere ideology upon social gerontology deserves a separate section. Several areas of social science research and theory concerning aging are imbued with gender-biased assumptions and language. I focus here on three such areas: caregiving, retirement, and widowhood (see also Szinovacz & Ekerdt on retirement, this volume; O'Bryant & Hansson on widowhood, this volume).

Caregiving

The idea that caregiving to elderly people by daughters is a "natural," almost biologically determined behavior of women permeates social gerontology. However, often forgotten is the fact that all the reported cases of female caregiving exist within patriarchal societies. It is possible that, as the strength of patriarchy decreases, which it appears to be doing in America, there will be major changes in personal and societal caregiving. A comparative analysis of traditional societies indicates some interesting differences among them and between them and more modern societies in who carries forth caregiving activities.

Numerous studies of Americans indicate that women, rather than men, do carry forth most of the caregiving, especially in the form of personal and emotional supports. All women are not expected to feel responsible for all elderly, however. We assume a "natural" direct line of responsibility from the daughter to her parents. This assumption ignores the shift of responsibility for aged parents from the son to the daughter in America and most of the world affected by modernization (Lopata, 1991b). Throughout much of Asia and the Middle East, which are still strongly patriarchal and patrilocal in culture and social organization, the son, not the daughter, has the closest relationship with the mother. The son inherits the property and the responsibility for his parents, whereas the daughter leaves home upon marriage and carries forth the care of the husband's parents, for whom he is responsible. Thus it made little sense for a mother in such a family system to invest emotionally and physically in an offspring who would leave and could never be of much help in later life. As Ross (1961) pointed out in her study of Indian families, the mother-son tie is known to be one of great love and affection. Of course, the son's wife, that is, the daughter-in-law, carries forth most of the personal care, but the son manages this care and is responsible for its enactment. Only with the breakup of the power of the male family line was the daughter freed from her main obligations to the in-laws. The result was a closer bond between her and the mother, whereas the son had to distance himself during his growth to maturity (Chodorow, 1978). It is rather ethnocentric for Americans to assume that the mother-daughter tie is inevitably the closest one, since that is not the case in so many societies. All patriarchal societies determine that women undertake the private care of others, however, which is exhausting and often unpleasant, no matter who the women are.

There is some debate among Americans as to the amount and quality differences in the care provided by sons and daughters. Most people assume that personal caregiving is a daughter's responsibility because women are supposed to be good at nurturance, personal care tasks, and household activities. Sons are expected to provide instrumental and supervisory support. Aronson (1992) subtitled her article on women's feelings, "But Who Else Is Going to Do It?" The cultural norms concerning the type of caregiving are definite, and the two types of support are often judged as being of equal value. Finley (1989), however, concluded that equating the care given to elderly people by men and women is possible only if men's activities are judged as more important than women's, and the institutionalization of women's emotional work takes for granted that they will do this "naturally." Only by such criteria can the contributions men make, which are much less personally demanding, be seen as "fair" by them and even by women and the society at large. The author concluded that change in the distribution of type and amount of care will be slow as long as the societal evaluation of men's contributions remains the same. Horowitz (1985) predicted: "The behavior of sons may eventually change with changes in sex-role socialization patterns, but we have yet to see this evidenced among our current cohorts" (p. 616). The point being made here is that the forms and intensity of caregiving by women and men are still consequences of patriarchal traditional and transitional times, not a "natural" consequence of biology. Many fathers of recent cohorts are extending much more personal care for their children than was true of men of the past. This may translate in the future into greater caregiving throughout the life course.

Retirement

The two-sphere ideology that reached its peak during the feminine mystique era (Friedan, 1963) permeated social gerontology literature on retirement. Most of the occupational world has been defined as masculine, and women's involvement has been viewed through the prism of their present or future role of mother, if not wife. For example, descriptions of retirement often contained the stereotypical view of the man as the only economic provider for the family (Cavan, 1962). It took Jessie Bernard (1983) to show how artificial this image was of the good provider achieving success in a world separated from the home but directed at supporting the household totally.

As late as the 1970s, the retirement literature focused on the alleged problems faced by men whose contributions to the employing organization were rejected, resulting in a loss of identity and life routine. According to this model, women were employed only by necessity, so that retirement simply brought them back home where their identities and responsibilities naturally belonged. Thus, they experienced fewer problems than retired men did.

Recent research on the career commitments of women indicates the need to revise the imagery of their retirement (Lopata, 1993c). There is no reason a woman should experience all the possible changes brought about by retirement to a lesser degree than a man does. The major factor influencing the degree of life disorganization from such an event is not gender but the degree of commitment to being employed, to a particular job, or to a career (Lopata, 1979a). Retirement can make fundamental changes in the same three areas of women's lives as men's—economic, social, and identity.

Economic changes

Until recently, economists and social scientists studying aging have not taken seriously the economic changes experienced by women upon their own retirement. Obviously, all people dependent upon their earnings for their lifestyle and other role involvements will experience change if the retirement income is inferior to that brought in by earnings. Most older women have not worked steadily through their lives and have not stayed with the same employer for a sufficient number of years to be fully vested, nor are they in portable programs often enough to receive any or adequate private pensions (Lopata & Brehm, 1986). Their employment history is also reflected in low Social Security benefits. As of now, there are no provisions by which part of the earnings of the husband is credited to the wife during the years in which she was involved in a two-person career, with the husband being the paid worker, or for the years of child rearing (Huber, 1990; Lopata & Brehm, 1986). Employed women's benefits were also often reduced if they were married to older men and retired early at the insistence of their retiring husbands. Women accustomed to earning at least some of the family income can feel belittled when the benefits they receive as wives of employed men outdistance the benefits they can receive as retired workers (see Harrington Meyer & Bellas, this volume, for more details).

Social changes

One can assume that occupationally involved women experience the same changes in their social lives with retirement as do men, but much more research has to be done to determine this. All employees become cut off from the employing organization as they lose contact with its day-by-day activities, especially if relations with coworkers had not been extended into nonwork spheres of life, as is often the case with women (Lopata, Barnewolt, & Miller, 1985). At the same time, interaction with other people such as neighbors, members of voluntary associations, and even family might have been curtailed during the years of occupational commitment. In this case retirement can result in the former employee's having to restructure her social support network. On the other side of the picture, cessation of full-time employment can open the door to independence, leisure, and the development of a whole new social life space. Allegedly, women are able to do this better than men (Berardo, 1970).

Retirement of a significant other can also have repercussive consequences upon the self, both by disorganizing the couple's established lifestyle and by creating the need to adjust to the adjustments of the partner. On the other hand, retirement can decrease problems and provide a new source of pleasant activity. The husband and wife can turn to each other in a revitalized marriage or simply go along parallel paths. Of course, many women at retirement are no longer, or never have been, married (Szinovacz & Ekerdt, this volume).

Identity changes

As stated earlier, the transitional true womanhood characterization assumes that women in retirement simply return home, where their identities were lodged all along. This position neglects the changes women might experience in their self-concept as a result of being employed. Many women work outside the home by choice, and even those who feel compelled to earn a living might become quite identified with the role of a paid worker in a particular job or occupation and pursue a career. It would be surprising if women did not develop such an identification and if their self-concept were not dependent upon these forms of identity (see Lopata, Barnewolt, & Miller, 1985; Lopata, 1993a, 1994). Many employed women would consider retirement into the role of full-time homemaker a status drop. On the other hand, and contrary to assumptions by many social scientists, many men see themselves as working for economic reasons alone and do not build their self-concept around their work involvement (Atchley, 1975). The assumption that women see their home as the dominion of their "queenship" (Cavan, 1962), whereas men define their home as foreign territory, is not supported by evidence.

Assumptions about the ease of retirement for women were based on studies conducted in previous decades that underplayed women's individualistic, rather than vicarious, sources of identity, feelings of competence, and positive self-concept in general (Lipman-Blumen & Leavitt, 1976). New generations of women are broadening their bases of identity into a variety of nonfamilial roles. The extent to which this expansion involves occupational roles will affect the degree of identity change with retirement. Greater flexibility of identity and social role involvement are undoubtedly trends for the future of both genders, encouraged by feminist and men's movements and by the tendency of Americans to see life as less contained within the first few decades than they did in the past (see Rubin, 1979).

Social scientists need to study in depth the changes in people's lives and in society's institutions to accommodate women's new commitments, as more and more of them enter demanding occupations.

An interesting commentary of recent times concerns two alleged problems in marriage arising from women's involvement in the world of paid work in later years of life. One problem is created when the wife earns more or is in a higher-status position than the husband. Both cases challenge the identity of a man who tries to live up to the image of the good provider (Bernard, 1981; Richardson, 1979). The other problem comes forth if the wife continues her occupational commitment even after the husband has retired, interfering with his desire for shared leisure or geographical mobility (Szinovacz, 1982).

Widowhood

The two-sphere ideology also enters discussions of widowhood. American society in its transitional stage, moving from the traditional to the modern stage, is uncomfortable about the husbandless woman, whether never married, divorced, or widowed. Women are still stigmatized by divorce more than men are (Gerstel, 1987). Widowhood carries with it an additional stigma of death (Lopata, forthcoming b).

Several aspects of the social gerontological treatment of widowhood bother this feminist symbolic interactionist. One is the lack of studies of widowers. Until I (see especially Lopata, 1973b, 1979b) started several research projects in the 1970s, the process and consequences of becoming widowed had been totally neglected except for Peter Marris's (1958) study in London and Felix Berardo's (1967, 1970) study in Washington state. My reason for focusing on widows was in terms of my previous research on American women. Actually, the situation of widows reflects the status of women in a society and the culture as well as the structure of the society itself. Luckily, studies of widows have now expanded even to other societies and cross-national comparisons are available (Lopata, 1987a, 1987b). Widowers are still relatively neglected.

Another feature of studies of widows is their portrayal as quite depressed and helpless with instrumental tasks within the home and with the world outside the home. Three assumptions underlie this portrayal of the widow, all increasingly outmoded by the life of women as they become more modernized. The first assumption is that women are limited to the private sphere of the home. The second is that past restrictions of stereotypically specialized knowledge and skills prevent learning new ways of mastering the environment and social relationships. The third assumption is that women obtain their whole identity and meaning of life only from family roles, so that the death of the husband, especially after the children have left home, deprives them of any meaning for the rest of their existence. This is a static view of widowhood, with the survivor unable to create or re-create any new identities and reality construction (Blieszner, 1993). Widows are no longer required to appear different from their married counterparts, whether by clothing or demeanor, but widows are seldom portrayed as competent, independent women enjoying a new stage of life after the heavy grief is over.

As with retirement, the degree of disorganization produced by the removal of the active role of wife from a woman's role cluster is influenced by many factors, especially by her dependence upon the circle of social relations of the role, upon her commitment to it, and upon the side bets, the role or relational investments, with which she supports it (Lopata, 1993a). How much of herself, in terms of identity, emotion, and lifestyle, did she invest in being a wife and the wife of that particular man? How important was the man in her life in general? What modifications are introduced in her other roles by the removal of that man as participant in the different social circles? What other circumstances of life are affected by the whole process of becoming and being a widow? What resources do different kinds of widows muster to build new lifestyles? How is widowhood different in small towns and large cities? Is it really true that African American widows of the lower class obtain much more social and emotional support from their church than do similar-class widows in a white community?

Unfortunately, many studies of the widow treat her in isolation from her social and physical environment. That is not how people live. The same questions can be asked about the degree of disorganization in the life of a widower, if we look at the total social life space, rather than just at skills of self-maintenance and social interaction. Modern society is encouraging and offering opportunities for multidimensional identities and involvements to old people, and growing old does not inevitably lead to passivity in building new identities and engagements. Thus, much is still to be learned about the meaning and effects of death and widowhood upon different kinds of men and women.

CONCLUSIONS: HETEROGENEITY AND CHANGES

The major problem of studies of old people is the stereotypical, homogenizing, problem-ridden image of this population. The aged are still seen more frequently as a problem than as a resource for the family and for society at large. Older women are especially likely to be portrayed as passive and inward and home-oriented and seldom as contributors to communities. They are studied as a drain on daughters and society, and all elderly are seen as receiving undue benefits at the expense of the young. Exceptions to these portrayals are found in the work of Hagestad (1987), Gutmann (1987), and Hudson (1987). These social scientists point to the importance of demographic changes and the failure of the society to take advantage of "a rapidly growing, vital older population" (Hagestad, 1987, p. 418). The stereotypes of old age, added to gender bias, prevent Americans, in general, and their gendered institutionalized agencies, in particular, from tapping into a resource of older adults to further many vital aspects of societal life.

The changes to which some social scientists are pointing as indexes of modernization's having effects upon Americans are numerous and have, or will have, tremendous effects upon future cohorts of the elderly, especially older women. Troll and her associates (1975) found that each one of three generations of women had greater cognitive complexity. Every study I have undertaken of women has documented the influence of education upon their self-concepts, expanded horizons, self-confidence, and their ability to initiate action vis-à-vis the world (e.g., see Lopata, 1971, 1973a, 1979b, 1994). Add to this an increase in occupational involvement, even in fields previously dominated by men, actual or potential economic independence or interdependence, decreased fertility and an expanded circle of assistants in the role of mother if it is entered into, health and vitality, and a long life.

The dramatic changes in the identities and social roles of American women will soon be reflected in the even greater heterogeneity of the elderly population than already exists. One of the sources of heterogeneity lies in family lifestyles throughout the family life course. Much attention is now being paid in the mass media to the decreasing frequency of the typical family of employed husband, full-time homemaking wife, and two children in the household. Commuter marriages, divorce, and widowhood involve independent living by women. Lesbian relationships of various intensity and duration affect life in old age, as do the social circles of never-married women. All sorts of combinations of primary relations are expanding. Flexibility of involvements and sequencing of role entrances and exits are making the lives of many people highly complex. Although poverty, health problems, and constrained life spaces still plague many Americans, life chances and cooperative efforts have bloomed recently and affect a growing proportion of women.

All these changes require new foci and methods in social gerontology. Studies show that social relations in all roles vary by social class, race, ethnicity, religion, education, occupation, urban-rural location, and so forth, but more research is needed on the effects of all these variations upon aging. We also need to learn more about elderly women of current times who have become leaders in social roles in the economic and political arenas. Knowledge of their approaches to those roles and their methods of supporting those roles through side bets can help social gerontologists to predict how these younger women might live their last few decades.

Although historical time, family time, and personal time are very different now than for the children of the Great Depression (Elder, 1974), some of that cohort of women were unaffected by societal restrictions placed on their gender in the past, and we can learn from them. There are so many questions that the older women who led more modern lives can help us answer in our attempt to predict the future. How are the relationships with spouses, children, and friends for publicly involved women different from those of women who have remained full-time homemakers? How will the lives of men be affected by the changes in the lives of women? We need to gain other answers from studies of some of the variant social arrangements. How are social relations among elderly lesbians or gay men different from those of straight men and women? The elderly people of the future are likely to have been in more than one marriage, requiring more knowledge about blended families of old people. How do remarried spouses and their families handle inheritance problems? Future elderly family members will probably have interacted with their children in different ways than have traditional parents, with use of day care and increasing community and employer responsibility for our youths. How will these differences affect parent-child relationships in old age? There is much to learn if we wish to understand aging and the family of the future, both from avant-garde older people and social units and from the middle-aged people of today.

Sociologists, psychologists, social gerontologists, and related scholars concerned with aging must anticipate changes in Americans and their gendered institutions, increasing heterogeneity, and the interweave between public and private lives. Feminist social scientists are drawing attention to the need to increase our understanding of the gendered aspects of human relationships, alongside other aspects of significance to our lives. As an optimist, I believe that the uncomfortable tightness of traditional roles, the restricted dependencies of the transitional times, and the somewhat narcissistic reaction to former restrictions in early modern times are being replaced—albeit very slowly—by increased feelings of community and responsibility on the part of autonomous individuals. This means that all social roles, throughout the whole life course, will undergo changes not understood as yet by the social scientists who, after all, grew up and lived much of their lives in transitional times.

NOTE

This is a modified version of a Distinguished Award Lecture presented at the Section on Sociology of Aging session at the American Sociological Association meetings on August 16, 1993, in Miami Beach, Florida. Thanks for help with earlier versions go to Rosemary Blieszner, Victoria Bedford, Judith Wittner, and Ruth Wallace.

REFERENCES

Acker, J. (1992). From sex roles to gendered institution. *Current Sociology, 21,* 565–569.

Aronson, J. (1992). Women's sense of responsibility for the care of old people: "But who else is going to do it?" *Gender and Society, 6,* 8–29.

Atchley, R. C. (1975). *Sociology of retirement.* Cambridge, MA: Schenkman.

Berardo, F. (1967). *Social adaptation to widowhood among a rural-urban aged population.* Washington State University: Agricultural Experiment Station Bulletin 689.

Berardo, F. (1970). Survivorship and social isolation: The case of the aged widower. *Family Coordinator, 19,* 11–25.

Bernard, J. (1981). *The female world.* New York: Free Press.

Bernard, J. (1983). The good provider role: Its rise and fall. In A. S. Skolnick & J. H. Skolnick (Eds.), *Family in transition* (4th ed., pp. 155–175). Boston: Little, Brown.

Bird, C. (in press). *On their own: Secrets of salty old women.*

Bleier, R. (1986). *Feminist approaches to science.* New York: Pergamon Press.

Blieszner, R. (1993). A socialist-feminist perspective on widowhood. *Journal of Aging Studies, 7,* 171–182.

Broverman, I. K., Broverman, D. M., Clarkson, F. E., Rosenkrantz, P. S., & Vogel, S. R. (1970). Sex role stereotypes and clinical judgements of mental health. *Journal of Consulting and Clinical Psychology, 34,* 1–7.

Cancian, F. (1987). *Love in America: Gender and self-development.* New York: Cambridge University Press.

Cavan, R. S. (1962). Self and role adjustment in old age. In A. Rose (Ed.), *Human behavior and social processes* (pp. 526–536). Boston: Houghton-Mifflin.

Chodorow, N. (1978). *The reproduction of mothering: Psychoanalysis and the sociology of gender.* Berkeley: University of California Press.

Daniels, A. K. (1988). *Invisible careers: Women community leaders in the volunteer world.* Chicago: University of Chicago Press.

Eichler, M. (1973). Women as personal dependents. In M. Stephenson (Ed.), *Women in Canada* (pp. 36–55). Toronto: New Press.

Elder, G. (1974). *Children of the Great Depression.* Chicago: University of Chicago Press.

Finley, N. J. (1989). Theories of family labor as applied to gender differences in caregiving for elderly parents. *Journal of Marriage and the Family, 51,* 79–86.

Fraser, N., & Nicholson, L. J. (1990). Social criticism without philosophy: An encounter between feminism and postmodernism. In L. J. Nicholson (Ed.), *Feminism/postmodernism* (pp. 19–38). New York: Routledge.

Friedan, B. (1963). *The feminine mystique.* New York: Norton.

Friedan, B. (1993). *The fountain of age.* New York: Simon & Schuster.

Gerstel, N. (1987). Divorce and stigma. *Social Problems, 34,* 172–186.

Gutmann, D. (1987). *Reclaimed powers: Toward a new psychology of men and women in later life.* New York: Basic Books.

Hagestad, G. O. (1987). Able elderly in the family context: Changes, chances and challenges. *Gerontologist, 27,* 417–422.

Harding, S. (1986). *The science question in feminism.* Ithaca: Cornell University Press.

Horowitz, A. (1985). Sons and daughters as caregivers to older parents: Differences in role performance and consequences. *Gerontologist, 25,* 612–617.

Huber, J. (1990). Macro-micro links in gender stratification. *American Sociological Review, 55,* 1–28.

Hudson, R. B. (1987). Tomorrow's able elders: Implications for the state. *Gerontologist, 27,* 405–409.

Inkeles, A. (1981). *Exploring individual modernity.* New York: Columbia University Press.

Inkeles, A., & Smith, D. H. (1974). *Becoming modern: Individual change in six developing countries.* Cambridge: Harvard University Press.

Lipman-Blumen, J., & Leavitt, H. J. (1976). Vicarious and direct achievement patterns in adulthood. *Counseling Psychologist, 6,* 26–32.

Lopata, H. Z. (1971). *Occupation: Housewife.* New York: Oxford University Press.

Lopata, H. Z. (1973a). The effect of schooling on social contacts of urban women. *American Journal of Sociology, 79,* 604–619.

Lopata, H. Z. (1973b). *Widowhood in an American city.* Cambridge, MA: Schenkman.

Lopata, H. Z. (1979a, April). *Sociological perspectives on the retirement of women.* Paper presented at the Symposium on Retirement in Honor of Leonard Breen, Purdue University.

Lopata, H. Z. (1979b). *Women as widows: Support systems.* New York: Elsevier.

Lopata, H. Z. (Ed.). (1987a). *Widows: The Middle East, Asia and the Pacific* (Vol. 1). Durham, NC: Duke University Press.

Lopata, H. Z. (Ed.). (1987b). *Widows: North America* (Vol. 2). Durham, NC: Duke University Press.

Lopata, H. Z. (1991a). Role theory. In J. R. Blau & N. Goodman (Eds.), *Social roles and social institutions: Essays in honor of Rose Laub Coser* (pp. 1–11). Boulder, CO: Westview Press.

Lopata, H. Z. (1991b). Which child? The consequences of social development on the support systems of widows. In B. B. Hess & E. W. Markson (Eds.), *Growing old in America* (pp. 39–49). New Brunswick, NJ: Transaction.

Lopata, H. Z. (1993a). Career commitment of American women: The issue of side bets. *Sociological Quarterly, 34,* 257–277.

Lopata, H. Z. (1993b, August). *Feminist perspectives in social gerontology.* Distinguished award lecture, Section on Sociology of Aging, American Sociological Association Annual Meeting, Miami Beach.

Lopata, H. Z. (1993c). The interweave of public and private: Women's challenge to American society. *Journal of Marriage and the Family, 55,* 176–190.

Lopata, H. Z. (1994). *Circles and settings: Role changes of American women.* Albany: State University of New York Press.

Lopata, H. Z. (forthcoming). *Current Widowhood: Myths and realities.* New York: Guilford Press.

Lopata, H. Z., Barnewolt, D., & Miller, D.A. (1985). *City women: Work, jobs, occupations, careers. Vol. 2, Chicago.* New York: Praeger.

Lopata, H. Z., & Brehm, H. (1986). *Widows and dependent wives: From social problem to federal policy.* New York: Praeger.

Lopata, H. Z., & Thorne, B. (1978). On the term "sex roles." *Signs, 3,* 718–721.

Marris, P. (1958). *Widows and their families.* London: Routledge & Kegan Paul.

Papanek, H. (1973). Men, women and work: Reflections on the two-person career. *American Journal of Sociology, 78,* 852–872.

Richardson, J. G. (1979). Wife occupational superiority and marital troubles: An examination of the hypothesis. *Journal of Marriage and the Family, 41*, 63–72.

Ross, A. (1961). *The Indian family in its urban setting.* Toronto: University of Toronto Press.

Rubin, L. B. (1979). *Women of a certain age.* New York: Harper & Row.

Smith, D. E. (1987). *The everyday world as problematic: A feminist sociology.* Boston: Northeastern University Press.

Smith, D. E. (1989). Sociological theory: Methods of writing patriarchy. In R. A. Wallace (Ed.), *Feminism and Sociological Theory* (pp. 34–64). Newbury Park, CA: Sage.

Stacey, J., & Thorne, B. (1985). The missing feminist revolution in sociology. *Social Problems, 32*, 301–316.

Szinovacz, M. (1982). *Women's retirement: Policy implications of recent research.* Beverly Hills, CA: Sage.

Troll, L. E., with Lycaki, H., & Smith, J. (1975). Development of the cognitively complex woman over the generations. In P. Bart et al., *No longer young: The older woman in America* (pp. 81–87). Ann Arbor: Institute of Gerontology, University of Michigan.

Wallace, R. (1989). Introduction. In R. Wallace (Ed.), *Feminism and sociological theory* (pp. 7–19). Newbury Park, CA: Sage.

Zuckerman, H., Cole, J. R., & Bruer, J. T. (Eds.). (1991). *The outer circle: Women in the scientific community.* New York: Norton.

7

Family Dynamics and the Leisure Experiences of Older Adults: Theoretical Viewpoints

Jay A. Mancini and Dan M. Sandifer

The benefits for healthy human development associated with productive leisure and with satisfying family relationships are quite similar, especially perhaps in the middle-life and aging years. In theory, leisure and recreation are main contexts in which people act and interact for the purposes of relaxation, renewal, personal development, and relationship enhancement. Most social institutions expect family relationships to anchor people in society and to be sources of comfort, understanding, intimacy, and social support. Despite similarities, however, the nexus of the family and leisure realms for aging people is neither clearly conceptualized nor adequately explored (Mancini & Blieszner, 1989). Our purpose is to focus on and explore the linkage of the family and leisure realms. We discuss the points of contact and note the functions of leisure and recreation for family life in adulthood. We also elaborate the leisure and family nexus through symbolic interaction and developmental theoretical lenses. We desire to interest the reader in the significance of the linkage between family and leisure in the lives of older adults and to provide a road map for research.

TIME, FAMILY, AND ADULT DEVELOPMENT

Time is the great organizer of daily life. Many commonly used expressions speak to various concepts of time. Among these expressions are "Time is on her side," "They are having the time of their lives," "I wouldn't give him the time of day," "It was a timely event," "His time ran out," "Time caught up with them," and so on. Kantor and Lehr (1975) said that the use of time is closely connected with life satisfaction or psychological well-being. Life satisfaction and well-being are commonly used terms in social gerontology, and their measurement is often included in research studies. Along with these global outcome concepts are intermediary concepts, that is, more specific outcomes that might tie into an overall outcome. These intermediary concepts include more particular satisfactions, such as relationship satisfaction and housing satisfaction, as well as particular outcomes that describe the nature of a personal relationship. From our perspective, one set of specific outcomes is found in Weiss's (1969) conceptualization of relationship functions. Framing human action and interaction in terms of relationship functions bridges social interaction and well-being quite effectively (Mancini & Blieszner, 1992). Consider, for example, the concept of attachment. Attachment is the opportunity to demonstrate emotions and feelings and to experience gain in feelings of security and connectedness with another person. Opportunities for attachment occur within the framework of time and are activity-oriented. Attachment is an important concept in understanding well-being because it represents a major, intense association between the individual and other individuals. Attachment brings the individual to another level of human existence, one of being connected and belonging. Leisure experiences provide a forum for the development and maintenance of attachment, which, in turn, is significant for well-being. A well-known expression that describes the effect of spending time together on family life is, "The family that plays together, stays together." Although this phrase is simplistic, its merit lies in its identification of attachment as impetus to keep people in the family interested in one another.

Usually researchers examine leisure activity in terms of the activity itself rather than the context in which it is done, such as with others in the family. Yet some research shows the significance of the family context. Kelly, Steinkamp, and Kelly (1987) found that for adults 75 years old and above, home-based and family activities were related more to well-being than activities done outside a family context. The importance that older people attach to recreation and leisure activity and the benefits that they can gain from it might have much to do with how family relationships are carried out. As examples, leisure can be a stage on which aspects of a family's history are replayed, can provide an opportunity for experimentation with new roles, can be a forum for continued strife, can be the place where relationship change occurs, and can be the arena in which a new relationship emerges between family members. Indeed, leisure activity harbors the potential for family *cohesion* and for relationship *dissonance* (Orthner & Mancini, 1980). The meaning of leisure can principally be either exhilarating and hopeful or onerous and discouraging. What might swing that meaning in either direction are the family dynamics that accompany spending time together (Orthner & Mancini, 1990).

Despite much research concerning family interaction in later life, especially with regard to aging parents and their adult children (Mancini, 1989; Mancini & Blieszner, 1989), the essential aspects of those relationships have yet to be captured. In particular, family interaction patterns and how they affect both the individual and the family group are fuzzy. We suggest that examination of intergenerational leisure experiences can provide some illumination of these family dynamics. For example, if people are playing games together, traveling together, or attending a spectator event, at least three processes are ongoing: action, interaction, and transaction. Individual family members are doing or saying things that provide chances for others to do and say things. In the course of doing and saying, interchanges of ideas, opinions, and feelings take place. Moreover, a shared reality develops, created by two or more people participating in the doing and saying of things. Laced throughout these events are assessments of the position each person might hold and the assignment of a grade on the merit of that position. Decision making and negotiation are required when participating with others in some activity. Negotiation may be as simple as deciding when to leave an event to get refreshments or as complex as the planning of a week-long trip (including where to stop, where to eat, and so on) and who pays for what. Decisions revolve around everyday, mundane points about which people interact and through which they sustain relationships. Thus the leisure context is a laboratory for observing family dynamics.

INDIVIDUAL AND FAMILY TRANSITIONS IN LATER LIFE

We believe that *transition* is an apt descriptor for family relationship and individual issues in later life. As the term suggests, the adulthood years are typified by movement and continued development. Family groups rarely are static entities for very long because their composition is always subject to variation, whether by design or by default. In the larger family group, transition occurs at several generational levels (from the oldest to the youngest generations) and at several family structure levels (including marital dyads, parent-child dyads, and other combinations of family relationships). Transitions that individuals make implicate others in the family; change that originates in one generation migrates into other generations. Examples of change that spills over from one family subgroup to another subgroup include a change in employment status, marital status (death of a spouse), or health status of an older adult; loss of an aging parent, the launching of children, and the leveling out of career development of a middle-aged adult; and education and career choices, increasing personal independence, and establishing a nuclear family among younger adults in the family. Because of the range of such events and also because of their critical nature, the search for the elements that hold a family together and that give a family its identity is an important one. We suggest that what happens with leisure and recreation is one of these elements.

LEISURE AND RECREATION RESEARCH

A review and discussion of aging and leisure were written by Cutler and Hendricks (1990), who took a life course perspective. Another excellent resource on the area is periodically found in *Activities, Adaptation & Aging,* a quarterly journal that published an aging and leisure bibliography seven times between 1985 and 1990. Our purpose here is not to repeat the information from these existing publications but to draw a few points from them as part of the backdrop to our discussion of theoretical directions.

Activity Patterns

Most investigations of what people do with their leisure time reveal that activity levels generally decline with age. The decline tends to be pronounced for activities requiring physical exertion and those that must be done outside the home. Sedentary activities and those typically done in the home change very little across the adult years. Leisure pursuits that are solitary in nature tend to increase with age. Despite these consistent general trends, analyses of the leisure patterns of older people must be open to a wide array of abilities, resources, and interests. Additionally, despite such activity changes over time, the 1982–83 Nationwide Recreation Survey revealed that older and younger people gave similar reasons for enjoying their favorite activities: enjoyment of nature and the outdoors; appreciation of peace, quiet, and solitude; affection for people with whom they do the activity; and the attraction of doing something new and different (U.S. Department of the Interior, 1986).

Quality Versus Quantity

Another consideration that sometimes escapes attention is a quality versus quantity comparison. Not only is what people actually do meaningful to them, but also what they think about what they do and what satisfaction they get from what they do are important. Studies by Ragheb and Griffith (1982) and by Mancini and Orthner (1980) demonstrated the significance of leisure satisfaction for individual well-being and cautioned against focusing exclusively on leisure participation information. More recently Russell (1987) reported that leisure satisfaction and well-being are positively related independent of gender, age, marital status, income, and health.

Issues of Context

Context is important in any discussion of family and leisure issues and especially so in discussions of older family members. In studies of aging, factors such as health, economic resources, and mobility must always be taken into account because they are *access variables* that often explain the behavior and lifestyle of older people. McGuire, Dottavio, and O'Leary (1986) found that health is the major reason that people 60 years of age and older cease doing outdoor recreation activities. The effects of economic resources on leisure participation are less clear, but obviously economically disadvantaged people cannot afford to participate in certain leisure pursuits. Economic factors are not pivotal in explaining why older people curtail outdoor activities, however (Cutler & Hendricks, 1990), indicating that activity type differences must be considered. Race is a context variable that often is not included in leisure and family studies, yet research has shown that it should be considered. Among older African Americans, leisure participation is influenced by socioeconomic factors and perceived health but not by actual chronic disease situation (Chin-Sang & Allen, 1991). Considerations of leisure and of family must be multicontextual because life is layered with contexts and because coping with life's many turns is related to being anchored in multiple contexts (Kelly, 1987). This chapter is essentially about multiple contexts—structural (e.g., family size), personal (e.g., health, wealth, gender, or race), or relational. One perspective on the relational context of life involves what people receive from interpersonal relationships. Kelly (1992) concluded that satisfaction with activities rests upon how well intimacy, communication, and community are enhanced.

PROVISIONS OF RELATIONSHIPS

Personal gains from relationships, whether with coworkers, children, or strangers, are rather mystifying and complex. Often people wonder why they spend time with certain others, especially when they are unclear about what they actually get from that spending of time. Any relationship—intimate or distant—does something for those involved in it. Gains from relationships may be on continua between good and bad, destructive and positive, meaningful and trivial, and short-lived and long-lasting.

Functional Specificity of Relationships

One approach to the question of what relationships provide has been conceptualized by Robert Weiss (1969). Weiss's theory is concerned with how interpersonal relationships function and what happens when relationship deficits occur. Weiss sought to deal generally with situations in which adults experienced a major life disruption (divorce and separation, retirement, death of a spouse). At the core of his framework are the relationship provisions of attachment, social integration, reliable alliance, guidance, reassurance of worth, and opportunity for nurturance. The basic thrust of Weiss's theory originated from the concepts of "fund of sociability" and "functional specificity" of relationships. The fund of sociability hypothesis suggests that adults have their relationship needs met in a variety of ways by any number of other people; what is important is the total amount of relationship provisions rather than particular provisions. The functional specificity hypothesis, in contrast, implies that adults require particular provisions from others; having a lot of one type of support does not offset the absence of other provisions. Weiss found more support for the functional specificity hypothesis than for the fund of sociability one. That is, particular adult needs can be satisfied only by interpersonal relationships, and, moreover, particular relationships address particular needs. Adults who are more satisfied with life, compared with those who are less satisfied, possess a variety of interpersonal relationships, that is, a network or constellation. Fully functioning persons have sets of relationships that provide them with opportunities to have their needs met as particular needs arise; these opportunities are the relationship functions mentioned before, reflecting what people provide to, and receive from others in human action and interaction (see Table 7.1). They are not mutually exclusive but, rather, constitute the relationship web. We consider them opportunities for adult development as well.

Table 7.1
Concepts on Which a Leisure- and Late-Life Family Theory Is Based

Relationship Functions: Attachment, social integration, opportunity for nurturance, reliable alliance, guidance, reassurance of worth.

Leisure Lifestyles: Time, activity patterns, leisure and recreation preferences, competence.

Symbolic Interaction: Self, meaning, role making, organismic involvement, role strain, quality of role enactment, ease of role transition, clarity of role expectations.

Family Development: Interdependence, selective boundary maintenance, ability to adapt to change, task performance, position, role, norms, positional career, role sequence, family career.

Relationship Web

Attachment (intimacy) is the opportunity to demonstrate emotions and feelings and, as a result, to experience gain in feelings of security and connectedness with another person. *Social integration* is the opportunity to share information, ideas, and experiences, which are the roots of companionship. Relationships are vehicles for social activity and social engagement, which, in turn, reinforce attachment. The process and result of sharing thoughts, feelings, and events become powerful dynamics in relationship development and maintenance. The *opportunity for nurturance* pertains to taking responsibility for a child and therefore experiencing a sense of being needed. A great deal of life's meaning comes from being needed by others. Though the theory as discussed by Weiss connects nurturance specifically with caring for a child, the concept is applicable to any relationship that involves the emotional and/or practical care of another. *Reassurance of worth* comes from opportunities to demonstrate competence and ability in a social role, to demonstrate value, and to be recognized for the value. Our interaction with others gives us information about how we are experienced so that we can estimate our worth somewhat through their eyes, as well as through our own. *Reliable alliance* (assistance) develops from opportunities to receive consistent assistance, provision of services, and resources. *Opportunity for guidance* comes from having relationships with people who can provide knowledge, advice, and expertise. Guidance is provided by people who are trusted, hold positions of authority, provide emotional support, or can assist in an action plan during a time of stress. These six relationship functions are essential for one's well-being, and they vary across individuals and across the life cycle. Weiss has maintained that the absence of these provisions or opportunities leads to distress. As examples, if attachment is absent, then loneliness and emotional isolation are likely to occur; life would feel less meaningful if nurturance opportunities are missing; lacking in reliable alliance leads to feelings of vulnerability, and so on (Mancini & Blieszner, 1992).

The framework provided by Weiss speaks to how interpersonal relationships function and the effects of deficits in them. The merit of this framework in our present discussion is that these provisions can be developed within the context of leisure and recreation (Mancini, 1984).

LEISURE LIFESTYLES: TIME, ACTIVITIES, PREFERENCES, AND COMPETENCE

Leisure and recreation can be understood through four interrelated lenses of time, activities, preferences, and competence (Mancini & Orthner, 1982). The components constitute a leisure lifestyle (see Table 7.1). How *time* itself is perceived is a predictor of how time is used and whether it is used for recreation. Perceptions of time control the organization of leisure because these viewpoints provide legitimacy to particular activities. Involved participation in leisure and recreation is influenced by whether the older person feels that nonwork pursuits have worth and are appropriate uses of time. Another dimension of time involves its future orientation. Older people who are less future-oriented might have quite a different perspective on how time should be used compared with those who are more future-oriented. For example, they might avoid new activities that require an extended learning period.

Three leisure *activity patterns* exist within time blocks. Each pattern reflects differing levels of contact and interaction with others. *Independent* activities are typically done alone and do not require the presence or participation of others (reading, watching television, walking, and contemplation are examples). Although independent activities could be done with others, their presence or absence does not affect the activities. *Parallel* activities are often independent activities done with others (watching television, attending sporting events and cultural events). *Parallel* activities include the potential for interpersonal interaction, but successful participation in the activity does not depend on that interaction. Some activities require interacting with others and are called *collaborative* (visiting with friends, many card or board games, team sports). People cannot engage in these activities without the cooperation and participation of others. These three activity patterns have various meanings for how people act and interact, and they allow for various relationship functions to emerge.

Preferences are the third part of a leisure lifestyle. Leisure activity and leisure preferences can be very different. In the case of older people, constraints associated with health, resources, and mobility might suppress a host of leisure preferences. Use of time, in part, depends on preferences, and such preferences are often intertwined with what people feel they are gaining from certain time uses. Of particular note regarding leisure preferences is whether older family members feel their preferences are considered by the family group and whether time is spent together out of choice or out of obligation.

Competence is the final aspect of our leisure lifestyle framework. Competence refers to whether or not older people feel effective participating in leisure and recreation. Feelings of competence direct how people behave in the presence of others, whether these others are strangers, friends, or family members. In adulthood unfamiliar activities might be avoided because of fearing the inability to master them, and they might be avoided even more so when one anticipates ability deficits related to aging (Lawton, Moss, & Fulcomer, 1986–87; Mobily, Lemke, & Gisin, 1991).

This second conceptual piece of our discussion of leisure, aging, and family has centered around a leisure lifestyle. How older family members structure their leisure time depends on how they define time itself, their typical activity patterns, what they prefer to do with their time, and how competent they feel in leisure and recreational pursuits. These four components are instructive for understanding the implications for family interaction and cohesion and for identifying how older people benefit from spending time with family.

Throughout the literature on recreation and leisure is a suggestion of the importance of studying meaning and perception for accurately understanding the use of time and studying the role that the life cycle plays in such an understanding. Roles and expectations permeate leisure behavior, even as they do virtually all aspects of adult life. For these reasons we now discuss the symbolic interaction and developmental family theories and present them as important lenses for knowing how family and leisure interact. These theoretical approaches concern themselves with meaning, perception, roles, expectations, transitions, and development.

THEORIES OF FAMILY DYNAMICS

Building upon our overview of a specific theory of relationship support and of lifestyle in a leisure and recreation framework, we move to folding into the discussion the various lenses on families that are offered by symbolic interaction and family development theories. Each of these family theories has something distinctive to add to our understanding of the leisure and family nexus (see Table 7.1).

Symbolic Interaction Theory

An excellent account of symbolic interaction as it applies to families is found in LaRossa and Reitzes (1993). This social-psychological perspective on family dynamics attaches a great deal of importance to meaning. People exist in a symbolic environment and both act upon, and react to, that environment. The *self* is central to the theory, in particular, how the self is developed and maintained. We discuss several concepts drawn from the theory that appear relevant to leisure and family issues in adulthood. *Role making* refers to the process by which individuals define situations and behave accordingly, in effect, constructing a role; this term speaks to the fluidity of roles. People in families make decisions about what is appropriate and functional in role performance. *Organismic involvement* is the level of energy that a role requires; some roles require little involvement whereas others require a person to become totally engrossed. A person's self is highly involved in some roles and not so much in others, and the meaning associated with the involvement is tied to a person's self-definition. Moreover, the evaluation of one's self in a particular role makes a difference in the intensity one experiences in the role. *Role strain* is an artifact of the difficulty one may have in fulfilling obligations. It results from unmet expectations associated with a role or a set of roles. The *quality of role enactment* is always in the minds of those within the role and those observing the role. People sense how well they are enacting a role from some recognized arbitrary benchmark or from comparisons with other people's performance. In adulthood various roles are active at any one time. In order to understand how families work, it is important to consider numerous roles in which adults participate, as well as the ease with which they move from one role to another (*ease of role transitions*). In a family, *consensus on role expectations* is important because such agreement will affect cooperation, communication, and cohesion. Also, clarity of role expectations is important because the degree to which expectations are muddled or identifiable influences one's role performance and one's satisfaction with that performance.

Family Development Theory

Family development theory is concerned with the process of change. Excellent reviews of this approach are found in Aldous (1978) and Mattessich and Hill (1987). We rely on the latter here. Family development theory includes three general categories of concepts: family systems, family structures, and orderly sequences. Several of these concepts are germane to examining leisure issues in adulthood. The systemic aspects of family life include *interdependence, selective boundary maintenance, ability to adapt to change,* and *task performance.* No one in a family lives or acts apart from others in the family. A family is a web of relationships. The connections and interconnections are many and complicated. Families are not insulated from outside influences but, rather, are partly receptive to those outer influences in the development of a family's history and identity. Outside factors, therefore, play some role. Families have a prominent adaptive character, both to the needs of people within a family and to the needs of the society and its culture. In the process of this adaptation a family adjusts its old patterns of behavior and creates new ones. A related aspect of family adaptation pertains to the survival of families. Families must behave in certain ways, that is, do certain things for their members, for their own well-being and for that of society. Family developmentalists usually discuss critical family tasks such as physical maintenance, socialization for family and societal roles, support of family morale, and motivation of family members to engage actively in roles. Family structure concepts of interest for our discussion are position, role, and norms. *Position* refers to a location within a social group, *role* refers to the expectations of behaviors and feelings that accompany a particular position, and *norms* are rules that guide behavioral conduct. In a family, grandmother is a position, and what people expect a grandmother to be like and what she actually does constitute the grandmother's role. *Positional career, role sequence,* and *family career* are time-oriented concepts reflecting orderly sequence. Over the life cycle of an individual and of a family, both the salience of various roles and the expectations associated with roles might change. Over time, therefore, families look different and act differently.

We have presented a brief overview of two family theories that have relevance for examining the significance for understanding leisure and recreation in adulthood. We return later to the symbolic interaction and developmental frameworks as we elaborate the leisure-family nexus.

IMPLICATIONS FOR RESEARCH: THEORETICAL ROAD MAPS

We have discussed four theoretical approaches so that issues of family and leisure might be better illuminated. Each approach provides a unique window; taken together, they suggest a wide range of questions. The relationship functions framework was originally created to explain relationship loss and recovery, the leisure lifestyles framework was developed to show the many levels of inquiry that are involved in analyzing time use, symbolic interaction theory emerged from an inquiry into how self and meaning are relevant to human development, and family development theory was designed to discuss change in the family system.

Relationship Functions

The leisure sciences field encompasses a strong emphasis on the benefits of leisure and recreation experiences (Driver, Brown, & Peterson, 1991). The relationship functions just discussed are benefits that result from interaction with others such as family members. Connecting the relationship functions approach to the leisure lifestyle framework yields the following questions. Generally, how does spending time with family affect closeness among various family members? Attachment or closeness is defined as connectedness and feeling secure with another person. Although it seems reasonable to assume that spending time together will enhance these feelings of belonging, it is difficult to know how much impact family leisure experience really has. It may well be that under particular conditions, a strong association between leisure experience and attachment to family members will emerge or endure. Among older adults it is possible, and some would say likely, that health is an important intervening factor in this association. Alternatively, an older person's friend network might play a relatively more important role in feelings of attachment than does family leisure.

A second relationship function that we highlight is reliable alliance. This function represents continuity in helpful behaviors involving provision of services, resources, and assistance. One question that remains open concerns the comparative significance of practical and emotional support, the former involving instrumental support services and the latter involving counsel and psychological assistance. How do activity patterns interact with feeling supported, or how do they engender other, nonrecreation supportive behaviors? Which dimensions of family leisure seem to detract from family cohesion? When speaking of family and leisure, researchers tend to overlook the downside of spending time together. Potential negative effects of family leisure include the exacerbation of ongoing interpersonal tensions, the heightening of unresolved conflicts and clashes, the draining of personal energy, incongruency with a person's leisure preferences, remorse when leisure experiences are interpersonally difficult, and problems in resolving the expectations of a positive leisure experience with actual negative experiences during leisure.

Another important research question is, Which relationship needs do family leisure experiences mostly address? There is no particular reason to expect that family leisure experiences uniformly affect the range of relationship functions that we have discussed. Also, the direction of influence of leisure on family, positive or negative, needs to be explored. To assume that spending time with family produces positive outcomes disregards other factors in a family's ecology, including a history of difficult interaction. Therefore, questions relating to the nature of the impact of leisure experience on family dynamics need to be examined. Research on older adults ought not to address a single life role, even one as significant as family member. Consequently other important social, personal, and interpersonal roles ought to be considered when viewing the leisure and family nexus.

Leisure Lifestyles

Several additional research questions that are more directly related to the leisure lifestyle framework remain to be explored. First, how does one's view of time relate to the use of family leisure, and, in turn, how is the quality of family life influenced? The prepotent sense of how one's time is appropriately and legitimately used cannot be ignored in research on leisure because such perceptions and feelings are gateways to behavior. Moreover, what role do leisure preferences play in the quality of family time? A close match between expectations and experience seems to promote well-being. In family groups, not everyone will have her or his leisure preferences met consistently. How much of an impact do unmet leisure needs have on the quality of individual or of family life? Another question is, How competent do older family members feel during family leisure experiences? Are they observers, rather than active participants? A principal goal of older adults is to maintain independence and competence as long as possible. Leisure experiences, whether with family, by oneself, or with others, have the potential to enhance feelings of competence. On the other hand, leisure experiences might foster feeling left out and incapable, especially if the activity is felt to be someone else's domain or preference.

Symbolic Interaction Theory

Symbolic interaction theory has alerted us to the significance of meaning in human action and interaction. McPherson (1991), while discussing aging and leisure benefits, noted that the meaning of an activity affects its impact on quality of life. What is the meaning that older people attach to family leisure experiences? Some feel that spending time with family is most important to them, and others feel less intense about family leisure experience, which differentially affects whether deficits in family leisure are experienced. How is a sense of self formed and maintained by family leisure experiences? How is this sense of self limited by fixed and rigid family leisure patterns?

Given our interest in the relation of leisure and family selves to family leisure experience, additional research questions emerge. For example, what level of personal energy is required of the older person to fully participate in family leisure? Focusing on the concept of organismic involvement, we note that some roles require little by way of involvement, whereas others, certainly those relating to family, can be engrossing. Do competing obligations constrain family leisure involvement, and how do these constraints affect the potential benefits of spending time with family? Across the generations in the family are many competing demands for how time could and should be used. As a result, spending time together might have a considerable obligatory component.

Another line of questioning involves notions of competence and flexibility. How well do families and their individual members enact the leisure role, and is leisure competence important for the family? Some roles are performed as expected whereas others are mishandled and contribute to family difficulties. This mishandling is especially likely if family members are inflexible. How readily do family members move from more rigid roles in their lives to more relaxed leisure roles? Ideally, leisure experiences provide opportunities for people to play rather than work and not to be bound to rigid expectations of behavior. In some families, however, people who occupy certain positions are not accorded the freedom "to be themselves." Do generations disagree about how the family structures its leisure time? Consensus is important for family functioning, especially when decision making is involved. In some family groups certain members make the decisions, and others are expected to fall in line; in others, decisions are negotiated. In both scenarios decisions are better received when family members agree with them. These observations are applicable to the decisions involved in the use of time for leisure activities.

Family Development Theory

Family development theory encourages researchers to examine the web of relationships in a family. This approach also leads to questioning how a family's history emerges and how its identity develops. What role do family leisure experiences play in family identity formation? How family members describe the family is linked, in part, to what family members do together. Often family members identify their family as artistic, musical, athletic, and so on. Events become the focus of the memory; therefore, leisure experience is significant for family identity and history.

Another question, parallel to what we have already discussed but at a slightly different level, is, How is a family member's view of his or her family enhanced or limited by spending time together? The family group image could be seen as good or bad, together or apart, backward or progressive, strife-ridden or cohesive. Another important dimension suggested by this approach concerns how family leisure alters overall family behavior patterns. Because spending time together gives a forum for interaction with others, including cooperation and competition, it becomes an opportunity for socialization. The spillover of one family subsystem into another leads to questions about the extent of that spillage. Further, how does this experience provide interpersonal learning that is transferred to situations outside leisure experiences? Because family development theory is concerned with change, a likely research strategy relates to examining how family and individual life cycle factors involve themselves with family leisure. For example, how is family leisure related to the launching of a child into adulthood? Roles inside and outside the family change as time passes and as development occurs. What place does family leisure experience have as developmental changes occur and as roles change? The life cycle variable should always be considered when looking at activities and their benefits.

CONCLUSIONS

We have suggested several research approaches that are related to the theories of relationship functions, leisure lifestyle, symbolic interaction, and family development. Our discussion is not exhaustive but exemplary of the range of inquiries that revolve around leisure and family issues in adulthood. Each theoretical approach suggests different dimensions of leisure and family relationships, and each points to increasing knowledge about two intricate spheres of life.

The significance of family relationships and of leisure and recreational activities for healthy adult development is almost universally agreed upon. For the most part, researchers have rarely coupled these domains of life in any detailed way. In this discussion, we have sought to address that deficiency by bringing into the literature on leisure and family a set of lenses that can be used for in-depth inquiries into the meaning of leisure for family life quality and for individual development. In many respects both the family and leisure realms are difficult to conceptualize; that is, they are fuzzy aspects of life. Numerous definitions of what *family* really is exist along with numerous viewpoints on what qualifies as *leisure*. Because the concepts are part and parcel of everyday life, their significance is often overlooked. Yet, when people are asked to identify what is meaningful to them, they often talk about their family relationships, and the descriptions of those relationships often revolve around doing things together. The leisure realm is a venue where the significance of family is developed.

146 Theoretical Frameworks and Research Methods

REFERENCES

Aldous, J. (1978). *Family careers: Developmental change in families*. New York: Wiley.

Brubaker, T. H. (1990). (Ed.). *Family relationships in later life* (2nd ed.). Newbury Park, CA: Sage.

Chin-Sang, V., & Allen, K. R. (1991). Leisure and the older black woman. *Journal of Gerontological Nursing, 17,* 30–34.

Cutler, S. J., & Hendricks, J. (1990). Leisure and time use across the life course. In R. H. Binstock & L. K. George (Eds.), *Handbook of aging and the social sciences* (3rd ed., pp. 169–185). San Diego: Academic Press.

Driver, B. L., Brown, P. J., & Peterson, G. L. (Eds.). (1991). *Benefits of leisure*. State College, PA: Venture.

Kantor, D., & Lehr, W. (1975). *Inside the family: Toward a theory of family process*. New York: Harper Colophon.

Kelly, J. R. (1987). *Peoria winter: Styles and resources in later life*. Lexington, MA: Lexington Books.

Kelly, J. R. (1992). Counterpoints in the sociology of leisure. *Leisure Sciences, 14,* 247–253.

Kelly, J. R., Steinkamp, M. W., & Kelly, J. R. (1987). Later-life satisfaction: Does leisure contribute? *Leisure Sciences, 9,* 189–200.

LaRossa, R., & Reitzes, D. C. (1993). Symbolic interactionism and family studies. In P. G. Boss, W. J. Doherty, R. LaRossa, W. R. Schumm, & S. K. Steinmetz (Eds.), *Sourcebook of family theories and methods* (pp. 135–166). New York: Plenum Press.

Lawton, M. P., Moss, M., & Fulcomer, M. (1986–87). Objective and subjective uses of time by older people. *International Journal of Aging and Human Development, 24,* 171–188.

Mancini, J. A. (1984). Leisure lifestyles and family dynamics in old age. In W. H. Quinn & G. A. Hughston (Eds.), *Independent aging: Family and social systems perspectives* (pp. 58–71). Rockville, MD: Aspen.

Mancini, J. A. (Ed.). (1989). *Aging parents and adult children*. Lexington, MA: Lexington Books.

Mancini, J. A., & Blieszner, R. (1989). Aging parents and adult children: Research themes in intergenerational relationships. *Journal of Marriage and the Family, 51,* 275–290.

Mancini, J. A., & Blieszner, R. (1992). Social provisions in adulthood: Concept and measurement in close relationships. *Journal of Gerontology: Psychological Sciences, 47,* P14–20.

Mancini, J. A., & Orthner, D. K. (1980). Situational influences on leisure satisfaction and morale in old age. *Journal of the American Geriatrics Society, 28,* 466–471.

Mancini, J. A., & Orthner, D. K. (1982). Leisure time, activities, preferences, and competence: Implications for the morale of older adults. *Journal of Applied Gerontology, 1,* 95–103.

Mattessich, P., & Hill, R. (1987). Life cycle and family development. In M. B.

Sussman & S. Steinmetz (Eds.), *Handbook of marriage and the family* (pp. 437–469). New York: Plenum Press.

McGuire, F. A., Dottavio, D., & O'Leary, J. T. (1986). Constraints to participation in outdoor recreation across the life span: A nationwide study of limiters and prohibitors. *Gerontologist, 26,* 538–544.

McPherson, B. D. (1991). Aging and leisure benefits: A life cycle perspective. In B. L. Driver, P. J. Brown, & G. L. Peterson (Eds.), *Benefits of leisure* (pp. 423–430). State College, PA: Venture.

Mobily, K. E., Lemke, J. H., & Gisin, G. J. (1991). The idea of leisure repertoire. *Journal of Applied Gerontology, 10,* 208–223.

Orthner, D. K., & Mancini, J. A. (1980). Leisure behavior and group dynamics: The case of the family. In S. E. Iso-Ahola (Ed.), *Social psychological perspectives on leisure and recreation* (pp. 307–328). Springfield, IL: Thomas.

Orthner, D. K., & Mancini, J. A. (1990). Leisure impacts on family interaction and cohesion. *Journal of Leisure Research, 22,* 125–137.

Ragheb, M. G., & Griffith, C. A. (1982). The contribution of leisure participation and leisure satisfaction to the life satisfaction of older persons. *Journal of Leisure Research, 14,* 295–306.

Rapoport, R., & Rapoport, R. (1975). *Leisure and the family life cycle.* London: Routledge & Kegan Paul.

Russell, R. V. (1987). The importance of recreation satisfaction and activity participation to the life satisfaction of age-segregated retirees. *Journal of Leisure Research, 19,* 273–283.

U.S. Department of the Interior. (1986). *1982–1983 nationwide recreation survey.* Washington, DC: U.S. Government Printing Office.

Weiss, R. S. (1969). The fund of sociability. *Trans-action, 6,* 36–43.

8

Methods and Analysis of Family Data

David J. Mangen

INTRODUCTION

Are the methodological and analysis issues associated with research on aging and the family sufficiently distinct as to warrant inclusion of a separate chapter in a publication such as this? In one very real sense, the answer is no. Research on aging and the family is subject to, and constrained by, exactly the same concerns that characterize all fields of social science inquiry. Given the goals of the research, the design must be characterized by strong internal and external validity, excellent measurement, and techniques of analysis appropriate to the hypotheses and data. This is no different from any other field. A chapter such as this is superfluous within this context, since many other excellent books are available that address these concerns from a strict methodological or statistical perspective.

If the scope of the work is expanded to include the linkages among the subject matter, existing theoretical perspectives, and the current trends in methods and analysis, then an entirely different conclusion is warranted. In this context, research on aging and the family is characterized by several unique issues that derive from these linkages.

I focus on several of these issues, illustrating some concerns and opportunities that I see in reviewing the field. My review is selective—not comprehensive—and thus subject to inevitable criticism that I have ignored some developments. I hope that my errors of omission do not detract from my discussion of these issues.

In the first substantive section of this chapter, I briefly review some of the major methodological and design issues, emphasizing some of the strengths and weaknesses of these approaches when used in research on aging and the family. Following that, I address the area of measurement— a topic that I consider central to research on aging and the family—and discuss several outstanding issues that revolve around explicitly linking theories of behavior to the process of measurement. Some of this discussion begins to overlap with the following section on statistical analysis. Finally, in the last section I attempt to integrate the different issues raised in the preceding sections.

DESIGN CONSIDERATIONS

At present, research in the area of aging and the family is dominated by a heavy reliance on classic survey research. To a lesser degree, in-depth qualitative research is used by some scholars to investigate family issues of aging. Pure experimental designs are rarely used. In this respect, the literature on aging and the family parallels that of gerontology and family studies.

I believe that the heavy reliance on survey research is a major limitation of current research on aging and the family. Almost any area of inquiry in the field of aging and the family, whether intergenerational relationships, husband-wife relations, nontraditional family forms, or the like, is confronted with a number of different research questions. What are the *dominant trends or characteristics* that describe aging families, what is the *process* by which these trends or patterns emerge, and—perhaps most important—*why do these trends emerge?* These questions illustrate in the abstract many of the typical research questions that face the field.

Over the course of a career, it seems reasonable to infer that a scholar emphasizing, for example, intergenerational relationships would seek to address these different questions and attempt to supply answers. In the terminology of formal theory construction, both operational and theoretical linkages would be provided. Can one research method effectively address all of these different questions? I doubt it. Yet scholars spent virtually their entire careers using just one general type of research methodology. Indeed, perhaps the dominant differentiation that characterizes research in the field of aging and the family is the split between the quantitative and the qualitative research camps. In short, *there is a tendency on the part of scholars in the field to adopt an ideological adherence to certain research methods and techniques of analysis that may not necessarily converge with, or extend, the theories they are investigating.*

Anyone who is familiar with my past work could, with considerable legitimacy, ask why I feel qualified to make this assertion. Almost all of my published work is clearly in the quantitative camp, heavily influenced by positivism, mostly restricted to classic survey research, and enamored with multivariate statistical modeling procedures. Because I have used these techniques so extensively, I am acutely aware of their limitations. At the same time, I appreciate the strengths and limitations of qualitative and experimental methods. My awareness has grown since I left academe. As a result of the demands of my clients, who are more interested in having their research questions answered in a cost-effective manner than in rigid adherence to ideological positions, I have been forced to use alternative research designs and, on occasion, develop some interesting hybrids.

In short, I believe that advancing current theory in the area of aging and the family requires greater flexibility on the part of researchers regarding the type of design that is used to address different research questions and a willingness to systematically use different designs at various stages of theoretical development. In order to illustrate this, I briefly review some of the major strengths and weaknesses of each design type and attempt to point out some of the ways in which that design is most effectively used. In many respects, the issues that I raise here are generic research issues that confront all social science inquiry, not just research on aging and the family; however, I attempt to concentrate my discussion and examples within this domain.

Classic Survey Research

Classic survey research is clearly the dominant trend in current literature on aging and the family. The design generally allows the researcher to gather a broad range of data that address many different issues and to do so in a reasonably structured form that is highly consistent across respondents. In Campbell and Stanley (1963) terms, the method has a high degree of *external validity* in that it is generalizable to broader populations, assuming good random sampling techniques and few problems with response bias.

The major limitation of classic survey research—at least from the perspective of the positivists—is the absence of strong internal validity. In Campbell and Stanley (1963) terms, this refers to the degree to which the design itself rules out competing explanations for any findings that emerge. Because most survey research has poor internal validity, a great deal of current survey research employs sophisticated multivariate statistical models. By employing statistical, as opposed to design-based, controls, the internal validity of the analysis is enhanced. Of course, it is impossible to control for everything. Only those variables that are known (or suspected) to influence the theoretical model and have been measured can be included in any multivariate tests. Our knowledge of most issues is certainly less than perfect; it is thus impossible to control for everything.

Survey research is, therefore, ideally suited to address questions of known importance and gather data on (1) the relative incidence and prevalence of these important characteristics in the broader population and (2) the important antecedents and consequences of these characteristics. These are very important and necessary parts of the process of theory building, but they are not the *only* part of the process. Survey research can effectively address these components.

Survey research is less effective, however, in understanding general issues of process or in answering the critical question of *why* different relationships among variables emerge. A survey could, for example, tell us that families that use active information search procedures to gather data about alternatives to institutionalization are less likely to send an aged parent to a nursing home and that more highly educated families are more likely to use active information search procedures. We speculate that education translates into a sense of mastery over the environment and a belief that it can be controlled; hence, information is sought and alternative decisions are reached. If we dig into the depths of the data, however, it is quite likely that some less well-educated persons use active information search strategies, and some well-educated ones do not. What, then, are the processes that lead to the formation of these strategies, and why? Look to the discussion section of almost any article using survey research, and the discussion of process and theoretical linkages is almost inevitably speculative at best. Yet developing theory requires that these concerns be addressed. I believe that alternative methods are better suited to address these issues.

Qualitative Methods

Researchers in tune with the qualitative research tradition (see, e.g., Gubrium & Wallace, 1990; Gubrium & Lynott, 1985; Hochschild, 1973; Murphy & Longino, 1992) question the validity of survey research—and positivism—from a more fundamental level than mere concerns about questionable design controls for internal validity. The fundamental nature of the critique lies in the rejection of the positivist assumption that standardized methods can be used to isolate underlying facts and that these facts can then be interrelated.

In essence, this is a criticism of measurement theory as applied to survey or experimental research in the positivist tradition. For the qualitative researchers, standardized questions or structured observations are inherently subject to great variation in interpretation among people. That variation is sufficiently great as to invalidate the entire measurement process. "Facts do not reside in absolute space, unencumbered by situational exigencies; data are not pure" (Murphy & Longino, 1992, p. 145).

Eschewing traditional empirical indicators, the qualitative tradition seeks to gather data of a more personal sort that are rich in detail and description. The positivists critique this approach as lacking both internal and external validity—even if it does make for more interesting reading. There is no guarantee that merely using a qualitative approach enhances the degree to which the subject's perspective of "fact" is understood. Only if the subject's world is entered can fact be understood, but guidelines for knowing when entry has been achieved are few (Murphy & Longino, 1992).

If the subject's perspective of fact is the only valid perspective, it is tempting to fall into highly particularistic forms of explanation. At its extreme, universal laws are impossible, because each case or subject has a law—dependent upon *its* facts—unto itself. To be sure, there may be *some* consistencies between the cases, but the consistency *could* be artificially imposed by a researcher who has failed to adequately understand the subject.

I thus reject qualitative methodologies as a panacea for addressing *all* issues necessary for a well-developed theory. In some areas, however, they can be invaluable. In conceptual explication, qualitative data are quite helpful in getting a grasp on the complexity that characterizes families who are defining events in their lives. In measurement, a preliminary qualitative approach assists in identifying the key terms and phrases that can be used to structure questions so that meaning is reasonably consistent across subjects. Finally, qualitative techniques can greatly assist in providing answers to the *how* and *why* questions needed for theoretical linkages, but only if the qualitative data are available for persons with known patterns. I return to this issue in the section on statistical analysis.

Experimental Methods

Use of experimental methods in research on the aging family is quite rare, even though a tradition of experimentalism exists in studies of the family (Straus & Tallman, 1971; Sussman, 1964). Although not classically viewed as topics within the domain of aging and family research, many of the research themes of this field are amenable to experimental research.

The tradition of experimentalism has, in my opinion, been subject to disproportionate criticism. It is attacked for lacking generalizability to larger populations. This criticism is largely justified but typically irrelevant. Generalization to a larger population is not the usual goal. Rather, the goal is a better understanding of process-related issues. Experimentalism, especially that conducted in a laboratory, is criticized because it is not real. This critique has more to do with the nature of the subject under investigation and the quality of the experiment than with any fundamental failure of the technique of experimentalism per se. If effectively designed, an experimental task can elicit realistic process-oriented data.

Witness the behavior of adults playing a simple game such as Monopoly. While everyone knows that the game is not real, the attraction of power and greed manifested by some players is quite often indicative of some basic, underlying characteristics they display in real life. Who behaves in an altruistic fashion, and under what circumstances? Who manipulates, and in what ways? On a somewhat more scientific level, I once had the opportunity to "fly" a Boeing 747 simulator used in pilot training. During this time, I was attached to instruments that took physiological readings. After "landing," I was able to review the data gathered while I was trying to land the plane with two engines out during a severe crosswind. I *knew* this was a simulator, but my pulse was 206, and my blood pressure on landing was 210 over 145. In short, my physiological body processes were reacting to an extremely stressful situation.

Admittedly, the airplane simulator was a special case that was backed up by an extensive set of visual, motion, thrust, and auditory cues. It was an excellent—and expensive—simulator. With recent advances in virtual reality, it will be possible to design simulators and experiments relevant to a range of aging and family issues and to introduce a significant level of reality into these experiments. I can envision experimental simulations designed to assess the decision-making process that families use when confronted with the need to institutionalize an aged family member or methods that investigate intergenerational conflict resolution strategies, environmental functioning, and other process-oriented questions. These simulations could be played out under a host of different experimental conditions, for example, resource-rich contexts versus deprived contexts, under highly complex systems of getting information versus centralized information brokers, with multiple stressful situations appearing both above and below in the intergenerational lineage, and so on.

Such laboratory experiments will, in all likelihood, not be generalizable to the broader population. External validity will be lacking. With an effectively designed experiment, using random assignment to treatment and control groups, it will be possible to randomize out all competing forms of explanation and have exemplary internal validity. What well-designed experiments can do, therefore, is address some of the different strategies and processes that people use under different structural circumstances. Assuming that some different strategies are typical, it then becomes the responsibility of the researcher to translate such findings into questions, dialogues, and the like that can be used in survey research to determine how often in the "real world" these strategies are used.

To this point the discussion of experimental design has assumed a context similar to the classic laboratory-oriented social psychological experiment, often using observational data collection techniques or computerized data collection procedures. This is not a *necessary* aspect of experimental research. In fact, the limitations on external validity can, in large part, be eliminated if the study is not restricted to a laboratory setting or if the lab is brought to the subject.

As a simple example, imagine a methodological study where the goal is to determine the effect of different response options on questionnaire measures. Because many questionnaire measures have an implied time referent of one year, this design is used as a control with experimental alternatives using six-month, three-month, and one-month time referents developed and used in the treatment cells. Clearly, differences are expected in the scores for the original coding system, but with proper extrapolation these could be converted to expected yearly frequencies. If a random sample of a known population is drawn and then randomly assigned to the different groups in the design, there is no a priori reason this study would not have sufficient external validity to permit generalization to a broader population.

Consolidation

I am suggesting that developing, testing, and refining theories on the aging family will be enhanced by using an integrated strategy that blends and uses various research methods tailored to the research questions, as opposed to the methodological inclinations of the researcher. Each method has its own strengths and weaknesses for addressing different types of research questions; capitalize on the strengths and compensate for the weaknesses of each method whenever possible.

It is impossible for me to identify a "correct" pattern for the sequential application of the different methods. In my own work, I have typically found it beneficial to start with qualitative research, follow it up with either survey or experimental designs, and then revisit the issues qualitatively after having a better grasp of dominant trends and/or operant processes. The cycle is then repeated but never completed.

Is it realistic to expect any one researcher—or even research team—to be proficient in all of these areas? On the abstract or philosophical level, I believe that the answer is an unqualified yes. On a practical level, perhaps not. Scholars investigating aging and the family issues are subject to all of the constraints that characterize the academic endeavor. Career advancement, funding, publication, and tenure are all important issues that influence the lives of individual scholars. If certain topics are "in vogue" with funding agencies, then the temptation to abandon one research program to pursue another that is more lucrative is great. If designing and carrying out an experiment will earn the ridicule of colleagues and deleteriously affect promotion opportunities, then the experiment will probably not be attempted. These are very real constraints that have nothing to do with the growth of the scientific endeavor but very much to do with the growth of individual careers.

The Issue of Time

Regardless of the research design used, addressing issues of time in age-related research is critical. These issues are very complex in the general research on aging; I believe that family considerations complicate the matter to a significant degree. Most discussions of the concept of time within aging research emphasize the age-period-cohort issue, with the usual recommendation and call for more longitudinal research or, better yet, cross-sequential research designs. Within the family, the general age-period-cohort model is complicated by the concept of generation.

For family research, the concept of generation has two important facets: (1) the lineage concept of generation as ranked position within the family and (2) the cohort-based concept of generation as shared historical experience (Bengtson, Cutler, Mangen, & Marshall, 1985). Regardless of the concept of generation that is used, the complications that are introduced into design and analysis are such that the basic model of the cross-sequential design exhibits fundamental theoretical weaknesses. That is, the design does not dovetail with the occurrence of events that are important to the research. To be sure, the logic of the design *as a methodological design* still works; it simply has a weak conceptual linkage to the theories that are employed.

Generation as Lineage

Within the family, the concept of generation is explicitly tied to an ordered position within the vertical family structure. Research on the relationships between family members of different generations occupies a central position in aging family research. Virtually every gerontological survey includes some minimal measures of the contact between aged parents and their offspring, and several studies have been conducted that use data from members of multiple generations (Bedford, 1992; Bengtson, 1975; Bengtson & Roberts, 1991; Hagestad, 1984; Hill, Foote, Aldous, Carlson, & MacDonald, 1970; Mangen, Bengtson, & Landry, 1988; Roberts & Bengtson, 1990), including longitudinal studies (Roberts & Bengtson, 1991; Silverstein & Bengston, 1991).

Generations as lineages introduce complexities into this research because the major changes of families as they age do not converge with the strict parallelism of the cross-sequential design. The logic of cross-sequential design requires that the time span associated with cohorts—roughly analogous to the generation concept—match up with periods of measurement. Figure 8.1 presents a simple example—assuming an age at marriage for the first or referent generation of 25 and using only one child born to each couple—that shows how quickly this strict parallelism becomes distorted. The equally spaced measurement periods of the cross-sequential design do not uniformly dovetail with the changes in lineage structure that occur, because the timing of the transitions is quite disparate both within and between families.

In Figure 8.1, the occurrence of a marriage is denoted with "M" and a birth with "B." The child of Family 1 was born relatively soon after their marriage—one year. We assume that child also married at age 25 and also began a family after one year. Thus, the original referent generation has become grandparents at age 52. If that G3 child follows an identical pat-

Figure 8.1
Generation as Lineage

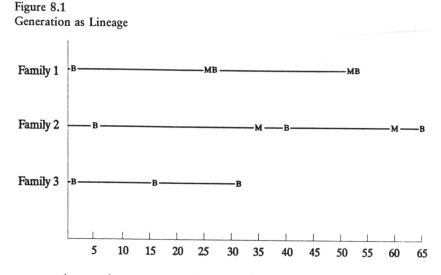

tern, we have a four-generation lineage when the original G1 is 78. Note that if data collection in the cross-sequential or longitudinal design occurs every five years, then the important transition states are "old news" and subject to recall error, or so far in the future that they may not yet be anticipated.

Contrast this with Family 2, where childbearing is postponed for a mere five years and where that child postpones marriage until age 30 and child-bearing until age 35. The age of the referent G1 generation upon achieving grandparenthood is 65. If that G3 child follows an identical pattern, the four-generation lineage will occur when the referent G1 is age 90. In this example, depending on the exact timing of the data collection effort, the longitudinal or cross-sequential design works reasonably well, in that the transition state is either imminent or recent.

Of course, the shifts can work the other way as well, as illustrated by Family 3. In this example, the child born to the G1 referent generation after one year gives birth at age 16. The grandparents in this example are only age 42. If the G3 child continues that pattern, the four-generation lineage would occur when the G1 is only 58, or before Family 2 has reached three-generation lineage status. Here, too, the timing of events is such that data collection efforts are likely to miss the critical moments of any transition.

In this simple example—where the ages of the referent generation at marriage are constrained to be equal and we look at only one child—the ages at which different generational positions within the family are achieved vary considerably and not nearly as neatly as the cross-sequential design requires. If we relax these assumptions and factor in the teenage pregnancy, postponement of marriage, and childbearing trends, then the example can become even sharper. Hagestad (1981) made this point quite clearly by pointing out the substantial age overlap between the generations in different three-generation studies.

This is not to say that longitudinal or cross-sequential research designed according to fixed periods of data gathering is without value to studies of aging and the family. On the contrary, variables can be developed (e.g., time since transition) that can be introduced as explanatory variables in any model of the transition process. Rather, the point is that the designs are not a panacea for existing research inadequacies. In studying the transition process, it may be better to develop a sample where considerable rapport is generated with the sample members and their cooperation gained in *soliciting from the researcher* interviews immediately before and after any transition is obtained. That is, the proximity to the event may be crucial.

Generation as Cohort

The other definition of generation that is useful for research on aging and the family is the concept of generation as cohort (Bengtson et al., 1985). Here, both from the context of cohort being defined as a group of persons with shared historical experiences and from Mannheim's definition of generation, the rigid fixed intervals associated with cross-sequential designs do not bear fruit. I am in concurrence with Marshall (1984), who stated that the concept of cohort is a methodological convenience, not a construction of social reality.

Figure 8.2 illustrates this process with some plausible definitions of generations since 1900. I recognize that others will disagree with me on the exact timing that I have identified for the shifts in generation. That is one of the significant problems with the concept of generation as cohort: generational boundaries become blurred. Many of the group that I have identified as the World War II small-birth cohort in fact identify with the boomer generation. Other "late boomers" born in the early 1960s actively resent being placed into that generation, describing them as a bunch of self-centered yuppies, and identify with Generation X. Similarly, the group I have defined as depression adolescents includes some persons who were probably too young to be significantly influenced by the depression per se but were more influenced by World War II.

A second key problem with the construct of generation as cohort reflects the typical linkage of cohorts to fixed intervals of birth years, usually defined in accordance with the census intervals. None of the generations I have identified are strictly defined by this methodological convenience, and only two of the generations are of equal width.

Finally, within the context of developing theory, I suspect that the concept of generation as cohort is useful from a descriptive perspective. It alerts researchers to the possibility that different age groups may have unique

Figure 8.2
Generation as Cohort

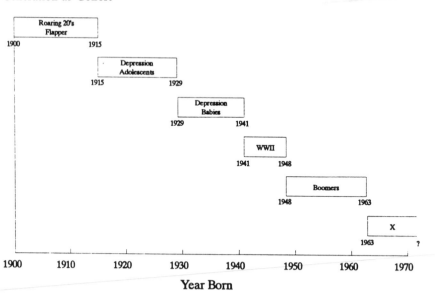

Year Born

social agendas dependent upon the historical epoch. From a strictly theoretical perspective, however, I suspect that there is less utility.

To illustrate this point, the primary use of the generation as cohort concept is that, depending upon the shared historical experiences of a generation, each cohort will display different levels of family characteristics, such as consensus with parents, geographic proximity to other family members, and the like. Furthermore, the interrelationships of important variables are often hypothesized to be different within the different generations, that is, a statistical interaction. Whereas this is a useful *descriptive* tool, does it assist in building theory? To merely assert a difference without describing the expected pattern of the difference is a weak theoretical statement. In short, the concept of generation as cohort provides an excellent null hypothesis but a minimal alternative hypothesis.

Perhaps if successive cohorts serve as proxies for macrosocial characteristics, and analysis is conducted using aggregate characteristics of the cohort as operational measures and the cohort as the unit of analysis, then generation as cohort may serve as a valuable theoretical tool in and of itself. The relationship of modernization to birthrates illustrates this approach quite well. For a great deal of research on the aging family, however, I suspect that the descriptive utility of generation as cohort does not translate into a powerful theoretical tool. The fundamental findings of the theory almost inevitably change as the next generation advances into the arena of social research, and the nature of the change cannot be predicted with great success.

MEASUREMENT IN AGING FAMILY RESEARCH

Measurement in research on the aging family has made considerable advances since the publication of *Research Instruments in Social Gerontology* (Mangen & Peterson, 1982a, 1982b, 1984). When we began that effort, it was often necessary to contact researchers directly to solicit information on reliability and validity tests; publications that reported such tests were comparatively few and far between. Now, reliability and validity data are reported within journal articles almost as a matter of course (see, e.g., Bedford, 1992; Depner & Ingersoll-Dayton, 1985; Gilford, 1984; Markides & Krause, 1985), and monographs (Mangen, Bengtson, & Landry, 1988) as well as journal publications (Kercher, 1992; Liang, 1985) explicitly devoted to measurement issues are seen as well.

While this constitutes a needed development, issues remain. Measurement issues central to the continued development of aging research include:

- The development of empirical indicators that have explicit theoretical linkages to the constructs that they purport to measure. This includes both specification of items from an existing theoretical structure as well as expansion and elaboration of constructs to capture the full complexity of the concept.
- Continued work on the testing and refinement of measures, including concern for all aspects of reliability and validity. Because validity is inherently a theoretical as opposed to statistical concern, there is some overlap of this point with the preceding one.
- Specification of measurement models that compare the model across relationships. In part, this is an emphasis on testing for more parsimonious measurement models.

Theoretical Linkages

Measurement is inherently the process of assigning rules of correspondence between observable measures and the underlying concepts that those observables are presumed to measure (Mangen, Peterson, & Sanders, 1982). Thus, depending upon the theoretical perspective that is brought to the research, the nature of those rules may be considerably different. Variations can plausibly exist in the types of indicators that are considered appropriate and the way in which the indicators are combined to form a composite measure.

I am normally loath to advocate development of new measures simply for the sake of developing a new measure, because the cumulation of evidence regarding an existing measure is inherently valuable. There are occasions, however, where it is clearly necessary to develop new measures simply because the types of indicators used in existing constructs do not have direct theoretical linkages with the underlying concept *as viewed by that theoretical perspective.*

For example, assume that the topic of interest is the affect that characterizes a parent-child relationship. From the symbolic interactionist perspective, an appropriate set of indicators might focus on the interpretation and meanings attached to the relationship and whether those meanings are defined in positive or gratifying terms. Conceptually, at least, it is plausible that the individual differences in meaning could result in a situation where objectively identical behaviors and relationships would be interpreted differently.

Contrast this with a more behaviorist theory such as exchange, where the key indicators might emphasize the occurrence of behaviors that are presumed to be rewarding and gratifying. As an elaboration, the assumption of whether those behaviors are rewarding could be measured as well. To illustrate this elaboration, consider the following item concerning the frequency of confiding in a parent-child relationship:

In the past month, how often has your mother confided in you?

- Not at all
- Once
- Twice
- 3–4 times
- 5 or more times

We may *assume* that having one's mother confide in you, or confiding in your mother, is interpreted positively within an exchange framework. For most persons it probably is. It is nonetheless an assumption that can be tested. For example:

How do you feel when your mother confides in you?

- I dislike it a great deal
- I dislike it
- Neutral
- I like it
- I like it a great deal

By moving to consideration of the interpretation that is applied to the exchange, elements of meaning are attached, and some aspects of the symbolic interactionist perspective are brought to bear on the measurements.

How can these data be transformed to capture affect? Specifically, if the responses to the frequency question are coded from 0 (not at all) through 4 (5 or more times), and the responses to the interpretation question are coded −2 (I dislike it a great deal) through +2 (I like it a great deal), then the multiplication of these variables yields a measure ranging from −8 for the joint occurrence of many episodes of confiding behavior that are interpreted negatively through +8 for the joint occurrence of many episodes of confiding behavior that are interpreted positively. A score of 0 is assigned to all persons who either never confide or react ambivalently.

The prior example illustrates an interactive measurement model at the item level. I am *not* attempting to claim that this is the correct way to measure affect; indeed, neither the questions nor the response options have been tested on any sample of which I am aware. Perhaps the response options for the interpretation question should vary from very uncomfortable to very comfortable, and the neutral point eliminated. These are very realistic options. What I am attempting to illustrate, however, is that the context of the theory that is brought to bear in addressing any research question has significant consequences for the types of questions that are asked and the rules of correspondence that link these questions to the underlying theoretical concept.

Another aspect of theoretical linkages involves the conceptual explication of the different dimensions and facets of a concept. Straus (1964) presented an excellent discussion of the procedures that may be used to explicate and develop a concept from a broad-based amorphous construct through dimensions and ultimately to the level of generating items or procedures for gathering data.

Conceptual explication can be employed at many different levels. Bengtson's (see, e.g., Bengtson & Schrader, 1982) description of solidarity as composed of six different dimensions constitutes conceptual explication at a very broad and descriptive level, taking the abstract and imprecise solidarity construct to a somewhat more specific set of dimensions. Each of these concepts can be further elaborated. Twenty dimensions were developed from the single exchange dimension in Bengtson's framework (Hancock, Mangen, & McChesney, 1988), and 12 dimensions were generated from the single familism component (Mangen & Westbrook, 1988). Perhaps the explication of these concepts into such detail is not necessary; the correlations among the specific dimensions could be so great that the concept has been shredded into minute pieces no longer resembling the whole. Further research will address these issues. What these papers illustrate is how the layers of a concept can be progressively peeled away like the layers of an onion, ultimately clarifying the specific empirical indicators that are needed. This assists item development by ensuring that items are specific to the dimension yet distinct from other closely related aspects of the concept.

Refinement of Measures

Under most circumstances, concern for the refinement of measures translates into issues of reliability and validity. Both of these are central to the measurement process. I have discussed generic issues of reliability and validity in other publications (Mangen et al., 1982; Mangen, 1986) and do not address these concerns here. Rather, I emphasize some specific issues germane to research on aging and the family. Fundamentally, most of these deal with different aspects of the validity of data used in aging family research, including:

- Potential patterns of response bias in research on the aging family. Given the highly personal nature of family life, to what extent are data gathered from respondents about themselves subject to distortion? Do respondents present their family life from a "rose-colored glasses" view of reality?
- Unit of analysis issues. Aging family research is seen at three different levels of analysis: individual, role-relationship, and the family unit. To what extent are errors introduced by single reports? How can multiple report data be analyzed?

Response Bias Issues

Are families as harmonious as the data suggest? On measures of closeness or affect in relationships, it would appear that families are extremely close (Gronvold, 1988). Indeed, on the basis of a considerable amount of published research, it would appear that most aspects of family solidarity are quite strong (Bengtson et al., 1985).

Are these findings accurate, or could response bias effects be manifested in the data? Evidence is not readily available, although the nature of the questions often asked in survey research suggests that response bias may be present. I illustrate this concern using the Positive Affect Index (Bengtson & Schrader, 1982; Gronvold, 1988), even though my comments are applicable to *many* other measures.

The Postive Affect Index has been used in a number of studies in addition to the original Southern California Three Generation study (e.g., Bedford, 1992; Markides & Krause, 1985), and longitudinal data are available (Richards, Bengtson, & Miller, 1989). The measure exhibits exemplary internal consistency reliability characteristics, a consistent factor structure across generations and role relationships, and reasonably high correlations with single-item indicators of affect (Gronvold, 1988). In short, most of the published data on reliability and validity are quite good.

In the original development sample, item mean scores on the 10 items are all quite high. Of the 60 generation- and role-specific item means reported by Gronvold (1988), almost all exceed 4.0 on the original 1–6 response coding. The conclusion appears to be straightforward: intergenerational affect is quite positive.

An analysis of item content reveals that all items are positively phrased, as might be expected from a Positive Affect Index. Specifically, respondents are asked how well they and their family members understand, like, and trust one another. Responses are given on a scale of (1) not well to (6) extremely well. Thus, none of the items *legitimate the expression of disagreement or conflict.* Affect is conceptualized only in the positive sense. Questions regarding arguments, conflict, and disagreements are not asked. Respondents are not afforded the opportunity to say that the relationship is terrible—merely not well.

If the conceptualization of affect is expanded to include both positive and negative questions, a single bipolar affect dimension could emerge. Alternatively, both positive and negative dimensions might emerge. Some families might have high scores on *both* the positive and negative dimensions (intense families) or low scores on both dimensions (disengaged). Perhaps the expression of conflict is so rare and/or idiosyncratic that the negative dimension items simply would not scale according to accepted psychometric criteria because the absence of variation would preclude meaningful covariation. Indeed, Bedford (1992) reported very low levels of expressed conflict between parents and children.

I suspect that a simple experimental study that used as its treatment a modified version of the Positive Affect Index—or any other positively phrased measure—that included several items legitimating the expression of conflict would show systematically lower mean scores for the *positively* phrased items. I suspect this would hold true even if few respondents endorsed the negatively phrased items. In short, the presence of the negatively phrased stimuli would encourage critical evaluation of the positive features of the relationship. This would reduce the skewness in the data, increase the variation, and, all other things being equal, probably increase the correlations with other measures.

The positive response bias that I suspect characterizes many measures might have no real consequences for the *relationships* unearthed by research on the aging family, except that the restricted variation will attenuate correlations. The key issue pertains to assessment of the *degree* of affect, intergenerational assistance, and so on that characterizes the family. Do we really believe the rosy picture painted by some measures? I do not intend to imply that families are inherently unstable, conflict-ridden groups, but I question the extremely positive scores when other data (e.g., Hagestad, 1984) suggest greater disenchantment.

I reiterate that these comments should be interpreted in a broad sense, not as an indictment of the Positive Affect Index. Acquiescence response set patterns as well as social desirability are very real problems in survey research (Mangen et al., 1982) and are not restricted to this measure. Similar comments can be made about many other parent-child research efforts (e.g., Cicirelli, 1980; Atkinson, Kivett, & Campbell, 1986) or husband-wife measures (see, e.g., Mangen, 1982, for a detailed review).

Varying stimulus magnitude and direction has long been recognized as fundamental criteria for developing good research instruments. Although including intensely phrased and negatively worded questions may require care in interview design, the potential benefits in fully tapping the range of the underlying concept would seem to warrant their inclusion. Too much work is restricted to positively phrased questions with relatively modest stimulus intensity.

Unit of Analysis

Research using only one informant to describe a family has long been criticized (Safilios-Rothschild, 1969; Hagestad, 1981; Bengtson et al., 1985). A considerable amount of research on aging and the family continues to use a single respondent to provide data about overall family relations. We can now report on some of the consequences of this approach by reporting correlations between different informants within the family. In a sense, this represents a form of interrater reliability. Selected findings include:

- *Parent-Child Association.* Contact between parents and children is an objective measure based on behavior and should be highly correlated. Mangen and Miller (1988) reported correlations of 0.41 to 0.75 between reports by different generations on the amount of contact they have with the other generation. The implication is that there are substantial discrepancies introduced by relying on one generation alone.

- *Parent-Child Affect.* As an evaluative assessment of the relationship, correlations between parent and child reports of affect should be moderately strong. Gronvold (1988) reported correlations for the Positive Affect Index. For directly adjacent generations, the correlations exceed 0.70. A correlation of 0.37 is reported for grandparent and grandchild affect. These correlations are actually quite strong, given that affect is an individually held property. Of course, the Positive Affect Index does include items about the attribution of feelings to the other.

- *Family Structure.* Using miles as a scale, McChesney and Mangen (1988) reported proximity correlations between the generations greater than 0.80. These increase to 0.90 if log transformations are used and to 0.94 or more if ordinal categories, derived from the original data, are used.

- *Familism Norms.* Bengtson, Mangen, and Landry (1984) reported very modest correlations, all less than 0.30, between the generations.

- *Exchanges of Assistance.* Using a highly abbreviated measure of exchange (Hancock et al., 1988), the total flow of exchanges—regardless of direction—formed single dimensions in modeling of intergenerational data. In part, this could be due to the very small number of items used in this analysis.

In summary, relying on the reports of a single informant in the family appears problematic under many circumstances. Moving to multiple informant data or using techniques designed to directly yield measures for the family as a whole (e.g., observational data) appears necessary to capture many family variables.

The role-relationship level of analysis continues to use individual-level data but links the responses of individuals within the family and analyzes the relationships among the different members of the family. For example, husband-wife observations may be linked or those of siblings or parents and children. The approach allows researchers to examine not only the characteristics of the multiple individuals within the role relationships but also their perception of the other (Thompson & Walker, 1982). Statistical modeling procedures are then used either (1) to develop family measures from the responses of all parties to the role relationship or (2) to model the relationships among the individuals (Thomson & Williams, 1982).

The role-relationship level of analysis holds considerable promise for analyzing data on the aging family, because the consistencies among the individuals within the family can be examined. Significantly, the discrepancies can also be examined. Analysis of data at this level is discussed in greater depth in the following sections of this chapter.

Moving to the family as the unit of analysis is a different matter, often requiring different techniques and attention to issues of measurement. The straightforward approach to developing family-level measures is briefly mentioned in the discussion of role-relationship analysis. If the reports of the different persons interviewed scale according to standard psychometric criteria, then simply combining responses into one scale is feasible.

Other family-level characteristics are less amenable to scaling via standard psychometric procedures, at least as the data are originally formulated. Take, for example, the concept of husband-wife consensus regarding child-rearing practices. We may ask both members of the dyad how much they are in agreement regarding number of children, discipline techniques, and the like. Such data would likely be skewed toward agreement, even if objectively significant differences exist. We may ask a number of different attitudinal measures and attempt to model not their actual scores on the items but some measure of the difference between the paired responses. Using this approach, it is best to have a number of different response options to the attitudinal questions because with few response options the potential for ties is quite great. Alternatively, a measure of consensus may be derived by estimating the correlation across items between responses for the husband and wife.

As suggested in the section on design issues, many aspects of family dynamics may be more effectively measured using techniques other than survey research. In particular, observational data (e.g., Conger, Elder, Simons, & Whitbeck, 1992; Simons, Beamon, Conger, & Chao, 1993) gathered in either an experimental or natural context may capture not only the actual level of agreement between spouses on different issues but the process by which consensus is negotiated or continued disagreement is managed.

Parismonious Measurement Models

I am heartened by the increased emphasis that researchers studying the aging family have given to issues of measurement. As researchers move to consider multiple family members, whether husband and wife, parents and children, or multiple siblings, the opportunity to test the comparability of measurement models across relationships emerges. If comparable models are sufficient for multiple relationships, then the more parsimonious explanation is preferable.

To illustrate the issues, assume a research project investigating parent-child affect. Further assume that this study is restricted to four-person families, including both husband and wife and two children, both of whom are assumed to be adolescents. In these families there are four intergenerational relationships, each of which can have affect expressed in two directions. That is, we are assuming that affect is an individual-level characteristic manifested in a specific role-relationship.

In Figure 8.3, a sample measurement model expressed in LISREL (Jöreskog & Sörbom, 1989) terms has been created. Three indicators of affect are answered by each respondent. The notation in Figure 8.3 is straightforward. $FC1_1$ refers to the *father* rating of the relationship with *child number 1,* with the subscript 1 referencing item 1. $MC1_1$ references the *mother's* rating of *child 1* on the same measure, while $C1F_1$ references the *First child's* evaluation of the *father* on the first item. Further assume that the items are identical, except for the appropriate referent individual. Each child completes six questions—three each about the mother and father—and each parent completes three questions about each of the children.

In Figure 8.3, ξ_1 through ξ_8 signify the unobserved measures or dimensions, δ_1 through δ_{24} are the errors of measurement, and λ_1 through λ_{24} are factor loadings or weights. Rather than complicate the representation of the model, the variances and covariances among the φ are simply represented by Φ. Assuming that the analysis will be conducted on a role-relationship level within the family (i.e., aggregation to a one-family measure is not desired), several different measurement models are relevant. Some example models that can be tested include:

- Strict parallel measures model. In the usual parallel measures model, the λ_i are equal, as are the δ_i. We use the term *strict parallel measures* to indicate that these

Figure 8.3
Sample Measurement Model

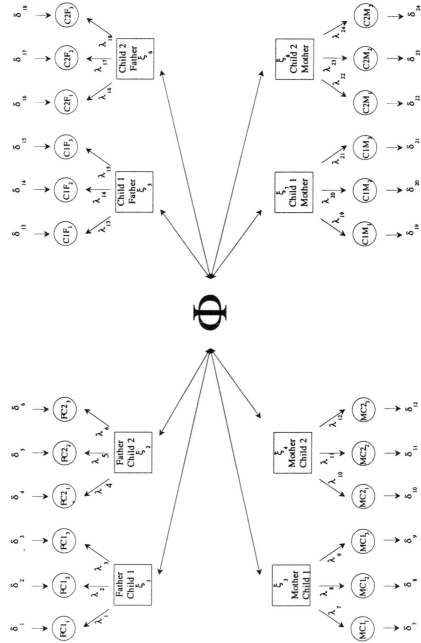

equality constraints apply across all measures for all relationships. This is a very restrictive model and tests whether all questions have the same significance for every relationship. A less restrictive form of this model demands only that the λ_i and δ_i constraints hold within each respondent's data for a given role relationship.

- Strict tau-equivalence model. In the tau-equivalence model, the λ_i are equal, but unique error variances (δ_i) are allowed. This is a slightly less restrictive model but still quite constrained. Here, too, the less restrictive version specific to each respondent and/or each role relationship is possible.

Both of these models are quite restrictive. Under most circumstances they will not adequately fit the data. Even then, however, they constitute useful benchmarks against which other elaborations can be compared. More theoretically interesting models include:

- Parental equality toward children. This model tests the equality of the coefficients for both husband and wife toward each of the children. In the terms of Figure 3, $\lambda_1 = \lambda_4 = \lambda_7 = \lambda_{10}$, $\lambda_2 = \lambda_5 = \lambda_8 = \lambda_{11}$, and $\lambda_3 = \lambda_6 = \lambda_9 = \lambda_{12}$. This model tests whether both parents weigh the same characteristics equally when reporting affect toward their children.

- Child equality toward parents. This model is comparable to the parental equality model, except that the emphasis is on the children's evaluation toward their parents. Specifically, $\lambda_{13} = \lambda_{16} = \lambda_{19} = \lambda_{22}$, $\lambda_{14} = \lambda_{17} = \lambda_{20} = \lambda_{23}$, and $\lambda_{15} = \lambda_{18} = \lambda_{21} = \lambda_{24}$.

- Reciprocated relationships. This model tests whether both parties to the relationship use the same relative emphasis for each measured attribute. In terms of the notation in Figure 8.3, the constraints include. $\lambda_1 = \lambda_{13}$, $\lambda_2 = \lambda_{14}$, $\lambda_3 = \lambda_{15}$ (for the father-child 1 relationship), $\lambda_4 = \lambda_{16}$, $\lambda_5 = \lambda_{17}$, $\lambda_6 = \lambda_{18}$ (for the father-child 2 relationship), $\lambda_7 = \lambda_{19}$, $\lambda_8 = \lambda_{20}$, $\lambda_9 = \lambda_{21}$ (for the mother-child 1 relationship), and $\lambda_{10} = \lambda_{22}$, $\lambda_{11} = \lambda_{23}$, $\lambda_{12} = \lambda_{24}$ (for the mother-child 2 relationship).

Variations on these themes are also plausible. Perhaps mothers distinctly evaluate their children, but more emotionally distant fathers "lump them together" and fail to do so. To test this would involve relaxing the constraints in the mother portion of the parental equality model. Perhaps two of the items within each dimension are subject to the equality restriction of any of the models, but the remainder are not. Any of these models are more parsimonious than the typical model that is estimated, which is:

- Congeneric Measures. In the congeneric measures model, no equality constraints are imposed on the λ_i and the δ_i, which are assumed to be different. If allowed to vary freely, some differences will inevitably be found, but whether these are *significant* differences is another matter.

This model is not parsimonious and *assumes* the greatest degree of differences among the different family members included in the study. Such a model may, in fact, be the best model to describe the data, but it is also the most complex. It is also typically the only model that is tested, thus increasing the likelihood of reporting measurement differences when none may exist.

Further variations and even greater theoretical relevance are possible if the gender of the children is also factored into the analysis suggested by Figure 8.3. Equality constraints for same-sex versus cross-sex relationships, depending upon the generational position, are interesting elaborations with relevance for understanding intergenerational dynamics. Age differences of parents and children can be examined as well.

If the specification of the model is changed, it is possible to test variations that take the unit of analysis to a different level. While the notation of Figure 8.3 is not correct to allow specification of a second-order factor analysis model, it is possible to do so. If a second-order factor analysis model fits the data, then a family measure, not a series of eight individual-level measures specific to the role relationship, is obtained. Alternatively, perhaps role-relationship measures explain the data well. Testing a model with four ξ that are defined by *both* respondents' data for that role relationship would test this hypothesis. For any of these variations, the elaborations of parallel measures, tau-equivalence, and congeneric measures models are also appropriate.

STATISTICAL ANALYSIS

As illustrated by the discussion of different measurement models, the statistical tools available for the analysis of family data have become increasingly sophisticated. Researchers studying the aging family are apt to use many different multivariate analysis procedures, ranging from multiple regression, factor analysis, and LISREL modeling through categorical modeling techniques and logistic regression with censored observations.

I am an advocate of the use of these techniques. They help to adjust for some of the basic limitations of the dominant survey-oriented methodology and as such are quite valuable for the field. I am concerned, however, about the overreliance that researchers place on the general linear model, as exemplified by the use of regression, LISREL modeling, and the like. It is not at all unusual for the typical study to report values of R^2 in the range of 0.10 to 0.40. While all social science research is clearly in the process of development, this clearly implies that there is much that we do not know.

Issues of measurement can contribute to the relatively low levels of explained variation by increasing random noise. Further, failure to specify all of the operant factors in a theoretical model will also lead to decreased explanation. The assumption of linear and additive relationships also needs to be questioned.

Efforts at formal theory construction (see, e.g., Burr, 1973; Burr, Hill,

Figure 8.4
Sample Causal Model

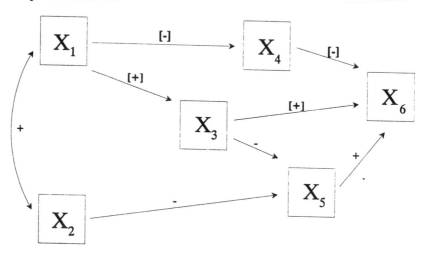

Nye, & Reiss, 1979) have often postulated relationships that are nonlinear and/or nonadditive. Unless explicitly specified, most tests using common multivariate procedures will not capture these effects. The assumption of additive relationships is questioned more frequently than the assumption of linearity. Indeed, much of the emphasis behind analyzing data in multigeneration families ultimately falls into a test for a statistical interaction by generation or role relationship.

The question of linearity is, however, more vexing. On one hand, while theories may suggest nonlinear trends, these trends may be obscured by random errors in the data. The mathematics to test power curves, exponential curves, and many other curve forms is readily available (Daniel & Wood, 1971) but very rarely used. It seems reasonable to expect that the relationship between intergenerational contact and affect is best described by a decelerating power curve or that the relationship between resource availability for one generation and resources received for another generation is an S-curve. While often discussed, such relationships are rarely tested. It may be the case that further detailed *description* is needed before effective *prediction* using nonlinear models can be achieved.

A promising avenue uses the strength of the linear model to isolate circumstances that warrant further examination by researchers. The approach involves looking at the dominant characteristics within the linear model and isolating those cases that do not match the assumed underlying linearity of the model. There are two ways to approach this process.

Figure 8.4 presents a content-free six-variable linear causal model of the sort seen in many studies of aging and the family. The variable X_i could be replaced with concepts from husband-wife relationships, sibling relationships, intergenerational relations—virtually any of the areas of research addressed in this book. Relationships between variables denoted by a [+] or [−] are assumed to be very strong relationships; unbracketed ± relationships are assumed to be statistically significant but less strong.

A pattern of findings like this would not be unusual. Typically, this would be the end of the story, except for the discussion and implications section of the article. It can be a new beginning. The *anomalies* to the model hold as much promise for aiding theoretical growth as the dominant trends. By virtue of being anomalies, they highlight those areas where improved understanding is needed.

Analysis of anomalies can take several forms. One statistical relationship can be the focus. If X_1 is geographic proximity and X_3 is intergenerational contact, then those cases that fall well above or below the predicted value for that *specific equation* may be more interesting than those where the actual and predicted values are reasonably close. Why do some family members avoid contact, even though they live close by, while others who are geographically distant manage to maintain face-to-face contact on a relatively frequent basis? Understanding these "errors" can, I believe, do much to advance overall knowledge.

A second strategy that can be used to investigate anomalies lies in a multivariate approach. In the example in Figure 8.4, four of the six variables occupy central positions in the model: X_1, X_3, X_4, and X_6. The other relationships are relatively weak. This subset of variables can be used in various cluster analysis techniques to isolate the groups of persons that fit the dominant trends and those that fit alternate or "deviant" trends.

Figure 8.5 presents an example of the sort of results that could be obtained from a cluster analysis of these data. The data in Figure 8.5 are presumed to be average standardized scores on the four measures central to the Figure 8.4 causal process. The cluster analysis procedure yields a series of five groups or types displaying unique patterns on the key variables in the linear causal model. In short, a typology has been developed that communicates the findings of the data from a different, not necessarily better, perspective.

Patterns 1–4 in Figure 8.5 illustrate groups or types of persons or families who are in keeping with the dominant trends isolated in the general linear analysis. Patterns 1 and 4 represent the extreme cases, and Patterns 2–3 illustrate moderate cases consistent with the trend. Consider, however, the pattern labeled anomaly. This group breaks away from, and does not fit, the dominant findings from the linear causal model; in fact, the group is contrarian. This segment warrants further examination.

Regardless of whether the focus is on a single relationship or on the multivariate pattern of relationships, the goal is the same. What are common themes that the members of the anomalous group or "error cases"

Figure 8.5
Clustering for Anomalies

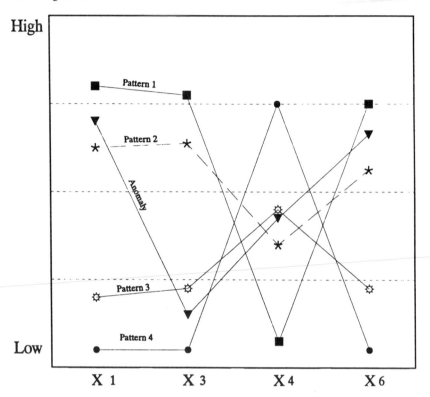

share that might plausibly explain the deviation from the primary trend in the data? Two different avenues can be used to explore this issue.

First, an in-depth exploration of existing research protocols is probably the best first step to use in examining these cases. Richards et al., (1989) used this approach in their analysis of changes over time in the quality of parent-child relations, although their analysis is not necessarily a deviant case analysis in the manner previously described. It is possible that a common theme may be isolated. Perhaps a variable statistically interacts with the entire process outlined in the general linear model. If this is the case, then this variable can be incorporated into the model via a set of cross-product interaction terms or through segmentation of the data set into multiple groups. The latter approach seems more useful in that the nature of the statistical interaction is more easily described.

The second strategy can be employed with both the anomalous cases and the dominant patterns outlined earlier with the cluster analysis approach. After having identified these unique patterns, families that represent the ideal types can be selected for further in-depth analysis, perhaps using qualitative or observational research techniques. In this context, ideal type means those cases closest to the type centroids obtained from the cluster analysis.

Conducting further qualitative research with respondents obviously requires going back to the subjects, securing their cooperation, and establishing rapport and dialogue along the lines discussed in the earlier section on qualitative methods. By doing this, however, the data are more refined, the subjects are to some degree known entities, and the tendency toward data overload that inhibits qualitative research can be minimized. Rather than having many cases in the qualitative analysis, some of whom are clearly idiosyncratic and fit no real pattern and others who are mixtures, the data gathering can emphasize cases that represent known regularities within the data. In essence, the clustering becomes a procedure for selecting cases that are most likely to yield fruitful qualitative data and supply answers to the vexing "how" and "why" questions that too often are left to speculation.

Advocates of qualitative methods might argue that selecting subjects in this way invalidates the methodology because structure has been imposed on the respondents prior to their participation in the new data-gathering effort. That is a legitimate, although I believe misplaced, criticism. The structure that has been imposed on these subjects is a definition of *who* and *what* they are, based upon the quantitative data. The qualitative data are not being gathered to address a question that has already been answered. The data are being gathered to determine *why* they manifest the patterns shown quantitatively and *how* the patterns developed. No a priori structure necessarily exists for those questions.

CONCLUSION

In this chapter I have attempted to review some different methodological and statistical issues in aging and family research. My review has been broad-based and has ignored many specific issues. In particular, issues pertaining to sampling of families and retention of the sample throughout the course of a longitudinal or cross-sequential study have been ignored. I have disproportionately emphasized the sociological tradition, especially that pertaining to the area of intergenerational relations, and have virtually ignored other areas of inquiry that are represented in other chapters of this book.

Research in the field of aging and the family has made great strides in the past decade. Both measurement and statistical analysis techniques have improved considerably, and a greater degree of theoretical specificity is seen throughout the field. These are encouraging trends that should be continued.

I am concerned, however, about what I see as a trend toward methodological and statistical orthodoxy. As would be expected, orthodoxy breeds the development of a "loyal opposition" who advance their framework. Both camps claim that their approach represents the "right way" to conduct research on the aging family. Given the state of knowledge in the field, such claims smack of hubris. All methods and all forms of analysis are needed to advance knowledge in this field. Premature closure is not warranted; methods used in combination may yield greater advances.

Within a chosen framework, I urge greater attention to the linkages of theory to method at all stages of the research process. Attention needs to be given to the fact that measurement is an inherently theoretical enterprise and that simply using existing measures without regard to the theoretical underpinnings of the measure will have consequences for the remainder of the analysis. At the same time, simply developing a new measure for the sake of doing so is inefficient and does not contribute to a cumulative body of knowledge. Techniques of statistical analysis need to be chosen carefully to reflect the fundamental hypotheses that are being tested in the research.

Statistical analysis techniques have grown in power and sophistication over the past 10 years, and more researchers are using these techniques. The techniques are powerful but virtually require that analysis becomes more and more technology-driven and further away from the underlying data. With greater distance from the data, it becomes tempting to focus on the success of the model and to ignore the model's failures, even though those failures indicate the avenues for continued theoretical growth. Multiple methods need to be used dynamically throughout the stages of the research in order to capitalize on the unique opportunities that are presented at each stage of the theory-research process.

The procedures that I outlined for analyzing cases with large residuals are, in part, technologically driven. The goal, however, is to return to the data in a more intimate sense. I suspect that it was more difficult to ignore large residuals when research involved using card-sorting machines to develop cross-tabulation tables, and "error cases" were indicated by the piles of punch cards that did not match the dominant trends in the data. Those piles demanded some attention; we need to return to considering those statistically deviant cases to advance knowledge.

Contributing to knowledge is, after all, what the research endeavor is all about. I believe that some of the steps I have outlined can assist researchers in fully exploiting their data and thus increase their contributions to this body of evidence.

REFERENCES

Atkinson, M., Kivett V., & Campbell, R. (1986). Intergenerational solidarity: An examination of a theoretical model. *Journal of Gerontology, 41,* 408–416.

Bedford, V. (1992). Memories of parental favoritism and the quality of parent-child ties in adulthood. *Journal of Gerontology: Social Sciences, 47,* S149–155.

Bengston, V. (1975). Generation and family effects in value socialization. *American Sociological Review, 40,* 358–371.

Bengston, V., Cutler, N., Mangen, D., & Marshall, V. (1985). Generations, cohorts, and relations between age groups. In R. Binstock & E. Shanas (Eds.), *Handbook of aging and the social sciences* (2nd ed., pp. 304–338). New York: Van Nostrand Reinhold.

Bengtson, V., Mangen, D., & Landry, P. (1984). The multi-generation family: Concepts and findings. In V. Garms-Homolová, E. M. Hoerning & D. Schaeffer (Eds.), *Intergenerational relationships* (pp. 63–80). Lewiston, NY: C. J. Hogrefe.

Bengtson, V., & Roberts, R. (1991). Intergenerational solidarity in aging families: An example of formal theory construction. *Journal of Marriage and the Family, 53,* 856–870.

Bengtson, V., & Schrader, S. (1982). Parent-child relations. In D. Mangen & W. Peterson (Eds.), *Research instruments in social gerontology* (Vol. 2, pp. 115–185). Minneapolis: University of Minnesota Press.

Burr, W. (1973). *Theory construction and the sociology of the family.* New York: Wiley.

Burr, W., Hill, R., Nye, F., & Reiss, I. (1979). *Contemporary theories about the family* (Vol. 1). New York: Free Press.

Campbell, D., & Stanley, J. (1963). *Experimental and quasi-experimental designs for research.* Chicago: Rand McNally.

Cicirelli, V. (1980). A comparison of college women's feelings toward their siblings and parents. *Journal of Marriage and the Family, 42,* 111–118.

Conger, R., Elder, G., Lorenz, F., Simons, R., & Whitbeck, L. (1992). A family process model of economic hardship and influences on adjustment of early adolescent boys. *Child Development, 63,* 526–541.

Daniel, C., & Wood, F. (1971). *Fitting equations to data.* New York: Wiley-Interscience.

Depner, C., & Ingersoll-Dayton, B. (1985). Conjugal social support: Patterns in later life. *Journal of Gerontology, 40,* 761–766.

Gilford, R. (1984). Contrasts in marital satisfaction throughout old age: An exchange theory analysis. *Journal of Gerontology, 39,* 325–333.

Gronvold, R. (1988). Measuring affectual solidarity. In D. Mangen, V. Bengtson, & P. Landry (Eds.), *Measurement of intergenerational relations* (pp. 74–97). Newbury Park, CA: Sage.

Gubrium, J., & Lynott, R. (1985). Alzheimer's disease as biographical works. In W. Peterson & J. Quadagno (Eds.), *Social bonds in later life.* Beverly Hills, CA: Sage.

Gubrium, J., & Wallace, J. (1990). Who theorizes age? *Ageing and Society, 10,* 131–149.

Hagestad, G. (1981). Problems and promises in the social psychology of intergenerational relations. In R. Fogel, E. Hatfield, S. Kiesler, & E. Shanas (Eds.), *Stability and change in the family* (pp. 11–46). New York: Academic Press.

Hagestad, G. (1984). Multi-generational families: Socialization, support, and strain.

In V. Garms-Homolová, E. M. Hoerning, & D. Schaeffer (Eds.), *Intergenerational relationships* (pp. 105–114). Lewiston, NY: C. J. Hogrefe.

Hancock, P., Mangen, D., & McChesney, K. (1988). The exchange dimension of solidarity: Measuring intergenerational exchange and functional solidarity. In D. Mangen, V. Bengtson, & P. Landry (Eds.), *Measurement of intergenerational relations* (pp. 156–186). Newbury Park, CA: Sage.

Hill, R. N., Foote, J., Aldous, R., Carlson, R., & MacDonald, R. (1970). *Family development in three generations.* Cambridge, MA: Schenkman.

Hochschild, A. (1973). *The unexpected community.* Englewood Cliffs, NJ: Prentice-Hall.

Jöreskog, K., & Sörbom, D. (1989). *LISREL VII user's guide.* Mooresville, IN: Scientific Software.

Kercher, K. (1992). Assessing subjective well-being in the old-old. *Research on Aging, 14,* 131–168.

Liang, J. (1985). A structural integration of the affect balance scale and the life satisfaction index A. *Journal of Gerontology, 40,* 552–561.

Mangen, D. (1982). Dyadic relations. In D. Mangen & W. Peterson (Eds.), *Research instruments in social gerontology* (vol. 2 pp. 43–114). Minneapolis: University of Minnesota Press.

Mangen, D. (1986). Measuring intergenerational family relations. *Research on Aging, 8,* 515–535.

Mangen, D., Bengtson, V., & Landry, P. (1988). *Measurement of intergenerational relations.* Newbury Park, CA: Sage.

Mangen, D., & Miller, R. (1988). Measuring intergenerational contact in the family. In D. Mangen, V. Bengtson, & P. Landry (Eds.), *Measurement of intergenerational relations* (pp. 98–125). Newbury Park, CA: Sage.

Mangen, D., & Peterson, W. (1982a). *Research instruments in social gerontology* (Vol. 1). Minneapolis: University of Minnesota Press.

Mangen, D., & Peterson, W. (1982b). *Research instruments in social gerontology* (Vol. 2). Minneapolis: University of Minnesota Press.

Mangen, D., & Peterson, W. (1984). *Research instruments in social gerontology* (Vol. 3). Minneapolis: University of Minnesota Press.

Mangen, D., Peterson, W., & Sanders, R. (1982). Introduction. In D. Mangen & W. Peterson (Eds.), *Research instruments in social gerontology* (Vol. 1, pp. 3–23). Minneapolis: University of Minnesota Press.

Mangen, D., & Westbrook, G. (1988). Measuring intergenerational norms. In D. Mangen, V. Bengtson, & P. Landry (Eds.), *Measurement of intergenerational relations* (pp. 187–206). Newbury Park, CA: Sage.

Markides, K., & Krause, N. (1985). Intergenerational solidarity and psychological well-being among older Mexican Americans: A three-generation study. *Journal of Gerontology, 40,* 390–392.

Marshall, V. (1984). Tendencies in generational research: From the generation to the cohort and back to the generation. In V. Garms-Homolová, E. M. Hoerning, & D. Schaeffer (Eds.), *Intergenerational relationships* (pp. 207–218). Lewiston, NY: C. J. Hogrefe.

McChesney, K., & Mangen, D. (1988). Measuring family structure. In D. Mangen, V. Bengtson, & P. Landry (Eds.), *Measurement of intergenerational relations* (pp. 56–73). Newbury Park, CA: Sage.

Murphy, J., & Longino, C. (1992). What is the justification for a qualitative approach to ageing studies? *Ageing and Society, 12,* 143–156.

Richards, L., Bengtson, V., & Miller, R. (1989). The "generation in the middle": Perceptions of changes in adults' intergenerational relationships. In K. Krepper & R. Lerner (Eds.), *Family systems and life-span developments* (pp. 341–366). Hillsdale, NJ: Erlbaum.

Roberts, R., & Bengtson, V. (1990). Is intergenerational solidarity a unidimensional construct? A second test of a formal model. *Journal of Gerontology: Social Sciences, 45,* S12–20.

Roberts, R., & Bengtson, V. (1991). Assessing familial and nonfamilial sources of parent-child attitude resemblance over two measurement occasions. In L. Collins & J. Horn (Eds.), *Best methods for the analysis of change: Recent advances, unanswered questions, future directions* (pp. 170–183). Washington, DC.: American Psychological Association.

Safilios-Rothschild, C. (1969). Family sociology or wives' family sociology? A cross-cultural examination of decision-making. *Journal of Marriage and the Family, 31,* 290–301.

Silverstein, M., & Bengtson, V. (1991). Do close parent-child relations reduce the mortality risk of older parents? *Journal of Health and Social Behavior, 32,* 382–395.

Simons, R., Beamon, J., Conger, R., & Chao, W. (1993). Stress, support, and antisocial behavior trait as determinants of emotional well-being and parenting practices among single mothers. *Journal of Marriage and the Family, 55,* 385–398.

Straus, M. (1964). Measuring families. In H. T. Christensen (Ed.), *Handbook of marriage and the family* (pp. 335–400). Chicago: Rand McNally.

Straus, M., & Tallman, I. (1971). SIMFAM: A technique for observational measurement and experimental study of families. In J. Aldous, T. Condon, R. Hill, M. Straus, & I. Tallman (Eds.), *Family problem solving: A symposium on theoretical, methodological, and substantive concerns.* Hinsdale, IL: Dryden Press.

Sussman, M. (1964). Experimental research. In H. T. Christensen (Ed.), *Handbook of marriage and the family* (pp. 275–299). Chicago: Rand McNally.

Thompson, L., & Walker, A. (1982). The dyad as the unit of analysis: Conceptual and methodological issues. *Journal of Marriage and the Family, 44,* 889–900.

Thomson, E., & Williams, R. (1982). Beyond wives' family sociology: A method for analyzing couple data. *Journal of Marriage and the Family, 44,* 999–1008.

Part III
FAMILY RELATIONSHIPS

9

Marriage and Close Relationships of the Marital Kind

Margaret Hellie Huyck

THE SCOPE OF INQUIRY

In this review I examine selected forms of voluntary, close relationships, usually between individuals of the same generation who are not closely linked genetically. The most common such relationship is marriage, recognized legally and socially as a distinctive relationship with rights and obligations. In addition, some adults have marital-like partnerships; these relationships might be heterosexual or homosexual. The relationships considered here all presume potential sexual sharing.

Because of increased longevity, less time in active childbearing and child rearing, and earlier retirement from the paid labor force, Swenson, Esker, and Kohlhepp (1984) argued that new stages of marriage are emerging. The new stages are (1) postchildbearing, preretirement, (2) post-child rearing, early retirement, and (3) post-child rearing, late retirement. Although the links to parenting are not applicable for all older adults, these phases correspond roughly with what are identified in the adult development literature as (1) middle age, (2) third age (or young-old), and (3) old age. These cover, potentially, 40 to 50 years of adult life.

The great majority of older adults have had some experience with marriage. For most groups, fewer than 10% of older adults never married; the greatest proportion of never-married adults is 15.5% among black men aged 45 to 55. The likelihood that a person is currently living with a spouse depends on age, sex, and race. According to the 1990 census data (U.S. Bureau of the Census, 1991), more than half of the men under 85, regardless of race or Hispanic origin, live with a wife. Over half of the white women under 75 and Hispanic-origin women under 65 are living with a husband; among black women, fewer than half are living with a husband by age 45. After age 85, barely half of men (35% to 49%) and a distinct minority of women (7% to 10%) live with a spouse (see also Dwyer, this volume).

Researchers do not agree on ways of understanding the current information on marital relationships in later life or on the assumptions that should guide future research. Theories and research reflect the complexity of the phenomena and the different disciplinary orientations of the researchers. Marriage or marital-like relationships are intensely personal; thus, some models have focused on the meanings of the relationship for the individuals involved and the variables that might account for differing experiences. This approach is most evident among psychoanalytic theorists. In their models, marriage is seen as one response to our human need to be attached to another person and overcome a sense of isolation (Bowlby, 1986). Some theorists see love relationships as examples of efforts either to continue (in a more mature form) the kind of good relationship experienced in very early life with the parent(s) or to establish a more satisfactory closeness (Huyck, 1994). A special feature of such close relationships is recognized as *projective identification*, or psychological division of labor, where partners look to each other to provide the emotional qualities they feel they lack or choose not to exercise. Many of these qualities are linked to maintaining a desired sense of gender identity (Farrell & Rosenberg, 1981). Because individuals come to a relationship with many idiosyncratic needs and fantasies, each couple evolves patterns of relating that have special meanings to them, even though the patterns might be contrary to those expected or displayed by others.

Marriage also involves social roles. This perspective leads to examination of each partner's role definition and role performance and how role expectations and role performance change over the lifetime (e.g., with retirement or illness) and over historical time (e.g., with redefinitions of feminine role behavior). Marital status is an index of one's place in the broader social system of legal, institutional, and informal access to resources. Other chapters in this handbook focus on some of those links, for example, between marital status and poverty for women and men as they age through later life (see Harrington Meyer & Bellas, this volume; Lopata, this volume). In this chapter I focus on the personal and relational aspects, with special attention to gender differences in the experience of marriage. Gender differences include social behaviors and the internal dispositions underlying them.

Critiques of life cycle studies of marital relations are available (e.g., Rollins, 1989). Many problems with the existing research base have been identified. For instance, researchers show little consensus on what constitutes a "long-term" marriage or relationship, with a range of 18 to 40 years or more for marriage and 10 years for homosexual partnership; usually only one partner provides data on the couple; most studies are cross-sectional, so that developmental changes are inferred, not demonstrated; and few studies have followed individuals into the third-age period or into old age. Some of the most interesting data, from longitudinal and other studies, are embedded in more holistic examinations of life structures, which nevertheless have several limitations. Even when a variable is ostensibly the same (such as marital satisfaction), the measures used might not be comparable. Particularly in studies of marital satisfaction and gender-role behaviors, measures have not controlled for social desirability biases that are inherent in self-report questionnaires. More standardized questionnaires might not be appropriate for later-life relationships, because they might focus more on parenting and less on health-related issues. In many studies, respondents are small groups of volunteers, and response rates in larger studies often have been low. Very few studies have included minority group respondents in sufficient numbers to assess their experiences, so it is questionable to generalize the findings to such groups. In cross-sectional studies of marital satisfaction, the age-linked patterns uncovered might reflect the attrition of some unhappy marriages due to divorce. Finally, although some of the relationships seem to be curvilinear over time (such as marital satisfaction over marital duration), researchers have typically used linear statistics to assess the relationships (see Mangen's discussion of this problem, this volume).

In the following section I describe marriages as experienced by women and men during the life phases of middle age, third age, and old age, followed by other close relationships, including heterosexual cohabiting couples, lesbian women, and gay male couples. Studies surveyed here focus on variables influencing marriage or marital-like experiences, such as sexuality, parenting, social status, ethnicity and culture, remarriage, retirement, health, and cohort effects. The review concludes with a brief overview of models for intervention in marital processes in later life.

MARRIAGES MIDDLE TO LATE LIFE

Midlife Marriages

Global marital satisfaction is the most heavily documented aspect of marriage. Cross-sectional studies, particularly those done prior to 1980, described either decline from young adulthood to midlife or a curvilinear pattern, with higher marital satisfaction among younger and older couples compared with middle-aged couples (Rollins, 1989). More recent analyses have included longitudinal data, larger, more representative samples, and efforts to control for selective attrition through divorce. These analyses suggest that no one pattern of satisfaction is associated with age or phase in the family cycle and that several styles of relating satisfactorily are evident at each phase of marriage (e.g., Skolnick, 1981).

Marriages and marital-like relationships are influenced by the expectations and opportunities that characterize the middle years generally (see Hunter & Sundel, 1989). For example, many couples emphasize role performance and the more instrumental aspects of the relationships; this emphasis, in part, reflects the substantial responsibilities in work, parenting, family care, and community leadership assumed by many persons during midlife. This emphasis contrasts with the more typical pleasure of young newlyweds associated with exploring each other and testing themselves in a new relationship (e.g., Lowenthal, Thurnher, Chiriboga, & Associates, 1975); young adulthood generally is characterized as a period for exploring opportunities and testing oneself.

Midlife marriages often reflect personality or interpersonal style changes, as wives become more self-confident and assertive and husbands become more dependent on the marriage for their sense of well-being and more willing to accommodate for the sake of preserving the peace (Farrell & Rosenberg, 1981; Huyck & Gutmann, 1992; Thurnher, 1976). Some husbands seem to feel that their masculine identity and status as head of the family are threatened by their wives' increased assertiveness within the marital relationship. Maintaining a sex-linked division of labor within the family seems to be particularly valued by middle-aged husbands, compared with younger and older men and women, because sex-typed tasks might serve to reaffirm gender identity. Some of the wives describe ways in which they collude with children to preserve the husband's sense of himself as being in charge within the family, while demanding their rights in areas they regard as crucial. One consequence might be reduced closeness; as Farrell and Rosenberg (1981) put it, "The couples seem more intent on not hurting or on protecting each other than in sharing experiences" (p. 125).

Husbands typically report more marital satisfaction than do wives (Rollins, 1989). Findings from qualitative studies suggest that this gender difference might reflect the willingness of husbands to idealize the situation and deny existing tensions as well as the wives' greater willingness to recognize problems and press for changes as the children are launched.

In the Berkeley Longitudinal Sample (Skolnick, 1981), marriages rated by experts as highly satisfactory were marked by strong affective commitment to the spouse rather than a utilitarian arrangement; such couples did not avoid conflict, and they did not expect perfection. Low-satisfaction marriages were marked by either conflict avoidance or serious conflicts resulting in hostility and tension. In one-quarter of the unsatisfying marriages, alcohol abuse was a major problem, but in most of the marriages there was no clear-cut problem. Some unsatisfactory marriages were held together by ambivalent mixtures of positive and negative feelings, and some were utilitarian arrangements.

Reports from clinicians working with middle-aged couples revealed several common problems (Nadelson, Polonsky, & Matthews, 1981). One problem was changes in the original implicit contract, particularly as to which partner was to be strong and which one was to be dependent. Other problems included unfulfilled goals, sexual problems, procreativity for couples who have not had children, reconstituted family issues, and physical disability.

Third-Age Marriages

The majority of older people rate their marriages as happy or very happy. No doubt this result reflects, in part, the selective survival of marriages that did not end in divorce. Several studies of couples who have celebrated a golden wedding anniversary emphasized the high marital satisfaction. It is important to note, however, that participants are volunteers and that husbands expressed even more satisfaction than did the wives (Field & Weishaus, 1992). Researchers employing cross-sectional designs have found that, compared with younger age groups, older couples reported fewer marital problems and were less likely to say they experienced negative sentiments, defined as sarcasm, disagreements, and anger. Older couples, however, were also less likely to report positive interactions than were young adults (Gilford & Bengtson, 1979).

Patterns in third-age marriages

Qualitative studies of marriage patterns during this period are embedded in several major longitudinal studies (Holahan, 1984; Kelly & Conley, 1987; Maas & Kuypers, 1974; Skolnick, 1981; Weishaus & Field, 1988) as well as in cross-sectional and single-age-group studies. The longitudinal databases are unique because they provide opportunities to assess continuity and change in individuals over a half century. The limitations of these studies are the relatively small samples and geographic and ethnic homogeneity. Most respondents are Caucasian and are drawn from the more advantaged socioeconomic groups. Nevertheless, the studies provide evidence for (1) the diversity of marriage patterns in later life, (2) the basic continuity in marriage styles over long periods of time, and (3) the links between marriage styles to personality characteristics evident in early adulthood.

Researchers have identified a variety of experiences of women and men in long-term marriages. Some husbands and some wives are primarily focused on the marital relationship, some focus on the general family relationship, and some are largely invested in activities outside the family setting. Satisfaction with the marital relationship varies within each of these styles, indicating that marital satisfaction cannot be predicted from marital style. Further, spouses do not necessarily describe themselves as following the same style.

The finding that marital patterns are generally stable might reflect the long-ranging impacts of basic personality dispositions. Researchers who identified varying styles of enduring marriages also differentiated later life-styles in terms of characteristics evident in young adulthood. For example, 70-year-old men who were highly involved in their families and expressed great satisfaction with their marriages had been distinguished in young adulthood by their willingness to express affection and to discuss conflict openly (Maas & Kuypers, 1974). The importance of a cluster of personality characteristics termed neuroticism (which includes generalized anxiety and negative mood) was evident in a major longitudinal study of marital relations, spanning a 45-year period from the engagement to old age (Kelly & Conley, 1987). One major variable distinguished the divorced from the still-married and the married-satisfied from the married-dissatisfied—neuroticism levels of both spouses (as rated in young adulthood by friends). In addition, low impulse control in the husband was related to less satisfactory marital outcomes, particularly predicting early divorce.

Late-Life Marriages

Information about marriages among the very old comes primarily from the longitudinal Berkeley Older Generation Study (Field & Weishaus, 1992). At the last wave in 1982–84, 17 couples of the Berkeley Older Generation Study were available for interviewing; they had been married for 50 to 69 years. For the analyses reported by Field and Weishaus, the Maas and Kuypers (1974) interviews were rerated to be consistent with earlier and later (1982–84) ratings. Changes in the marital relationship between the two assessment periods, young-old and old-old, were then explored. Several shifts during the 15 years were noted. For instance, many respondents reported increased satisfaction and feelings of closeness in old age (47% of the women and 37% of the men), along with generally stable ratings of marital adjustment. Compared with the earlier period, marital satisfaction in advanced old age was more linked to contact with children (with more maritally satisfied couples having more contact) and to frequency of club and church activities (with maritally satisfied couples having less involvement). Weishaus and Field (1988) examined all case records for the past 50+ years for all 17 couples, using these qualitative data to construct a dynamic taxonomy to describe the course of marriage throughout adulthood. The most common pattern was curvilinear (n = 7, 41%), with satisfaction high in young adulthood, dipping in midlife, and increasing in later life. The depth, timing, and the duration of the dip varied across couples.

OTHER CLOSE RELATIONSHIPS IN LATER LIFE

Heterosexual Cohabitation

Although it has become more common for younger people to live together as a precursor to marriage (to the same or another partner), it is not clear how many older individuals are choosing this means of relating. One clue comes from the U.S. Bureau of the Census (1991). When all men in a particular age group are used as a reference, unmarried heterosexual cohabitation is clearly unusual, representing less than 1% of the middle-aged or older men. Similarly, fewer than 1% of the women in each of the older age groups are living with an unrelated adult. Based on other research evidence, it is likely that these groups include individuals who have never married, are currently in transition out of a marriage, are contemplating marriage, would marry but are concerned about not being able to collect on a late spouse's Social Security benefits, have adult children who strongly object to a remarriage, or are concerned about other responsibilities in a later-life marriage (Macklin, 1987). Note, however, that census data do not permit assessment of whether the individuals sharing households are in the kinds of close relationships considered in this chapter. Cohabitating elders have not been much studied. The general conclusion from younger adults is that cohabitors have a clearer sense of the need for personal time than those who move into marriage (Blumstein & Schwartz, 1983); it is not clear whether this applies to older adults.

Same-Sex Romantic Relationships in Middle and Later Life

Critique of the knowledge base

Systematic attention to same-sex romantic relationships emerged in the 1970s as one aspect of sex and gender liberation movements; attention to older gay males and lesbian females became part of that renewed focus (Kimmel, 1990). In part, this recent attention reflects the substantial historical and generational differences in how homosexual partnerships have been regarded in the larger society. Homosexual couples who are now middle-aged and older grew up in an era in which homosexuality was viewed as an abnormal perversion, with little social or familial support for openness about such desires or activities; their relationships are marked by the larger social realities, and their relative absence in the research literature is one clue of their invisibility. Most of the major studies comparing heterosexual, gay, and lesbian couples have included few homosexual couples over 50 (e.g., Blumstein & Schwartz, 1983). Much of the research on homosexual couples resembles early research on heterosexual couples, marked by small samples of volunteers, nearly all Caucasian, with data from one partner, and utilizing anonymous surveys and questionnaires rather than intensive interviews of couples.

Estimates of prevalence

The problem in estimating the number of same-sex partnerships is that the definition of *homosexual* is not clear (Peplau & Cochran, 1990). The disagreements center around the relative importance of sex, what is included as sex (e.g., whether genital arousal is required), and whether the emotional experience of love is required. Using self-definitions undifferentiated by age, estimates are that 40% to 60% of homosexual males and 75% of lesbian females consider themselves to be in a relationship (though degree of closeness is not specified). Of these, approximately half of the gay males and perhaps three-fourths of the lesbians live together (Peplau & Cochran, 1990). Because persons who are now older are less likely to be open about a homosexual orientation, these estimates are probably more accurate for younger persons than for older persons. Another estimate is available in census data on persons living with an unrelated same-sex partner. These living arrangements include approximately .5% of the men and .5% of the women in each age group (U.S. Bureau of the Census, 1991). Some of the individuals who are living together might not define themselves as couples, and others who are living apart probably do consider themselves coupled.

General patterns in longer-term same-sex relationships

Most homosexual persons report that they desire a steady, loving, long-term romantic relationship (Bell & Weinberg, 1978). An early large-scale study of homosexual men and women in the San Francisco area documented a variety of couple lifestyles. The couples varied in the extent to which their social life was shared with their partner and in their level of satisfaction with the relationship (Bell & Weinberg, 1978). In the relatively few studies comparing individuals in heterosexual, gay, and lesbian relationships who are similar in age and other salient social characteristics, findings are similar for partners on global satisfaction with the relationship, levels of love felt, the importance of satisfaction with sexual aspects of the relationship, and personal adjustment or mental health (Peplau & Cochran, 1990).

Homosexual couples who are now middle-aged or older have been described as more likely to interact with their partners in ways that seem similar to gender-differentiated styles; such relationships seem modeled after heterosexual relationships prevalent in their age group, with a clear division of labor and one partner regarded as more dominant. In contrast, younger middle-aged partners in enduring homosexual relations tend to emphasize role flexibility, taking turns, and equity (Maracek, Finn, & Cardell, 1988).

Some problems seem to be distinctive for same-sex couples. Pressures that are exerted to keep a heterosexual marriage intact are often exerted to break up a homosexual relationship. For instance, social barriers against dismantling marriages and against formalizing homosexual relationships are evident in the legal, social, and (typically) familial spheres (Dynes, 1990; Peplau & Cochran, 1990). In later life, special problems arise in handling issues such as inheritance, openness to health care providers, and obtaining support for bereavement when a partner is ill or dies (Kimmel, 1990). Some aspects of the relationship seem linked to gender, leading us to examine lesbian female and gay male relationships separately.

The evidence suggests that many women who define themselves in middle and later life as lesbians have had prior experiences with marriage; one survey estimated that 25% to 30% of the lesbians had been married (Bell & Weinberg, 1978). Coupled lesbians have fewer complaints of loneliness than do heterosexual married women (Bell & Weinberg, 1978). Some authors suggest that middle-aged lesbians are advantaged compared with middle-aged heterosexual women because they are more likely to have a partner with whom they expect to grow old, to share the same life expectancy curve, to be less threatened by physical appearance changes, to have been employed and accumulated their own financial security, and to be involved in shared couple activities than are heterosexual or homosexual male couples. Further, lesbians often have a close network of friends for support when a partner leaves or dies (e.g., Raphael & Robinson, 1984). On the other hand, lesbian couples share experiences of growing up female and of devalued social status (Burch, 1987; Kirkpatrick, 1989). Clinicians often report that heterosexual wives complain about loneliness, emotional distance, and lack of communication; lesbian partners might struggle with more intensity and sharing than are comfortable (Kirkpatrick, 1989).

Gay men who maintain long-term relationships are likely to live in proximity to other gay men, who provide opportunities for contact and a supportive community. Gay men who live in rural areas or small towns are likely to keep their sexual orientation secret and to have episodic, short-term homosexual relationships (Dynes, 1990). Given a supportive homosexual community, long-term relationships can be sustained. Several studies revealed a generation gap whereby older gay men expect mentor/protégé relationships marked by age and status discrepancies, and younger gay men prefer age peers for partners (Dynes, 1990). One issue in age-discrepant relationships is making the transition from the youthful lover to the older sponsor, an issue likely to emerge in early midlife (Liebert, 1989).

SEXUALITY

Critique of the Knowledge Base

Socially sanctioned sexual sharing is an explicit component of marriages and marital-like relationships. Sexual feelings and sexual behavior are complex, drawing on physical responses evoked in an interpersonal context. Responses in any current situation are affected by a lifelong sense of what it means to be touched and kissed and to penetrate or be penetrated in intercourse. Because many aspects of sexual expression are intrinsically satisfying, sharing sexuality has the potential to forge and affirm a pleasure bond. On the other hand, sexual behaviors might become associated with feeling physical or psychological pain.

Ideally, in this section I would like to review a rich literature describing the ways in which sexuality is important to a relationship at various phases. Unfortunately, social science databases focus more narrowly on general level of interest in sexual behavior, incidence of specific sexual behaviors (especially heterosexual intercourse), and some standard variables associated with maintenance or decline in sexual interest and activity with advancing age.

There are more exhortations about the desirability of maintaining sexual activity than there are realistic assessments of sexual relationships in later life. Up to the early 1980s, virtually all the studies on later-life sexuality included only Caucasians, neglected possible sexual experiences outside marriage, and focused on individual, rather than interactional, measures. The definition of *sexually active* ranges widely. A national survey of respondents 60 and over used a report of intercourse with spouse during the past month to indicate active status (Marsiglio & Donnelly, 1991), whereas in another study very old respondents were described as sexually active if they had fantasized or daydreamed at least once in the past year about being close, affectionate, and intimate with the opposite sex (Bretchneider & McCoy, 1988). Given this range, it is crucial to note just what is being described.

Research on Interest and Activity

The general finding is that avowed interest in sex is quite stable throughout adulthood and old age, with men indicating stronger interest than women, on the average, and with individual differences maintained throughout life (Garza & Dressel, 1983). These patterns are seen in heterosexual and homosexual couples, although the database is much more adequate for heterosexuals. Sexual activity declines faster than interest. Within heterosexual couples the decline is gradual, unless serious health problems interfere (George & Weiler, 1981). In a national study of married persons over 60, 53% of all respondents and 44% of those over 65 said they had sexual relations with their spouse in the past month; these are probably high-end estimates of activity, because 34% of the respondents refused to answer the question. Only 24% of the men over 75 said they were sexually active (Marsiglio & Donnelly, 1991). Volunteers recruited to describe later-life sexuality report more interest and activity than recorded in other samples. Satisfaction with the sexual relationship is strongly associated with relationship satisfaction among heterosexual, gay male, and lesbian couples (Blumstein & Schwartz, 1983; Field & Weishaus, 1992; Skolnick, 1981). When marital sexual relations cease, both husbands and wives agree that it is the husband who has lost interest or capability (Garza & Dressel, 1983).

Little current research is available on patterns of sexual activity among middle-aged and older lesbians and gay men. The minimal findings available for younger middle-aged homosexuals suggest that lesbian couples have less frequent sex than other types of couples. Gay male couples begin their relationships with the highest frequencies of sexual activity, which drops after a few years to a level lower than that of heterosexual couples in comparable-length relationships but higher than that of lesbian couples (Blumstein & Schwartz, 1983).

Patterns of sexual activity outside the couple relationship also seem to vary. Some researchers suggest that among the younger and middle-aged gay male couples, sexual activities outside the relationship seem to be expected and tolerated (McWhirter & Mattison, 1984). Lesbian women tend to have emotionally involved outside affairs that are likely to break up the original couple (Nichols, 1987). Patterns among heterosexuals have changed over the past three decades. Younger cohorts of heterosexual men and women engage in sexual affairs in approximately equal proportions. Such affairs are likely to be kept secret and to be deeply disturbing to the relationship if disclosed. Among older cohorts, men are more likely than women to have had extramarital affairs (Blumstein & Schwartz, 1983).

Factors Affecting Sexual Patterns

Clearly, the most important factors affecting sexual patterns are gender and age. Men are likely to feel demasculinized if they do not experience sexual desire and (to a somewhat lesser extent) sexual activity. Women usually feel feminine even if they do not feel sexual desire and are not sexually active. In addition, individual differences in drive strength and comfort with sexuality seem stable across the years. Although the levels of desire and activity decline in old age, the most interested and active men in old age are those who were also more erotically engaged when they were young men. Continuity is less marked for women, largely because in heterosexual unions women's sexual interest and activity seem closely tied to those of their partner; it is not clear whether this pattern will be found for contemporary young women as they grow older.

Masters and Johnson (1970) documented the basic normal physiological changes in the sexual response cycle, pointing out that men showed significant changes in erectile capacity. Women's changes of lessened lubrication are relatively easy to compensate, and most retain the capacity to be orgasmic and multiorgasmic. More problematic than the normal age-related changes are dysfunctions linked to health. Arthritis, prostate enlargement, and medication side effects are among the health problems that can affect sexual desire and responsivity. But even given medical problems, the key elements in a couple's sexual expression seem to be high sexual drive and the man's confidence that he will be successful sexually (Creti & Libman, 1989). Sexual activities also obviously depend upon opportunities for the couple to have sufficient time and privacy.

OTHER INFLUENCES ON MARRIAGE IN MIDDLE AND LATER LIFE

Parenting

The majority of middle-aged and older married couples and a minority of homosexual couples have living children. Relationships between adult children and their parents are covered more fully elsewhere (see Robertson, this volume; Suitor, Pillemer, Keeton, & Robison, this volume). The focus here is on evidence concerning the ways in which children affect the marriage or couple relationship. Four themes are evident. First, having children and grandchildren is part of the generalized enjoyment of family, particularly as the burdens of direct responsibility for offspring phase out. Men are especially likely to talk about the family as a collective unit, rather than focus on separate relationships (Huyck, 1989; Thurnher, 1976). Second, relationships with children can provide an alternative source of gratification when the marriage relationship is not very rewarding, providing an overall sense of satisfaction with family life. This pattern seems to be more evident for working-class women, who generally are less satisfied with the marriage relationship and more invested in mothering compared with middle-class women (Farrell & Rosenberg, 1981; Maas & Kuypers, 1974). Third, responsibilities for children might distract from an otherwise satisfying couple relationship. Pressures involved in launching children into adulthood or caring for dependent adult children have been linked to reduced companionship time available to the couple and hence to lessened marital satisfaction (Spanier, Lewis, & Cole, 1975). Dealing with children in blended families (heterosexual or homosexual) can present problems for the marriage at any stage. Approval of adult children has been linked to successful remarriages in later life (Vermer, Coleman, Ganong, & Cooper, 1989). Finally, responsibility for dependent children has been proposed as a major influence in emphasizing gender-role distinctions in the marriage (Gutmann, 1987). In the parental imperative model, fathers suppress their own desires to be passive and be nurtured in order to be good providers of physical security (the distinctively paternal form of nurturing) for their families; mothers suppress their own desires to be competitive and manage their own lives in order to provide emotional security for vulnerable children and to keep the father attached to the family unit. As children become independent, each parent can reclaim repressed aspects of the self. Support for this model as it applies to the midlife marriage relationship was evident in our research, where wives who no longer had younger children (under 24) living at home were more likely to be openly assertive within the marriage, compared with wives who had younger children still at home (Huyck & Gutmann, 1992).

Social Status

One obvious impact of socioeconomic status is that it affects the resources available to the couple to pursue companionate activities, if they desire to do so. In addition, power and status wielded outside the couple unit may influence relationships within the couple. In couples where the husband has a higher-status occupation, the wives are more likely to defer to him (Blumstein & Schwartz, 1983) and to be husband-centered rather than child- or activity-centered (Lopata & Barnewolt, 1984).

Ethnicity and Culture

Few researchers have directed attention specifically to the ways in which ethnicity and culture affect marriage or other couple relationships in middle and later life. Evidence about general patterns of family life suggests that some differences might emerge. The impact of ethnicity is likely to be greatest among recent immigrants (e.g., Wilkerson, 1987). Johnson (this volume) discusses such issues further.

Remarriage

Most of the research cited previously did not yield distinctions between persons who are in their first marriage and those who have remarried. Results of some studies indicate that divorced and widowed persons engage in dating behavior (Bulcroft & Bulcroft, 1991). Men are substantially more likely to remarry than are women, divorced persons are somewhat more likely to remarry than are widowed persons, and African Americans are less likely to remarry than are Caucasians (Brubaker, 1985). The few studies of remarriage indicate that late-life remarriages are more likely to be successful when partners are in good health and have adequate incomes, when friends and relatives support the remarriage, and when partners have had a successful first marriage (Bengtson, Rosenthal, & Burton, 1990).

Retirement

The impact of retirement from paid employment on the marriage seems to vary. Some researchers report that retirement improves marital quality after an initial period of adjustment (Atchley, 1976). Other researchers find little impact (e.g., Ekerdt & Vinick, 1991) or slightly negative effects of retirement on marriage (Lee & Shehan, 1989). See Lopata (this volume) and Szinovacz and Ekerdt (this volume) for more details.

Illness

Older persons are more likely than younger ones to experience illness requiring hospitalization, although they are no more likely than people in other age groups to experience illness of one week or more involving activity limitation or illness of a family member (Hughes, Blazer, & George, 1988). Nevertheless, the impact of serious illness on the marriage relationship has been extensively researched (see Dwyer, this volume; Travis, this volume). In spite of the extensive research on caregiving, conclusions about the implications for marriage of late-life illness must be tentative because most studies have used nonrepresentative, volunteer samples and have relied on cross-sectional designs (Gatz, Bengtson, & Blum, 1990). For married persons, the spouse is the most likely caregiver. Some spouses report intensified feelings of commitment, closeness, and love as a result of caregiving (e.g., Fitting, Rabins, Lucas, & Eastham, 1986). Some women feel particularly burdened by their awareness of the changed marital relationship and are reluctant to tell the ailing husband what to do. Men, more than women, approach caregiving during illness like a project and are comfortable delegating tasks (e.g., Miller, 1987). Some authors suggest that illness and impairment have less impact on late-life marriages than on earlier-life marriages (Johnson, 1985).

Cohort Effects

One of the major questions in all cross-sectional and longitudinal analyses is whether observed age differences reflect cohort effects and whether patterns observed in this decade will be reliable predictors for coming decades. In this context, we want to know whether we have described the natural life course of marriages or close relationships. There is no clear-cut answer, but several lines of research suggest that some aspects of marriage are changing, whereas others are not.

Generally, marriage quality seems to be improving. The strongest evidence for this comes in the studies of Middletown, initially in 1924–25, in 1935, and in 1976–78 (Caplow, Bahr, Chadwick, Hill, & Williamson, 1982). Although the data were not analyzed separately for marriage by life stage, the researchers described marriages in the 1920s as dreary for both husbands and wives, with limited companionship, strained sexual relations, and substantial evidence of husbands' cruelty, adultery, and abandonment. In the 1970s marriages were substantially improved, with greater companionship, communication, and satisfaction. The social class differences so evident earlier had abated, and battered wives were encouraged and helped to leave bad marriages.

Changing attitudes about what constitutes a good marriage are also evident in research comparing the Terman Gifted Study sample at age 30 in 1940 with a comparable sample of 30-year-olds in 1981 (Holahan, 1984). Contemporary women were more egalitarian in attitudes toward marital role relationships than were the Terman women at the same age, although the Terman women by 1981 had become nearly as egalitarian as the young women. This finding suggests that sociohistorical change reinforces developmental changes. Cohort differences were much more evident among the men. Although contemporary young men were just as likely as the Terman young men to wish they could "wear the pants" in the family, they endorsed more active parenting roles and greater emotional expressiveness than did the young adult Terman sample men. The contemporary men and women expressed less satisfaction with their marriages than had the Terman sample as young adults, suggesting that the changing ideology about marriage might be inducing new tensions for the advantaged persons represented in these samples (as compared with residents of Middletown).

Other research documents the changing patterns of age at marriage, age differences between spouses, divorce, and expectations about marriage relationships. One prediction is that the "marital union" of the past is giving way to a "marital partnership" of the future, which will accommodate informal as well as formal marriages, less dependence between spouses, greater egalitarianism, lower fertility, and higher levels of divorce (Schoen, Urton, Woodrow, & Baj, 1985). To the extent that such patterns evolve, ripple effects will occur for relationships in middle and later life. One area where changes are evident is in sexuality; younger cohorts of participants in the Duke Longitudinal Studies are more sexually active than were earlier-born cohorts at the same ages (George & Weiler, 1981), and women who are now entering middle age seem to have more sex and more orgasms than did their grandmothers (Luria & Meade, 1984). How the greater comfort with sexuality will affect later-life relationships is not clear. Although some of these changes can be appropriately described as cohort effects, efforts to explain marriage relationships using cohort frameworks have been limited.

ENHANCING RELATIONSHIPS

The preceding review has provided many clues about the kinds of strains and problems experienced in some marriages and homosexual relationships during the middle years and later. Psychotherapy is not a common treatment among persons who are now old, and marital therapy is even less common than personal therapy. The reluctance to seek help might be a reflection of the strength of old people, as survivors. Reluctance to seek help may also reflect the assumption that nothing can be done about problems that occur during old age. Therapists are challenged to combat these negative stereotypes. The cohorts of currently older adults grew up in times when seeking psychotherapeutic help was unusual and stigmatizing. Although the field of marriage counseling has burgeoned in recent decades, relatively little attention has been paid to the kinds of distinctive issues that sometimes emerge in later life or to the ways in which recurrent problems may take on different forms.

One model for late-life marital intervention lists developmental tasks of the mature-stage marriage. These tasks include redefining intimacy, interactional patterns, and roles; setting new goals; validating all stages of the marriage; fostering the ability to live together without undue concern about illness or death of either spouse; providing nurturing care even if the physical or mental problems of a spouse limit the ability to reciprocate; developing the capacity to mourn losses while maintaining a meaningful relationship; letting go when the spouse dies or is unable to function; and acquiring the ability to view oneself as a separate individual whose life will have meaning even in the face of illness or death of one's spouse (Wolinsky, 1990). Other psychodynamic models emphasize the ways in which normal developmental transitions, such as women's becoming more assertive and managerial around midlife, can have serious repercussions in the marriage when either spouse is particularly threatened by these changes due to psychological defenses formed much earlier in life (Gutmann, 1991). In such models, the focus is less on a losses-of-aging perspective and more on how developmental gains can be experienced as catastrophic. Therapy in such cases focuses on the unconscious fears associated with otherwise normal changes and emphasizes ways in which the current situation is not the same as the earlier, traumatic one.

A variety of interventions have been shown to be effective in working with relationship problems presented by older couples. Special issues in providing counseling and therapy for gay male and lesbian female clients have been identified recently, such as differentiating among problems that stem from negative feelings about the homosexual self, from social attitudes and discrimination, and from issues not related to sexual orientation (Committee on Lesbian and Gay Concerns, 1990). Very little attention has been directed toward providing couple counseling specifically with these clients.

As diverse forms of close, supportive relationships are seen as normal in middle and later life, it would be desirable for a full range of appropriate counseling and therapy services to become available. Couples who are now entering middle age are likely to be much more comfortable seeking and using such services and to hold the expectation that the services will be sensitive to their particular circumstances. It will be a major challenge to identify and implement appropriate interventions, because they require an appreciation of the complex systems reflected in marriages and other close relationships. The knowledge base to support such planning must be stronger than it is now, and it must be much more attuned to describing differential patterns of relationship. Researchers should drop any quest for one formula for "a happy marriage," particularly in terms of its usefulness for practice. Close relationships of the sort described in this review combine the most idiosyncratic, personalized, and irrational interactions along with versions of widely shared, mundane patterns of behavior. The fact that couples share some sorts of behaviors has beguiled some researchers into thinking that the hidden truths about relationships over time will be revealed only by developing the perfectly standardized measurement of marital satisfaction. It is far more likely that we will discover the patterns of relationship that sustain or stress individuals at various points in the life course by listening carefully to couples' own experiences and the meanings they attribute to their experiences. Because the meanings are not standard, the measures probably cannot be standardized in the sense that we now define standardization. We need more specificity about the desires evoked in romantic relationships and the ways in which relationships are experienced as fulfilling or thwarting those desires. We have clues of the relationship varieties we might find, particularly in some of the qualitative, longitudinal studies. We need careful studies of the relationships of the diverse groups of ethnic and cultural heritage. We have much to do.

REFERENCES

Atchley, R. (1976). *The sociology of retirement.* Cambridge, MA: Schenkman.

Bell, A. P., & Weinberg, M. S. (1978). *Homosexualities: A study of diversity among men and women.* New York: Simon & Schuster.

Bengtson, V. L., Rosenthal, C., & Burton, L. (1990). Families and aging: Diversity and heterogeneity. In R. Binstock & L. George (Eds.), *Handbook of aging and the social sciences* (3rd ed., pp. 263–287). San Diego: Academic Press.

Blumstein, P., & Schwartz, P. (1983). *American couples: Money, work, sex.* New York: William Morrow.

Bowlby, J. (1986). *Attachment, life-span, and old age.* (Ed. J. Munnichs & B. Misen.) Deventer, Netherlands: Van Loghum Slaterus.

Bretchneider, J., & McCoy, N. (1988). Sexual interest and behavior in healthy 80- to 102-year olds. *Archives of Sexual Behavior, 17,* 109–129.

Brubaker, T. (1985). *Later life families.* Beverly Hills, CA: Sage.

Bulcroft, R., & Bulcroft, K. (1991). The nature and functions of dating in later life. *Research on Aging, 13,* 244–260.

Burch, B. (1987). Barriers to intimacy: Conflicts over power, dependency and nurturing in lesbian relationships. In Boston Lesbian Psychological Collective, *Lesbian psychologies* (pp. 126–141). Chicago: University of Illinois Press.

Caplow, T., Bahr, H., Chadwick, B., Hill, R., & Williamson, M. H. (1982). *Middletown families: Fifty years of change and continuity.* Minneapolis: University of Minnesota Press.

Committee on Lesbian and Gay Concerns. (1990). *Bias in psychotherapy with lesbians and gay men* (Final Report). Washington, DC: American Psychological Association.

Creti, L., & Libman, E. (1989). Cognitions and sexual expression in the aging. *Journal of Sex and Marital Therapy, 15,* 83–101.

Dynes, W. R. (Ed.). (1990). *Encyclopedia of homosexuality.* New York: Garland.

Ekerdt, D. J., & Vinick, B. H. (1991). Marital complaints in husband-working and husband-retired couples. *Research on Aging, 13,* 364–382.

Farrell, M. P., & Rosenberg, S. D. (1981). *Men at midlife.* Boston: Auburn House.

Field, D., & Weishaus, S. (1992). Marriage over half a century: A longitudinal study. In M. Bloom (Ed.), *Changing lives* (pp. 269–273). Columbia: University of South Carolina Press.

Fitting, M., Rabins, P., Lucas, M. J., & Eastham, J. (1986). Caring for dementia patients: A comparison of husbands and wives. *Gerontologist, 26,* 248–252.

Garza, J., & Dressel, P. (1983). Sexuality and later life marriages. In T. Brubaker (Ed.), *Family relationships in later life* (pp. 91–108). Beverly Hills, CA: Sage.

Gatz, M., Bengtson, V. L., & Blum, M. J. (1990). Caregiving families. In J. Birren & K. W. Schaie (Eds.), *Handbook of the psychology of aging* (3rd ed., pp. 404–426). San Diego: Academic Press.

George, L. K., & Weiler, S. J. (1981). Sexuality in middle and late life: The effects of age, cohort, and gender. *Archives of General Psychiatry, 38,* 919–923.

Gilford, R., & Bengtson, V. (1979). Measuring marital satisfaction in three generations: Positive and negative dimensions. *Journal of Marriage and the Family, 41,* 387–398.

Gutmann, D. L. (1987). *Reclaimed powers: Toward a new psychology of men and women in later life.* New York: Basic Books.

Gutmann, D. L. (1991, February). *Patterns of psychological vulnerability to developmental shifts in middle-aged and older husbands.* Paper presented at the International Conference on Gender and the Family, Brigham Young University, Provo, Utah.

Holahan, C. K. (1984). Marital attitudes over 40 years: A longitudinal and cohort analysis. *Journal of Gerontology, 38,* 49–57.

Hughes, D. C., Blazer, D., & George, L. (1988). Age differences in life events. *International Journal of Aging and Human Development, 27,* 207–220.

Hunter, S., & Sundel, M. (Eds.). (1989). *Midlife myths: Issues, findings, and practice implications.* Newbury Park, CA: Sage.

Huyck, M. H. (1989). Midlife parental imperatives. In R. Kalish (Ed.), *Midlife loss* (pp. 115–148). Newbury Park, CA: Sage.

Huyck, M. H. (1994). The relevance of psychodynamic theory for understanding gender among older women. In B. F. Turner & L. E. Troll (Eds.), *Women growing older: Psychological perspectives* (pp. 202–238). Newbury Park, CA: Sage.

Huyck, M. H., & Gutmann, D. L. (1992). Thirtysomething years of marriage: Understanding experiences of women and men in enduring family relationships. *Family Perspective, 26,* 249–265.

Johnson, C. L. (1985). Impact of illness on late-life marriages. *Journal of Marriage and the Family, 47,* 165–172.

Kelly, E., & Conley, J. (1987). Personality and compatibility: A prospective analysis of marital stability and satisfaction. *Journal of Personality and Social Psychology, 52,* 27–40.

Kimmel, D. (1990). *Adulthood and aging: An interdisciplinary, developmental view.* New York: Wiley.

Kirkpatrick, M. (1989). Lesbians: A different middle age? In J. M. Oldham & R. S. Liebert (Eds.), *The middle years: New psychoanalytic perspectives* (pp. 135–148). New Haven, CT: Yale University Press.

Lee, G. R., & Shehan, C. L. (1989). Retirement and marital satisfaction. *Journal of Gerontology: Social Sciences, 44,* S226–230.

Liebert, R. S. (1989). Middle aged homosexual men: Issues in treatment. In J. M. Oldham & R. S. Liebert (Eds.), *The middle years: New psychoanalytic perspectives* (pp. 149–159). New Haven, CT: Yale University Press.

Lopata, H. Z., & Barnewolt, D. (1984). The middle years: Changes and variations in social role commitments. In G. Baruch & J. Brooks-Gunn (Eds.), *Women in midlife* (pp. 83–108). New York: Plenum.

Lowenthal, M. F., Thurnher, M., Chiriboga, D., & Associates. (1975). *Four stages of life: A comparative study of women and men facing transitions.* San Francisco: Jossey-Bass.

Luria, Z., & Meade, R. (1984). Sexuality and the middle-aged woman. In G. Baruch & J. Brooks-Gunn (Eds.), *Women in midlife* (pp. 371–397). New York: Plenum Press.

Maas, H., & Kuypers, J. (1974). *From thirty to seventy.* San Francisco: Jossey-Bass.

Macklin, E. D. (1987). Nontraditional family forms. In M. B. Sussman & S. K. Steinmetz (Eds.), *Handbook of marriage and the family* (pp. 317–353). New York: Plenum Press.

Maracek, J., Finn, S. & Cardell, M. (1988). Gender roles in the relationships of lesbians and gay men. In J. DeCecco (Ed.), *Gay relationships* (pp. 169–175). New York: Harrington Park Press.

Marsiglio, W., & Donnelly, D. (1991). Sexual relations in later life: A national study of married persons. *Journal of Gerontology: Social Sciences, 46,* S338–344.

Masters, W. H., & Johnson, V. E. (1970). *Human sexual inadequacy.* Boston: Little, Brown.

McWhirter, D., & Mattison, A. (1984). *The male couple: How relationships develop.* Englewood Cliffs, NJ: Prentice-Hall.

Miller, B. (1987). Gender and control among spouses of the cognitively impaired. *Gerontologist, 27,* 447–453.

Nadelson, C., Polonsky, D., & Matthews, M. A. (1981). Marriage problems and marital therapy in the middle-aged. In J. Howells (Ed.), *Modern perspectives in the psychiatry of middle age* (pp. 337–352). New York: Brunner/Mazel.

Nichols, M. (1987). Lesbian sexuality. In Boston Lesbian Psychologists Collective, *Lesbian psychologies* (pp. 97–125). Chicago: University of Illinois Press.

Peplau, L. A., & Cochran, S. D. (1990). A relationship perspective on homosexuality. In D. P. McWhirter, S. Sanders, & J. Reinisch (Eds.), *Homosexuality/heterosexuality: Concepts of sexual orientation* (pp. 321–349). New York: Oxford University Press.

Raphael, S., & Robinson, M. (1984). The older lesbian: Love relationships and friendship patterns. In T. Darty & S. Potter (Eds.), *Women-identified women* (pp. 67–82). Palo Alto, CA: Mayfield.

Rollins, B. C. (1989). Marital quality at midlife. In S. Hunter & M. Sundel (Eds.), *Midlife myths: Issues, findings and practical implications* (pp. 184–194). Newbury Park, CA: Sage.

Schoen, R., Urton, W., Woodrow, K., & Baj, J. (1985). Marriage and divorce in twentieth century American cohorts. *Demography, 22,* 101–114.

Skolnick, A. (1981). Married lives: Longitudinal perspectives on marriage. In D. H. Eichorn, J. A. Clausen, N. Haan, M. P. Honzik, & P. H. Mussen (Eds.), *Present and past in middle life* (pp. 269–298). New York: Academic Press.

Spanier, G. B., Lewis, R. A., & Cole, C. L. (1975). Marital adjustment over the family life cycle: The issue of curvilinearity. *Journal of Marriage and the Family, 37,* 263–275.

Swenson, C., Esker, R. & Kohlhepp, K. (1984). Five factors in long term marriages. *Lifestyles, 7,* 94–106.

Thurnher, M. (1976). Midlife marriage: Sex differences in evaluation and perspectives. *International Journal of Aging and Human Development, 7,* 129–135.

U.S. Bureau of the Census. (1991). *Marital status and living arrangements: March, 1990.* (Current Population Reports, Series P-20, No. 450). Washington, DC: U.S. Government Printing Office.

Vermer, E., Coleman, M., Ganong, L. H., & Cooper, H. (1989). Marital satisfaction in remarriage: A metaanalysis. *Journal of Marriage and the Family, 51,* 713–725.

Weishaus, S., & Field, D. (1988). A half century of marriage: Continuity or change? *Journal of Marriage and the Family, 50,* 763–774.

Wilkerson, D. (1987). Ethnicity. In M. B. Sussman & S. K. Steinmetz (Eds.), *Handbook of marriage and the family* (pp. 183–210). New York: Plenum Press.

Wolinsky, M. A. (1990). *Heart of wisdom: Marital counseling with older and elderly couples.* New York: Brunner/Mazel.

10

Sibling Relationships in Middle and Old Age

Victoria Hilkevitch Bedford

"You know the profit to me, all these years, from your support?" "But Ifat," I said with sudden tears, "to have you as sister is a high honor of my life!" Then we rose and turned to other things, conscious of having uttered all that could be said.
—Sara Suleri, *Meatless Days,* 1987

Although siblings would seem to be an obvious part of any family, only in the past decade has the sibling relationship been routinely differentiated in social research on adults from other kinship ties. Following a gradual recognition that relationships with original family members continue through old age (Troll, 1971), the presumed obscurity of siblings after adolescence (Bernard, 1942) was replaced with the recognition that the sibling tie persists throughout life. Several researchers have documented that this persistent tie is often highly valued in middle and old age (Cicirelli, 1985; Cumming & Schneider, 1961; Gold, 1989a, 1989b). Subsequently, sibling researchers have attempted to map the nature of this important tie, to discern why the tie is so important, and to understand sources of variability in the important aspects of the relationship. The purpose of this chapter is to take stock of this effort by updating and elaborating upon other recent reviews of this literature (Bedford, 1989c, 1993c; Cicirelli, 1993).

The chapter begins with a broad definition of siblings within which the scope of current studies can be located. Next, I examine sibling relationships from two perspectives—their position and function in the personal network of the individual and their nature as a personal relationship. The emphasis here is on sources of variability in the personal benefits and costs accrued from sibling relationships.

WHAT IS A SIBLING?

Siblings are assumed to be offspring of the same parents, thereby sharing, on average, 50% of the same genes (Scarr & Grajek, 1982; Weisner, 1989). In fact, many siblings do not meet this criterion. Using anthropological terminology, there are siblings by adoption, who lack the biological link; "part-siblings" (stepsiblings), who share one biological parent; and "quasisiblings," who have different biological parents not married to each other but living together (Weisner, 1989, p. 12). Siblings can also be socially designated; these "fictive" siblings achieve their status in a formal ritual in some societies (Marshall, 1983) and informally in others. Finally, in some societies biological siblings are not limited to the nuclear family; they include cousins as well (Marshall, 1983). Most adult sibling scholarship is limited to biological and adopted siblings; nothing is known, as yet, about other kinds of siblings.

THE PLACE OF SIBLINGS IN PERSONAL NETWORKS

In this section, the full siblingship (all brothers and sisters within one family) is the unit of analysis. These studies are concerned with the part played by siblings in meeting the social support needs of a person, often in comparison with other categories of relationships. Much of this research is descriptive, providing information about the content of siblings' contributions and the proportion of particular categories of social support supplied by siblings. There has been some attempt to account for these descriptive findings by examining whether gender, social class, or ethnic membership makes a difference. Given the enormous quantity of data needed to construct personal networks, it is not surprising that age comparisons are rare. Discrete studies of older adults, however, provide some absolute data about this family relationship in later life that are used to help interpret some preliminary results on age differences.

Social Support from the Sibling Group

Network analyses lend some justification to studying relationships by category (e.g., sibling, friend, parent), because they reveal meaningful differences between such categories, at least in the case of social support. Specifically, various social support provisions are not simply spread across different relationships; they are often found to cluster around specific categories of relationships. In other words, in most categories of network members, people provide a few specialized functions (Fehr & Perlman, 1985; Wellman & Wortley, 1989). Although overlap among relationship categories does occur (e.g., Dykstra, 1993), people in each category also provide some unique forms of social support.

Recently, network analysts have compared contributions of members who are family and nonfamily and the different relationship categories within these broad classifications (e.g., adult children, siblings, neighbors and friends). Wellman and Wortley (1989) sampled networks of Canadians living in East York, in which the modal person was aged 40 and living with a spouse and school-aged children. On average, kin made up 9% of all "actual" ties ($n = 35$), meaning both weak and strong ties. Further, immediate kin (parents, adult children, and siblings) made up 30% of all active ties ($n = 6$), where active ties included both intimates (those outside the home with whom a respondent feels closest) and significants (those with whom respondents are in touch in their daily life and who are significant in their life but not intimate). Siblings were the most numerous of active immediate kin (21%, including siblings-in-law), followed by parents (7%, including parents-in-law) and children (2%). Friends and neighbors constituted nearly half the active ties (48%).

In this sample, many characteristics differentiated kin from nonkin and siblings from other kin; some of these distinctions replicate findings from other studies. Kin had known each other an average of 35 years, which is nearly three times as long as nonkin. Kinship ties were also more dense (known to one another) whereas nonkin were loosely connected, if connected at all. Finally, kin were not voluntarily chosen, which resulted in their having fewer desired characteristics than friends have (Wellman & Wortley, 1989).

Within the kinship classification, differences between relationship categories emerged. Findings indicated that, whereas parents and adult children had the most supportive of all active ties (providing high levels of both material and emotional support), siblings actually provided more support than parents did, but simply because there were more siblings (individually, siblings provided less than parents did). Interestingly, in-laws were included in each category, because their support provisions clustered together, no doubt because social exchanges occurred between couples or households, not between individuals. This same context for exchange probably contributed to the lack of sex differences within each relationship category. Comparing support provided by siblings with that provided by others, Wellman and Wortley (1989) drew the following conclusions: (1) Siblings comprise 24% of all emotionally supportive relationships, because there are so many more of them in most networks. The proportion of sisters and sisters-in-law who provide emotional support is second to mothers and daughters who provide the most. (2) Siblings together provide 21% of all services, more than parents and children, but any one sibling provides fewer services than parents, children, and neighbors, and no more than kin and co-workers, due to their greater geographic distance. When geographically near, siblings are particularly likely to provide services (e.g., Scott, 1983). (3) Few network members, including siblings, provide financial aid. The few exchanges that occur are between parents and adult children. (4) Siblings are more likely to be companions than other kin are. Despite their common age and interests, though, they do not provide the companionship of friends, mostly because they live farther away than do friends (see Connidis & Davies, 1990). (5) Siblings, like other kin, are better at maintaining active long-distance relationships than are friends. In general, immediate kin are the only network members who can be intimates when needed, whether or not their company is usually sought or enjoyed.

Siblings, in summary, resemble kith more than kin in some ways, such as providing companionship, and siblings resemble kin more than kith in others ways, such as providing emotional support (see Adams, 1967, for theoretical comparisons). Findings from a study of old people (aged 65 to 75) in the Netherlands help to bring the overlap between siblings and friends into focus. Dykstra (1993) found that emotional supportiveness varied by consanguinity for kin (in the order of spouse, child, sibling, other kin) and by degree of friendship for friends (in the order of best friend, close acquaintance, superficial acquaintance). In terms of absolute level of emotional supportiveness provided, the sibling group resembled the close acquaintance group most nearly.

Do these average proportions of siblings support apply to old people? Using a very large sample of men and women aged 50 to 90 ($n = 4,400$), Dykstra (1993) demonstrated that the proportion of siblings in the active network varied with age according to marital status. Whereas the proportion of siblings remained constant for those who never married, the proportion decreased somewhat for the formerly married and for those cohabitating with their partner. In fact, only the proportion of neighbors increased. Whether the changes in the proportion of siblings are accompanied by a decrease in their social support awaits further analyses. Findings from American sibling research, however, indicate a decline in instrumental help in old age (Bedford, 1989d; Gold, 1989a).

Sources of Variation

What accounts for variation in the proportion of social support contributed by the siblings group? The emotional support and companionship for which siblings are sought in North American and European communities (the First World), as revealed in network studies, are unlikely to be primary needs unlike in the Second and Third worlds, where access to those with power or those able to help obtain food and shelter are essential (Wellman & Wortley, 1990). For instance, in the Philippine Highlands, where family self-reliance is necessary to ensure family welfare (no other institutions are available), siblings are an important source of economic aid (Peterson, 1990) in contrast to North American communities, where siblings rarely provide economic aid (e.g., Wellman, 1990).

Ethnicity also contributes to variation in the social support provided by siblings. Comparing low-income Mexican Americans, African Americans, and Anglos, ranging in age from 60 to 91 years, exchange activities with siblings (instrumental and expressive) differed significantly, even though the economic needs of the three groups were similar. Specifically, African American siblings both received and gave the most help (54% and 53%, respectively), followed by Mexican Americans (44% and 41%, respectively) and Anglos (36% and 38%, respectively) (Myers & Dickerson, 1990). The high reliance of African Americans on siblings was confirmed by the results of a large survey of mostly southern, urban dwellers, aged 17 to 95 years, with low family incomes. Comparing the proportion of respondents who called upon their siblings in an emergency, blacks were far more likely to do so than were whites and Hispanics (Taylor, Chatters, & Mays, 1988).

Other influences on whether one calls on a sibling have been examined. Not surprisingly, the number of siblings is significant; the more siblings, the more one is likely to call on one as a confidant, for instance (Connidis & Davies, 1992). The availability of other family relationships also makes a difference. For instance, the greater the number of grown children, the less likely one is to confide in a sibling (Connidis & Davies, 1992). Also, those who have a child geographically near are less likely to name a sibling as a confidant than are those whose children live at a distance. Geographical distance from sibling was not considered in these comparisons (Connidis & Davies, 1990).

Studies of the influence of marital status on sibling interaction and feelings yield mixed results. Marital status can influence the support function of siblings, such that the never married and previously married turn to siblings more than do those who are married (e.g., Connidis & Davies, 1990; O'Bryant, 1988; Scott, 1990). In the study by Taylor and colleagues described earlier, based on multivariate analyses, only the status of never married (for both black men and women) predicted turning to siblings in emergencies (Taylor et al., 1988), not the status of formerly married. Connidis and Davies (1990) had similar results with respect to confiding, but for women only. In a later analysis of the same data, however, the authors identified variables that mediated the apparent relation between marital status and sibling support. For their sample of 400 community-residing old people in London, Canada, the number of children and proximity to sibling accounted for the greater number of single women who confided in their sibling, not being single (Connidis & Davies, 1992).

PERSONAL RELATIONSHIPS WITH SIBLINGS

In most sibling studies, a single dyad is the unit of analysis (e.g., Bedford, 1989a; Gold, 1989b; Suggs, 1989). Pragmatic factors, no doubt, contribute to this focus, but justification also comes from evidence that personal well-being might be related to close personal relationships, rather than to support networks as a whole (Levitt, 1991).

Personal relations research is concerned with the development of relationships (Morgan, 1990)—how relationships are initiated, maintained, and terminated. These processes have different meanings in relationships with kin than in those with nonkin, because kinship ties are ascribed; one can neither select a sibling (excepting fictive siblings) nor divorce one. Even the rare adult who breaks off communication with a sibling usually keeps informed about her or him through intermediaries (Allan, 1977). Sibling ties differ from other kin ties such as parent-child relations with respect to active maintenance, however, because norms of obligation are weaker for siblings (Adams, 1967; Lerner, Somers, Reid, Chiriboga, & Tierney, 1991). Having multiple siblings allows for still more selectivity and discretion concerning content and frequency of interaction with any particular sibling (Connidis, 1992). Yet, the ease of sustaining the sibling relationship at some minimal level might be its greatest value. The fact that sibling bonds cannot be severed and that their duration is unusually long (covering most of the life span) seems to provide siblings with a sense of security that proves to be especially important in old age (Cicirelli, 1977).

Separation from Sibling

Despite their persistence, ties to siblings seem to wane temporarily sometime during the first half of adulthood (Bank & Kahn, 1982), especially between brothers (Adams, 1968). Adams (1968) found the relationship to be constrained largely by different values and interests during this period. Although this lull in the relationship was once assumed to mark its termination (Bernard, 1942), such an assumption proved to be shortsighted; after preoccupations with the procreative family subside, sibling involvement generally resumes (e.g., Gold, 1989b; Bedford, 1989a, 1989b). Little is known about the processes underlying the cessation and reactivation of the relationship, but clinical interviews suggest that adults continue to be emotionally involved with their siblings while the overt relationship lies dormant (Bank & Kahn, 1982).

For very close siblings, one salient issue during the period in which interaction attenuates is sibling loss. Based upon attachment theory, separation from the attachment figure is a threat to felt security (Bowlby, 1979). That separation from the sibling should be experienced so poignantly at this time might be due to the fact that siblings do not have a normative period to separate psychologically as do parents and children during adolescence. A rupture in the sibling relationship, therefore, is imposed from without by later life events (Siemon, 1980). Even so, it is not clear that all siblings successfully differentiate from each other at this time. For instance, same-sex twins, even those who are successful adults, typically fail to achieve psychological differentiation (Schave & Ciriello, 1983).

For most close siblings, however, concerns over sibling separation subside after the period of active parenting and career building. Using thematic analyses of adults' stories in response to ambiguous scenes depicting a pair of separating siblings, men and women of the "empty nest" had significantly fewer themes of separation and differentiation between the siblings than did those in the child-rearing phase (Bedford, 1989a). Perhaps separation issues are no longer as important because the relationship has resumed or, perhaps, because older adults have come to accept theirs and their siblings' autonomy.

Benefits of the Sibling Relationship

Positive affect

Positive social experiences seem to have less bearing on well-being than negative social experiences (Rook, 1984), at least in the short term (Vinokur & van Ryn, 1993). Assuming relationship satisfaction is a beneficial experience in its own right (Mancini & Blieszner, 1989), however, feeling good about a sibling is a rewarding experience. Results of studies on the positive social experiences of sibling relationships are consistent. Overall, older adults rate the relationship to be very positive (Cicirelli, 1985; Cumming & Schneider, 1961; Scott, 1983). Gold (1989a), who classified sibling dyads of old people into typologies, found, in a middle-class white sample, that about 85% of the dyads with one or two sisters and about 63% of brother pairs had positive types of relationships (intimate, congenial, or loyal), as did 95% of a comparable sample of blacks (Gold, 1990). Nonetheless, positive ratings have been found to be lower in the 20-to-45 age range (Adams, 1968) and for white males in general (e.g., Gold, 1989a). It appears, then, that adults like their siblings, especially in the second half of adulthood. Whether the sibling's gender is also related to having a more positive relationship is somewhat controversial, as discussed later.

Only a few studies have probed for sources of variation in positive feelings toward siblings. In one study of 65 middle-class midwesterners, aged 29 to 68 years, less emotional closeness existed between brothers compared with sisters, but further analyses revealed that several variables mediated the gender differences. Men and women felt closer to the sibling who was older (not younger) than themselves, who was less healthy (moderately rather than very healthy), who interacted with them more frequently, and whose educational level was less disparate from their own (Bedford, 1990b).

Association

Suggs (1989), too, found that gender was not predictive of positive social outcomes with siblings. She examined determinants of association, meaning the number of different shared activities during the past year. For a sample of 400 elderly, rural, white people living in North Carolina, association was strongly accounted for by the variety of help exchanged within the dyad, by residential propinquity, and by the degree of value consensus. For blacks in the same region, mutual helping and residential propinquity were also the most important predictors of association, but not value similarity. Instead, the black subjects associated with siblings who were discrepant in age (associating more with a younger sibling) and discrepant in education level (associating more with a less-educated sibling). To summarize, whites chose to associate with siblings who resembled themselves (shared life values), whereas blacks chose siblings who differed from themselves demographically (younger and less educated).

In spite of the racial differences found by Suggs, predictors of positive social outcomes were unique for siblings compared with other relationships. Whereas association between parents and children is determined by obligation and sex linkage (Bengtson, 1976, cited by Suggs, 1989), neither of these variables was significant for siblings (Suggs, 1989). The contribution of educational disparity to positive social outcomes with siblings varies by study. Wellman and Wortley (1990) found that the amount of social support provided by network members in total was not related to educational disparity, whereas Bedford (1990b) found that a lack of disparity predicted greater emotional closeness, and Suggs (1989) found that greater disparity was related to association between black siblings.

Attachment

Attachment is also a positive social outcome. Attachment is evidenced in solace-seeking and solace-dispensing behaviors and feelings when one member of the dyad is distressed. Because mere proximity to an attachment figure brings solace, indicators of attachment are seeking proximity when distressed, protesting separation, and rejoicing at reunion after separation. Because older children and adults can invoke an attachment figure symbolically by thinking about him or her, these actual behaviors might not be overtly manifested, but the same feelings about separations and need for proximity when distressed probably occur across the life span (Bowlby, 1988).

Siblings have received little attention as attachment figures, compared with parents. This neglect is probably because parents are assumed to be the primary attachment figures and because attachment figures are those who are perceived to be stronger and wiser than oneself (Bowlby, 1988). This assumption that siblings play a secondary or substitute role to parents has been challenged as ethnocentric (Peterson, 1990) and even erroneous in dominant Western societies (Downing, 1988). In fact, middle-class preschoolers frequently proffer care to their baby sibling in the absence of parents, suggesting that sibling attachment relationships form very early (e.g., Stewart, 1983) and that siblings can function in complementary, as well as in egalitarian, ways toward one another (Peterson, 1990).

Sibling attachment as manifested by the intensity of grief at the death of a sibling in late life is highly variable across dyads (Moss & Moss, 1989). In a recent attempt to account for variability in sibling attachment to an age-near, like-gender, middle- to old-aged sibling, strong predictors were birth order (the younger member of the dyad sought out the older when distressed), early experience in the relationship (being favored by father precluded being an attachment figure), and the subjects' characteristic expectations about self and other in close relationships (securely and preoccupied attachment styles predicted more attachment) (Bedford, 1993a). Whether siblings actually satisfy attachment needs of adults requires evidence that they contribute to personal well-being, which is the next social benefit to be discussed.

Well-being

Friends' contribution to well-being in old age has been easier to document than family members' (e.g., Mancini & Blieszner, 1989). For instance, contact frequency with siblings showed no relation whatsoever to morale in a large, representative sample (Lee & Ihinger-Tallman, 1980). For recent widows, however, O'Bryant (1988) found that contact with sisters, but not brothers, predicted a more positive affect state. But, McGhee (1985) found that for rural aged women, simply having a sister live nearby, but not rate of contact with her, was associated with life satisfaction. Recently, attachment theory was used to explain the connection between having a sibling and well-being. Assuming secure attachment feelings are represented by degree of closeness, Cicirelli (1989) found that the closer men and women over 65 felt to their sisters (based on the average rating for all sisters in a siblingship), the fewer symptoms of depression they had. Finally, a comparison of same-sex sibling pairs revealed that the sibling relationship affected the well-being for sister pairs only: the more women anticipated having negative feelings toward their sister upon reuniting with her after a long separation, the more negative was their affective state in general. Because other negative feelings toward the sister were not related to affect state, this finding is not likely to be explained by a generally negative response tendency (Bedford, 1993b). Common to all these studies is the exclusive contribution *sisters* make to well-being in later life.

Costs of the Sibling Relationship

Negative feelings

The concern of family gerontology with well-being delayed consideration of the dark side of family relationships (Morgan,1990). Another problem is the difficulty obtaining reliable data about feelings that adults are not proud to admit to having (Bedford, 1989a, 1989b). Use of supportive discussion groups (Ross & Milgram, 1982), clinical interviews (Lowenthal, Thurnher, & Chiriboga, 1975), and projective stories (Bedford, 1989a) has uncovered considerable conflict and negative feelings despite the highly positive self-report ratings previously documented (Bedford, 1989b).

Sex differences in sibling conflict are noteworthy. Based on projective techniques, women's stories about sisters had more themes about conflict than did men's stories about brothers (Bedford, 1989a). Further, ratings of interview data showed more conflict between sisters than other sex combinations (Lowenthal et al., 1975). High levels of conflict between sisters have been attributed to the greater intensity of feeling in the relationship (Lowenthal et al., 1975), but they might also be influenced by the "culture's devaluation of female characteristics," which women themselves might incorporate (McGoldrick, 1989, p. 245). Women, however, devalued brothers as well as sisters (more than men did), judging from the egocentric bias of their ratings of siblings' contribution to parent care. Perhaps the greater cost of parent care to sisters than to brothers accounted for this finding (Lerner et al., 1991).

One developmental task of old age is the resolution of sibling rivalry (Goetting, 1986). Lower negative ratings of siblings by older subjects (Cicirelli, 1985) could be interpreted as the successful completion of this task. In a cross-sectional analysis of adults of all ages, Bedford (1989d) found that the intensity of felt conflict actually increased with age in response to some elicitors, but the likelihood of these elicitors occurring decreased precipitously with age. Perhaps old people take precautions to avoid known sources of conflict in order to optimize their interactions (Carstensen, 1992). The "decreases" in sibling conflict could also reflect cohort differences, given that most studies are cross-sectional. Stearns (1988) presumed that cohorts born before 1920 must have experienced less jealousy and rivalry toward siblings than those born between 1920 and 1960. Demographic changes and family practices after 1920 created a fertile environment for intense rivalry between siblings. These changes included more intense maternal affection, less severe discipline, the use of hospitals for delivery of infants, and smaller families.

Caring for Siblings

Because siblings rarely function as primary caregivers for one another, sibling care has almost never been studied. Now that the need for informal caregivers for frail old people is increasing, some scholars have considered the potential of siblings to fill this role. The broader topic of sibling help has been reviewed in detail elsewhere (see Cicirelli, 1992b). In this section, the focus is on the newest studies about the delivery of primary care to old people by siblings.

In Western societies, parents take care of their adult children who are dependent. As aged parents' health declines, the decision by a well sibling to take over that care usually determines whether a developmentally disabled sibling (Seltzer, Begun, Seltzer, & Krauss, 1991) or mentally ill sibling (Horowitz, Tessler, Fisher, & Gamache, 1993) will be institutionalized. In these same societies, spouses typically care for dependent elders, and in their absence an adult child takes over (see Dwyer, this volume). When neither spouse, child, nor daughter-in-law is available, apparently no norms prescribe responsibilities for delivering care to dependent old people.

The incidence of siblings as primary caregivers of siblings is relatively rare. In a sample of primary caregivers of 256 physician-referred elderly dementia patients, only 3% were siblings, constituting just under 20% of those not cared for by spouse or child (Suitor & Pillemer, 1993). In the National Long Term Care Survey, about 8% of those who participated in the 1982 and 1984 waves of data collection said a sibling was the main source of care at some time during the study (Cicirelli, Coward, & Dwyer, 1992). Similarly, 7% of the primary caregivers in the National Hospice Study were siblings (McHorney & Mor, 1988).

Many conditions are likely to mitigate against sibling care to frail elders. These appear to be the failing health of a sibling who is also old, lack of residential propinquity, and the absence of social norms obligating sibling responsibility (which varies by ethnicity), to name a few (Avioli, 1989). In a longitudinal study of siblings who provided long-term care to elders, some of the reasons for ceasing caregiving gave credence to these speculations. For instance, people ceased to care for those siblings whose age was more advanced (by implication, the caregiver was also older and in worse health), and they ceased to care for siblings who moved away (Cicirelli et al., 1992).

Several conditions seem to support the likelihood of siblings to proffer care to a dependent elder. The absence or unavailability of a spouse or child is, surely, primary. Also, although the sibling tie has a strong voluntary component, most old people appear to have very positive feelings about their siblings, as discussed earlier. In addition, siblings have a shared family history to bind them emotionally, and, finally, biological siblings are thought to be motivated to protect their common gene pool (Cicirelli, 1989). Although this latter reason might seem inappropriate in the case of postchildbearing women, those women often contribute to protection of the common gene pool by caring for grandchildren (see Robertson, this volume) and contribute to the welfare of their children. Data from the long-term care survey mentioned before supported the availability hypothesis: caregivers were more likely to be without a spouse (had disrupted marriages or were never married) and had fewer children (Cicirelli et al., 1992).

The psychological risks of sibling care were recently documented in a study controlling for age by comparing sibling and spousal care of old people (Mui & Morrow-Howell, 1993). Both siblings and spouses experienced considerable strain, and spouses more so, but only siblings suffered when the relationship was qualitatively poorer, and siblings suffered more than spouses from lack of respite and from perceived conflict in their personal life. One might expect considerable strain to both spouse and elder sibling caregivers for gender-related reasons. Most caregivers are women (e.g., 85% in Mui and Morrow-Howell's sample of siblings), and women in later life show the desire to relinquish their predominantly nurturing roles in favor of autonomous strivings (see Huyck, this volume). The formerly married women might have already cared for a frail husband, perhaps their parents and parents-in-law, and might relish a chance for independence (Bedford, 1989d; Cohler & Grunebaum, 1981). Despite these commonalities, sibling caregivers reacted more to certain stressors, such as conflict in the relationship, than did spouses. Perhaps the differences lie in the spouse's greater sense of moral obligation, as well as differences in the kinds of social networks available to caregiving spouses and siblings (Mui & Morrow-Howell, 1993).

SPECIAL ISSUES

Many potential sources of variation between sibling relationships are possible, but two sources have particular relevance for later-life families— gender and life events. Gender is an important consideration because women dominate the ranks of the old. Life events and their impact on sibling relationships hold a key to understanding the plasticity of sibling relationships and their emergent qualities during the course of adulthood.

Influences of Gender

The literature contains much disagreement on the influence of gender on sibling relationships. In some studies, sex differences are a function of the "femaleness" of the dyad (the more females included in the dyad, the more intimate, and so on) (Gold, 1989b; Suggs, 1989). In other studies, differences derive from the partners' gender likeness (like-sex dyads are closer than cross-sex dyads) (Gold, 1989a). In still other studies, the importance of gender interacts with developmental period; for instance, if gender becomes less relevant with age (Cicirelli, 1992b), then gender differences might be greater earlier in adulthood than in old age.

In several studies, relationships with sisters were emotionally closer than those with brothers (Adams, 1968; Cicirelli, 1993; Gold, 1989b), but Connidis (1989) found that the gender composition of sibling dyads did not predict whether a sibling was considered to be a friend or a confidant. Femaleness of a sibling dyad (whether composed of none, one, or two women) was an important differentiating characteristic of sibling typologies. Gold (1989a) found that the loyal type of sibling relationship in old age was modal across gender, but sisters were more than twice as likely to be found in the intimate relationship type, more than four times as likely to be in the congenial type, and about one-eighth as likely to be in the apathetic type as were other gender combinations (see Scott, 1990, for comparable findings).

Across ages, same-sex sibling pairs are noted throughout the literature for the intense feelings they have for one another, whether positive or negative (e.g., Bank & Kahn, 1982). For some, the same-sex tie might be "the most stressful, volatile, ambivalent one we will ever know" (Downing, 1988, p. 12). Based on clinical and literary sources, whether same-sex sibling pairs are male or female appears to affect the partners' level of emotional interdependence, which is related to the intensity of their interidentification (Bank & Kahn, 1982). A common theme is that interidentification is problematic for sister pairs, but not for brother pairs (Downing, 1988). This sex difference has been attributed to the socialization of girls to have an identity as the "receptacle for the needs of others," rather than the individual identity encouraged in boys (McGoldrick, 1989, p. 244).

Influences of Life Events

A nondeterministic view of human behavior poses that change is possible at any time in life due to the impact of life events, continued cognitive and personality development, and so forth. This position presupposes that the environment influences behavior (feelings and thoughts included) as well as, or in interaction with, personal characteristics, such as personality traits. If we are to understand whether sibling relationships are different in later years than earlier in life, then the relative contribution of early and contemporary experiences to the relationship should be examined. A few studies have addressed this issue.

Apparently, experiences early in life persist to influence some aspects of the sibling relationships during the second half of adulthood. Early patterns of cooperation are thought to account for sharing responsibilities of parent care (Tonti, 1988), and reactivation of early conflicts is thought to account for conflicts that arise over parent care (Allan, 1977; Bedford, 1989d; Matthews & Rosner, 1988; Suitor & Pillemer, 1993). As mentioned earlier, attachment in middle and old age was strongly predicted by differential paternal affection in childhood, early established attachment styles, and early interaction patterns based on birth order (Bedford, 1993a). These findings are not surprising, given that sibling expectancies are established early in life and considering how difficult it is to change expectancies about family relationships once they are established (Levitt, 1991). Although extreme violations of expectations can change relationships (Levitt, 1991), sibling interaction in adulthood is sufficiently infrequent that few opportunities for change are available (Bedford, 1989d).

Variability in sibling relationships has also been examined with respect to specific life events. Results vary among studies, no doubt due to incomparable methodologies, such as whether the unit of analysis is one dyad or the sibling network. The effect of marriage on sibling relationships is especially controversial. In one study, respondents whose sibling was married (all respondents were married) and respondents who worked longer hours felt less conflict toward the sibling than those whose sibling was not married and who worked less (Bedford, 1990b). These findings suggest that having multiple roles lessens expectations or dilutes the intensity of emotional involvement with siblings. Ross (1981), on the other hand, found that marriage, like most events that are socially determined (move from home, divorce) detracted from the relationship. Connidis's (1992) results supported this finding; she found marriage, "an event which creates a relatively closed subsystem," was more likely to be followed by reduced closeness and contact than any other event (p. 980). Divorce also yielded mixed results. Ross found divorce to have a negative influence on sibling relationships, whereas Connidis's sample reported increased closeness and support following divorce.

One might question whether adults' perceptions of the influences of life events on their sibling relationship are accurate. I explored this question by comparing perceived effects of events on feelings toward a sibling with differences in affect ratings toward this sibling before and after the event. Seventy-five percent of the respondents' perceptions were in agreement with the direction of change. Respondents' subjective appraisal of the effect of life events on their sibling relationship, therefore, seem to be fairly accurate (Bedford, 1990a).

Parent care is the most researched of any event experienced by siblings and has been reviewed recently (Cicirelli, 1992a, 1992b). This review is limited to just one aspect, the effect of parent care on sibling relationships. The data indicate that parent care has immediate consequences for the sibling relationship, both positive and negative, from the perspective of the primary caregiver and the subsidiary siblings, but primarily for women (Brody, 1990; Cicirelli, 1992a; Suitor & Pillemer, 1993).

In terms of the positive impact of parent care on siblings, Brody (1990) found that many rewarding interactions were the consequence of caring for a parent. For instance, both primary caregivers of institutionalized parents and their local siblings (those living nearby) felt reassured that they could depend on a sibling to help their parent. Siblings also felt that their sibling, whether the primary caregiver or her local sibling, understood the nature of their caregiving efforts. These siblings also felt rewarded by the socioemotional support and approval their siblings showed them. Sisters, however, experienced more rewards from such interactions than did brothers.

In another study that also included distant siblings (those who lived far from the primary caregiver), 82% of all respondents said that a sibling had been very dependable when needed (Schoonover, Brody, Hoffman, & Kleban, 1988). Using a network approach, Suitor and Pillemer (1993) did not find that siblings provided the emotional support described by Brody (1990); sibling support was primarily instrumental. Comparing the support rendered to the primary caregiver by a sibling and by other network members, Suitor and Pillemer (1993) found that friends were more emotionally supportive than were sisters or brothers.

Despite the positive social outcomes of parent care for siblings, siblings also contribute to caregiving strain (e.g., Brody, 1990; Matthews & Rosner, 1988; Suitor & Pillemer, 1993). Many sibling interactions that are related to parent care are negative, which compounds the strains inherent to parental caregiving. Not only primary caregivers suffer from parent care, however; their local sisters also suffer considerably, although their local brothers experience little discomfort (Brody, 1990). From the perspective of the primary caregiver, in Suitor and Pillemer's (1993) study, siblings were by far the greatest source of interpersonal stress. Siblings were unusual compared with most network members, however, because they were a source of support as well as conflict, whereas most network members were either consistently supportive or troublesome to the primary caregiver. Of the geographically distant siblings (distant from the primary caregiver), only sisters, not brothers, experienced interpersonal conflict (Brody, 1990; Schoonover et al., 1988). No doubt distant sisters felt this conflict because they were more likely to be the primary caregiver's target of unfairness than were distant brothers. Also, distant sisters reported that problems in the relationship caused them more strain than brothers reported.

Due to a lack of long-term longitudinal data, it is not known whether these positive and negative feelings toward siblings in response to events such as parent care are typical for a particular relationship, whether they are a temporary response to the event, or whether they are the inception of a lasting shift in feelings toward the sibling. Matthews and Rosner (1988) found that conflict among siblings caring for parents was a continuation of the old relationship and, therefore, did not represent a change in the relationship at all. Over half (62%) of Cicirelli's (1992a) respondents also reported no change in close feelings toward their siblings as a result of parent care, but of the 38% who felt a change in the relationship, more than twice as many felt closer (25%) than less close (12%). Whether these changes were lasting remains to be seen, however. Only Ross (1981) actually collected data on the longevity of changes in response to life events. Retrospectively, subjects claimed that the effects of the events they named lasted at least 10 years. Clearly, little is known, then, about the long-term impact of life events on sibling relationships.

WHERE DO WE GO FROM HERE?

Despite the many studies cited here and in other reviews, enormous gaps in knowledge about sibling relationships remain, even at the descriptive level. Because sibling research is rarely funded, most investigators use small samples or tack a few questions onto studies designed for other purposes. The small-sample studies have successfully launched the field with their careful and innovative methods and their intensive investigation of individuals' relationships, but their generalizability is greatly restricted. Although some progress has been made, little is known about the variation in sibling relationships across racial, ethnic, and social-economic status.

Macroanalytic Studies

Large surveys, devoted expressly to sibling issues, are needed. Although much progress can be seen with the availability of new data from national surveys, more probing questions are required. For instance, learning about the appropriateness of sibling caregivers calls for more sophistication than demographic descriptions of the participants and single-item ratings of the quality of the relationship. Research designs must include detailed questions that test deliberate hypotheses, and either use psychometrically sound instruments or include multiple measures that allow for post hoc tests of validity. Further, qualitative data must be gathered on subsamples of survey respondents in order to make meaningful interpretations of findings (see Mangen, this volume) and to allow new theories to emerge.

Microanalytic Studies

In addition to learning more about intersibling variability, more information is needed on intrasibling variability. Age differences and effects of life events on the relationship are merely a few examples of intrasibling variability considered in this chapter. Because of the strains that arise during sibling care and parent care, new research should address how these strains are generated. More information is also needed on whether the same positive relationships are the ones that become conflict-laden when joint tasks are pursued (e.g., Allan, 1977) or whether continuity in the functioning of the relationship can be expected (e.g., Matthew & Rosner, 1988). Finally, theories, methods, coding, and data analytic techniques are needed to help formulate and guide research that will address intrasibling variability.

Theory

Given the dearth of theory in general family research, it is surprising how many theories have guided studies of sibling relationships. Some of these include adaptations of intergenerational solidarity (Gold, 1989a; Suggs, 1989), role theory (role demand overload, role engulfment, and so on) (Mui & Morrow-Howell, 1993), attachment (Cicirelli, 1989; Bedford, 1993b), hierarchical-compensatory and task-specific models (Connidis & Davies, 1990, 1992), and complementarity and substitutability models (Peterson, 1990). Preliminary attempts at model building have also commenced (e.g., Bedford, 1989d). Perhaps the most comprehensive theory that has promise for understanding sibling affect and the well-being potential of the relationship is attachment theory. Its focus on the solace-providing aspects of relationships, however, might prove to be too limiting, because play and companionship also appear to be important aspects of some sibling relationships. The potential of attachment theory for furthering understanding of sibling separation effects has yet to be tapped fully, however. Theoretical guidance for understanding the processes underlying sibling conflict, its resolution, activation, and reactivation is especially needed.

Methods

Methods used in sibling research have not captured the processes of continuity and change within dyads. Researchers in other disciplines are developing promising technologies that could be adapted to sibling research. Given the powerful effect that the symbolic relationship holds for siblings, methods need to transcend actual interactions. Experience sampling (e.g., Larson & Csikszentmihalyi, 1983) and single and double diaries (Auhagen, 1990) could be used to chart relational processes in both active and latent relationships by recording interactions (actual and in thought) and responses to them as soon as possible. Very little is known about actual interactions between siblings. Live observations and video and auditory recordings are possibilities for sibling sets that can be brought together. For geographically dispersed samples, however, conference calls could be recorded, and respondents might be willing to make video recordings of their reunions and interactions themselves, especially if they have access to the equipment and instructions for its use. Perhaps respondents and their siblings would be willing to undertake prescribed tasks during their reunions before the camera.

Coding and analyses

The coding and analyzing of data can also be enriched by adapting methods of other disciplines. To understand interactional processes, both affective and cognitive processes can be coded from the recordings of interactions and the texts of their content. To understand the processes underlying the symbolic relationship, these coding schemes can also be applied to video recordings made during personal interviews while respondents talk about their siblings.

The Social Context of Sibling Relationships

Researchers of social support have made great strides in understanding the social context in which sibling relationships are enacted and the relative position of siblings in the social lives of old people. Relational properties other than social support should be targeted too, however, in order to have a better sense of siblings' place in personal networks. Perhaps the space occupied by siblings in latent networks would reveal something about their influence on their members. Auhagen's (1990) comparisons of time spent thinking about siblings versus friends might be a step in this direction. Also, it might be helpful to investigate the transition of siblings from latent to active network members and how and why these transitions occur or fail to occur when siblings are needed.

Conclusions

These recommendations largely concern understanding the causes of variability within and between sibling relationships. Parents, siblings, adult children of old parents with siblings, therapists, and policymakers could all benefit from the knowledge such studies could generate. Implementation of strategies based on this knowledge should guide decision making by all involved that will be in the best interests of this lifelong relationship and its individual members.

REFERENCES

Adams, B. (1967). Interaction theory and the social network. *Sociometry, 30,* 64–78.
Adams, B. (1968). *Kinship in an urban setting.* Chicago: Markham.
Allan, G. (1977). Sibling solidarity. *Journal of Marriage and the Family, 39,* 177–184.
Auhagen, A. E. (1990, July). *Friendship and sibling dyads in everyday life: A study with the new method of double diary.* Paper presented at the Fifth International Conference on Personal Relationships, Oxford, England.
Avioli, P. S. (1989). The social support functions of siblings in later life: A theoretical model. *American Behavioral Scientist, 33,* 45–57.
Bank, S. P., & Kahn, M. D. (1982). *The sibling bond.* New York: Basic Books.
Bedford, V. H. (1989a). A comparison of thematic apperceptions of sibling affiliation, conflict, and separation at two periods of adulthood. *International Journal of Aging and Human Development, 28,* 53–66.
Bedford, V. H. (1989b). Sibling ambivalence in adulthood. *Journal of Family Issues, 10,* 211–224.
Bedford, V. H. (1989c). Sibling research in historical perspective: The discovery of a forgotten relationship. *American Behavioral Scientist, 33,* 6–18.

Bedford, V. H. (1989d). Understanding the value of siblings in old age; A proposed model. *American Behavioral Scientist, 33*, 33–44.

Bedford, V. H. (1990a, July). *Changing affect toward siblings and the transition to old age.* Paper presented at the Second International Conference on the Future of Adult Life, Leeuwenhorst Conference Center, the Netherlands.

Bedford, V. H. (1990b). Predictors of variation in positive and negative affect toward adult siblings. *Family Perspectives, 24*, 245–262.

Bedford, V. H. (1992, November). *Siblings as attachment figures in adulthood.* In R. Blieszner (Chair), *The family context of health challenges in an aging society.* Symposium conducted at the Annual Scientific Meetings of the Gerontological Society of America, Washington, DC.

Bedford, V. H. (1993a, August). *Attachment, intimacy and other relational links to well-being: Which apply to sibling relationships?* In V. H. Bedford (Chair), *Social support revisited: Costs and benefits of personal relationships.* Symposium conducted at the annual convention of the American Psychological Association, Toronto.

Bedford, V. H. (1993b). *Attachment to a sibling in adulthood: Predisposing conditions.* Manuscript submitted for publication.

Bedford, V. H. (1993c). Geschwisterbeziehungen im Erwachsenenalter [Relationships between adult siblings]. In A. E. Auhagen & M. von Salisch (Eds.), *Zwischenmenschliche Beziehungen* [Interpersonal Relationships] (pp. 119–141). Göttingen, Germany: Hogrefe.

Bernard, J. (1942). *American family behavior.* New York: Harper.

Bowlby, J. (1979). *The making and breaking of affectional bonds.* London: Tavistock.

Bowlby, J. (1988). Developmental psychiatry comes of age. *American Journal of Psychiatry, 145*, 1–10.

Brody, E. M. (1990). *Women-in-the-middle: Their parent care years.* New York: Springer Publishing Co.

Carstensen, L. L. (1992). Social and emotional patterns in adulthood: Support for socioemotional selectivity theory. *Psychology and Aging, 7*, 331–338.

Cicirelli, V. G. (1977). Relationship of siblings to the elderly person's feelings and concerns. *Journal of Gerontology, 131*, 317–322.

Cicirelli, V. G. (1985). Sibling relationships throughout the life cycle. In L. L'Abate (Ed.) *Handbook of family psychology and therapy* (Vol. 1, pp. 177–214). Homewood, IL: Dorsey Press.

Cicirelli, V. G. (1989). Feelings of attachment to siblings and well-being in later life. *Psychology and Aging, 4*, 211–216.

Cicirelli, V. G. (1992a). *Family caregiving: Autonomous and paternalistic decision making.* Newbury Park, CA: Sage.

Cicirelli, V. G. (1992b). Siblings as caregivers in middle and old age. In J. W. Dwyer & R. T. Coward (Eds.), *Gender, families, and elder care* (pp. 84–101). Newbury Park, CA: Sage.

Cicirelli, V. G. (1993). Sibling relationships in adulthood. *Marriage and Family Review, 16*(3/4), 291–310.

Cicirelli, V. G., Coward, R. T., & Dwyer, J. W. (1992). Siblings as caregivers for impaired elders. *Research on Aging, 14*, 331–350.

Cohler, B. J., & Grunebaum, H. U. (1981). *Mothers, grandmothers, and daughters.* New York: Wiley.

Connidis, I. A. (1989). Siblings as friends in later life. *American Behavioral Scientist, 33,* 81–93.

Connidis, I. A. (1992). Life transitions and the adult sibling tie: A qualitative study. *Journal of Marriage and the Family, 54,* 972–982.

Connidis, I. A., & Davies, L. (1990). Confidants and companions in later life: The place of family and friends. *Journal of Gerontology: Social Sciences, 45,* S141–149.

Connidis, I. A., & Davies, L. (1992). Confidants and companions: Choices in later life. *Journal of Gerontology: Social Sciences, 47,* S115–122.

Cumming, E., & Schneider, D. M. (1961). Sibling solidarity: A property of American kinship. *American Anthropologist, 63,* 498–507.

Downing, C. (1988). *Psyche's sisters: Reimagining the meaning of sisterhood.* San Francisco: Harper & Row.

Dykstra, P. A. (1993). The differential availability of relationships and the provision and effectiveness of support to older adults. *Journal of Social and Personal Relationships, 10,* 355–570.

Fehr, B., & Perlman, D. (1985). The family as a social network and support system. In L. L'Abate (Ed.), *The handbook of family psychology and therapy* (Vol. 1, pp. 323–356). Homewood, IL: Dorsey Press.

Goetting, A. (1986). The developmental tasks of siblingship over the life cycle. *Journal of Marriage and the Family, 48,* 703–714.

Gold, D. T. (1989a). Generational solidarity: Conceptual antecedents and consequences. *American Behavioral Scientist, 33,* 19–32.

Gold, D. T. (1989b). Sibling relationships in old age: A typology. *International Journal of Aging and Human Development, 28,* 37–51.

Gold, D. T. (1990). Late-life sibling relationships: Does race affect typological distribution? *Gerontologist, 30,* 741–748.

Horowitz, A. V., Tessler, R. C., Fisher, G. A., & Gamache, G. M. (1993). The role of adult siblings in providing social support to the severely mentally ill. *Journal of Marriage and the Family, 54,* 233–241.

Larson, R., & Csikszentmihalyi, M. (1983). The experience sampling method. In H. Reis (Ed.), *New directions for naturalistic methods in the behavioral sciences* (pp. 41–56). San Francisco: Jossey-Bass.

Lee, G. R., & Ihinger-Tallman, M. (1980). Sibling interaction and morale: The effects of family relations on older people. *Research on Aging, 2,* 367–391.

Lerner, M. J., Somers, D. G., Reid, D., Chiriboga, D., & Tierney, M. (1991). Adult children as caregivers: Egocentric biases in judgments of sibling contributions. *Gerontologist, 31,* 746–755.

Levitt, M. J. (1991). Attachment and close relationships: A life-span perspective. In J. L. Gewirtz & W. M. Kurtines (Eds.), *Intersections with attachment* (pp. 183–206). Hillsdale, NJ: Erlbaum.

Lowenthal, M. F., Thurnher, M., & Chiriboga, D. (1975). *Four stages of life.* San Francisco: Jossey-Bass.

Mancini, J. A., & Blieszner, R. (1989). Aging parents and adult children: Current and prospective social science research themes. *Journal of Marriage and the Family, 51,* 275–290.

Marshall, M. (1983). *Siblingship in Oceania* (Monograph No. 8). New York: University Press of America.

Matthews, S. H., & Rosner, T. T. (1988). Shared filial responsibility: The family as the primary caregiver. *Journal of Marriage and the Family, 50,* 185–195.

McGhee, J. L. (1985). The effects of siblings on the life satisfaction of the rural elderly. *Journal of Marriage and the Family, 49,* 85–95.

McGoldrick, M. (1989). Sisters. In M. McGoldrick, C. M. Anderson, & F. Walsh (Eds.), *Women in families* (pp. 244–266). New York: Norton.

McHorney, C. A., & Mor, V. (1988). Predictors of bereavement depression and its health services consequences. *Medical Care, 26,* 882–893.

Morgan, D. L. (1990). Combining the strengths of social networks, social support, and personal relationships. In S. Duck (Ed.), *Personal relationships and social support* (pp. 190–215). Newbury Park, CA: Sage.

Moss, S. Z., & Moss, M. S. (1989). The impact of the death of an elderly sibling: Some considerations of a normative loss: Antecedents and consequences. *American Behavioral Scientist, 33,* 94–106.

Mui, A. C., & Morrow-Howell, N. (1993). Sources of emotional strain among the oldest caregivers: Differential experiences of siblings and spouses. *Research on Aging, 15,* 50–69.

Myers, D. R., & Dickerson, B. E. (1990). Intragenerational interdependence among older, low-income African American, Mexican American, and Anglo siblings. *Family Perspective, 24,* 217–243.

O'Bryant, S. L. (1988). Sibling support and older widows' well-being. *Journal of Marriage and the Family, 50,* 173–184.

Peterson, J. T. (1990). Sibling exchanges and complementarity in the Philippine Highlands. *Journal of Marriage and the Family, 52,* 441–451.

Rook, K. S. (1984). The negative side of social interaction: Impact on psychological well-being. *Journal of Personality and Social Psychology, 46,* 1097–1108.

Ross, H. G. (1981, August). *Critical incidents and their perceived consequences in adult sibling relationships.* Paper presented at the annual convention of the American Psychological Association, Los Angeles.

Ross, H. G., & Milgram, J. I. (1982). Important variables in adult sibling relationships: A qualitative study. In M. E. Lamb & B. Sutton-Smith (Eds.), *Sibling relationships: Their nature and significance across the lifespan* (pp. 225–249). Hillsdale, NJ: Erlbaum.

Scarr, S., & Grajek, S. (1982). Similarities and differences among siblings. In M. E. Lamb & B. Sutton-Smith (Eds.), *Sibling relationships: Their nature and significance across the lifespan* (pp. 357–382). Hillsdale, NJ: Erlbaum.

Schave, B., & Ciriello, J. (1983). *Identity and intimacy in twins.* New York: Praeger.

Schoonover, C. G., Brody, E. M., Hoffman, C., & Kleban, M. H. (1988). Parent care and geographically distant children. *Research on Aging, 10,* 472–292.

Scott, J. P. (1983). Siblings and other kin. In T. Brubaker (Ed.), *Family relationships in later life* (pp. 47–62). Newbury Park, CA: Sage.

Scott, J. P. (1990). Siblings' interaction in later life. In T. Burbaker (Ed.), *Family relationships in later life* (2nd ed., pp. 86–99). Newbury Park, CA: Sage.

Seltzer, G. B., Begun, A., Seltzer, M. M., & Krauss, M. W. (1991). Adults with mental retardation and their aging mothers: Impact of siblings. *Family Relations, 40,* 310–317.

Siemon, M. (1980). The separation-individuation process in adult twins. *American Journal of Psychotherapy, 34,* 1–14.

Stearns, P. N. (1988). The rise of sibling jealousy in the twentieth century. In C. Z. Stearns & P. N. Stearns (Eds.), *Emotion and social change* (pp. 193–222). New York: Holmes & Meier.

Stewart, R. B. (1983). Sibling attachment relationships: Child-infant interactions in the strange situation. *Developmental Psychology, 19,* 192–199.

Suggs, P. K. (1989). Predictors of association among siblings: A black/white comparison. *American Behavioral Scientist, 33,* 70–80.

Suitor, J. J., & Pillemer, K. (1993). Support and interpersonal stress in the social networks of married daughters caring for parents with dementia. *Journal of Gerontology: Social Sciences, 48,* S1–8.

Suleri, S. (1987). *Meatless days.* Chicago: University of Chicago Press.

Taylor, R. J., Chatters, L. M., & Mays, V. M. (1988). Parents, children, siblings, in-laws, and non-kin as sources of emergency assistance to black Americans. *Family Relations, 37,* 298–304.

Tonti, M. (1988). Relationships among adult siblings who care for their aged parents. In M. D. Kahn & K. G. Lewis (Eds.), *Siblings in therapy: Life span and clinical issues* (pp. 417–434). New York: Norton.

Troll, L. E. (1971). A decade review. *Journal of Marriage and the Family, 33,* 263–290.

Vinokur, A. D., & van Ryn, M. (1993). Social support and undermining in close relationship: Their independent effects on the mental health of unemployed persons. *Journal of Personality and Social Psychology, 65,* 350–359.

Weisner, T. S. (1989). Comparing sibling relationships across cultures. In P. G. Zukow (Ed.), *Sibling interaction across cultures: Theoretical and methodological issues* (pp. 11–25). New York: Springer-Verlag.

Wellman, B. (1990). The place of kinfolk in personal community networks. *Marriage and Family Review, 15,* 195–228.

Wellman, B., & Wortley, S. (1989). Brothers' keepers: Situating kinship relations in broader networks of social support. *Sociological Perspectives, 32,* 273–306.

Wellman, B., & Wortley, S. (1990). Different strokes from different folks: Which community ties provide what social support? *American Journal of Sociology, 96,* 558–588.

11

Aged Parents and Aging Children: Determinants of Relationship Quality

J. Jill Suitor, Karl Pillemer, Shirley Keeton,
and Julie Robison

In any attempt to understand parent-child relations in later life, two fundamental themes emerge. The first of these highlights family solidarity and views adult children and aged parents as primary sources of both emotional and instrumental support for one another. In contrast, the second theme focuses on the potential for conflict with, and abandonment of, the elderly, perhaps reflecting generalized societal fears about the welfare of the aged. At different historical points, one of the themes has tended to be particularly dominant, whereas the other has receded into the background.

Academic gerontology has experienced a shift between these themes, from an early view that the isolated nuclear family alienated its elderly members, to a more recent wave of studies documenting the responsible behavior of children toward elderly relatives (cf. Shanas, 1979). Current perspectives now attempt to integrate both views, recognizing that the aging family is the locus of both conflict and consensus.

In this chapter, we take such an integrative approach, beginning by reviewing historical trends that form the context for understanding variations in the quality of intergenerational relations in contemporary society. We then present a conceptual framework that identifies likely determinants of the quality of parent-child relations in the later years. We address the following questions: What factors contribute to positive relations between the generations in later life? In contrast, what are predictors of poor relationships?

Exploration of these issues is important from the perspective of basic research, as well as policy and practice. It is clear that negative parent-child relationships can lead to distress among both the elderly and their offspring (Pillemer & Suitor, 1991; Umberson, 1992). It is also likely that negative relationships inhibit exchange of support between the generations, such as ongoing care for aged parents (Brody, 1990).

SOCIETAL CONTEXT OF PARENT-ADULT CHILD RELATIONSHIPS

The way in which the themes of conflict and consensus are worked out in late-life families has been affected by striking changes in the age structure of American society. First, average life span has increased dramatically, which means that family members will spend more time than ever before occupying intergenerational family roles. For example, over the past 150 years, the proportion of late-middle-aged and elderly women with one or more surviving parents has increased substantially. In 1800 a 60-year-old woman had about a 3% chance of having a living parent, but by 1980 her chances had increased to 60% (Watkins, Menken, & Bongaarts, 1987).

The lengthened life span can provide opportunities for positive family involvement by elderly persons. However, increased life expectancy also leads to a greater likelihood that families will spend longer periods of time caring for disabled elderly relatives. Coupled with declining fertility, this development indicates that larger numbers of elderly people will be cared for by fewer offspring. Adult children, in turn, will bear the costs of caring for aged parents, with fewer siblings to assist them (Treas & Bengtson, 1988).

Second, women's increased participation in the labor force and their return to college in great numbers are likely to affect intergenerational relations. To be sure, the acquisition of these nonfamilial roles provides new and enriching opportunities for women; however, it is likely to alter the time that has traditionally been devoted to "kinkeeping" between the generations (Moen, Dempster-McClain, & Williams, 1992) and may produce value dissimilarities between the generations (Pillemer & Suitor, 1992; Suitor, 1987).

Third, unprecedented geographic mobility also has affected intergenerational relations, in that it causes children to be widely dispersed. This is important because physical proximity is a major factor in determining the frequency of contact with kin. Numerous studies have found that the frequency of intergenerational contact is greatly affected by geographical distance, with more distant children interacting less often with parents and often reporting less closeness to parents (DeWit & Frankel, 1988). A similar pattern has been found in relationships with grandchildren (Cherlin & Furstenburg, 1986). Research has established that few older people are totally isolated from kin (Pillemer & Suitor, 1992); however, geographical mobility has created a subset of older persons who lack networks of supportive family relationships.

A fourth long-term historical change affecting parent-child relations in later life is the massive decline in intergenerational coresidence. In 1910, the majority of older women in the United States lived with adult children. Over half of married women and over three-quarters of widows with living children resided with at least one child (Elman & Uhlenberg, 1992). This has declined to less than 15% in both categories in contemporary society (Bumpass & Sweet, 1987). Further, in prior eras, many of the elderly had their own minor children living with them, because mothers continued to give birth far later in life than in contemporary society. The extended "empty nest" common today was virtually unknown prior to this century (Laslett, 1991).

Although this trend might be reversed somewhat by current high divorce rates and poor economic conditions, which have led to the return of adult children to the parental home (Suitor & Pillemer, 1987), it has already produced a large number of elderly people (especially widows) living alone. In just the 30 years between 1950 and 1980, the percentage of women aged 65 years and above who headed a household in which there were no kin increased from 18% to 42% (Treas & Bengtson, 1988).

A final trend is worthy of mention: the increasingly voluntary nature of parent-child relations in later life. That is, elderly parents' relationships with grown children are characterized by choice, rather than by an obligation to remain together (Foner, 1986; Hess & Waring, 1978; Suitor & Pillemer, 1987). In the past, control of family resources was a major method of ensuring contact with, and care by, children. In contemporary society, the young are dependent on the labor market for their livelihood, rather than on elderly parents (Myles, 1989). Further, norms of filial responsibility were more clearly articulated in the past. At present, the amount and nature of parent-child contact and the degree of mutual aid between the generations tend to be individually negotiated, with only limited guidance from society.

A FRAMEWORK FOR UNDERSTANDING THE QUALITY OF PARENT-CHILD RELATIONS IN LATER LIFE

In developing a framework of determinants of elderly parent-adult child relationship quality, we follow House (1989) in our view that it is important to examine both social structural and psychological determinants of relationship quality. Such a perspective can help to reduce the overemphasis on problems of family caregiving in discussions of intergenerational relations.

Discussions of parent-child relationships in later life are often framed around parental dependency, role reversal, parents moving in with children because of illness, and related topics. As we have discussed elsewhere (Pillemer & Suitor, 1991), this view has become such a dominant paradigm in the field that it has tended to obscure other important research questions. It does not take into account, nor is it able to explain, relationships in which parents are in good health—a state that characterizes a majority of the aged population. It also fails to recognize that adult children are likely to affect their *parents,* as well as the reverse.

For this reason, we treat increased parental dependency not as the dominant theme in intergenerational relations in later life but as one factor among a number that affect the parent-child relationship. This allows for the construction of a more exhaustive conceptual framework to understand determinants of relationship quality.

These determinants can be organized into three general sets of factors: social structural positions, status transitions, and stressful life events and resulting changes in dependency.

Social Structural Positions and Intergenerational Relations

The past two decades have seen the development of a greater focus on the effects of social structural factors in explaining family relationships. It has been demonstrated that the social structural positions of both parents and children are crucial to an understanding of intergenerational relations. In this section, we treat three social structural positions that play a particularly important role in determining the quality of parent-child relations in later life. These are age, gender, and race.

Age

Theories of adult development and intergenerational relations suggest that the age of the adult child affects the quality of parent-child relations. This literature argues that as adult children become older, less conflict and greater closeness occur in the parent-child relationship. Specifically, these theories maintain that maturational changes are likely to reduce differences between parents and adult children, thus minimizing the bases for conflict between them. For example, Bengtson (1979) suggested that as children mature, their orientations become more similar to those of their parents, whereas Blenkner (1965) proposed that adult children's identification with their parents increases as part of the process of developing "filial maturity." Similarly, Hagestad (1987) posited both that differences between parents and children become muted across time and that there is greater tolerance for differences that remain.

Data collected from both adult children and elderly parents also suggest more harmonious relations when children are older. Cicirelli (1981) reported a negative relationship between adult children's ages and their reports of conflict with their parents. Likewise, in a study of elderly parents' relations with their middle-aged children, Aldous and her colleagues (Aldous, Klaus, & Klein, 1985) found that both fathers and mothers were more likely to report that they used their older, rather than their younger, children as confidants. Further, Hagestad's (1986) interviews with middle-generation mothers indicated that they expected their children's maturation to result in the same increases in understanding they had experienced with their own mothers upon reaching adulthood. Last, Suitor and Pillemer (1987, 1988) found adult children's age to be negatively related to parent-child conflict when adult children returned to, or continued to live in, their elderly parents' homes. Taken together, this literature demonstrates quite consistently that the quality of adult child-parent relations increases with the child's age.

Gender

A review of the literature suggests that the gender of both parent and child affects intergenerational relations. Studies of the effects of gender consistently demonstrate stronger affectional ties between mothers and daughters than any other combination. For example, mothers report more positive affect with adult daughters than sons (Angres, 1975; Rossi & Rossi, 1990), are more likely to rely on daughters than sons as confidants and comforters (Aldous et al., 1985; Lopata, 1979), and are less likely to become angry (Lopata, 1979) or disappointed (Aldous et al., 1985) with daughters. In turn, adult daughters report greater feelings of closeness to mothers than fathers (Adams, 1968; Cicirelli, 1981; Rossi & Rossi, 1990) and are more likely to rely on mothers as confidants (Suitor, 1984).

The literature on other parent-child gender combinations suggests that there is greater closeness and less conflict in both mother-son and father-daughter pairs than in father-son pairs. The preponderance of studies of intergenerational relations has found that adult sons report greater closeness to mothers than to fathers (Adams, 1968; Lowenthal, Thurnher, & Chiriboga, 1975; see Rossi & Rossi, 1990 for an exception), whereas fathers report greater closeness in their relationships with their daughters than with their sons (Aldous et al., 1985; Miller, Bengtson, & Richards, 1987; Rossi & Rossi, 1990).

Race

The literature on ethnic diversity in families in the later years has grown considerably during the past decade. Most of this work has focused on differences between black and white families; however, both Hispanic and Asian families have also received attention.

The literature has revealed some consistent differences in intergenerational relations between black and white families. In particular, elderly blacks are substantially more likely than whites to live in two- and three-generational households (Chatters & Taylor, 1990; Mitchell & Register, 1984; Kivett, 1991) and to be involved in their grandchildren's day-to-day activities (Cherlin & Furstenburg, 1986; Kivett, 1991).

Further, there is reason to hypothesize greater closeness and less intergenerational conflict in black than nonblack families. Willie (1988) argued that older blacks are less insistent that younger family members adhere to their elders' customs than are nonblacks, which might reduce the basis for conflict over intergenerational value discrepancies. The few studies that have investigated this issue have not provided a consistent picture. For example, Johnson and Barer (1990) found that elderly black parents were more likely than white parents to rely on adult children for emotional support; however, Umberson (1992) found no differences in black parents' or adult children's reports of parent-child relationship strain and somewhat greater parental dissatisfaction among black than nonblack parents. Thus, further investigation is necessary to determine whether there are consistent differences in closeness between black and nonblack parents and adult children.

The literature is more consistent in demonstrating that many of the same factors play a role in explaining parent-adult child relations in both black and white families. In particular, both gender and proximity have been found to be similarly important in explaining intergenerational relations in black and white families (cf. Spitze & Miner, 1992, regarding gender; and Spitze & Miner, 1992, and Taylor & Chatters, 1991, regarding proximity).

Parent-adult child relations among Hispanics appear to differ from those of both blacks and whites. For example, parent-adult child contact is more frequent among Hispanics than among whites (Dowd & Bengtson, 1978; Lubben & Becerra, 1987; Mindel, 1980) or blacks (Lubben & Becerra, 1987), and Hispanic elderly are more likely to live with their adult children than are blacks or whites (Lubben & Becerra, 1987; Markides & Mindel, 1987). Further, several studies suggest greater intrafamily support in Hispanic than non-Hispanic families (cf. Markides & Mindel, 1987, for a review). However, because most of these studies did not separate the role of adult children from that of other close family members, it is difficult to determine with certainty whether parent-child relations are closer in Hispanic than in non-Hispanic families.

Although the population of Asian elderly is growing rapidly in the United States, there is relatively little literature on parent-adult child relations among these ethnic groups. The literature that exists suggests inconsistencies in the patterns of parent-child relations among Asian-American families. On one hand, filial piety is still normative (Lum, 1983; Markides & Mindel, 1987), and parent-adult child coresidence is common (Lubben & Becerra, 1987), yet Chinese American parents who do not live with their children have *lower* frequency of contact with them than do black, white, or Hispanic parents (Lubben & Becerra, 1987). Further, value differences that might lead to conflict between parents and children are increasingly common in Asian families (cf. Chen, 1979; Lum, 1983).

STATUS TRANSITIONS AND THE QUALITY AND CONTENT OF PARENT-CHILD RELATIONS

Changes in either parents' or children's social structural positions might have profound effects on intergenerational relations. In this section, we discuss transitions that are experienced by adult children and those experienced by elderly parents. Further, we make an important distinction between two types of transitions: those that are normative—that is, socially acceptable and expected to occur at a given time—and those that are nonnormative.

Adult Children's Transitions

Effects of normative transitions

Numerous studies over the past three decades have found a consistent pattern of increased intergenerational closeness and contact when children experience normative transitions. For example, parents and adult children appear to become closer when children establish separate households (Roberts, Richards, & Bengtson, 1991), marry (Fischer, 1986; Komarovsky, 1962; Suitor & Pillemer, 1988; Young & Willmott, 1957), and become parents (Belsky & Rovine, 1984; Fischer, 1981, 1986; McCannell, 1987; Young & Willmott, 1957).

In part there is a positive change in intergenerational relations when adult children experience these normative transitions, because such transitions confirm that the adult child is conforming to societal norms regarding maturational development. An often neglected point is that normative transitions also improve parent-child relations because these transitions increase the number of social structural positions that adult children share with their parents.

Effects of nonnormative transitions

Considering that normative transitions generally intensify affectional bonds, it is not surprising to find that *nonnormative* transitions often affect adult child-parent relations detrimentally. Evidence for this point comes from recent studies of such transitions on the part of children. Hagestad (1986) found that mothers of adult children tended to have strong developmental expectations for children (see also Greene & Boxer, 1982). They form plans for their children and assume that these will be fulfilled in the long run. They hope that their children will "grow up, establish themselves as functioning adults, and become important supports" (Hagestad, 1986, p. 685). Mothers of children who were not "on schedule" in becoming independent adults experienced strain and a sense of personal failure. To some extent, they felt that they could not carry on with their own lives until their children progressed successfully. Children who have not successfully negotiated leaving the parental home and becoming independent serve as a reminder that parents have not achieved their task of socialization (Aldous, 1978).

Theories of status similarity (cf. Homans, 1950; Lazarsfeld & Merton, 1954; Newcomb, 1961) suggest that nonnormative transitions would be the most likely to have a detrimental effect on parent-child relations when the transition decreases similarity between the children and parents. This argument received support from Suitor's (1987) study of married women who returned to school while raising families. Suitor found that the daughters' return to school created stress in relationships in which the daughters educationally surpassed their elderly mothers, primarily because the transition created value differences between these mothers and daughters.

Other nonnormative transitions may have detrimental effects on parent-child relations, perhaps because they violate the parents' expectations or increase children's demands on elderly parents. Recent studies of adult children's job loss support this argument. For example, Newman (1988) found that relations between middle-class sons and their parents often became strained when the sons lost their jobs. Further, Aquilino and Supple (1991) found that adult children's unemployment was one of the best predictors of conflict with parents when the generations shared a home.

Nonnormative transitions that neither create value dissimilarities nor challenge the parents' values appear to have little or no impact on parent-adult child relations. For example, it appears that adult children's return to their parents' homes creates little distress in the parent-child relationship (Aquilino & Supple, 1991; Suitor & Pillemer, 1988) and has little effect on parents' marital relationships (Suitor & Pillemer, 1987) or psychological well-being (Pillemer & Suitor, 1991). In fact, more than two-thirds of the parents in Aquilino and Supple's (1991) study reported high levels of satisfaction with their children's coresidence. Further, both Aquilino and Supple's (1991) and Suitor and Pillemer's (1987) studies suggest that coresidence is not disruptive in the absence of high levels of parent-child conflict.

The preponderance of the literature suggests that divorce also has little or no deleterious effect on the quality of parent-child relations (Anspach, 1976; Cicirelli, 1986b; Johnson, 1988; Spanier & Thompson, 1987; see Umberson, 1992, for an exception), even when the divorce precipitates a return to the parents' home (Aquilino & Supple, 1991; Newman, 1988). In fact, some findings suggest that there might even be an increase in parent-adult child closeness following the child's divorce (Ahrons & Bowman, 1982; Cicirelli, 1986b), particularly when daughters maintain custody of their children (Sprey & Matthews, 1982). Further, there appears to be an increase in parents' support to children—particularly daughters—during the period immediately following the divorce (Cicirelli, 1986b; Isaacs &

Leon, 1986; Johnson, 1988). This increase in support from the older to the younger generation is generally asymmetric, because this is a time when there is often a decrease in daughters' support to parents (Cicirelli, 1983).

Parents' Transitions

Effects of normative transitions

Both retirement and widowhood have been identified as normative transitions that have potential for affecting relationships between parents and adult children (Remnet, 1987). However, there is no consensus on the type or extent of these effects.

For example, Ragan (1979) suggested that parental retirement might represent a major crisis for adult children because it could signify that parents can lose their productive roles and eventually die. She also argued that children might fear that the resulting decrease in parental income would require them to assume financial responsibility for their parents while they are still supporting their own children.

Others argue that these fears are not necessarily founded. According to McCallum (1986), "[T]he support required from children in coping with retirement is not intensive, and often involves pleasant interaction and can be managed from a distance" (p. 136), and, broadly speaking, the adjustment made by the family network following retirement is likely to include increased participation by the retiree.

Empirical findings on this issue are mixed. Whereas Wan (1982) found that retirement did not affect intergenerational relations, Broese van Groenou and van Tilburg (1993) found an increase in contact with kin following retirement in the Netherlands. The inconsistency in these findings suggests that there might be cultural variation in the effects of retirement; however, further research must be completed to determine whether this is the case.

In contrast to retirement, the widowhood of a parent involves a direct change in the lives of adult children. Widowhood marks a drastic change in the life of the surviving spouse and has been found to be the most stressful of all life events (Holmes & Rahe, 1967). Whereas the entire family generally responds positively by providing support (Anderson, 1984; McCallum, 1986; Wan, 1982), adult children are a particularly important source of emotional support and instrumental assistance to the surviving parent during this time (Chappell, 1983; Lopata, 1979; McCallum, 1986; Pitcher & Larson, 1989; Shanas, 1979). Further, there appears to be a general pattern of stability and continuity in parent-child relationships following widowhood (Anderson, 1984; Dean, Matt, & Wood, 1992; Ferraro, 1984; Umberson, 1992).

Taken together, this line of research suggests that parents' normative transitions have relatively little effect on parent-child relations and that any effects that occur improve, rather than threaten, the quality of the relationship.

Effects of parent's nonnormative transitions

Divorce is among the most common nonnormative transitions in the lives of parents of adult children. Although parental divorce at any point in the life course is likely to have consequences for the parent-child relationship, until recently research in this area focused on divorces among people under the age of 35 and on short-term marriages (Pett, Lang, & Gander, 1992). However, recent increases in divorce among couples in the middle and later years (Uhlenberg, Cooney, & Boyd, 1990) have bolstered interest in parent-adult child relations following the termination of their parents' marriage in the later years.

The preponderance of this work has shown that the detrimental effects of parental divorce on intergenerational relations continue throughout the life course. For example, White (1992) found that both divorced and remarried parents provide less emotional support to their adult children and report lower levels of parent-child solidarity than do parents who have not divorced. Umberson (1992) also found divorce to have detrimental effects on the parent-adult child relationship, with divorced parents reporting less frequent contact and greater strain in their relations with their adult children.

Divorce does not appear to affect the intergenerational relationships of men and women equally; this transition has been found to be particularly detrimental to the relationships between fathers and their children (Bulcroft & Bulcroft, 1991; Cooney & Uhlenberg, 1990; Seltzer & Bianchi, 1988; Smyer & Hofland, 1982).

STRESSFUL LIFE EVENTS AND DEPENDENCY

Early research on infancy, childhood, and adolescence presumed the unidirectional influence of parents on children (Bell, 1979; Steinberg, 1988). In the past decade, however, researchers have moved toward a more bidirectional view of family influence in studying the early stages of the family life cycle. Such a perspective is greatly needed in the study of parent-child relations in later life as well. As noted earlier, the predominance of the view that highlights parental dependency and resulting stress for caregivers has limited our understanding of parent-child relations in later life.

However, recent research indicates that adult children and elderly parents have strong reciprocal effects on one another. In particular, negative events in the lives of *either* children and parents affect their relationship and, in turn, affect psychological well-being. In this section, we first examine the impact of stressful life events and adult children's dependency on the parent-child relationship. We then explore the impact of declining health of parents and resulting dependency on caregiving children.

Effects of Children on Parents

Direct investigations of the effects of adult children on elderly parents are relatively uncommon. In fact, research on the psychological well-being of the elderly had not typically included variables related to parent-child interaction. However, several recent studies have begun to shed light on this issue.

Consistent with more general research on the negative effects of social interaction, problems experienced by adult children and contact with children during these periods can detrimentally affect elderly parents' well-being. For example, Pillemer and Suitor (1991) found that parents whose adult children had mental, physical, or substance abuse or stress-related problems experienced greater depression than did parents whose children did not have these problems. This relationship was unaffected by the parent's gender or whether the parent and child shared a home. Greenberg and Becker (1988), in a small exploratory study of elderly married couples, found similar results.

Further, parents of mentally ill adults experience both substantial psychological distress and reduced marital quality resulting from problems associated with their children's bizarre and threatening behaviors (Cook, 1988; Cook & Cohler, 1986; Cook, Hoffschmidt, Cohler, & Pickett, 1992; Gubman & Tessler, 1987). Violence and abuse by adult children are particularly distressing to elderly parents (Pillemer & Prescott, 1989; Pillemer & Suitor, 1988).

Morale can also suffer if adult children's problems require parents to continue to provide them with care and support. Such continued assistance is associated with increased psychological distress among the elderly (cf. Cohler & Grunebaum, 1981; Hess & Waring, 1987; Mutran & Reitzes, 1984; Rosow, 1967). Thus, to the extent that problems experienced by children lead to their increased dependency, the quality of the relationship tends to decline, and decrements in psychological well-being can result.

Effects of Parents on Children: Family Caregiving

As the elderly population grows, so will the number of family members involved in their care. It is estimated that approximately 2.2 million people currently provide unpaid help to elderly disabled relatives and that these individuals provide 80% of the care received by the frail elderly. Of these individuals, more than one-third are adult children (Stone, Cafferatas & Sangl, 1987).

Declines in parents' health and resulting dependency can lead to distress among adult children. In a recent exhaustive review, Schulz, Visintainer, & Williamson (1990) concluded that caregivers experience increased depression and demoralization, as well as increased psychiatric illness. Although the evidence is less clear, caregivers also appear to be more vulnerable to physical illness.

Although numerous studies have been conducted on the effects of caregiving on adult children's psychological and physical well-being, less research has examined the impact of parental ill health and dependency on the *quality* of the parent-child relationship. Further, the research that does exist does not provide an entirely consistent picture of the effects of caregiving on relationship quality. Several studies indicate that declines in parents' health often result in decreased closeness and attachment between them and their adult children (Baruch & Barnett, 1983; Cicirelli, 1981, 1983; Mindel & Wright, 1982); however, other research suggests that caregiving is more likely to have positive than negative consequences on relationship quality. For example, Walker, Shin, and Bird (1990) found that half of daughters reported positive effects of caregiving on their relationships with their mothers, and only 5% reported negative effects. Almost half of the mothers also reported positive effects of caregiving, whereas only two reported negative effects. Similarly, Schultz and colleagues (Schultz et al., 1990) found that a sizable minority of caregivers reported greater closeness as the result of the increased dependency of their elderly parents.

There are theoretical bases for suggesting that the motivation of adult child caregivers is related to relationship quality. Three major theories of caregiving motivation have been proposed, each of which would be expected to have different effects on relationship quality.

The first involves the norm of reciprocity, which is incorporated into both exchange theory and equity theory (George, 1986; Cicirelli, 1991). According to these theories, adult children care for their parents because (1) they wish to repay their parents for the years their parents spent caring for them or (2) they expect to receive some reward in the future, most commonly, an inheritance.

Second, researchers have also used social obligation theory to frame research on adult child caregiving. In this perspective, adult children are motivated by societal expectations that they will care for their parents with no consideration for reciprocity or for the distress or disruption it might create in their own lives (George, 1986; Jarrett, 1985).

Finally, attachment theory has been employed to explain the motivation of adult child caregivers, primarily by Cicirelli (1986a, 1991). In this view, the attachment relationship formed between parents and infants endures across the life span. Just as the infant seeks to protect his or her attachment figure once the attachment bond has formed, the adult child wants to protect the parent whose life is threatened by sickness or injury (Cicirelli, 1991).

We suggest that adult children who are motivated by attachment, rather than exchange or obligation, would experience better-quality relationships. Although caregiving relationships may begin with a significant amount of reciprocity in various forms, caregiving often extends to the latest stages of disability or illness, in which case caregivers perform their role without any obvious reciprocation from their elderly parents. For these reasons, we expect that caregivers who are primarily motivated by exchange would experience declines in relationship quality as the exchange becomes progressively more inequitable. Similarly, caregiving that results from obligation might result in lower relationship quality, because the duration of caregiving might extend the period of felt obligation.

Although research on the connection between caregiver motivation and the quality of parent-child relations is limited, some recent work provides support for our argument. Walker, Walker, Pratt, Shin, and Jones (1990) found substantially better relationships between daughters and dependent mothers when daughters were motivated by feelings of "affection, closeness, and enjoyment of the relationship" (p. 52) than when they were motivated by obligation.

In addition to its impact on relationship quality, attachment motivation appears to lead to better outcomes in other areas, as well. Brody (1990) reported that less strain was experienced when there was a history of prior love and affection. Further, Williamson and Schulz (1990) found that greater closeness prior to the onset of dementia resulted in less burden during caregiving. Taken together, it appears that the effect of caregiving on the quality of parent-child relations is greatly dependent upon several factors associated with the quality of the relationship prior to caregiving and the reasons adult children began providing care to their parents.

CONCLUSION

Our goal in this chapter has been to review selected literature on elderly parent-adult child relationships, with a special focus on factors that contribute to the quality of those relationships. We believe that such a focus serves as a useful framework to organize research on this topic, especially because questions regarding the amount and patterns of parent-child contact have increasingly been resolved (Mancini & Blieszner, 1989).

In this chapter we have proposed a conceptual framework for understanding parent-child relations that included three factors: social structural positions, status transitions, and life events and resulting dependency. Clearly, this model is not exhaustive. Many additional variables could be included under each of the various factors. For example, a number of variables might modify the effect of caregiving on parent-adult child relationship quality, including gender of both parent and child and coresidence of the generations. Space considerations obviously limit the degree to which such additional variables can be discussed; we hope that future investigations will expand the model.

We believe that one particularly useful approach would be to consider parent-adult child relationship quality as an intervening variable. For example, researchers frequently investigate the effects of status transitions on physical and psychological well-being in the middle and later years without considering the possible mediating effects of intergenerational relationship quality. However, evidence suggests that this factor might serve as a critical mediator between stressors and well-being outcomes. We believe that such an approach would greatly enhance understanding of the role of parent-child relations for both generations.

In conclusion, investigation of the quality of parent-child relationships in later life should be a major priority for researchers. As this discussion has indicated, poor-quality relationships can have deleterious effects on physical and mental health for both parents and adult children. Further, negative relationships can lead to unwillingness to provide care for family members and hence greater dependence on public resources. Thus, from both basic research and applied perspectives, the issue is likely to be a highly worthwhile one for further study.

ACKNOWLEDGMENT

Preparation of this chapter was supported in part by a grant from the National Institute of Mental Health to the first two authors (1 R01 MH42163).

REFERENCES

Adams, B. N. (1968). *Kinship in an urban setting.* Chicago: Markham.

Ahrons, C. R., & Bowman, M. E. (1982). Changes in family relationships following divorce of adult child: Grandmothers' perceptions. *Journal of Divorce, 5,* 49–68.

Aldous, J. (1978). *Family careers: Developmental changes in families.* New York: Wiley.

Aldous, J., Klaus, E., & Klein, D. M. (1985). The understanding heart: Aging parents and their favorite child. *Child Development, 56,* 303–316.

Anderson, T. B. (1984). Widowhood as a life transition: Its impact on kinship ties. *Journal of Marriage and the Family, 46,* 105–114.

Angres, S. (1975). *Intergenerational relations and value congruence between young adults and their mothers.* Unpublished Ph.D. dissertation, University of Chicago.

Anspach, D. F. (1976). Kinship and divorce. *Journal of Marriage and the Family* 38, 323–330.

Aquilino, W. S., & Supple, K. (1991). Parent-child relations and parents' satisfaction with living arrangements when adult children live at home. *Journal of Marriage and the Family, 53,* 13–27.

Baruch, G., & Barnett, R. C. (1983). Adult daughters' relationships with their mothers. *Journal of Marriage and the Family, 45,* 601–606.

Becerra, R. M. (1983). The Mexican-American: Aging in a changing culture. In R. L. McNeely & J. L. Colen (Eds.), *Aging in minority groups* (pp. 108–118). Beverly Hills, CA: Sage.

Bell, R. Q. (1979). Parent, child, and reciprocal influences. *American Psychologist, 34,* 821–826.

Belsky, J., & Rovine, M. (1984). Social network contact, family support, and the transition to parenthood. *Journal of Marriage and the Family, 45,* 567–579.

Bengtson, V. L. (1979). Research perspectives on intergenerational interaction. In P. K. Ragan (Ed.), *Aging parents* (pp. 37–57). Los Angeles: University of Southern California Press.

Bengtson, V. L., Rosenthal C., & Burton, L. (1990). Families and aging: Diversity and heterogeneity. In R. H. Binstock & L. George (Eds.), *Handbook of aging and the social sciences* (3rd ed., pp. 263–287). San Diego: Academic Press.

Blenkner, M. (1965). Social work and family in later life, with some thoughts on filial maturity. In E. Shanas & G. Streib (Eds.), *Social structure and the family: Generational relations* (pp. 46–59). Englewood Cliffs, NJ: Prentice-Hall.

Brody, E. M. (1985). Parent care as a normative family stress. *Gerontologist, 25,* 19–29.

Brody, E. M. (1990). *Women in the middle: Their parent-care years.* New York: Springer Publishing Co.

Broese van Groenou, M. I., & van Tilburg, T. G. (1993, February). *Mapping changes in networks following retirement: A comparison of two identification methods.* Paper presented at the International Sunbelt Social Network Conference, Tampa.

Bulcroft, K. A., & Bulcroft, R. A. (1991). The timing of divorce: Effects on parent-child relationships in later life. *Research on Aging, 13,* 226–243.

Bumpass, L. L., & Sweet, J. A. (1987). *American families and households.* New York: Russell Sage Foundation.

Chappell, N. L. (1983). Informal support networks among the elderly. *Research on Aging, 5,* 77–100.

Chatters, L. M., & Taylor, R. J. (1990). Social integration. In Z. Harel, E. A. McKinney, & M. Williams (Eds.), *Black aged* (pp. 82–99). Newbury Park, CA: Sage.

Chen, P. N. (1979). A study of Chinese-American elderly residing in hotel rooms. *Social Casework, 60,* 89–95.

Cherlin, A. J., & Furstenburg, F. F., Jr. (1986). *The new American grandparent: A place in the family, a life apart.* New York: Basic Books.

Cicirelli, V. G. (1981). *Helping elderly parents: Role of adult children.* Boston: Auburn House.

Cicirelli, V. G. (1983). A comparison of helping behavior to elderly parents of adult children with intact and disrupted marriages. *Gerontologist, 23,* 619–625.

Cicirelli, V. G. (1986a). The helping relationship and family neglect in later life. In

K. A. Pillemer & R. S. Wolf (Eds.), *Elder abuse: Conflict in the family* (pp. 49–66). Dover, MA: Auburn House.

Cicirelli, V. G. (1986b). The relationship of divorced adult children with their elderly parents. *Journal of Divorce, 9,* 39–54.

Cicirelli, V. G. (1991). Attachment theory in old age: Protection of the attached figure. In K. Pillemer & K. McCartney (Eds), *Parent-child relations throughout life* (pp. 25–41). Hillsdale, NJ: Erlbaum.

Cohler, B. J., & Grunebaum, H. U. (1981). *Mothers, grandmothers and daughters: Personality and childcare in three generation families.* New York: Wiley.

Cook, J. (1988). Who "mothers" the chronically mentally ill? *Family Relations, 37,* 42–49.

Cook, J., & Cohler, B. J. (1986). Reciprocal socialization and the care of offspring with cancer and with schizophrenia. In N. Datan, A. Greene, & H. Reese (Eds.), *Life-span development psychology: Intergenerational relations* (pp. 223–243). Hillsdale, NJ: Erlbaum.

Cook, J., Hoffschmidt, S., Cohler, B. J., & Pickett, S. (1992). Marital satisfaction among parents of the severely mentally ill living in the community. *American Journal of Orthopsychiatry, 62,* 552–563.

Cooney, T. M., & Uhlenberg, P. (1990). The role of divorce in men's relations with their adult children after mid-life. *Journal of Marriage and the Family, 52,* 677–688.

Dean, A., Matt, G. E., & Wood, P. (1992). The effects of widowhood on social support from significant others. *Journal of Community Psychology, 20,* 309–325.

Dewit, D. J., & Frankel, B. G. (1988). Geographic distance and intergenerational contact: A critical assessment and review of the literature. *Journal of Aging Studies, 2,* 25–43.

Dowd, J., & Bengtson, V. L. (1978). Aging in minority populations: An examination of the double jeopardy hypothesis. *Journal of Gerontology, 33,* 427–436.

Elman, C., & Uhlenberg, P. (1992, November). *Early twentieth century coresidence of elderly women and their children.* Paper presented at the Annual Scientific Meeting of the Gerontological Society of America, Washington, DC.

Ferraro, K. F. (1984). Widowhood and social participation in later life. *Research on Aging, 6,* 451–468.

Fischer, L. R. (1981). Transitions in the mother-daughter relationship. *Journal of Marriage and the Family, 43,* 613–622.

Fischer, L. R. (1986). *Linked lives: Adult daughters and their mothers.* New York: Harper & Row.

Foner, A. (1986). *Aging and old age: New perspectives.* Englewood Cliffs, NJ: Prentice-Hall.

George, L. K. (1986). Caregiver burden: Conflict between norms of reciprocity and solidarity. In K. Pillemer & R. Wolf (Eds.), *Elder abuse: conflict in the family* (pp. 67–92). Dover, MA: Auburn House.

Greenberg, J. S., & Becker, M. (1988). Aging parents as family resources. *Gerontologist, 28,* 786–791.

Greene, A. L., & Boxer, A. M. (1982). Daughters and sons as young adults: Restructuring the ties that bind. In N. Datan, A. Greene, & H. Reese (Eds.),

Life-span developmental psychology: Intergenerational relations (pp. 125–149). Hillsdale, NJ: Erlbaum.

Gubman, G., & Tessler, R. (1987). The impact of mental illness on families. *Journal of Family Issues, 8,* 226–245.

Hagestad, G. O. (1986). Dimensions of time and the family. *American Behavioral Scientist, 29,* 679–694.

Hagestad, G. O. (1987). Able elderly in the family contact: Changes, chances, and challenges. *Gerontologist, 27,* 417–428.

Hess, B. B., & Waring, J. H. (1978). Changing patterns of aging and family bonds in later life. *Family Coordinator, 27,* 303–314.

Hofferth, S. L. (1984). Kin networks, race, and family structure. *Journal of Marriage and the Family, 46,* 791–806.

Holmes, T. H., & Rahe, R. H. (1967). The social readjustment rating scale. *Journal of Psychosomatic Research, 11,* 213–218.

Homans, G. C. (1950). *Social behavior: Its elementary forms.* New York: Harcourt Brace Jovanovich.

House, J. S. (1989). Social structure and interpersonal relations: A discussion of Alice Rossi's chapter. In K. W. Schaie & C. Schooler (Eds.), *Social structure and aging: Psychological processes* (pp. 237–243). Hillsdale, NJ: Erlbaum.

Isaacs, M. B., & Leon, G. H. (1986). Social networks, divorce, and adjustment: A tale of three generations. *Journal of Divorce, 9,* 1–16.

Jarrett, W. H. (1985). Caregiving within kinship systems: Is affection really necessary? *Gerontologist, 25,* 55–61.

Johnson, C. L. (1988). Postdivorce reorganization of relationships between divorcing children and their parents. *Journal of Marriage and the Family, 50,* 221–231.

Johnson, C. L., & Barer, B. M. (1990). Families and networks among older inner-city blacks. *Gerontologist, 30,* 726–733.

Kivett, V. R. (1991). Centrality of the grandfather role among older rural black and white men. *Journal of Gerontology: Social Sciences, 46,* S250–258.

Komarovsky, M. (1962). *Blue-collar marriage.* New York: Random House.

Laslett, P. (1991). *A fresh map of life.* Cambridge: Harvard University Press.

Lazarsfeld, P. F., & Merton, R. K. (1954). Friendship as a social process: A substantive and methodological analysis. In M. Berger et al. (Eds.), *Freedom and control in modern society* (pp. 18–66). New York: Litton.

Lopata, H. Z. (1979). *Women as widows: Support systems.* New York: Elsevier.

Lowenthal, M. F., Thurnher, M., & Chiriboga, D. (1975). *Four stages of life.* San Francisco: Jossey-Bass.

Lubben, J. E., & Becerra, R. M. (1987). Social support among black, Mexican, and Chinese elderly. In D. E. Gelfand & C. M. Barresi (Eds.), *Ethnic dimensions of aging* (pp. 130–144). New York: Springer Publishing Co.

Lum, D. (1983). Asian-Americans and their aged. In R. L. McNeely & J. L. Colen (Eds.), *Aging in minority groups* (pp. 84–94). Beverly Hills, CA: Sage.

McCallum, J. (1986). Retirement and widowhood transitions. In H. L. Kendig (Ed.), *Ageing and families* (pp. 129–148). Sydney: Allen & Unwin.

Mancini, J. A., & Blieszner, R. (1989). Aging parents and adult children: Research themes in intergenerational relations. *Journal of Marriage and the Family, 51,* 275–290.

Markides, K. S., & Krause, N. (1985). Intergenerational solidarity and psychological well-being among older Mexican Americans: A three-generation study. *Journal of Gerontology, 40,* 506–511.

Markides, K. S., & Mindel, C. H. (1987). *Aging and ethnicity.* Beverly Hills, CA: Sage.

McCannell, K. (1987). Social networks and the transition to motherhood. In R. Milardo (Ed.), *Families and social networks* (pp. 83–106). Beverly Hills, CA: Sage.

Miller, R. B., Bengtson, V. L., & Richards, L. (1987, August). *Patterns and predictors of parent-child relationships in aging families.* Paper presented at the Annual Meeting of the American Sociological Association, Chicago.

Mindel, C. (1980). Extended families among urban Mexican Americans, anglos, and blacks. *Hispanic Journal of Behavioral Sciences, 2,* 21–34.

Mindel, C. H., & Wright, R., Jr. (1982). Satisfaction in multigenerational households. *Journal of Gerontology, 37,* 483–489.

Mitchell, J. S., & Register, J. C. (1984). An exploration of family interaction with the elderly by race, socioeconomic status and residence. *Gerontologist, 24,* 48–54.

Moen, P., Dempster-McClain, D., & Williams, R. M., Jr. (1992). Successful aging: A life-course perspective on women's multiple roles and health. *American Journal of Sociology, 97,* 1612–1638.

Mutran, E., & Reitzes, D. C. (1984). Intergenerational support activities and well-being among the elderly: A convergence of exchange and symbolic interaction perspectives. *American Sociological Review, 49,* 117–130.

Myles, John. (1989). *Old age in the welfare state.* Lawrence: University Press of Kansas.

Newcomb, T. M. (1961). *The acquaintance process.* New York: Holt, Rinehart, & Winston.

Newman, K. S. (1988). *Falling from grace: The experience of downward mobility in the American middle class.* New York: Free Press.

Pett, M. A., Lang, N., & Gander, A. (1992). Late-life divorce: Its impact on family rituals. *Journal of Family Issues, 14,* 526–552.

Pillemer, K., & Prescott, D. (1989). Psychological effects of elder abuse: A research note. *Journal of Elder Abuse and Neglect, 1,* 65–73.

Pillemer, K., & Suitor, J. J. (1988). Elder abuse. In V. Van Hasselt, H. Bellack, R. Morrison, & M. Hersen (Eds.), *Handbook of Family Violence* (pp. 247–270). New York: Plenum Press.

Pillemer, K., & Suitor, J. J. (1991). "Will I ever escape my child's problems?" Effects of adult children's problems on elderly parents. *Journal of Marriage and the Family, 53,* 585–594.

Pillemer, K., & Suitor, J. J. (1992). Intergenerational relations. In E. F. Borgatta & M. F. Borgatta (Eds.), *Encyclopedia of sociology* (pp. 949–955). New York: Macmillan.

Pitcher, B. L., & Larson, D. C. (1989). Elderly widowhood. In S. J. Bahr & E. T. Peterson (Eds.), *Aging and the family* (pp. 59–81). Lexington, MA: Lexington Books.

Ragan, P. K. (1979). *Aging parents.* Los Angeles: University of Southern California Press.

Remnet, V. L. (1987). How adult children respond to role transitions in the lives of their aging parents. *Educational Gerontology, 13*, 341–355.

Roberts, R.E.L., Richards, L. N., & Bengtson, V. L. (1991). Intergenerational solidarity in families: Untangling the ties that bind. *Marriage and Family Review 16*, 11–46.

Rosow, I. (1967). *Social integration and the aged.* New York: Free Press.

Rossi, A. S., & Rossi, P. H. (1990). *Of human bonding: Parent-child relations across the life course.* New York: Aldine de Gruyter.

Schulz, R., Visintainer, P., & Williamson, G. M. (1990). Psychiatric and physical morbidity effects of caregiving. *Journal of Gerontology: Psychological Sciences, 45*, P181–191.

Seltzer, J. A., & Bianchi, S. M. (1988). Children's contact with absent parents. *Journal of Marriage and the Family, 50*, 663–77.

Shanas, E. (1979). The family as a social support system in old age. *Gerontologist, 19*, 169–174.

Smyer, M. A., & Hofland, B. F. (1982). Divorce and family support in later life. *Journal of Family Issues, 3*, 61–77.

Spanier, G. B., & Thompson, L. (1987). *Parting: The aftermath of separation and divorce.* Beverly Hills, CA: Sage.

Spitze, G., & Miner, S. (1992). Gender differences in adult child contact among black elderly parents. *Gerontologist, 32*, 213–218.

Sprey, J. S., & Matthews, S. H. (1982). Contemporary grandparenthood: A systematic transition. *Annuals of the American Academy of Political and Social Sciences, 464*, 91–103.

Stack, C. B. (1986). Sex roles and survival strategies in an urban black community. In R. Staples (Ed.), *The black family.* Belmont, CA: Wadsworth.

Steinberg, L. (1988). Reciprocal relations between parent-child and pubertal maturation. *Developmental Psychology, 24*, 122–128.

Stone, R., Cafferata, G. L., & Sangl, J. (1987). Caregivers of the frail elderly: A national profile. *Gerontologist 26*, 616–626.

Suitor, J. J. (1984, September). *Family members' support for married mothers' return to school.* Paper presented at the Annual Meeting of the New York State Council on Family Relations, Ithaca.

Suitor, J. J. (1987). Mother daughter relations when married daughters return to school: Effects of status similarity. *Journal of Marriage and the Family, 49*, 435–444.

Suitor, J. J., & Pillemer, K. (1987). The presence of adult children: A source of stress for elderly couples' marriages? *Journal of Marriage and the Family, 49*, 717–725.

Suitor, J. J., & Pillemer, K. (1988). Explaining conflict when adult children and their elderly parents live together. *Journal of Marriage and the Family, 50*, 1037–1047.

Tate, N. (1983). The black aging experience. In R. L. McNeely & J. L. Colen (Eds.), *Aging in minority groups* (pp. 95–107). Beverly Hills, CA: Sage.

Taylor, R. J. (1986). Receipt of support from family among black Americans: Demographic and familial differences. *Journal of Marriage and the Family, 48*, 67–77.

Taylor, R. J., & Chatters, L. M. (1991). Extended family networks of older black adults. *Journal of Gerontology: Social Sciences, 46,* S210–217.

Treas, J., & Bengtson, V. L. (1988). The family in later years. In M. B. Sussman & S. K. Steinmetz (Eds.), *Handbook of marriage and the family* (pp. 625–650). New York: Plenum Press.

Uhlenberg, P., Cooney, T. M., & Boyd, R. (1990). Divorce for women after midlife. *Journal of Gerontology: Social Sciences, 45,* S3–S11.

Umberson, D. (1992). Relationships between adult children and their parents: Psychological consequences for both generations. *Journal of Marriage and the Family, 54,* 664–674.

Walker, A. J., Pratt, C. C., Shin, H., & Jones, L. J. (1990). Motives for parental caregiving and relationship quality. *Family Relations, 39,* 51–56.

Walker, A. J., Shin, H., & Bird, D. N. (1990). Perceptions of relationship change and caregiver satisfaction. *Family Relations, 39,* 147–152.

Wan, T.T.H. (1982). *Stressful life events, social-support network and gerontological health.* Lexington, MA: D. C. Heath.

Watkins, S. C., Menken, J. A., & Bongaarts, J. (1987). Demographic foundations of family change. *American Sociological Review, 52,* 346–358.

White, L. (1992). The effect of parental divorce and remarriage on parental support for adult children. *Journal of Family Issues, 13,* 234–250.

Williamson, G. M., & Schulz, R. (1990). Relationship orientation, quality of prior relationship, and distress among caregivers of Alzheimer's patients. *Psychology and Aging, 5,* 502–509.

Willie, C. V. (1988). *Black and white families: A study of complementarity.* Dix Hills, NY: General Hall.

Young, M., & Willmott, P. (1957). *Family and kinship in East London.* Baltimore: Penguin.

12

Grandparenting in an Era of Rapid Change

Joan F. Robertson

At a time when the question of what defines a family has taken on a particular public urgency because so many economic and social benefits are tied to family status, family policy researchers agree on two characteristics unique to the concept of family—birth and generational ties (Zimmerman, 1992). This chapter addresses generational ties, particularly, grandparenthood. It begins with a discussion of current realities regarding grandparenting, family, and community life as social and economic changes in American society have affected family members, especially grandparents and grandchildren. The next section characterizes the state of the art with respect to knowledge on grandparenting per se, a review that is necessary because the often-cited reference (Bengtson & Robertson, 1985) is out of print. A third section presents some salient theoretical and methodological issues in the grandparent-grandchild research. This discussion is not intended to be exhaustive but rather to pull together information that could encourage creative new approaches for examining grandparent phenomena. It is important to look to research experiences of the past as we craft creative designs for future work. The final section of this chapter deals with research needs for the future. The hope is that this discussion will inspire others to examine the dynamic subtleties and nuances of intergenerational research. The need for rigorous longitudinal research, using multiple design strategies and samples spanning three, four, or five generations of cohorts, remains unfulfilled.

CURRENT REALITIES ON GRANDPARENTING, FAMILY, AND COMMUNITY LIFE

A resurgence of interest has surfaced over the past 15 years in the status, functions, and roles of grandparents in family and community life. Two interrelated realities support this. First, the American family has been transformed by dramatic social, economic, and demographic changes. Family problems related to substance abuse, crime, child abuse and neglect, out-of-wedlock childbearing among teenagers, the divorce rate, the number of single-parent families, and poverty have been increasing. These changes have profoundly affected family roles and relationships and seriously affected children (National Commission on Children, 1991). It is perhaps no coincidence that 3.2 million children are living with grandparents (U.S. Bureau of the Census, 1991)—an increase of more than 40% in approximately the past decade—or that 2 million of these children live in households with grandparents but no parent. One can argue that the magnitude of the problem is also reflected in the number of out-of-home placements of children. For example, by 1992 the Child Welfare League of America reported that over 430,000 children were separated from their parents and had been placed in foster care, an increase of approximately 56% within the last decade. This was the period when kinship care (i.e., protective placement of children with family members) emerged as a form of foster care. Grandparents are the relatives most frequently used in these out-of-home placements (Child Welfare League of America, 1992).

A second reality has been the rapid momentum of "grandparent rights," a movement that has received steady attention in the media and the courts. Recently, for example, a newsmagazine reported that "millions of grandparents have stepped into the breach to rescue children from faltering families, drugs, abuse and violent crime" (Creighton, 1991, p. 80). A poignant theme in the article was that the elaborate system of child protection and support agencies was hindering, rather than helping, beleaguered grandparents' taking full responsibility for their grandchildren without legal or custodial protection. Newspapers frequently carry stories of grandparents whose cases for visitation rights with grandchildren are being heard before the higher courts. (Segal, 1992a, 1992b). The current public policy definition of a family can be interpreted to the detriment of the rights of relatives, and grandparents are challenging this situation by suing for visitation and legal rights to grandchildren (Zimmerman, 1992). As a result of such grandparents' actions, legal statutes are being revisited (McCrimmon & Howell, 1989). Also, grandparents from across the country testified at a congressional forum in Washington, D.C., in their efforts to preserve family rights with respect to grandchildren (Dunn & Robertson, 1991). Wacker (this volume) provides a detailed discussion of grandparenting and legal issues.

The state of knowledge about generational interdependence is a vital issue in light of these realities. But it is also important to bear in mind that the roles, functions, and attendant woes of grandparents in family and community life are not without a prior history. In fact, generational interdependence has always been operational in American society. Grandparenthood is one of the oldest social roles in the human experience (Bengtson, 1985). Generational interdependence must be viewed from a historical perspective as a family's generational structure changes over time. Given recent dramatic changes in American society, it is an appropriate time to address three interrelated questions. Have the mutual obligations and responsibilities felt by younger and older generations shifted over time? Have kinship connections and exchanges altered with changes in generational structures? Is it still the case that Americans and public policy sunder the three- and four-generation family and split grandparents from grandchildren (Guttmann, 1985)? Such questions are being discussed by scholars of generational phenomena, who assume the stance that current political conflicts over generational equity are presaged and shaped by changes in the demographic structure of society with concomitant social, economic, and political changes (Bengtson & Achenbaum, 1993).

THE STATE OF THE ART IN KNOWLEDGE
ABOUT GRANDPARENTING

Grandparenthood continues to be a topic that interests the general public and researchers. Although very few grandparents were alive at the turn of the century, this is no longer the case. With increases in life expectancy, 75% of older adults in the late 1970s were experiencing grandparenthood, and 50%, great-grandparenthood (Shanas, 1980). A more recent study (Hagestad, 1988) reported similar figures for the eastern United States. Several decades of research have been devoted to the study of grandparenthood, providing a foundation for future studies (e.g., Bengtson & Robertson, 1985; Bengtson, 1989; Hagestad & Burton, 1986; Hagestad, 1988); approximately 25 new journal articles have been published since 1985. These efforts have resulted in a relatively modest increment in the production of new information, a point discussed later.

Information about grandparenthood comes from three sources. One source is informal norms and myths about grandparenting perpetuated through popular literature and the mass media (Creighton, 1991; Hagestad & Cogley, cited in Hagestad, 1985). A second source consists of two types of broader family life studies. Some family life research focuses on the exchange of reciprocal helping resources between older family members and their adult children (Eggebeen & Hogan, 1990; Litwak & Kulis, 1987; Mindel, 1980; Mutran, 1985). These provide useful information but render only an indirect assessment of the significance of grandparenting in family life. Other types of broader family studies address the status of grandparents by examining the relationship of aging parents and their adult children. If the status of grandparent is central to the older person, investigators presume that it influences the quantity and quality of intergenerational contacts (Aldous, 1987; Brubaker, 1990). A third major source of information consists of studies that focus specifically on the subject of grandparenthood. This research highlights socialization for the grandparenting role and the meaning of grandparenthood for grandparents and their family members.

Informal Norms and Myths

Creighton (1991) and Hagestad and Cogley (cited in Hagestad, 1985) provided the best examples of the perpetuation of informal norms and myths about grandparenthood in popular literature. Creighton blended poignant and readable prose with statistics and photographs to portray grandparents as "silent saviors" who rescue grandchildren from "faltering families" and inadequate or ineffective child protection and support services. Hagestad presented data from a study of images of grandmothers in *Good Housekeeping* magazine from the 1880s to the 1970s. Images of grandmothers shifted over the years from the "pedestal to the peripatetic." The kindly, aged, or passive grandmother who rocks and knits with quiet resignation has been gradually replaced by an active, midlife juggler who arranges matrices of roles and schedules (Bengtson, 1985, p. 13).

Studies of Family Life: Exchanges and Status of Grandparents

The importance of grandparenting in family life is often assessed indirectly in broader family studies concerned mainly with intergenerational exchanges or the status of aging parents and their relationships with their adult children. Investigations presume frequent contact and helping to signify that grandparents are valued members of the family and that, conversely, a paucity of such interactions suggests a lesser importance of grandparenthood in family life. Review of two studies illustrates this perspective.

In a recent test of theoretical formulations based on evolutionary theory, Eggebeen and Hogan (1990) investigated intergenerational giving. They measured giving by the number of exchanges between older parents and their adult children (e.g., child care, monetary and material resources, household assistance, companionship, and advice). Data were drawn from the 1987–1988 National Survey of Families and Households. The survey included interviews with a representative sample of 13,017 subjects aged 19 and older (Sweet, Bumpass, & Call, 1988). Three findings from the Eggebeen and Hogan (1990) study have implications for those who assume that exchanges per se indicate the importance of grandparents in family life. These are that (1) generational exchanges are not widely evident in American society; (2) when they do take place, exchanges between the generations differ by age, gender, family structure, ethnicity, and social structure; and (3) although frequent, contacts between young adult parents of varying ethnic backgrounds with nonresident older parents are not characterized by a high level of regular exchange. These findings appear to contradict much of the earlier research. The authors further reported that poor people were less frequently involved in exchanges than persons with higher income; Mexican Americans and blacks were less involved than whites in all forms of exchanges. Eggebeen and Hogan (1990) stated that "even among single black mothers with young children, the focus of so much earlier, small-scale research, the advantages in kin support claimed for blacks does not occur" (p. 230). On the basis of the data from this study, one could assume that grandparents feel no obligation to assist younger generations and that grandparenting is not especially important to family life.

Caution is in order, however. This survey has advantages and disadvantages for speculative inferences about grandparenting phenomena. It provides a representative national sample permitting assessment of variation in intergenerational exchanges by gender, age, socioeconomic situation, family structure, the availability and proximity of kin, or life situations. As is typical for surveys, however, the design strategy yields a breadth of information at the expense of depth of information. It does not speak to the quality of the exchanges or the meaning of the exchanges for those involved. Researchers of intergenerational phenomena have challenged the usefulness of quantity and frequency measures in this regard (Rosow, 1967; Robertson, 1977).

Aldous (1987) used a sample of middle-class elderly and near-elderly people to assess whether the status of grandparenthood was central in their life. She hypothesized a direct relationship between the importance of grandparent status to older parents and their level of involvement with adult children and grandchildren. Aldous found that older nonresident parents, particularly females, had frequent contact with their adult children but that these parents selectively initiated the helping contacts. Grandparents provided episodic support that was concentrated in times of need (e.g., child care in situations such as illness in the adult child's family).

It is important to note that both of these studies used quantity and frequency of helping behaviors as measures of exchange or involvement. Measures such as the frequency of contacts, the number of exchanges, and the availability or proximity of kin do not reflect the motivation behind helping exchanges and are not good indicators of the extent or quality of relationships. Neither do they address the real or symbolic meaning individuals might attribute to the exchanges they provide as members of a generational cohort within an extended family system. Years ago, Robertson (1977), using data from random samples of grandmothers and their spouses (Wood & Robertson, 1976), reported that although grandparents engaged in 14 unique types of behavior exchanges with families and grandchildren, they engaged in only 3 with a high degree of frequency. These frequent behaviors were initiated by the parent or the grandchild, more often by the parent. The type of helping exchange and who initiated the exchange were more important variables than frequency of exchange. The most frequent exchange was child care. Most grandparents wanted to be involved in family life, especially with grandchildren. They chose not to be involved out of fear that their initiation of exchanges would be seen by the parent generation as meddlesome, intrusive, or inappropriate (Robertson, 1977). Researchers studying intergenerational helping patterns need to probe more deeply than is possible with quantity and frequency measures. It is necessary to move beyond survey indicators by using a blend of quantitative and qualitative strategies to obtain richer in-depth data that capture the subtleties of family life (see Mangen, this volume). If grandparents go to extremes to avoid meddling in family life, one would expect to find less evidence of contact and helping exchanges except under specific circumstances such as special occasions or at the request of the middle generation.

Studies of Grandparenthood

Other scholars have spoken tacitly or directly to grandparenting in reviewing research on late-life families, relationships between adult children and older parents, and other intergenerational relationships (Bengtson, 1989; Brubaker, 1990; Mancini & Blieszner, 1989). The portrayal of grandparenthood is complex. One finds in this literature a multitude of metaphors and other identifiers for the real and symbolic functions or roles that grandparents have assumed in family and community life. Historically, enactment of the role of grandparent has yielded a number of benefits for younger people and a sense of purpose for older adults—vital functions at times when the social fabric is weakened by pressing social problems. Researchers have seen grandparents as full-time caregivers of disabled and dependent children of parents with drug or other serious problems (Burton, 1992; Child Welfare League of America, 1992; Minkler, Rose, & Price, 1992; Robertson, in press; Seligman, 1991); silent saviors of children from faltering families and inadequate protective service systems (Creighton, 1991); child-care providers for infants and toddlers of employed parents (Presser, 1989); the second line of defense serving as a safety net for children whose parents are unable or unwilling to provide care (Kornhaber, 1985); stabilizers for grandchildren and parents at times of divorce and remarriage (Barranti, 1985); companions for young people (Cherlin & Furstenberg, 1986); disciplinarians of children when the mother is an unmarried adolescent or when she enters the workforce following divorce (Cherlin & Furstenberg, 1986); family watchdogs or national guard of the family (Hagestad, 1985; Troll, 1985); models of the generative chain to which the family belongs (McCready, 1985); wardens and conveyers of culture (Barranti, 1985; Guttmann, 1985); stress buffers, arbitrators, and conveyers of family legacy (Bengtson, 1985; Hagestad, 1985); and kinkeepers and guardians (Frazier, 1939).

Approximately 25 citations have been added to the grandparent literature since 1985; nevertheless, the state of the art remains tentative, incomplete, and contradictory (Robertson, Tice, & Loeb, 1985). Aside from those on legal issues, three types of studies dominate the literature. What follows is an update of the 1985 review by Robertson, Tice, and Loeb under the topical headings of grandparenting and socialization; grandparenting and reciprocity; and grandparenting, personhood, and the life course.

Grandparenting and socialization

Grandparents have socialized younger generations for many years. The earliest information about grandparenting and family dynamics came from anthropological (Apple, 1956; Nadel, 1951; Radcliffe-Brown, 1952) and sociological studies (Albrecht, 1954; Lajewski, 1959; Young, 1954). These were followed by the often-cited Neugarten and Weinstein (1964) study, "The Changing American Grandparent." Grandparenting emerged as a fruitful area of inquiry in the late 1960s and flourished thereafter. The first group of grandparent researchers were mentored either by Neugarten or by her protégés.

With few exceptions (Kornhaber, 1985; Wechsler, 1985), the research of the 1970s was grounded in life course, generational, and socialization theoretical perspectives. Most of the researchers assumed that older generations function as the bearers and conveyers of culture and history; that role transitions occur over the life course; that transitions or timing of roles is shaped not by persons, but by age norms and the individual's phase of the life course in a given historical period; and that older persons transmit knowledge, skills, and experience to the young to ensure the perpetuation and maintenance of social equilibrium. Older generations, deliberately or incidentally, serve as reference groups and models for society, families, and individuals. Hence, grandparents function as microcosms of the family and the broader community. They perpetuate and transmit real and symbolic functions and role behaviors that reflect both ascribed and achieved statuses. Members of younger generations receive and incorporate socialization experiences from grandparents into their repertoire; hence, the young help in socializing older adults into their roles as grandparents.

Researchers working from these perspectives have reported a number of important, conceptually distinct, but interrelated dimensions within grandparenting and family life. These concepts, which are rooted in the work of Bengtson and Hagestad, are diversity and symbolism (Bengtson, 1985; Hagestad, 1985); timing, continuity, and connectedness (Burton & Bengtson, 1985; Hagestad, 1985; Hagstad & Burton, 1986); and reciprocity or generational interdependence (Bengtson, 1985; Burton & Bengtson, 1985; Hagestad, 1985). Bengtson (1985), integrating the varied intellectual agendas of scholars whose work is described in Bengtson and Robertson (1985), characterized the diverse ways in which older adults assume and enact the role of grandparenthood. For example, he compared and contrasted grandparents by historical period, by gender, and by ethnicity and culture. In addition, he discussed the salience of symbolic meanings that different individuals and cohort generation members attach to the role, meanings that reflect the importance of the role for them. Hagestad (1985) also discussed diversity and continuity using data from her study of three generations. She reported that older adults bring to the role of grandparent a unique set of historical and experiential events that shape the meaning and essence of the life course for them (i.e., they have developed a life script that they often pass on to the young). Grandparents provide a lineage link that puts younger generations in touch with their family history. Hence, grandparents provide family connectedness or continuity. This perspective is supported by McCready (1985). He studied grandparenthood using national samples of grandparents from different white ethnic groups. He reported that grandparents provide real and symbolic models that put grandchildren in touch with the generative chain to which the family belongs.

Finally, some researchers have reported that transitions to grandparenthood are different from other role transitions, as grandparents have no control over the timing of the event (Troll, 1985). This has prompted others to study the importance of normative versus nonnormative entry into the grandparent role for black women (Burton & Bengtson, 1985). Black women who became grandmothers at a young age, mostly those in the mid- to upper 30-year-old range, were not happy with being a grandparent so early in life.

Grandparenting and reciprocity

In addition to role modeling and the transmission of knowledge, values, and skills, historical evidence shows that since the era of old New England, grandparents have helped adult children and grandchildren in times of need (Bengtson & Robertson, 1985; Demos, 1978). They have provided child care when parents worked outside the home, given support to adult children and grandchildren when family structure changed as a result of divorce or remarriage, and undertaken primary caregiving for grandchildren when parents were unable or unwilling to do so (Bengtson & Robertson, 1985).

Presser (1989) studied grandparents' provision of child care using data from a national representative sample of working mothers aged 19 to 26 years from the 1984 Youth Cohort of the National Longitudinal Survey of Labor Market Experience. Caring for children is a strong indicator of the extent to which grandmothers help their adult children. Presser reported that 59% of the mothers in the study were employed full-time and relied solely on grandmothers for child care for infants and toddlers. One-third of grandmothers providing child care were also employed full-time outside the home. Grandmothers juggled employment schedules around the hours they cared for children. Nonemployed grandmothers who provided care had particularly limited financial means. They received cash payments from their adult children for the child care. Both the employed and nonemployed grandmothers who provided child care for grandchildren needed money. Acknowledging the limits of the study, Presser concluded that, in general, grandmothers need income. This finding provides an additional insight that was not evident in previous research. Many grandmothers who provide child care also work full-time. Grandmothers' assistance with care to their grandchildren increases their workload. The increasing prevalence of full-time employment of grandmothers might preclude the availability of grandmothers to help with child care of young children in the future (Presser, 1989). (Unfortunately, the study did not address whether grandfathers assisted in these child-care functions.) This could pose a problem for families with young children and a challenge for policymakers and those concerned about the welfare of young children. For example, it has been projected that 14.6 million preschool children will have parents in the workforce by 1995—73% more than in 1980 and 35% more than in 1985 (Hofferth & Phillips, 1987).

The prevalence of divorce and remarriage might also affect grandparenting and reciprocity. Johnson (1988) examined functions that grandparents assumed during and following divorce to ascertain whether family reorganization affected the status of grandparents and whether grandparents were a source of comfort to grandchildren. She used anthropological strategies with two generations in 50 divorcing middle-class families, selected from public divorce records in the San Francisco Bay area, and followed subjects for 40 months. Half her subjects were paternal grandmothers, and half were maternal grandmothers. Most of the grandmothers provided major moral support for adult children and for grandchildren, tempering the strain in their children's families. The amount of assistance declined over time, mostly for the paternal grandmothers. Grandparents drew clear boundaries between parenting and grandparenting. They preferred voluntary short-term functions to long-term arrangements in order to avoid parenting functions; they enjoyed freedom from parenting and made great effort to protect that freedom. Johnson and Barer (1987) also undertook a study of kinship reorganization aimed at examining whether marital instability and divorce affected the status and kinship networks of grandparents. They obtained data from interviews with a sample of 50 parent-grandmother dyads from middle-class families with "additional information from individuals along the divorce and remarriage chains" (p. 330). Nearly half (48%) of grandparent kinship networks had expanded. This was especially the case for paternal grandmothers, who retained relationships with former daughters-in-law in addition to gaining new relatives as a result of blended family restructuring.

Additionally, as noted, many grandparents are assuming full-time primary care functions for dependent children. Some of these children are in "kincare or relative care" foster home placements arranged by the public child welfare system. Little is known about full-time grandparent caregiving of dependent grandchildren, emphasizing the pressing need for more information on this topic. Does the assumption of full-time primary caregiving for dependent grandchildren have stressful or negative consequences for the grandparent or the grandchild? What effect does full-time primary child care have on the physical and mental health and the economic well-being of older adults? Do the age and the behavior status of grandchildren affect these impacts? How does full-time primary caregiving affect the work or other responsibilities of grandparents? How does it affect grandchildren?

Two studies have offered information on lower-class and working-class African American extended families in which grandparents functioned as primary caregivers for grandchildren of drug-dependent parents. Minkler et al., (1992) used a purposive sample of 71 caregiver grandmothers to study the effect of surrogate parenting on the physical and emotional health status of the grandmothers. They found that caregivers de-emphasized their own physical and emotional health concerns to protect the security of grandchildren, specifically from fears of foster home placement. Burton (1992) interviewed 60 grandparent caregivers (10 males and 50 females) from two black urban communities. Using ethnographic strategies, she examined the costs and benefits of caregiving, the service needs of caregivers, and the contextual, familial, and individual stressors that caregivers faced. Those interviewed experienced neighborhood problems, drug traffic fears, economic problems, fears about the children's safety outdoors, problems with other drug-dependent family members, responsibilities for older kinfolk, and stress and sacrifices due to a myriad of problems related to drug addiction in the family. They also experienced rewards, such as the love and attention they received from the children. They felt satisfaction from knowing that they were able to protect their grandchildren from the foster care system or drug-dependent parents. However, many expressed a need for more instrumental support from church, community, and governmental agencies.

Seligman (1991), in an issue-oriented paper, discussed the hopes, fears, and adaptations of grandparents of children with chronic pediatric disability. He observed that the impact of childhood disability on grandparents has largely been ignored. After reviewing the roles and meaning of grandparenthood, he explored the impact of a disabled child on grandparents and discussed ways in which grandparents could provide emotional and instrumental support to the child's parents or ways in which they might be a source of stress.

Clearly, grandparents have provided emotional and instrumental assistance for grandchildren in a number of ways over the years, and a sizable number are now primary caregivers. Grandparent advocates have argued the need for information and supports to buffer the stressors and burdens that accompany grandparent caregiving of dependent children. At the present time, much is left to speculation. This is unfortunate at a time when the number of children placed with grandparents and other kin in surrogate parenting and foster home situations has been steadily increasing.

Grandparenting, personhood, and the life course

Most scholars who have studied grandparents within the contexts of personhood and the life course agree that grandparents constitute a diverse mixture of personalities and styles of behavior. This diversity reflects societal expectations and attitudes about the role and is reinforced by family and related life contexts that shape the meaning of grandparenthood for each individual. According to Troll's (1985) psychosocial perspective, grandparenting is shaped by the synchronicity of its timing with other events and processes within a person's life. The meaning and behaviors one attributes to the role are framed by the complementarity of psychological and social development that occurs simultaneously with other life events (i.e., those affiliated with marital, filial, and work statuses). The resultant diversity in styles of grandparenting leads to a conceptualization of the role as a career track along the continuum of individual development.

Hagestad and Burton (1986) employed a life course perspective to explain grandparent phenomena. They posited that lives within the family are interwoven and interdependent with life careers. Thus grandparenthood can best be described within "life webs" (i.e., the web of relationships that give personal meaning to the roles individuals assume at various phases of the life course). Kivnick (1985) provided yet another perspective on grandparenthood in its relationship to life review processes. She identified five distinct dimensions of meaning that grandparents bring to the role: role centrality, valued eldership, immortality through clan, reinvolvement with personal past, and indulgence. Using social well-being, psychiatric, and role abdication perspectives, Kornhaber (1985) also explored the personal significance of grandparenting for individuals. He suggested that grandparents help grandchildren, families, and the community maintain crucial social and emotional connections at times when the social fabric is threatened. Hence, grandparenting is essential for the well-being of young people and for generational transmission of family values and social connectedness. Guttmann (1985) suggested that the meaning of grandparenthood is derived from societal expectations and norms that reflect the value of elders as wardens or conveyers of culture. As a consequence of age, status, and life experiences, grandparents function as the living repositories of the effects of social change. Wardens of culture are essential for society because they foster age integration and provide appropriate status for elders. Failure explicitly to recognize the status and functions of older people results in deculturation and loss of culture (Guttmann, 1985).

THEORETICAL AND METHODOLOGICAL ISSUES

The 1960s and 1970s were decades of expansionism for basic and applied research in family gerontology as research funding increased. The 1980s and thereafter represent an era of retreat and regression for research because of fiscal constraints, as predicted by Berardo (1981). Some of the limitations in the state of the art in grandparent research might reflect this reality. With this caveat, what legacy does existing grandparent research offer for the future?

Quantitative research on grandparenthood, a delimited area of family study, lags behind other areas of social and behavioral science research in methodological sophistication. A modest increment in the production of new information has occurred, but knowledge about grandparenthood remains tentative and incomplete. For the most part, the state of the art is descriptive rather than explanatory. Existing basic and applied studies suffer from a number of theoretical, conceptual, design, sampling, and measurement problems.

Beginning with theoretical and conceptual issues, the work of Bengtson (1985, 1989), Burton and Bengtson (1985), Cherlin and Furstenberg (1986), Hagestad (1985), Hagestad and Burton (1986), Robertson (1977), and Troll (1985) was guided by intergenerational and life span perspectives. These researchers have offered a rich blend of quantitative and qualitative data from which to generate and test specific hypotheses. For example, most of the research revealed sharp contrasts or differences between the meaning and behaviors of grandfathers and grandmothers. What is the relationship between the gender of the grandparent and the types of assistance provided for grandchildren? Are contemporary grandparents who are actively employed willing or able to provide assistance to adult children at times of family stress? Does grandparent child care or full-time caregiving of dependent grandchildren affect the well-being of the grandparent? The majority of studies on grandparenting have provided some fruitful information. Most were limited. They were not grounded in systematic theory and often used methodologies that limited generalization of the findings.

Most of the research from the late 1980s and the early 1990s is applied in nature—guided by service, practical, or popular emphases rather than by systematic theory (Barranti, 1985; Blau, 1984; Burton, 1992; Chaloff, 1982; Langer, 1990; McCrimmon & Howell, 1989; Minkler et al., 1992; Tinsey & Park, 1984). This type of research can stimulate exploration; it often renders rich insights and hypotheses for further study. It does little to advance the scientific state of the art, however. Although it is possible to inductively derive theoretical propositions ex post facto from research motivated by service or practical needs, service-based research is seldom used for systematic and cumulative scientific knowledge building. If such knowledge building about grandparent phenomena is a goal, studies that develop and test theoretical propositions are needed.

Turning to methodological issues, the designs and types of samples employed to study grandparenting have various strengths and limitations. Some researchers (Hagestad, 1985; Bengtson, 1985; Burton & Bengtson, 1985; Cherlin & Furstenberg, 1986) used longitudinal, three- and four-generation nonrandom samples. Those efforts yielded some of the richest and most creative in-depth perspectives for understanding salient dimensions of grandparenting. Unfortunately, the nature of the samples and concerns about validity and reliability of study indexes pose limitations.

Other investigators have studied grandparenthood using cross-sectional designs with national samples. A major benefit of these studies was a breadth of suggestive data that had not been reported previously. For example, McCready (1985) provided new information about grandparents from various white immigrant and nonimmigrant ethnic backgrounds, Cherlin and Furstenberg (1986) used a more comprehensive sample than had Robertson (1977) to examine the variable styles of grandparenting, and Presser (1989) discussed the implications of employment data on mothers and grandmothers for the need for child-care providers for preschool children. Moreover, the Cherlin and Furstenberg (1986) study had good theory, appropriate sampling procedures, and well-explicated results. These studies have limitations as well. In all three cases, the investigators conducted secondary analyses of data collected for other purposes, necessitating cautious interpretation of the results. The cross-sectional designs and the restricted age range of the Presser (1989) sample preclude generalization of the findings.

A third set of researchers used smaller random samples of primarily working-class grandmothers and grandfathers in a midwestern community (Robertson, 1977; Wood & Robertson, 1975). The studies were grounded theoretically, the samples were appropriate, and the results were well explicated; but generalizations were limited to working-class grandparents with characteristics similar to those of the respondents. To examine a series of functional and expressive service exchanges between the generations, Langer (1990) used a random sample of noninstitutionalized Jewish grandparents 65 and older (from a Miami Beach apartment complex) with at least one adult grandchild. The limitations of the research are self-evident. Others (Johnson, 1988; Johnson & Barer, 1987) studied grandparent phenomena by focusing on changes in family structure, emotional history data (Kornhaber, 1985), or the functions and burdens of black grandparents assuming primary caregiving responsibilities for dependent grandchildren of drug-addicted parents (Burton, 1992; Minkler et al., 1992). Restrictive service or treatment samples were used. These studies were informative, but they lacked theoretical grounding and had measurement problems; thus, their value is primarily exploratory.

RESEARCH NEEDS FOR THE FUTURE

Problems often provide opportunities for change. Certainly, theoretically grounded longitudinal research on grandparenthood would be most valuable. This should blend qualitative and quantitative design strategies and use samples of three or four generations of cohorts. Although limitations in the state of the art exist, it is important to emphasize that much has been accomplished. Researchers have enriched the field with considerable exploratory data and a number of fruitful concepts for describing grandparent phenomena. This knowledge base might be used creatively to develop and test specific propositions about grandparenthood using life course, ecological, or family theoretical perspectives or a combination of these.

Bronfenbrenner's (1979) ecological perspective of human development included a challenging spatial imagery that provides a fruitful way for examining how individual and family life are nested in a variety of interlocking systems in the broader social environment. He offered a number of ready-made propositions for testing how near and distant environmental systems affect individual development and behavior; I am applying these to the current knowledge base on grandparenting with the aim of generating grandparent- and family-specific propositions for testing. The Bronfenbrenner theoretical perspective is not unlike the life webs framework of Hagestad and Burton (1986).

A number of substantive challenges also need to be addressed. Within the reality of scarce funding, it is still possible to conduct a number of small-scale studies on substantive topical areas with special populations or in given geographic areas. These types of studies are necessary to begin the tedious process of building a more systematic and cumulative knowledge base, an essential goal for advancing the state of the art.

Many research issues are important and timely. For example, additional studies of grandparenting in families of color are needed, especially because most research on families of color has focused on families with problems rather than on the strengths, potential, and resiliency of these families. Another important topic is grandfatherhood. Research on grandfathers has barely begun, and the existing studies deal with grandfathers only in conjunction with their female counterparts. Grandfatherhood needs to be studied in its own right.

A third crucial research topic is grandparental child care. Despite census statistics showing that millions of grandparents function as the primary caregivers of dependent children, some researchers, as noted earlier, have suggested that kinship exchanges between older parents and their adult children have become less evident than in the past. Why does this discrepancy exist? How many grandparents in the general population are primary caregivers of grandchildren? How many of them constitute the subset of the population receiving some type of assistance from the public welfare system? What are the some of the differences between these two groups of grandparents? How do child-caring grandparents who receive public welfare benefits differ from those who do not? What social, economic, and institutional supports are available for grandparents who care for dependent grandchildren? What are the supportive linkages that caregivers have with other kin, informal social systems, social service systems, the workplace, schools, or health systems? What are the burdens, costs, and benefits for grandparents who assume child-care functions at varying points in the life cycle? Are these roles more frequently assumed by grandmothers than by grandfathers? How many primary caregiver grandparents are employed full-time of part-time? How many of them are providing care to a spouse or dependent adult child who is seriously mentally ill, substance-dependent, or developmentally disabled? How do all these circumstances affect the general well-being of grandparents?

Finally, research addressing the impact both of services provided through the private sector and of public policies on family life, particularly intergenerational relationships, is needed. Information is not available on the contributions of grandparents and other older adults to children and families through volunteer work, on the extent of assistance to caregiving grandparents provided by the private sector, or on the management strategies of grandparents who do not receive public benefits to support their caregiving activities. Study of these neglected topics will provide greater understanding and appreciation of the full range of grandparental activities and experiences.

REFERENCES

Albrecht, R. (1954). The parental responsibilities of grandparents. *Marriage and Family Living, 26,* 201–204.

Aldous, J. (1987). New views on the family life of the elderly and the near elderly. *Journal of Marriage and the Family, 49,* 227–234.

Apple, D. (1956). The social structure of grandparenthood. *American Anthropologist, 58,* 656–663.

Barranti, C. C. (1985). The grandparent-grandchild relationship: Family resource in an era of voluntary bonds. *Family Relations, 34,* 343–352.

Bengtson, V. L. (1985). Diversity and symbolism in grandparental roles. In V. L. Bengtson & J. F. Robertson (Eds.), *Grandparenthood* (pp. 11–26). Beverly Hills, CA: Sage.

Bengtson, V. L. (1989). The problem of generations: Age group contrasts, continuities, and social change. In V. L. Bengtson (Ed.), *The course of later life: Research and reflections* (pp. 25–54). New York: Springer Publishing Co.

Bengston, V. L., & Achenbaum, W. A. (Eds.). (1993). *The changing contract across generations.* New York: Aldine de Gruyter.

Bengtson, V. L., & Robertson, J. F. (Eds.). (1985). *Grandparenthood.* Beverly Hills, CA: Sage.

Berardo, F. M. (1981). Family research and theory: Emergent topics in the 1970s and prospects for the 1980s. *Journal of Marriage and the Family, 45,* 251–257.

Blau, T. H. (1984). An evaluative study of the role of the grandparent in the best interests of the child. *American Journal of Family Therapy, 12,* 46–50.

Bronfenbrenner, U. (1979). *The ecology of human development: Experiments by nature and design.* Cambridge: Harvard University Press.

Brubaker, T. H. (1990). Families in later life: A burgeoning research area. *Journal of Marriage and the Family, 52,* 959–981.

Burton, L. M. (1992). Black grandparents rearing children of drug-addicted parents: Stressors, outcomes and social service needs. *Gerontologist, 32,* 744–751.

Burton, L. M., & Bengtson, V. L. (1985). Black grandmothers: Issues of timing and continuity of roles. In V. L. Bengtson & J. F. Robertson (Eds.), *Grandparenthood* (pp. 61–78). Beverly Hills, CA: Sage.

Chaloff, M. B. (1982). Grandparents' statutory visitation rights and rights of adoptive parents. *Brooklyn Law Review, 49,* 149–171.

Cherlin, A. J., & Furstenberg, F. F. (1985). Styles and strategies of grandparenting. In V. L. Bengtson & J. F. Robertson (Eds.), *Grandparenthood* (pp. 97–116). Beverly Hills, CA: Sage.

Cherlin, A. J., & Furstenberg, F. F. (1986). *The new American grandparent.* New York: Basic Books.

Child Welfare League of America. (1992). *North American Kinship Care: Policy and Practice Committee* (Draft #3). Washington, DC: Author.

Creighton, L. L. (1991, December 16). The silent saviors. *U. S. News and World Report,* pp. 80–89.

Demos, J. (1978). Old age in early New England. In J. Demos and S. S. Boocock (Eds.), *Historical and sociological essays on the family* (pp. 248–285). Chicago: University of Chicago Press.

Dunn, E., & Robertson, J. F. (1991, October 2). *Testimony presented at hearing before the Subcommittee on Human Services of the Select Committee on Aging, U.S. House of Representatives.* Madison: University of Wisconsin, School of Social Work.

Eggebeen, D. J., & Hogan, D. P. (1990). Giving between generations in American families. *Human Nature, 1,* 211–232.

Frazier, F. E. (1939). *The Negro family in the United States.* Chicago: University of Chicago Press.

Guttmann, David. I. (1985). Deculturation and the American grandparent. In V. L. Bengtson & J. F. Robertson (Eds.), *Grandparenthood* (pp. 173–182). Beverly Hills, CA: Sage.

Hagestad, G. O. (1985). Continuity and connectedness. In V. L. Bengtson & J. F. Robertson (Eds.), *Grandparenthood* (pp. 31–48). Beverly Hills, CA: Sage.

Hagestad, G. O. (1988). Demographic change and the life course: Some emerging trends in the family realm. *Family Relations, 37,* 405–410.

Hagestad, G. O., & Burton, L. (1986). Grandparenthood, life context, and family development. *American Behavioral Scientist, 29,* 474–484.

Hofferth, S. L., & Phillips, D. A. (1987). Child care in the United States. *Journal of Marriage and the Family, 49,* 559–571.

Johnson, C. L. (1988). Active and latent functions of grandparenting during the divorce process. *Gerontologist, 28,* 185–191.

Johnson, C. L., & Barer, B. M. (1987). Marital instability and the changing kinship networks of grandparents. *Gerontologist, 27,* 330–335.

Kivnick, H. Q. (1985). Grandparenthood and mental health. In V. L. Bengtson & J. F. Robertson (Eds.), *Grandparenthood* (pp. 211–224). Beverly Hills, CA: Sage.

Kornhaber, A. (1985). Grandparenthood and the new social contract. In V. L. Bengtson & J. R. Robertson (Eds.), *Grandparenthood* (pp. 159–172). Beverly Hills, CA: Sage.

Lajewski, H. C. (1959). Working mothers and their arrangements for the care of their children. *Social Security Bulletin, 22,* 8–13.

Langer, N. (1990) Grandparents and their adult children: What they do for one another. *Journal of Aging and Human Development, 31,* 101–110.

Litwak, E., & Kulis, S. (1987). Technology, proximity, and measures of kin support. *Journal of Marriage and the Family, 49,* 649–662.

Mancini, J. A., & Blieszner, R. (1989). Aging parents and their adult children: Research themes in intergenerational relationships. *Journal of Marriage and the Family, 51,* 275–290.

McCready, W. (1985). Styles of grandparenting among white ethnics. In V. L. Bengtson & J. F. Robertson (Eds.), *Grandparenthood* (pp. 49–60). Beverly Hills, CA: Sage.

McCrimmon, C. A., & Howell, R. J. (1989). Grandparents' legal rights to visitation in the fifty states and the District of Columbia. *Bulletin Academy Psychiatry Law, 17,* 355–366.

Mindel, C. H. (1980). Extended familism among urban Mexican Americans, Anglos, and blacks. *Hispanic Journal of Behavioral Sciences, 2,* 21–34.

Minkler, M., Rose, K., & Price, M. (1992). The physical and emotional health of grandmothers raising grandchildren in the crack cocaine epidemic. *Gerontologist, 32,* 752–760.

Mutran, E. (1985). Intergeneration support among blacks and whites: Response to culture or to socioeconomic differences. *Journal of Gerontology, 40,* 382–389.

Nadel, S. F. (1951). *The social foundations of social anthropology.* Glencoe, IL: Free Press.

National Commission on Children. (1991). *Final report.* Washington, DC: U.S. Government Printing Office.

Neugarten, B., & Weinstein, K. (1964). The changing American grandparent. *Journal of Marriage and the Family, 26,* 199–204.

Presser, H. B. (1989). Some economic complexities of child care provided by grandmothers. *Journal of Marriage and the Family, 51,* 581–591.

Radcliffe-Brown, A. R. (1952). *Structure and function in primitive society*. London: Cohen & West.

Robertson, J. F. (1977). Grandmotherhood: A study of role conceptions. *Journal of Marriage and the Family, 39*, 165–174.

Robertson, J. F. (in press). *Grandparents parenting grandchildren*. Chicago: Applied Center for Gerontology.

Robertson, J. F., Tice, C. H., & Loeb, L. (1985). Grandparenthood: From knowledge to programs and policy. In V. L. Bengtson & J. F. Robertson (Eds.), *Grandparenthood* (pp. 211–224). Beverly Hills, CA: Sage.

Rosow, I. (1967). *Social integration of the aged*. New York: Free Press.

Segal, C. (1992a, March 22). Grandparents fight for rights. *Wisconsin State Journal*, pp. 11–11A.

Segal, C. (1992b, March 24). Court hears grandparents. *Wisconsin State Journal*, p. 6.

Seligman, M. (1991). Grandparents of disabled grandchildren: Hopes, fears, and adaptation. *Journal of Contemporary Human Services, 72*, 147–152.

Shanas, E. (1980). Older people and their families: The new pioneers. *Journal of Marriage and the Family, 42*, 9–15.

Sweet, J. A., Bumpass, L., & Call, V. (1988). *The design and content of the national survey of families and household* (Working paper no. 1). Madison: University of Wisconsin, Center for Demography Ecology.

Tinsey, B. R., & Park, R. D. (1984). Grandparents as support and socialization agents. In M. Lewis (Ed.), *Beyond the dyad* (pp. 161–194). New York: Plenum Press.

Troll, L. E. (1985). The contingencies of grandparenting. In V. L. Bengtson & J. F. Robertson (Eds.), *Grandparenthood* (pp. 135–149). Beverly Hills, CA: Sage.

U.S. Bureau of the Census. (1991). *Current population reports: Marital status and living arrangements: March 1990*. (Series P-20 No. 450). Washington, DC: U.S. Government Printing Office.

Wechsler, H. L. (1985). Judaic perspectives on grandparenthood. In V. L. Bengtson & J. F. Robertson (Eds.), *Grandparenthood* (pp. 185–194). Beverly Hills, CA: Sage.

Wood, V., & Robertson, J. F. (1976). The significance of grandparenthood. In J. Gubrium (Ed.), *Time, roles, and self in old age* (pp. 265–278). New York: Behavioral Publications.

Young, M. (1954). The role of extended families in a disaster. *Human Relations, 7*, 189–204.

Zimmerman, S. L. (1992). *Family policies and family well being*. Newbury Park, CA: Sage.

Part IV

THE CONTEXT OF FAMILY LIFE

13

U.S. Old-Age Policy and the Family

Madonna Harrington Meyer and
Marcia L. Bellas

Although images of elderly persons as isolated and lonely still abound, nearly all are part of family networks (Shanas, 1979). Relatives provide many types of aid to elderly family members, most notably financial assistance and informal care. Consequently, policies that determine the extent of public support available to elderly persons, particularly policies that establish eligibility guidelines for poverty-based support, have important consequences for family members of all ages. In this chapter we examine the impact of four major government programs—Social Security, Supplemental Security Income (SSI), Medicare, and Medicaid—on aged people and their families. Because the impact of public policy on families is, to a large extent, a function of social class, gender, and race, within each section we give special attention to variations resulting from these stratifying characteristics.

THE U.S. OLD-AGE WELFARE STATE

The U.S. welfare state is generally regarded as fragmented and incomplete. A vehement adherence to the liberal work ethic prevents us from developing the sorts of comprehensive social welfare programs enjoyed by other Western democracies (Myles, 1984; Quadagno, 1988a; Acker, 1988; Esping-Andersen, 1989). U.S. policymakers and voters alike maintain what Katz (1986) referred to as the convenient fiction that poverty is not an economic misfortune but a moral failure. Requests for assistance are regarded as symptomatic of individual rather than societal shortcomings. One notable exception is the U.S. old-age welfare state. Historically regarded as the deserving poor, the aged have shrinking incomes and expanding needs, particularly health care, through no fault of their own (Marmor, 1970; Katz, 1986; Quadagno, 1988a, 1990). In response to a variety of historical and social factors, the U.S. government has implemented numerous public policies to address the needs of elderly persons that are not available to other age groups.

Social provision is generally based on one of two opposing principles: (1) social assistance or (2) social insurance. Social assistance programs target only those with the greatest financial need. Early social assistance programs placed the burden of caring for the aged, disabled, and otherwise unemployed squarely on the shoulders of families. Benefits provided temporary subsistence only when families failed (Katz, 1986; Myles, 1988). The reigning principle of less eligibility meant that treatment of the poor should be less desirable than treatment of the lowest wage earners in order to discourage reliance on social assistance (Myles, 1988). Therefore, gatekeeping was, and continues to be, an important element of social assistance programs (Katz, 1986). Over time, yesterday's poor laws have given way to today's "means-tested" programs, which provide basic services only to those who demonstrate that they have no other means of support (Beeghley, 1989). Reliance on social assistance is associated with degradation, humiliation, and persistent poverty (Adams, Meiners, & Burwell, 1992; Harrington Meyer, 1994; Katz, 1986; Esping-Anderson, 1989).

Contemporary social welfare programs are increasingly designed to provide a form of social insurance. In contrast to social assistance programs, social insurance programs distribute benefits to citizens regardless of financial need. The goal of programs that provide universal benefits is not subsistence, but wage replacement and continuity of living standards over the life course (Myles, 1988). Unlike social assistance programs, social insurance programs distribute the burden of caring for the aged, disabled, and otherwise unemployed across all citizens rather than concentrating responsibility on individual families. Whereas social assistance programs are politically divisive, pitting tax-paying contributors against welfare recipients, social insurance programs enjoy broad-based political support because all who contribute benefit from the program (Esping-Andersen, 1989; Quadagno 1988a).

Social insurance and social assistance programs now exist side by side in the U.S. old-age welfare state. Social insurance programs, namely Social Security and Medicare, provide monthly income and limited health care to nearly all elderly persons. Social assistance programs, such as Supplemental Security Income (SSI) and Medicaid, provide monthly income and health care only to the poorest of the aged.

SOCIAL SECURITY

When Congress passed the Social Security Act of 1935, providing monthly public pensions to the aged, the permanently blind, and the disabled, the elderly were disproportionately poor. Now, to a great extent *because* of Social Security, the poverty rate among persons aged 65 and over has dropped below the national average (Beeghley, 1989). Social Security initially excluded workers in many occupations, including agriculture and domestic service, as well as the self-employed and those employed by religious, charitable, and educational organizations (Quadagno, 1984; Abramovitz, 1988). These exclusions eliminated from coverage nearly one-half of all workers and nearly all women and blacks. Over time, Social Security incorporated most of these categories of workers and, in 1992, provided monthly benefits to more than 82% of the aged (Social Security Administration, 1992). Although originally designed as an income supplement, Social Security is the primary source of income for many older Americans, particularly those who are poor (Quadagno, 1988b; Harrington Meyer, 1990). Among all elderly persons, Social Security provides 40% of total income. For those with incomes below the federal poverty line, Social Security provides 70% of total income (Harrington Meyer, 1990).

Social Security is a universal program in the sense that coverage is extensive, and benefits are based on contributions or family relationships rather than financial need. Eligibility for Social Security is generally determined by one's relationship to the labor force (Olson, 1982; Harrington Meyer, 1990; Esping-Andersen, 1990). Maximum benefits, $1,147 per month in 1994, are available only to those with lengthy and continuous labor force participation in higher-paying jobs. Those with interrupted participation and lower-paying jobs are penalized substantially. Blacks, plagued by significantly higher unemployment rates and segregation into lower-paying jobs, receive smaller benefits than whites on average (Davis, 1978; Hochschild, 1988; Quadagno, 1987). Women of all races, burdened by the conflicting demands of waged and unwaged labor, persistent sex segregation in the labor force, and wages averaging only two-thirds those of men, receive the lowest benefits of all (O'Rand & Henretta, 1982; Reskin & Hartmann, 1986). Thus eligibility rules maximally benefit white men (Olson, 1982; Quadagno, 1988a).

Social Security benefits are funded through a regressive income tax system. In 1994, workers paid 6.2% of their earnings to Social Security on any income below $60,600 (Social Security Administration, 1994). Because earnings above the $60,600 ceiling are not subject to Social Security taxes, lower-income earners contribute a larger proportion of their total earnings to Social Security than higher-income earners, while ultimately receiving the smallest benefits. Racial differences in median income suggest that blacks are hardest hit by the regressive tax structure. Davis (1978) demonstrated that 100% of the median annual income for black families, compared with 70% of the median annual income for white families, is subject to Social Security taxes.

Although reduced Social Security benefits are now available at age 62 and full benefits at age 65, by the year 2027 full benefits will not be available until age 67. This policy change is based on increased longevity and is intended to delay retirement. The degree to which it will do so is unclear, however, given the increasing trend toward early retirement (Hess, 1991). Delaying eligibility for full Social Security benefits will most certainly increase economic hardship for those who are forced out of the labor force by layoffs or poor health (Harrington Meyer & Quadagno, 1990). Delaying benefits also magnifies one source of racial bias already built into the system. Because older blacks and Hispanics have lower life expectancies than whites (black male life expectancy at birth is just under 66 years), their chances of ever drawing benefits are considerably fewer (Harrington Meyer, 1990; Hess, 1991).

Worker Benefits

To qualify for Social Security, a worker must have contributed to Social Security for at least 40 quarters or 10 years (Greenberg, 1978). The quarters need not be consecutive, so eligibility is not compromised when women interrupt waged labor to rear children or to perform other unpaid domestic work (Harrington Meyer, 1990). Such disruptions do, however, affect benefit size, which is based on earnings averaged over 35 years—the number of years between age 21 and 62, minus the five lowest earning years (Greenberg, 1978; Burkhauser & Holden, 1982). Because women's average earnings are lower than men's and because women are more likely than men to interrupt waged labor, women's Social Security benefits average just 76% of men's (Reskin & Hartmann, 1986; Social Security Administration, 1992). Thus, women are penalized for conforming to a role that they are strongly encouraged to assume—unpaid household worker—and their disadvantaged economic position carries into old age (Arendell & Estes, 1991).

Spousal Benefits

Initially, only those who contributed to Social Security were eligible to receive benefits. In 1939, Congress extended coverage to spouses and widows, as well as to the blind and permanently disabled. Women married for at least 20 years to a qualified retired worker could receive a spousal "allowance" equal to one-half their husbands' benefit. In 1950, Congress extended spousal benefits to the husbands of retired women workers and in 1972 reduced the length of a qualifying marriage to 10 years. Nonetheless, of all spousal beneficiaries, 99% are women (Social Security Administration, 1992). Married women's spousal benefits are equal to one-half of their current husband's benefits. Divorced women qualify for one-half the amount of their ex-husband's benefits, provided the marriage lasted at least 10 years.

The establishment of spousal benefits created a dual eligibility structure based on either beneficiaries' own or their spouses' earnings record, whichever provides the greater benefit (Harrington Meyer, 1990; Social Security Administration, 1992). Because husbands typically earn substantially more than their wives, most men receive benefits based on their work records, whereas the majority of women receive spousal benefits. Consequently, despite the apparent gender neutrality of spousal benefits, women are vulnerable to changes in family status in a way that men typically are not (Harrington Meyer, 1990). Women married fewer than 10 years receive no compensation, regardless of any direct or indirect contributions they made to their husbands' earnings. In addition, divorced women who qualify for spousal benefits forfeit previous claims if they are remarried when they apply for benefits. Moreover, if married men choose not to apply for Social Security benefits, their wives will not receive spousal benefits. Ostensibly created to protect women with limited histories of paid labor, the structure of spousal benefits highlights and reinforces women's dependence on men's earnings across the life course.

Dual Entitlement

As women's labor force participation increases, more women are dually entitled for Social Security benefits. In other words, they qualify on the basis of both their own and their husbands' work records. The proportion of women who are dually entitled has more than doubled since 1970 (Social Security Administration, 1992). Nonetheless, women who are dually entitled often receive larger benefits through spousal, rather than through worker, entitlement. For example, of new women beneficiaries in 1982, 60% received spousal, rather than worker, benefits (Social Security Administration, 1985). Holden (1982) reported that 84% of dually entitled women who had any zero-earnings quarters were eligible for spousal benefits greater than their worker benefits.

Dual entitlement is increasingly under fire precisely because so many women receive the spousal benefit—a benefit to which they would have been entitled even if they had never contributed to Social Security. Thus the contributions married women make as workers appear unnecessary and unfair. Aware of the rising controversy, the Social Security Administration describes dually entitled women who draw spousal benefits as receiving a "combined benefit" (Social Security Administration, 1985). This is misleading because, in fact, these women would be entitled to the same benefit amount had they never participated in the labor force. Although the spousal benefit provides essential economic security to women with low lifetime earnings, some suggest that it also acts as a working wife's penalty (Burkhauser & Holden, 1982). By implementing payment policies that optimally benefit those with traditional family arrangements, U.S. old-age policies encourage and reward women's economic dependence (Pascall, 1986; Acker, 1988; Harrington Meyer, 1900; Miller, 1990).

Widow/Widower Benefits

In 1939, Congress added widows' benefits to the Social Security Act. Policymakers recognized that widowhood is often accompanied by a pronounced decline in income and marked by poverty, particularly for women (Lopata & Brehm, 1986). Congress first created surviving spouse benefits for women, then extended coverage to men in 1950. However, because men's worker benefits are typically higher than their wives', few men actually receive this benefit. In 1990, 99% of all nondisabled widow/widower beneficiaries were women (Social Security Administration, 1992). Initially, beneficiaries received 75% of their deceased spouses' Social Security benefit (Social Security Administration, 1992). In 1972, the benefit was raised to 100%. Divorced persons may also receive widow/widower benefits following the death of a former spouse provided the marriage lasted at least 10 years. Because women are more likely to be widowed and because divorcées are among the poorest of the elderly, increased benefits provide welcome economic relief for many older women (Harrington Meyer, 1990).

The Earnings Test

The Social Security earnings test restricts the wages that retired beneficiaries may earn and still qualify for full benefits. Originally, beneficiaries could not earn more than $15 per month without losing the entire benefit. In 1994, beneficiaries aged 65 to 69 years and older could earn up to $11,160 per year (regardless of the amount of their benefit), after which they forfeited $1 for every $3 earned (Social Security Administration, 1994). Those between 62 and 65 years of age could earn up to $8,040 per year, after which benefits decreased $1 for every $2 earned. There are no limits on earned income for those 70 and older and no limits on unearned income from assets and investments at any age (Olson, 1982). Consequently, families with smaller Social Security benefits are doubly disadvantaged by the earnings test. They are most likely to need additional earnings to supplement their benefits and least likely to have income-producing assets or investments.

The earnings test applies to both the retired worker and the spousal beneficiary. Because spousal benefits equal one-half of worker benefits, spousal benefits are reduced when the earnings test is applied to worker benefits even though the spouse may not be employed or have access to the worker's wages. The same scenario applied to divorced persons until 1983, when Congress enacted the Independently Entitled Divorced Spouse Benefit measure (Social Security Administration, 1992). This act permits divorced women to receive a spousal benefit equal to one-half their ex-husband's benefit amount after age 62, even if the former husband never applies for benefits. Under this same measure, her benefit will remain at one-half her former husband's benefit even if his wages surpass the earnings ceiling. That married women's spousal benefits are subject to the earnings test while divorced women's benefits are not stems from the assumption that married women share in their husband's income while divorced women do not benefit from their ex-husband's earnings.

Despite the gender-neutral language used to describe Social Security benefits, men typically receive worker benefits whereas most women receive spousal and widow/widower benefits. Because spousal benefits typically exceed women's worker benefits, women are, in a sense, rewarded for their dependence, but at the level of only one-half that of their husband. Furthermore, worker benefits are based on contributions and are therefore earned and unaffected by subsequent changes in family status. In contrast, spousal and widow/widower benefits are determined by family relationships (Quadagno, 1990). Women are therefore vulnerable to changes in family status that may affect their eligibility and benefit size. Benefits are structured to assist maximally workers with continuous labor force participation and high wages. Moreover, regressive taxation and the earnings test are least detrimental to the highest earners. On these measures, the most disadvantaged workers are most disadvantaged by the Social Security system.

SUPPLEMENTAL SECURITY INCOME

In 1972, Congress eliminated the Social Security minimum benefit, as well as a series of federal-state programs, and created the federally administered Supplemental Security Income program (SSI). In 1991, nearly 1.5 million aged persons received SSI. One-half of SSI recipients are ineligible for Social Security benefits; the remainder receive Social Security benefits below the SSI income limit. Because women live longer than men on average and because they are more likely to be poor, three-fourths of elderly SSI recipients are women (Social Security Administration, 1992).

Like many poverty-based programs, SSI is underused by older people. Researchers consistently report that just over one-half of elderly persons entitled to SSI benefits actually receive them (U.S. Senate Select Committee on Aging, 1984). Underuse is related, at least in part, to SSI's modest benefits and strict income and asset regulations and to the stigma associated with social assistance programs. In 1991, average old-age monthly SSI payments were $221. The median old-age monthly benefit was approximately $160 (i.e., one-half of all SSI beneficiaries received less than $160). Total monthly income for older individuals cannot exceed $434, while aged couples must have monthly incomes below $652 (Social Security Administration, 1992). Assets, excluding a house, car, and burial fund under certain conditions, must be below $2,000 for older individuals living independently, whereas older couples must have less than $3,000 in assets. Benefits for those who are not living independently—that is, residing in another person's household such as an adult child's—are reduced by one-third under the assumption that other household members provide in-kind benefits. Under federal guidelines, those who qualify for SSI receive enough benefits to raise their monthly incomes to 77% of the federal poverty line. Many states supplement SSI to raise benefits above the federal benefit level, but only a few states provide enough of a supplement even to meet the poverty line (Neuschler, 1987; Margolis, 1990).

Unlike the Social Security earnings test, which overlooks unearned income, SSI counts all earned and unearned income in determining eligibility. The first $65 of earned income, along with an additional $20, is disregarded each month. Any additional earnings decrease benefits by $1 for every $2 earned. Unearned income decreases benefits by $1 for every $1 received. The distinction between earned and unearned income is more than semantic. Margolis (1990) described a 73-year-old widow who lost her eligibility for SSI when she began baby-sitting for her two school-aged grandchildren. The children's parents carefully set her monthly salary at $65 so as not to interfere with the SSI earnings test. Because family members paid the wages, however, SSI officials deemed them a gift (and therefore unearned) and retracted her eligibility. Only after more than a year of review and appeal did the Social Security Administration overturn the decision and restore her eligibility.

In contrast to Social Security, a universal program, the strict income and asset limits of SSI characterize poverty-based social assistance programs. Although SSI benefits are indexed to inflation and have risen steadily since the program began, neither the asset limit nor the income disregard is adjusted for inflation. In fact both amounts have increased only slightly since the program began (Social Security Administration, 1992). Thus, by failing to adjust for 20 years of inflation, eligibility requirements have become more stringent by default rather than through explicit policy changes.

Of particular concern to the families of elderly recipients is the requirement that SSI be discontinued upon institutionalization (Olson, 1982). Nursing home residents are generally ineligible for SSI unless Medicaid pays at least 50% of their care. Prior to 1986, SSI recipients lost benefits entirely during nursing home stays of even one month. Since 1987, institutionalized recipients may receive SSI for up to three months if benefits are needed to maintain a home (Social Security Administration, 1992). Once the three-month grace period has elapsed, SSI benefits to nursing home residents receiving Medicaid are limited to $30 per individual, the equivalent of the personal needs allowance permitted all Medicaid recipients (Harrington Meyer, 1991). Those who remain in nursing homes for more than three months often risk losing their place of residence and might be forced into permanent institutionalization (Olson, 1982).

MEDICARE

Medicare has provided universal health care benefits to the aged, blind, and permanently disabled since 1965. Medicare is funded, in part, through payroll taxes of 1.45% on all earnings (the 1993 ceiling, $135,000 per year, was eliminated in 1994) (Social Security Administration, 1994). Before the program began, just 56% of the aged had hospital insurance. In 1992, at least 97% of all older persons in the United States had coverage because all who qualify for Social Security are eligible for Medicare. Medicare Part A coverage is compulsory insurance for hospital inpatient services. For an additional premium, deducted directly from the Social Security check, Medicare Part B provides supplemental coverage for physician and related services.

Although Medicare is nearly universal in terms of eligibility, it is hardly comprehensive in its coverage. Recent estimates indicate that Medicare pays for just 44% of all old-age health care costs (Brown, 1984; Holden & Smeeding, 1990). Gaps in Medicare coverage include long-term care, preventive care, Medicare Part B premiums, deductibles, copayments, and any fees that surpass allowable charges. As a result, three-fourths of older people obtain at least one supplemental private health insurance, or Medigap, package (Iglehart, 1992). Despite Medicare and Medigap policies, older people pay higher out-of-pocket health care expenses than any other age group (Davis, 1986). In 1965, elderly people spent 15% of their annual incomes on health care expenses. This percentage declined following implementation of Medicare, but by 1990 expenses approached 19%. Each year, one-third of the near-poor elderly population is reduced to the federal poverty line by out-of-pocket health care expenses alone (Commonwealth Fund, 1987). Moon (1987a) contended that the increase in Medicare's cost-sharing provisions is substantial enough to deter some from seeking care. Out-of-pocket health care costs continue to rise for the elderly despite Medicare's soaring budget, which topped $100 billion in 1990. The majority of Medicare expenditures go to a small fraction of beneficiaries (Iglehart, 1992). Average benefits in 1990 were $4,000, yet 20% of Medicare enrollees received no benefits at all while another 20% accounted for 80% of program expenditures.

Prospective Payment System (DRGs)

Between 1965 and 1983, Medicare reimbursed hospitals and doctors retrospectively on a cost-plus-profit basis. Health care costs skyrocketed, quadrupling in one 10-year period alone (Iglehart, 1992; Brown, 1984).

Physicians and hospitals enjoyed unparalleled profits while the elderly received unprecedented, and often unwarranted, medical care (Brown, 1984). In the early 1980s, as medical care costs continued to rise faster than inflation, the Health Care Financing Administration (HCFA) implemented cost-containment measures such as Medicare's prospective payment system (PPS). Under this system, physicians categorize patients into diagnostic related groupings (DRGs) based on their condition. Medicare then reimburses hospitals the average cost of care for patients in these diagnostic categories (Fischer & Eustis, 1989).

DRGs have forced hospitals to contain costs and curb unnecessary treatments somewhat. Early fears that the quality of inpatient care would decline are so far unsubstantiated (Iglehart, 1992). Evidence suggests, however, that hospitals have sustained their profits by releasing older patients "quicker and sicker," with profound implications for family members (U.S. House Select Committee on Aging, 1986; Estes, 1989; Fischer & Eustis, 1989). For example, average hospital stays declined by 18% between 1981 and 1991. Shorter stays are generally interpreted as a positive outcome, but in the 20-month period following implementation of DRGs, HCFA reported 4,724 cases of premature discharge and inappropriate transfers (U.S. House Select Committee on Aging, 1986). Committee hearings before the U.S. House Select Committee on Aging (1986) provided numerous case descriptions of hospital responses to DRGs. For example, Mary Fisher of the American Nurses' Association recounted the effect of DRGs on the family of one elderly woman.

A 68-year-old woman with amyotrophic lateral sclerosis (ALS; Lou Gehrig's disease) and nine additional diagnoses was discharged home directly from the medical intensive care unit, with 13 pages of care instructions for her family. She had a tracheotomy and was on a ventilator, required tube feedings, was on nine medications (including an anticoagulant medicator that involved daily injections) and needed special skincare. No nursing home would take her because she was respirator-dependent. She was, therefore, totally dependent on her husband and one of her children for care beyond the daily and sometimes twice daily visits by the community health nurse. This dependency had a very negative impact on the family, to the degree that officials from protective services had to be called in to deal with spouse abuse. While cases of spousal abuse are rare, many families experience frustration and guilt at their inability to provide the highly technical care that the patient requires. Prior to PPS, this woman probably would not have gone home before her death from ALS (U.S. House Select Committee on Aging, 1986, p. 139).

In response to DRGs, hospitals are exporting less profitable work to the home where others, primarily women, perform without pay what is sometimes highly technical work (Harrington Meyer, 1994). Glazer (1990) described how informal caregiving has evolved from housekeeping and minor nursing to encompass complex nursing regimes once performed only in hospitals, including chemotherapy, apnea monitoring, phototherapy, and tube feeding. Formal care providers, such as visiting nurses, used to make frequent and relatively lengthy visits to perform a variety of services. Recent cost-containment efforts have doubled home care providers' caseloads, causing them to shorten their visits and limit the tenure of their relationships with clients (Glazer, 1990). With little time to spare, nurses and aides focus on preparing family members to provide care in their absence.

In the wake of DRGs, Medicare coverage of community long-term care, including nursing services, chore services, personal care, and homemaking, remains meager. Just 3% of the Medicare budget goes to community-based care (U.S. Senate Select Committee on Aging, 1988). Community care is limited in duration and provided only to those deemed rehabilitatable and housebound. Consequently, informal caregivers provide 80% to 90% of all community-based care (U.S. Senate Select Committee on Aging, 1988). Estes (1989) calculated that since the implementation of DRGs in 1983, family caregivers have assumed responsibility for 21 million days of care that previously would have been hospital days. Glazer (1990) estimated that the medical industry saves $10 billion in wages annually because of the labor of unpaid family workers. For every $120 in publicly funded long-term care, family members provide $287 worth of unpaid services (Glazer, 1990). Although family members (typically, wives and daughters) have always cared for elderly persons, Social Security and Medicare transferred some of this responsibility from the family to the state. The reduction in payment for formal caregiving associated with Medicare's cost-containment measures has shifted more responsibility to families, increasing the dependence of elderly persons on informal caregivers (Fischer & Eustis, 1989; Harrington Meyer, 1994).

The effects of this shift are most strongly felt by women. Women have significantly higher rates of chronic illness, longer life expectancies, and fewer resources in old age than men have; thus, women pose the greatest demand for long-term care. In addition, as unpaid care providers, women perform about 75% of all informal caregiving (U.S. Senate Select Committee on Aging, 1988). Studies of caregiver strain and burden indicate that women experience greater strain than men do because they spend more time in caregiving, assume the more tedious aspects of caregiving, and are significantly more likely to maintain their own households (Brody, 1981; Horowitz, 1985; Stone, Cafferata, & Sangl, 1987). The demands associated with caregiving are compounded when the caregiver is also employed (Montgomery & Kamo, 1989; Anastas, Gibeau, & Larson, 1990). Stone et al. (1987) found for a national sample of caregivers that 30% were employed. An additional 9% had left their jobs to care for an aged parent, with obvious ramifications for their economic security (see Brody, Kleban, Johnson, Hoffman, & Schoonover, 1987). Many informal caregivers of both sexes are themselves aged. Their own health concerns and the financial constraints associated with old age put this group at particular risk of any detrimental effects of caregiving (Cantor, 1983); see Dwyer, this volume, and Travis, this volume, for additional information about informal caregiving and effects on family members. Transferring nursing services from hospitals to informal family caregivers without increasing community support services shifts financial and emotional costs from society at large to individual families, often with devastating results.

To relieve caregiver burden, some advocates for elderly persons debate the pros and cons of following international precedent by providing direct government subsidies to informal caregivers (Linsk, Keigher, Simon-Rusinowitz, & England, 1992). Others call for an expansion of Medicare's coverage of community-based long-term care to reverse the trend of increasing reliance on informal care (Moon, 1987b; Glazer, 1990). Policy discussions surround the need to increase support to informal caregivers in the form of education, day care, home health care, respite, and other services (Cantor, 1983; Kola & Dunkle, 1988; Scharlach & Boyd, 1989). Because many caregivers are employed, those who advocate policy changes also call for greater empathy and support from employers (Cantor, 1983; Kola & Dunkle, 1988; Anastas et al., 1990). Employed caregivers are more likely than other employees to miss work, to take time off, and to suffer from fatigue (Scharlach & Boyd, 1989; Anastas et al., 1990). Not surprisingly, then, employed caregivers report that flexible work hours and the ability to take time off for family illness are particularly helpful policies (Scharlach & Boyd, 1989). Other programs such as job sharing and part-time options, adult day care, counseling, and information services that deal with gerontological issues might also assist employed caregivers (Cantor, 1983; Scharlach & Boyd, 1989; Anastas et al., 1990). The recently enacted Family Leave Bill requires employers to permit employees up to 12 weeks off without pay to care for frail older relatives. These proposals could be beneficial to family members responding to acute episodes, such as a broken hip, but given the lengthy tenure of most informal caregiving relationships and the economic status of many informal caregivers, 12 weeks of unpaid leave is not often a meaningful option.

MEDICAID

In 1965, Congress created the Medicaid program in conjunction with Medicare. Although intended to provide health care to poor persons of all ages, Medicaid dollars are disproportionately directed toward aged and institutionalized individuals. Persons aged 65 and older constitute 12% of the total U.S. population but account for at least 50% of Medicaid expenditures (Eustis, Greenberg, & Patten, 1985). Three-fourths of this amount goes to nursing home care alone, although only 5% of the elderly reside in nursing homes at any given time. After elderly persons themselves, Medicaid is the principal payer of nursing home care. This nation spent roughly $54 billion on nursing home care in 1990, and Medicaid paid 42% of the cost (Harrington, 1991; U.S. Senate Select Committee on Aging, 1988). Despite these staggering figures, only one-third of the poor elderly actually receive Medicaid (Neuschler, 1987; Margolis, 1990).

Like other social assistance programs, eligibility for Medicaid is based on family assets and income. Assets include savings and checking accounts, stocks, bonds, mutual funds, and any form of property that can be converted to cash. Under specified conditions, certain assets are excluded, including a home, a car, some life insurance policies, burial space, and funds up to $1,500 per person. Remaining assets must total less than $2,000 for a single person and $3,000 per elderly couple (Social Security Administration, 1992). Income restrictions are more varied and complex than asset guidelines. Generally, states must provide Medicaid coverage to the *categorically needy*—those who qualify for SSI and whose incomes fall below 77% of the federal poverty line (Neuschler, 1987; Tilly & Brunner, 1987). In addition, states may provide coverage to the *medically needy*—those who can demonstrate for a period of one to six months that income minus medical expenses leaves a monthly income near or below the SSI limit.

Reliance on poverty-based welfare programs is generally regarded as stigmatizing and degrading, a humiliation to be avoided if possible (Katz, 1986; Branch, Friedman, Cohen, Smith, & Socholitzky, 1988; U.S. Senate Select Committee on Aging, 1988; Adams et al., 1992). Although Medicaid provides medical care to those with few resources, eligibility is often accompanied by discrimination, restricted access to medical care, and lower-quality care (Brown, 1984; Katz, 1986; Wallace, 1990; Margolis, 1990). The government reimburses health care providers at a lower rate and often at a slower pace than private insurers or payers. Consequently, many providers refuse Medicaid recipients altogether. Brown (1984) reported that one-fifth of all physicians refuse to see Medicaid patients, and just 6% of physicians care for one-third of Medicaid patients. Nursing homes often discriminate against applicants with Medicaid coverage. When Medicaid recipients are admitted, they often find that their accommodations are more cramped and barren and their treatment is less comprehensive than private payers experience (Margolis, 1990). Moreover, because Medicaid recipients living in nursing homes are wards of the state, recipients' entire monthly incomes, save a small personal needs allowance, go toward paying monthly nursing home bills (Harrington Meyer, 1991). Left with only $30 to $70 (depending on the state), many nursing home residents cannot afford basic necessities such as clothing, haircuts, transportation, and even some medical expenses. If family members cannot pay for these items, the elderly person must do without them.

Spenddown

Spenddown has received considerable attention in the gerontological literature and in public policy debates because it is so troublesome for families. Spenddown represents the loss of economic and social status in old age (Harrington Meyer, 1994). When individuals are ineligible for Medicaid because of excess income or assets, they might deplete those resources to become eligible. In the process of spending down, many older people go without needed medical care and home improvements before ultimately relying on Medicaid to meet their health care needs. Although spenddown can occur among those living in the community, it is most common in nursing homes. Adams et al. (1992) concluded that between 20% and 25% of those who enter nursing homes as private payers convert to Medicaid before discharge, that most who spend down do so within one year of nursing home admission, and that women are at somewhat greater risk than men of spending down in nursing homes (Liu & Manton, 1989; Liu, Doty, & Manton, 1990; Spence & Weiner, 1990).

The Medicaid Gap

When Medicaid applicants do not qualify for coverage because of excess assets, they can deplete them by paying additional medical bills. When applicants are ineligible because their monthly income exceeds Medicaid's limit, in many instances they can never qualify for Medicaid (Quadagno, Harrington Meyer, & Turner, 1991). Only 30 states provide coverage to the medically needy in nursing homes whose incomes—after medical expenses—fall below an established threshold (Neuschler, 1987). The remaining 20 states do not provide coverage to the medically needy. In these states, older people whose incomes exceed the income test never qualify for Medicaid regardless of how high their health care costs soar. These families are caught in the Medicaid gap. One study of Florida residents caught in the Medicaid gap revealed how devastating this can be for the elderly and their families (Quadagno et al., 1991). Some families were able to contribute enough money to cover the Medicaid gap, enabling the older relative to remain in a nursing home. However, lower-income families were generally unable to sustain financial support and removed the older person from the nursing home to provide round-the-clock informal care.

Spousal Impoverishment

Many older people unwittingly impoverish their spouses in the process of spending down to become eligible for Medicaid coverage, particularly when one spouse enters a nursing home and the other remains in the community (Harrington Meyer, 1994). Spousal impoverishment is most likely to affect women for several reasons. First, 32% of men in nursing homes are married, compared with 11% of women. Thus older men are three times more likely than older women to have a spouse in the community who may become impoverished (Commonwealth Fund, 1988). Second, whereas younger couples may increasingly stress joint ownership of marital properties, older couples were more likely to place much of their property in the husband's name only. Historically, when determining Medicaid eligibility for nursing home residents, states used federal "name on the instrument" rules, through which ownership was assigned only to the spouse whose name was on the check, account, or title. Over time, some states began to apply community property guidelines, while others deemed all joint properties the sole property of the institutionalized spouse. In 1988, the Medicare Catastrophic Coverage Act eliminated state variation in the division of spousal income and assets. Congress later repealed the bill but kept the provision stipulating that all assets be available to the institutionalized spouse. A noninstitutionalized spouse may, however, retain a "monthly allowance" of at least 150% of the federal poverty line, and one-half or $12,000 of the couple's assets, whichever is greater (Carpenter, 1988). Thus the provision is aimed at easing impoverishment without eliminating spousal responsibility. However, in a simulated analysis, Holden and Smeeding (1990) found little reduction in the risk of impoverishment. Additionally, they found that the real beneficiaries of the legislative change were middle- and upper-class women, who are more likely than lower-class women to be married in old age and to have income and assets approaching the new ceilings. This demonstrates that tinkering with a poverty-based program might produce little real benefit, as well as unforeseen consequences (Harrington Meyer, 1994).

CONCLUSIONS

Unlike other Western democracies, the United States restricts its social insurance programs to elderly persons. Social Security and Medicare boast near-universal participation rates and are widely praised for improving the social and economic status of the aged (Marmor, 1970; Brown, 1984; Quadagno, 1988b; Minkler, 1991). Yet these programs provide incomplete coverage. For those with tenuous relationships to the labor force or substantial long-term care needs, benefits are far from comprehensive. Women, blacks, Hispanics, and the poor are particularly vulnerable under current guidelines. Two need-based programs—SSI and Medicaid—provide safety nets of sorts. The poorest of the poor may qualify for SSI benefits to bring their incomes up to 77% of the federal poverty line. One-third of the aged poor receive health care benefits through Medicaid. However, the majority of poor elderly persons do not receive assistance via these poverty-based programs, and those who do must wrestle with gaps in coverage, discrimination, and the stigma that accompanies reliance on welfare. A fragmented old-age welfare state places much of the responsibility for the care of older people on the shoulders of family members, mainly women, with profound consequences.

Historically, policymakers and laypersons alike have regarded the elderly as the deserving poor (Marmor, 1970; Katz, 1986; Quadagno, 1988a). By the late 1970s, however, troubled economic times spurred many policy-makers to question age as a basis for determining eligibility (Neugarten, 1982; Preston, 1984). Despite gaps in coverage, some believe that existing programs are too comprehensive. Opponents of Social Security and Medicare have launched a three-pronged attack aimed at restoring an exclusively poverty-based welfare state. Some charge that universal programs provide benefits to middle- and upper-class persons who could manage without them, whereas lower-income elderly receive insufficient aid (Neugarten, 1982; Binstock, 1991). Binstock (1991), for example, argued that if, in a declining economy, the only choices are to ration resources by age or by need, need is the lesser of two evils. Others pit the improved economic condition of the elderly against the deteriorating economic conditions of children (Longman, 1982; Preston, 1984). In this scenario, the elderly are regarded as "greedy geezers" who are taking food from the mouths of babes. Still others are concerned that those who currently contribute to the Social Security and Medicare trust fund will reap few rewards when they become old because the program will go bankrupt under the strain of aging baby boomers (Longman, 1985). This final attack focuses on the varying demographic characteristics of generations and on issues of generational equity. Longman argued that as longevity increases and fertility rates decline, too few workers will contribute to Social Security and Medicare to support expanding numbers of older persons.

We find counterarguments, just as numerous, to be more persuasive. Social Security and Medicare have greatly improved the social, political, and economic well-being of the elderly (Minkler, 1991). Though the poverty rate among the elderly is now slightly below that for the population as a whole, eliminating these programs would restore higher poverty rates. Wallace and Estes (1991) estimated that eliminating Social Security would increase the poverty rate among the elderly from 12.4% to 48%. Furthermore, several nations with higher percentages of older persons and more generous welfare provisions than the United States (e.g., Sweden and Japan) are not unduly burdened and report little evidence of intergenerational hostility (Myles, 1984). Finally, universal programs are less stigmatizing than need-based programs. They are therefore more popular politically and less likely to be slashed during economic downturns (Myles, 1984; Esping-Andersen, 1989; Quadagno, 1990, 1991).

As a nation we are at a crossroads, balancing the costs and benefits of social assistance versus social insurance. Some favor turning back the clock to the supposed efficiencies of a targeted, poverty-based old-age welfare state. Others prefer to forge ahead, developing a comprehensive universal welfare state for all ages. Those who support the first alternative might not recognize that Social Security and Medicare have socialized financial responsibility for the aged, taking the direct burden from younger generations. Even under the current mix of social assistance and social insurance programs, many families report almost unbearable levels of burden. A return to an exclusively poverty-based old-age welfare state promises to magnify the burden on families. In contrast, through pooled risk and shared responsibility, expanded universal old-age benefits could relieve families of at least some of the burden.

NOTE

We thank Jill Quadagno, Barbara Lingg, Mary Ann Prucnell, Liza Pavalko, Catherine Ross, Ralph Bellas, John Tichenor, Rosemary Blieszner, and Victoria Bedford for their assistance and suggestions.

REFERENCES

Abramovitz, M. (1988). *Regulating the lives of women: Social welfare policy from colonial times to the present.* Boston: South End Press.

Acker, J. (1988). Class, gender, and the relations of distributions. *Signs, 13,* 473–497.

Adams, K., Meiners, M., & Burwell, B. (1992). *A synthesis and critique of studies on Medicaid asset spenddown.* Report by the Office of Family, Community and Long Term Care Policy. Office of the Assistant Secretary for Planning and Evaluation. Washington, DC: Department of Health and Human Services.

Anastas, J., Gibeau, J., & Larson, P. (1990). Working families and eldercare: A national perspective in an aging America. *Social Work, 35,* 405–411.

Arendell, T., & Estes, C. (1991). Older women in the post-Reagan era. In M. Minkler & C. Estes (Eds.), *Critical perspectives on aging: The political and moral economy of growing old* (pp. 209–226). New York: Baywood.

Beeghley, L. (1989). *The structure of social stratification in the United States.* Needham Heights, MA: Allyn & Bacon.

Binstock, R. (1991). Aging, politics, and public policy. In B. Hess & E. Markson (Eds.), *Growing old in America* (pp. 325–340). New Brunswick, NJ: Transaction.

Branch, L., Friedman, D., Cohen, M., Smith, N., & Socholitzky, E. (1988). Impoverishing the elderly: A case study of the financial risk of spend-down among Massachusetts elderly people. *Gerontologist, 28,* 648–652.

Brody, E. (1981). Women in the middle and family help to older people. *Gerontologist, 21,* 471–480.

Brody, E., Kleban, M., Johnson, P., Hoffman, C., & Schoonover, C. (1987). Work status and parent care: A comparison of four groups of women. *Gerontologist, 27,* 201–208.

Brown, R. (1984). Medicare and Medicaid: The process, value and limits of health care reform. In M. Minkler & C. Estes (Eds.), *Readings in the political economy of aging* (pp. 117–143). New York: Baywood.

Burkhauser, R., & Holden, K. (1982). *A challenge to Social Security: The changing roles of women and men in American society.* New York: Academic Press.

Cantor, M. (1983). Strain among caregivers: A study of experience in the United States. *Gerontologist, 23,* 597–604.

Carpenter, L. (1988). Medicaid eligibility for persons in nursing homes. *Health Care Financing Review, 10,* 67–77.

Commonwealth Fund. (1987). *Medicare's poor.* Washington, DC: Commission on Elderly People Living Alone.

Commonwealth Fund. (1988). *Aging alone: Profiles and projections.* Washington, DC: Commission on Elderly People Living Alone.

Coward, R., & Dwyer, J. (1990). The association of gender, sibling network composition and patterns of parent care by adult children. *Research on Aging, 12,* 158–181.

Davis, F. (1978). *The black community's Social Security.* Washington, DC: University Press of America.

Davis, K. (1986). Paying the health care bills of an aging population. In A. Pifer & L. Bronte (Eds.), *Our aging society* (pp. 299–318). New York: Norton.

Esping-Andersen, G. (1989). The three political economies of the welfare state. *Canadian Review of Sociology and Anthropology, 26,* 10–36.

Esping-Anderson, G. (1990). *The three worlds of welfare capitalism.* Cambridge: Polity.

Estes, C. (1989). Aging, health and social policy: Crises and crossroads. *Journal of Aging and Social Policy, 1,* 17–32.

Eustis, N., Greenberg, J., & Patten, S. (1985). *Long term care for older persons: A policy perspective.* Monterey, CA: Brooks, Cole.

Fischer, L., & Eustis, N. (1989). Quicker and sicker: How changes in Medicare affect the elderly and their families. *Journal of Geriatric Psychiatry, 22,* 163–191.

Glazer, N. (1990). The home as workshop: Women as amateur nurses and medical care providers. *Gender & Society, 4,* 479–499.

Greenberg, J. (1978). *The old age survivors and disability insurance (OASDI) system: A general overview of the social problem* (HS 7094 U.S. Report No. 78–200 EPW). Washington, DC: U.S. Government Printing Office.

Harrington, C. (1991). The nursing home industry: A structural analysis. In M. Minkler & C. Estes (Eds.), *Critical perspectives on aging: The political and moral economy of growing old* (pp. 153–164). New York: Baywood.

Harrington Meyer, M. (1990). Family status and poverty among older women: The gendered distribution of retirement income in the United States. *Social Problems, 37,* 551–563.

Harrington Meyer, M. (1991). Political organization of the frail elderly. In B. Hess & E. Markson (Eds.), *Growing old in America* (pp. 363–376). Brunswick, NJ: Transaction.

Harrington Meyer, M. (1994). Gender, race and the distribution of social resources: Medicaid use among the frail elderly. *Gender & Society, 8,* 8–28.

Harrington Meyer, M., & Quadagno, J. (1990). Ending a career in a declining industry: The retirement experience of male autoworkers. *Sociological Perspectives, 33,* 51–62.

Hess, B. (1991). Growing old in America in the 1990s. In B. Hess & E. Markson (Eds.), *Growing old in America* (pp. 5–22). New Brunswick, NJ: Transaction.

Hochschild, J. (1988). Race, class, power, and the American welfare state. In A. Gutmann (Ed.), *Democracy and the welfare state* (pp. 157–184). Princeton, NJ: Princeton University Press.

Holden, K. (1982). Supplemental OASI benefits to homemakers through current spouse benefits, a homemaker credit, and child-care drop-out years. In R. Burkhauser & K. Holden (Eds.), *A challenge to Social Security: The changing roles of women and men in American society* (pp. 41–72). New York Academic Press.

Holden, K., & Smeeding, T. (1990). The poor, the rich and the insecure elderly caught in between. *Millbank Quarterly, 68,* 191–219.

Horowitz, A. (1985). Sons and daughters as caregivers to older parents: Differences in role performance and consequences. *Gerontologist, 25,* 612–617.

Iglehart, J. (1992). Health policy report: The American health care system—Medicare. *New England Journal of Medicine, 327,* 1467–1472.

Katz, M. (1986). *In the shadow of the poorhouse: A social history of welfare in America.* New York: Basic Books.

Kola, L., & Dunkle, R. (1988). Eldercare in the workplace. *Social Casework, 69,* 569–574.

Linsk, N., Keigher, S., Simon-Rusinowitz, L., & England, S. (1992). *Wages for the caring: Compensating family care of the elderly.* Westport, CT: Greenwood.

Liu, K., Doty, P., & Manton, K. (1990). Medicaid spenddown in nursing homes. *Gerontologist, 30,* 7–15.

Liu, K., & Manton, K. G. (1989). The effect of nursing home use on Medicaid eligibility. *Gerontologist, 29,* 59–66.

Longman, P. (1982, November). Taking America to the cleaners. *Washington Monthly,* pp. 24–30.

Longman, P. (1985, June). Justice between generations. *Atlantic Monthly,* pp. 73–81.

Lopata, H., & Brehm, H. (1986). *Widows and dependent wives: From social problem to federal program.* New York: Praeger.

Margolis, R. (1990). *Risking old age in America.* Boulder, CO: Westview.

Marmor, T. (1970). *The politics of Medicare.* New York: Aldine.

Miller, D. (1990). *Women and social welfare: A feminist analysis.* New York: Praeger.

Minkler, M. (1991). Generational equity and the new victim blaming. In M. Minkler & C. Estes (Eds.), *Critical perspectives on aging: The political and moral economy of growing old* (pp. 67–80). New York: Baywood.

Montgomery, R., & Kamo, Y. (1989). Parent care by sons and daughters. In J. Mancini (Ed.), *Aging parents and adult children* (pp. 213–230). Lexington, MA: Lexington Books.

Moon, M. (1987a). The elderly's access to health care services: The crude and subtle impacts of Medicare changes. *Social Justice Research, 1,* 361–375.

Moon, M. (1987b). Increases in beneficiary burdens: Direct and indirect effects. In M. Pauly & W. Kissick (Eds.), *Lessons from the first twenty years of Medicare* (pp. 321–339). Philadelphia: University of Pennsylvania Press.

Myles, J. (1984). Conflict, crisis and the future of old age security. In M. Minkler & C. Estes (Eds.), *Readings in the political economy of aging* (pp. 168–176). New York: Baywood.

Myles, J. (1988). Decline or impasse? The current state of the welfare state. *Studies in Political Economy, 26,* 73–107. Boston: Little, Brown.

Neugarten, B. (1982). Policy for the 1980s: Age or need entitlement? In B. Neugarten (Ed.), *Age or need? Public policies for older people* (pp. 19–32). Newbury Park, CA: Sage.

Neuschler, E. (1987). *Medicaid eligibility for the elderly in need of long term care.* (Contract No. 86–26). Washington, DC: National Governor's Association, Congressional Research Service.

Olson, L. K. (1982). *The political economy of aging.* New York: Columbia University Press.

O'Rand, A., & Henretta, J. (1982). Delayed career entry, industrial pension structure and early retirement in a cohort of unmarried women. *American Sociological Review, 47,* 365–373.

Pascall, G. (1986). *Social policy: A feminist critique.* London: Tavistock.

Pauly, M. (1980). Introduction. In M. Pauly (Ed.), *National health insurance: What now? What later? What never?* Washington, DC: American Enterprise Institute for Public Policy Research.

Preston, S. (1984). Children and the elderly in the U.S. *Scientific American, 251,* 44–49.

Quadagno, J. (1984). Welfare capitalism and the Social Security Act of 1935. *American Sociological Review, 49,* 632–647.

Quadagno, J. (1987). Theories of the welfare state. *Annual Review of Sociology, 13,* 109–128.

Quadagno, J. (1988a). *The transformation of old age security.* Chicago: University of Chicago Press.

Quadagno, J. (1988b). Women's access to pensions and the structure of eligibility rules: Systems of production and reproduction. *Sociological Quarterly, 29,* 541–558.

Quadagno, J. (1990). Race, class and gender in the U.S. welfare state: Nixon's failed family assistance plan. *American Sociological Review, 55,* 11–28.

Quadagno, J. (1991). Interest-group politics and the future of U.S. Social Security. In J. Myles & J. Quadagno (Eds.), *States, labor markets and the future of old age policy* (pp. 36–58). Philadelphia: Temple University Press.

Quadagno, J., Harrington Meyer, M., & Turner, B. (1991). Falling into the Medicaid gap: The hidden long term care dilemma. *Gerontologist, 31,* 521–526.

Reskin, B., & Hartmann, H. (1986). *Women's work and men's work: Sex segregation on the job.* Washington, DC: National Academy of Sciences Press.

Scharlach, A., & Boyd, S. (1989). Caregiving and employment: Results of an employee survey. *Gerontologist, 29,* 382–387.

Shanas, E. (1979). The family as a support system in old age. *Gerontologist, 19*, 169–174.

Shaver, S. (1983). Sex and money in the welfare state. In C. Baldcock & B. Cass (Eds.), *Women, social welfare and the state in Australia* (pp. 146–163). Sydney: Allen & Unwin.

Spence, D., & Weiner, J., (1990). Estimating the extent of Medicaid spenddown in nursing homes. *Journal of Health Politics, Policy and Law, 15*, 607–626.

Social Security Administration. (1985). *1982 new beneficiary survey: Women and Social Security, 48*, 17–26. Washington DC: U.S. Department of Health and Human Services.

Social Security Administration. (1992). *Social Security bulletin annual statistical supplement.* Washington, DC: Health Care Financing Administration.

Social Security Administration. (1994). *Social Security bulletin annual statistical supplement.* Washington, DC: Health Care Financing Administration.

Stone, R., Cafferata, G., & Sangl, J. (1987). Caregivers of the frail elderly: A national profile. *Gerontologist, 27*, 616–626.

Tilly, J., & Brunner, D. (1987). *Medicaid eligibility and its effect on the elderly* (Publication #8605). Washington, DC: American Association of Retired Persons.

U.S. House Select Committee on Aging. (1985). *Twentieth anniversary of Medicare and Medicaid: Americans still at risk* (Publication No. 99–538). Washington, DC: U.S. Government Printing Office.

U.S. House Select Committee on Aging. (1986). *Out sooner and sicker: Myth or Medicare crisis?* (Publication No. 99–591). Washington, DC: U.S. Government Printing Office.

U.S. House Select Committee on Aging. (1988). *An assault on Medicare and Medicaid in the 1980s: The legacy of an administration* (Publication No. 100–679). Washington, DC: U.S. Government Printing Office.

U.S. Senate Select Committee on Aging. (1984). *The Supplemental Security Income program: A 10-year overview.* Washington, DC: U.S. Government Printing Office.

U.S. Senate Select Committee on Aging. (1988). *Developments in aging, 1987: Vol. 3, The long term care challenge.* Washington, DC: U.S. Government Printing Office.

Wallace, S. (1990). Race versus class in the health care of African American elderly. *Social Problems, 37*, 517–534.

Wallace, S., & Estes, C. (1991). Health policy for the elderly. In B. Hess & E. Markson (Eds.), *Growing old in America* (pp. 569–588). New Brunswick, NJ: Transaction.

14

Legal Issues and Family Involvement in Later-Life Families

Robbyn R. Wacker

Gerontologists investigate many different aspects of later-life families, such as the role of grandparents within the extended family, widowhood and social support networks, divorce and well-being, and declining health and the role of family caregivers. Although researchers tend to examine these issues using a social or psychological perspective, each issue potentially involves a number of legal concerns. For example, after the divorce of a child, the ex-son- or daughter-in-law might refuse to let the grandparents visit grandchildren; the government might deny retirement income benefits to a surviving or divorced spouse; and, when physical or mental capacity wanes, family members might seek a guardianship in order to make personal and financial decisions on behalf of their older impaired relatives. Furthermore, when older family members encounter various legal concerns or problems, adult children, spouses, and other kin are likely to be involved in some way. This chapter has four purposes: to demonstrate the importance of studying legal issues in later-life families; to identify various legal problems facing later-life families; to consider ways in which family members, particularly adult children, become involved when legal problems arise; and to identify topics for future research in law and aging.

THE IMPORTANCE OF STUDYING LEGAL PROBLEMS OF LATER-LIFE FAMILIES

Studying the different legal concerns of later-life families is timely in light of the rapid growth in the older population. Given that 13% of the population will be 65 or older at the turn of the century, with the percentage rising to 17.7% by the year 2020 (Spencer, 1989), a significant portion of the population may encounter legal concerns unique to later life. Indeed, evidence suggests that legal problems have an impact on large numbers of the current cohort of older adults, especially low-income seniors. In fiscal year 1989, $16.4 million of Title III funds were spent for legal services, benefiting approximately 305,000 older adults (U.S. Senate Special Committee on Aging, 1991b).

Legal problems might have a different impact on the lives of older adults when compared with the younger population who encounter similar issues. For example, adults of all ages can be victims of crime and consumer fraud. It can be argued, however, that the financial and social impact of such legal problems is most severe for older adults. For example, although older adults are less likely to be victims of crime than those in the general population, they are more likely to suffer serious injuries when assaulted (Covey & Menard, 1988; Lawton, Nahemow, Yaffe, & Feldman, 1976; O'Keefe & Reid-Nash, 1985), which severely limit any activities outside the home. Similarly, elderly victims of consumer fraud who are on a fixed or limited income might find the loss of income more financially devastating and irreplaceable (Malinchak & Wright, 1978) than do younger victims.

The likelihood of encountering legal difficulties increases as one enters later life and experiences the many role transitions contained within these stages. For example, in the transition from labor force participation to retirement, older adults must deal with the complexities and ever-changing regulations of government bureaucracies in order to receive Medicare, Social Security, and other benefits. Mistakes in reporting income and denial or termination of benefits become legal problems. The death of a spouse can result in problems with collecting pensions and other benefits and with administering the estate. Widowhood and the loss of a second income can create a number of potential legal problems, such as the inability to pay financial obligations and property taxes. For those older adults with diminished mental and physical health, the capacity to carry on personal and financial matters can become impaired. Such impairment necessitates execution of advanced directives or petitioning of a guardianship for financial matters or health care decision making by others. Finally, facing the prospect of dying and death, many older adults begin to contemplate and make known their preferences regarding life-sustaining procedures. Although these conditions are not exclusively unique to older adults, they are more likely to affect elderly persons than any other age group.

Finally, studying legal problems of later-life families can expand our understanding regarding the ways in which older family members receive assistance from kin when legal problems occur. Research in the last two decades has established that older adults do not exist separately and in isolation from their family members (see Suitor et al., this volume). The legal problems encountered by older adults are likely to occur in an intergenerational context, with some measure of support and assistance coming from family members. Studies of the caregiving activities provided to older adults substantiate the assistance of the family network in legal matters. Montgomery and Kamo (1989) and Stoller and Earl (1983) reported that caregiving sons and daughters provided assistance with banking and legal matters, and Cicirelli (1992) reported that middle-aged adult child caregivers, most often, sons, mediated activities in legal and financial matters and with government agencies. Scott (1983), in reporting support activities of siblings and other kin, found that a small percentage of grandchildren and siblings also provided legal assistance to older family members, as did brothers of widows in O'Bryant's research (1988).

Family members also are more directly involved in legal matters affecting older persons in their family. For example, family members participate in the process of obtaining guardianship of their parents (Wacker & Keith, 1992), informally serve as a substitute decision maker (Fowler, 1984; Kapp, 1987), or, in a less positive role, are accused of acts of elder abuse against their parents (Pillemer & Finkelhor, 1988). Therefore, based on the few studies conducted, evidence suggests that family members occupy different roles in situations involving either legal planning or action.

Although Cohen (1978) remarked in an editorial in *The Gerontologist* that "[t]here is a growing recognition among lawyers and more recently among gerontologists, that there are serious areas of inquiry and research in aging and law which address critical areas of social significance" (p. 229), few sociolegal studies involving the aged have been conducted. Further, the few existing studies have not addressed possible consequences of legal problems on familial relationships, the nature of the impact, or the role family members play when a legal concern arises.

CONCEPTUAL FRAMEWORK

I discuss the legal problems of later-life families by subdividing them into two broad categories based on the type of family involvement that is likely to occur within each of the different legal issues. The first category of legal issues directly involves immediate family members. Primary family involvement in legal problems requires active, long-term participation, usually by adult children, who play an important, significant, or influential role.

The second category of legal concerns incorporates secondary family involvement. These legal problems are characterized by short-term participation of family members as advisers or advocates. For example, adult children or siblings might offer advice on solving legal problems, serve as mediators, or act on behalf of older adults in seeking a resolution to a legal problem. Conversely, secondary family involvement also occurs when elderly parents inform their adult children of legal decisions that will require their children's involvement at some point in the future, such as administering an estate or supervising living will directives.

The distinction between primary and secondary family involvement in a legal matter is not in all cases static or clear-cut. Family members who start out simply as advisers might find that over time it is necessary to occupy a primary role in trying to resolve the issue. Nevertheless, certain differences in family involvement exist in the various legal problems faced by later-life families. The distinction between primary and secondary family involvement enables movement from a mere description of the legal problems to examination of legal issues from within a family context. Note, however, that much of the discussion about family involvement is hypothetical because of the dearth of studies on the role family members play when legal concerns arise. Framing the discussion of legal issues within the context of the family system points to new research directions that can fill some of the gaps in the legal gerontology literature.

LEGAL ISSUES HAVING PRIMARY FAMILY INVOLVEMENT

Two legal problems—grandparent visitation and substitute decision making—are examples of legal issues having primary family involvement. In these situations, immediate family members take a direct role in matters of determining and negotiating grandparent visitation rights and acting as substitute decision makers.

Grandparent Visitation

The makeup of the family unit has undergone important changes during this century. Individuals can now expect to live well into their seventh decade, and almost all older adults with children are grandparents (Brubaker, 1985). In addition, approximately half of all marriages end in divorce (Glick, 1984). These two factors combine to create a unique circumstance for older adults, their children, and grandchildren: divorce increases the possibility that intergenerational relations might be disrupted. Furthermore, other events, such as the death of a parent, the adoption of a grandchild by a relative or stranger, and the termination of parental rights, can place the relationship between grandparent and grandchild in jeopardy.

Grandparent visitation rights first appeared in court almost 100 years ago and established a legal precedent on both parental and grandparental rights and roles within the family. In 1894, the appellate court ruled in the case of *Succession of Reiss* that grandparent visitation was a moral, not a legal, obligation, and, as such, parents were not legally forced to allow such visitation (Wilhite, 1987). The common law developed throughout the years has held that parents have the right to determine the care, management, and companionships of their children, including contacts with grandparents (Burns, 1991). Without statutory law authorizing grandparent visitation, grandparents were often not successful in gaining access to their grandchildren.

In the last decade, however, the enactment of grandparent visitation statutes challenged the legal precedent that granted parents the sole decision regarding grandparent visitation. By 1991 all 50 states had such legislation (Burns, 1991), and they vary with regard to who can petition for visitation rights, the circumstances that must be present before the court grants visitation rights, and the application of the "best interests" standard for the grandchild (Wilhite, 1987). Divorce, separation, and death of the parent(s) are the most common circumstances that must be present in order for grandparents to petition for visitation rights (Burns, 1991). In other instances, such as the adoption of grandchildren by strangers, by other relatives, or by stepparents or children born out of wedlock, there is no uniformity of law among states (Burns, 1991). Presently, no states allow grandparents to petition for visitation rights when the children live in intact households.

The focus of research in this area has been on the patterns of interaction between grandparents and grandchildren following a divorce (Bray & Berger, 1990; Johnson, 1985). Only a few sociolegal studies regarding the number of grandparents who have been denied visitation rights or who use the courts to secure visitation rights have been conducted. English investigators have ascertained how many custodial or noncustodial parents have denied grandparents visitation with their grandchildren. For example, Kaganas and Piper (1990) reported that in spite of having laws allowing grandparents to petition for visitation rights, few English grandparents used the legal process that affords them access to their grandchildren. Lowe and Douglas (1989) surveyed 87 grandparents who were members of Grandparent Federation (a group concerned with advocating for grandparent rights in England) to examine the nature of the dispute regarding grandparent visitation and the actions taken. They reported that in private law disputes, the most often cited reasons given for the family dispute were divorce and death. Furthermore, the majority of grandparents sought only access to, rather than custody of, their grandchildren, and 12 of the 46 who were advised to take legal action chose not to do so. Reasons for not pursuing visitation rights were the inability to obtain legal aid, the cost of pursuing the action in court, and the wish to avoid making the family situation worse.

As adult children, parents, and in-laws renegotiate family roles after marital disruptions, family members clearly play a primary role in grandparent visitation. Seeking to establish grandparent visitation rights through the court might imply that the renegotiation of these roles has failed in some way. A number of questions, however, remain to be investigated. Why do some grandparents who are denied access to their grandchildren use the legal system while others do not? Is the relationship between the grandparent-grandchild altered in any way after visitation is awarded? Does the salience of the grandparent role within the family network predict which grandparents pursue access to grandchildren through the judicial system?

Substitute Decision Making

Perhaps one of the most difficult times for both older adults and their families comes when elders' physical and mental capacities decline to such an extent that activities of daily living are impaired. With such limitations come decreased autonomy and new forms of dependence, including the relinquishing of personal and financial decision making to significant others. As life expectancy increases, the potential need for substitute decision makers in later life also increases.

It is well established that individuals have the legal right to make autonomous decisions regarding all aspects of personal, health, and financial actions. The right to self-determination in health care, for example, is expressed in the doctrine of informed consent. Before health care professionals provide medical treatment, patients must be informed of the diagnosis, treatment options, and consequences, and the patients must then voluntarily agree to the proposed treatment. In the process of obtaining informed consent, patients must have the mental competency to understand the diagnosis and prognosis of the illness and treatments. Informed consent may not be given by anyone other than competent patients (see Kapp, 1987, for a review); when they are unable to give informed consent, family members play a primary role in acting as substitute decision makers on their behalf.

If an elderly person cannot give consent, customary practice and the law provide several methods of recognizing significant others as substitute decision makers. First, family members often step forward informally to assume responsibility for making decisions. A growing body of literature suggests that family members both influence and make decisions regarding the care of their relatives (Cicirelli, 1992; Keith, 1983). Health care professionals often rely on family members to assist in making health and personal care decisions without seeking a formal appointment by the court. Second, family members may be formally appointed as substitute decision makers in one of two ways. Older adults can execute legal documents that convey their wishes regarding financial, personal, and health care decisions. These documents, referred to as advanced directives, must be executed while one is still competent and remain valid in the event of incapacity. An example of advanced directives that place a family member in the primary role of a substitute decision maker includes a durable power of attorney and a durable power of attorney for health care. A person can also become a formally recognized substitute decision maker by being appointed as a guardian or conservator through a court. Such appointees become responsible for personal and financial decisions when the court determines the older adult is no longer competent to make decisions on his or her own behalf. Advanced directives and guardianships formalize the substitute decision-maker role within the family unit, and these individuals become actively involved in decisions regarding the personal, financial, and health care matters of older family members.

Durable Power of Attorney

A durable power of attorney allows the "principal" to designate an "agent" to act on his or her behalf, typically in financial matters, such as paying bills or managing other matters the principal designates (see Stiegel, Hurme, & Stone, 1991, for a complete discussion and state-by-state review). Unlike the generic power of attorney, which becomes invalid once the individual is incompetent, the durable power of attorney continues to be valid. The creation of a durable power of attorney does not require court intervention, and no automatic judicial oversight of the agent's activities occurs. All 50 states have statutes authorizing the use of a durable power of attorney (Stiegel et al., 1991).

When originally conceived, the durable power of attorney authorized financial decision making and did not specifically authorize the agent to make health care decisions. In many states, statutes are silent regarding the use of a durable power of attorney for health care decision making, but Stiegel et al. (1991) reported that legal opinion has authorized its use as such. A number of states have enacted legislation that specifically authorizes the use of durable power of attorney for health care decisions.

The number of older adults who have executed a durable power of attorney is unknown, but whites and those who are well educated are more likely than others to do so (Alexander, 1991). Anecdotal information suggests that family members are often called upon to become agents under powers of attorney. Empirical documentation is lacking on the number of older adults who use durable powers of attorney, as well as the duration and scope of the activities performed by family members under the auspices of this directive.

Guardianships and Conservatorships

All states have statutes under which an individual can obtain the legal authority to make personal or financial decisions on behalf of an allegedly incompetent individual, referred to as the ward. Although the terminology varies by state, in general, a guardianship authorizes an individual to make personal decisions for a ward such as determining the ward's residence, health care needs, and any other personal needs. In contrast, a conservatorship authorizes an individual to take care of financial matters such as administering real estate and financial accounts for a ward. The court can appoint a guardianship and a conservatorship simultaneously on behalf of an incompetent individual. These appointments can be temporary or permanent, limited or complete in scope. The individual desiring to become a guardian over another must file a petition with the appropriate court stating the reasons a guardianship or conservatorship (hereinafter referred to as guardianship) is needed, and she or he must present evidence proving that the potential ward is in fact incompetent and in need of a substitute decision maker.

The process of obtaining guardianships for elderly persons has been the subject of critical commentary and, more recently, the subject of empirical investigation (Bulcroft, Kielkopf, & Tripp, 1991; Iris, 1988; Keith & Wacker, 1993). Legal and academic scholars have criticized the guardianship process for its lack of adequate notice of the guardianship hearing, the informal and nonadversarial nature of the hearings, the absence of an objective standard of incapacity, the lack of adequate representation for the allegedly incompetent individual, the almost exclusive appointment of a plenary or full guardian, and the failure to oversee the guardian's activities. The concern about guardianships stems, in part, from the fact that the appointment of a guardian is the most restrictive substitute decision-making intervention that exists. The formal appointment of a guardian represents the loss of control and self-determination for the allegedly incompetent individual. For example, the ward automatically loses such personal freedoms as the right to marry, vote, or enter into a contract and is likely to lose the right to make financial and health care decisions.

Hidden from much of the discussion, however, are the guardians themselves. Sociolegal studies have provided information about guardians—who they are and what activities they perform. Empirical evidence revealed that guardians were most often adult children who were previously involved in caregiving activities before becoming guardians (Bulcroft et al., 1991; Keith & Wacker, in press). Furthermore, recent research by Keith and Wacker (in press) confirmed that family members play a primary role in the guardianship process. In their study of 387 guardians in Iowa, Missouri, and Colorado, family members were actively involved in the decision to seek a guardianship and in the selection of who among family members should be the guardian. In 81% of the cases, family members agreed that they should petition for a guardianship, and in 90%, they agreed about who should be appointed as guardian. Despite this high level of agreement, many guardians indicated they would have preferred more opportunities to talk over the problems of their ward with other family members. The study also showed that guardians were quite active in providing various forms of assistance to their wards, with the majority spending between two and seven hours per week providing care. They made personal visits, provided emotional support, filed forms, completed paperwork, and purchased personal items. In general, then, family members are highly involved in the decision to pursue guardianship, but the majority of caregiving activities are the responsibility of one legal caregiver.

Scholars can investigate many other aspects about guardianships of the elderly that remain unanswered. Researchers have called for more studies that examine the benefits older adults and their families obtain by having a guardianship (Hommel, 1992) and for the use of family and sociological theory to guide future guardianship studies (Bulcroft, 1992). We turn now to legal concerns of later-life families in which family members play a secondary role.

LEGAL ISSUES HAVING SECONDARY FAMILY INVOLVEMENT

Whereas the preceding examples illustrate direct involvement of family members in the legal affairs of their older relatives, other issues arise that involve family members less directly. In this secondary role, aged parents might inform adult children of a decision or an act that has taken place and the legal role they expect offspring to play in the future, as with a living will. Alternatively, family members might provide advice or information about the options available to resolve a legal problem, encourage aged persons to seek legal advice, or act as mediators and advocates with an agency. Legal problems of later-life families having secondary family involvement are wills, living wills, legal concerns associated with long-term care such as admissions agreements and residents' rights, government benefits, and consumer fraud.

Wills

The disposition of one's estate is both a legal and a social act reflecting the perception of equity and exchange between family members and significant others. Legally, the disposition of property upon death is governed by state law providing guidance for those who die with and without a will. When one dies intestate, or without having executed a will, state law directs the division of any property belonging to the estate. For example, a surviving spouse may inherit an entire estate or be entitled to only half of the estate, with the other half divided equally among any surviving children. In the absence of a surviving spouse, the court divides the estate among the surviving children or the deceased child's children. The probate of assets for an intestate estate can be complicated, time-consuming, and subject to conflicts among family members regarding the value and rightful ownership of the property. In contrast, a written will directs the appointment of a personal representative to administer the estate and directs the division of assets to beneficiaries according to the wishes of the deceased person. Designating the administrator of the estate and specifying division of property among beneficiaries reduce some of the potential conflict among family members.

How people divide their estate reflects a lifetime of attitudes and perceptions about past and present familial relationships, although contemporary inheritance patterns have received little attention by researchers. One recent study, however, by Tsuya and Martin (1992) investigated Japanese elderly's attitudes toward inheritance patterns. The results indicated that 21% of the respondents felt the inheritance should go to the eldest son, and 22% indicated that all children should share the inheritance equally, whereas 44% felt parental property should go to the family member who takes care of the parent. In addition, respondents living with married children, having low educational levels, and living in traditional agricultural areas were more likely to prefer that parental property go to the eldest son, reflecting a more traditional inheritance pattern.

How are family members involved in the process of making a will? One can only speculate that, in some instances, family members are merely recipients of the estate and are not consulted or informed of the decision to make a will or how to distribute the estate. Older adults might simply inform family members that a will exists and tell them of its whereabouts. In contrast, older adults might give family members the details regarding the disposition of property or seek their advice regarding how to distribute the property.

Drawing from the few contemporary studies on inheritance patterns, researchers can investigate a number of areas. These include identification of social and psychological barriers that influence the decision to execute a will, examination of how surviving family members negotiate the disposition of personal and real property contained in the estate when specific directions do not exist, and identification of the nature of the strategy used (e.g., familial equity) to justify the patterns of inheritance contained in the will among family members.

Living Wills

Living wills provide the legal mechanism enabling individuals, while still competent, to express their wishes regarding life-sustaining treatment. Living wills are quite narrow in scope because they authorize the withdrawal of certain life-sustaining procedures only in situations where the individual has a terminal illness or is comatose (Alexander, 1991). Forty-two states have passed living will statutes, and although these laws vary by state, they define medical conditions to which the statute applies, the types of life support systems, such as respirators and ventilators, that can be withdrawn, the procedures needed to execute or revoke a valid living will, and the obligations of physicians to comply with the request (Sabatino & Gottlich, 1991).

Much attention has been given to living wills through the media, due in part to the two well-known cases of Karen Quinlan and Nancy Cruzan (for case law see *In re Quinlan,* 355, A.2nd 647, *Cruzan v. Harmon,* 760 S.W. 2nd 408; see Moody, 1992, for a general discussion) and by health and social professionals, yet the number of older adults who have executed living wills remains low. In a study of 70 older veterans, Sugarman, Weinberger, and Samsa (1992) found that only 4% had executed living wills, although 57% had heard of living wills before they were interviewed for the study. Similarly, Gamble, McDonald, and Lichstein (1991), in their study of 75 older adults attending a congregate meal site, found that none of the research participants had signed a living will, and High (1988) reported that only 18% of elderly respondents had executed living wills. The small percentage of older adults who have signed a living will does not correspond to the percentage who have discussed their wishes with family members. Gamble et al. (1991) reported that even though no one in their sample had executed a living will, 45% had discussed their wishes regarding life-sustaining procedures with a family member. Due in part to the high numbers of older adults who verbally inform family members of their wishes, scholars assert that family members are best suited to become substitute decision makers in the absence of a living will and should have the authority to be appointed as such (High, 1988, 1991; Jecker, 1990; King, 1991). The Supreme Court, however, ruled in the Cruzan case that the family did not have the presumptive right to make decisions for incompetent family members without any preexisting directives (King, 1991). High (1991) postulated that this turn away from granting family members the surrogate decision-making role without a written directive is perpetuating a "second myth" about families. The first myth was that families abandon their elderly members (Shanas, 1979); the second assumes that family members are not capable of making decisions that are in the best interests of their relatives.

In response to the dilemma of whom to appoint as substitute decision makers in the absence of living wills, a few states have passed laws authorizing spouses, family members, and significant others to direct medical care for incapacitated persons whose wishes are unknown. At least 14 states have enacted such legislation identifying substitute decision makers in order of priority (Vignery, 1989).

Processes surrounding the discussion and creation of living wills are probably similar to the ways families handle the disposition of personal property. As the empirical evidence suggests, older adults appear to be more comfortable simply informing family members of their wishes, should they ever need life-sustaining treatment, than executing formal documents. But whether wishes about life-sustaining treatment are formally or informally conveyed, family members will be counted on at a later date to ensure that these wishes are carried out.

Admissions Agreements and Resident's Rights

Whereas 5% of older adults reside in long-term care facilities at any one time (approximately 1.5 million persons), 43% of adults aged 65 or older can expect to stay in a long-term care facility at least once in their lives (Murtaugh, Kemper, & Spillman, 1990). Families go to great lengths to keep an elderly member from entering a nursing home, and the decision to relinquish caregiving activities to a long-term care facility is a difficult one (Brody, 1978; Smallegan, 1985). Because of the salience of emotional and, possibly, financial issues surrounding admission to a long-term care facility, the older adult and his or her family might overlook the importance of understanding the provisions of the admissions agreement.

A handful of studies evaluating the legality of provisions contained in nursing home admissions agreements has appeared in the last 10 years (e.g., Ambrogi & Leonard, 1988; Wacker, 1985; see Ambrogi, 1990, for a list of states that have reviewed long-term care agreements). The results of these studies pointed to numerous illegalities and problems. First, many admissions agreements did not disclose detailed information regarding the basic services provided and the costs of those services or the costs of extra services. Second, in some cases, admission was contingent on obtaining a signature of a responsible party. Although this requirement is illegal in any facility participating in the Medicare and Medicaid programs (Ambrogi, 1990), many family members willingly agree to become responsible parties. Signing as responsible parties or guarantors could make the signers legally responsible for any financial liabilities of the resident. Third, some admissions agreements required the applicant to remain a private-pay resident for a certain length of time before becoming a Medicaid resident. Such a provision can cause undue financial stress on older adults who, if unable to remain private-pay, would have to be discharged or rely on family members to pay the cost of care. Fourth, many of the contracts contained illegal or questionable clauses that, in effect, waived the facility from any liability for personal injury or property damage. Finally, some of the contracts contained reasons for discharge or transfer that the courts may not find permissible under the law.

When these illegalities are discovered, family members may be called upon to advocate for, or negotiate, a resolution to the problem because many older adults entering long-term care facilities have multiple physical and mental impairments that limit their ability to fully comprehend the admissions agreement. Unfortunately, if problems do occur with the provisions set forth under an admissions agreement, many older adults and their family members are unaware that they might have valid legal challenges to those contracts. Once admitted to a long-term care facility, older adults and families will find that there are a number of federal and state laws governing the operations of long-term care facilities, and these laws are designed to protect the rights of the resident and promote a high standard of care. Under the most recent nursing home reform law enacted by Congress in 1987, the Omnibus Reconciliation Act, nursing homes must provide care and services to residents in such a way that the facilities promote and maintain residents' physical, social, and mental well-being (Eldeman, 1990). The new law retained and expanded many of the previous laws governing residents' rights that protect quality of physical care provided, matters of privacy and confidentiality, and issues of self-determination (see Strauss, Wolf, & Schilling, 1990, for an in-depth review). In addition, federal and state laws prohibit facilities from discriminating against Medicaid residents in the type of care provided, transferring or discharging residents once they are no longer private-pay clients, and refusing to admit Medicaid residents (Strauss et al., 1990).

Family members and residents must deal with the possible consequences of discrimination, and a number of remedies can be pursued. Family members or residents who believe there has been a violation can file a grievance through the facility, send a report to the long-term care ombudsman and/ or the state agency that conducts the inspection, and seek legal recourse through the courts. Of course, many barriers prohibit the filing of complaints, including the unwillingness or inability to tackle a complicated and time-consuming grievance process, fear of reprisal, or belief that the situation will not change. Family members, no doubt, play an important role in ensuring the rights of their family members once they are residing in long-term care facilities. Many residents of long-term care facilities are visited regularly by family members. In one study, the average number of visits by family in a one-month period was twelve (York & Caslyn, 1977). Family members who visit regularly are in a position to observe improprieties. Indeed, family members are most often the ones who file grievances with long-term care ombudsmen (V. Fraser, personal communication, January 13, 1993). To what extent family members are involved in filing grievances and the impact such discrimination has on families remain to be investigated.

Government Benefits

Ninety percent or 40 million of older adults receive some income from Social Security, and approximately 4.7 million receive income from Supplemental Security Income (Grad, 1990; U.S. Senate Special Committee on Aging, 1991b). For many of these older adults, applying for, and receiving, these benefits can result in a number of legal problems.

Considering the complex and complicated regulations that govern the administration of these programs, it is not surprising that a number of legal problems can arise. First, individuals are ineligible for Social Security and Supplemental Security Income benefits for many reasons, including the lack of proof regarding age, marital status or work history, and failure to meet Social Security's definition of disability. Furthermore, eligibility requirements for Supplemental Security Income (SSI) benefits are that the recipient must be aged, blind or disabled, and have a financial need. Social Security will terminate SSI benefits if a recipient's income or asset level exceeds predesignated amounts.

Statistics indicate that many older adults do encounter problems in collecting benefits under both Social Security and SSI. For example, during March 1981 and June 1983, under orders from the Reagan administration to reexamine current Social Security disability beneficiaries, the Social Security Administration (SSA) reviewed 1.13 million recipients' cases, and approximately 50% of these reviews resulted in the termination of benefits (U.S. Senate Special Committee on Aging, 1984). Only half the beneficiaries appealed the termination decision, but of those who appealed, 67% were reinstated to the program. In 1987 and 1988, over 185,000 SSI recipients had their benefits eliminated because of their failure to respond to requests for information concerning eligibility status, and a review of these cases revealed that SSA improperly terminated the eligibility of many recipients (U.S. Senate Special Committee on Aging, 1991b).

Overpayment of benefits is another common problem experienced by Social Security and Supplemental Security Income beneficiaries. Such errors can occur either because of a mistake in computing the amount of payment due to beneficiaries by Social Security staff or because of inaccuracy in reporting earned income by beneficiaries. Because many older adults receive benefits from more than one income program, each having different reporting requirements, an overpayment can result when beneficiaries fail to report changes to both agencies. Regardless of who is at fault for the overpayment, the Social Security Administration is authorized to recoup the amount determined to be paid in error unless the beneficiary can prove that collecting the overpayment would cause an undue hardship. Overpayments are quite frequent; one source estimated that in one year 2 million Social Security or Supplemental Security Income recipients received overpayment notices (Legal Services Corporation, 1981). Given that 14% of older adults depend on Social Security as their sole or major source of income, and individuals who receive SSI have annual incomes of less than $4,884 (Grad, 1990; U.S. Special Committee on Aging, 1991b), any reduction, termination, or denial of benefits could be financially devastating.

It is likely that many older adults do not appeal adverse decisions regarding their benefits either because they are intimidated by the bureaucracy or because they do not understand how the appeal process works or that an appeal is possible. When they do appeal such decisions, they typically turn to family members for assistance. Research on caregiving activities indicates that family members mediate with agencies to secure services on behalf of their older family members (e.g., Stone, Cafferata, & Sangl,

1987). Family members are likely to play a key role in resolving the eligibility or overpayment problem by intervening to provide missing information, clarifying income status, filling out appeal forms, or finding legal assistance in challenging the adverse decision.

Consumer Fraud

According to a report presented to the U.S. House Select Committee on Aging (1986), older adults constitute approximately 60% of all health-related fraud victims and 30% of all white-collar crime victims. Older adults are more likely than others to be victims of consumer fraud for a variety of reasons. First, physical frailty or mental impairments might leave older adults at a disadvantage when dealing with persistent salespersons. Second, elderly homebound persons might appreciate opportunities to shop at home as well as the company of friendly salespersons. Third, older adults with low incomes are especially susceptible to specious opportunities to increase their incomes, take advantage of promised low prices, or send away for prize money. Consumer fraud against elderly persons is particularly widespread in the areas of health care, home repairs, and mail fraud. Family members are apt to be involved in pursuing legal remedies to such fraud.

Health Care

Older adults spend more money on health care than any other age group. They have more visits to physicians and hospitals and use twice as many prescription drugs compared with younger adults (U.S. Senate Special Committee on Aging, 1991a). Out-of-pocket spending by older adults on health care averaged $1,540 in 1987 (Waldo, Sonnefeld, McKusick, & Arnett, 1989). Although Medicare pays for some health care costs, many older adults purchase supplemental health care coverage through what are commonly known as Medigap policies. Approximately three out of four older adults have purchased Medigap policies and pay an average of $600 per month on premiums (U.S. House of Representative Select Committee on Aging, 1986). Medigap insurance coverage provides an important supplement to cover health care expenses, but abuses have occurred in the selling of such policies. Concerns about the high costs of health care and declines in physical health make older adults vulnerable targets of fraudulent sales tactics. For example, some buy multiple policies because they believe that more polices will provide greater coverage. One elderly woman had purchased 28 policies, including 4 from one company alone (U.S. House of Representative Select Committee on Aging, 1986). Insurance companies will not pay duplicate claims; therefore, having more than one policy is worthless. Other fraudulent sales tactics include the unnecessary replacement of existing policies, falsification of applications, misrepresentation of policy coverage, and forgery. Many states have enacted protective legislation requiring full disclosure of coverage, an explanation of coverage in relation to Medicare, and an indication that insurers have evaluated the appropriateness and nonduplicative nature of the policy (U.S. House of Representative Select Committee on Aging, 1986). Most states provide legal recourse through state insurance commissioners and consumer fraud statutes.

Home Repair

The majority of older adults have lived in their own homes more than 20 years (Atchley, 1991). Forty-three percent of the homes owned by those 65 years of age and older were built before 1950, and 15% were built before 1920; 1.3 million housing units with persons aged 65 or older as householders had flaws in the plumbing, kitchen, physical structure, common areas, heating, or electrical systems (U.S. Bureau of Census, 1989). No doubt many of these homes are in need of repair. Although many older adults rely on family members or volunteer agencies to assist with home repairs, others hire private companies to do the work.

Problems can occur when workers make unnecessary repairs, when workers receive payment but never complete the work, or when workers make only superficial repairs, leaving the original problem intact. One widowed woman, aged 84, was in the process of paying $50,000 to have a leaky toilet fixed, although the actual repair cost was estimated to be $150 ("Widow," 1984). Home repair frauds are difficult to prosecute as those responsible move from town to town and are difficult to apprehend.

Mail Fraud

Because of their eagerness to increase their incomes, older adults who live near or below the poverty level may be easy targets of mail fraud schemes that offer phony business opportunities or money-making schemes. In these schemes, fraudulent businesses tell older consumers to invest start-up monies to buy the materials needed to make the goods that the business promises to purchase. The finished products are never bought, and the money invested is never returned (U.S. Senate Special Committee on Aging, 1987).

Clearly, consumer fraud of all kinds affects the most vulnerable of the aged, particularly those with limited economic, physical, or mental capacities. Because victims of these schemes often do not report incidents of consumer fraud, perhaps due to embarrassment or lack of knowledge about reporting mechanisms, the number of elderly victims of consumer fraud is unknown. Anecdotal evidence suggests, however, that family members and bank personnel are often the ones who discover the fraud and intervene to remedy the situation.

DIRECTIONS FOR FUTURE RESEARCH

This chapter highlighted some of the legal problems facing later-life families by using family involvement as the organizing framework and to propose some direction for future research. Although there is a great deal written by legal scholars about the types of legal problems older adults encounter, it is nevertheless apparent by the lack of sociolegal studies that numerous possibilities for future research exist. Indeed, sociolegal issues of later-life families remain one of the most unexplored topics in the field of gerontology. Suggestions for future areas of inquiry follow.

First, it is necessary to build a knowledge base about the legal problems of older adults. Investigators could begin by identifying how many older adults experience the legal problems discussed in this chapter, as well as other legal concerns in areas of employment and housing. Included in this knowledge base should be information regarding the utilization of legal assistance by older adults when a legal problem arises. Specifically, problems of access and utilization might occur because older adults do not know what legal rights they have in a given situation; they might be uncomfortable using the legal system as a way to resolve problems; they might wish to avoid the embarrassment of admitting that they have a legal problem; or they might not recognize their problem as a legal problem for which they have a right to legal redress (Edelstein, 1990). Furthermore, researchers must use heterogeneous samples of older adults to identify different patterns of legal problems and to identify variables that differentially influence access and utilization of legal assistance according to race, ethnicity, social class, rural/urban residence, and gender. In addition, scholars should identify the impact legal problems have on the financial, emotional, and social well-being of the older adult and the immediate family. Finally, researchers should begin to identify the precise role family members play when legal concerns arise. The caregiving literature provides us with a hint of evidence that family members do assist with legal decision making, yet this information is limited to the activities of frail elders and their caregivers. Many questions remain unanswered. How do family members assist in legal matters before they assume a caregiver role? How does such assistance differ for selected family members when a spouse is available to provide assistance compared with those who are single? Do peers such as friends and siblings play a more important role than adult children in providing advice, given that they might experience similar problems?

Second, once researchers gather descriptive information about the legal problems of older adults, they must develop empirical studies grounded in appropriate theoretical perspectives. For example, research using equity or exchange theory might lead to a better understanding of family network process, including how estates are divided among family members or how an adult child is selected to be a substitute decision maker. Using the functionalist perspective, one might examine whether families seek a guardianship of older members in order to facilitate a smooth transition of decision-making power to others in the family, thereby reducing any dysfunction with regard to who makes what decisions within the family unit. In contrast, using conflict theory might lead to an examination of power and control issues within the family. Perhaps guardianships are sought in order to control the resources of an older adult who no longer has the power needed within the family unit to maintain that control.

Third, numerous sociolegal issues exist on a macrolevel that researchers could examine. For example using the age-stratification model (Riley, 1977), one can examine how statutory laws deal with older adults compared with persons in other age groups. Many laws are age-based, including those that specify who can vote, hold office, obtain a driver's license, or consume alcoholic beverages. Under many laws elderly individuals as a subgroup are recipients of certain benefits and are seen as being in need of special protections. For example, some states have more severe penalties for those convicted of criminal acts and consumer fraud against aged adults than for those perpetrating such crimes against younger individuals (Schaffner & McCaffrey, 1990). Moreover, older adults might be eligible to receive special property or income tax allowances, and they might qualify for home equity conversion, whereas younger adults cannot participate in such programs. Laws protect elderly people from financial and physical abuse apart from the protection afforded the general population. Implied in many of these laws is the assumption that certain economic and physical conditions are normative and expected in later life (e.g., financial problems, frailty, and vulnerability), thereby justifying the existence of such distinctions based on age. As Kapp (1990) pointed out, older adults have two images under the law, which deems them, on one hand, as physically and financially vulnerable and therefore in need of special protections and, on the other hand, as independent and in need of protection against external interference. The question of whether the law *should* create special protections for older adults and what benefits or disadvantages older adults experience as a result of their differential treatment needs to be explored. Indeed, this question is timely in an era in which programs for older adults are being challenged by those who espouse generational equity.

Researchers can also apply various theoretical perspectives as another means of examining the enactment and impact of elder laws. Parsons (1980) suggested that the legal system acts as a mechanism of social control, and laws themselves are concerns, patterns, and norms applied to the acts and roles of individuals. As such, how do laws affecting elderly citizens also regulate their behavior and maintain the functioning of society and/or the family?

Use of conflict theory can offer additional insights into the legal problems of older adults. Perhaps many of the legal issues outlined in this chapter affect older adults and certain subpopulations of older adults more often than other age groups because older adults as a whole occupy a less powerful position in society than younger adults. According to Turk (1980), effectively defending an individual's legal rights is contingent on the control of legal resources, and the most powerful members of society are able to secure these legal resources. Frail older adults, those with low incomes, and those living in institutions cannot easily access the legal resources needed to protect their rights. No doubt other social and psychological theoretical perspectives could be employed to examine a wide variety of legal issues of concern to later-life families.

Finally, greater attention to the application of laws concerning older adults is needed. Such research could compare what the law is designed to accomplish in theory with the actual outcome of such a law. By identifying the disparity between the stated purpose of the law and the outcome, such information could serve as an impetus for changing the law or the procedure. Recent research on guardianships of elderly wards serves as an example of such research. Under guardianship law, individuals are entitled to be represented by an attorney, to be present at the hearing, and to cross-examine witnesses, yet empirical research demonstrated that, in practice, those rights were not being transferred to actual cases. This flurry of research and criticism by scholars has served as a basis for change in both the procedural and substantive guardianship laws. Applied social science research could examine the legal procedures regarding protective service, elder abuse, and grandparent visitation laws.

In closing, my goal was to describe a few of the legal problems encountered by older adults and their families. It should be readily apparent that a dearth of relevant empirical literature exists. Indeed, gerontologists, practicing attorneys, legal scholars, and older adults and their families can all benefit from increased empirical activity in the area of elder law.

NOTE

I wish to thank Victoria H. Bedford and Rosemary Blieszner for helpful criticisms of earlier drafts. Responsibility for content, however, remains solely with me.

REFERENCES

Alexander, G. J. (1991). Time for a new law on health care advanced directives. *The Hastings Law Journal, 42,* 755–778.

Ambrogi, D. M. (1990). Legal issues in nursing home admissions. *Law, Medicine and Health Care, 18,* 254–262.

Ambrogi, D. M., & Leonard, F. (1988). *Nursing home admission agreements: State studies, national recommendations.* San Francisco: California Law Center on Long Term Care.

Atchley, R. C. (1991). *Social forces and aging.* Belmont, CA: Wadsworth.

Bray, J. H., & Berger, S. H. (1990). Noncustodial father and paternal grandparent relationships in stepfamilies. *Family Relations, 39,* 414–419.

Brody, E. (1978). The aging of the family. *Annals of the American Academy of Political and Social Sciences, 438,* 13–27.

Brubaker, T. H. (1985). *Later life families.* Beverly Hills, CA: Sage.

Bulcroft, K. (1992, November). *Outcomes of legal guardianship for the elderly.* Paper presented at the 45th Annual Scientific Meeting of the Gerontological Society of America, Washington, DC.

Bulcroft, K., Kielkopf, M. R., & Tripp, K. (1991). Elderly wards and their legal guardians: Analysis of county probate records in Ohio and Washington. *Gerontologist, 31,* 156–164.

Burns, E. M. (1991). Grandparent visitation rights: Is it time for the pendulum to fall? *Family Law Quarterly, 25,* 60–81.

Cicirelli, V. G. (1992). *Family caregiving: Autonomous and paternalistic decision making.* Beverly Hills, CA: Sage.

Cohen, E. S. (1978). Editorial: Law and aging, lawyers and gerontologist. *Gerontologist, 18,* 229.

Covey, H. C., & Menard, S. (1988). Trends in elderly criminal victimization from 1973 to 1984. *Research on Aging, 10,* 329–341.

Eldeman, T. S. (1990). The nursing home reform law: Issues for litigation. *Clearinghouse Review. 24,* 545–550.

Edelstein, S. (1990). *Legal issues and resources: A guide for Area Agencies on Aging.* Washington, DC: American Bar Association Commission on Legal Problems of the Elderly.

Fowler, M. (1984). Appointing an agent to make medical treatment choices. *Columbia Law Review, 88,* 985–998.

Gamble, E. R., McDonald, P. J., & Lichstein, P. R. (1991). Knowledge, attitudes, and behavior of elderly persons regarding living wills. *Archives of Internal Medicine, 151,* 277–280.

Glick, P. (1984). Marriage, divorce, and living arrangements: Prospective changes. *Journal of Family Issues, 5,* 7–26.

Grad, S. (1990). *Income of the population 55 or over, 1988.* Pub. no. 13-11871, June 1990. Washington, DC: Social Security Administration.

High, D. M. (1988). All in the family: Extended autonomy and expectations in surrogate health care decision making. *Gerontologist, 28, Supplement,* 46–52.

High, D. M. (1991). A new myth about families of older persons? *Gerontologist, 31,* 611–618.

Hommel, P. A. (1992, November). *Resorting to guardianship: A study of the use of alternatives to guardianship by petitioners.* Paper presented at the 45th Annual Scientific Meeting of the Gerontological Society of America, Washington, DC.

Iris, M. A. (1988). Guardianship of the elderly: A multi-perspective view of the decision-making process. *Gerontologist, 28, Supplement,* 39–45.

Jecker, N. S. (1990). The role of intimate others in medical decision making. *Gerontologist, 30,* 65–71.

Johnson, C. (1985). Grandparenting options in divorcing families: An anthropological perspective. In V. Bengston & J. F. Robertson (Eds.), *Grandparenthood* (pp. 81–96). Beverly Hills, CA: Sage.

Kaganas, F., & Piper, C. (1990). Grandparents and the limits of the law. *International Journal of Law and the Family, 4,* 27–51.

Kapp, M. B. (1987). *Preventing malpractice in long term care: Strategies for risk management.* New York: Springer.

Kapp, M. B. (1990). Law and aging: Special persons, special treatment? *Law, Medicine and Health Care, 18,* 290–292.

Keith, P. M. (1983). Patterns of assistance among parents and the childless in very old age: Implications for practice. *Journal of Gerontological Social Work, 6,* 49–59.

Keith, P. M., & Wacker, R. R. (1993). Implementation of recommended guardianship practices and outcomes of hearings for older persons. *Gerontologist, 33,* 81–87.

Keith, P. M., & Wacker, R. R. (in press). *Older wards and their guardians.* New York: Praeger.

King, P. A. (1991). The authority of families to make medical decisions for incompetent patients after the *Cruzan* decision. *Law, Medicine and Health Care, 19,* 76–79.

Lawton, M. P., Nahemow, L., Yaffe, S., & Feldman, S. (1976). Psychological aspects of crime and fear of crime. In J. Goldsmith & S. S. Goldsmith (Eds.), *Crime and the elderly* (pp. 21–29). Lexington, MA: Lexington Books.

Legal Services Corporation. (1981). Fact sheet: *Legal problems of the elderly.* Washington, DC: Legal Services Corporation.

Lowe, N., & Douglas, G. (1989). The grandparent–grandchild relationship in English law. In J. Eekelaar & D. Pearl (Eds.), *An aging world: Dilemmas and challenges for law and social policy* (pp. 755–774). Oxford: Clarendon Press.

Malinchak, A. A., & Wright, D. (1978). Older Americans and crime: The scope of elderly crime victims. *Aging, 281,* 10–16.

Montgomery, R.V.J., & Kamo, Y. (1989). Parent care by sons and daughters. In J. A. Mancini (Ed.), *Aging parents and adult children* (pp. 213–230). Lexington, MA: Lexington Books.

Moody, H. R. (1992). *Ethics in an aging society.* Baltimore, MD: Johns Hopkins University Press.

Murtaugh, C., Kemper, P., & Spillman, B. (1990). The risk of nursing home use in later life. *Medical Care, 28,* 952–962.

O'Bryant, S. L. (1988). Sibling support and older widows' well-being. *Journal of Marriage and the Family, 50,* 173–183.

O'Keefe, G. J., & Reid-Nash, K. (1985, November). *Fear of crime and crime prevention competence among the elderly.* Paper presented at the Annual Convention of the American Psychological Association, Los Angeles.

Parsons, T. (1980). The law and social control. In W. M. Evans (Ed.), *The sociology of law.* New York: Free Press.

Pillemer, K., & Finkelhor, D. (1988), The prevalence of elder abuse: A random sample survey. *Gerontologist, 28, 51–57.*

Riley, M. W. (1977). Age strata in social systems. In R. H. Binstock & E. Shanas (Eds.), *Handbook of aging and the social sciences.* New York: Van Nostrand Reinhold.

Sabatino, C. P., & Gottlich, V. (1991). Seeking self-determination in the Patient Self-Determination Act. *Clearinghouse Review, 25, 639–647.*

Schaffner, A., & McCaffrey, J. W. (1990). Financial exploitation of the elderly. *Loyola Consumer Law Report, 2, 32–39.*

Scott, J. P. (1983). Siblings and other kin. In T. Brubaker (Ed.), *Family relationships in late life.* (pp. 47–62). Newbury Park, CA: Sage.

Shanas, E. (1979). The family as a social support system in old age. *Gerontologist, 19, 169–174.*

Smallegan, M. (1985). There was nothing else to do: Needs for care before nursing home admission. *Gerontologist, 25, 364–369.*

Spencer, G. (1989). Projections of the population of the United States, by age, sex and race: 1988 to 2080. *Current Populations Reports Series,* P-25, No. 1018. Washington, DC: U.S. Bureau of the Census.

Stiegel, L. A., Hurme, S. B., & Stone, M. (1991). Durable powers of attorney: An analysis of state statutes. *Clearinghouse Review, 25, 690–707.*

Stoller, E. P., & Earl, L. L. (1983). Help with activities of daily living: Sources of social support for the noninstitutionalized elderly. *Gerontologist, 23, 64–70.*

Stone, R., Cafferata, G. L., & Sangl, J. (1987). Caregivers of the frail elderly: A national profile. *Gerontologist, 27, 616–626.*

Strauss, P. J., Wolf, R., & Shilling, D. (1990). *Aging and the law.* Chicago: Commerce Clearing House.

Sugarman, J., Weinberger, M., & Samsa, G. (1992). Factors associated with veterans' decisions about living wills. *Archives of Internal Medicine, 152, 343–347.*

Tsuya, N. O., & Martin, L. G. (1992). Living arrangements of elderly Japanese and attitudes toward inheritance. *Journal of Gerontology: Social Sciences, 47, S45–54.*

Turk, A. T. (1980). Law as a weapon in social conflict. In W. M. Evans (Ed.), *The sociology of law* (pp. 105–120). New York: Free Press.

U.S. Bureau of the Census & U.S. Department of Housing & Urban Development. (1989, December). American housing survey for the United States in 1987. *Current Housing Reports,* series H-150-87. Washington, DC: U.S. Government Printing Office.

U.S. House of Representatives, Select Committee on Aging. (1986). *Catastrophic health insurance: The medigap crisis.* Pub. No. 99-587. Washington, DC: U.S. Government Printing Office.

U.S. Senate, Special Committee on Aging. (1984). *Discrimination against the poor and disabled in nursing homes.* Washington, DC: U.S. Government Printing Office.

U.S. Senate, Special Committee on Aging. (1987). *Direct mail solicitations to the elderly.* Pub. No. 100–633. Washington, DC: U.S. Government Printing Office.

U.S. Senate, Special Committee on Aging. (1991a). *Aging America: Trends and projections* (1991 edition). Washington, DC: U.S. Department of Health and Human Services.

U.S. Senate, Special Committee on Aging. (1991b). *Developments in aging: 1990* (Vol. 1). Washington, DC: U.S. Government Printing Office.

Vignery, B. (1989). Legislative trends in nonjudicial surrogate health care decision making. *Clearinghouse Review, 23,* 422–425.

Wacker, R. R. (1985). *Long term care admission agreements in Colorado: A review.* Denver: Advocacy Assistance Program.

Wacker, R. R., & Keith, P. M. (1992). *Who comforts the comforters? Older wards and their guardians.* Paper presented at meetings of the Midwest Sociological Society, Kansas City, MO.

Waldo, D. R., Sonnefeld, D. R., McKusick, D. R., & Arnett, R. H. III. (1989). Health expenditures by age group, 1977 and 1987 [Special issue]. *Health Care Financing Review, 10* (4).

Widow, 84, almost pays firm $50,000 to fix leaky toilet. (1984, September 13). *Des Moines Register,* p. 15A.

Wilhite, M. (1987). Children, parents and grandparents: Balancing the rights of association and control. *American Journal of Family Law, 1,* 473–489.

York, J. L., & Caslyn, R. J. (1977). Family involvement in nursing homes. *Gerontologist, 17,* 500–505.

15

Cultural Diversity in the Late-Life Family

Colleen L. Johnson

Beyond research on racial variations, the study of broader cultural diversity in the late-life family is in a preliminary stage. In fact, social gerontology has developed in the United States without consistent attention to ethnic groups (Manuel, 1982; McNeely & Colen, 1983). With the exception of a chapter on race and ethnicity (Markides, Liang, & Jackson, 1990), the most recent *Handbook on Aging and the Social Sciences* (Binstock & George, 1990) included only a few passing references to ethnic variations among older people. Moreover, in their introduction to a recent collection of articles on ethnicity and aging (Gelfand & Barresi, 1987), the editors did not include the family as one of their primary interests. Such a situation occurs at a time when ethnogerontology is espoused as a new field in aging research (Jackson & Ensley, 1990–1991) and when it is commonly recognized that ethnic group membership, whether racial or immigrant groups, exerts far-reaching effects on health, socioeconomic status, family life, and social supports (Blau, Oser, & Stephens, 1979). Consequently, students of this subject must conclude that investigations on cultural diversity have not kept pace with other areas of aging research (Usui, 1989).

Four explanations can account for this gap in aging research. First, as Markides and his colleagues (1990) pointed out, the almost exclusive attention given to disadvantaged and minority older people has taken place at the expense of examining the aging process in other American ethnic groups. In agreement, Holzberg (1982) stressed the importance of dissociating ethnic characteristics from the imperatives of social class because, irrespective of their social position, the ethnic group may function as an integrative force and a compensatory buffer that facilitates adaptation of its elderly members. Consequently, it is productive to study such adaptive elements in various cultural backgrounds that are not necessarily related to poverty and racism. In fact, a widespread interest in the double- or triple-jeopardy hypotheses persists, even though there is little empirical support for its propositions (Dowd & Bengtson, 1978; Cantor, 1979; Gratton, 1987; Jackson & Ensley, 1990–1991; Markides, 1983). This emphasis on a jeopardy, arising when social class, minority status, and aging intersect, occurs at the same time there are few empirical studies of ethnic groups other than blacks and Hispanics (Cohler & Lieberman, 1979).

Second, the processes of assimilation and acculturation that entail taking on the characteristics of the dominant group have long dominated the conceptual approaches to ethnicity. In an opposing view, Michael Novak's book *The Rise of the Unmeltable Ethnics* (1972) describes how European Catholic groups have staked their claims as bona fide ethnics, rejecting the stance taken by some sociologists that they had blended into a general working class. The processes of assimilation and acculturation, consequently, have not been a linear progression from being ethnic to becoming Americans. Ethnicity continues to be an emergent phenomenon that is dynamic and ever-changing (Yancy, Erickson, & Juliani, 1976). For example, cultural pluralism has occurred, such as with Irish Americans, where individuals retain some elements of their ethnic background at the same time that they move into the mainstream of American society (Kennedy, 1973).

Third, the study of diversity also is impeded, because the concept of *ethnicity* as an alternate to *minority* eludes consensus on a precise definition and a relevant theoretical framework. As Irving Howe (1977) commented, "No one quite knows what ethnicity means. That's why it is a very useful term" (p. 68). Others have referred to it as a murky subject (Greeley, 1974), an obscure emotional force (Freud, cited in Erikson, 1976), or "a search for primordial affinities and attachments, a massive tribalization" (Isaacs, 1975, p. 30). Objective criteria for identifying members of an ethnic group are through selective trait indexing, an approach that seeks commonalities such as language, food preferences, and rituals. Compilers of the *Harvard Encyclopedia of American Ethnic Groups* (Thernstrom, Orlov, & Handlin, 1980), however, contended that the concept of ethnicity must be pragmatic and focused on specific analytic problems. In exploring cultural diversity in the late-life family, factors of particular interest are the supportive capacities of ethnic families and values that promote attachment and affiliation (Driedger & Chappell, 1987).

Fourth, methodological problems also are apparent in the study of ethnic diversity in America. Even though the subtleties of ethnic behaviors evident on a daily basis are more amenable to study by qualitative ethnographic approaches, the gerontological literature is dominated by survey research and multivariate statistical analyses (Bastida, 1987). Investigators typically use socioeconomic status, race, and ethnicity as independent variables, a practice that obscures their significance. As a result, such practices marginalize important points of differentiation by making them merely historical or residual categories (Holzberg, 1982).

This neglect comes at a time when demographers predict that the numbers of ethnic elderly will increase in the future because of increased longevity and the recent waves of immigration (Manton, 1990). In 1900, one-third of the population in the United States were foreign-born, most of whom were European Catholics and Jews. The survivors from this group constitute a large proportion of the older population today. Although the proportion of foreign-born people had decreased to 6% by 1980, the large number of immigrants during the 1980s will gradually increase their numbers. In 1980, 84% of the nonwhite elderly were African Americans. If future elderly in ethnic groups have higher life expectancy in old age, as has been found among blacks, then these numbers will increase even more. In fact, there were 885,000 Hispanic elderly in 1985, with a fourfold increase in these numbers predicted in the future (Gelfand & Yee, 1991; Manton, 1990).

Ethnicity as a cultural category provides a lens through which individuals experience, define, and interpret their world. As a social category, an ethnic group functions as one of the primary units of social organization, so ethnic forces undoubtedly shape the aging process. The family is a particularly appropriate institution to study, because it bridges other social institutions and the less-institutionalized areas of daily life (LeVine, 1973). Families provide the primary setting through which the culture is defined and interpreted (Luborsky & Rubinstein, 1987). As a unit of social structure, families provide a source of social integration for the aged and the primary source of any needed supports. As the family socializes children, norms are instilled that influence the position of older family members. Thus, ethnic diversity affects the status of older generations, and the family is an arena where ethnic behaviors are often most prominent.

I define ethnic group membership by both social and cultural criteria. Individuals are members of ethnic groups if they stake a claim to membership in that group as a basis of their identity, if they share the norms and values of the group, and if ethnic group membership is one organizing principle in their social life. As the following illustrates, ethnic factors in family life are most evident in the cultural domain, in the family's structure and functioning, and in the nuclear family's position in an extended network of kin and friends.

THE CHANGING AMERICAN FAMILY

In reading descriptions of ethnic families, one comes away with the impression that, with a few exceptions, traditionalism, along with high familism, characterizes the immigrant family in most groups (Mindel, Haberstein, & Roosevelt, 1988; Rosenthal, 1983). Generational change is also a prominent theme, with the second generation in the United States exhibiting diverse family types and the third generation moving toward the

American nuclear model. In any case, the traditional family type has a hierarchical structure, with the old dominant over the young and males dominant over females. Such values as respect, obligation, and interdependence represent the cultural domain of ethnic family life. Also under the rubric of traditionalism, the nuclear family has been submerged into the kinship system. A cross-cultural survey, for example, found that the position of members of the older generation is more advantageous in a traditional family system than in the nuclear family (Cowgill & Holmes, 1972). Whereas the traditional family exists among recent immigrant groups such as the Vietnamese, such a family type is difficult to sustain in American urban culture (Tran, 1988). Consequently, members of succeeding generations generally modify traditional family patterns.

In contrast to the traditional family type, the Parsonian nuclear model long dominated the scholarly thinking on the American family (Parsons, 1965). This nuclear "ideal" family is conceptualized as a domestic unit consisting of husband, wife, and children. It is more egalitarian in structure than the traditional family, but it retains a gender-based division of labor, with men focusing on instrumentalism and women on the expressive sphere of family life. This family type, moreover, is a private, autonomous unit relatively isolated from the kinship system. Such a family, according to Parsons and his followers, has turned over instrumental functions to other institutions and has become specialized in the emotional functions of socializing children and stabilizing the adult personality.

Since the rise of the feminist movement in the 1960s, the nuclear family type has been widely condemned as a social unit that repressed and exploited women (Fass, 1993). Paralleling the spiraling divorce rate beginning in the early 1960s, the proportion of intact nuclear families has declined as more and more children live in one-parent households. Additionally, families in the inner city have had to devise variant family forms in order to adapt to stressors of lower-class living. Today an unprecedented number of young adults have foregone marriage altogether, and unmarried adults of all ages are likely to live alone.

Parsons (1942) himself perceptively pointed out that, although the nuclear family model was suited to the needs of industrial society, it had two points of strain: the position of the aged and the status of women. Older family members, he maintained, were vulnerable, because they were structurally isolated from the families of their children and their kinship group. Because they maintained separate households and their children were geographically mobile, they had to turn to community institutions for help.

The *opportune family* is used here to identify some alternatives to the nuclear family. These families result when the nuclear ideal has been rejected either ideologically or out of practical necessity. Individuals espousing new-age philosophy in the quest for self-actualization commonly find the nuclear family too constraining or incompatible with their values (Johnson, 1988). Others must abandon the nuclear family ideal because of divorce, poverty, sexual preferences, and, under some conditions, the stresses of immigration. These newer family forms are individual-centered, with elastic and ever-changing boundaries. Relationships are optional and directed by spontaneous personal decisions. Here the status of older people is especially equivocal, because family life is determined on the basis of personal choices rather than by conventional or traditional norms. Nevertheless, such flexibility permits the formation of family-like bonds, with fictive kin potentially providing support to older members.

A THEORETICAL PERSPECTIVE ON LATE-LIFE ETHNIC FAMILIES

Given the prolongation of life of older adults today, families are likely to have three or four extant generations as more older members survive. Because increased longevity is not necessarily associated with decreased morbidity, increasing numbers of older people are likely to need assistance from their families. Consequently, what is the status of aged individuals in these diverse family types? Which types of families work best in maintaining optimal social integration and well-being for their older members?

The following sections address these questions by approaching the review of the literature on ethnic families with three assumptions. First, I assume that the cultural domain includes norms and values that offer directives regarding the strength of family ties and the priorities given to family members over others. Such orientations, in turn, also determine attitudes toward aging family members. Second, the family's structure and functions are, in part, a result of the normative directives that shape family roles and relationships. Third, following the anthropological approaches to the study of social networks by Barth (1969) and Bott (1971), networks in which families participate consist not only of social relationships but also of normative boundaries. The degree of connectedness of networks therefore influences the extent to which ethnic family norms and subsequent structural characteristics are reinforced, modified, or rejected. Illustrations come mostly, but not exclusively, from the most frequently researched family types. Because of the great variation in family structure among Native American groups and the dearth of studies, I have omitted them from this review.

Cultural Dimensions

The concept of *culture* used here incorporates both the symbolic and experiential world and the specialized valuative criteria of norms and values. Virtually all ethnic groups have value orientations that influence the status of aged family members. These include values that calibrate independence, interdependence, or dependence, those that influence evaluations on age hierarchies or egalitarianism, and those that emphasize a sociocentric versus an egocentric orientation. Moreover, these valuative criteria define the optimal degree of attachment of individuals to the nuclear family and the strength of the family's connection to the kinship group. The cultural domain also influences the extent to which particular family types act as agents of change or sources of stability.

All societies prescribe some norms of mutual responsibility between older people and their adult children (Cowgill & Holmes, 1972). By most status criteria, however, the position of older people is determined, in part, by that group's value orientation. The generic value orientation theory of Kluckhohn and Strodtbeck (1961) was widely used in the past to encompass the enormous variations in values among American ethnic groups. Of particular relevance to the status of older people are the relational orientations, which range from individual, to lineal, to collateral. Dominant American values place a strong emphasis on individualism, independence, and self-reliance. Such values have been compared and contrasted with some ethnic groups, such as Irish Americans and African Americans, who place an emphasis on collateral relationships and egalitarian values. Others, such as Hispanic and Asian groups, place a strong emphasis on lineal or intergenerational relationships that are usually reinforced by hierarchical values (Kluckhohn & Strodtbeck, 1961; Papajohn & Spiegel 1975; Woehrer, 1978, 1982).

In contrast to whites and African Americans in the United States, for whom norms of filial responsibility are implicit at best (Hanson, Sauer, & Seelbach, 1983), Asian American groups are still influenced by Confucian moral principles that clearly articulate values enhancing the status of aged people (Benedict, 1946; De Vos, 1989). In its ideal form, many members of these groups continue to endorse ancestor worship and filial piety. Even after death, aged family members may be enshrined in altars in the home, where daily prayers are said. Norms of obligation are explicit, and the younger generations are pressured to be obedient and respectful. Strong identification with the family and the obligation to uphold its honor are emphasized; members are condemned if they bring shame to the family. Patrilineal and patriarchal family structures are also outgrowths of these Asian traditions.

Japanese American families have preserved, to some extent, the Japanese value of dependency, *amaeru*, which encourages the preservation of special dependent relationships with others (Doi, 1973; Kitano, 1970; Johnson, 1977; Johnson, 1993). Osako (1979) suggested that the *issei*, or immigrant generation, accept their dependency upon their children and grandchildren as an effective mechanism of coping with the upward mobility of the younger generations. *Enryo* is another Japanese normative guideline, which concerns patterns of deference and modesty (Johnson & Johnson, 1975;

Kitano, 1970). These patterns are easily carried over into respectful attitudes toward members of the older generation. Obviously, such a subcultural background stands in stark contrast to the dominant American culture, and, not surprisingly, intergenerational tensions are prominent as succeeding generations modify their value orientations. In fact, the *nisei* in Hawaii, members of the second generation, described themselves as "the sucker generation" who felt trapped between the demands for filial piety from their parents and the increasing Westernization of their children (Johnson, 1976, 1977). Despite this fact, however, the third generation in Hawaii, the *sansei*, were more kinship-oriented than their parents, suggesting that a weakening of traditional values might not necessarily undermine family ties but, rather, could indicate that a different form of intergenerational solidarity is emerging (Johnson, 1977). As I discuss in a later section, shifts in inheritance patterns also can be an impetus for some of these changes.

Researchers on European Catholic groups also draw contrasts between American values regarding independence and distance from the family and the compelling family ties in various ethnic groups. For example, Yugoslavian families (Simic, 1977) and Eastern Europeans in general are particularly noted for intimacy and interdependence among family members (Krickus, 1980). Cohler and Lieberman (1979) traced the closeness between generations among European Americans to the cooperative familism of peasant cultures of Eastern and Southern Europe. Italian Americans, most of whom originated in the peasant culture of southern Italy, place a strong emphasis on respect for elders (Johnson, 1978, 1985). Moreover, the family is dishonored in the community if children place elderly members in nursing homes. To Italian Americans, nursing homes are for those who have no families. Hispanics also are reluctant to use long-term care facilities (Burr & Mulcher, 1992). In all, the traditional family with its strong norms of filial responsibility usually provides extensive support to older members.

A number of commentators have pointed out that higher socioeconomic status among ethnic Americans has been associated with diminishing ethnic family behaviors (Cantor, 1979). As might be expected, achievement values are likely to have an indirect effect on the status of older parents. Among Jewish Americans, for example, achievement is strongly emphasized even if it conflicts with filial obligations (Thomas & Wister, 1984). Greek Americans, with their emphasis on achievement, have experienced high rates of both upward mobility and intermarriage. Although they continue to express the filial ideals, their parents usually live apart from them (Kourvetaris, 1988; Welts, 1982). Likewise, Japanese Americans have been viewed as a model group who share the achievement values of the American middle class (Caudill & De Vos, 1956). Rather than increased distance between parents and adult children, they appear to have escaped a widening generation gap through preserving continuity in filial norms (Johnson, 1977;

Osako, 1979). In fact, most Asian groups place a strong emphasis on education, but it is likely that the resulting achievement is seen to benefit the family rather than the individual, as is typical in Western society. Where upward mobility entails geographic mobility, it is nonetheless increasingly likely that elderly family members are separated from their children and grandchildren.

Family Structure and Functioning

With worldwide industrialization, the nuclear family, at least until recently, was becoming both the statistical and cultural norm (Goode, 1970). Aside from recent immigrant groups, the households of most American families in the child-rearing years are either a nuclear or an abbreviated nuclear form (Suitor, Pillemer, Keeton, & Robison, this volume). Ethnic differentials in rates of fertility, marriage, divorce, and mortality in particular ethnic groups influence the probability that older people will have a spouse or child in their old age (Himes, 1992). Consequently, groups such as Hispanics, who have large families and high rates of marriage, will have more family resources available to aged family members. These groups can be contrasted to most Jewish Americans, who have been noted for their small family size. In 1980, their fertility rate was below the level needed to replace their population, and the rate was still declining (Della Pergola, 1980). Thus, one can predict that there will be fewer Jewish children to care for aged family members in the future.

For the country as a whole, one in four adults today is not married, a significant increase over the past two decades. Increased numbers in all age groups do not live in family units (National Center for Health Statistics, 1991), a trend that will obviously have an impact on the families of older people (see Dwyer, this volume). This trend is already apparent in a study by Himes (1992), who looked at the availability of future caregivers for the elderly. Among older African Americans, only 20% of the women 65 years and older in 1990 were married with children, in contrast to 30% of the white women. After 85 years of age, a leveling occurs, when only 6% of African American women and 7% of white women are married and have one child. Whereas more men than women are married, African American men in both age groups are notably less likely than white men to have both a spouse and child.

In old age, the large numbers of people living alone mean that the family as a domestic unit is less prevalent (Johnson & Troll, 1992). As a result, older individuals, who are predominantly women, live in one-person households and do not always carry on family relations on a daily basis. The living situation in later life, thus, is of considerable interest. For researchers of minority groups, household composition is the most easily accessed and objective indicator of ethnic variations. Household composition varies among groups (Kinsella, this volume), particularly in the propensity of children to incorporate their parents into their own nuclear household. Clarke and Neidert (1992), in a study of older Americans of European origin, found that those from Southern and Eastern Europe were more likely to live with relatives than were those from Northwestern Europe.

Some debate is ongoing as to whether household composition results from economic forces or from the cultural context in which decisions are made (Angel & Tienda, 1982). On one hand, Lacayo (1991) contended that poverty is a key determinant of the living situation of older people. Angel and Tienda (1982) also maintained that extended households are responses to poverty among African Americans and Hispanics. Such claims, however, are incongruent with Himes's findings (1992) that older African Americans, many of whom live below the poverty line, are more likely than whites to live alone. Her findings are more consistent, on the other hand, with studies by Pelham and Clark (1987) and Mutcher (1990), who found that, among widowed women, African Americans and whites tend to live alone, whereas Asians and Hispanics live with others. Even those unmarried African Americans who suffer declines in functioning continue living alone. Likewise, wide ethnic differences are found in living arrangements in California, with more elderly Chinese living with others than whites and African Americans (Lubben & Becerra, 1987).

In view of these mixed findings, one must be cautious about overemphasizing living arrangements as an ethnic trait, because that variable fails to tap the cultural domain. In comparisons made in Canada, Thomas and Wister (1984) found that older English people are more likely to live separately from their children than are their French counterparts, and older Jewish people are far more likely than Italians to live alone. Such patterns, they suggested, reflect differing normative beliefs, namely, that the Italians and the French have stronger filial values, which most likely make adult children more amenable to incorporating their elderly parents into their households. They contrasted this pattern to that of the English, who value their privacy and independence, and to that of Jewish Canadians, who permit their achievement orientation to supersede filial obligations.

Household composition, although reflecting ethnic variations, also does not indicate the level of closeness among family members. For example, even those older adults who live alone usually have at least one child living nearby and staying in frequent contact (Shanas, 1979). Chinese Americans tend to have semiextended families in which the aged who live alone remain in close proximity to their children (Huang, 1981). The modern Western family's relationship to the kinship system has been described as intimate at a distance (Rosenmayr & Kockeis, 1963), in contrast to the structured intimacy commonly observed in ethnic families. Structured intimacy results when both cultural directives, such as filial responsibility, and structural factors, such as proximity to kin, create strong social bonds quite different from those that are intimate but socially distant (Kiefer, 1971). Fandetti and Gelfand (1976) found, for example, that intergenerational assistance is likely to be high among Catholic European Americans. Some exceptions exist, however; Irish Americans live farther from their parents than do Poles and Italians (Cohler, 1982).

Gender roles vary significantly among different ethnic groups. African American women have been noted for the strength and stability of their family roles, and today the granny continues to be extolled (Lesnoff-Caravaglia, 1982). Among immigrant groups, norms regarding the traditional female role of subservience to men were difficult to sustain in this country because of the need for women to work outside the home (Lopata, 1988). In some family systems, such as the Irish American, women had always held strong positions. Likewise, earlier in this century, Jewish immigrant women exercised considerable power as they performed the instrumental roles in the family while men were absorbed in religious life (Blau, 1969). Thus it is likely today that the family roles of older women have been shaped, at least in part, by their earlier status in the family. Independence can be a function of family structure, with egalitarian families having relatively independent and autonomous women and traditional hierarchical families having women who remain dependent upon their husband and children.

The Social Network

The study of social networks can reveal the extent to which the nuclear family is connected to the broader kinship unit. Where interactions and reciprocity are frequent, older members are usually more integrated into an extended family (Johnson, 1977; Troll, 1986). Empirically, one can observe a range of such connectedness from active, sociable extended families that incorporate the older generations into their activities to families in which the old live out their lives relatively remote from the lives of their children, grandchildren, and other relatives.

One factor influencing ethnic variations in kinship networks concerns the structural emphasis on vertical intergenerational ties or collateral age-similar ties (Kluckhohn & Strodtbeck, 1961; Woehrer, 1978, 1982), an emphasis that creates differing types of helping networks for aged family members. The generational emphasis in networks is commonly found among Asian and Hispanic families, where the prominence accorded to intergenerational relationships reinforces bonds among parents, children, and grandchildren. This structural emphasis on vertical organization tends to be hierarchical, with the elderly parents retaining some power. In contrast, the collateral emphasis places a priority on marriage above the intergenerational bond. Collateral priorities also highlight the sibling tie or accentuate the importance of friends. For example, the nuclear family model of the dominant group is noted for its collateral emphasis, and it is also found among Irish and African American families. In fact, members of the latter groups tend to consider relatives as friends (Woehrer, 1978).

Some exceptions to these typologies include Italian Americans, who endorse strong filial values and a hierarchical organization. In the past, parents who were adapting to the stress of immigration had usually come to this country in a chain migration with their siblings and other extended family members. Relatives were likely to live on the same block or even in the same building. Parents and aunts and uncles were often too distracted adjusting to their new lives to attend to the needs of their children as individuals. Instead they dealt collectively with a group of their children and nieces and nephews, all of whom shared in family activities. In the process, strong sibling and collateral relationships formed at the same time that the age hierarchy was preserved (Johnson, 1982).

Network theory is particularly useful in interpreting the forces of stability and change in contemporary ethnic families. I assume, in agreement with Barth (1969), that when individuals ascribe themselves as members of an ethnic group, they agree on the dominant norms of that group. For practical purposes, the boundary of an ethnic group is a social network consisting of sets of social relationships between family members and others (Bott, 1971). Where these networks are connected, that is, where individuals in the network also have relationships with each other, they tend to agree on the norms that govern family relationships. If consensus is present, individuals are pressured to conform to family expectations. Where members of the same ethnic group constitute a family's network, pressures to conform to the ethnic group's norms are also strong. As a consequence, ethnic norms usually continue to shape the performance of family roles.

Within most ethnic groups, subsequent generations have assimilated, at least in part, into occupational and community institutions of the dominant society (Mindel, Wright, & Starrett, 1986). These boundaries are elastic, with individuals crossing back and forth to associate with members outside their group. In such cases, new norms and values are generally introduced that eventually act as agents of change. If members of an ethnic group continue to maintain their primary relationships within the ethnic group, however, some characteristics of the ethnic family are likely to continue, a situation sometimes referred to as nine-to-five assimilation (Hannerz, 1974).

Ethnic boundaries are more connected when individuals remain embedded in ethnic neighborhoods, religious institutions, and community associations. As assimilation progresses, however, variations in the family are likely to occur in a given ethnic group. As associations become more heterogeneous over time and with succeeding generations, the intermarriage rate generally rises. Then one can predict changes in the family, a process I describe in the following section.

FORCES OF STABILITY AND CHANGE

Traditional Family Systems

Most evidence suggests that helping networks are stronger in the traditional family, with its vertical emphasis on intergenerational relationships, than in collateral family types (Cantor & Little, 1985; Weeks & Cuellar, 1981). As noted, elements of traditionalism are most prominent today in Asian, Hispanic, and some European Catholic families. Although Chinese families are so varied because of the length of time in this country and the varied rates of social mobility, evidence suggests that the elders still have a favored place in the family (Wong, 1988). One study found that 68% of aged Chinese turn to the family for support and that as many as 90% believe children should support their elders (Cheng, 1978).

Among the Japanese Americans in Hawaii, strong emphasis is placed upon norms of respect, filial obligation, reciprocity, and dependence upon family (Johnson, 1976, 1977). Such continuities take place even with structural changes in inheritance patterns. Now all children usually share the inheritance from the parents as well as the responsibility for older parents, unlike the past, when the eldest son assumed full responsibility and received the inheritance. Such persistence of filial attentiveness is also evident on the mainland, where 20% of the older Japanese American parents receive part of their income from their children, a sharp contrast to the American norm, where the flow of aid generally goes from parent to adult child (Montero, 1979).

Debate continues about the claims that Hispanics are still embedded in close-knit families (Markides & Mindel, 1987). Conflicting views are perhaps related to the fact that Spanish-speaking individuals do not constitute a monolithic group but rather trace their origins to Mexico, the Caribbean, and Central or South America. Hispanics have also settled in different areas of the country, and they are considered to be going through differing stages in their transition to American culture (Halpern, 1990). Cantor (1979) found stronger helping patterns among most Puerto Ricans when contrasted to whites or African Americans in New York City. She predicted, however, that these differences would disappear with changing economic resources (Cantor & Little, 1985). Most studies report that Hispanics, in comparison to whites and African Americans, have higher levels of family solidarity, with the elderly members more integrated into their extended families (Becerra, 1983; Falicov, 1982; Sanches-Ayendez, 1988). Others have described the high familism and traditionalism among Hispanics (Maldonado, 1979). At least among Mexican Americans in the Southwest, however, parents expect more help from their children than children are willing to give (Markides, Boldt, & Ray, 1986), a finding that might reflect the strains commonly found in traditional families in this country, where members of the younger generation have changing conceptions of their responsibilities.

Among Italian American immigrants, traditionalism, or the old-fashioned way, was most pronounced. Traditionalism included strong priorities to the family at the expense of individual interests and was accompanied by overt respect for elders. Child rearing was, and remains today, a blend of strict controls and high maternal nurturance that mothers have used to advance the interests and solidarity of the family (Johnson, 1985). Third-generation Italian Americans recognize the limitations of some aspects of traditionalism, so it is not surprising that only 13% live in three-generation households. Nevertheless, adult children still accord parents a high status and take responsibility for their care (Johnson, 1985; Squier & Quadagno, 1988). Thus, despite high rates of intermarriage and social mobility, norms of filial responsibility remain strong, and Italian American elderly are generally well integrated into the extended family. These continuities are particularly evident among those Italian Americans who remain embedded in Italian neighborhoods and in social networks that are predominantly Italian.

Perhaps the best example of both the strengths and weaknesses of the traditional family system can be observed among recent Asian immigrant groups. Most Koreans came after 1965, and unlike other immigrant groups, most had professional and technical occupations (Min, 1988). They have larger households, yet a lower fertility rate, than the national average. One-half live in some form of the extended family, mostly with one or both of their parents. A study of Koreans in New York City, however, indicates that the parent-child relationship may be changing and becoming similar to the dominant American pattern (Koh & Bell, 1987).

Southeast Asian refugees who recently arrived in this country have experienced far-reaching effects on their families. Whether the family is a consistent source of support to their aged relatives in this country has not been determined (Weinstein-Shr & Henkin, 1991).

The potential for family conflict is enormous among the recent immigrants and refugees. Aged parents who accompany their children have routinely suffered serious disadvantages, such as loss of assets and lower status. For example, the Vietnamese elderly live in extended families, but during the day their children and grandchildren are at work or at school (Tran, 1988). Their dislocations are magnified, because the elderly, who customarily do not speak English, are isolated and homebound much of the day. Similar problems have been reported among the Hmong immigrants (Hays, 1987).

The Nuclear Family Model

The nuclear family as an ideal type might be an outcome of assimilation. It occurs among middle-class African Americans and among members of other groups who discard features of their ethnic family configuration but still identify themselves culturally as members of the ethnic group. Changes in the traditional family generally occur with succeeding generations, particularly as a result of social and geographic mobility and intermarriage. Such structural changes also tend to change the personnel in the family's social network as more individuals outside the ethnic group are included. In heterogeneous networks, outsiders introduce new values that can change the status of the aged. This process, nevertheless, is not uniform because of differential exposure to ethnic institutions. Prominent examples are found among Irish and Jewish Americans, whose family types appear to be related to the strength of their religious affiliation (Horgan, 1988; Farber, Mindel, & Lazarwitz, 1988).

Historically, the Irish American family never resembled the kinship systems of the traditional families previously described (Horgan, 1988). In rural Ireland, one son inherited the land, while other children dispersed to cities and to America to seek their livelihood (Arensberg & Kimball, 1968). Consequently, single women, as well as men, immigrated alone to this country in the mid-nineteenth century, and the families they formed were more egalitarian in their gender roles than those from Southern and Eastern Europe. Irishwomen were viewed as morally and spiritually superior to men and, in their matriarchal status, were a stabilizing force in the family (Greeley, 1972). They were also noted for their relative coldness in child rearing, a starkly different view than the romanticized view of the warm, loving Italian American mother (Greeley, 1972; McGoldrick, 1982).

Irish Americans, according to Horgan (1988), have developed a wide range of family situations, depending upon their level of assimilation, upward mobility, and affiliation with the Catholic church. One of these family types arises among the enclaved Irish Americans of working-class background whose lives revolve around the family, the neighborhood, and the Catholic church. The second family situation includes the Irish in professional or managerial occupations who have families and lifestyles quite similar to those of mainstream, middle-class Americans. Other middle-class Irish remain close to the church, but they advocate a reformed church that favors abortion and other liberal issues. Members of the final group either married other Catholics and blended into a Catholic melting pot or married Protestants and blended into the mainstream.

Greeley's 1977 survey of American Catholics reported that the Irish had the largest family size, which potentially provides more children for aged parents. Despite this, they had the lowest proportion of children among the Catholic groups who visited their parents at least weekly even when they were living in proximity. In fact, the Irish patterns of contact were more similar to those of Protestants and Jews than to those of other Catholic groups. No more recent surveys are available regarding the status of the elderly in Irish American families, but one would expect that it would vary depending upon the extent to which the Catholic church and the Irish community provide conservative influences upon families.

Researchers on Jewish American families also use religious affiliation, rather than generation succession in this country, to map changes in the family (Farber, Mindel, & Lazerwitz, 1988). Family diversity among Jews, as evidenced by intermarriage and divorce, appears to be linear, ranging from low rates in Orthodox groups, to higher rates among Conservative and Reform Jews, to the highest rates among those with no religious preference. A Phoenix study (Farber et al., 1988) found that Jews who were more religious had more contacts with parents. Yet scattered reports (cited in Farber et al., 1988), mostly at least 20 years old, show that extended family solidarity remains strong among Jewish Americans. Most likely, the tendency of members of the extended family to live in proximity facilitated this solidarity. The kinship structure of the Jewish American family emphasizes collateral ties, and, like middle-class Irish American, Jewish Americans have adopted the nuclear family model of the dominant group. At the same time, within the cultural domain, they identify strongly with their ethnic background and, in most cases, their religious heritage. Like members of the dominant group, however, ties to parents are probably strong but do not usually have the intense and obligatory quality found in more traditional family systems.

The Opportune Family

Having never endorsed strict norms on family obligations, Americans in the dominant group have always had an element of choice in shaping their family relationships to suit their wishes and needs (Furstenberg, 1981). The current era of revolutionary changes has witnessed altered gender roles, serial monogamy, changing sexual preferences, and, in some cases, the desire to return to bucolic communal rural life. I have labeled these contemporary versions as the *opportune family,* in which individuals exercise options regarding their households, their mutual responsibilities, and their significant relationships.

As a consequence, alternative family types emerge as another point of diversity in family life. Divorce and its aftermath entail complicated processes of family reorganization. In the process of marital changes, individuals can selectively accumulate relatives through marriage, divorce, and remarriage. The end results are the blended families that have complex family forms but only vaguely specified rights and obligations (Johnson, 1988). In these circumstances, with new and changing guidelines, the status of the grandparent generation is variable and most likely negotiable.

Other opportune families arise out of necessity, such as among inner-city African Americans, who are adapting to various problems created by single parenthood, poverty, and racism. Severe economic conditions are typical in the inner cities, with as many as 45% of black men being unemployed (Staples, 1988). This deprivation has undermined marriage and resulted in an ephemeral male-female bond. As a consequence, the majority of black females are not married, and a large proportion of their children have no contact with their fathers. Although such figures are usually indicators of family disorganization, ethnographic researchers have pointed to the capacities of black families to adapt to severe economic hardships (Hannerz, 1969; Liebow, 1967; Stack, 1974; Willie, 1988). The loose-knit family structure of low-income blacks results in resilient and flexible networks that also potentially serve the needs of the elderly members.

Comparative studies demonstrate that blacks have larger extended families than whites, a higher frequency of kin-based households (Choi, 1991; Hofferth, 1984; George, 1988; Gratton, 1987), and higher levels of social support to older family members (George, 1988; Taylor & Chatters, 1986; Taylor, 1988; Mutran, 1985; Petchers & Milligan, 1987). Contradictory findings come from some researchers, however, who challenge the viability of these kin networks (Mindel et al., 1986; George, 1988; Smerglia, Deimling, & Barresi, 1988). African Americans with higher socioeconomic status are more effective providers of supports to their elderly parents than are the less advantaged (Mutran, 1985; Taylor, 1988). This pattern might be related to the fact that children of the poor are usually poor themselves and too distracted to provide for their parents (Johnson & Barer, 1990).

For most black elderly, the presence of a child generally elicits a large helping network (Taylor, 1986). Consequently, the lower fertility of older, single black women can leave them with few family resources. We found in our study of inner-city older people that African Americans are often without supportive children, but they still have more active support networks than whites (Johnson & Barer, 1990). Sibling ties are also strong in African American families and, in turn, maximize collateral ties (Gold, 1990). Furthermore, black families readily create fictive kin by turning good friends into relatives and by adopting foster or "play" children, those defined as "like a child to me." Networks are also strengthened collaterally with fellow church members, who can substitute for absent family members (Johnson & Barer, 1990). Given a heavy reliance on formal supports among these inner-city residents, irrespective of family involvement, older African Americans are able to withdraw from the problems in the daily lives of their children and grandchildren and mold a social network of relatives, fictive kin, and friends that serves them well in late life.

CONCLUSIONS

Other than the current research on minority groups such as African Americans, reports on cultural diversity among older people in the United States are spotty, and often the studies have been methodologically inadequate. Moreover, much of the research on cultural diversity does not deal specifically with aging and the family. Given these deficiencies, a review of the literature by necessity is uneven in its coverage of specific groups, and, in some cases, the results are quite dated. Thus, the central question posed here—in the midst of great diversity in this country, what kind of family works best for the older generation?—can be only partially answered.

I have reviewed family types beginning with the traditional family, which was, and still is, prominent among immigrants from around the world. Traditionalism results in a hierarchical family that gives power and authority to the older generation. Norms of respect and obligation are prominent, as is high familism. Such a family type understandably collides with the dominant American values, so children and grandchildren of immigrants have modified some aspects of traditionalism. They are likely to live in nuclear families yet remain closely attached to their parents. Evidence suggests that, despite changes and the potential for conflict, elderly family members enjoy a favored position in the traditional family, because family members are still more likely to adhere to filial norms than do white Protestants and African Americans.

Despite its critics, most Americans strive to maintain a nuclear family. Members of the older generation in such a family system are generally detached from the families of their children physically and often emotionally. This family has become the common form among the dominant group as well as with middle-class African, Irish, and Jewish Americans. Variations in families appear to be influenced by the level of upward mobility, the strength of religious affiliation, and the degree of submersion in the ethnic community, all factors that influence the status of older people.

This analysis has drawn upon network theory to identify forces of stability and change in ethnic families. Namely, I propose that when family members are embedded in the extended family and ethnic community, ethnic norms on family life persist. When members of an ethnic group move into mainstream America in their work and community associations, their social networks come to include individuals from other groups in the society who introduce new norms of family life. However, if their networks contain mostly fellow ethnics, conservative forces can still operate. Thus, assimilation is not always a steady progression to some dominant American family form.

African Americans are a distinctive case because the devastating effects of racism and poverty are likely to affect those older people in inner cities. In response to these adverse conditions, African Americans are noted for their flexible family systems, here called the opportune family, a form that provides a strong source of integration. Although less likely to have a spouse or child as a supporter, elderly African Americans can usually draw upon relatives, friends, and fictive kin who serve them well in their old age. Moving beyond the nuclear family, then, groups can potentially adopt alternate family forms as they capitalize on the relative freedom American culture permits in defining the boundaries of the family system.

It should be emphasized that no ethnic group has abandoned its older members or rejected some responsibility for them. At the same time and given the pressures of immigration and minority status, it would be inaccurate to conclude that close-knit families can take care of their elderly people without formal services (Gratton, 1988). Families in this country are constantly changing as they adapt to external conditions and changing cultural determinants, with their older members likewise responding to the same contemporary forces as do their children and grandchildren.

NOTE

The author wishes to thank Sandra Hyde for her assistance in preparing the bibliography. Barbara Barer, Frank Johnson, and Lillian Troll made helpful comments on an earlier version, but the responsibility for the content is entirely my own.

REFERENCES

Adams, J. P. (1980). Service arrangements preferred by minority elderly: A cross-cultural survey. *Journal of Gerontological Social Work, 3,* 39–57.

Angel, R., & Tienda, M. (1982). Determinants of extended household structure: Cultural pattern or economic need? *American Journal of Sociology, 87,* 1360–1383.

Arensberg, C. M., & Kimball, S. T. (1968). *Family and community in Ireland.* Cambridge: Harvard University Press.

Barth, R. (1969). *Ethnic groups and boundaries.* Boston: Little, Brown.

Bastida, E. (1987). Issues of conceptual discourse in ethnic research and practice. In D. E. Gelfand & C. M. Barresi (Eds.), *Ethnic dimensions of aging* (pp. 51–63). New York: Springer.

Becerra, R. M. (1983). The Mexican-American: Aging in a changing culture. In R. L. McNeely & J. L. Colen (Eds.), *Aging in minority groups* (pp. 108–118). Beverly Hills, CA: Sage.

Benedict, R. (1946). *The chrysanthemum and the sword: Patterns of Japanese culture.* Boston: Houghton Mifflin.

Binstock, R., & George, L. (Eds.). (1990). *Handbook of aging and the social sciences.* New York: Academic Press.

Blau, Z. (1969). In defense of the Jewish mother. In P. Rose (Ed.), *The ghetto and beyond: Essays on Jewish life in this country* (pp. 57–68). New York: Random House.

Blau, Z., Oser, G. T., & Stephens, R. C. (1979). Aging, social class, and ethnicity. *Pacific Sociological Review, 22,* 501–525.

Bott, E. (1971). *Family and social network.* New York: Free Press.

Burr, J. A., & Mulcher, J. E. (1992). The living arrangements of unmarried elderly Hispanic females. *Demography, 29,* 93–112.

Cantor, M. H. (1979). The informal support system of New York's inner city elderly: Is ethnicity a factor? In D. E. Gelfand & A. J. Kutzik (Eds.), *Ethnicity and aging* (pp. 153–174). New York: Springer.

Cantor, M. H., & Little, V. (1985). Aging and social care. In R. H. Binstock & L. K. George (Eds.), *Handbook of aging and the social sciences* (3rd ed., pp. 745–781). New York: Van Nostrand Reinhold.

Caudill, W., & De Vos, G. (1956). Achievement, culture, and personality: The case of the Japanese Americans. *American Anthropologist, 58,* 1102–1126.

Cheng, E. (1978). *The elder Chinese.* San Diego, CA: Campanile Press.

Choi, N. G. (1991). Racial differences in the determinants of living arrangements of widowed and divorced elderly women. *Gerontologist, 31,* 496–504.

Clarke, T. C., & Neidert, L. J. (1992). Living arrangements of the elderly: An examination of differences according to ancestry and generation. *Gerontologist 32:* 796–804.

Cohler, B. J. (1982). Stress or support: Relations between older women from three European groups and their relatives. In R. C. Manuel (Ed.), *Minority aging: Sociological and social psychological issues* (pp. 115–122). Westport, CT: Greenwood Press.

Cohler, B. J., & Lieberman, M. A. (1979). Personality change across the second half of life: Findings from a study of Irish, Italian, and Polish-American men and women. In D. E. Gelfand, & A. J. Kutzik (Eds.), *Ethnicity and aging: Theory, research and policy* (pp. 227–245). New York: Springer Publishing Co.

Cowgill, D. O., & Holmes, L. D. (Eds.). (1972). *Aging and modernization.* New York: Appleton Century-Crofts.

Della Pergola, S. (1980). Patterns of Jewish American fertility. *Demography, 17,* 261–273.

De Vos, G. (1989). *Confucian family socialization: The religion, morality, and aesthetics of propriety.* Working paper, Department of Anthropology, University of California, Berkeley.

Doi, T. (1973). *Anatomy of dependence.* New York: Kodansha International.

Dowd, J. J., & Bengtson, V. L. (1978). Aging in minority populations: An examination of the double jeopardy hypothesis. *Journal of Gerontology, 33,* 427–436.

Driedger, L., & Chappell, N. (1987). *Aging and ethnicity: Toward an interface.* Toronto: Butterworths.

Erikson, E. (1976). The concept of identity in race relations: Notes and queries. In A. Deshefsky (Ed.), *Ethnic identity in society* (pp. 54–71). Chicago: Rand McNally.

Falicov, C. J. (1982). Mexican families. In M. McGoldrick, J. K. Pearse, & J. Giordano (Eds.), *Ethnicity and family therapy* (pp. 134–161). New York: Guilford Press.

Fandetti, D. V., & Gelfand, D. E. (1976). Care of the aged: Attitudes in white ethnic families. *Gerontologist, 16,* 544–549.

Farber, B. (1981). *Conceptions of kinship.* New York: Elsevier.

Farber, B., Mindel, C. H., & Lazerwitz, B. (1988). The Jewish American family. In C. H. Mindel, R. W. Haberstein, & W. Roosevelt, Jr. (Eds.), *Ethnic families in America* (3rd ed., pp. 400–437). New York: Elsevier.

Fass, P. (1993). Perspectives on family theory: Families in history and beyond. In P. Cowan, D. Field, D. Hanson, A. Skolnick, & G. Swanson (Eds.), *Family, self, and society: Toward a new agenda for family research* (pp. 143–152). Hillsdale, NJ: Erlbaum.

Furstenberg, F. (1981). Remarriage and intergenerational relations. In J. March (Ed.), *Aging: Stability and change in the family* (pp. 115–142). New York: Academic Press.

Gelfand, D. E. (1989). Immigration, aging, and intergenerational relationships. *Gerontologist, 29,* 366–372.

Gelfand, D. E., & Barresi, C. M. (Eds.). (1987). *Ethnic dimensions of aging.* New York: Springer Publishing Co.

Gelfand, D. E., & Yee, B. W. (1991). Influences of immigration, migration, and acculturation on the fabric of aging in America: Trends and forces. *Generations, Fall/Winter,* 7–10.

George, L. (1988). Social participation in later life: Black-white differences. In J. S. Jackson (Ed.), *The black American elderly* (pp. 99–128). New York: Springer Publishing Co.

Gibson, R. C. (1989). Minority aging research: Opportunity and challenge. *Journal of Gerontology: Social Sciences, 44,* S2–3.

Gold, D. T. (1990). Late-life sibling relationships: Does race affect typological distribution? *Gerontologist, 30,* 741–748.

Goode, W. (1970). *World revolution and family patterns.* New York: Free Press.

Gratton, B. (1987). Familism among the black and Mexican-American elderly: Myth or reality? *Journal of Aging Studies, 1,* 19–32.

Gratton, B. (1988). Family support systems and minority elderly: A cautionary analysis. *Journal of Gerontological Social Work, 13,* 81–93.

Greeley, A. M. (1972). *That most distressful nation: The taming of the American Irish.* Chicago: Quadrangle Books.

Greeley, A. M. (1974). *Ethnicity in the United States: A preliminary reconnaissance.* New York: Wiley.

Greeley, A. M. (1977). *The American Catholic: A social portrait.* New York: Basic Books.

Halpern, R. H. (1990). Aging and minority cultures: A comparison of three groups. *Journal of Cross-Cultural Gerontology, 5,* 395–404.

Hannerz, U. (1969). *Soulside: Inquiries into the ghetto culture and community.* New York: Columbia University Press.

Hannerz, U. (1974). Ethnicity and opportunity in urban America. In A. Cohen (Ed.), *Urban ethnicity* (pp. 37–76). London: Tavistock.

Hanson, S., Sauer, W., & Seelbach, W. (1983). Racial and cohort variations in filial responsibility norms. *Gerontologist, 23,* 26–31.

Hays, C. L. (1987). Two worlds in conflict: The elderly Hmong in the United States. In D. E. Gelfand & C. M. Barresi (Eds.), *Ethnic dimensions of aging* (pp. 79–95). New York: Springer Publishing Co.

Himes, C. (1992). The future caregivers: Projected family structures of older people. *Journal of Gerontology: Social Sciences, 47,* S17–S26.

Hofferth, S. L. (1984). Kin networks, race and family structures. *Journal of Marriage and the Family, 46,* 791–806.

Holzberg, C. (1982). Ethnicity and aging: Anthropological perspectives on more than just the minority elderly. *Gerontologist, 22,* 249–257.

Horgan, E. S. (1988). The American Catholic Irish family. In C. H. Mindel, R. W. Haberstein, & W. Roosevelt, Jr. (Eds.), *Ethnic families in America* (3rd ed., pp. 45–75). New York: Elsevier.

Howe, I. (1977). The limits of ethnicity. *New Republic,* June 25, 17–19.

Huang, L. J. (1981). The Chinese American family. In C. H. Mindel & R. B. Haberstein (Eds.), *Ethnic families in America* (pp. 230–257). New York: Elsevier.

Isaacs, H. (1975). Basic group identity: The idols of the tribe. In N. Glazer & D. Moynihan (Eds.), *Ethnicity: Theory and experience* (pp. 29–52). Cambridge: Harvard University Press.

Jackson, J. J., & Ensley, D. E. (1990–1991). Ethnogerontology's status and complementary and conflicting and cultural concerns for American minority elders. *Journal of Minority Aging, 12,* 41–78.

Johnson, C. L. (1976). The principle of generations among Japanese in Honolulu. *Ethnic Groups, 1,* 13–35.

Johnson, C. L. (1977). Interdependence, reciprocity and indebtedness: An analysis of Japanese American kinship relations. *Journal of Marriage and the Family, 39,* 351–363.

Johnson, C. L. (1978). Family support systems of elderly Italian Americans. *Journal of Minority Aging, 3,* 34–41.

Johnson, C. L. (1982). Sibling solidarity: Its origins and functioning in Italian-Americans. *Journal of Marriage and the Family, 44* (1), 155–167.

Johnson, C. L. (1985). *Growing up and growing old in Italian-American families.* New Brunswick, NJ: Rutgers University Press.

Johnson, C. L. (1988). *Ex-Familia: Grandparents, parents and children adjust to divorce.* New Brunswick, NJ: Rutgers University Press.

Johnson, C. L., & Barer, B. M. (1990). Families and networks among older inner-city blacks. *Gerontologist, 30,* 726–733.

Johnson, C. L., & Johnson, F. (1975). Interaction rules and ethnicity. *Social Forces, 54,* 452–466.

Johnson, C. L., Troll, L. (1992). Family functions in late life. *Journal of Gerontology: Social Sciences, 47,* S66–S72.

Johnson, F. A. (1993). *Dependency and Japanese socialization.* New York: New York University Press.

Kennedy, R. E. (1973). *The Irish emigration, marriages and fertility.* Berkeley: University of California Press.

Kiefer, C. (1971). Notes on anthropology and the minority aged. *Gerontologist, 11,* 94–98.

Kitano, H. H. L. (1970). *The Japanese American.* Englewood Cliffs, NJ: Prentice-Hall.

Kluckhohn, F., & Strodtbeck, F. (1961). *Variations in value orientations.* New York: Harper & Row.

Koh, J., & Bell, W. (1987). Korean living arrangements in the United States: Intergenerational relations and living arrangements. *Gerontologist, 27,* 66–71.

Kourvetaris, G. (1988). The Greek American family. In C. Mindel, R. Haberstein,

& R. Wright (Eds.), *Ethnic families in America* (pp. 76–108). New York: Elsevier.

Krickus, M. A. (1980). The status of East European women in the family: Tradition and change. In *Conference on the educational and occupational needs of white ethnic women* (pp. 76–96). Washington, DC: National Institute of Education.

Lacayo, C. (1991). Living arrangements and social environment among ethnic minority elderly. *Generations, Fall/Winter*, 43–46.

Lesnoff-Caravaglia, G. (1982). The black "granny" and the Soviet "babushka": Commonalities and contrasts. In R. C. Manuel (Ed.), *Minority aging: Sociological and social psychological issues* (pp. 109–114). Westport, CT: Greenwood Press.

LeVine, R. (1973). *Culture, behavior, and personality.* Chicago: Aldine.

Liebow, E. (1967). *Tally's corner: A study of negro street corner men.* Boston: Little, Brown.

Lopata, H. (1988). The Polish American family. In C. Mindel, R. Haberstein, & R. Wright (Eds.), *Ethnic families in America* (pp. 17–44). New York: Elsevier.

Lubben, J. E., & Becerra, R. M. (1987). Social support among black, Mexican, and Chinese elderly. In D. E. Gelfand & C. M. Barresi (Eds.), *Ethnic dimensions of aging* (pp. 130–144). New York: Springer Publishing Co.

Luborsky, M., & Rubenstein, R. L. (1987). Ethnicity and lifetimes: Self-concepts and situational contexts of ethnic identity in late life. In D. E. Gelfand & C. M. Barresi (Eds.), *Ethnic dimensions of aging* (pp. 18–34). New York: Springer Publishing Co.

Maldonado, D., Jr. (1979). Aging in the Chicano context. In D. E. Gelfand & A. J. Kutzik (Eds.), *Ethnicity and aging* (pp. 175–183). New York: Springer Publishing Co.

Maldonado, D., Jr. (1989). The Latino elderly living alone: The invisible poor. *California Sociologist, 12,* 8–21.

Manton, K. (1990). Mentality and morbidity. In R. Binstock & L. George (Eds.). *Handbook of aging and the social sciences* (3rd ed. pp. 64–90). San Diego: Academic Press.

Manuel, R. C. (Ed.). (1982). *Minority aging: Sociological and social psychological issues.* Westport, CT: Greenwood Press.

Markides, K. S. (1983). Minority aging. In M. W. Riley, B. B. Hess, & K. Bond (Eds.), *Aging in society: Selected reviews of recent research* (pp. 115–137). Hillsdale, NJ: Lawrence Erlbaum Associates.

Markides, K. S., Boldt, J. S., & Ray, L. A. (1986). Sources of helping and intergenerational solidarity: A three-generations study of Mexican Americans. *Journal of Gerontology, 41,* 506–511.

Markides, K., Liang, J., & Jackson, J. S. (1990). Race, ethnicity, and aging. In R. Binstock & L. George (Eds.), *Handbook of aging and the social sciences* (3rd ed., pp. 112–129). San Diego: Academic Press.

Markides, K. S., & Mindel, C. H. (1987). *Aging and ethnicity* (Vol. 63, Sage library of social research). Newbury Park, CA: Sage.

McGoldrick, M. (1982). Irish families. In M. McGoldrick, J. K. Pearse, & J. Giordano (Eds.), *Ethnicity and family therapy* (pp. 310–339). New York: Guilford Press.

McNeely, R. L., & Colen, J. L. (1983). *Aging in minority groups.* Beverly Hills, CA: Sage.

Min, P. G. (1988). The Korean American family. In C. H. Mindel, R. W. Haberstein, & W. Roosevelt, Jr. (Eds.), *Ethnic families in America* (3rd ed., pp. 199–229). New York: Elsevier.

Mindel, C. H., Wright, R., & Starrett, R. A. (1986). Informal and formal health and social support systems of black and white elderly. *Gerontologist, 26,* 279–285.

Mindel, C. H., Haberstein, R. W., & Roosevelt, W., Jr. (Eds.). (1988). *Ethnic families in America* (3rd ed.). New York: Elsevier.

Mitchell, J., & Regisler, J. (1984). An exploration of family interactions with the elderly by race, socioeconomic status and residence. *Gerontologist 24,* 382–389.

Montero, D. (1979). *Vietnamese Americans: Patterns of resettlement and socioeconomic adaptation in the United States.* Boulder, CO: Westview Press.

Mutcher, J. E. (1990). Household composition among the nonmarried elderly. A comparison of black and white women. *Research on Aging, 12,* 487–506.

Mutran, E. (1985). Intergenerational family support among blacks and whites: Response to culture or to socioeconomic differences. *Journal of Gerontology, 40,* 382–389.

National Center for Health Statistics. (1991). *Vital and Health Statistics* (Vol. 40, No. 7). Hyattsville, MD: Public Health Service.

Novak, M. (1972). *The rise of the unmeltable ethnics.* New York: Macmillan.

Osako, M. M. (1979). Aging and family among Japanese Americans: The role of ethnic tradition in the adjustment to old age. *Gerontologist, 19,* 448–455.

Papajohn, J., & Spiegel, J. (1975). *Transactions in families.* San Francisco: Jossey-Bass.

Parsons, T. (1942). Age and sex in the social structure of the United States. *American Sociological Review, 7,* 604–616.

Parsons, T. (1965). The normal American family. In S. Farber (Ed.), *Man and civilization* (pp. 31–50). New York: McGraw-Hill.

Pelham, A. O., & Clark, W. F. (1987). Widowhood among low income racial and ethnic groups in California. In H. Lopata (Ed.), *Widows: North America* (Vol. 2, pp. 191–222). Durham, NC: Duke University Press.

Petchers, M. K., & Milligan, S. E. (1987). Social networks and social support among black urban elderly: A health care resource. *Social Work in Health Care, 12,* 103–117.

Rosenmayr, L., & Kockeis, E. (1963). Propositions for a sociological theory of aging and the family. *International Social Science Journal, 15,* 410–426.

Rosenthal, C. J. (1983). Aging, ethnicity and the family: Beyond the modernization thesis. *Canadian Ethnic Studies, 15,* 1–16.

Sanchez-Ayendez, M. (1988). The Puerto-Rican American family. In C. H. Mindel, R. W. Haberstein, & W. Roosevelt, Jr. (Eds.), *Ethnic families in America* (3rd ed., pp. 173–198). New York: Elsevier.

Shanas, E. (1979). Social myth as hypothesis: The case of family relations of old people. *Gerontologist, 19,* 3–9.

Simic, A. (1977). Winners and losers: Aging Yugoslavs in a changing world. In B. Meyerhoff & A. Simic (Eds.), *Life course—aging: Cultural variations in growing old* (pp. 77–106). Beverly Hills, CA: Sage.

Smerglia, V. L., Deimling, G. T., & Barresi, C. M. (1988). Black/white family comparisons in helping and decision-making networks of impaired elderly. *Family Relations, 37,* 305–309.

Squier, D. A., & Quadagno, J. (1988). The Italian American family. In C. H. Mindel, R. W. Haberstein, & W. Roosevelt, Jr. (Eds.), *Ethnic families in America* (3rd ed., pp. 109–137). New York: Elsevier.

Stack, C. (1974). *All our kin: Strategies for survival in a black community.* New York: Harper & Row.

Staples, R. (1988). The black American family. In C. H. Mindel, R. W. Haberstein, & W. Roosevelt, Jr. (Eds.), *Ethnic families in America* (3rd ed., pp. 303–324). New York: Elsevier.

Taylor, R. J. (1986). Receipt of support from family among black Americans: Demographic and familial differences. *Journal of Marriage and the Family, 48,* 67–77.

Taylor, R. J. (1988). Aging and supportive relationships among black Americans. In J. Jackson (Ed.), *The black American elderly.* New York: Springer Publishing Co.

Taylor, R. J. (1991). Extended family networks of older black adults. *Journal of Gerontology, 46,* S210–217.

Taylor, R. J., & Chatters, L. M. (1986). Patterns of informal support to elderly black adults: Family, friends, and church members. *Social Work, 31,* 432–438.

Thernstrom, S., Orlov, A., & Handlin, O. (1980). *Harvard encyclopedia of American ethnic groups.* Cambridge: Harvard University Press.

Thomas, K., & Wister, A. (1984). Living arrangements of older women: The ethnic dimension. *Journal of Marriage and the Family, 46,* 301–311.

Tran, T. V. (1988). The Vietnamese American family. In C. H. Mindel, R. W. Haberstein, & W. Roosevelt, Jr. (Eds.), *Ethnic families in America* (3rd ed., pp. 276–302). New York: Elsevier.

Troll, L. (1986). *Family issues in current gerontology.* New York: Springer Publishing Co.

Usui, W. M. (1989). Challenges in the development of ethnogerontology. *Gerontologist, 29,* 566–568.

Weeks, J. R., & Cuellar, J. (1981). The role of family members with helping networks of older people. *Gerontologist, 21,* 388–394.

Weinstein-Shr, G., & Henkin, N. Z. (1991). Continuity and change: Intergenerational relations in Southeast Asian refugee families. *Marriage and Family Review, 16,* 351–367.

Welts, E. P. (1982). Greek families. In M. McGoldrick, J. K. Pearse, & J. Giordano (Eds.), *Ethnicity and family therapy* (pp. 269–287). New York: Guilford Press.

Willie, C. V. (1988). *A new look at black families.* Dix Hills, NY: General Hall.

Woehrer, C. E. (1978). Cultural pluralism in American families: The influence of ethnicity on social aspects of aging. *Family Coordinator. 27,* 329–339.

Woeher, C. E. (1982). The influence of ethnic families on intergenerational relationships and later life transitions. *Annals, American Academy of Political and Social Sciences, 464,* 65–78.

Wong, M. G., (1988). The Chinese American family. In C. H. Mindel, R. W. Haberstein, & W. Roosevelt, Jr. (Eds.), *Ethnic families in America* (3rd ed., pp. 230–257). New York: Elsevier.

Woroby, J. L., & Angel, R. J. (1990) Poverty and health: Older minority women and the rise of the female-headed household. *Journal of Health and Social Behavior, 31,* 370–383.

Yancy, W. L., Erickson, E. P., & Juliani, R. (1976). Emergent ethnicity: A review and reformulation. *American Sociological Review, 41,* 391–403.

16

Aging and Kinship in Rural Context

B. Jan McCulloch

INTRODUCTION

The title of this chapter implies that there is something distinctively different about aging and family life experiences in rural areas. What evidence do we have to suggest that this is, indeed, the case? Contextually, distinctions include individual as well as community characteristics that provide a unique backdrop for the examination of family and aging. Rural residents, for example, are characterized as having more fatalistic attitudes, greater suspicion of governmental and agency assistance, and greater investment in the maintenance of self and family independence (Buckwalter, Smith, & Caston, 1994). At the community level, geographic barriers, limited economic opportunity, and limited availability and/or access to public transportation, formal service delivery, and mental and physical health care services characterize the context in which an increasing number of rural residents experience family life and aging.

As defined by the Census Bureau, *rural* refers to areas in and surrounding places with 2,500 inhabitants or fewer, a designation that captures persons living in areas of low population density and size. *Nonmetropolitan areas,* on the other hand, are defined as counties outside metropolitan areas (U.S. Senate Special Committee on Aging, 1992). For the purposes of this chapter, rural and nonmetropolitan classifications are combined.

Romantic perceptions of an idyllic rural lifestyle that provides spatial, community, and interpersonal benefits to residents pervade public impressions and have been noted as problematic by some scholars (Coward, McLaughlin, Duncan, & Bull, 1994; Fitchen, 1991; Rowles, 1991). Rural elders, for example, are stereotyped as having large and supportive friendship networks in contrast to stereotypic depictions of urban elders who rarely even know their neighbors (Stoller & Lee, 1994). Rural/urban comparative descriptions, such as lower costs of living, stronger and larger kinship and community ties, and less environmental stress for rural residents, hamper understanding of the realities of rural family life and aging and contribute to multiple myths regarding the advantages of rurality. As rural studies increase and as these studies move beyond descriptive presentations, a consistent body of knowledge notes the importance of examining the complexities of aging and kinship specific to the rural environmental context. For example, the openness and geographic dispersion so valued in romantic perceptions of rurality often mean that older adults and families with limited individual and community resources are more socially isolated; must travel greater distances for goods, services, and medical care; and are less likely to have public transportation as an alternative to car ownership and maintenance when compared with older adults and families in urban contexts (Coward, 1987; U.S. Congress, 1990).

From a purely demographic perspective, approximately 8 million elders, or 29% of older Americans, live in rural areas (U.S. Senate Special Committee on Aging, 1992). The largest proportion of these older adults, approximately 91%, lives in rural small towns and villages or in nonfarm open country. Additionally, elders in small villages, with residential numbers between 1,000 and 2,500, constitute the largest population segment when compared with all other age groups (Scheidt & Norris-Baker, 1990). During the 1970s and 1980s, a significant number of in-migrants, particularly young-old adults, moved to retirement or recreational rural areas, seeking retirement areas with lower costs of living and idyllic environmental surroundings. These in-migrants differed from long-term rural residents in that they relocated to rural areas with greater financial resources and better overall health (Glasgow & Reeder, 1990).

Note, however, that generalizations from purely objective measures of life status, such as cost of living indexes and relative access to social and formal services, also oversimplify characterizations of aging and kinship in rural areas. In general, older rural adults and long-term or permanent rural residents express satisfaction with their lifestyle and would rather remain in a rural area than relocate to urban centers where increased community and formal support services could improve access to community resources (Ansello, 1980). Fear of urban crime, close ties to community, and strong ties to the land, particularly among farm families, are a few of the factors important to older adults and families when they are asked about their satisfaction with rural living. In addition, the in-migration of retirees to selected rural areas during the 1970s and 1980s suggests the persistent perceptions of a rural lifestyle advantage (Johansen & Fuguitt, 1990).

In this chapter, I provide an overview of research examining aging and kinship in the rural context. Because comprehensive reviews of research on older rural adults and kinship have been published (e.g., Lee & Cassidy, 1981, 1985; Powers, Keith, & Goudy, 1981), the primary focus of this chapter is on key considerations that investigators of aging and kinship in rural areas should address. Specific objectives include discussions of (1) rural/urban comparisons of the status of older adults and family life, (2) the importance of addressing heterogeneity when examining aging and kinship in rural context, (3) examinations of the relationship of environmental factors to aging and kinship in rural areas, (4) theoretical and methodological issues regarding research on rural aging and kinship, and (5) suggestions for future research and policy agendas in this area.

RURAL/URBAN COMPARISONS

Specific to issues discussed here, older rural adults have been compared with urban residents across several dimensions, including health, socioeconomic status, and family context. Although these comparisons oversimplify the diversity known to exist within rural environments, they do provide information useful to the discussion of family and aging in rural areas.

Rural/Urban Comparisons of Older Adult Health and Socioeconomic Status

Rural/urban comparisons of elders' health status have provided considerable evidence supporting the disadvantaged general health of older rural adults. Although rural and urban elders experienced the same kinds of physical health problems, rural older adults reported greater incidences of chronic illness (Glasgow & Beale, 1985; Krout, 1986, 1988; U.S. Congress, 1990) and greater numbers of conditions that limited activity and required hospitalization (Glasgow & Beale, 1985). Rural elders also reported greater incidences of specific diseases, such as arthritis, heart disease, hypertension, emphysema, ulcers, kidney and thyroid problems, and visual and hearing problems, than urban dwellers experienced (Geller, 1989). Information about mental health in rural areas remains scant (Wagenfeld, 1990), but existing findings indicate some support for hypotheses positing residential differences. Recent studies indicated that factors associated with increasingly difficult economic situations, such as declining employment in rural manufacturing, mining, and farming, and fewer opportunities to develop effective coping strategies have contributed to higher than average rates of depression and other mental health problems in rural areas (Bergland, 1988; Buckwalter et al., 1994). Additionally, some have suggested that the characteristics of different environmental areas, such as population stability and levels of available support from both formal and informal sources, are important correlates of depression (O'Hara, Kohout, & Wallace, 1985). With regard to dementia, a mental health problem of particular importance to all elders, data remain unavailable for rural/urban comparisons of illness prevalence (Buckwalter et al., 1994). It is estimated, however, that scarce resources in rural areas, including professional and nonprofessional staff who could deliver specialized services, contribute to expected difficulties in diagnosis as well as difficulties in the provision of family assistance (Buckwalter et al., 1994).

Indicators of socioeconomic status, including levels of poverty among older rural adults and educational and employment disadvantages, underscore the economic disadvantage characteristic of many rural areas, particularly those localities relatively isolated from urban centers. Educational attainment, a resource positively related to older adult employment opportunities and subsequent retirement resources, also remains lower in rural areas (Cordes, 1989). The interrelationship of educational, employment, and subsequent retirement resources in both current and future cohorts of rural elders remains consistent predictors of poor quality of life. Rural areas, when compared with urban ones, have disproportionately large numbers of older persons living in poverty (Coward, 1987; Glasgow, 1988; Rural Sociological Society Task Force on Persistent Rural Poverty, 1993). Age and residence interact to increase the numbers of older rural adults living with inadequate financial resources. For example, one-half of all older Americans who live in poverty reside in rural areas and small towns (Coward, 1987; Glasgow & Beale, 1985), with monthly Social Security benefits averaging $60 less for rural elders as compared with urban ones (U.S. Senate Special Committee on Aging, 1992). In addition, potential sources of assistance, such as federally funded Supplemental Security Income (SSI) and Food Stamp programs, continue to be underutilized by many eligible elders (American Association of Retired Persons, 1991a, 1991b).

Rural/Urban Comparisons of Family Context

Kinship ties and attitudes about family

Investigators comparing the lifestyles of rural and urban families noted more traditional family values among rural than among urban residents, with both men and women expressing more conservative attitudes toward women's participation in the workplace and marital stability (Hennon & Brubaker, 1986; Powers et al., 1981; Rosenfeld, 1985; Scanzoni & Arnett, 1988). Traditional family values were demonstrated by greater gender-role differentiation among husbands and wives in rural areas as compared with those in urban communities (Scanzoni & Arnett, 1988). For example, rural women, compared with urban ones, were more likely to be married, had more children, lived in larger families, completed their families earlier, and placed greater importance on strong community and family ties (Brown, 1981). Rural women, historically and currently, have been described as having pride in their rural heritage and culture, continuing traditions of self-care, and demonstrating strong family attachment and community involvement (Bigbee, 1986; Kivett, 1990). Historical accounts indicated the pivotal role rural women played in the preservation of family traditions, with their roles in family and community affected only in marginal ways by the occupational and community activities of male family members (Kivett, 1990).

In addition, divorce rates remain lower in rural areas, as compared with urban ones, particularly among farm couples (Coward, Cutler, & Schmidt, 1989; Lee & Cassidy, 1985). Note, however, that the lower divorce rates characteristic of rural areas do not coincide with higher levels of marital satisfaction. In fact, evidence suggests no significant differences in rural/ urban couples' marital satisfaction or adjustment (Lee & Cassidy, 1985). Although some moderation in these attitudes has occurred, significant rural/ urban family value differences continue to exist (Dorfman & Heckert, 1988; Dorfman & Hill, 1986; Lee, 1986). Rural elders and their families, in general, remain more conservative and place greater importance on family and community interaction as compared with urban families, who place greater value on the economic and cultural aspects of community life (Heller, Quesada, Harvey, & Warner, 1981; Hennon & Brubaker, 1986).

Support for elderly family members

Romantic views of rurality and the maintenance of more conservative values have contributed to perceptions that older adults living in rural areas have larger and stronger informal networks, including kinship networks, than do those in urban areas. Studies show, however, that characterizations of rural areas as peaceful oases that envelop elders in supportive networks and provide buffers against stresses and hardships are not accurate (Coward et al., 1994; Fitchen, 1991). For example, Crowell, George, Blazer, and Landerman (1986) found that rural residence was differentially related to the effects of stress and hardship on depression, with younger rural residents receiving benefits whereas middle-aged and older adults did not. In fact, rural older adults, especially unmarried males, ex-farmers, and persons living in small towns, are disadvantaged when compared with urban residents in the amounts of available family support and interaction they have with family members and others (Lee, 1988; Lee & Cassidy, 1981, 1985).

Older rural adult marital status and proximity to kin

The availability of marital partners and proximate kin is associated with older adults' ability to remain in their communities as well as their quality of life and health status, particularly that of functional health (Coward et al., 1994). With regard to the importance of marital partners, older married adults are happier, more satisfied, and in better physical and mental health than widowed or unmarried older adults (Reiss & Lee, 1988). Additionally, older married adults are less likely to skip meals (Davis, Murphy, & Neuhaus, 1988) and are less anxious about the availability of support during illness or emergency situations (Fengler, Danigelis, & Little, 1983). Marital partners also are reported as the most dependable caregivers for persons experiencing difficulties with daily living tasks (Stoller, 1992). In light of these marital status advantages for all elders, regardless of residence, what issues are unique to the rural context?

First, when rural/urban elders were compared across age by residence groupings, rural elders in the groups 65 to 74 years, 75 to 84 years, and 85 or more years of age were more likely than urban elders to be married (Coward et al., 1994), a finding suggesting a "marital advantage" for rural elders. Primary caregivers in rural areas are, in fact, more likely to be spouses, but they also are more likely to provide care with fewer personal, financial, and community resources when compared with urban caregivers (Stone, 1991). Although these findings indicate that rural elders have the support and intimacy noted as marital advantages, caution should be used when interpreting the effects of such advantages. First, the greater likelihood of being married might not actually work to the advantage of rural elders, particularly older women, if they care for spouses when they have inadequate financial resources and when they are likely to continue caregiving, because of limited personal and community support, until their own health is jeopardized. Greene (1984), for example, reported the greater likelihood that rural elders were institutionalized at younger ages than urban ones, suggesting the personal and economic difficulties of providing care for frail and dependent family members in rural areas. Second, the assumption that older rural adults are more socially secure because greater proportions of them are married, an artifact partially due to age, actually may leave rural older adults disadvantaged when widowhood is experienced and the number of available proximate family members is less than that for urban elders.

Specific to rural/urban differences in living arrangements, few significant differences have been noted. Coward and associates (1994) reported no significant differences in the living arrangements of rural and noncentral city elders. Rural elders differed significantly from central city elders, however, with rural older adults more likely to live in husband/wife households. With advancing age across all residential types, the proportion of elders living alone increased, with greater than 40% living alone in the 85+ age category.

As older rural adults advance in age and experience greater likelihood of widowhood, the geographic dispersion of proximate kin places them at risk for inadequate informal support and social isolation. The importance of proximity to informal support has been a consistent finding in studies examining assistance to older adults. Family propinquity increases the amount and type of social interaction, including face-to-face parent-child interactions and other types of informal support available to older rural adults (Kivett, 1985; Mercier, Paulson, & Morris, 1988). Note, however, that differences in the propinquity of family members occur not only between rural and urban older adults but also within rural environments. Older rural nonfarm adults, representing the majority of the rural older population, are the least likely across residential categories (urban, rural farm, and rural nonfarm) to have children nearby, placing them at most risk for inadequate informal support (Dwyer, Lee, & Coward, 1990; Lee, 1988).

The possibility of inadequate informal support is particularly important in light of the underutilization of formal services by rural elders and their families. Rural families, even during final health crises, continue to rely very little on formal assistance (Kivett & McCulloch, 1989, 1992). Longitudinal results showed that families became increasingly more important to older rural adults, particularly in meeting the daily needs of frail elders and in times of emergency. By very old age (defined as 75 years of age and older), approximately one in every four very old rural adults needed the assistance of a primary caregiver for accomplishment of activities of daily living (Kivett & McCulloch, 1989). Across residential categories, urban elders with mild impairment in activities of daily living in large cities were more likely to live with a child than rural elders who also had mild impairments, a further example of the increased likelihood that rural elders will have inadequate amounts of informal support (Lee, Dwyer, & Coward, 1990).

Intergenerational exchange

Rural and urban older adults also differ in the amounts of help and association they exchange, even when other factors such as proximity to adult children, gender, and marital status are controlled (Scott & Roberto, 1988). For example, older rural adults exchanged more help during times of illness and participated in more vacation visits and reunions with children than urban ones. Older rural men provided more financial aid to their children than urban ones provided. Rates of interaction among married farm men and their fathers were significantly higher than father-son interactions across other occupational/residential categories (Klatsky, 1972). Compared with the networks of urban residents, the helping networks in rural areas consist primarily of informal helpers, largely representing help from family members (Blieszner, McAuley, Newhouse, & Mancini, 1987; Coward, Cutler, & Mullens, 1990). Many investigators, however, have expressed concern about the effects of young adult out-migration and the increase in rural female labor force participation on the numbers and availability of family members for informal support (Matthews & Rosner, 1988; Tennstedt, McKinlay, & Sullivan, 1989).

HETEROGENEITY OF RURAL FAMILIES

Although the preceding summary has provided a brief overview of findings about rural aging and family life, the heterogeneity among rural populations makes generalizations difficult. Variant patterns of family interaction have been found in rural areas, with aging and family life across rural environments representing geographically, culturally, and regionally diverse phenomena (Lee, 1988; Rowles, 1988). For example, farm families differ from rural nonfarm families, rural minority families experience aging differently than the rural majority population, and different regions of the country exhibit differential family values, attitudes, and behaviors. Additionally, rural environments differ by their relationship to metropolitan areas, their rural developmental and industrial context, and the amounts and types of in- and out-migration that occur within specific rural environments. Recognition of these rural differences is important for family scholars as well as for professionals practicing in rural areas. For example, study results based on assumptions of rural homogeneity, in either conceptual or operational terms, overgeneralize findings and, thereby, mask contextual information important to the development and implementation of public policy and service delivery in specific rural areas (Deavers, 1992).

Farm versus Nonfarm Families

Relatively few aging and kinship studies have been conducted specific to farm versus nonfarm differences in rural areas. Evidence suggests, however, that not only do older rural adults differ individually across social, economic and occupational, and health dimensions when farm/nonfarm distinctions are examined, but the experience these elders have within their families also differs.

Less than 5% of the total rural population can be classified as farming-dependent (Bigbee, 1986; Coward, 1987; Lee, 1986). Family ownership, however, remains the dominant type of farm ownership, as compared with agribusiness operations, with many rural farm men and women working extra off-farm jobs to maintain an agrarian lifestyle (Rosenfeld, 1985). Although rural/urban comparisons about aging and kinship have revealed few differences, one of the most interesting outcomes of recent research has been the detection of differences in the experiences of aging and family life between farm and nonfarm rural residents (Lee & Cassidy, 1981, 1985). For example, some scholars suggest that, in an industrial society that separates work and family roles, farm families are theoretically different from other family types (Rosenfeld, 1985). Compared with other families, farm families are distinguished by the overlap between farm family and business activities, the intergenerational nature of the family business, the wife's role in the farming enterprise, and the more fluid role boundaries that accompany the meshing of farm and family roles (Davis-Brown & Salamon, 1988; Olson & Schellenberg, 1986).

Specific to individual risks, farming has been identified as one of the most hazardous occupations, and farmers and their families continue in this working environment with little or no state or federal labor regulations (Emanuel, Draves, & Nycz, 1990). Farming differs from other occupations in that children and adolescents under the age of 18 and elders over the age of 65 actively operate machinery and distribute chemicals, herbicides, and pesticides (U.S. Bureau of the Census, 1989), and all family members, regardless of the degree to which they participate in farming operations, are exposed to the hazards of the farm work environment (Cordes & Rea, 1988). Exposure to herbicides and pesticides, for instance, has been linked to malignant lymphoma, lymphatic leukemia, and stomach and bladder cancers (Coye, 1986). The problems of accidents and illnesses for older farmers frequently are compounded by remote work sites and consequent long distances to medical care and, with aging, the possibility of effects from drug interaction, slower reaction time, fatigue, and sight and hearing impairments. Cogbill, Busch, and Stiers (1985) reported that farmers injured from tractor overturns lie in the field an average of one hour and 40 minutes before they are found. Still others report that a large proportion of farm injuries are treated only at home, with no follow-up consultation by professional medical personnel (Kohn, 1988; Rosenblatt & Lasley, 1991), with Kohn reporting that injuries as serious as broken backs were treated in such a manner.

It is likely that the increased risks experienced by older adults living on farms, particularly those who continue to participate in the farming enterprise, affect individual as well as family responsibilities, both in type and extent of care and in the expenses needed to provide care when health problems occur. Little or no information, however, is currently available of such a specific nature, particularly information about family caregiving differences between farm and nonfarm residents. Specific to family health expenditures, however, studies examining public/private health insurance do indicate that significantly higher numbers of rural residents rely either on health insurance coverage purchased outside the workplace or on insurance coverage that tends to require higher premiums and provides benefits that are less comprehensive than the coverage purchasable within the workplace (Patton, Nycz, & Schmelzer, 1990). The high cost of insurance coverage purchased outside the workplace affect the amounts of out-of-pocket expenses older rural adults and their families must expend for gaps in health coverage, and these costs also increase the numbers of rural residents who are uninsured, a figure estimated to be as high as 53% for some rural counties (Patton et al., 1990). The inability of rural elders and families to purchase private insurance coverage, coupled with a general resistance to public assistance, may help to explain the amounts of home care noted in occupational injury studies of the farm population.

Within-rural comparisons also showed notable farm/nonfarm differences with regard to family characteristics, such as family interaction and family propinquity (Lee, 1988; Lee & Cassidy, 1981, 1985). Rural farm residents, for example, had relatively high levels of interaction with kin and lived in close proximity to both children and grandchildren when compared with elders living in other rural areas or in small towns or in cities. On the other hand, rural nonfarm residents ranked at or near the bottom across residential categories in family propinquity and kin interaction, placing these older adults, the majority of rural residents, at the greatest risk of inadequate proximate family support (Lee, 1988; Lee & Cassidy, 1981, 1985; Lee et al., 1990). Older in-migrants might be particularly disadvantaged in this regard, especially when they retire to areas where they have had little or no previous family or occupational connection.

Racial/Ethnic Diversity

Rural minority families often live in ethnic and cultural isolation, with many elders residing in culturally intact enclaves (Hawkes, Kutner, Wells, Christopherson, & Almirol, 1981). Despite the serious risks and lifelong consequences of poor educational and employment opportunities for rural minority individuals, few researchers specifically have addressed rural aging and kinship issues in the context of cultural and ethnic diversity. Diverse cultural and ethnic patterns interact with environmental factors, such as limited employment and educational opportunities and community resources, to affect aging and kinship (see also Johnson, this volume).

Rural minorities have consistently ranked among the most severely economically disadvantaged groups (Kivett, 1993; Rural Sociological Task Force on Persistent Rural Poverty, 1993), a characteristic that, coupled with the underutilization of public assistance typical of rural residents, elevates their risk of health problems (Jensen & Tienda, 1989). When poverty rates in rural areas were examined by racial/ethnic groups, minority rural residents consistently experienced greater proportions of economic hardship. Using 1989 figures, the percentages of elders living in poverty were reported as 40% for African Americans, 35% for Hispanics, 30% for American Indians, and 13% for whites (Rural Sociological Society Task Force on Persistent Rural Poverty, 1993).

The specific groups and proportion of minority elders residing in rural areas vary. For example, the largest elderly minority population, constituting approximately 6% of the older adults in rural areas, is that of African Americans. Although African American elders outnumber other ethnic/racial elders living in rural areas, a greater proportion of Native American older adults are rural residents, 52%, as compared with proportions for

Asian/Pacific Islanders or Hispanic Americans (10%), blacks (20%), and the majority population (white, 26%) (American Association of Retired Persons, 1987).

Minority groups, regardless of residential location, have long-standing histories of oppression with regard to the majority population and federal and local governments. Aging and family life for elders in specific rural minority groups, therefore, remain unique. Two culturally specific examples for Native American elders illustrate this uniqueness. First, Native American elders remain fearful that, when they become dependent, they will be permanently relocated off reservations to hospitals, nursing homes, or long-term care facilities perceived as demonstrating little awareness of, or concern for, tribal customs, laws, and lifestyles (Edwards & Egbert-Edwards, 1990). Second, Native American elders have unique concerns about economic dependency. Family resources are affected by cultural values and expectations as well as by fears and suspicions about governmental assistance that continues to be perceived as unfair and untrustworthy by Native American elders and their family members (Edwards & Egbert-Edwards, 1990).

Regional Differences in Aging and Kinship

Regional differences also contribute to rural diversity. Many early studies of rural aging were conducted in the eastern and southern regions of the country. These regionally specific studies were generalized to all rural areas and contributed to the widely held perception that rural elders in general received greater family and informal support than urban older adults received. Subsequent studies have shown regional differences in degrees of familism and cohesiveness among rural families. Heller and associates (1981) found that two family systems existed in the United States: one, an extended-kin or family-as-group form, was found in the East (Virginia), and a primary-kin or nuclear family type was found in midwestern (Ohio) and western (Nevada) samples. The higher levels of extended-kin interaction previously reported as characteristic of all rural families may, in fact, be particularistic to the eastern and southern regions of the country, and nuclear family ties may be more characteristic of the Midwest and West.

THEORETICAL AND METHODOLOGICAL ISSUES

Previous sections of this chapter have highlighted issues of particular importance to the examination and interpretation of aging and kinship relationships within a specific environmental context, rural America. Many investigators have provided descriptions of specific aspects of rural aging and family relations. Others have developed exploratory hypotheses regarding the relationships of various factors to aging and kinship in rural environments. The majority of these investigations have not been grounded in theoretical frameworks. Thus, researchers have rarely attended to the explication of causal mechanisms. If progress is to be made regarding the study of rural aging and kinship, contextual variables must be integrated within current theoretical frameworks.

Theoretical Integration of Place

Several phenomena contributing to the distinctiveness within rural environments and underscoring the need for studies that focus on aging and family diversity could be included in existing conceptual frameworks. One of these phenomena is place, a construct that represents the sociocultural context in which persons interact with their families and grow old. *Place* is defined as the land, community, or home location to which one is attached, and it has special meaning for many older rural adults and their families, particularly for those whose families have remained in an area over several generations.

Previous regional studies provide insights for the operationalization of place constructs. Norris-Baker and Scheidt's work, for example, examined the importance of place dependency to the experience of growing old in small rural Kansas towns (Norris-Baker & Scheidt, 1989; Scheidt & Norris-Baker, 1989). They examined the interrelationship of personal identity and place identity, using a contextual view of environmental stress that integrates environmental and social change within the context of historical, developmental, and nondevelopmental factors. Constructs that might serve as proxies for environmental context include subjective indicators such as the degree of attachment older adults have for place or older adults' history of generational ties to the land. Objective indicators include rates of elderly in-migration, young adult out-migration, rates of economic growth, and community tax base.

In brief, the diversity and the special meaning of place known to exist in rural areas should be included in theoretical frameworks used to examine the experience of aging and family life in rural areas. The development and understanding of the contextual relevance of aging and family in rural areas, however, depend on the integration of the causal linkage of place into existing theoretical frameworks (Newby & Buttel, 1980). The application of aging and kinship hypotheses is strengthened by the integration of environmental factors. Consistent evidence of environmental differences across rural areas, as well as rural/urban differences, particularly when health and financial resources are examined, points to the importance of this convergence. Thus, understanding of the experiences of aging and family life in rural areas will not be significantly increased without greater theoretical integration of the diversity that characterizes rural environments.

Methodological Issues

Although not singularly important to the study of rural aging and kinship, examinations of social phenomena in rural areas can benefit from attention to several methodological issues. Improvement in four specific domains, including rural operationalization, rural sample selection, study design, and unit of analysis, will strengthen the likelihood that hypotheses can be tested within a more inclusive contextual framework that increases the generalizability of findings and accounts for noted within-rural differences.

Operationalization of rural concepts

The use of a rural/urban dichotomy is problematic when issues such as aging and kinship are examined because the differences that exist across the continuum of residence should be reflected in both sampling and analysis stages (Coward et al., 1994; Deavers, 1992). Depending on the focus of study, it also might be important to include place characteristics that represent sociocultural, ecological, and occupational dimensions of the experience of aging and family life in diverse rural areas (Miller & Luloff, 1981). Deavers (1992) outlined three characteristics that set rural areas apart from urban ones: (1) the small scale and low density of rural areas, (2) the distance rural areas are from urban centers, and (3) the specialization of rural economies.

No consensus regarding the operational definition of rural, or nonmetropolitan, has emerged (Coward et al., 1994). Four operational strategies have been used by scholars in attempts to more accurately describe the diversity of rural areas. First, census definitions have been used to differentiate rural areas by defining rural places as small towns, villages, and open country with fewer than 2,500 residents. Second, Standard Metropolitan Statistical Area (SMSA) definitions have been used to define nonmetropolitan areas as those not a part of standard metropolitan areas, a classification that allows for the identification of rural communities within metropolitan areas. Third, rural areas have been conceptualized on a continuum along with other residential types, with anchors on the continuum defined as farm/open country at one end and large urban centers, such as New York City, at the other end (Coward et al., 1994). Fourth, the Economic Research Service-U.S. Department of Agriculture (ERS-USDA) has developed a typology that should prove helpful to aging and kinship scholars in that it provides a mixture of economic, social, and political dimensions important in differentiating rural communities (Deavers, 1992).

Sample selection

Second, it is important to recognize the continued value of both nationally representative and regional studies. Some issues, particularly those that are comparative in nature, require examination with national, representative samples of elders and families. To date, however, the majority of existing national samples do not contain adequate numbers of rural respondents to meet power and analysis assumptions or do not provide the information needed to make detailed environmental distinctions. For example, in a secondary analysis of existing data, one might begin with a very large sample but end up with empty cells or disproportionately sized residential groups as a result of subsample selection. Coward, Cutler, and Mullens (1990) underscored this problem in their examination of residential differences in rural/urban helping networks. After dividing representative national data into residential categories, including SMSA central cities, SMSA noncentral cities, and non-SMSA areas, they acknowledged that a further refinement of rural or non-SMSA areas would have been desirable, but only 56 of the total number of respondents (1,265) selected for their analysis lived on farms. In the future, national sampling frames should be designed to provide adequate numbers of rural minority elders, elders in different residential categories (e.g., farm/nonfarm, villages, small towns), and elders from different rural regions.

On the other hand, samples from smaller geographic areas can be advantageous for in-depth examinations of specific rural aging and kinship issues. For example, Kivett's studies provide longitudinal information about the aging and final health crises of older rural adults in a rural, isolated area (Kivett & McCulloch, 1989; Kivett & Suggs, 1986). The most recent of these studies provided a 13-year account of rural elders' aging in place and included information on both surviving and nonsurviving elders (Kivett & McCulloch, 1989). Kivett and associates collected information from public records, community informants, surrogate family members, and primary caregivers of very old survivors, sources that would be difficult to tap in large national samples. Regional studies could be strengthened, however, by greater attention to the possible effects of geographic location and regional differences on aging and kinship relationships. To date, however, most regional investigations provide general demographic sample profiles. Few provide the needed integration of environmental context effects on outcomes.

In addition, regional studies are suitable for examinations that integrate multiple-method research strategies. Rank (1988), for example, suggested that the combination of several techniques, such as the embedding of in-depth interviews within surveys and the addition of survey research components to fieldwork, provided a more comprehensive picture of family phenomena than that provided by a singular method. The in-depth qualities and richness characteristic of qualitative methodology complement quantitative data. On the other hand, the generalizability and reliability characteristic of quantitative studies enhance information collected with qualitative methods. Specific to the issues discussed here, the use of multiple methods of data collection would be especially helpful because they would provide comprehensive ways of examining rural heterogeneity and rural reality versus myth in investigations of aging and kinship in rural areas.

Study design

A common issue in social gerontology, that of cross-sectional versus longitudinal design, also is important in studies of aging and family life in rural context. Although a few national (e.g., Coward & Dwyer, 1991) and regional (e.g., Kivett & McCulloch, 1989, 1992; Kivett & Suggs, 1986) longitudinal rural studies have been conducted, more are needed. Several issues, such as the types and amounts of rural family interaction and support, the difficulties that elders have with community resources and health care access, and the patterns of caregiving among diverse rural populations, point to the importance of being able to disentangle rural advantage myths and provide a better understanding of the changes that occur in the context of a changing and often declining community environment. The incorporation of cross-sequential designs that address attrition problems and provide within- and across-wave comparisons is an excellent way of overcoming the limitations of both cross-sectional and longitudinal designs (Schaie, 1983, but see Mangen, this volume, for limitations of cross-sequential designs). As with gerontology as a whole, the vast majority of conclusions about aging in rural contexts have been based on cross-sectional data. The numbers of rural elders and continued increases in life expectancy require the same imperative for longitudinal data as called for in other areas of gerontology and family studies.

Unit of analysis

Additionally, a dearth of studies specific to rural aging and family life has been conducted that examines aging and family issues using dyadic or family data. Comparing results across individual and dyadic units of analysis shows that reporting varies by the perceptions of individual family members (Anderson & McCulloch, 1993; Godwin & Scanzoni, 1989; Thompson & Williams, 1982). These findings underscore the importance of (1) identifying individual family members' perceptual differences regarding family constructs and relationships and (2) investigating appropriate ways of incorporating "extra" data from multiple family members. For example, should family data be the average of the responses of husband and wife (e.g., Bagozzi & Van Loo, 1981), the respecification of one family member model with additional family members (e.g., Fried & Udry, 1979), or the simultaneous estimation of individual family members' reports about family constructs and relationships (e.g., Anderson & McCulloch, 1993; Godwin & Scanzoni, 1989; Thompson & Williams, 1982)?

In particular, dyadic and family data are needed to clarify understanding of caregiving responsibilities and filial expectations, caregiving stress and burden, and older adult and family perceptions of informal network availability and support. It is possible that previous results, based largely on reports from only one family member, might not accurately represent phenomena of interest, particularly when proximate kin are scarcer than expected, as is often the case in rural areas. Dyadic examinations might be especially revealing in rural areas as the out-migration of many younger family members affects filial expectations, the number of available proximate kin, and the delivery of care to frail older family members.

CONCLUSIONS AND FUTURE DIRECTIONS

The purpose of this chapter has been the presentation of unique properties about aging and kinship in rural areas. Disparities exist between rural and urban areas, revealing that the aging of rural residents differs in important ways from that of urban dwellers. Many older rural adults, although often viewing their situations in a positive light, must cope with limited personal, family, and community resources. These limitations affect quality of life and contribute to difficulties with the availability of goods and services, access to health care, and the receipt of family and community support. Additionally, heterogeneity exists within rural areas, including differences in aging and family life across geographic regions, racial/ethnic minority and majority groups, and farm/nonfarm residence.

Distinctions within rural communities have been inadequately addressed in previous studies, contributing to three specific shortcomings in the understanding and use of information about rural aging and kinship. First, the limited attention given to the identification of differences has contributed to oversimplified and, in some instances, erroneous descriptions of older adults and families in rural areas. Second, generalizations about rural areas, without consideration of diversity, have contributed to limited theoretical explanations about aging and kinship in rural areas. Third, the overgeneralization of rural findings to all rural areas has contributed to ineffective public policy development, program implementation, and service delivery.

Future Directions

Studies that specifically address issues of diversity not only will contribute to understanding patterns of aging and kinship within rural communities but also will provide the basis for effective public policy and intervention. What patterns of family support exist across residential categories, and what are the implications of these patterns for policies and programs? Little is known about the aging of racial/ethnic minority elders in the rural context. Are adequate numbers of proximate kin available to minority elder residents? Are caregiving responsibilities different across rural racial/ethnic groups? Do macroenvironmental factors affect rural elders and families differently when regional, racial/ethnic, and farm/nonfarm contextual issues are analyzed? Additionally, virtually nothing is known about alternative family and individual lifestyles in rural areas. How do ever-single, gay, and lesbian people experience aging in rural areas, places that are characterized as less accepting of alternative lifestyles? Methodologically, how useful are standard instruments in assessing attitudes and behaviors across culturally, regionally, and residentially diverse rural residents?

Just as important, greater attention must be paid to the use of theoretical frameworks in the explication of causal pathways for rural aging and kinship issues. Using even the simplest definition of theory, a set of statements and propositions that explain phenomena, it becomes clear that greater understanding of the experiences of aging and family life will come from the integration of environmental propositions with traditional social and psychological frameworks. For example, what effects do contextual factors have on the hypothesized relationships among intergenerational solidarity dimensions, association, consensus, and helping behavior (Bengtson, Olander, & Haddad, 1976)? Does the diversity in rural areas affect the process of caregiver selection; that is, does the substitution principle (Horowitz, 1985; Shanas, 1979) noted in studies of caregivers in general also apply across farm/nonfarm and racial/ethnic groups? In addition, how does the overlap of work and family roles characteristic among farm families affect intergenerational helping and deferred reciprocity?

The integration of diversity and theory should provide more realistic guidelines for the development of workable rural public policy and a better understanding of the ways in which practitioners can deliver services to older rural adults and their families across diverse regions and cultures. Research on service delivery in rural areas consistently underscores the problems of transposing urban public policy and service delivery models to rural areas. Moreover, economic concerns and increases in the numbers of persons who need services underscore the importance of policies that recognize social and cultural barriers across diverse environmental contexts. Such barriers increase the likelihood that older rural adults and their families will underutilize services.

In conclusion, the focus of this chapter was on aging and kinship within a specific population subgroup, rural elderly adults. The cornerstone of the discussion was the importance of recognizing heterogeneity within rural environments. If greater understanding of aging and kinship in rural areas is to be achieved, investigators must not only note these differences but also incorporate a means of testing the effects of these differences in examinations of issues such as informal support, caregiving, and intergenerational interaction. This incorporation is needed at multiple levels, including integration of contextual factors in theory testing and use of research designs and sampling frames that provide mechanisms for detecting such differences. Events occurring in the last decade, such as the farm crisis, the loss of manufacturing jobs, and the continued problems of delivering services and health care to rural residents, further underscore the importance of increasing understanding of this specific population subgroup. The evidence, presented here and elsewhere, indicates that much remains to be examined with regard to aging and kinship in rural areas.

REFERENCES

American Association of Retired Persons. (1987). *A portrait of older Americans.* Washington, DC: Author.

American Association of Retired Persons. (1991a). *Food stamp program: A review of participation rates and outreach activities.* Washington, DC: Author.

American Association of Retired Persons. (1991b). *Supplemental security income (SSI): A review of participation rates and outreach activities.* Washington, DC: Author.

Anderson, T. B., & McCulloch, B. J. (1993). Conjugal support: Factor structure for older husbands and wives. *Journal of Gerontology: Social Sciences, 48,* S133–142.

Ansello, E. F. (1980). Special considerations in rural aging. *Educational Gerontology, 5,* 343–354.

Bagozzi, R. P., & Van Loo, M. F. (1981). Decision-making and fertility: A theory of exchange in the family. In T. K. Burch (Ed.), *Demographic behavior: Interdisciplinary perspectives on decision-making* (pp. 91–124). Boulder, CO: Westview Press.

Bengtson, V. L., Olander, E. B., & Haddad, A. A. (1976). The "generation gap" and aging family members: Toward a conceptual model. In J. Gubrium (Ed.), *Time, roles, and the self in old age* (pp. 237–263). New York: Human Science.

Bergland, B. (1988). Rural mental health: Report of the national action commission on the mental health of rural Americans. *Journal of Rural Community Psychology, 9,* 29–39.

Bigbee, J. L. (1986). Rural-urban differences in hardiness, stress, and illness among women. (Doctoral dissertation, University of Texas at Austin, 1985). *Dissertation Abstracts International, 46,* 4405.

Blieszner, R., McAuley, W. J., Newhouse, J., & Mancini, J. A. (1987). Rural-urban differences in service use by older adults. In T. H. Brubaker (Ed.), *Aging, health and family: Long-term care* (pp. 162–174). Newbury Park, CA: Sage.

Brown, D. L. (1981). A quarter century of trends and changes in the demographic structure of American families. In R. T. Coward & W. M. Smith, Jr. (Eds.), *The family in rural society* (pp. 9–25). Boulder, CO: Westview Press.

Buckwalter, K. C., Smith, M., & Caston, C. (1994). Mental and social health of the rural elderly. In R. T. Coward, G. Kukulka, C. N. Bull, & J. M. Galliher (Eds.), *Health services for rural elders* (pp. 203–232). New York: Springer Publishing Co.

Cogbill, T., Busch, H., & Stiers, G. (1985). Farm accidents in children. *Pediatrics, 76,* 562–566.

Cordes, D. H., & Rea, D. F. (1988). Health hazards of farming. *American Family Physician, 38,* 233–244.

Cordes, S. M. (1989). The changing rural environment and the relationship between health services and rural development. *Health Services Research, 23,* 757–784.

Coward, R. T. (1987). Poverty and aging in rural America. *Human Services in the Rural Environmental, 10,* 41–49.

Coward, R. T., Cutler, S. J., & Mullens, R. A. (1990). Residential differences in the comparisons of the helping networks of impaired elders. *Family Relations, 39,* 44–50.

Coward, R. T., Cutler, S. J., & Schmidt, F. (1989). Differences in the household composition of elders by age, gender, and area of residence. *Gerontologist, 29,* 814–821.

Coward, R. T., & Dwyer, J. W. (1991). *Health programs and services for elders in rural America: A review of the life circumstances and formal services that affect the health and well-being of elders.* Kansas, City, MO: National Resources Center for Rural Elderly.

Coward, R. T., McLaughlin, D. K., Duncan, R. P., & Bull, C. N. (1994). An overview of health and aging in rural America. In R. T. Coward, G. Kukulka, C. N. Bull, & J. M. Galliher (Eds.), *Health services for rural elders* (pp. 1–32). New York: Springer Publishing Co.

Coward, R. T., Miller, M. K., & Dwyer, J. W. (1990). Rural America in the 1980s: A context for rural health research. *Journal of Rural Health, 6,* 357–363.

Coye, M. J. (1986). The health effects of agriculture production: II. The health of the community. *Journal of Public Health Policy, 7,* 340–354.

Crowell, Jr., B. A., George, L. K., Blazer, D., & Landerman, R. (1986). Psychosocial risk factors and urban and rural differences in the prevalence of major depression. *British Journal of Psychiatry, 149,* 307–314.

Davis, M. A., Murphy, S. P., & Newhaus, J. M. (1988). Living arrangements and eating behaviors of older adults in the United States. *Journal of Gerontology: Social Sciences, 43,* S96–98.

Davis-Brown, K., & Salamon, S. (1988). Farm families in crisis: An application of stress theory to farm family research. In R. Marotz-Baden, C. B. Hennon, & T. H. Brubaker (Eds.), *Families in rural America: Stress, adaptation and revitalization* (pp. 47–55). St. Paul, MN: National Council on Family Relations.

Deavers, K. (1992). What is rural? *Policy Studies Journal, 2,* 184–189.

Dorfman, L. T., & Heckert, D. A. (1988). Egalitarianism in retired rural couples: Household tasks, decision making, and leisure activities. In R. Marotz-Baden, C. B. Hennon, & T. H. Brubaker (Eds.), *Families in rural America: Stress, adaptation and revitalization* (pp. 85–92). St. Paul, MN: National Council on Family Relations.

Dorfman, L. T., & Hill, E. A. (1986, November). *Rural housewives and retirement: Joint decision-making matters.* Paper presented at the 38th Annual Scientific Meeting of the Gerontological Society of America, New Orleans.

Dwyer, J., Lee, G. R., & Coward, R. T. (1990). The health status, health services utilization and support networks of the rural elderly: A decade review. *Journal of Rural Health, 6,* 379–398.

Edwards, E. D., & Egbert-Edwards, M. (1990). Family care and the native American elderly. In M. S. Harper (Ed.), *Minority aging: Essential curricula content for selected health and allied health professions* (pp. 145–163). DHHS Publication No. HRS (P-DV-90-4). Washington, DC: Health Resources and Services Administration, Department of Health and Human Services.

Emanuel, D. A., Draves, D. L., & Nycz, G. R. (1990). Occupational health services for farmers. *American Journal of Industrial Medicine, 18,* 149–162.

Fengler, A. P., Danigelis, N., & Little, V. C. (1983). Later life satisfaction and household structure: Living with others and living alone. *Aging and Society, 3,* 357–377.

Fitchen, J. M. (1991). *Endangered spaces, enduring places: Change, identity, and survival in rural America.* Boulder, CO: Westview Press.

Fried, E. S., & Udry, J. R. (1979). Wives' and husbands' expected costs and benefits of childbearing as predictors of pregnancy. *Social Biology, 26,* 265–274.

Geller, J. M. (1989). The rural health paradox. *Earth Matters, 38,* 19–23.

Glasgow, N. (1988). *The nonmetro elderly: Economic and demographic status.* RDRR No. 70, Economic Research Service. Washington, DC: U.S. Department of Agriculture.

Glasgow, N., & Beale, C. L. (1985). Rural elderly in demographic perspective. *Rural Development Perspectives, 2,* 22–26.

Glasgow, N., & Reeder, R. J. (1990). Economic and fiscal implications of nonmetropolitan retirement migration. *Journal of Applied Gerontology, 9,* 433–451.

Godwin, D. D., & Scanzoni, J. (1989). Couple consensus during marital joint decision-making: A context, process, outcome model. *Journal of Marriage and the Family, 51,* 943–956.

Greene, V. (1984). Premature institutionalization among the rural elderly in Arizona. *Public Health Reports, 99,* 58–62.

Hawkes, G. R., Kutner, N. G., Wells, M. J., Christopherson, V. A., & Almirol, E. B. (1981). Families in cultural islands. In R. T. Coward & W. M. Smith, Jr. (Eds.), *The family in rural society* (pp. 87–126). Boulder, CO: Westview Press.

Heller, P. L., Quesada, G. M., Harvey, D. L., & Warner, L. G. (1981). Rural familism: Interregional analysis. In R. T. Coward & W. M. Smith, Jr. (Eds.), *The family in rural society* (pp. 73–85). Boulder, CO: Westview Press.

Hennon, C. B., & Brubaker, T. H. (1986). Rural families: Characteristics and conceptualization. In R. Marotz-Baden, C. B. Hennon, & T. H. Brubaker (Eds.), *Families in rural America: Stress, adaptation and revitalization* (pp. 1–9). St. Paul, MN: National Council on Family Relations.

Horowitz, A. (1985). Family caregiving to the frail elderly. In M. P. Lawton & G. L. Maddox (Eds.), *Annual Review of Gerontology and Geriatrics, 5,* 194–246.

Jensen, L., & Tienda, M. (1989). Nonmetropolitan minority families in the United States: Trends in racial and ethnic economic stratification, 1959–1986. *Rural Sociology, 54,* 509–532.

Johansen, H. E., & Fuguitt, G. V. (1990). The changing rural village. *Rural Development Perspective, 7,* 2–6.

Kivett, V. R. (1985). Consanguinity and kin level: Their relative importance to the helping networks of older adults. *Journal of Gerontology, 40,* 228–234.

Kivett, V. R. (1990). Older rural women: Mythical, forebearing, and unsung. *Journal of Rural Community Psychology, 11,* 83–101.

Kivett, V. R. (1993). Informal supports among older rural minorities. In C. N. Bull (Ed.), *Aging in rural America* (pp. 204–215). Newbury Park, CA: Sage.

Kivett, V. R., & McCulloch, B. J. (1989). *Support networks of the very old: Rural caregivers and receivers (Caswell III, 1976–1989).* Final Report to AARP Andrus Foundation. Greensboro: University of North Carolina.

Kivett, V. R., & McCulloch, B. J. (1992). Older rural nonsurvivors: Their prediction and terminal care. *Journal of Applied Gerontology, 11,* 407–424.

Kivett, V. R., & Suggs, P. K. (1986). *Caswell revisited: A ten-year follow-up on the rural by-passed elderly.* Final Report to AARP Foundation. Greensboro: University of North Carolina at Greensboro.

Klatsky, S. R. (1972). *Patterns of contact with relatives.* Washington, DC: American Sociological Association.

Kohn, H. (1988). *The last farmer.* New York: Summit.

Krout, J. A. (1986). *The aged in rural America.* Westport, CT: Greenwood Press.

Krout, J. A. (1988). Rural versus urban differences in elderly parents' contact with their children. *Gerontologist, 28,* 198–203.

Lee, G. R. (1986). *Rural families: Stereotypes and reality.* Studies prepared for the use of the Subcommittee on Agriculture and Transportation of the Joint Economic Committee, Congress of the United States. Washington, DC: U.S. Government Printing Office.

Lee, G. R. (1988). Kinship ties among older people: The residence factor. In R. Marotz-Baden, C. B. Hennon, & T. H. Brubaker (Eds.), *Families in rural America: Stress, adaptation and revitalization* (pp. 176–182). St. Paul, MN: National Council on Family Relations.

Lee, G. R., & Cassidy, M. L. (1981). Kinship systems and extended family ties. In R. T. Coward & W. M. Smith, Jr. (Eds.), *The family in rural society* (pp. 57–71). Boulder, CO: Westview Press.

Lee, G. R. & Cassidy, M. L. (1985). Family and kinship relations of the rural elderly. In R. T. Coward & G. R. Lee (Eds.), *The elderly in rural society: Every fourth elder* (pp. 151–169). New York: Springer Publishing Co.

Lee, G. R., Dwyer, J. W., & Coward, R. T. (1990). Residential location and proximity to children among impaired elderly parents. *Rural Sociology, 55,* 579–589.

Matthews, S. H., & Rosner, T. T. (1988). Shared filial responsibility and the family as the primary caregiver. *Journal of Marriage and the Family, 50,* 185–195.

Mercier, J. M., Paulson, L., & Morris, E. W. (1988). Rural and urban elderly: Differences in the quality of the parent-child relationship. In R. Marotz-Baden, C. B. Hennon, & T. H. Brubaker (Eds.), *Families in rural America: Stress, adaptation and revitalization* (pp. 168–175). St. Paul, MN: National Council on Family Relations.

Miller, M. K., & Luloff, A. E. (1981). Who is rural? A typological approach to the examination of rurality. *Rural Sociology, 46,* 608–625.

Newby, H., & Buttel, F. H. (1980). Toward a critical rural sociology. In F. H.

Buttel & H. Newby (Eds.), *The rural sociology of advanced societies: Critical perspectives* (pp. 1–35). Montclair, NJ: Allanheld.

Norris-Baker, C., & Scheidt, R. J. (1989, November). *The meaning of place among older residents of small dying towns: A transactional approach.* Paper presented at the Annual Meeting of the Gerontological Society of America, Minneapolis.

O'Hara, M. W., Kohout, F. J., & Wallace, R. B. (1985). Depression among the rural elderly: A study of prevalence and correlates. *Journal of Nervous and Mental Disease, 173,* 582–589.

Olson, K. R., & Schellenberg, R. P. (1986). Farm stressors. *American Journal of Community Psychology, 14,* 555–569.

Patton, L. T., Nycz, G. R., & Schmelzer, J. R. (1990). *Health insurance coverage in early 1987: A metro-nonmetro county chartbook.* Marshfield: Wisconsin Rural Health Research Center.

Powers, E., Keith, P., & Goudy, W. J. (1981). Family networks of the rural aged. In R. T. Coward & W. S. Smith (Eds.), *The family in rural society* (pp. 199–217). Boulder, CO: Westview Press.

Rank, M. R. (1988). Racial differences in length of welfare use. *Social Forces, 66,* 1080–1101.

Reiss, I. L., & Lee, G. R. (1988). *Family systems in America* (4th ed.). New York: Holt, Rinehart, & Winston.

Rosenblatt, P. C., & Lasley, P. (1991). Perspective on farm accident statistics. *Journal of Rural Health, 7,* 51–62.

Rosenfeld, R. A. (1985). *Farm women: Work, farm, and family in the United States.* Chapel Hill: University of North Carolina Press.

Rowles, G. D. (1988). What's rural about rural aging? An Appalachian perspective. *Journal of Rural Studies, 4,* 115–124.

Rowles, G. D. (1991). Changing health culture in rural Appalachia: Implications for serving the elderly. *Journal of Aging Studies, 5,* 375–389.

Rural Sociological Society Task Force on Persistent Rural Poverty. (1993). *Persistent poverty in rural America.* Boulder, CO: Westview Press.

Scanzoni, J., & Arnett, C. (1988). Policy implications derived from a study of rural and urban marriages. In R. Marotz-Baden, C. B. Hennon, & T. H. Brubaker (Eds.), *Families in rural America: Stress, adaptation and revitalization* (pp. 270–280). St. Paul, MN: National Council on Family Relations.

Schaie, K. W. (1983). What can we learn from the longitudinal study of adult psychological development? In K. W. Schaie (Ed.), *Longitudinal studies of adult development* (pp. 1–19). New York: Guilford Press.

Scheidt, R. J., & Norris-Baker, C. (1989, August). *Small town to ghost town? Rural elderly at risk.* Paper presented at the 97th Annual Meeting of the American Psychological Association, New Orleans.

Scheidt, R. J., & Norris-Baker, L. (1990). A transactional approach to environmental stress among older residents of rural communities: Introduction to a special issue. *Journal of Rural Community Psychology, 11,* 5–30.

Scott, J. P., & Roberto, K. A. (1988). Informal supports of older adults: A rural-urban comparison. In R. Marotz-Baden, C. B. Hennon, & T. H. Brubaker (Eds.), *Families in rural America: Stress, adaptation and revitalization* (pp. 183–191). St. Paul, MN: National Council on Family Relations.

Shanas, E. (1979). Older people and their families: The new pioneers. *Journal of Marriage and the Family, 42,* 9–15.

Stoller, E. P. (1992). Gender differences in the experiences of caregiving spouses. In J. W. Dwyer & R. T. Coward (Eds.), *Gender, families, and elder care* (pp. 49–64). Newbury Park, CA: Sage.

Stoller, E. P., & Lee, G. R. (1994). Informal care. In R. T. Coward, G. Kukulka, C. N. Bull, & J. M. Galliher (Eds.), *Health services for rural elders* (pp. 33–64). New York: Springer Publishing Co.

Stone, R. I. (1991, July). *Rural caregiving: Implications for the aging network.* Presented at the National Symposium on the future of aging in rural America, National Resource Center for Rural Elderly, Kansas City, MO.

Tennstedt, S., McKinlay, J., & Sullivan, L. (1989). Informal care for frail elders: The role of secondary caregivers. *Gerontologist, 29,* 677–683.

Thompson, E., & Williams, R. (1982). Beyond wives' family sociology: A method for analyzing couple data. *Journal of Marriage and the Family, 44,* 999–1008.

U.S. Bureau of the Census. (1989). *Statistical abstract of the United States, 1988.* Washington, DC: U.S. Government Printing Office.

U.S. Congress. (1990). *Health care in rural America: Summary.* Office of Technology Assessment. Washington, DC: U.S. Government Printing Office.

U.S. Senate Special Committee on Aging. (1992). *Common beliefs about the rural elderly: Myth or fact?* Washington, DC: U.S. Government Printing Office, Serial No. 102-N.

Wagenfeld, M. O. (1990). Mental health and rural America: A decade review. *Journal of Rural Health, 4,* 507–522.

17

Convoys of Social Relations: Family and Friendships within a Life Span Context

Toni C. Antonucci and Hiroko Akiyama

It is now well known that one must view social support as a subset of the broader concept of social relations and that any true understanding of this concept must be considered within a life span perspective (Schulz & Rau, 1985). In this chapter, the life span concept of convoys of social support is expanded (Plath, 1980; Kahn, 1979; Kahn & Antonucci, 1980), and the nature of social relations among family and friends throughout adulthood and old age is explored. The chapter begins with a theoretical discussion of the role of family and friends throughout life, especially in old age. Through a consideration of the convoy model of social relations, social relations as a developmental phenomenon is emphasized. A selected review of the literature examining the characteristics of social relations and the effects of social relations on the health and well-being of the elderly is provided. Where relevant, data from the recently completed study of social relations over the life course are incorporated. The chapter concludes with a consideration of how to best utilize one's convoy of family and friendship relations in planning for a successful old age that realistically anticipates and meets the challenges of aging.

A LIFE COURSE PERSPECTIVE OF SOCIAL RELATIONS

Kahn and Antonucci (1980) developed the concept of convoys of social relations to expand upon previous conceptualizations of the term *convoy* within a social relations context (e.g., Plath, 1975). Their work focused on incorporating the relatively new theoretical perspective of life span developmental psychology as well as the psychological literature in the areas of attachment, social roles, and social support. In essence, Kahn and Antonucci attempted to provide an organizing framework for the emerging plethora of empirical research concerning the social support relations of adults.

The convoy model emphasizes recognition of the importance of social relations and their longitudinal character, including variation both with the specific individuals involved and with the specific types of relationships.

Although several researchers have utilized the convoy model within the context of ongoing empirical research (Antonucci & Akiyama, 1987b; Baltes, Mayer, Helmchen, & Steinhagen-Thiessen, in press; Ingersoll-Dayton & Antonucci, 1988; Levitt, 1991; Sonderen, Ormel, Brilman, & van den Heuvel, 1990), only quite recently have scholars offered additional theoretical examinations of the concept (e.g., Antonucci, 1994; Levitt, Coffman, & Guacci, in press). Other investigators have considered the fundamental processes and mechanisms involved in the interpersonal and intrapersonal aspects of social relations (Antonucci & Jackson, 1987; Brehm, 1984; Cohen, 1988; Coyne & Bolger, 1990; House, Landis, & Umberson, 1988; Pearlin & Turner, 1987; Sarason, Sarason, & Pierce, in press), as well as the possibility that age and gender differences in convoys of social relations might systematically reinforce different behavioral characteristics in older and younger people or men and women (Antonucci & Akiyama, 1987a, 1987b). In this chapter the question of age differences in social relationships among family members and friends is specifically addressed.

According to the convoy model, individuals move through their lifetimes surrounded by people who are close and important to them and who have a critical influence on their life and well-being. Kahn and Antonucci (1980) have consistently argued that this influence may be either positive or negative. In this life span model, the importance of relationships' building upon interactive sequences in a manner quite similar to that described in the infancy literature is emphasized. The infancy literature has traditionally stressed the development of qualitatively positive (or negative) relationships through the accumulation of mother-child interactions (Ainsworth, Blehar, Waters, & Wall, 1978). Much as attachment theorists argue that this accumulation of interactive sequences develops qualitatively distinct attachment types that can be either securely attached, anxiously avoidant, or ambivalently attached (i.e., either positive or negative), so too, can the accumulation of social relations across the life span have the same cumulative positive or negative effects.

This does not, however, mean to suggest a fatalistic projectory. Although some consistencies might occur in the types or styles of relationships people seek and experience in their lifetimes, all relationships are not of the same quality. The manner in which social relations accumulate and change over time is not yet well articulated nor well understood but is critical for understanding the long-term trajectory of social relations. Intraindividual, as well as interindividual, differences in social relations are important to understanding the role of different types of relationships in the maintenance of older adults' health and well-being.

SOCIAL RELATIONS AS A
DEVELOPMENTAL PHENOMENON

Social relations are a developmental phenomenon both interindividually and intraindividually. The term *interindividual development* suggests that relationships between individuals develop over time. An obvious example is the relationship individuals have with their parents. Babies' relationships with their parents are special and unique. As the babies grow into childhood, adolescence, adulthood, and later maturity, these original relationships remain important but also evolve, develop, and change in important ways. This point is particularly critical as more and more 60- and 70-year-olds continue to have relationships with their 80- and 90-year-old parents. Assessing the continuity and the change in these relationships is critical to understanding the bases for present and future interactions. As increased research focuses attention on the nature of social relations among older people, the longevity of these relationships must not be overlooked. Interpreted as an interindividual phenomenon, this means that many exchanges—reciprocal and nonreciprocal, positive and negative—experienced in the past are important to how people interpret the present. Friends or marital partners of 40 years and parents or siblings of 60 or 70 years have had ample time to experience a complex web of interrelationships, which are likely to result in feelings of cumulative goodwill or long-term conflict. A relationship with a relative could be forever marred or cemented by an event that took place many years earlier. Most people who work with elderly adults have recognized this phenomenon in many elderly people's approach to problem solving.

Intraindividual development (i.e., the change that takes place within an individual over time) also affects how one experiences old age. For the young person, intraindividual development often refers to the development of skills such as cognitive or physical ability. But the same types of changes are also experienced by older people on both similar and different dimensions. As people get older, they are increasingly likely to experience intraindividual changes in a wide array of areas, including, for example, physical changes, cognitive limitations, social changes, and health problems. Each of these intraindividual developments affects how the individual experiences the present and future. People change, as do relationships, but rarely without taking their personal history and family and friendship experiences with them. To neglect studying these changes would leave a very incomplete picture of social relationships among elderly people. Fortunately, recent empirical literature has offered considerable insights concerning relations with family and friends in later life.

METHODOLOGICAL AND DEFINITIONAL ISSUES

Before turning to an overview of the literature on family and friendship relationships among elderly adults, a brief review of several methodological and definitional issues is necessary. As several authors have noted, these issues influence both collection and interpretation of the data (Antonucci, 1990; Dean, Kolodny, Wood, & Ensel, 1989; Heitzmann & Kaplan, 1988; House & Kahn, 1985; Lubben, 1988; Orth-Gomer & Unden, 1987; Sonderen et al., 1990; Weinberger, 1987). Fortunately and unfortunately, the subject of social relations has colloquial meaning for almost everyone. Consequently, the literature contains a greater lapse in definitional and methodological rigor than might be tolerated in most scientific endeavors. As a result, everyone knows what a social relationship is, but there is no generally agreed upon definition of these relationships. For example, social relationships might be defined as relationships with people with whom you feel close, those who are important to you, those who do things with you, those who do things for you, those who are related to you, or those with whom you spend a lot of time. Although there might be a great deal of overlap in the persons named with the use of each of these definitions, it is clear that there would not necessarily be acceptable test-retest reliability with the use of these different definitions. At the same time, there is no reason to argue that any of these definitions is wrong. Depending on the nature of the relationship of interest, any one of these definitions might be appropriate.

A parallel problem exists methodologically because definition often drives measurement. One could reasonably ask for a list of role relationships, that is, a list of parents, siblings, children, spouse, friends, neighborhoods, coworkers. If one were seeking emotional or geographical closeness, however, eliciting names of those in particular role relationships might not provide the most direct route to assessing people who could provide help with instrumental tasks or with whom the individual might enjoy engaging in leisure activities.

Finally, the purpose of the research once again biases the type of data collected and, therefore, the information acquired. At least two types of research investigations in the field of social relations, specifically, social support, have dominated. The first explores the characteristics of social ties or social relations. These studies described the number and types of social networks, network members, and exchanges between members. This is the research conducted in the tradition of Boissevain (1974), Bott (1957), Fischer (1982), and Wellman and Wortley (1989). The second type of study focuses on the associations among social support, health, and well-being. This work has been the focus of both gerontological and epidemiological researchers (Berkman & Syme, 1979; Blazer, 1982; House, Robbins, & Metzner, 1982; see House et al., 1988, for a review). These studies have offered important insights into the maintenance of health and well-being among the elderly. The following review of the literature is loosely organized around these two types of research, with an emphasis on the family and friendship relationships of elderly people.

CHARACTERISTICS OF SOCIAL RELATIONS

Several studies now available provide descriptions of social relations among older adults, using sophisticated measures and representative samples. The findings of these studies are influenced, as outlined before, by both the measures utilized and the purpose of the investigation.

Structure of Social Relations

Virtually every study, regardless of the measurement technique utilized, reports that most elderly adults are well entrenched in a network or convoy of people who are very important to them. Most of these social networks consist of both family and friends relationships that have existed for a long time (Morgan, 1988; Stoller & Pugliesi, 1988; Wellman, 1990). Social isolation is rare, but its effects are usually devastating in terms of poorer mental and physical health status and increased likelihood of institutionalization and mortality (cf. Berkman & Syme, 1979; Chappell & Badger, 1989).

The most basic characteristic of social relations that has been described in the literature is size of the personal network. Of course, the way information about social relations is solicited distinctly influences the estimate of network size. Various data sources indicate that elderly adults have substantial family and friendship ties. Wellman (1990) reported that most research has identified a range of between 14 and 23 persons as significant active ties or personal network members. Wellman and Wortley (1989) estimated that their East York Canadian sample of adults had an average of approximately 137 "socially close intimates" and 210 "somewhat less-intimate, significant persons" with whom they were in active contact. Only about 4 to 7 of these ties would actually be considered close and supportive intimates, however. In their national sample of men and women over 50 years of age, Antonucci and Akiyama (1987b) reported an average of 8.9 network members, with an average of 3.5 very close intimates, 3.5 close intimates and only 1.9 less close intimates. Size of network did not differ across age groups. In their study of the elderly (aged 60 to 95 years) in Jerusalem, Auslander and Litwin (1991) reported an average of 6.34 people to whom the respondent could turn for support. A study of the elderly in southwestern France (Fuhrer, Antonucci, & Dartigues, 1992) indicated that most respondents reported eight or more people in their network, though this was more true of the youngest group (65 to 74 years, 51%), than of the other two age groups (75 to 84 years, 44%; over 85 years, 39%). This summary of studies from around the world reinforces House and Kahn's (1985) conclusion that assessment of 5 to 10 network members generally includes most significant relationships.

The personal networks of older adults include a significant proportion of both family and friends. The exact wording of the question greatly influences the nature of the response and the proportion of friends to family. Generally speaking, most network studies indicate that at least half of the active ties are kin relationships. If the question focuses on close and intimate relationships, the proportion of family can be much higher. Antonucci and Akiyama (1987b) reported that over 80% of their elderly respondents' networks consisted of family members, including spouse, children, siblings, and other kin. Their more recent study of social relations of people aged 13 to 94 years similarly indicated that family members occupy a sizable proportion of everyone's network, from 75% for teenagers to over 80% for all other adults (Antonucci & Akiyama, 1993). Not only are family members numerous in most people's convoy, but they also occupy positions of prominence. Over 90% of the respondents of all ages nominated a family member as the person closest to them. Intergenerational family research indicates that people feel closest to same-generation family members, next closest to adjacent-generation family members, and least close to nonadjacent-generation family members (Antonucci & Akiyama, 1991). Wellman (1990) also found that family members constituted at least half the network members of his East York Canadian sample, even when the definition included a broad general question about active ties or people with whom one has contact. Intergenerational family ties are clearly strong and important in the lives of older adults across most ethnic groups in the United States and around the world (Bengtson, Rosenthal, & Burton, 1990; Hagestad, 1988; Kendig, Hashimoto, & Coppard, 1992; Hermalin, Ofstedal, & Lee, 1992; Lawrence, Bennett, & Markides, 1992; Peterson & Peterson, 1988; Spitze & Logan, 1990; Taylor & Chatters, 1991).

Researchers have also examined relations among extended family members. For example, siblings appear to be a unique example of extended social relations (Bedford, 1989, 1992; Gold, 1989). Connidis (1989; Connidis & Davies, 1990) outlined the special nature of this relationship, noting that sibling ties are not like any other long-term family or friendship relationship. Sibling relationships vary widely and are often strongly influenced by geographic proximity and life circumstances. Most siblings, however, seem to experience some feelings of solidarity, especially when faced with family or personal crises (Cicirelli, 1985a, 1985b, 1989). Both Bedford (1989) and Gold (1989) offered topologies that help organize the nature of sibling relationships in adulthood. This work can best be summarized by noting that, depending on specific life circumstances, sibling relationships can exhibit a level of intimacy similar to that between spouses or best friends or, on the contrary, can be relatively distant, even hostile.

Although family relations are important to elderly people, it is clear that friends are also important social relations. Some investigators have examined the nature of friendship relationships, in particular, attending to the important characteristics of friendships at different ages (Jones & Vaughan, 1990). Valued characteristics of friendships do not seem to change greatly with age. These include enjoyment, understanding, trust, affection, respect, acceptance, spontaneity (Davis & Todd, 1985). Friendship interactions seem to be dictated by the requirement of pleasure whereas family interactions involve daily needs and routine tasks. The unique qualities of interactions with friends facilitate transcendence of mundane daily realities. Thus, it is critical to identify the differential contributions of specific family members and friends to the well-being of individuals. An example of recent developments in this area is the Blieszner and Adams (1992) model of adult friendship. Their model incorporates structural, cultural, and historical context and includes both sociological and psychological perspectives on friendship. It incorporates the effects of stage of life course and stage of development as well as other social and individual characteristics as important factors influencing friendship patterns. The model is helpful in its recognition of the complex array of characteristics that influence interpersonal relationships, in this case, friendship. A similar model could easily be developed with special attention given to the additional unique characteristics of family relationships such as ascribed membership and lifelong duration.

Data consistently indicate that although family members are close and intimate members of most elderly people's network, friends are named as the people with whom they enjoy spending time, engage in leisure activities, and have daily or frequent contact and who have the most significant positive impact on well-being. Data from our recent social relations over the life course study indicate that the proportion of same-sex friends reported did not change across age groups from the teen years through old age. Thus, although the absolute number of social relations is smaller in succeeding age groups, the role of friends appears to remain important throughout life, as will be noted once again when the associations between social relations and well-being are considered. A substantial number of studies now exist documenting the importance of friends in the lives of elderly people (cf. Adams & Blieszner, 1989; Blieszner & Adams, 1992).

Function of Social Relations

Another well-examined characteristic of social relations is their function, that is, the actual interactions or support exchanges indicating who does what for whom. This research provides some insight into the different roles that friendship and family relationships occupy. Cantor (1979; see also Litwak, 1985; Connidis & Davis, 1990; Roberto & Scott, 1984) first suggested a support hierarchy of exchanges from preferred sources. For example, friends are expected to provide companionship and short-term crisis intervention whereas family members are expected to provide more significant resources when necessary and long-term support for chronic needs (see Travis, this volume). Such data reinforce the idea of differential roles (e.g., of confidants versus companions) of each support network member. The issue is further complicated by life course issues such as lifelong childlessness or divorce or never-married status (Troll & Johnson, 1992). People who become widows are different in network characteristics from people who have never married. Their strategy for acquiring and maintaining social ties with age is fundamentally affected by these life course differences (Lopata, 1988). Nevertheless, although friendships remain important to well-being into late life, certain concomitants of age, especially advanced age, have been shown to negatively affect friendship relationships. These are best summarized as role losses such as those signaled by retirement and widowhood. Poor health, especially in the form of functional limitations, can also have a negative impact on social relations since it limits the flexibility and ability of the person to maintain contact with others (Allan & Adams, 1989).

Similarly, certain characteristics of support exchanges seem to change with age while others remain quite stable over time. For example, family members clearly exchange instrumental and emotional support (Rossi & Rossi, 1990) and usually in a bidirectional manner both within and across generations (Antonucci, 1990; Bengtson et al., 1990). Because caregiving is a specific type of support often exchanged within the family, it is not difficult to note clear age differences in caregiving needs. For example, the grandparents of young children often provide sick care or general day care for their grandchildren, while the adult children, especially daughters, of older people are often the primary caregivers of sick or functionally limited elders (Fischer, 1991; Walker, Martin, & Jones, 1992). Hamon and Blieszner (1990) showed that both generations believe that emotional support is an important resource from adult children to elderly parents. Parents, however, disapprove of living with their children, receiving money from them, or having the children adjust their schedules to suit their parents. Everyone seems to agree that emotional support from adult children to their parents is a very important resource exchange (Mancini & Blieszner, 1989).

Note that gender differences predominate in terms of both quantity and styles of relationships in family and friend relationships (cf. Krause & Keith, 1989; Shumaker & Hill, 1991; Wright, 1989). Investigators have often documented that women have more social relationships than men. Their relationships tend to be more intimate and to involve a greater number of exchanges. Men, on the other hand, tend to have social relations primarily tied to, and through, their spouse. Their relationships tend to be more distant and less intimate. Much debate has focused on the meaning of these differences and whether they imply a superiority in social relations for women. Recent work, however, has suggested that women may, in fact, be burdened by these relationships and exchanges, given findings suggesting that along with the presence of relationships, woman often feel demands being placed on them (Antonucci, 1994; Walker et al., 1992).

SOCIAL RELATIONS, HEALTH, AND WELL-BEING

Having established that relationships are continual and life span in nature, it is time to consider the impact of family and friendship relationships on the well-being of older adults. The relative influence of these types of relationships on the well-being of old people has presented something of an anomaly to researchers for some years. Scholars know, of course, that both sets of relationships are important. Early (e.g., Arling, 1976; Blau, 1973; Rosow, 1967) and later researchers (Crohan & Antonucci, 1989; Larson, Mannell, & Zuzanek, 1986; Lee & Shehan, 1989), using both simple and more sophisticated designs and samples, have documented that friend relationships, but not family relationships, have a significant positive effect on the psychological well-being of aged people. At the same time, they have also documented that adults who have no family or who have poor relationships with family have much lower levels of general well-being than others (Thompson & Heller, 1990).

Antonucci (1985) hypothesized that this apparent paradox could be understood within the context of obligatory versus optional relationships. Family relationships are obligatory; therefore, they are sorely missed when absent. Reporting that elderly women with low perceived family support had poor psychological well-being regardless of perceived support from friends, Thompson and Heller (1990) documented embarrassment and shame among women who felt that family members did not value them or offer assistance. On the other hand, friend relationships are optional. Their presence, therefore, represents a volitional positive contribution to one's social interactions. Family should be available; thus, their absence is felt as a deficit. Friends do not have to be available; therefore, their presence is so much more a benefit.

Distinctions in formation and maintenance of family versus friend relationships can also be understood in the context of obligatory and optional relationships. Family relationships are ascribed. People cannot choose or substitute their parents, siblings, and children. Also, they cannot easily terminate family relationships, even when such relationships are a constant source of stress and are detrimental to well-being. By contrast, to a much larger degree, people establish and maintain friendship relations by mutual choice based on a consensus of common experiences, interests, values, affection, and reciprocity. Individuals involved in friendship relations both choose their friends and are chosen as friends. Being chosen as a friend indicates to individuals that they possess desirable qualities, inducing other people to choose them as friends over many other alternative individuals. This feeling of being attractive and desirable enhances emotional well-being (Lee & Ishii-Kuntz, 1987). Furthermore, unlike family relations, problematic friend relations can usually be terminated. These differences in formation and maintenance of family and friend relationships argue for the importance of investigating negative as well as positive aspects of the relationships in studying the influence of family and friends on well-being of individuals.

The differential influence of family and friendships on well-being might be more attributable to role than to relationships. Because, for the most part, family members are not matched on age or sex, the relationship one has with family members is not typically a peer relationship. Cohort differences in family relations create differences in lifestyle, values, attitudes, and interests, or the so-called generation gap, that can become the source of conflicts (Bengtson & Cutler, 1976; Mutran & Reitzes, 1984).

Larson et al. (1986) presented an alternative perspective on the differential contribution of family and friend relationships to well-being. They argued that family members provide day-to-day physical and emotional assistance and serve as sources of security and insulation against threats and losses. Thus, family relationships contribute to well-being within a global time frame, as a general state dependent on an individual's overall security and satisfaction. By contrast, friend relations primarily influence immediate well-being. Friends are less likely than kin to provide long-term support or attend to global needs. Instead, they are most significant as a source of enjoyment.

The role of the marital relationship vis-à-vis the effects of family and friend relationships on well-being is unclear. On one hand, marriage is clearly a family relation and deeply embedded in family ties of obligation. On the other hand, spouses are typically in the same cohort and generation. It is the only family relation that is not ascribed but formed on the basis of mutual choice. An interesting question is whether marriage affects well-being as friendship does or as family relations do. Data clearly indicate the fundamentally significant influence of marital satisfaction on well-being (Andrews & Withey, 1976; Campbell, Converse, & Rodgers, 1976; Veroff, Douvan, & Kulka, 1981), but much less is known about the evolution of this relationship. Some research has documented different phases of marital relationships, including the honeymoon phase with high levels of satisfaction, the early child-rearing phase with decreased marital satisfaction, and the late-life, postparenting phase of renewed partnership and companionship (Lupri & Frideres, 1981; Spanier, Lewis, and Coles, 1975). Some research has shown that viewing one's spouse as a best friend is an important factor in marital happiness (Bengtson et al., 1990), suggesting the blending of both family and friendship characteristics in the marital relationship.

The quality of social relations, rather than the structural characteristics of these relations, has the most significant effect on well-being. This finding has begun to appear consistently in the literature (cf. George, Blazer, Hughes, & Fowler, 1989; Oxman, Berkman, Kasl, Freeman, & Barrett, 1992). Our study of social relations over the life course indicates that people not satisfied with their social relations reported higher levels of depressive symptomatology at all ages than those who were satisfied. Younger people were much more likely than older people to report that others get on their nerves. This is equally true of relationships with mother, father, spouse, children, other family, and friends. These results are quite consistent with Bedford's (1989) theoretical model concerning the special nature of sibling relationships in old age and Carstensen's (1991) theory of optimization suggesting that as people age, they are increasingly selective about the relationships in which they choose to invest. Thus, older adults might have fewer people who get on their nerves simply because they do not maintain or invest in relationships that are irritating to them. Similarly, for all age groups, people report that family members get on their nerves more than friends do. This seems consistent with the fact that family relations are ascribed and friendship relations are voluntary; irritating friend relationships can be terminated but similarly unsatisfactory family relationships cannot.

People who reported that others in their network get on their nerves were more likely to be depressed than those who did not have network members getting on their nerves. Among adults, having a spouse or children who got on their nerves had a much more negative impact on mental health than all other such problematic social relationships.

USING CONVOYS OF SOCIAL RELATIONS TO PLAN FOR A SUCCESSFUL OLD AGE

Our review of the literature and the preliminary data available from the recently completed study, social relations over the life course, offer compelling evidence that both family and friends represent important components of a person's convoy of social relations and have a significant impact on their well-being over the entire life course. Friends and family occupy different, though sometimes overlapping, roles in the complex web of social relations, regardless of age.

Our examination of negative as well as positive aspects of the network suggests additional insights. Older people were more satisfied with the quality of their support relationships than were younger people. At all ages, people who are not satisfied with their relationships had lower levels of well-being as reflected in their higher levels of depressive symptomatology.

Older people were much less likely to report that convoy members get on their nerves than younger people were. The data also indicate that people of all ages were more likely to have family members than friends who get on their nerves. We suggest that this distinction reflects the obligatory nature of family relations and the voluntary nature of friendship relations (Adams, 1967; Allan & Adams, 1989). A particularly complex issue is whether a spouse is more like a family member or more like a friend. A spouse is usually a member of the same cohort, a confidant, and a companion. The data suggest that a spouse represents the best of family and friendship relationships. When this is not the case, however, the impact on the individual's well-being is significant.

Our investigation and brief review of the literature suggest that convoys of social relations offer potentially useful vehicles for achieving a successful old age. Although the challenges of old age are many, it seems clear that family and friends can be very helpful in meeting these challenges. Most people of all ages are surrounded by a convoy of family and friends. Even though older people have fewer family and friendship relationships than younger people have, they tend to be more satisfied with those that they do have than are younger people. For both older and younger people, family and friends are important to mental health. People should be encouraged to develop and maintain high-quality social relations. Social and government policy must be designed not to interfere with, but rather to strengthen, these relationships. Future research must be directed at explicating exactly what the individual and community can do to maintain and optimize the social relations of elderly persons, thus contributing to the their overall health and well-being.

REFERENCES

Adams, B. N. (1967). Interaction theory and the social network. *Sociometry, 30,* 64–78.

Adams, R. G. (1987). Patterns of network change: A longitudinal study of friendships of elderly women. *Gerontologist, 27,* 222–227.

Adams, R. G., & Blieszner, R. (Eds.). (1989). *Older adult friendship: Structure and process.* Newbury Park, CA: Sage.

Andrews, F., & Withey, S. (1976). *Social indicators of well-being.* New York: Plenum Press.

Ainsworth, M. S., Blehar, M. C., Waters, E., & Wall, S. (1978). *Patterns of attachment: A psychological study of the strange situation.* Hillsdale, NJ: Erlbaum.

Allan, G. A., & Adams, R. G. (1989). Aging and the structure of friendship. In R. G. Adams & R. Blieszner (Eds.), *Older adult friendship: Structure and process* (pp. 45–65). Newbury Park, CA: Sage.

Antonucci, T. C. (1985). Personal characteristics, social support, and social behavior. In R. H. Binstock & E. Shanas (Eds.), *Handbook of aging and the social sciences* (2nd ed., pp. 94–128). New York: Van Nostrand Reinhold.

Antonucci, T. C. (1990). Social supports and social relationships. In R. H. Binstock & L. K. George (Eds.), *Handbook of aging and the social sciences* (3rd ed., pp. 205–227). San Diego: Academic Press.

Antonucci, T. C. (1994). A life-span view of women's social relations. In B. F. Turner & L. E. Troll (Eds.), *Women growing older: Psychological perspectives* (pp. 239–269). Newbury Park, CA: Sage.

Antonucci, T. C., & Akiyama, H. (1987a). An examination of sex differences in social support among older men and women. *Sex Roles, 17,* 737–749.

Antonucci, T. C., & Akiyama, H. (1987b). Social networks in adult life and a preliminary examination of the convoy model. *Journal of Gerontology, 42,* 519–527.

Antonucci, T. C., & Akiyama, H. (1991). Convoys of social support: Generational issues. *Marriage and Family Review, 16,* 103–124.

Antonucci, T. C., & Akiyama, H. (1993, August). *Sex differences in friendship over the life course.* Paper presented at the 101st Annual American Psychological Association Convention, Toronto, Ontario.

Antonucci, T. C., & Jackson, J. S. (1987). Social support, interpersonal efficacy, and health. In L. L. Carstensen & B. A. Edelstein (Eds.), *Handbook of clinical gerontology* (pp. 291–311). New York: Pergamon Press.

Arling, G. (1976). The elderly widow and her family, neighbors, and friends. *Journal of Marriage and the Family, 38,* 757–768.

Auslander, G. K., & Litwin, H. (1991). Social networks, social support, and self-ratings of health among the elderly. *Journal of Aging and Health, 3,* 493–519.

Baltes, P. B., Mayer, K. U., Helmchen, H., & Steinhagen-Thiessen, E. (1993). The Berlin Aging Study (BASE): Overview and design. *Ageing and Society, 13,* 483–515.

Bedford, V. H. (1989). Understanding the value of siblings in old age: A proposed model. *American Behavioral Scientist, 38,* 756–768.

Bedford, V. H. (1992). Memories of parental favoritism and the quality of parent-child ties. *Journal of Gerontology: Social Sciences, 47,* S149–155.

Bengtson, V. L., & Cutler, N. E. (1976). Generations and intergenerational relations: Perspectives on age groups and social change. In R. H. Binstock & E. Shanas (Eds.), *Handbook of aging and the social sciences* (pp. 130–159). New York: Van Nostrand Reinhold.

Bengtson, V. L., Rosenthal, C. L., & Burton, L. (1990). Families and aging: Diversity and heterogeneity. In R. H. Binstock & L. K. George (Eds.), *Handbook of aging and the social sciences* (3rd ed., pp. 263–287). San Diego: Academic Press.

Berkman, L. F., & Syme, S. L. (1979). Social networks, host resistance, and mortality: A nine-year follow-up study of Alameda County residents. *American Journal of Epidemiology, 109,* 186–204.

Blau, Z. S. (1973). *Old age in a changing society.* New York: New Viewpoints.

Blazer, D. G. (1982). Social support and mortality in an elderly community population. *American Journal of Epidemiology, 115,* 684–694.

Blieszner, R., & Adams, R. (1992). *Adult friendship.* Newbury Park, CA: Sage.

Boissevain, J. (1974). *Friends of friends: Networks, manipulators, and coalitions.* Oxford: Blackwell.

Bott, E. (1957). *Family and social networks.* London: Tavistock.

Brehm, S. (1984). Social support processes. In J. C. Masters & K. Yarkin-Levin (Eds.), *Boundary areas in social and developmental psychology* (pp. 108–129). Orlando: Academic Press.

Campbell, A., Converse, P. E., & Rodgers, W. L. (1976). *The quality of American life.* New York: Russell Sage Foundation.

Cantor, M. (1979). Neighbors and friends: An overlooked resource in the informal support system. *Research on Aging, 1,* 434–463.

Carstensen, L. L. (1991). Social and emotional patterns in adulthood: Support for socioemotional selectivity theory. *Psychology and Aging, 7,* 331–338.

Chappell, N. L., & Badger, M. (1989). Social isolation and well-being. *Journal of Gerontology: Social Sciences, 44,* S169–176.

Cicirelli, V. G. (1985a). The role of siblings as family caregivers. In W. J. Sauer & R. T. Coward (Eds.), *Social support networks and the care of the elderly* (pp. 93–107). New York: Springer Publishing Co.

Cicirelli, V. G. (1985b). Sibling relationships throughout the life cycle. In L. L'Abate (Ed.), *Handbook of family psychology* (pp. 177–214). Homewood, IL: Dorsey Press.

Cicirelli, V. G. (1989). Feelings of attachment to siblings and well-being in later life. *Psychology and Aging, 4,* 211–216.

Cohen, S. (1988). Psychosocial models of the role of social support in the etiology of physical disease. *Health Psychology, 7,* 269–297.

Connidis, I. A. (1989). *Family ties and aging.* Toronto: Butterworths.

Connidis, I. A., & Davies, L. (1990). Confidants and companions in later life: The place of family and friends. *Journal of Gerontology: Social Sciences, 45,* S141–149.

Coyne, J. C., & Bolger, N. (1990). Doing without social support as an explanatory concept. *Journal of Social and Clinical Psychology, 9,* 148–158.

Crohan, S. E., & Antonucci, T. C. (1989). Friends as a source of social support in old age. In R. G. Adams & R. Blieszner (Eds.), *Older adult friendship: Structure and process* (pp. 129–146). Newbury Park, CA: Sage.

Davis, K. E., & Todd, M. J. (1985). Assessing friendship: Prototypes, paradigm cases and relationship description. In S. Duck & D. Perlman (Eds.), *Understanding personal relationships* (pp. 17–37). London: Sage.

Dean, A., Kolodny, B., Wood, P., & Ensel, W. M. (1989). Measuring the communication of social support from adult children. *Journal of Gerontology: Social Sciences, 44,* S71–79.

Fischer, C. (1982). *To dwell among friends.* Berkeley: University of California Press.

Fischer, L. R. (1991). Between mothers and daughters. In S. K. Pfeifer & M. B. Sussman (Eds.), *Families: Intergenerational and generational connections* (pp. 237–248). New York: Haworth Press.

Fuhrer, R., Antonucci, T. C., & Dartigues, J. F. (1992). The co-occurrence of depressive symptoms and cognitive impairment in a French community sample: Are there gender differences? *European Archives of Psychiatry and Clinical Neurosciences, 242,* 161–171.

George, L. K., Blazer, D. G., Hughes, D. C., & Fowler, N. (1989). Social support and the outcome of major depression. *British Journal of Psychiatry, 154,* 478–485.

Gold, D. T. (1989). Sibling relationships in old age: A topology. *International Journal of Aging and Human Development, 28,* 37–51.

Hagestad, G. O. (1988). Demographic change and the life course: Some emerging trends in the family realm. *Family Relations, 37,* 405–410.

Hamon, R. R., & Blieszner, R. (1990). Filial responsibility expectations among adult child-older parent pairs. *Journal of Gerontology: Psychological Sciences, 45,* P110–112.

Heitzmann, C. A., & Kaplan, R. M. (1988). Assessment of methods for measuring social support. *Health Psychology, 7,* 75–101.

Hermalin, A. I., Ofstedal, M. B., & Lee, M. L. (1992, April). *Characteristics of children and intergenerational transfers.* Paper presented at the Annual Meeting of the Population Association of America, Denver. University of Michigan, Research Report No. 92–21.

House, J. S., & Kahn, R. L. (1985). Measurement concepts of social support. In S. Cohen & S. L. Syme (Eds.), *Social support and health* (pp. 83–108). New York: Academic Press.

House, J. S., Landis, K. R., & Umberson, D. (1988). Social relationships and health. *Science, 241,* 540–545.

House, J., Robbins, C., & Metzner, M. (1982). The association of social relationships and activities with mortality: Prospective evidence from the Tecumseh Community Health Study. *American Journal of Epidemiology, 116,* 123–140.

House, J. S., Umberson, D., & Landis, K. R. (1988). Structures and processes of social support. *Annual Review of Sociology, 14,* 293–318.

Ingersoll-Dayton, B., & Antonucci, T. C. (1988). Reciprocal and non-reciprocal social support: Contrasting side of intimate relationships. *Journal of Gerontology: Social Sciences, 43,* S65–73.

Jones, D. C., & Vaughan, K. (1990). Close friendships among senior adults. *Psychology and Aging, 3,* 451–457.

Kahn, R. L. (1979). Aging and social support. In M. W. Riley (Ed.), *Aging from birth to death* (pp. 77–91). Boulder, CO: Westview Press.

Kahn, R. L., & Antonucci, T. C. (1980). Convoys over the life course: Attachment, roles, and social support. In P. B. Baltes & O. Brim (Eds.), *Life-span development and behavior* (Vol. 3, pp. 253–286). New York: Academic Press.

Kendig, H., Hashimoto, A., & Coppard, L. C. (Eds.). (1992). *Family support for the elderly: The international experience.* New York: Oxford University Press.

Krause, N., & Keith, V. (1989). Gender differences in social support among older adults. *Sex Roles, 21,* 609–628.

Larson, R., Mannell, R., & Zuzanek, J. (1986). Daily well-being of older adults with friends and family. *Psychology and Aging, 1,* 117–126.

Lawrence, R. H., Bennett, J. M., & Markides, K. S. (1992). Perceived intergenerational solidarity and psychological distress among older Mexican Americans. *Journal of Gerontology: Social Sciences, 47,* S55–65.

Lee, G. R., & Ishii-Kuntz, M. (1987). Social interaction, loneliness, and emotional well-being among the elderly. *Research on Aging, 9,* 459–482.

Lee, G. R., & Shehan, C. L. (1989). Social relations and the self-esteem of older persons. *Research on Aging, 11,* 427–442.

Levitt, M. J. (1991). Attachment and close relationships: A life span perspective. In J. L. Gewirtz & W. F. Kurtines (Eds.), *Intersections with attachment* (pp. 183–206). Hillsdale, NJ: Erlbaum.

Levitt, M. J., Coffman, S., & Guacci, M. A. (in press). Attachment relationships and life transitions: An expectancy model. In M. B. Sperling & W. H. Berman (Eds.), *Attachment in adults: Theory, assessment and treatment.* New York: Guilford Press.

Litwak, E. (1985). *Helping the elderly: The complementary roles of networks and formal systems.* New York: Guilford Press.

Lopata, H. Z. (1988). Support systems of American urban widowhood. *Journal of Social Issues, 44,* 113–128.

Lubben, J. E. (1988). Assessing social networks among elderly populations. *Journal of Family and Community Health, 8,* 42–51.

Lupri, E., & Frideres, J. (1981). The quality of marriage and the passage of time: Marital satisfaction over the family life cycle. *Canadian Journal of Sociology, 6,* 283–305.

Mancini, J. A., & Blieszner, R. (1989). Aging parents and adult children: Research themes in intergenerational relations. *Journal of Marriage and the Family, 51,* 275–290.

Morgan, D. (1988). Age differences in social network participation. *Journal of Gerontology: Social Sciences, 43,* S129–137.

Mutran, E., & Reitzes, D. (1984). Intergenerational support activities and well-being. *American Sociological Review, 49,* 117–130.

Orth-Gomer, K., & Unden, A. L. (1987). The measurement of social support in population surveys. *Social Science and Medicine, 24,* 83–94.

Oxman, T. C., Berkman, L. F., Kasl, S., Freeman, D. H., & Barrett, J. (1992). Social support and depressive symptoms in the elderly. *American Journal of Epidemiology, 135,* 356–368.

Pearlin, L. I., & Turner, H. A. (1987). The family as a context of the stress process. In S. Kasl & C. L. Cooper (Eds.), *Stress and health issues in research methodology* (pp. 143–165). Chichester: Wiley.

Peterson, C. C., & Peterson, J. L. (1988). Older men's and women's relationship with adult kin: How equitable are they? *International Journal of Aging and Human Development, 27,* 221–231.

Plath, D. (1975, February). *Aging and social support.* Paper presented to the Committee on Work and Personality in the Middle Years, Social Science Research Council, New York, NY.

Plath, D. W. (1980). *Long engagements: Maturity in modern Japan.* Stanford, CA: Stanford University Press.

Roberto, K., & Scott, J. (1984). Friendships of older men and women: Exchange patterns and satisfaction. *Psychology and Aging, 1,* 103–109.

Roberto, K. A., & Scott, J. P. (1986). Friendships among older men and women: Exchange patterns and satisfaction. *Psychology of Aging, 1,* 103–109.

Rosow, I. (1967). *Social integration of the aged.* New York: Free Press.

Rossi, A. F., & Rossi, P. H. (1990). *Of human bonding: Parent-child relations across the life course.* New York: Aldine DeGruyter.

Sarason, I. G., Sarason, B. R., & Pierce, G. R. (in press). Relationship specific social support: Toward a model for the analysis of supportive interaction. In B. R. Burleson, T. C. Albrecht, & I. G. Sarason (Eds.), *The communication of social support: Messages, interactions, relationships, and community.* Newbury Park, CA: Sage.

Schulz, R., & Rau, M. T. (1985). Social support through the life course. In S. Cohen & S. L. Syme (Eds.), *Social support and health* (pp. 129–149). New York: Academic Press.

Shumaker, S. A., & Hill, D. R. (1991). Gender differences in social support and health. *Health Psychology, 10,* 102–111.

Sonderen, E. V., Ormel, J., Brilman, E., & van den Heuvel, C.V.L. (1990). Personal network delineation: A comparison of the exchange, affective, and role relation approach. In C.P.M. Knipscheer & T. C. Antonucci (Eds.), *Social network research* (pp. 101–120). Amsterdam/Lisse: Swets & Zeitlinger.

Spanier, G. B., Lewis, R. A., & Coles, C. L. (1975). Marital adjustment over the family life cycle: The issue of curvilinearity. *Journal of Marriage and the Family, 37,* 263–275.

Spitze, G., & Logan, J. (1990). Sons, daughters, and intergenerational social support. *Journal of Marriage and the Family, 52,* 420–430.

Stoller, E. P., & Pugliesi, K. L. (1988). Informal networks of community based elderly. *Research on Aging, 10,* 499–516.

Taylor, R. J., & Chatters, L. M. (1991). Extended family networks of older black adults. *Journal of Gerontology: Social Sciences, 46,* S210–217.

Thompson, M. G., & Heller, K. (1990). Facets of support related to well-being: Quantitative social isolation and perceived family support in a sample of elderly women. *Psychology and Aging, 5,* 535–544.

Troll, L., & Johnson, C. L. (1992). Family functioning in late life. *Journal of Gerontology: Social Sciences, 47,* S66–72.

Veroff, J., Douvan, E., & Kulka, R. (1981). *The inner American.* New York: Basic Books.

Walker, A. J., Martin, S. K., & Jones, L. L. (1992). The benefits and costs of caregiving and care receiving for daughters and mothers. *Journal of Gerontology: Social Sciences, 47,* S130–139.

Weinberger, M. (1987). Assessing social support in elderly adults. *Social Science and Medicine, 25,* 1029–1045.

Wellman, B. (1990). The place of kinfolk in personal community networks. *Marriage and Family Review, 15,* 195–228.

Wellman, B., & Wortley, S. (1989). Brothers' keepers: Situating kinship relations in broader networks of social support. *Sociological Perspectives, 32,* 273–306.

Wright, P. H. (1989). Gender differences in adults' same- and cross-gender friendships. In R. G. Adams & R. Blieszner (Eds.), *Older adult friendship: Structure and process* (pp. 197–221). Newbury Park, CA: Sage.

Part V

TURNING POINTS AND INTERVENTIONS

18

Families and Retirement

Maximiliane Szinovacz and David J. Ekerdt

INTRODUCTION

Work and family are the two great involvements of adulthood, and rarely are roles, events, and transitions in one sphere without implications for the other. Research shows, for example, that parents' occupational position influences their child-rearing values, that women's employment status affects their participation in household work, and that spouses' occupational obligations relate to the time they spend with each other and the quality of their marital relationship (see Piotrowski, Rapoport, & Rapoport, 1987; Spitze, 1988 for reviews).

Awareness of the ways that work and family careers are intertwined, generated primarily from studies of young and middle adulthood, is now beginning to enter the retirement literature. Past research has been characterized by an individualistic approach, in which the marital and family contexts of retirement experience were frequently overlooked (Szinovacz, Ekerdt, & Vinick, 1992a). Some recent research endeavors, nevertheless, have started to overcome the individualist and isolationist biases of the past. Foremost among these are attempts to establish the impact of past and present family responsibilities on retirement timing decisions and retirement benefits, as well as investigations of the effect of retirement on marital relations and household roles. Many potential routes of inquiry into retirement-family linkages remain unexplored, however.

In this chapter we first lay out the theoretical assumptions underpinning our claim that family and retirement experiences are intricately linked. Next we describe certain population trends that increasingly compel attention to family retirement issues. We review the empirical evidence about these issues, discussing, in turn, various family influences on the retirement process, then what is known about retirement effects on marriage and family relationships. We also explain ways by which retirement institutions have significant bearing on the entire life course and on intergenerational responsibilities. We finish by noting promising methods and issues for further research. Along the way, we note many examples of known and suspected links between family and retirement experiences, and we invite the reader to imagine yet others.

FAMILY RELATIONSHIPS AND RETIREMENT: A THEORETICAL FRAMEWORK

Our theoretical framework for assessing family-retirement linkages builds on assumptions of diverse sociological and social-psychological theories. The eclectic nature of this theoretical framework corresponds with the interdisciplinary character of gerontological and family research, as well as the complexity of family-retirement linkages. Specifically, we derive major assumptions from systems, role, exchange/equity, life course, and political economy perspectives (see also Szinovacz, 1989a; Szinovacz et al., 1992a).

The first assumption, derived from systems and role theories, asserts mutual influence among family members. *Individuals' retirement transitions and experiences affect, and are affected by, not only their own attitudes, role expectations, and behaviors but also those of their family members.* This implies that (1) retirement is planned and timed with an awareness of other family members (especially one's spouse) and influenced by family-related circumstances and responsibilities (e.g., care needs of relatives); (2) expectations regarding family responsibilities and the performance of family roles may change after retirement (e.g., child care provided by retired grandparents); (3) retirement-related changes in individuals' attitudes or behaviors are likely to influence other family members (e.g., renewed affection for a newly retired spouse); and (4) family characteristics (such as the health of the spouse or marital troubles of adult children) may color an individual's experience with retirement.

The second assumption is based on exchange, equity, and role theories. *Retirement as a status transition alters the distribution of resources and labor among family members. These alterations may result in changes in family members' power, exchange relationships, and their perceptions of equity.* Retirement may alter expectations about, and the implementation of, a specific division of housework between spouses or the division of care activities for frail parents among siblings and siblings-in-law. Such changes in role expectations and in the distribution of labor also may result in a reevaluation of relationship equity or fairness. Employed wives, for example, might resent retired husbands who fail to carry a fair share of the housework. In addition, retirement itself, as well as income losses upon retirement, can be expected to alter power relationships among family members. Because employment status and income serve as important power bases, retirees' power may be reduced, especially vis-à-vis still-employed spouses and extended kin. Such shifts in power also may alter the nature of exchanges among family members (e.g., from material gifts to service contributions).

According to the third assumption, *retirement plans, decisions, adaptation, and postretirement activities are contingent on the accumulation and timing of other life events, including events pertaining to family members.* Concurrent family-related events (e.g., illness or death of family members, divorce, birth of grandchildren) can influence retirement transition processes and postretirement experiences. Retirement timing decisions may hinge on family events, for instance, when care needs of relatives require earlier-than-planned retirement. Furthermore, family events may determine postretirement activities and lifestyles, as when the birth of grandchildren sets retirees off on extended visits.

The fourth assumption arises from a life course perspective: *past family responsibilities and events influence individuals' retirement transition processes and their postretirement experiences.* Family-related work interruptions and past changes in family life and relationships (e.g., divorce, widowhood) shape occupational careers and, with them, the eventual decision to retire, the level of pension income, and the style of retired life. For instance, midlife divorce can reduce women's income and the prospects of sharing in a spouse's pension, and these reductions may force delayed retirement in the later years.

Fifth, *government programs for old-age support and retirement are consequential not only for work careers but also for the course and quality of family life among all cohorts, as well as relationships between generations.* The mechanisms and arrangements that finance retirement—Social Security and supplementary pensions—are designed to regulate the size of, and flow of resources through, the labor market and thus exert social control by channeling adults toward continuous work histories and timely retirements. However, Social Security and pension programs also tend to reinforce traditional family and gender roles, and they affect intergenerational relationships and supports. Because the welfare state assumes a great share of responsibility for the economic support of older people, intergenerational ties are constituted by voluntary interaction rather than economic obligation.

Taken together, these assumptions imply a complex cascade of mutual influences between the work-retirement career and the family career. As shown in Figure 18.1, adequate assessment of family-retirement linkages must consider concurrent reciprocal relationships between employment experiences and family events and relationships, as well as causal linkages between the two domains over time. For example, spouses' work histories can create a certain style of marital accommodation and practical problem

Figure 18.1
A Model of Family-Retirement Linkages

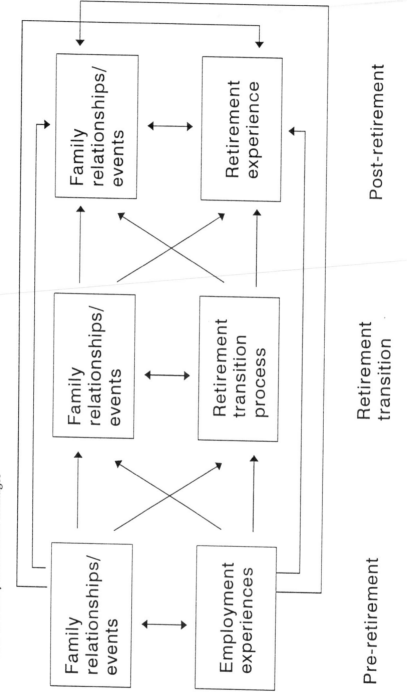

Family relationships/events

Employment experiences

Family relationships/events

Retirement transition process

Family relationships/events

Retirement experience

Pre-retirement

Retirement transition

Post-retirement

solving; these characteristics may, in turn, guide spouses' retirement timing decisions; and both streams of experience—enduring marital quality and the circumstances of retirement—may then affect postretirement relationships as well as each spouse's retirement activities. To date, researchers have focused mainly on selected and relatively simple family-retirement linkages (e.g., the impact of family events on retirement timing or the effect of retirement on marital ties) but have yet to limn the complex chains of circumstances suggested by Figure 18.1.

DEMOGRAPHIC TRENDS

In this section we explore some implications of demographic changes for the retirement experience of individuals and their families (see also Kinsella, this volume). During this century, the percentage of the population surviving from birth to age 65 has doubled, from 41% in 1900 to 79% in 1988. Life expectancy at age 55 has increased from 17 years for men and 18 years for women in 1910, to 22 years for men and 26 years for women in 1988 (National Center for Health Statistics, 1991). These changes mean, first, that more individuals historically, especially women, now make the retirement transition as members of couples and experience widow(er)hood later, as a postretirement event. For example, whereas about one-quarter of women aged 55 to 64 years were widowed in 1960, this proportion dropped to 17.2% by 1990 (U.S. Bureau of the Census, 1960, 1991a). This increased survivorship is partially offset by family structural changes, however, especially increases in the divorce rate. A second consequence of the increase in life expectancy is that many individuals in the pre- and postretirement years still have living parents who may require care and economic support. Such care responsibility can affect the timing of retirement as well as postretirement lifestyle.

Greater variety in family structure is another trend in retirement-age groups. Most notable is the recent decline in married-couple households, especially among nonwhites of retirement age. Between 1970 and 1990 the proportion of nonwhite males aged 55 to 64 years in married-couple households fell from 77.3% to 61.3%. The proportion of nonwhite females aged 55 to 64 years living in married-couple households declined from 47.7% to 42.3%. These declines were paralleled by increases in other living arrangements (U.S. Bureau of the Census, 1971, 1991a). This trend will doubtless increase and extend to more population groups as the high-divorce cohorts reach retirement age. The potential impact of such family structural change and of diverse living arrangements on the retirement experience is as yet little understood. The precarious financial situation of many divorced people (especially women) and their lack of spousal supports, however, may render this group particularly vulnerable during later life.

Another family structural change likely to bear on future generations of retirees is the trend toward delayed marriage and delayed parenthood among young and middle-aged adults. Most of today's retirees completed childbearing in their 20s, and few of them have dependent children at the time of retirement (Hayward & Liu, 1992). Moreover, most of their children will have reached middle age and have teenage offspring when the parents retire. As the age gap between generations increases, more retirees will have dependent children on the eve of retirement, and more will have either very young or no grandchildren at all by the time they retire. This trend is likely to alter not only the economic exchange potential between generations but also the extent and kinds of social support.

Two truly profound changes for the retirement experience are the increases in women's labor force participation and the trend toward early retirement. As shown in the top panels of Figure 18.2, labor force participation rates for married and other (ever-married) women aged 45 to 64 years increased dramatically over the past four decades (from 22% to 57% for married and from 50% to 65% for "other" women). By 1990, about two-thirds of women aged 45 to 54 years and well over one-half of women aged 55 to 59 years were in the labor force (U.S. Bureau of the Census, 1992). At the same time, among persons 65 and older there was a pronounced trend toward nonparticipation for all groups except married females (lower panel of Figure 18.2). These patterns hold across racial groups (U.S. Department of Labor, 1988).

Combined with the increases in longevity, these labor force trends mean that retirement has become—for those who are married—a couple phenomenon (Szinovacz et al., 1992a). More individuals reach retirement while they are still married, and a growing proportion of couples faces the retirement of both spouses. Indeed, the dual-earner pattern now predominates among couples approaching retirement age. In 1991, 42.9% of Hispanic married couples aged 50 to 54 years were dual earners, as were 54.7% of black couples and 61.2% of white couples in the same age group (U.S. Bureau of the Census, 1991b). This raises such issues as how couples time their labor force exits in relation to each other and how spouses anticipate and adapt to each other's retirement.

Overall, these demographic trends portend significant changes in the retirement process. For those who are married, retirement will become more of a couple experience, requiring decisions on spouses' retirement timing and mutual adaptation to each other's retirement. Increased numbers of divorced men and women will enter retirement, and a greater diversity in the living arrangements, household structure, and family obligations of retirees will occur. Changes in family structure as well as in the age gap between generations also may alter for future retirees the intergenerational calculus of support and obligation.

Figure 18.2
Labor Force Participation, by Marital Status and Sex: 1950–1990

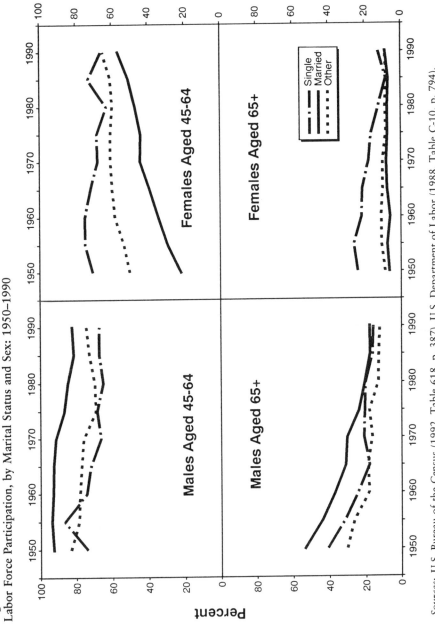

Sources: U.S. Bureau of the Census (1992, Table 618, p. 387), U.S. Department of Labor (1988, Table C-10, p. 794).

Note: "Other" persons are widowed, divorced, separated, or married with spouse absent.

FAMILY-RETIREMENT LINKAGES: EVIDENCE FROM PAST RESEARCH

Our theoretical framework posits intertwined family and retirement experiences. In the following sections we provide examples from past research that demonstrate such family-retirement linkages. For reasons of clarity, we first address family effects on retirement and then summarize retirement effects on family relationships. Keep in mind, however, that this approach oversimplifies many family-retirement linkages (see Figure 18.1), even though it is representative of current research treatments. We discuss more complex relationships among family and retirement experiences in the final section on needed research.

Family Effects on Retirement

Timing of retirement

Retirement timing depends on many things, including wages and pension status, health, occupational characteristics, and, not least, marital and family contexts (Parnes, 1988). In this last regard, studies have implicated marital status, spouse's employment, and family obligations in the timing of retirement. Figure 18.2 shows how retirement (labor force nonparticipation) varies by marital status. Married men are more likely than nonmarried men to be employed at all ages. Among women, however, nonmarried and especially divorced women tend to delay retirement, and they are also more apt than married women to report plans for postponed retirement or plans not to retire at all (Hatch & Thompson, 1992; Morgan, 1992). This pattern reflects the often precarious financial situation of divorced or widowed women in mid- and later life (Fethke, 1989; Weitzman, 1985), which may force them to remain longer in the labor force than their married counterparts. Furthermore, married women frequently adjust their retirement timing to that of their often older husbands, thus retiring relatively early (Campione, 1987; Hurd, 1990; Szinovacz, 1989b).

Another set of studies has focused on couples' retirement timing patterns (Henretta & O'Rand, 1983; Hurd, 1990; O'Rand, Henretta, & Krecker, 1992). These investigations confirm that spouses time their retirement in relation to each other and tend to opt for joint retirement unless adverse circumstances preclude or render the joint retirement option too costly. Such circumstances include both early family experiences (e.g., work interruptions during the child-rearing years, divorce) as well as current family conditions (e.g., presence of dependent children, health limitations of the spouse, or age difference between spouses).

Evidence also links some retirement decisions of individuals and couples to women's caregiving responsibilities. Studies demonstrate consistently that the caregiving needs of relatives lead at least some women to quit the labor force, to retire early, and to retire jointly with their spouses rather than to continue working after the husband's retirement (Brody, Kleban, Johnsen, Hoffman, & Schoonover, 1987; Hatch & Thompson, 1992; O'Rand et al., 1992; Scharlach & Boyd, 1989).

Retirement benefits and income

Changes in marital status before and after retirement can affect pension prospects and retirement income. Although widowed individuals are entitled to survivor benefits, this amount may not be sufficient to cover living expenses, and it applies only to individuals aged 60 and over unless they have dependent children in the household (Burkhauser & Holden, 1982). Furthermore, both divorce and widowhood can mean the loss of income from the spouse's private pension, if any.

Effects of divorce and widowhood, however, are not uniformly untoward. Marital disruption at midlife may prompt women, in particular, to enter the labor force or seek a better-paying job. In so doing they can improve their economic position and pension prospects, offsetting somewhat the lost access to some or all of the former spouse's retirement income (DeViney & Solomon, 1990).

Postretirement experience

Studies that illustrate family effects on postretirement adaptation and activities show that the experience of retired life varies depending on the sort of kin convoy that accompanies individuals over the retirement process—whether people are married, have children and grandchildren, have surviving parents, or rely on ties to siblings. For example, being married yields more positive retirement attitudes, higher retirement satisfaction, and better postretirement adaptation than being unmarried (Atchley, 1982; Seccombe & Lee, 1986). Social and emotional support from spouses is particularly important for married men (Keith, Hill, Goudy, & Powers, 1984; Lawton, Moss, & Kleban, 1984; Szinovacz, 1992), making their quality of retired life vulnerable to disruptions of this support by spousal illness or death (Bossé, Aldwin, Levenson, & Workman-Daniels, 1991).

Unmarried persons (especially men), who often lack close relationships with kin, are more likely to feel the loss of social commerce from work colleagues (Keith, 1986; Rubinstein, 1987; Szinovacz, 1992). Dorfman and Moffett (1987) reported that retention of preretirement friends and social contacts plays a more important role for the life satisfaction of widowed than married women who are retired. Similarly, visiting with relatives has a more pronounced effect on the retirement adaptation of widowed, as compared with married, women (Szinovacz, 1992).

Some evidence also reveals that family life events surrounding the retirement transition affect postretirement adaptation and activities. Retirement that is motivated by family events (e.g., caregiving needs caused by illness of spouse or parents) might be viewed as untimely and result in adaptation problems (Szinovacz, 1989b). Such family needs can eclipse and perhaps spoil the retirement experience, keeping individuals from enjoying the activities they had foreseen (Szinovacz & Washo, 1992; Vinick & Ekerdt, 1991). Experience of other life events and losses can affect the perceived eventfulness of retirement as a critical transition (Matthews & Brown, 1987).

The coordination of retirement timing among dual-earner couples can have consequences for the postretirement experience. Generally, spouses seem to prefer joint retirement, and the dual-retired pattern seems to gratify couples (Gilford, 1984; O'Rand et al., 1992). Studying men, Wan and Ferraro (1985) concluded that dual retirement satisfies husbands because a retired spouse provides consensual validation to the retirement role. If the husband retires first, however, marital strain may occur. Indeed, the pattern of employed wives with retired husbands has been linked to various adaptation problems (e.g., lower marital satisfaction, spousal disagreements), though the dimensions of this asynchrony remain to be more fully described (Keith & Schafer, 1986; Keith, Powers, & Goudy, 1981; Lee & Shehan, 1989; Szinovacz, 1989b). The overall trend reported in these studies is hardly surprising, considering that the husband-retired/wife-employed pattern runs counter to the traditional gender roles held by the cohorts under study.

Few investigators have taken the long view illustrated in Figure 18.1 that would see the retirement experience as an outcome of enduring marital and family relationships. For example, conflictual marriages might produce fewer joint retirements and, later, more apparent marital difficulties when both partners eventually find themselves at home together. Similarly, preretirement relationships with adult children or other family members can influence plans for, and engagement in, postretirement activities. For example, retirees with close relationships to extended family may opt to move closer to kin after retirement and center retirement activities on social commerce with kin rather than on personal pursuits (Cuba, 1992).

Retirement Effects on Marital and Family Relationships

The effect-of-retirement study is a genre of aging research that, among other important topics, has sifted retirement effects for such standard marriage research themes as housework, marital quality, and power. Compared with this body of work, fewer efforts have been made to study retirement's implications for kin relationships.

Division of household work

Some conclusions about retirement and housework have been fairly well established among recent cohorts (Dorfman, 1992). Retirement does not seriously alter the preretirement division of household work along traditional gender lines. Rather, partners remain responsible for their respective feminine and masculine tasks (Brubaker & Hennon, 1982; Szinovacz, 1980, 1989a; Vinick & Ekerdt, 1989). This gender-differentiated pattern persists despite expectations of greater role sharing, especially on the part of wives (Ade-Ridder & Brubaker, 1988; Brubaker & Hennon, 1982).

At the same time, some retired husbands participate more in household work and female tasks—"helping" their wives—and for these couples the division of labor could be said to become more egalitarian after retirement (Dorfman, 1992; Dorfman & Heckert, 1988; Keith & Schafer, 1986; Palmore, Burchett, Fillenbaum, George, & Wallman, 1985). Retired husbands also help more when wives remain employed or are in poor health (Brubaker, 1985; Keith, Dobson, Goudy, & Powers, 1981; Szinovacz, 1989a). Yet the total effort expended on household tasks, even if shared more evenly, might actually increase for women because retired wives as well as husbands devote more time to homemaking and maintenance (Dorfman & Heckert, 1988; Palmore et al., 1985; Szinovacz, 1980, 1989a). One important point about tasks and sharing is that they depend on the past and current employment status of both partners (Szinovacz & Harpster, in press).

An egalitarian division of labor is gratifying to couples in retirement (Keith et al., 1981a, 1981b; Hill & Dorfman, 1982), although this association between task sharing and satisfaction in retirement probably has a basis in enduring marital style. Too much help by the husband may induce marital tensions, however. For example, the husband's presence in the wife's domain as well as his increased scrutiny of her housework performance can increase perceptions of conflict and disenchantment among both partners (Keith & Schafer, 1986, 1991). Other research shows that husbands and wives attach different meanings to their postretirement household activities. Whereas women seem to gain some satisfaction from instrumental aspects of housework (having a *really* clean house, creative cooking), men seem to profit from household work if they see it as a contribution to their spouse or if they lack opportunities for other involvements (Szinovacz, 1992).

Marital quality

A growing body of research discourages the idea that retirement is a serious threat to marital quality (Anderson, 1992; Atchley, 1992; Ekerdt & Vinick, 1991; Lee & Shehan, 1989; Szinovacz, 1980; Vinick & Ekerdt,

1991). Though these findings proceed from research designs that have not always been strong methodologically, they nonetheless consistently point to the continuity of marital quality over the retirement transition. It is interesting to note, as well, that many couples anticipate more retirement-related changes in activities and more problems in retirement than they actually experience (Vinick & Ekerdt, 1992). Thus, retirement is not likely to wreck the marriages of older couples, nor is it likely to resurrect them.

Although retirement does not generally have big effects on marital quality, it is not inconsequential. Indeed, qualitative, in-depth analyses suggest that retirement affects marital relationships in various ways, both positively and negatively. Positive changes brought about by retirement include increased freedom to develop joint endeavors, increased companionship, fewer time pressures, and a more relaxed atmosphere at home. Spouses engaging in joint decision making and shared activities are especially likely to benefit from retirement. In addition, support from the spouse, confirmation of the retiree's self-concept, and adjustment to the retired spouse's needs seem important prerequisites for marital adjustment after retirement (Atchley, 1992; Dorfman & Hill, 1986; Dorfman & Heckert, 1988; Dorfman, Heckert, Hill, & Kohout, 1988; Hill & Dorfman, 1982; Szinovacz, 1980; Vinick & Ekerdt, 1991).

Considerable popular lore about the disruptiveness of retirement prevails (Harbert, Vinick, & Ekerdt, 1992), and research studies, too, have recorded the marital complaints of spouses. The dominant theme is wives' complaints about husbands being underfoot and about a lack of privacy and too much togetherness (Dorfman & Hill, 1986; Hill & Dorfman, 1982; Keating & Cole, 1980; Vinick & Ekerdt, 1991). In addition to this problem of impingement, Vinick and Ekerdt (1991) have also detected the dismay of some husbands about their wives' humdrum routines and narrow interests. Though abundant, anecdotes and observations about retirement-related marital strain are not easy to evaluate. Is retirement broadly troubling to marriages—something that survey research fails to support—or do these reports reflect the temporary issues and manageable matters that occur as spouses realign roles to which they have long been accustomed? Impingement anecdotes are part of the social construction of retirement (Ekerdt & Vinick, 1991; Vinick & Ekerdt, 1991); this subject awaits more skilled interpretive analysis.

Equity, decision making, and power

From a power or exchange perspective, retirement would be expected to reduce one's economic resources and erode one's relative power in the relationship (Blumberg & Coleman, 1989; Blumstein & Schwartz, 1991; Szinovacz, 1987). If husbands' participation in housework is viewed as an indicator of wives' power to obtain help from their husbands (Hartmann, 1981), then studies showing an increase in husbands' housework after retirement would substantiate his loss of power after retirement. Several studies suggest, however, that wives in traditional households often are ambivalent about, if not opposed to, husbands' help with housework (Dorfman, 1992), so that a shifting division of labor is not an unambiguous indicator of wives' relative power advantage.

Similarly, a reduction of husbands' power after his retirement should lead to more egalitarian decision making between spouses, enhanced perceptions of marital equity (especially for wives), and reduced feelings of marital power on the part of husbands. Existing research fails to offer conclusive evidence on these issues. Regarding marital power, Strauss, Aldrich, and Lipman (1976) found a retirement-related sense of loss in relative family status, especially among lower-class men. Joint decision making, especially concerning finances and running the household, does seem to rise after retirement (Dorfman & Heckert, 1988). Does this signal a shift in spouses' power relationships, or is it merely a by-product of increased time together and joint involvements? Perceptions of marital equity (fairness) appear to be largely unaffected by the work-retirement status of either spouse or by the perpetuation of traditional responsibilities after retirement (Keith & Schafer, 1991; Keith, Wacker, & Schafer, 1992). As with marital quality, the strengths and resiliency of long-term marriages seem to check the presumed disruptiveness of retirement.

Relationships with extended kin

More research could profitably be conducted on the relationship between retirement and kin ties in later life. Although ample research on the kin relationships and social supports of the elderly has been conducted, work-retirement status has rarely been used as an explanatory variable (for a critique of this approach see Spitze, 1988). Even when a study population is wholly of retirement age, employment history might still be relevant to current family relationships.

Do kinship relationships and other social ties change upon retirement? As might be expected, retirement leads to a decline in contacts with work colleagues (Bossé, Aldwin, Levenson, Workman-Daniels, & Ekerdt, 1990; Francis, 1990) and to a decrease in organization membership, especially for men in higher socioeconomic status groups (Palmore et al., 1985). Whether, to what extent, and how quickly these social losses are overcome through substitution of other friends or relatives remains unclear. Some studies indicate that retirees increase the time spent with friends and kin (Dorfman & Mertens, 1990; Palmore et al., 1985; Roberto & Kimboko, 1989; Vinick & Ekerdt, 1989), but others indicate some social withdrawal and dissatisfaction with social relationships, at least shortly after retirement (Richardson & Kilty, 1991).

Other evidence shows that the types of exchanges among kin and the meaning of kin relationships may change after retirement. Streib's (1958) early research on the retirement experience found a shift toward more child care by retired grandparents. More recent studies show that retirees do provide financial supports to both their parents and children (Morgan, 1983; Seccombe, 1988). Just as the time afforded by retirement can be a resource for married couples, retirement can free individuals to devote themselves to family relationships. Increased contact, visiting, and help can flow willingly from retirees to their parents and adult children. Vinick and Ekerdt (1989) reported one retiree's even building a house for his newly married son. However, kin can also claim retirees' time (e.g., for daily care of grandchildren or to take over caregiving responsibilities from still-employed siblings) to the point of perhaps spoiling the retirement experience (Brubaker & Brubaker, 1992; Miller & Cavanaugh, 1990; Vinick & Ekerdt, 1991).

Although retirement migration is still not common, research on the relocation decisions and experiences of elderly migrants illustrates the intertwining of retirement and family relationships (Cuba, 1989; Cuba & Longino, 1991). Whereas long-distance moves might be expected to attenuate kin ties, regional moves can be undertaken with a view to maintaining established patterns of family life. In shorter-distance moves, kin stay within reach. If the destination is located in an attractive or resort-type area, the new home can function explicitly as a "drawing card" for visits from family and friends. Cuba (1992), examining marital status differences, found a tendency for unmarried retirees, primarily women, to make amenity moves in the direction of kin, whereas couples were more likely to stress climate and leisure motives for moving.

RETIREMENT POLICY AND THE FAMILY

What allows people to retire is the ability to obtain a stream of income that replaces the wages or salary obtained from employment. Historically, for individuals fortunate to live long enough, retirement income was arranged privately, either through lifelong family strategies designed to secure financial resources for the later years or through direct economic dependence on the younger generation. With the emergence of the modern welfare state, the responsibility for economic support of older people has shifted, in part, from the family onto the state and onto employers, who supply Social Security and other pensions (Myles, 1989). The present societal arrangements that support retirement income have far-reaching implications for work and family careers. In this section, we discuss how retirement institutions affect the social control of behavior within intertwined work and family careers and also how relationships between generations are affected by retirement policy. The reader is referred to Harrington Meyer and Bellas (this volume) for a detailed discussion of modern welfare state programs and policy as they affect the family.

The Regulation of the Life Course

Social Security and pensions serve as social control mechanisms in several ways. One primary policy goal of these arrangements is to induce older workers to retire. These programs and plans serve to solve the abeyance problem of labor markets, the potential surplus of workers (Guillemard, 1983; Mirkin, 1987; Mizruchi 1983), by mandating or encouraging withdrawal from the labor force at a predetermined age. Social Security earnings tests, age-based eligibility regulations, early retirement incentives, and, in some sectors, mandatory retirement policies all ensure "timely" retirement. Though the timing of retirement can vary and is apparently voluntary, the event of retirement is nearly universal for older workers (Henretta, 1992). The prospect and event of retirement, of course, set in motion the numerous, immediate family-retirement linkages noted in the previous section. The retirement imperative also poses potential difficulties when family careers do not conform to bureaucratic timetables for withdrawal from work. A partner's illness, dependent children in the household, or the not-yet pension eligibility of a spouse can pull individuals toward off-time retirements that are undesirably early or late by common standards (Hanks, 1990; O'Rand et al., 1992).

Decades before they prompt retirement, Social Security and pensions also regulate individuals' work behaviors as well as their job mobility. Prevailing Social Security regulations in the United States as well as in most other industrialized nations link retirement benefit eligibility and benefit levels to past work experience (Burkhauser & Holden, 1982; O'Grady-LeShane & Williamson, 1992). In the United States, discontinuous work patterns and early retirement are circumstances that result in lowered benefits. Consequently, work interruptions and early retirements that are family-related (and largely socially approved) exact a homemaking and child-care penalty on retirement benefits (Chen, 1988). Employers' or private pensions also require work continuity. These devices—essentially, deferred wages—exist to bind workers to jobs. The vesting requirements of most pension plans can preclude eligibility for those individuals who interrupted work, changed jobs, or left the labor force early due to family obligations and commitments (O'Rand, 1988; Quadagno, 1988).

Retirement financing arrangements, therefore, reward continuous attachment to the labor force, occupation, and employer. For a married couple with family obligations, their best interests are served by a household division of labor that assures at least one spouse's ability to compile an uninterrupted history of employment. Because women characteristically carry the main responsibility for child rearing and care of ill relatives, women yield to, and support, the continuous employment of husbands, a strategy that can earn good pension prospects for the household if the marriage remains intact, but eroded prospects for the wife if the marriage dissolves

(Harrington Meyer & Bellas, this volume). For single parents, the duty to compile a continuous work career is not relaxed, even when family responsibilities are pressing. Thus, current Social Security and pension programs, on one hand, reinforce traditional gender roles but, on the other hand, penalize wives for work disruptions devoted to family care (Brocas, 1988; Wolff, 1988).

The favor shown to married couples is a feature of the public pension regulations of many industrialized countries. Most nations provide a spouse supplement to the wage earner's benefit, only a few offer dependent spouse and survivor benefits to the divorced or persons in nontraditional unions, and the majority penalize workers for work interruptions. Moreover, some countries restrict survivor benefits to widows and set differential minimum pension ages for men and women (O'Grady-LeShane & Williamson, 1992). Several changes in Social Security and pensions rules have been proposed that would not only address the gender inequities of the program but also leave retirement institutions less intrusive upon family careers. These include credits for child-care years, survivor benefits to divorcees and perhaps unmarried partners, and the general portability of pensions. Experts agree that Social Security and pension policies will have to pay greater tribute to the diversity of the older population and adapt to changes in women's roles and family structure (Allen, Clark, & McDermed, 1988; Brocas, 1988; Chen, 1988; Moon, 1988; O'Grady-LeShane & Williamson, 1992; Wolff, 1988).

Intergenerational Obligations and Relations

Retirement institutions channel the work careers of adults with implications for marital and family careers. Another important observation about retirement financing, mainly the welfare state system of Social Security, is that it affects the structure of obligations between generations, though how it does so is a matter of some debate.

The late 1970s saw the beginning of a broad campaign to undermine public support for the welfare state. As this campaign unfolded, the charge was made that Social Security policies enriched an elderly middle class at the expense of children in disadvantaged families. Regressive payroll taxes were draining needed income from young families; these young workers themselves stood little chance to enjoy someday the same retirement benefits because large baby boom cohorts would eventually cripple the program. The demand for intergenerational (more correctly, intercohort) equity made considerable political headway (Longman, 1987; Quadagno, 1991). Proposed correctives included cuts in Social Security taxes and benefits and increased reliance on private pensions, asset accumulation, and individual retirement plans as bases of old-age economic security.

The merits of these arguments have been examined elsewhere (Binstock,

1991; Kingson, Hirshorn, & Cornman, 1986; Quadagno, 1991). The debate, nonetheless, has helped articulate ways that Social Security facilitates the fulfillment of family responsibilities—parents to children, and adult children to aging parents. We note some of them here.

First, Social Security (along with the private pensions it calls forth) encourages people to retire, thus reducing unemployment and opening up jobs in the labor market that can be filled by younger workers in their family-formation years. Second, the consumption careers of households would be quite different without the Social Security promise. Although its payroll taxes reduce the income of households with children, those taxes earn an entitlement to later retirement income and help stabilize retirement planning. Free of the need to finance their own retirement wholly from savings or employment—an uncertain calculation—parents are freed to invest in the present support and education of children. Third, by maintaining Social Security and other programs for old-age security (e.g., Medicare), the state assumes financial responsibility for the aged. When aging parents are not economically beholden to the wealth of their children and can maintain independent households, intergenerational relationships can be founded on sentiment and affection that are uncomplicated by financial obligation and the strain it engenders. Voluntary emotional bonds, rather than material duty, can tie older people with their adult children and grandchildren (Kingson et al., 1986; Knipscheer, 1988; Quadagno & McClellan, 1989).

Historical research does not encourage the notion that abolishing Social Security would be a pro-children policy. Until the middle of this century, economic support for the elderly was secured through several mechanisms, among them the accumulation of assets and property, the pooling of family members' wages to secure household wealth in midlife, detailed retirement contracts with children that guaranteed the transmission of property, direct dependence of older people on children and other family members, and community relief and charity. Evidence suggests that family-based economic support for the elderly involved considerable sacrifices on the part of the younger generation (especially in terms of reduced education due to early labor force activity, marital opportunities foregone, or the delay of economic independence due to late land transfers) and constituted a source of intergenerational conflict (Gratton & Rotondo, 1992; Held, 1982).

Family-based strategies for old-age support are vulnerable to sudden shifts in fortune and lack long-term reliability. Even in the preindustrial period, support for the elderly was not exclusively a family responsibility. Diverse forms for community and public relief were widespread, including supports by the church, by towns, or by landholders (Atchley, 1982; Evans & Williamson, 1991; Laslett, 1977; Quadagno & Janzen, 1987; Thomson, 1989). If both family and community strategies failed, poverty and reliance on charity were often inevitable consequences. Indeed, high poverty rates among older people well into the mid-twentieth century testify to their uncertain and vulnerable economic situation when public pension entitlements are low or limited (Quadagno, 1991).

Current data on intergenerational relations indicate families' willingness to provide economic support in times of need, but this is also paired with a preference for state-based regular economic support of the elderly (Cicirelli, 1981; Treas & Spence, 1989). In all, a Social Security program reduced in size or scope promises few advantages for families' ability to meet intergenerational responsibilities. Household budgets would have to balance the present support and educational expenses of children with parents' heightened obligation to save for retirement. Proposals to cut Social Security would erode the old-age safety net of the great majority of middle- and lower-income families and force upon them intergenerational economic dependencies that most do not desire and that many can ill afford.

FUTURE RESEARCH NEEDS

Two paths of research design, each informing the other, hold the promise that further research on family-retirement linkages can converge on sounder, surer conclusions. In one course of research, investigators will have greater access to population-based data from large-scale prospective studies, in particular, waves of the National Survey of Families and Households and the new Health and Retirement Survey. Findings from data sources such as these gain authority from the representativeness of the samples and the ability to follow cases over time. The size of such samples also affords investigators the power to study population subgroups that are of special interest (Szinovacz et al., 1992a, 1992b). The other promising course of research on the family-retirement experience lies in the pursuit of qualitative studies. The highly selected measures used in large-scale omnibus studies simply cannot address many important research questions, nor can they adroitly sift people's interpretation of their experience. Qualitative methods are well suited to understanding processes by which couples and families create and sustain their own realities across the retirement transition (Daly, 1992). Whatever the method chosen, exploration of family-retirement issues must remain incomplete unless researchers include dyadic and family-level measures in their research designs.

As for content, several topics should be added to the current agenda of family-retirement research. First, the field needs additional research about family influences on the retirement process and retired life. How do long-established styles of marital and kin relations shape retirement planning, timing, migration, and postretirement activities?

Second, investigators should address aspects of marriage other than spouses' division of housework and marital quality. To date we know little and understand less about such issues as perceptions of equity, marital gratifications and conflicts, time use and sharing of activities, or shifts in marital power relations upon retirement (Atchley, 1992). In addition, these studies will have to be conducted with consideration for the employment-retirement status of both spouses.

Third, expanded research into ties with extended kin would be welcome. Such research should not be restricted to studies of retirement effects on the frequency of kin contacts. Rather, it seems essential to explore whether extended family members' expectations for kin contacts and supports change upon retirement (i.e., can relatives claim retirees' time?), whether and how retirement-related increases or decreases in kin contacts affect the quality of kin relationships, or to what extent interactions with adult children and other kin substitute for the social commerce of the workplace (Francis, 1990).

Fourth, given current changes in family structure, more attention should be directed at retirees involved in alternative family lifestyles. As yet, we know practically nothing about the retirement experiences of homosexual or cohabiting couples and very little about those of the never-married and divorced (Barresi & Hunt, 1990; Lipman, 1986). We also need to establish how family-retirement linkages occur within groups that differ by racial or ethnic background, socioeconomic status, or rural-urban residence (Belgrave, 1988; Dorfman, 1992; Gibson, 1987; Hatch, 1991; Taeuber, 1990). Attention to these diverse situations and circumstances will reveal the full dimensions of family retirement issues.

A fifth avenue for future inquiry is the assessment of family-related inequities in retirement benefits and policies. It has become abundantly clear that current policies favor individuals involved in traditional family arrangements and especially penalize women for their involvement in family work. We need more research, however, on how such policies will affect future cohorts of retirees who are even more likely than today's retirees to approach and enter retirement as members of nontraditional family arrangements. Can we foresee which of the many current proposals to reduce inequities in Social Security and pension coverage are most likely to succeed?

Finally, and perhaps most important, future research should pay full tribute to the complexity of family-retirement linkages (as outlined in Figure 18.1). The field needs more than the mere accumulation of additional empirical evidence. Unless guided by theory, future research efforts will lack the integration necessary to understand adequately the rich interplay between family and retirement experiences. The life course approach used in some very recent studies (O'Rand et al., 1992) is an important step in this direction, but other theoretical perspectives are necessary as well. To the extent that we use the clarifying power of theory, shed the bias that favors research on individuals only, study longer skeins of work and family careers, range across larger and more diversified samples, look deeper into people's experience, and acknowledge the sociopolitical context of later family life, there will someday be much more to tell about retirement and families.

NOTE

This chapter was funded in part by a grant of the AARP-Andrus Foundation to Maximiliane Szinovacz. Paula Harpster, master's student at Old Dominion University, compiled and calculated the census data.

REFERENCES

Ade-Ridder, L., & Brubaker, T. H. (1988). Expected and reported division of responsibility of household tasks among older wives in two residential settings. *Journal of Consumer Studies and Home Economics, 12,* 59–70.

Allen, S. G., Clark, R. L., & McDermed, A. (1988). The pension cost of changing jobs. *Research on Aging, 10,* 459–471.

Anderson, T. B. (1992). Conjugal support among working-wife and retired-wife couples. In M. Szinovacz, D. Ekerdt, & B. H. Vinick (Eds.), *Families and retirement* (pp. 174–188). Newbury Park, CA: Sage.

Atchley, R. C. (1982). The process of retirement: Comparing women and men. In M. Szinovacz (Ed.), *Women's retirement: Policy implications of recent research* (pp. 153–168). Beverly Hills, CA: Sage.

Atchley, R. C. (1992). Retirement and marital satisfaction. In M. Szinovacz, D. Ekerdt, & B. H. Vinick (Eds.), *Families and retirement* (pp. 145–158). Newbury Park, CA: Sage.

Barresi, C. M., & Hunt, K. (1990). The unmarried elderly: Age, sex, and ethnicity. In T. H. Brubaker (Ed.), *Family relationships in later life* (2nd ed., pp. 169–192). Newbury Park, CA: Sage.

Belgrave, L. L. (1988). The effects of race differences in work history, work attitudes, economic resources, and health on women's retirement. *Research on Aging, 10,* 383–388.

Binstock, R. H. (1991). Aging, politics, and public policy. In B. Hess & E. Markson (Eds.), *Growing old in America* (4th ed., pp. 325–340). New Brunswick, NJ: Transaction.

Blumberg, R. L., & Coleman, M. T. (1989). A theoretical look at the gender balance of power in the American couple. *Journal of Family Issues, 10,* 225–250.

Blumstein, P., & Schwartz, P. (1991). Money and ideology: Their impact on power and the division of household labor. In R. L. Blumberg (Ed.), *Gender, family, and economy: The triple overlap* (pp. 261–288). Newbury Park, CA: Sage.

Bossé, R., Aldwin, C. M., Levenson, M. R., & Workman-Daniels, K. (1991). How stressful is retirement: Findings from the Normative Aging Study. *Journal of Gerontology: Psychological Sciences, 46,* P9–14.

Bossé, R., Aldwin, C. M., Levenson, M. R., Workman-Daniels, K., & Ekerdt, D. J. (1990). Differences in social support among retirees and workers: Findings from the Normative Aging Study. *Psychology of Aging, 5,* 41–47.

Brocas, A. (1988). Equal treatment of men and women in social security: An overview. *International Social Security Review, 41,* 231–249.

Brody, E. M., Kleban, M. H., Johnsen, P. T., Hoffman, C., & Schoonover, C. B. (1987). Work status and parent care: A comparison of four groups of women. *Gerontologist, 27,* 201–208.

Brubaker, E., & Brubaker, T. H. (1992). The context of retired women as caregivers. In M. Szinovacz, D. J. Ekerdt, & B. H. Vinick (Eds.), *Families and retirement* (pp. 222–235). Newbury Park, CA: Sage.

Brubaker, T. H. (1985). *Later life families.* Beverly Hills, CA: Sage.

Brubaker, T. H., & Hennon, C. B. (1982). Responsibility for household tasks: Comparing dual-earner and dual-retired marriages. In M. Szinovacz (Ed.), *Women's retirement: Policy implications of recent research* (pp. 205–219). Beverly Hills, CA: Sage.

Burkhauser, R. V., & Holden, K. D. (1982). Introduction. In R. V. Burkhauser & K. C. Holden (Eds.), *A challenge to Social Security* (pp. 1–20). New York: Academic Press.

Campione, W. A. (1987). The married woman's retirement decision: A methodological comparison. *Journal of Gerontology, 42,* 381–386.

Chen, Y.-P. (1988). Better options for work and retirement: Some suggestions for improving economic security mechanisms for old age. *Annual Review of Gerontology and Geriatrics, 8,* 189–216.

Cicirelli, V. G. (1981). *Helping elderly parents: The role of adult children.* Boston: Auburn House.

Cuba, L. (1989). Retiring to vacationland. *Generations, 13*(2):63–67.

Cuba, L. (1992). Family and retirement in the context of elderly migration. In M. Szinovacz, D. J. Ekerdt, & B. H. Vinick (Eds.), *Families and retirement* (pp. 205–221). Newbury Park, CA: Sage.

Cuba, L., & Longino, C. F., Jr. (1991). Regional retirement migration: The case of Cape Cod. *Journal of Gerontology: Social Sciences, 46,* S33–42.

Daly, K. (1992). The fit between qualitative research and characteristics of families. In J. F. Gilgun, K. Daly, & G. Handel (Eds.), *Qualitative methods in family research* (pp. 3–11). Newbury Park, CA: Sage.

DeViney, S., & Solomon, J. C. (1990, November). *Gender, economic structure, family career, and retirement income.* Paper presented at the meeting of the Gerontological Society of America, Boston.

Dorfman, L. T. (1992). Couples in retirement: Division of household work. In M. Szinovacz, D. J. Ekerdt, & B. H. Vinick (Eds.), *Families and retirement* (pp. 159–173). Newbury Park, CA: Sage.

Dorfman, L. T., & Heckert, D. A. (1988). Egalitarianism in retired rural couples: Household tasks, decision-making, and leisure activities. *Family Relations, 37,* 73–78.

Dorfman, L. T., Heckert, D. A., Hill, E. A., & Kohout, F. J. (1988). Retirement satisfaction in rural husbands and wives. *Rural Sociology, 53,* 25–39.

Dorfman, L. T., & Hill, E. A. (1986). Rural housewives and retirement: Joint decision-making matters. *Family Relations, 35,* 507–514.

Dorfman, L. T., & Mertens, C. E. (1990). Kinship relations in retired rural men and women. *Family Relations, 39,* 166–173.

Dorfman, L. T., & Moffett, M. M. (1987). Retirement satisfaction in married and widowed rural women. *Gerontologist, 27,* 215–221.

Ekerdt, D. J., & Vinick, B. H. (1991). Marital complaints in husband-working and husband-retired couples. *Research on Aging, 13,* 364–382.

Evans, L., & Williamson, J. B. (1991). Old age dependency in historical perspective. In B. B. Hess & E. Markson (Eds.), *Growing old in America* (4th ed., pp. 525–530). New Brunswick, NJ: Transaction Books.

Fethke, C. C. (1989). Life-cycle models of saving and the effect of the timing of divorce on retirement economic well-being. *Journal of Gerontology: Social Sciences, 44,* S121–128.

Francis, D. (1990). The significance of work friends in later life. *Journal of Aging Studies, 4,* 405–424.

Gibson, R. C. (1987). Reconceptualizing retirement for black Americans. *Gerontologist, 27,* 691–698.

Gilford, R. (1984). Contrasts in marital satisfaction throughout old age: An exchange theory analysis. *Journal of Gerontology, 39,* 325–333.

Gratton, B., & Rotondo, F. M. (1992). The "family fund": Strategies for security in old age in the industrial era. In M. Szinovacz, D. J. Ekerdt, & B. H. Vinick (Eds.), *Families and retirement* (pp. 51–63). Newbury Park, CA: Sage.

Guillemard, A.-M. (Ed.). (1983). *Old age and the welfare state.* London: Sage.

Hanks, R. S. (1990). *Defining issues of timing and control in incentive based early retirement.* Paper presented at the 12th World Congress of Sociology, Madrid, Spain.

Harbert, E., Vinick, B. H., & Ekerdt, D. J. (1992). Marriage and retirement: Advice to couples in popular literature. In J. F. Gilgun, K. Daly, & G. Handel (Eds.), *Qualitative methods in family research* (pp. 263–278). Newbury Park, CA: Sage.

Hartmann, H. I. (1981). The family as the locus of gender, class, and political struggle: The example of housework. *Signs, 6,* 366–394.

Hatch, L. R. (1991). Informal support patterns of older African-American and white women: Examining effects of family, paid work, and religious participation. *Research on Aging, 13,* 144–170.

Hatch, L. R., & Thompson, A. (1992). Family responsibilities and women's retirement. In M. Szinovacz, D. J. Ekerdt, & B. H. Vinick (Eds.), *Families and retirement* (pp. 99–113). Newbury Park, CA: Sage.

Hayward, M. D., & Liu, M. (1992). Men and women in their retirement years: A demographic profile. In M. Szinovacz, D. J. Ekerdt, & B. H. Vinick (Eds.), *Families and retirement* (pp. 23–50). Newbury Park, CA: Sage.

Held, T. (1982). Rural retirement arrangements in seventeenth-to-nineteenth-century Austria: A cross-community analysis. *Journal of Family History, 7,* 227–254.

Henretta, J. C. (1992). Uniformity and diversity: Life course institutionalization and late-life work exit. *Sociological Quarterly, 33,* 265–279.

Henretta, J. C., & O'Rand, A. M. (1983). Joint retirement in the dual worker family. *Social Forces, 62,* 504–520.

Hill, E. A., & Dorfman, L. T. (1982). Reactions of housewives to the retirement of their husbands. *Family Relations, 31,* 195–200.

Hurd, Michael D. (1990). The joint retirement decision of husbands and wives. In

D. A. Wise (Ed.), *Issues in the economics of aging* (pp. 231–258). Chicago: University of Chicago Press.

Keating, N., & Cole, P. (1980). What do I do with him 24 hours a day? Changes in the housewife role after retirement. *Gerontologist, 20,* 84–89.

Keith, P. M. (1986). The social context and resources of the unmarried in old age. *International Journal of Aging and Human Development, 23,* 81–96.

Keith, P. M., Dobson, C. D., Goudy, W. J., & Powers, E. A. (1981). Older men: Occupation, employment status, household involvement, and well-being. *Journal of Family Issues, 2,* 336–349.

Keith, P. M., Hill, K., Goudy, W. J., & Powers, E. A. (1984). Confidants and well-being: A note on male friendship in old age. *Gerontologist, 24,* 318–320.

Keith, P. M., Powers, E. A., & Goudy, W. J. (1981). Older men in employed and retired families. *Alternative Lifestyles, 4,* 228–241.

Keith, P. M., & Schafer, R. B. (1986). Housework, disagreement, and depression among younger and older couples. *American Behavioral Scientist, 29,* 405–422.

Keith, P. M., & Schafer, R. B. (1991). *Relationships and well-being over the life stages.* New York: Praeger.

Keith, P. M., Wacker, R. R., & Schafer, R. B. (1992). Equity in older families. In M. Szinovacz, D. J. Ekerdt, & B. H. Vinick (Eds.), *Families and retirement* (pp. 189–201). Newbury Park, CA: Sage.

Kingson, E. R., Hirshorn, B. A., & Cornman, J. M. (1986). *Ties that bind: The interdependence of generations.* Washington, DC: Seven Locks Press.

Knipscheer, C.P.M. (1988). Temporal embeddedness and aging within the multi-generational family: The case of grandparenting. In J. E. Birren & V. L. Bengtson (Eds.), *Emergent theories of aging* (pp. 426–446). New York: Springer Publishing Co.

Laslett, P. (1977). *Family life and illicit love in earlier generations.* Cambridge: Cambridge University Press.

Lawton, M. P., Moss, M., & Kleban, M. H. (1984). Marital status, living arrangements, and the well-being of older people. *Research on Aging, 6,* 323–345.

Lee, G. R., & Shehan, C. L. (1989). Retirement and marital satisfaction. *Journal of Gerontology: Social Sciences, 44,* S226–230.

Lipman, A. (1986). Homosexual relationships. *Generations, 10*(4), 51–54.

Longman, P. (1987). *Born to pay: The new politics of aging in America.* Boston: Houghton Mifflin.

Matthews, A. M., & Brown, K. H. (1987). Retirement as a critical life event. *Research on Aging, 9,* 548–571.

Miller, S. S., & Cavanaugh, J. C. (1990). The meaning of grandparenthood and its relationship to demographic, relationship, and social participation variables. *Journal of Gerontology: Psychological Sciences, 45,* P244–247.

Mirkin, B. A. (1987). Early retirement as a labor force policy: An international overview. *Monthly Labor Review, 110*(3), 19–33.

Mizruchi, E. H. (1983). Abeyance processes, social policy and aging. In A.-M. Guillemard (Ed.), *Old age and the welfare state* (pp. 45–52). London: Sage.

Moon, M. (1988). The economic situation of older Americans: Emerging wealth and continuing hardship. *Annual Review of Gerontology and Geriatrics, 8,* 102–131.

Morgan, L. A. (1983). Intergenerational financial support: Retirement age males, 1971–1975. *Gerontologist, 23,* 160–166.

Morgan, L. A. (1992). Marital status and retirement plans: Do widowhood and divorce make a difference? In M. Szinovacz, D. J. Ekerdt, & B. H. Vinick (Eds.), *Families and retirement* (pp. 114–126). Newbury Park, CA: Sage.

Myles, J. (1989). *Old age in the welfare state: The political economy of public pensions* (rev. ed.). Lawrence: University Press of Kansas.

National Center for Health Statistics. (1991). *Vital statistics of the United States, 1988;* Vol. 2, Sec. 6, life tables. Washington, DC: Public Health Service.

O'Grady-LeShane, R., & Williamson, J. B. (1992). Family provisions in old-age pensions: Twenty industrial nations. In M. Szinovacz, D. J. Ekerdt, & B. H. Vinick (Eds.), *Families and retirement* (pp. 64–77). Newbury Park, CA: Sage.

O'Rand, A. M. (1988). Convergence, institutionalization, and bifurcation: Gender and the pension acquisition process. *Annual Review of Gerontology and Geriatrics, 8,* 132–155.

O'Rand, A. M., Henretta, J. C., & Krecker, M. L. (1992). Family pathways to retirement. In M. Szinovacz, D. J. Ekerdt, & B. H. Vinick (Eds.), *Families and retirement* (pp. 81–98). Newbury Park, CA: Sage.

Palmore, E. B., Burchett, B. M., Fillenbaum, G. G., George, L. K., & Wallman, L. M. (1985). *Retirement: Causes and consequences.* New York: Springer Publishing Co.

Parnes, H. S. (1988). The retirement decision. In M. E. Borus, H. S. Parnes, S. H. Sandell, & B. Seidman (Eds.), *The older worker* (pp. 115–159). Madison, WI: Industrial Relations Research Association.

Piotrowski, C., Rapoport, R. N., & Rapoport, R. (1987). Families and work. In M. B. Sussman & S. K. Steinmetz (Eds.), *Handbook of marriage and the family* (pp. 251–284). New York: Plenum Press.

Quadagno, J. (1988). Women's access to pensions and the structure of eligibility rules: Systems of production and reproduction. *Sociological Quarterly, 29,* 541–558.

Quadagno, J. (1991). Generational equity and the politics of the welfare state. In B. Hess & E. W. Markson (Eds.), *Growing old in America* (4th ed., pp. 341–352). New Brunswick, NJ: Transaction.

Quadagno, J., & Janzen, J. M. (1987). Old age security and the family life course: A case study of nineteenth-century Mennonite immigrants to Kansas. *Journal of Aging Studies, 1,* 33–49.

Quadagno, J., & McClellan, S. (1989). The other functions of retirement. *Generations, 13*(2): 7–10.

Richardson, V., & Kilty, K. M. (1991). Adjustment to retirement: Continuity vs. discontinuity. *International Journal of Aging and Human Development, 33,* 151–169.

Roberto, K. A., & Kimboko, P. J. (1989). Friendship in later life: Definitions and maintenance patterns. *International Journal of Aging and Human Development, 28,* 9–19.

Rubinstein, S. L. (1987). Never-married elderly as a social type: Re-evaluating some images. *Gerontologist, 27,* 108–113.

Scharlach, A. E., & Boyd, S. L. (1989). Caregiving and employment: Results of an employee survey. *Gerontologist, 29,* 382–387.

Seccombe, K. (1988). Financial assistance from elderly retirement-age sons to their aging parents. *Research on Aging, 10,* 102–118.

Seccombe, K., & Lee, G. R. (1986). Gender differences in retirement satisfaction and its antecedents. *Research on Aging, 8,* 426–440.

Spitze, G. (1988). Women's employment and family relations: A review. *Journal of Marriage and the Family, 50,* 595–618.

Strauss, H., Aldrich, B. W., & Lipman, A. (1976). Retirement and perceived status loss: An inquiry into some objective and subjective problems produced by aging. In J. F. Gubrium (Ed.), *Time, role, and self in old age* (pp. 220–232). New York: Human Sciences Press.

Streib, G. F. (1958). Family patterns in retirement. *Journal of Social Issues, 14,* 46–60.

Szinovacz, M. (1980). Female retirement: Effects on spousal roles and marital adjustment. *Journal of Family Issues, 3,* 423–438.

Szinovacz, M. (1987). Family power. In M. B. Sussman & S. K. Steinmetz (Eds.), *Handbook of marriage and the family* (pp. 651–693). New York: Praeger.

Szinovacz, M. (1989a). Decision-making on retirement timing. In D. Brinberg & J. Jaccard (Eds.), *Dyadic decision making* (pp. 286–310). New York: Springer Publishing Co.

Szinovacz, M. (1989b). Retirement, couples, and household work. In S. J. Bahr & E. T. Peterson (Eds.), *Aging and the family* (pp. 33–58). Lexington, MA: Lexington Books.

Szinovacz, M. (1992). Social activities and retirement adaptation: Gender and family variations. In M. Szinovacz, D. J. Ekerdt, & B. H. Vinick (Eds.), *Families and retirement* (pp. 236–253). Newbury Park, CA: Sage.

Szinovacz, M., Ekerdt, D. J., & Vinick, B. H. (1992a). Families and retirement: Conceptual and methodological issues. In M. Szinovacz, D. J. Ekerdt, & B. H. Vinick (Eds.), *Families and retirement* (pp. 1–19). Newbury Park, CA: Sage.

Szinovacz, M., Ekerdt, D. J., & Vinick, B. H. (1992b). Families and retirement: Avenues for future research. In M. Szinovacz, D. J. Ekerdt, & B. H. Vinick (Eds.), *Families and retirement* (pp. 254–261). Newbury Park, CA: Sage.

Szinovacz, M., & Harpster, P. (in press). Couples' employment/retirement status and the division of household tasks. *Journal of Gerontology: Social Sciences.*

Szinovacz, M., & Washo, C. (1992). Gender differences in exposure to life events and adaptation to retirement. *Journal of Gerontology: Social Sciences, 47,* S191–196.

Taeuber, C. (1990). Diversity: The dramatic reality. In S. A. Bass, E. A. Kutza, & F. M. Torres-Gil (Eds.), *Diversity in aging* (pp. 1–45). Glenview, IL: Scott, Foresman.

Thomson, D. (1989). The intergenerational contract—Under pressure from population aging. In J. Eekelaar & D. Pearl (Eds.), *An aging world: Dilemmas and challenges for law and social policy* (pp. 369–388). Oxford, U.K.: Clarendon Press.

Treas, J., & Spence, M. (1989). Intergenerational economic obligations in the welfare state. In J. A. Mancini (Ed.), *Aging parents and adult children* (pp. 181–195). Lexington, MA: Lexington Books.

U.S. Bureau of the Census. (1960). Marital status and family status: March 1960.

Current population reports: Population characteristics, Series P-20, no. 105. Washington, DC: U.S. Government Printing Office.

U.S. Bureau of the Census. (1971). Marital status and family status: March 1970. *Current population reports: Population characteristics,* Series P-20, no. 212. Washington, DC: U.S. Government Printing Office.

U.S. Bureau of the Census. (1991a). Marital status and living arrangements: March 1990. *Current population reports: Population characteristics,* Series P-20, no. 450. Washington, DC: U.S. Government Printing Office.

U.S. Bureau of the Census. (1991b). Household and family characteristics: March 1991. *Current population reports: Population characteristics,* Series P-20, no. 458. Washington, DC: U.S. Government Printing Office.

U.S. Bureau of the Census. (1992). *Statistical abstract of the United States: 1992.* (112th ed.). Washington, DC: U.S. Government Printing Office.

U.S. Department of Labor, Bureau of Labor Statistics. (1988). *Labor force statistics derived from the current population survey, 1948–87.* Washington, DC: U.S. Government Printing Office.

Vinick, B. H., & Ekerdt, D. J. (1989). Retirement and the family. *Generations, 13*(2), 53–56.

Vinick, B. H., & Ekerdt, D. J. (1991). The transition to retirement: Responses of husbands and wives. In B. B. Hess & E. Markson (Eds.), *Growing old in America* (4th ed., pp. 305–317). New Brunswick, NJ: Transaction.

Vinick, B. H., & Ekerdt, D. J. (1992). Couples view retirement activities: Expectation versus experience. In M. Szinovacz, D. J. Ekerdt, & B. H. Vinick (Eds.), *Families and retirement* (pp. 129–144). Newbury Park, CA: Sage.

Wan, T.T.H., & Ferraro, K. F. (1985). Retirement attitudes of married couples in later life. In T.T.H. Wan (Ed.), *Well-being of the elderly* (pp. 75–88). Lexington, MA: Lexington Books.

Weitzman, L. (1985). *The divorce revolution.* New York: Free Press.

Wolff, N. (1988). Women and the equity of the Social Security program. *Journal of Aging Studies, 2,* 357–377.

19

The Effects of Illness on the Family

Jeffrey W. Dwyer

INTRODUCTION

The ontogenetic fallacy that there is a necessary and invariant relationship between aging and poor health has influenced much of the family gerontology literature (Stahl & Feller, 1990). Old age is often associated with frailty and decrements in physical functioning (Streib, 1983), and later family life course stages are typically defined in terms of health rather than the social characteristics (e.g., marriage, children, empty nest) that denote earlier stages (Atchley, 1985). Although biological age and health are clearly linked, biographical age (Callahan, 1987), the experience and timing of events over the life course (Henretta, 1992), and present social context (Dannefer, 1984) are also important dimensions of old age. Definitions of aging that assume an inevitable linkage between old age and disease-related disabilities unaffected by the social context within which aging takes place are problematic because they negatively influence perceptions of the elderly (Steuart, 1985), expectations of family care providers (Minkler & Stone, 1985), and social and public policies (Older Women's League, 1989).

Health, like age, is not a purely biological concept (Weeks, 1981). The World Health Organization (1958), for example, defines health as a state of complete physical, mental, and social well-being, rather than simply the absence of disease or infirmity. This comprehensive definition underscores the biological, social, and psychological dimensions of health but also reinforces the perception that perfect health is probably incompatible with the process of living (Dubos, 1959). Because of the difficulties associated with defining and measuring health, other concepts are frequently used to describe nonhealth. *Disease* is a label usually legitimated by health professionals that has biological connotations (Friedson, 1970); *illness* is "a social state created by self-evaluation" (Stahl & Fuller, 1990, p. 22) that might or might not be associated with disease; and *sickness* is a social role, generally distinguished by the inability to carry out expected tasks, that also places certain obligations and expectations on others (Parsons, 1951). These distinctions are important because many public programs for elders (e.g., Medicare and Medicaid) are associated with the presence of disease, yet a diagnosed medical condition is not necessarily coincident with the need for caregiving assistance.

Like age and health, characterizations of the family must be multidimensional. Definitions of the family usually include some aspects of their structure, function, and stage in the family life cycle. Individuals of any age can be involved in single- or multigenerational families that span a range of structural types. Hence, families that experience multiple marriages and short-term generational relationships (i.e., stepchildren, stepgrandchildren), the inclusion of fictive kin, and other variations are increasingly the norm. Diversity in family structure and organization implies that the ability to respond to the needs of a chronically ill older family member is variable and family-specific.

In this chapter I explore the impact of changing social context on the provision of long-term care to impaired older people by family members. The review begins by introducing characteristics of the elder, the family, and society that shape the environment within which elder care is provided. Changes in social structure that influence the effects of chronic impairment on the family over time are then discussed. Next, the implications of chronic illness for family members are explored. Finally, future research needs are discussed.

THE STRUCTURE OF FAMILY CAREGIVING

Family caregiving typically refers to the caregiving work of family members that is "rendered for the well-being of older individuals who, because of chronic physical or mental illness, cannot perform such activities for themselves" (Hooyman, 1992, p. 182). Caregiving is usually motivated by love and affection, a desire to reciprocate for past assistance, or normative obligations associated with spousal or filial responsibility (Doty, 1986). The lifelong interactions and immediate circumstances that affect caregiving attitudes and behaviors are varied yet are influenced by characteristics of the impaired elder, the family caregiver(s), and the social context within which care is provided.

Impaired Elders

During the twentieth century the leading causes of death for people age 65 and older have changed dramatically. In 1900 older people were most likely to die from influenza/pneumonia or tuberculosis. Today, however, the leading causes of death are diseases of the heart and malignancies, conditions that are often preceded by long periods of chronic impairment (Crandall, 1991). Lubkin (1986) defined chronic illness as "the irreversible presence, accumulation, or latency of disease states or impairments" (p. 6) that require the intervention of the total human environment in order to maximize functioning. Chronic illnesses affect individuals and families throughout the life cycle, but the incidence and prevalence of long-term functioning decrements are especially pronounced among elderly adults. The type of disease, stage of the illness, and level of incapacity are all critical components of the need for care and the ability of the potential caregiving network to respond (Rolland, 1988).

Because the same illness or disease can have different consequences for how individuals carry out routine daily tasks (World Health Organization, 1959), elders' health status is often measured in terms of functional ability. Assessing impairments in activities of daily living (ADLs) (e.g., personal care tasks such as bathing, toileting, eating, and dressing) or instrumental activities of daily living (IADLs) (e.g., tasks such as shopping, housework, managing money) "provide[s] a more practical and parsimonious means of estimating general long-term care requirements than coping with the complex of morbid conditions and disabilities that actually characterize an individual's health state" (Sangl, 1985, p. 93). Moreover, measures of ADL and IADL functioning help to define the conditions under which reciprocal family exchanges are initiated and the transition is made into a caregiving relationship (Horowitz, 1985).

Although estimates vary depending on the definition of impairment used, between 6 and 10 million functionally impaired elders were living in the United States in the late 1980s (Wiener, Hanley, Clark, & Van Nostrand, 1990). Moreover, the "intriguing finding . . . that individuals along the full impairment continuum . . . live in nursing homes and in the community" (Newman, Struyk, Wright, & Rice, 1990, p. 173) has focused attention on the elder, family, and societal characteristics that underlie long-term care decisions. Despite the fact that approximately 5% of the population aged 65 years and over are in a nursing home at any given time, at a cost in 1990 of approximately $50 billion (Levit, Lazenby, Cowan, & Letsch, 1991), 80% of elders in need of long-term care live in the community and receive most or all of their assistance from family and friends (Scanlon, 1988).

The social framework within which caregiving occurs has particularly deleterious consequences for women, minorities, and the poor. Because they live longer, marry at younger ages, and are less likely to experience a non-fatal chronic condition than men, most elderly people in need of long-term care are women (Lee, 1992). Minority elders are more likely than their white counterparts to experience functional disabilities (Markides & Mindel, 1987), but they are less likely to be institutionalized (Newman et al.,

1990) and no more likely than nonminority elders to receive assistance from children (Mindel, Wright, & Starrett, 1986) or to live in a shared household with kin (Soldo, Wolf, & Agree, 1990). Elders with higher incomes receive more home health care (Kane, 1989) and are more likely to be placed in an institution with better-quality care than those with lower incomes (Rivlin, Wiener, Hanley, & Spence, 1988). In addition, elders who own a home are at lower risk of being institutionalized than nonhomeowners because they are more likely to be able to purchase home care (Hanley, Alecxih, Wiener, & Kennell, 1990) and are frequently able to adapt to functional limitations when in familiar surroundings (Struyk & Katsura, 1988). Hence, long-term care options and decisions must be considered within a framework that acknowledges the role of gender in the context of intergenerational family exchanges.

Family Caregivers

Impaired older people are usually cared for by a primary caregiver who provides regular assistance with ADLs and IADLs (Sangl, 1985), organizes the supplemental assistance of other formal and informal providers (Matthews & Rosner, 1988), and facilitates and mediates interaction with the bureaucracies that control access to services and benefits (Streib, 1983; see also Travis, this volume). The likelihood of becoming a caregiver follows a hierarchical pattern (Horowitz, 1985). If a spouse is available, he or she usually becomes the primary caregiver (Stoller, 1992). When a spouse is not present or is unable to provide care because of his or her own disabilities, an adult child typically assumes responsibility (Montgomery, 1992). Finally, in the absence of a spouse or adult child, other family members (e.g., siblings, grandchildren) usually provide care. Although caregiving is often portrayed as a specific activity associated with the provision of assistance, the role of family caregiver becomes a significant social role, with accompanying norms and expectations, when an individual assumes primary responsibility for the care of an elderly relative (Suitor & Pillemer, 1990).

Although spouses and adult children are identified as caregivers in approximately equal proportions (35.5% and 38.4%, respectively), the nature of the caregiving work they perform is decidedly different (Stone, Cafferata, & Sangl, 1987). Spouses are likely to be sole care providers and to be responsible for assisting with ADLs (Stoller, 1992). Conversely, adult children are more likely to be primary caregivers receiving supplemental assistance from other formal or informal providers (Tennstedt, McKinlay, & Sullivan, 1989).

Caregiving is both a profound personal experience with positive emotional and psychological dimensions and an oppressive social institution that can impede relationships and activities as well as threaten economic independence (Abel, 1986). Eighty percent of the frail elderly who live in the community are cared for by women who must frequently fulfill the dual roles of full-time labor force participant and primary caregiver simultaneously (Dwyer & Coward, 1992). Although most employed female caregivers adapt to these multiple responsibilities by sacrificing their personal time, modifying work demands, or maintaining rigid schedules (Seccombe, 1992), significant numbers are forced to quit work, reduce the number of hours worked, or take time off without pay because of their caregiving obligations (Stone et al., 1987).

Social Context

The reliance on family members for the care of impaired elders is a relatively recent phenomenon. In the early twentieth century only 3 million people in the United States were over age 65 (U.S. Bureau of the Census, 1975), elders were in generally good health (Dahlin, 1980), and more than 50% of middle-aged couples had no living parents (Uhlenberg, 1980). As industrialization increased, however, employment opportunities declined, and older people with limited economic resources became a vulnerable population in need of societal intervention. Support for aged persons initiated by the social programs of the 1930s (Axinn & Stern, 1985) largely absolved families of financial responsibility for providing care to their disabled elderly members (Fischer, 1978). The myth that elderly people were isolated and abandoned by their families during this period was perpetuated by some social observers, but later research revealed that older people were an integral part of a modified extended family system (Litwak, 1965) and that a primary function of families was to provide security for adults in later life (Sussman, 1965).

Public acceptance of financial responsibility for disabled older people continued until the economic decline of the late 1970s, and rapid growth in the older population converged to exceed the ability of government to provide care. According to Hooyman (1990) the response of policymakers during the last decade to the social problem posed by large numbers of frail elders has been to transfer caregiving work from the public to the private sphere "based on the erroneous assumption that informal structures for providing care are underutilized and simply need to be activated" (p. 223). One manifestation of this emphasis is that social expectations regarding the obligation of family members to care for older relatives have been reinforced by laws that provide standards for caregiving responsibilities (Suitor & Pillemer, 1990).

FAMILY CAREGIVING AND THE LIFE COURSE

Life course research emphasizes the common historical experience of individuals who are in the same cohort (Hareven, 1978), provides a frame-

work for understanding variability in the uniformity and diversity of life
course transitions and their timing (Henretta, 1992), focuses on the interconnectedness of early- and late-life transitions (Streib & Binstock, 1990),
and acknowledges that the timing and sequencing of transitions vary by
social strata (e.g., gender, race, and class) for individuals who experience
similar historical periods (Dannefer, 1988). The life course perspective has
been central to the study of family transitions for several decades (Elder,
1992; see also Hareven, this volume) but has been underutilized in caregiving research. In this section several population trends are reviewed.
Independently, these trends reveal changes in population characteristics
over time that have profound implications for elders, potential family care
providers, and society in general. Collectively, they provide a comprehensive picture of the future impact of illness on family caregiving.

Population Aging

Elderly people now number more than 30 million, the ratio of women
to men is 146:100, and many people over age 65 still have living parents
(Coward, Horne, & Dwyer, 1992). Moreover, by the year 2060 (see Figure
19.1), the over-65 population will more than double, the population aged
85 years and older will increase from approximately 3 to 18 million (U.S.
Bureau of the Census, 1989), and the ratio of older women to men will
continue to increase (Rivlin et al., 1988). Hence, the need for long-term
care and the predominance of women as both care receivers and care providers will increase dramatically during the next century. (For a more in-
depth look at this and related population trends, see Kinsella, this volume).

Incidence of Chronic Conditions

Beyond sheer size, the trends in population aging depicted in Figure 19.1
have important implications for family caregiving because the incidence of
disabling and chronic conditions (Verbrugge, 1989) and the risk of nursing
home admission increase substantially with age (Hanley et al., 1990). The
estimates and projections presented in Figure 19.2 show, for example, that
the total community disabled and institutionalized populations will increase
from nearly 6 million in 1980 to approximately 20 million in 2060. The
largest increases will occur in the community-ADL and nursing home populations. Hence, the burden of providing personal care to frail family members will affect greater numbers of families well into the twenty-first
century.

Total Fertility Rate

As the proportion of elders who are women and unmarried increases,
their likelihood that relying on adult children, usually daughters, to provide

Figure 19.1
Actual and Projected Population of the United States Age 65 and Older, by Sex: 1900–2060

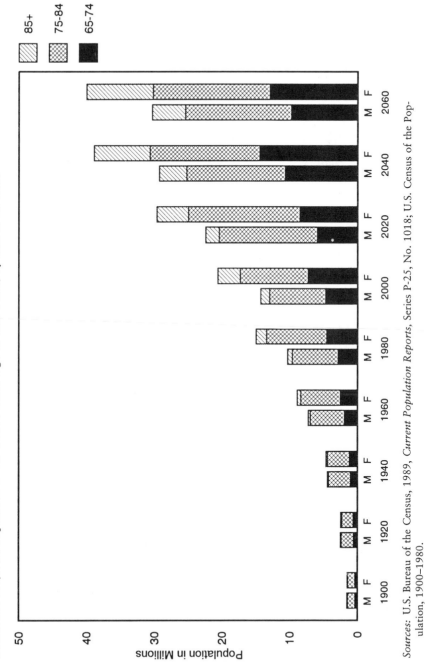

Sources: U.S. Bureau of the Census, 1989, *Current Population Reports*, Series P-25, No. 1018; U.S. Census of the Population, 1900–1980.

Figure 19.2
Estimates and Projections of the Community Disabled and Institutionalized Populations Age 65 and Older, by Sex: 1980–2060

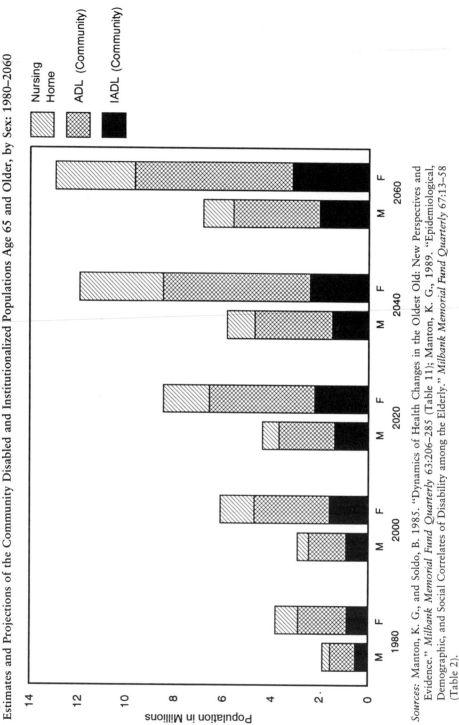

Sources: Manton, K. G., and Soldo, B. 1985. "Dynamics of Health Changes in the Oldest Old: New Perspectives and Evidence." Milbank Memorial Fund Quarterly 63:206–285 (Table 11); Manton, K. G., 1989. "Epidemiological, Demographic, and Social Correlates of Disability among the Elderly." Milbank Memorial Fund Quarterly 67:13–58 (Table 2).

care will also increase (Coward et al., 1992). Among a sample of functionally impaired elders, for example, both the total number of children (Lee,
Dwyer, & Coward, 1990) and the presence of a daughter (Dwyer & Coward, 1991) were strong predictors of receiving assistance. Yet, as shown in
Figure 19.3, the availability of children has declined dramatically during
the twentieth century. Since 1900, the total fertility rate for black women
has declined from more than 6.0 to 2.4, while the comparable rate for
white women has been reduced from 4.7 to 1.8. Low fertility rates among
cohorts of elders who will be disabled and living in the community in
increasing numbers will place them at risk of needing formal assistance (i.e.,
in-home nursing care, institutionalization) or relying on other types of informal providers (i.e., neighbors, friends, grandchildren) who may be unable or unwilling to provide extensive care over long periods of time.

Divorce Rate

The rising divorce rate throughout the twentieth century also has important implications for family caregiving. The date in Figure 19.4 show
the proportion of marriages initiated in selected years that have ended, or
are expected to end, in divorce. Spouses are the first line of defense when
an elder becomes impaired (Horowitz, 1985), and the ongoing, personal
nature of the tasks they perform are often carried out based on norms and
obligations associated with the marital role. For many spouse caregivers,
providing assistance is an act of love intended to repay years of support,
love, and assistance provided by the impaired partner. Due to the reliance
on spouses as caregivers and the expectations associated with long-term
marital relationships, elders who become disabled while divorced or who
are married for the second or third time might be disadvantaged with regard to the availability of caregivers or the type of care a long-term spouse
is willing to provide (Stoller, 1992). Similarly, a high divorce rate among
adult children might reduce their availability as care providers, especially
in the case of daughters, who disproportionately experience the economic
consequences of marital dissolution and might be forced into the full-time
labor force. Yet, although women shoulder the short-term consequences of
divorce, Goldscheider (1990) argued that males are at risk of being without
a marital partner or children willing to care for them in old age.

Female Labor Force Participation

Inasmuch as daughters are the chief source of care for impaired older
people who do not have a spouse, changes in competing responsibilities
over time are likely to affect their ability to provide care. Labor market
activity is now the norm for women in nearly all demographic groups. The
data presented in Figure 19.5 reveal that, especially for white women, labor

Figure 19.3
Total Fertility Rate for Women, 15–44 Years of Age, by Race: 1900–1990

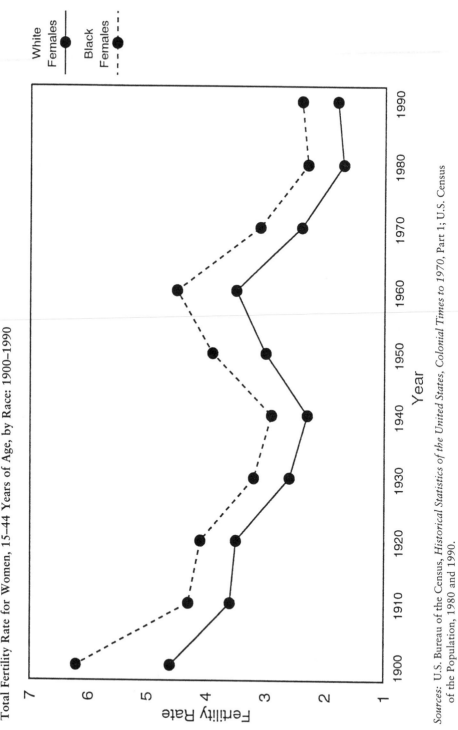

Sources: U.S. Bureau of the Census, *Historical Statistics of the United States, Colonial Times to 1970*, Part 1; U.S. Census of the Population, 1980 and 1990.

Figure 19.4
Actual and Projected Percentage of Marriages Begun in Each Year Ending in Divorce, 1900–1990

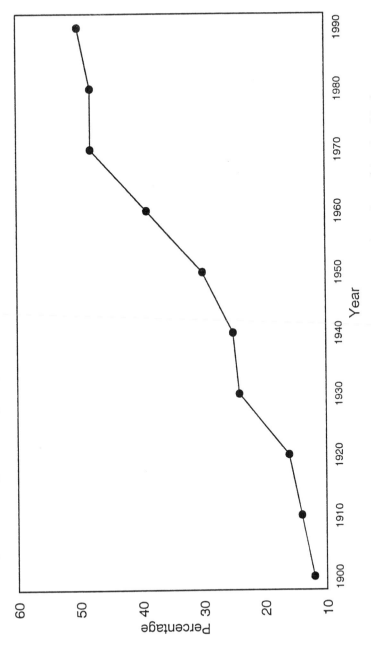

Sources: Preston, Samuel H., and McDonald, J. 1979. "The Incidence of Divorce within Cohorts of American Marriages Contracted Since the Civil War." *Demography* 16:1–25; Weed, James 1980. "National Estimates of Dissolution and Survivorship." National Center for Health Statistics, Series 3, No. 19, Washington, D.C.: CPO; Bumpass, Larry L. 1990. "What's Happening to the Family? Interactions Between Demographic and Institutional Change." *Demography* 27:483–498.

Figure 19.5
Female Labor Force Participation Rate, by Race: 1900–1990

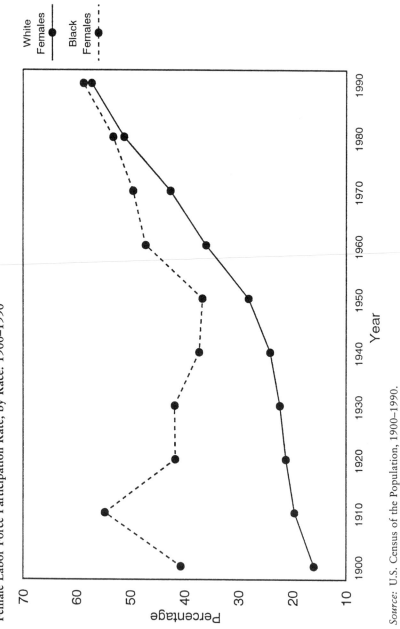

Source: U.S. Census of the Population, 1900–1990.

force participation has increased steadily throughout the last century. High rates of labor force participation by women are likely to reduce the numbers who are available to provide the type of frequent, personal, and long-term care that will be needed as the older disabled population expands. In particular, by the year 2000, more than 75% of women aged 45 to 54 years and approximately 50% of women aged 55 to 64 years will be in the labor force (Shank, 1988). In light of the advancing age of the elderly population, these are the women most likely to be called on to provide care to impaired parents.

Potential Family Caregivers

Figure 19.6 shows the projected distribution of family structures (i.e., four combinations of the presence or absence of marriage and children) for elders aged 85 years and older from 1980 to 2020 by race and sex. The data reveal that women in general and black women in particular are at highest risk of being unmarried with no children (Himes, 1992). In the year 2000, for example, approximately 30% of black women aged 85 years and older will be unmarried and have no children. In the year 2020, the proportion of elders across categories who are unmarried and have no children will decline, while the proportion who are not married but who have at least one child will increase. This shift will occur because these elders are predominantly the parents of the baby boom that occurred in the mid-twentieth century. These data show that a variety of factors are likely to influence the social context of caregiving over time.

THE IMPACT OF ILLNESS

The transition from health to impairment by older people affects nearly every aspect of their lives. Illness-related restrictions on activities (Lubkin, 1986), psychological problems associated with increasing dependency and feelings of powerlessness (Lee, 1985), and the alteration of relationships with family members (Leventhal, Leventhal, & Nguyen, 1985) are especially problematic. In addition, elders are often faced with expending their financial resources in order to acquire necessary medical care and other types of assistance.

Impaired elderly people appear to be particularly concerned with the inability to participate in the kinds of reciprocal exchanges that characterize intergenerational family relationships throughout the life course. Although the amount and direction of the exchange should be based on the relative resources available to the generations and be balanced over time, the extent of the assistance required by many elders sometimes exceeds these norms. Stoller (1985) found, for example, that "the inability to reciprocate, rather

Figure 19.6
Actual and Projected Distribution of Family States for the Population Age 85+, by Sex and Race: 1980–2020

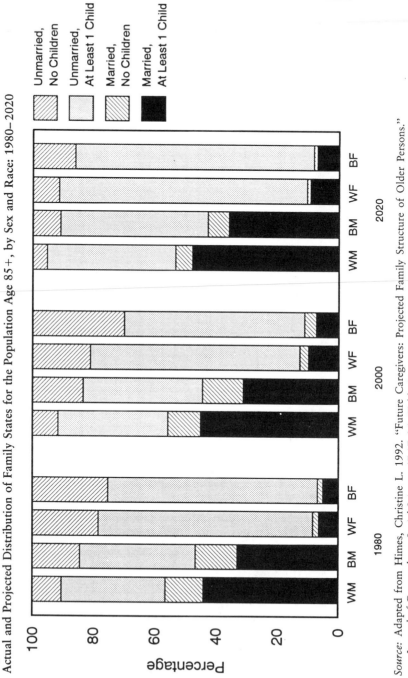

Source: Adapted from Himes, Christine L. 1992. "Future Caregivers: Projected Family Structure of Older Persons."
Journal of Gerontology: Social Sciences 47:17–26. (Table 9).

than the need for assistance, undermines the morale of the older person" (p. 341).

Numerous authors have argued that relying on families as the principal source of community-based long-term care for the impaired aged compromises their well-being in the process (see Qualls, this volume). Caregivers of ADL-impaired elders provide an average of four hours of care each day and assist with a variety of household and personal care tasks (Stone et al., 1987), yet they do so at great cost. Spouses typically continue caregiving regardless of the costs until deterioration of their own health prevents them from providing needed assistance. Although spouses are less likely than other caregivers (e.g., adult children) to encounter competing demands from other roles (Hess & Soldo, 1985), they do experience high levels of burden and restrictions on personal freedom (Horowitz, 1985).

Adult children, due in large part to their often simultaneous commitments to marriage, the labor force, and child rearing, experience a range of physical, social, and emotional consequences resulting from caregiving (Montgomery, 1992). In particular, adult daughters frequently must rearrange work schedules, impose on their own familial obligations, and provide financial assistance in order to facilitate adequate care (Stone et al., 1987). Depending on the nature of the underlying disease condition, some adult children must also learn special skills and perform relatively invasive procedures that are medically necessary but may violate intergenerational contact and relationship taboos (Montgomery, 1992).

FUTURE RESEARCH NEEDS

Demographic trends suggest that the chronically impaired older population in the United States will encounter an ever-changing constellation of family caregiving structures over time. Research is needed on the dynamics underlying long-term care decisions and the consequences that redound to elders, family caregivers, and society. In addition, data that can be used by policymakers and practitioners to inform and formulate effective policies and intervention strategies will be especially important in the future. Thus, the following discussion centers on five specific areas of research that will increase understanding of the relationship between the experience of illness by older people and the provision of care by family members.

First, more research is needed that characterizes disabled elders as active, rather than passive, participants in the caregiving relationship. To date, little emphasis has been placed on the ability of impaired older people to reciprocate the care they receive from a caregiver. Even severely disabled elders can provide emotional support and financial assistance and perform specific tasks (e.g., baby-sitting, housekeeping) that can reduce the impact of caregiving on the caregiver. Specifically, data should be gathered from caregiver-care recipient dyads that (1) focus on the types of activities, tasks, and assistance that are interpreted as supportive by both the caregiver and the disabled elder; (2) measure socioemotional outcomes for the caregiver and elder from a multidimensional perspective; and (3) explore the interrelationships among caregiver outcomes (i.e., stress and burden), elder outcomes (i.e., happiness and satisfaction), and the provision of assistance. To the extent that intervention strategies can be devised that encourage and assist elders in attempts to provide reciprocal support, the negative impact of caregiving on the caregiver is likely to be reduced, and the psychological well-being of the elder might be enhanced.

Second, as the trends reported earlier in this chapter suggest, family history might have a tremendous impact on caregiving choices and outcomes. The nature of the parent-child relationship during early life cycle stages; the frequency and timing of events such as divorce, remarriage, and labor force entry and exit; and the corollary experiences of other family members are likely to influence caregiving experience in later life. Bedford (1992) found, for example, that memories of being the least-favored child affected the quality of the parent-child bond for adult children. Because caregiving behaviors are based, at least in part, on feelings of affection, early life experiences that reduce affection might influence the likelihood of providing parent care. Moreover, parent-child separation at early life cycle stages due to divorce might weaken these bonds and reduce the sense of obligation to provide caregiving assistance to the separated parent at later stages (Goldscheider, 1990). Greater understanding of these issues would be gained through study of the interconnectedness of early- and late-life events that might influence the propensity to provide care.

Third, caregiving situations are too frequently viewed as static, rather than fluid, even though the need for assistance can span several years (Stone et al., 1987). Using data from the 1982–1984 National Long-Term Care Survey, Dwyer, Henretta, Coward, and Barton (1992) showed that approximately one-half of adult children change their caregiving commitment over a two-year period and that different factors predict the initiation and the discontinuance of caregiving. As the number of elders who experience chronic illness for extended periods increases, more attention should be given to the changing family constellation that is available and capable of providing care. Qualitative longitudinal studies that document the patterns of helping among informal caregivers would provide important information for developing large-scale studies to better measure these changes.

Fourth, stratification in caregiving by fundamental social characteristics is increasingly apparent. Specifically, differences by gender, race, class, and even age (e.g., the young-old, old-old, and oldest-old) should be highlighted in future research. This emphasis will present several interesting challenges. Researchers must (1) include sufficient numbers of people in various social strata, by oversampling when necessary, to permit appropriate analyses; (2) estimate empirical models separately by significant population characteristics rather than simply including them as controls in more general models; and (3) account for interactions between two or more of these social indicators in their impact on various outcomes. Himes's (1992) research on family structures, for example, showed that important differences are apparent when the data are separated by both sex and race.

Finally, as new diseases and illnesses affect the general population, they might require responses by both formal and informal care providers. For example, although diseases such as acquired immunodeficiency syndrome (AIDS) are more prevalent among younger persons, older people do become infected. Moreover, the loss of children to this disease might affect later caregiving options of their parents by reducing the size of the child network available to assist them. As treatments are introduced that prolong the conversion period from infection with human immunodeficiency virus (HIV) to AIDS, more people might carry the virus into old age. The presence of HIV positive people in the older population will present new challenges to family caregivers, formal care providers, and policymakers.

NOTE

Work on this chapter was supported by a fellowship (1992) from the Brookdale Foundation. Please address all correspondence to Jeffrey W. Dwyer, Ph.D., Institute of Gerontology, Wayne State University, 87 East Ferry, Detroit, MI 48202.

REFERENCES

Abel, E. K. (1986). Adult daughters and care for the elderly. *Feminist Studies, 12,* 479–497.

Atchley, R. C. (1985). *Social forces and aging.* Belmont, CA: Wadsworth.

Axinn, J., & Stern, M. J. (1985). Age and dependency: Children and the aged in American social policy. *Milbank Memorial Fund Quarterly, 63,* 648–670.

Bedford, V. H. (1992). Memories of parental favoritism and the quality of parent-child ties in adulthood. *Journal of Gerontology: Social Sciences, 47,* S149–155.

Callahan, D. (1987). Terminating treatment: Age as a standard. *Hastings Center Report, 17,* 21–25.

Coward, R. T., Horne, C., & Dwyer, J. W. (1992). Demographic perspectives on gender and family caregiving. In J. W. Dwyer & R. T. Coward (Eds.), *Gender, families, and elder care* (pp. 18–33). Newbury Park, CA: Sage.

Crandall, R. C. (1991). *Gerontology: A behavioral science approach* (2nd ed.). New York: McGraw-Hill.

Dahlin, M. (1980). Perspectives on the family life of the elderly in 1900. *Gerontologist, 20,* 99–107.

Dannefer, D. (1984). Adult development and social theory: A pragmatic reappraisal. *American Sociological Review, 49,* 100–116.

Dannefer, D. (1988). What's in a name? An account of the neglect of variability in the study of aging. In J. E. Birren & V. L. Bengtson (Eds.), *Emergent theories of the family* (pp. 356–384). New York: Springer Publishing Co.

Doty, P. (1986). Family care of the elderly: The role of public policy. *Milbank Memorial Fund Quarterly, 64,* 34–75.

Dubos, R. (1959). *Mirage of health.* New York: Doubleday.

Dwyer, J. W., & Coward, R. T. (1991). A multivariate comparison of the involvement of adult sons versus daughters in the care of impaired parents. *Journal of Gerontology: Social Sciences, 46,* S259–269.

Dwyer, J. W., & Coward, R. T. (Eds.). (1992). *Gender, families, and elder care.* Newbury Park, CA: Sage.

Dwyer, J. W., Henretta, J. C., Coward, R. T., & Barton, A. J. (1992). Changes in the helping behaviors of adult children as caregivers. *Research on Aging, 14,* 351–375.

Elder, G. H., Jr. (1992). The life course. In E. F. Borgatta & M. L. Borgatta (Eds.), *The encyclopedia of sociology* (Vol. 3, pp. 1120–1130). New York: Macmillan.

Fischer, D. H. (1978). *Growing old in America.* New York: Oxford University Press.

Friedson, E. (1970). *Professional dominance: The social structure of medical care.* New York: Atherton.

Goldscheider, F. K. (1990). The aging of the gender revolution. *Research on Aging, 12,* 531–545.

Hanley, R. J., Alecxih, L.M.B., Wiener, J. M., & Kennell, D. L. (1990). Predicting elderly nursing home admissions. *Research on Aging, 12,* 199–228.

Hareven, T. K. (1978). Historical changes in the life course and the family. In J. Yinger & S. J. Cutler (Eds.), *Major social issues: Multidisciplinary view* (pp. 338–345). New York: Free Press.

Henretta, J. C. (1992). Uniformity and diversity: Life course institutionalization and late-life work exit. *Sociological Quarterly, 33,* 265–279.

Hess, B. B., & Soldo, B. (1985). Husband and wife networks. In W. J. Sauer & R. T. Coward (Eds.), *Social support networks and the care of the elderly* (pp. 67–92). New York: Springer Publishing Co.

Himes, C. L. (1992). Future caregivers: Projected family structures of older persons. *Journal of Gerontology: Social Sciences, 47,* S17–26.

Hooyman, N. (1990). Women as caregivers to the elderly. In D. E. Biegel & A. Blum (Eds.), *Aging and caregiving: Theory, research, and policy* (pp. 221–241). Newbury Park, CA: Sage.

Hooyman, N. R. (1992). Social policy and gender inequities in caregiving. In J. W. Dwyer & R. T. Coward (Eds.), *Gender, families, and elder care* (pp. 181–201). Newbury Park, CA: Sage.

Horowitz, A. (1985). Family caregiving to the elderly. *Annual Review of Gerontology and Geriatrics, 5,* 194–246.

Kane, R. L. (1989). The home care crisis of the nineties. *Gerontologist, 29,* 24–31.

Lee, G. R. (1985). Kinship and social support of the elderly: The case of the United States. *Ageing and Society, 5,* 19–38.

Lee, G. R. (1992). Gender differences in family caregiving: A fact in search of a theory. In J. W. Dwyer & R. T. Coward (Eds.), *Gender, families, and elder care* (pp. 120–131). Newbury Park, CA: Sage.

Lee, G. R., Dwyer, J. W., & Coward, R. T. (1990). Residential location and proximity to children among impaired elderly parents. *Rural Sociology, 55*, 579–589.

Leventhal, H., Leventhal, E. A., & Nguyen, T. V. (1985). Reactions of families to illness: Theoretical models and perspectives. In D. C. Turk & R. D. Kerns (Eds.), *Health, illness, and families: A life-span perspective* (pp. 108–145). New York: Wiley.

Levit, K. R., Lazenby, H. C., Cowan, C. A., & Letsch, S. W. (1991). National health expenditures, 1990. *Health Care Financing Review, 13*, 29–54.

Litwak, E. (1965). Extended kin relations in an industrial democratic society. In E. Shanas & G. F. Streib (Eds.), *Social structure and the family* (pp. 290–323). Englewood Cliffs, NJ: Prentice-Hall.

Lubkin, I. M. (1986). *Chronic illness: Impact and interventions.* Boston: Jones & Bartlett.

Markides, K. S., & Mindel, C. H. (1987). *Aging and ethnicity.* Newbury Park, CA: Sage.

Matthews, S. H., & Rosner, T. T. (1988). Shared filial responsibility: The family as the primary caregiver. *Journal of Marriage and the Family, 50*, 185–195.

Mindel, C. H., Wright, R., & Starrett, R. (1986). Informal and formal social and health service use by black and white elderly: A comparative cost approach. *Gerontologist, 26*, 279–285.

Minkler, M., & Stone, R. (1985). The feminization of poverty and older women. *Gerontologist, 25*, 351–357.

Montgomery, R.J.V. (1992). Gender differences in patterns of child-parent caregiving relationships. In J. W. Dwyer & R. T. Coward (Eds.), *Gender, families, and elder care* (pp. 65–83). Newbury Park, CA: Sage.

Newman, S. J., Struyk, R., Wright, P., & Rice, M. (1990). Overwhelming odds: Caregiving and the risk of institutionalization. *Journal of Gerontology: Social Sciences, 45*, S173–183.

Older Women's League. (1989). *Failing America's caregivers.* Washington, DC: Author.

O'Rand, A. M. (1990). Stratification and the life course. In R. H. Binstock & L. K. George (Eds.), *Handbook of aging and the social sciences* (Vol. 3, pp. 130–148). San Diego: Academic Press.

Parsons, T. (1951). *The social system.* Glencoe, IL: Free Press.

Rivlin, A. M., Wiener, J. M., Hanley, R. J., & Spence, D. A. (1988). *Caring for the disabled elderly: Who will pay?* Washington, DC: Brookings Institution.

Rolland, J. S. (1988). A conceptual model of chronic and life threatening illness and its impact on families. In C. S. Chilman, E. W. Nunnally, & F. W. Cox (Eds.), *Chronic illness and disability* (pp. 17–68). Newbury Park, CA: Sage.

Sangl, J. (1985). The family support system of the elderly. In R. J. Vogel & H. C. Palmer (Eds.), *Long-term care: Perspectives from research and demonstration* (pp. 307–336). Rockville, MD: Aspen.

Scanlon, W. J. (1988). A perspective on long-term care for the elderly. *Health Care Financing Review* (Annual Suppl.), 7–15.

Seccombe, K. (1992). Employment, the family, and employer-based policies. In J. W. Dwyer & R. T. Coward (Eds.), *Gender, families, and elder care* (pp. 165–180). Newbury Park, CA: Sage.

Shank, S. E. (1988). Women and the labor market: The link grows stronger. *Monthly Labor Review, 3,* 3–8.

Soldo, B., Wolf, D., & Agree, E. (1990). Family, households and care arrangements of frail older women: A structural analysis. *Journal of Gerontology: Social Sciences, 45,* S238–249.

Stahl, S. M., & Feller, J. R. (1990). Old equals sick: An ontogenetic fallacy. In S. M. Stahl (Ed.), *The legacy of longevity* (pp. 21–34). Newbury Park, CA: Sage.

Steuart, G. W. (1985). Social and behavioral change strategies. In H. T. Phillips & S. A. Gaylord (Eds.), *Aging and public health* (pp. 217–247). New York: Springer Publishing Co.

Stoller, E. P. (1985). Exchange patterns in the informal networks of the elderly: The impact of reciprocity on morale. *Journal of Marriage and the Family, 47,* 335–342.

Stoller, E. P. (1992). Gender differences in the experiences of caregiving spouses. In J. W. Dwyer & R. T. Coward (Eds.), *Gender, families, and elder care* (pp. 49–64). Newbury Park, CA: Sage.

Stoller, E. P., & Pugliesi, K. L. (1989). Other roles of caregivers: Competing responsibilities or supportive resources. *Journal of Gerontology: Social Sciences, 44,* S231–238.

Stone, R., Cafferata, G. L., & Sangl, J. (1987). Caregivers of the frail elderly: A national profile. *Gerontologist, 27,* 616–626.

Streib, G. F. (1983). The frail elderly: Research dilemmas and research opportunities. *Gerontologist, 23,* 40–44.

Streib, G. F., & Binstock, R. H. (1990). Aging and the social sciences: Changes in the field. In R. H. Binstock & L. K. George (Eds.), *Handbook of aging and the social sciences* (Vol. 3, pp. 1–18). San Diego: Academic Press.

Struyk, R., & Katsura, H. (1988). *Aging at home: How the elderly adjust their housing consumption without moving.* New York: Haworth Press.

Suitor, J. J., & Pillemer, K. (1990). Transition to the status of family caregiver: A new framework for studying social support and well-being. In S. M. Stahl (Ed.), *The legacy of longevity* (pp. 310–320). Newbury Park, CA: Sage.

Sussman, M. B. (1965). Relationship of adult children to their parents in the United States. In E. Shanas & G. F. Streib (Eds.), *Social structure and the family* (pp. 62–92). Englewood Cliffs, NJ: Prentice-Hall.

Tennstedt, S., McKinlay, J., & Sullivan, L. (1989). Informal care for frail elders: The role of secondary caregivers. *Gerontologist, 29,* 677–683.

Uhlenberg, P. (1980). Death and the family. *Journal of Family History, 5,* 313–320.

U. S. Bureau of the Census. (1975). *Historical statistics of the United States, colonial times to 1970, bicentennial edition, part 2.* Washington, DC: U. S. Government Printing Office.

U. S. Bureau of the Census. (1989). *Projections of the population of the United States by age, sex, and race.* Current Population Reports, Series P-25, No. 1018. Washington DC: U. S. Government Printing Office.

Verbrugge, L. M. (1989). Gender, aging, and health. In K. S. Markides (Ed.), *Aging and health* (pp. 23–78). Newbury Park, CA: Sage.

Weeks, J. R. (1981). *Population: Introduction to concepts and issues.* Belmont, CA: Wadsworth.

Wiener, J. M., Hanley, R. J., Clark, R., & Van Nostrand, J. F. (1990). Measuring the activities of daily living: Comparisons across national surveys. *Journal of Gerontology: Social Sciences, 45,* S229–237.

World Health Organization. (1958). Constitution of the W.H.O., Annex I. *The First Ten Years of the World Health Organization.* Geneva: Author.

World Health Organization. (1959). *The public aspects of the aging of the population.* Report of an advisory group. Copenhagen: World Health Organization, Regional Office for Europe.

20

Death and Bereavement

Miriam S. Moss and Sidney Z. Moss

Older persons as family members are no strangers to death and bereavement. They experience more deaths of persons close to them, go to more funerals (Kalish & Reynolds, 1976), talk and think more about death (Wass & Myers, 1982), and probably have had more personal and family brushes with death than middle-aged or younger persons have experienced. Persons over age 65 represented 72% of all deaths in the United States in 1990 (U.S. Bureau of the Census, 1990), although they constituted less than 13% of the population. Most old persons have close family members who would be affected by their death.

In this chapter we discuss two main interrelated topics: first, the impact on close family members of the death of old persons, and second, the impact on old persons of the death of close family members. Throughout our discussion, it is important to keep in mind that old persons are a heterogeneous group. Although many demographic characteristics of elderly adults might be particularly salient to bereavement, they have received little research attention and thus are minimally dealt with in this chapter. These include age, gender, health, ethnicity, socioeconomic status, and characteristics of the terminal illness. Old persons' attitudes toward their own dying and coming to terms with their own death are also not covered in this chapter, although considerable literature on these topics is available (Kübler-Ross, 1969; Schulz & Schlarb, 1987–88; Tobin, 1991).

Behavioral scientists have noted the paucity of research and theory about death and bereavement over the life course (Osterweis, Solomon, & Green, 1984) and have emphasized spousal death for persons under age 65 (Stroebe, Stroebe, & Hansson, 1993; also see O'Bryant and Hansson, this volume). The fields of gerontology and thanatology (the study of death and dying) have minimal overlap. The few who have tried to bridge the two disciplines include Kalish (1987), Kastenbaum (1969), Lund (1989), Marshall (1986), Moss and Moss (1989b), and Wass and Myers (1982). The challenge for this chapter is to begin to chart the meaning of nonspousal deaths for older persons and their families.

In addition to the dyadic ties between parent and child (see Suitor, Pillemer, Keeton, & Robison, this volume), husband and wife (see Huyck, this volume), or siblings (see Bedford, this volume), strong ties to the family as a whole usually occur. Built upon lifelong interactions, family ties continue over the lifetime, and we suggest they persist beyond death (Levitt, 1991; Moss & Moss, 1989a). Thus, the death or the bereavement of an old person can have considerable impact on individuals and families within and across generations (Troll, 1986).

THEORIES OF BEREAVEMENT

Bereavement, our focus here, refers to an individual's and family's multidimensional responses to death. The more limited term *grief* refers primarily to emotional responses to loss. Theories of bereavement have generally been derived from clinical and research experience with middle-aged or young family members (Raphael, 1987; Rando, 1993; Stroebe et al., 1993). They have rarely been tested on the bereaved of deceased elderly people. Mainstream theories are best represented by Freud (1957) and Bowlby (1980).

Freud emphasized the significance of the early childhood experience with mother as the paradigm for later relationships. When the loved other has died, a wish to maintain the tie continues. Confronted by the reality of that loss over time, the person gradually decathects, withdrawing emotional energy (libido) from the deceased person. This process enables the survivor to establish new relationships and thus recover from the loss. Bowlby (1980) stressed that close family ties involve strong, primary attachments that provide a base for mutual security and protectiveness. When an attachment figure dies, the survivor actively seeks to retrieve the lost person. The painful process of searching, yearning, and despair eventually is resolved through detachment and reorganization, allowing the survivor to develop new ties. Reorganization involves a shift in the survivor's assumptive world to a new sense of reality in experiencing life without the deceased (Parkes, 1988).

Following Freud and Bowlby, clinicians have viewed bereavement within a medical model. They have suggested that failure to decathect from a deceased person might signal complicated bereavement and require treatment (Rando, 1993). Alternative views of the process of bereavement, also generated by bereavement of younger persons, have been suggested by behavioral researchers and death educators, such as Klass (1988), Silverman and Worden (1992), and Wortman and Silver (1992). They frame the process of bereavement in different terms. They highlight several themes in fam-

ily bereavement that recur in our discussion: (1) bereavement is a normative
life process, rather than an illness necessitating recovery or treatment; (2)
rather than specific phases or stages, individuals find many ways to traverse
the transition of bereavement and encompass family losses; (3) holding on
to the deceased is a core theme in family bereavement; and (4) bereavement
is an active process in which the survivor makes choices about how to
respond to the loss emotionally, cognitively, and behaviorally (Attig, 1991).

IMPACT OF DEATH ON THE FAMILY

Little is known about the dynamics of a family when a member of any
age or generation dies. During the process of bereavement, shifts in family
roles and expectations occur (Walsh & McGoldrick, 1991). Emotional
shock waves can affect each individual, each generation, and the family
system as a whole. The death of a family member usually leaves an empty
space. A new person might step into the role, or the family might close
ranks. In either event, the family structure will be modified, because there
is no substitute for the deceased member. The death of a family member
represents both the loss of a family's link with the past and the loss of
future interactions (Hagestad & Neugarten, 1985). Even after death, however, a sense of the presence of the deceased person might persist and remain meaningful in the lives of the survivors.

IMPACT OF THE DEATH OF OLD PERSONS

In this section we explore the impact of the death of an elderly member
on the family. One characteristic of the deceased person that determines
the family's response is age. It is not surprising that after a death, one of
the first questions asked is, "How old was your relative?" First, we examine
two themes that are often salient: (1) anticipation of the death and (2)
disfranchisement of bereavement. Then we discuss a prototypical death of
an old person—the death of a parent—and its potential impact on a middle-aged child.

Anticipation

Quality of life varies widely in the final year (Lawton, Moss, & Glicksman, 1991). An old person's loss of physical or mental functioning can
trigger family bereavement for incremental losses well before the death,
which Kowalski (1986) refers to as partial grief.

The death of an old person is often anticipated even in the absence of
chronic illness (Owen, Fulton, & Markusen, 1982–83). Bass and Bowman
(1990) reported on various ways that caregivers prepare for an old person's
death, ranging from spending more time with the dying person (80%), to

discussing the funeral (44%) or their feelings with the dying person (29%), to helping relatives plan for a future life without the dying person (22%). For deaths in general, no consistent evidence shows that anticipation of the loss, or partial grief, affects the quality of later responses to bereavement (Rando, 1986). The few studies specific to older persons, focused on widows, similarly found that anticipatory bereavement is complex and has no consistent effect after the death (Lund, 1989).

Although relatives often interact with elders toward the end of life in their "final career" of dying (Marshall & Levy, 1990, p. 249), anticipation of death might or might not be openly shared with other family members or with the dying person. In a retrospective study of the last year of life of 200 community-dwelling old people, 30% of the next of kin reported a period of time when both they and the dying person knew about the seriousness of the condition but did not admit it to each other. Forty-one percent said they did not talk about the death at all with the old person; of those who did discuss it, 75% said it was always the dying person who brought up the topic (Moss, 1984). The authors' ongoing research of 50 adult children of elderly nursing home residents indicates that although children seldom or never talked with their parent about the parent's dying (76%), they did have thoughts about the possibility of the parent's death "sometimes" or "a lot" (86%). Little else is known about whether or how family members discuss a relative's impending death.

Disfranchisement

Kalish and Reynolds (1976) found that the death of an old person was thought by many to be the least tragic of deaths. Kastenbaum (1969) noted a pecking order in which the death of the oldest family member is expected prior to the death of younger family members. Even before death an old person might be treated as socially dead if he or she has severe dementia or is otherwise unable to communicate. If a death seems fair and timely, it may be less socially disruptive, and it is not surprising that families mark such a death with fewer funeral rituals (Owen et al., 1982–83).

In general, U.S. society frowns on expressions of grief in bereavement and encourages denial of, and self-control over, such emotions. If the lives and deaths of old persons tend to have reduced social value, when an old person dies, people tend to devalue the grief of the survivors. This is an example of disfranchised grief, which Doka (1989) defined as "a loss that is not or cannot be openly, publicly mourned, or socially supported" (p. 4). Thus, it might be socially inappropriate to have a long, intense, personally upsetting, and familially disruptive process of bereavement for an old family member (Moss & Moss, 1989b). The death of an old person might elicit less empathy and less "vicarious grief" (Kastenbaum, 1987, p. 447) by family and friends.

DEATH OF AN ELDERLY PARENT

Most old people do have a living child; thus, most who die have surviving children. The focus here is limited to the dyad of deceased parent and surviving child because of the lack of literature on, and the complexity of, a broader family approach.

First we examine the impact of the death of an elderly parent, comparing it with other deaths and then suggesting that it is a normative transition engendering grief and affecting the self and the family. We highlight the potential effect of background characteristics of the parent and child, the quality of their relationship, and the context of the parent's death.

Comparable Deaths

Differential responses to the death of different family members occur (Osterweis et al., 1984). A few investigators have compared groups of bereaved persons who had lost a parent, a child, or a spouse (Bass, Noelker, Townsend, & Deimling, 1990; Owen et al., 1982–83; Sanders, 1979–80). In general, when different responses to bereavement in the three groups were found, the intensity of response was greater for the death of a child than for a spouse and greater for a spouse than for a parent. For example, Sanders (1979–1980) studied survivors of a random sample of deaths (picked from obituaries) and found, two months after the death, that the 35 sons and daughters (mean age = 39 years) tended to have fewer physical symptoms and, in general, lower intensity of bereavement than the 53 bereaved spouses reported. Similarly, Owen et al. (1982–83), comparing survivors of parental (N = 39), child (N = 85), and spouse death (N = 434), found that adult children reported the least depression, the least preoccupation with the deceased, and the lowest proportion of somatic complaints after the death. None of these investigators suggest, however, that parental death has an insignificant impact.

A Normative Transition

As suggested by the notion of the pecking order of death and confirmed by the research previously discussed, death of an old parent is a normative life course transition for middle-aged persons (Hagestad & Neugarten, 1985). Winsborough (1980) defined the onset of a life cycle transition for a cohort as the point when 25% of the members have experienced it, and the completion of the transition when 75% have experienced it. He found that the transition of mother's death occurred for the 1920 birth cohort between their ages 35 and 59 (a period of 24 years). For the 1970 birth cohort, he projected that the transition would occur between the ages of 49 and 64 (over only 15 years). Thus, parental death is becoming a more clearly defined life course transition. In addition, Winsborough (1980) estimated that in 1920, 47% of women aged 50 had a living mother, whereas in 1970, the figure was 73%. Uhlenberg (1980) also reported that parental deaths are occurring later in the life of children: in 1900, 24% of children up to the age of 15 had a parent die, but by 1976 the figure had dropped to 5%.

In spite of the frequency of the death of old parents, only in the last decade has the beginning of a body of knowledge emerged about how adults perceive and respond to the death of a parent. The meaning and impact of this death have been minimally explored not only because the parent is old but because the bereaved are generally middle-aged persons, a life period that as a whole is infrequently studied. Responses to these deaths might be particularly disfranchised because it is expected and acceptable that parents will predecease children.

Impact of Parent Death on Middle-Aged Children

Researchers of parental death have begun to explore its impact on the adult child's emotions and sense of self and on her or his family relationships. Further, investigators have examined bereavement as it relates to characteristics of the child and parent, the quality of the parent-child relationship, and the context of the death.

Emotional response to death

Scharlach (1991) used newspaper ads to recruit 220 adults (median age = 47 years) who had a parent (median age = 74 years) die in the previous one to five years. He found that these adult children had a range of persistent emotional responses, such as being upset, crying, having painful memories, experiencing loneliness, and being preoccupied with thoughts of the parent.

Depression has been used as a primary outcome measure of the emotional response to the death of a close family member. It is important to stress, however, that measures of depression and grief are not interchangeable and differ in significant ways among widowed persons and probably among other bereaved people, as well. Umberson (1990) undertook secondary analyses of a national two-wave panel study of persons aged 24 years and over. Within this group, 207 persons had experienced the death of a parent over the two-and-half-year study period. Controlling for demographic characteristics and baseline measures of various aspects of the child's well-being, she found that filial bereavement was associated with increased levels of depression from pre- to postdeath. Norris and Murrell (1990) conducted a longitudinal study of a stratified area probability sample of 1,429 persons over age 55 years. Their subanalysis of the 58 persons whose parent died showed no transient or persistent changes in depression from the initial levels prior to the death. Thus, research on the impact of parental loss on depression has yielded conflicting findings.

Impact on self

Parental death affects the sense of self in a variety of ways. Robbins (1990) held lengthy qualitative interviews with 10 middle-class daughters aged 35 to 55 years, recruited from women's networks. She examined the relationship between the meanings that the daughter assigned to parental loss and the daughter's personal autonomy. The findings revealed that death led to increases in the daughter's positive view of her own self and world and to shifts in her view of her mother and their tie. In contrast, Umberson (1990) found that parental death was associated with decreased personal mastery, although it had no effect on other measures of self.

The death of a parent can also represent the loss of a natural buffer against the adult child's own death and the movement of the child to be next in line, closer to death (Kowalski, 1986; Scharlach, 1991). For example, Douglas (1990–91) analyzed qualitative interviews with 40 middle-aged children who reported an increased sense of personal mortality after the death of one or both parents. But Galloway (1990), in a retrospective study of 19 bereaved adult children of younger parents (mean age at death = 58), found that although they felt more vulnerable, with an increased sense of personal finitude, children were supported in their bereavement by warm memories as well as religious and philosophical views.

Impact on the family

There is a paucity of research on the impact of an elderly parent's death on the bereaved family. Umberson (1991), analyzing data from a large national sample, found that bereavement was not associated with changes in family relationships with a surviving parent, with the adult child's own children, or with other kin. The adult children's marital relationships, however, were affected negatively at the time they were measured up to 30 months after parental death. Douglas (1990–91) also reported increased marital difficulties, as did Guttman (1991) in her clinical study. Rosenthal (1985) found that if the deceased person had a central role such as the head of the clan or kinkeeper, that person's death caused a ripple effect in the same and younger generations.

Background characteristics

A number of background characteristics of adult children and their parents are associated with the impact of bereavement. Umberson (1990) found that neither age, gender, nor marital status of the child had an independent effect on depression following the death but that being younger or unmarried was independently associated with poorer adaptation to the death. Also, the death of a mother was associated with higher levels of depression and poorer adaptation to the death (compared with death of a father). Further, the death of the first parent had more impact on depression than the death of the remaining parent. Scharlach (1991) and Moss, Moss, Rubinstein, and Resch (1992–93) also found that younger adult children were more affected by grief than were older adult children. Scharlach further reported that daughter's initial reaction to the father's death was more intense than that of sons. Both Umberson (1990) and Scharlach (1991) found that children with higher levels of income and education appeared to be more affected by a parent's death than those with lower socioeconomic status. This is congruent with Wortman and Silver's (1992) finding that economically comfortable people with assumptions about a benign world might be particularly vulnerable to difficulties in adjusting to family deaths.

Quality of the parent-child tie

In studying the relationship between the quality of the parent-child ties and bereavement outcomes, investigators have rarely used uniform measures, and thus it is not surprising that they report seemingly conflicting findings. For example, Umberson (1990) found that the more emotional support the mother provided to the adult child prior to her death, the greater the depression and poorer the child's adaptation after the death. Popek and Scharlach's (1991) analysis of 46 mother-daughter dyads yielded different findings. They reported that close and mutually accepting mother-daughter ties were associated with resolution of the death and acceptance of the loss. Scharlach (1991) also found that lack of filial autonomy, but not other dimensions of the parent-child tie such as attachment and assistance, was a consistent independent predictor of grief.

Context of the death

Our ongoing research on the contexts of death and the process of bereavement involves 107 middle-aged daughters who recently experienced the death of their widowed mother. We examined seven multi-item indexes of bereavement outcomes: grief (emotional response to death and loneliness), somatic responses (health or health-related practices), acceptance (timeliness and fairness of the death), finitude (perceptions of closeness to one's own death), comfort (feeling good about memories), reunion (expectations about future togetherness with mother), and guilt (regrets about care and time with mother) (Moss et al., 1992–93). None of the outcomes are significantly correlated with all of the others. We compared bereavement across four contexts of the death: *heavy caregiving* to coresident mothers, *nursing home* resident mothers, geographically *distant* mothers, and *light caregiving* to relatively independent proximate mothers. Although the four groups of daughters did not differ on measures of somatic responses, finitude, comfort, and guilt, the light caregivers showed significantly more grief, less acceptance, and more thoughts of future reunion than did those with mothers in nursing homes. These findings underscore the value of distinguishing between multiple dimensions of bereavement outcomes and analyzing how each operates in different contexts of parental death.

Klapper, Moss, Moss, and Rubinstein (1994) analyzed the interface between the social-cultural context of the loss and the intrapersonal expression of bereavement. The results yielded the concept of selfish grief, in which the daughter controls her expression of deep sadness because it would be selfish to wish her mother to continue to live and suffer. Rubinstein (in press) described three themes in the daughters' narratives of their mothers' deaths: the centrality of medical care, the pervasiveness of ageism, and the difficulties of terminal care.

Bass and his colleagues, in a prospective study of caregivers, described the process of bereavement for 55 adult children (mean age = 51 years). Overall, the subjective aspects of the process of caregiving were associated with bereavement outcomes more than was the support the caregiver received after the death (Bass, Bowman, & Noelker, 1991). Those who perceived caregiving as more difficult reported greater bereavement strain after death (Bass & Bowman, 1990). Further, other evidence suggests that caregivers' well-being improves in the year following death (George & Gwyther, 1984). Again the context of the death can play a major role in the process of bereavement.

Summary

Although studies of the death of an elderly parent use a range of methodologies, findings yield some congruence: the intensity of the impact of the death on the well-being of the child is rarely pathological; the death has some effect on family relationships, particularly marriage; predeath experiences (e.g., quality of parent-child tie, appraisal of caregiving, anticipation of the death) have an impact on the child's reaction to the death; positive outcomes are reflected in personal growth; it is important to examine the pattern of bereavement outcomes rather than a single indicator such as grief; and the context of the death plays an important role in bereavement.

WHEN AN OLD PERSON IS BEREAVED

How do old persons respond to the death of family members? Bereavement surely has a strong effect on psychological distress and might require more adjustment for an old person than any other life event. We suggest, however, that the basic processes and outcomes of bereavement are relevant across the life cycle.

Multiple Losses

Old age is replete with multiple and sequential losses. Although the family deaths that are the focus of this chapter exclude spousal death, it is important to stress that many persons 65 years of age and over have been widowed. Some would argue that mastery of the experience of stressful events in the past can reduce the impact of later stressful events. For instance, this mastery might lead to developing a worldview that facilitates adaptation to later losses (Wortman & Silver, 1992). Conversely, the impact of multiple losses might have a cumulative negative effect (Norris & Murrell, 1990).

Disfranchisement

Societal ageism can be internalized by older persons as they devalue themselves and their feelings. If the bereaved person and the deceased are both old, then the grief might be doubly disfranchised. Kalish (1987) suggested that when older persons evidence normal responses to bereavement such as lack of energy, confusion, loneliness, and social withdrawal, these behaviors are sometimes interpreted as problems reflective of old age. Again, bereavement of old persons may be disfranchised.

The bereavement experienced by old persons might be devalued if it is seen as secondary to the bereavement of younger family members. For example, if a married adult child of an old person dies, family and friends might be most concerned about the grieving widowed spouse and disfranchise the parental mourner.

The remainder of this section focuses on themes that are beginning to emerge in research on the differential responses of elderly persons to the death of family members from different generations: a very old parent, a sibling, and a child. Although many aspects of bereavement are similar across these losses, each has distinct characteristics.

Death of an Old Person's Parent

Ten percent of persons who have reached the age of 65 years have at least one living parent, and 10% of persons over age 65 have a living child who is also over 65 years old (Brody, 1990). Yet, the only discussion of parent death for old persons in the literature is by Kalish (1987). Old persons' parents are probably beyond their mid-80s and might have serious chronic diseases. Thus, the elderly child has had time to think and talk about the possibility of the parent's death. Kalish (1987) suggested that this anticipation can contribute to an increasing emotional distance from elderly parents and after death lead to "a minimal destructive impact on the surviving elderly adult children" (p. 35).

On the other hand, when very old parents die, issues of generational succession, awareness of finitude, and possibly a sense of orphanhood arise. The themes in parental loss experienced by middle-aged persons (described earlier) might well apply to filial grief of the elderly.

Death of an Elderly Sibling

Probably the most normative death experienced by elderly persons is of a sibling (Perkins & Harris, 1990). Almost four-fifths (77%) of a large random sample of older persons had a living sibling, and over two-fifths had experienced sibling death since they were 60 years of age (Moss & Moss, 1989c).

Sibling ties generally represent the longest family bond over a lifetime (see Bedford, this volume). Why has the death of an adult sibling received so little research attention? Few adults share a household with a sibling, and few siblings are primary caregivers to frail and dependent elderly persons. Clinicians probably ignore the impact of adult sibling death because few persons seek counseling around issues of sibling ties. When adults die, the members of their nuclear family (spouse and children) are expected to be the most affected. Murrell and Himmelfarb (1989) placed siblings out of the category of "attachment bereavement," indicating that this tie is secondary to spousal, parental, and child deaths. Thus, when an elderly sibling dies, few social supports for the recognition of the loss or the expression of grief are available. Yet few would suggest that sibling bonds are without importance in the lives of old persons or that sibling deaths occur with no impact.

Sibling death has a considerable impact on middle-aged survivors (Perkins & Harris, 1990). At that time associations and reminiscences with surviving siblings provide comfort and strengthen the shared tie with the deceased sister or brother (Rosenblatt & Elde, 1990). Moss and Moss (1989c) interviewed 20 older persons (mean age = 77 years) about a sibling who had died since the respondent was age 60. They concluded that the tie with the deceased sibling continues and has an impact on the survivor's identity, sense of vulnerability, and the meaning of family.

Sibling death affects the sense of identity insofar as the sibling was central to the development of the self. Siblings might have represented a source of personal validation and a standard for personal comparison. Loss of that person would be felt as a depletion of self. Surviving siblings might, however, feel a sense of mastery in having been able to handle the death of a significant family member. Thus, the experience could simultaneously weaken and strengthen the survivor's sense of identity.

As with parental death, when an age peer dies, one often is faced with the shortened distance to one's own death. The biogenetic bond of siblings could lead the survivors to expect similar health conditions and patterns of terminal decline. Sibling death might generate feelings of partial grief for incremental losses in one's self. Although Moss and Moss (1989c) expected that the death of a younger sibling would be more difficult than death of an older sibling because it is considered off-time and that the death of the last surviving sibling would particularly trigger one's view of personal finitude, neither hypothesis was confirmed. As Kalish (1985) suggested, a sense of renewed resiliency might emerge in the survivor who is able to say, "It wasn't me" with relief and pleasure as well as guilt. Thus, sibling death can both increase and decrease one's personal sense of vulnerability.

A sense of family incompleteness might result from sibling death, and family ties might be weakened. But sibling death might also increase family closeness (Ross & Milgram, 1982). Moss and Moss (1989c) noted that ties with the surviving spouse and children of the deceased sibling were actually strengthened.

Death of an Adult Child

In the expected rhythm of life, children do not die before their parents. Yet, this event does occur all too frequently. A secondary analysis of a national probability sample of 3,996 elderly persons found that 10% of all persons who had ever been parents had a child die when the parent was at least 60 years old (Moss, Lesher, & Moss, 1986–87). Another study projected that 25% of all women over the age of 65 years who have an adult son will experience the death of a son (Metropolitan Life Insurance, 1977). Several researchers who compared the impact of a child's death with that of a spouse or a parent found that the death of a child leads to more intense reactions such as despair, somatization, anger, and guilt than do other deaths (Owen et al., 1982–83; Sanders, 1979–80).

There has been some research on the impact of a child's death on parents across the life cycle. Klass (1988), studying a self-help group of parents of young children who had died, suggested that the loss of a child is manifested as a threat to self. The parents frequently used a metaphor of amputation and saw absence and emptiness in their lives. He found that the process of internalization of the representation of the deceased child gives enriched remembrance, which tends to alleviate sorrow and provide comfort.

Research on adult child deaths is beginning to emerge (Margolis et al., 1988). Israeli studies of deaths of adult children who were war casualties are inconclusive: although Levav, Lubner, and Adler (1988) found no evidence for increased mortality of middle-aged parents, Rubin (1991–92) reported that 4 to 13 years after the child's death, bereaved parents had more anxiety than nonbereaved parents.

Studies of old parents whose children have died are rare. Lesher and Bergey (1988) interviewed 18 nursing home residents (mean age = 87 years) whose child had died an average of six years previously. Sixty-nine percent reported that the death had changed their everyday life "a great deal," and clinical interviews revealed some evidence of increasing psychological distress, sometimes of long duration. Goodman, Rubinstein, Alexander, and Luborsky's (1991) analysis of qualitative interviews with a small number of Jewish (12) and non-Jewish (17) elderly women indicated that Jews were more depressed, expressed more grief, and felt greater centrality of the loss than non-Jews. They suggest that the nature and strength of the mother-child tie affect the mother's response to the death of a child and that these phenomena are culturally determined.

Overall, six themes are particularly associated with the death of an adult child: (1) untimeliness, or the feeling of parents that their worldview has been shattered; (2) a strong biosocial bond has been broken that may represent a severe threat to one's identity as a protective parent; (3) survivor guilt is profound; (4) family relationships can be affected, perhaps weakening the marriage and shifting the parents' relationship with their surviving children and with the offspring of the deceased child; (5) loss of social and instrumental supports as providers of care in old age; and (6) with expected legacies and generativity unfulfilled, the future might take on different meanings for the bereaved parent.

FUTURE RESEARCH

Methods

Several methodological approaches are recommended to throw additional light on the interface among old age, death, and the family. For example, prospective longitudinal studies that cover shorter intervals between measures will enhance understanding of bereavement not as an event but as a process that extends over a long time period. Study samples that are large and representative of target populations will permit multivariate analyses. Qualitative research that focuses on the multiple meanings of the death and on the bereaved person's cognitive, emotional, and behavioral responses will bring a greater depth of understanding of the process. Accessible and reliable multidimensional measures of bereavement will facilitate comparability of research findings. Finally, interviews with multiple family members will foster development of typologies of family responses to bereavement.

Topics

We suggest three groups of topics for future research: the processes and outcomes of bereavement, the context of the loss, and family dynamics of bereavement.

The processes of bereavement

Studies that further delineate normative bereavement typologies involving older persons will enhance understanding of the bereavement process across the life course. How do the dimensions of bereavement relate to each other? In what ways do people anticipate death, and what is the impact of anticipation on subsequent aspects of bereavement? What factors control or facilitate expression of bereavement? Do people have role models for responses to bereavement? What are the positive and negative aspects of bereavement that affect self and others? How do individual bereavement processes and outcomes change over time?

Context of the loss

An examination of the psychosocial context of death adds to the understanding of the process of bereavement. How is bereavement affected by such characteristics of the deceased person as role in the family, experience of terminal illness, suddenness of the death, living arrangement? How is bereavement affected by the survivor's age, gender, ethnicity, religion, health, psychological well-being, developmental stage, and quality of the relationship with the deceased? How do other life events, including sequential and concurrent losses, affect bereavement? How are the characteristics of family caregiving associated with bereavement?

Family dynamics of bereavement

It is a challenge to researchers and clinicians to understand how a family responds to the death of a member. To what extent do old persons think or talk about the impact of their potential deaths on the continuity and functioning of their families? How do individual family members respond to, and evaluate, the appropriateness of each other's expression of bereavement? How are family bereavement traditions and rituals developed and maintained? How do family members, individually and collectively, maintain their ties with deceased members?

SUMMARY AND IMPLICATIONS

We have highlighted the multidimensional aspects of bereavement in response to the death of an old person as well as for old persons who themselves are bereaved. Although many persons express deep emotions of grief, other processes of bereavement, such as cognitive shifts in view of the self, the family, and the world, are also significant. The death or bereavement of an old person tends to be socially devalued, and thus the expression of the impact is disfranchised. Generalities that can be drawn about bereavement of and for elderly persons are that it is often a normative experience, it includes both emotional and cognitive elements, it has both negative and positive characteristics, it often requires active responses involving choice, it has an impact on the individual survivor as well as the family as a whole, and it is best understood as a transition from having a specific living family member to not having that living family member, rather than as a process of recovery (as in the medical model).

Professionals in both physical and mental health fields who work with families should be sensitive to the impact on their clients of the death of close old family members as well as the complex processes of bereavement in old age. Professionals must consider these processes when they interact with old persons and their families concerning anticipation of a death, plans for terminal care, and the reaction of survivors. The staff of acute- or long-term-care facilities who frequently experience deaths must learn to work effectively with individuals and families who anticipate or experience the death of their unique family members.

REFERENCES

Attig, T. (1991). The importance of conceiving of grief as an active process. *Death Studies, 15,* 385–393.

Bass, D. M., & Bowman, K. (1990). The impact of an aged relative's death on the family. In K. F. Ferraro (Ed.), *Gerontology: Perspectives and issues* (pp. 333–356). New York: Springer Publishing Co.

Bass, D. M., Bowman, K., & Noelker, L. S. (1991). The influence of caregiving and bereavement support on adjusting to an older relative's death. *Gerontologist, 31,* 32–42.

Bass, D. M., Noelker, L. S., Townsend, A. L., & Deimling, G. T. (1990). Losing a relative: Perceptual differences between spouses and adult children. *Omega, 21,* 21–40.

Bowlby, J. (1980). *Attachment and loss* (Vol. 3). New York: Basic Books.

Brody, E. M. (1990). *Women in the middle: Their parent-care years.* New York: Springer Publishing Co.

Doka, K. J. (1989). Disenfranchised grief. In K. Doka (Ed.), *Disenfranchised grief* (pp. 3–11). Lexington, MA: Lexington Books.

Douglas, J. D. (1990–91). Patterns of change following parent death in midlife adults. *Omega, 22,* 123–137.

Freud, S. (1957). Mourning and melancholia. In J. Strachey (Ed.), *Complete psychological works* (Standard ed., Vol. 14, pp. 243–258). London: Hogarth Press.

Galloway, S. C. (1990). Young adult's reactions to the death of a parent. *Oncology Nursing Forum, 17,* 899–904.

George, L., & Gwyther, L. (1984, November). *The dynamics of caregiver burden: Changes in caregiver well-being over time.* Paper presented at the Annual Scientific Meeting of the Gerontological Society of America, San Antonio, TX.

Goodman, M., Rubinstein, R., Alexander, B., & Luborsky, M. (1991). Cultural differences among elderly women in coping with the death of an adult child. *Journal of Gerontology: Social Sciences, 46,* S321–329.

Guttman, H. A. (1991). Parental death as a precipitant of marital conflict. *Journal of Marital and Family Therapy, 17,* 81–87.

Hagestad, G. O., & Neugarten, B. L. (1985). Age and the life course, In R. H. Binstock & E. Shanas (Eds.), *Handbook of aging and the social sciences* (2nd ed., pp. 35–61). New York: Van Nostrand Reinhold.

Kalish, R. A. (1985). The social context of death and dying. In R. H. Binstock & E. Shanas (Eds.), *Handbook of aging and the social sciences* (2nd ed., pp. 149–170). New York: Van Nostrand Reinhold.

Kalish, R. A. (1987). Older people and grief. *Generations, 11,* 33–38.

Kalish, R. A. & Reynolds, D. K. (1976). *Death and ethnicity: A psychocultural study.* Los Angeles: University of Southern California Press.

Kastenbaum, R. (1969). Death and bereavement in later life. In A. H. Kutscher (Ed.), *Death and bereavement in later life* (pp. 27–54). Springfield, IL: C. C. Thomas.

Kastenbaum, R. (1987). Vicarious grief: An intergenerational phenomenon? *Death Studies, 11,* 447–453.

Kastenbaum, R. (1987–88). Theory, research and application: Some critical issues for thanatology. *Omega, 18,* 397–410.

Klapper, J., Moss, S., Moss, M. S., & Rubinstein, R. (1994). The social context of grief among adult daughters who have lost a parent. *Journal of Aging Studies, 8,* 29–43.

Klass, D. (1988). *Parental grief: Solace and resolution.* New York: Springer Publishing Co.

Kowalski, N. C. (1986). Anticipating the death of an elderly parent. In T. A. Rando (Ed.), *Loss and anticipatory grief* (pp. 187–199). Lexington, MA: Lexington Books.

Kubler-Ross, E. (1969). *On death and dying.* New York: Macmillan.

Lawton, M. P., Moss, M., & Glicksman, A. (1991). The quality of the last year of life of older persons. *Milbank Quarterly, 68,* 1–28.

Lesher, E. L., & Bergey, K. J. (1988). Bereaved elderly mothers: Changes in health, functional activities, family cohesion and psychological well-being. *International Journal of Aging and Human Development, 26,* 81–90.

Levav, I., Lubner, M., & Adler, I. (1988). The bereaved parents of adult children: A case study. In O. S. Margolis, A. H. Kutscher, E. Marcus, H. C. Raether, V. R. Pine, & I. B. Seeland (Eds.), *Grief and loss of an adult child* (pp. 71–82). Westport, CT: Praeger.

Levitt, M. J. (1991). Attachment and close relationships: A life span perspective. In J. L. Gewirtz & W. M. Kurtines (Eds.), *Intersections with attachment* (pp. 183–206). Hillsdale, NJ: Erlbaum.

Lund, D. A. (1989). Conclusions about bereavement in later life and implications for interventions and future research. In D. A. Lund (Ed.), *Older bereaved spouses* (pp. 217–231). New York: Hemisphere Press.

Margolis, O. S., Kutscher, A. H., Marcus, E., Raether, H. C., Pine, V. R., & Seeland, I. B. (1988). *Grief and the loss of an adult child.* Westport, CT: Praeger.

Marshall, V. W. (1986). A sociological perspective on aging and dying. In V. W. Marshall (Ed.), *Later life: The social psychology of aging* (pp. 125–146). Beverly Hills, CA: Sage.

Marshall, V. W., & Levy, J. A. (1990). Aging and dying. In R. H. Binstock & L. K. George (Eds.), *Handbook of aging and the social sciences* (3rd ed., pp. 245–260). San Diego: Academic Press.

Metropolitan Life Insurance Company. (1977). Current patterns of dependency. *Statistical Bulletin of Metropolitan Life Insurance Company, 58.*

Moss, M. S. (1984). *The last year of life: Initial findings.* Unpublished manuscript. Philadelphia Geriatric Center, Philadelphia.

Moss, M. S., Lesher, E., & Moss, S. Z. (1986–87). The impact of the death of an adult child on elderly parents. *Omega, 17,* 209–218.

Moss, M. S., & Moss, S. Z. (1989a). The death of a parent. In R. A. Kalish (Ed.), *Midlife loss* (pp. 89–114). Newbury Park, CA: Sage.

Moss, M. S., & Moss, S. Z. (1989b). Death of the very old. In K. Doka (Ed.), *Disenfranchised grief: Recognizing hidden sorrow* (pp. 213–227). Lexington, MA: Lexington Books.

Moss, M. S., Moss, S. Z., Rubinstein, R., & Resch, N. (1992–93). Impact of elderly mother's death on middle aged daughters. *International Journal of Aging and Human Development, 37,* 1–22.

Moss, S. Z., & Moss, M. S. (1989). The impact of the death of an elderly sibling. *American Behavioral Scientist, 33,* 94–106.

Murrell, S. A., & Himmelfarb, S. (1989). Effects of attachment bereavement and the pre-event conditions on subsequent depressive symptoms in older adults. *Psychology of Aging, 4,* 166–172.

Norris, F. H., & Murrell, S. A. (1990). Social support, life events and stress as modifiers of adjustment to bereavement by older adults. *Psychology in Aging, 5,* 429–436.

Osterweis, M., Solomon, F., & Green, M. (Eds.). (1984). *Bereavement: Reactions, consequences and care.* Washington, DC: National Academy Press.

Owen, G., Fulton, R., & Markusen, E. (1982–83). Death at a distance: A study of family survivors. *Omega, 13,* 191–225.

Parkes, C. M. (1988). Bereavement as a psychosocial transition: Processes of adaptation to change. *Journal of Social Issues, 44,* 53–65.

Perkins, W. H., & Harris, L. B. (1990). Familial bereavement and health in adult life course perspective. *Journal of Marriage and the Family, 52,* 233–241.

Popek, P., & Scharlach, A. E. (1991). Adult daughters' relationship with their mothers and reactions to the mothers' deaths. *Journal of Women and Aging, 3,* 79–96.

Rando, T. A. (1986). A comprehensive analysis of anticipatory grief: Perspective, processes, promises, and problems. In T. A. Rando (Ed.), *Loss and anticipatory grief* (pp. 3–37). Lexington, MA: D. C. Heath.

Rando, T. A. (1993). *Treatment of complicated mourning.* Champaign, IL: Research Press.

Raphael, B. (1987). Current state of research in the field of bereavement. *Israel Journal of Psychiatry and Related Sciences, 1–2,* 5–32.

Robbins, M. A. (1990). *Midlife women and death of mother.* New York: Peter Lang.

Rosenblatt, P., & Elde, C. (1990). Shared reminiscences about a deceased parent: Implications for grief education and grief counseling. *Family Relations, 39,* 206–210.

Rosenthal, C. J. (1985). Kinkeeping in the familial division of labor. *Journal of Marriage and the Family, 47,* 965–974.

Ross, H. G., & Milgram, J. I. (1982). Important variables in adult sibling relationships: A qualitative study. In M. E. Lamb & B. Sutton-Smith (Eds.), *Sibling relationships: Their nature and significance over the life span* (pp. 225–249). Hillsdale, NJ: Erlbaum.

Rubin, S. S. (1991–92). Adult child loss and the two track model of bereavement. *Omega, 24,* 183–202.

Rubinstein, R. L. (in press). Narratives of elder parental death: A structural and cultural analysis. *Medical Anthropology Quarterly.*

Sanders, C. M. (1979–80). A comparison of adult bereavement in the death of a spouse, child and parent. *Omega, 10,* 303–322.

Scharlach, A. E. (1991). Factors associated with filial grief following the death of an elderly parent. *American Journal of Orthopsychiatry, 61,* 307–312.

Schulz, R., & Schlarb, J. (1987–88). Two decades of research on dying: What do we know about the patient? *Omega, 18,* 299–317.

Silverman, P. R., & Worden, J. W. (1992). Children's reactions in the early months after the death of a parent. *American Journal of Orthopsychiatry, 62,* 93–104.

Stroebe, M. S., Stroebe, W., & Hansson, R. O. (1993). *Handbook of bereavement: Theory, research and intervention.* New York: Cambridge University Press.

Tobin, S. S. (1991). *Personhood in advanced old age.* New York: Springer Publishing Co.

Troll, L. E. (1986). *Family issues in current gerontology.* New York: Springer Publishing Co.

Uhlenberg, P. (1980). Death and the family. *Journal of Family History, 5,* 313–320.

Umberson, D. (1990, November). *The impact of death of a parent on adult children's psychological well being: A prospective study.* Paper presented at Annual Scientific Meeting of the Gerontological Society of America, Boston.

Umberson, D. (1991, November). *Impact of a parent's death on adult children's relationships.* Paper presented at Annual Scientific Meeting of the Gerontological Society of America, San Francisco.

U.S. Bureau of the Census. (1990). *1990 census of population and housing: Summary population and housing characteristics.* Washington, DC: U.S. Government Printing Office.

Walsh, F., & McGoldrick, M. (Eds.). (1991). *Living beyond loss.* New York: Norton.

Wass, H., & Myers, J. E. (1982). Psychosocial aspects of death among the elderly: A review of the literature. *Personnel and Guidance Journal, 61,* 131–137.

Winsborough, H. H. (1980). A demographic approach to the life cycle. In K. W. Back (Ed.), *Life course: Integrative theories and exemplary populations* (pp. 65–77). Boulder, CO: Westview Press.

Wortman, C., & Silver, R. C. (1992). Reconsidering assumptions about coping with loss: An overview of current research. In L. Montado, S. H. Filipp, & M. J. Lerner (Eds.), *Life crises and experiences of loss in adulthood* (pp. 341–365). Hillside, NJ: Erlbaum.

21

Widowhood

Shirley L. O'Bryant and Robert O. Hansson

The study of the psychosocial phenomenon of widowhood has been a major undertaking by researchers for the last three decades; thus, in this chapter on widowhood and the family, it is impossible to cover all the important contributions past and present researchers have made toward understanding widowhood. Out of necessity, we limit our citations to those that are most recent or provide unique information about widowhood. In the first section of this chapter, we briefly summarize the bereavement experience of older persons. The main portion of the chapter then focuses on the implications of widowhood in later life for the family system.

THE BEREAVEMENT EXPERIENCE OF OLDER PERSONS

Researchers and clinicians have learned much about the experience of bereavement in general: its potentially complex symptomatology, physical and mental health consequences, processes associated with recovery, and so on. Although grief reactions reflect immense diversity across individuals and cultures, they are widely associated with increased incidence of emotional distress, physical illness, physician visits, use of psychotropic medication, hospitalization, and mortality (Stroebe & Stroebe, 1987; Stroebe, Stroebe, & Hansson, 1993).

Bereavement studies, for the most part, have not focused exclusively on older persons; however, recent longitudinal studies suggest that bereavement reactions among older samples generally parallel findings on broader populations (e.g., Gallagher-Thompson, Futterman, Farberow, Thompson, & Peterson, 1993; Lund, 1989). A number of important themes also emerge from recent research on older bereaved men and women, of which three are discussed here. They are resiliency, age as a risk factor, and multiple stresses at widowhood.

First, older bereaved persons, like their younger counterparts, appear quite resilient over the long term. For example, in a longitudinal study of persons over age 65, McCrae and Costa (1988) found those widowed during the study did not differ from married controls at a 10-year follow-up on measures of general well-being, depressive symptoms, or rated health, although the widows had suffered significant reductions in income and were more likely to be institutionalized.

Studies of shorter time span, however, provide a finer-grained analysis of the course of bereavement among older adults. For example, Thompson, Gallagher-Thompson, Futterman, Gilewski, and Peterson (1991) assessed recently widowed older adults (and a control group) over a 30-month period. At two months post-loss, the widowed sample exhibited significantly elevated symptoms of emotional distress and depression and a decline in physical health (including increased likelihood of a new or worsened illness and increased medication). By two years post-loss, however, assessments of general psychological distress, depressive symptoms, and health complaints had diminished to nonsignificant levels. In contrast, grief-specific feelings and experiences (e.g., loneliness, yearning, missing the deceased) remained high for extended periods of time. Similar findings with older widowed persons have been reported by Lund (1989) and Lund, Caserta, and Dimond (1993). For example, Lund and colleagues (1993) estimated that, at two years' post-loss, over 80% of widowed respondents had recovered satisfactorily, over 70% reported having learned new skills for living during their bereavement, and only 12% had felt it necessary to seek professional help. Such findings were particularly encouraging, given that over 70% of widowed respondents reported the loss of their spouse to have been the most stressful event of their lives. This pattern of resiliency closely parallels findings among younger widowed populations (Stroebe & Stroebe, 1993), although, at any age, a small percentage of bereaved persons continues to experience clinically relevant symptoms for extended periods of time (Lopata, 1988; Lund et al., 1993; Stroebe & Stroebe, 1993; Thompson et al., 1991).

Second, the preponderance of findings on age as a risk factor for poor bereavement outcome suggests that it is actually younger widowed individuals (Stroebe & Stroebe, 1987) and younger families (Hansson, Fairchild, Vanzetti, & Harris, 1992) who are at greater risk for negative outcome than are older individuals and families. This pattern presumably reflects the likelihood that death in later life is less unexpected and is seen as less unfair than death in the early years of life. (See Moss & Moss, this volume for a full treatment of attitudes toward the death of old people.)

Third, spousal bereavement is one of many problematic life events that tend to cluster in later life. Resulting emotional and physical distress might well interact with, or exacerbate, existing age-related problems with illness or disability. Moreover, at such a time, the loss of an integral member of the social and economic family unit might jeopardize the survivor's ability to live independently. The loss of a caregiver might force decisions about involuntary relocation to the home of a child or to an institution. Like the onset of a dramatic physical disability in old age, widowhood might assume symbolic proportions, marking "the line between not being old and being old" (Kemp, 1985).

During this period, newly widowed people might feel they lack skills for independent living, and they might be reluctant to make needed decisions (e.g., selling a house, reorganizing finances, or forming new relationships)— particularly when such decisions might conflict with the expectations of family members or the wishes of the deceased (Lund et al., 1993). Such complexity can present a tremendous adaptive challenge for both the bereaved individual and the family system for years to come. We now turn to the research on how older widowed persons and their families deal with these issues.

DEMOGRAPHICS OF WIDOWHOOD

Widowed, noninstitutionalized persons constitute 50% of the elderly population in the United States or approximately 13.5 million Americans. Older blacks are more likely to be widowed and to remain widowed as a result of racial differences in both death rates and remarriage rates. Of all women age 65 and over, almost 70% are widowed; of all men in the same age group, only 22% are widowed (U.S. Bureau of the Census, 1984). The mean age at widowhood is 66 years for women and 69 years for men; the mean duration of widowhood for men is about 6 years whereas for women it is approximately 15 years. These demographic figures reflect three facts: (1) in the general population, women live longer than men, (2) women are generally younger than their husbands and, therefore, are likely to outlive them; and (3) widowers are more likely to remarry than are widows, thus shortening the time they spend in a widowed state.

FAMILY CHARACTERISTICS AND THE WIDOWED

Certain characteristics of families affect the ability, desire, and need for family members to interact with, and respond to, a widowed relative. For example, the size of the family should be considered when assessing the availability of support; it is reduced by at least one—the deceased—at the time of the death. Furthermore, the deceased person's "side of the family" (the in-laws) usually withdraws from the widowed person's support system (Wan & Odell, 1983). In addition, family contact and support are affected by the geographical proximity of kin.

The gender of the widowed person's adult children is also an important consideration. For example, older widows and their daughters appear to have better relationships than older widowers and their sons (Adams, 1968). Furthermore, having children of only one gender apparently places limitations on the types of support a widowed parent receives. O'Bryant (1988a) found that older widows with no sons receive significantly less assistance with traditionally male household tasks (e.g., home and car repairs) than widows with sons, and Horowitz (1985) found that frail widowed parents without daughters receive less extensive caregiving than do those with daughters.

Because of the prevalence of adult children in the support systems of widowed persons, particular concern has been expressed about childless widowed persons. O'Bryant (1985, 1987) reported that childless widows, when compared with widowed mothers, have less contact with other family members, receive less frequent family assistance, and might not have comparable friend and neighbor support systems. There is, however, other evidence that suggests that Canadian childless widows have developed networks of other relatives and unrelated persons that might compensate for the absence of children (Martin Matthews, 1991). Because more married adults in the future might opt to remain childless, further research is needed in this area.

LIVING ARRANGEMENTS

The majority of older widows and widowers live alone. Factors that contribute to widowed persons' living alone include younger age, higher income, more education, childlessness, and being a homeowner (Chevan, 1987; O'Bryant, 1987). White widows appear most likely to live alone, followed by blacks, Hispanics, and Asians, respectively (Pelham & Clark, 1987). Older urban widows are more likely to live alone than are older rural widows.

Widows living alone are more likely than married couples to view their income as inadequate and their transportation needs as unmet. They are also more likely to report that no one would care for them in an emergency (Fengler, Danigelis, & Little, 1983). Despite such problems, however, most widows want to live alone rather than live with family members. Their reasons include retaining their freedom, avoiding the problems of sharing the kitchen and housework, and avoiding disagreements about child rearing (Lopata, 1973). Some widows who live alone compensate for diminished family contact by increasing contacts with friends and neighbors (Alwin, Converse, & Martin, 1985). Others, however, relish their solitude; consequently, it is a mistake for social scientists to equate an older person's living alone with lonesomeness and/or social isolation.

The death of a spouse often raises concerns about housing arrangements and pressures to relocate. An older widow might be unable to meet mortgage payments on a reduced income or to perform household maintenance. She might feel vulnerable to neighborhood crime or might simply wish to live closer to family. Relocation, however, might be problematic if the older person is in poor health or is very attached to his or her home (O'Bryant & Murray, 1986).

Widows appear more likely to move closer to their family members, rather than move into the same residence with them (O'Bryant & Murray, 1986). Coresidence of parents and adult children is not a normative pattern in the United States, as "independent living" is clearly preferred by both generations (Fengler et al., 1983). In recent decades the number of elderly who live in the same household with their children or other kin has declined. Nevertheless, widowhood increases the probability that a person will live with a child by 11% (Crimmins & Ingegneri, 1990). For white widows, living with others appears to be the consequence of poverty status and not of preference. Conversely, nonwhite widows are more likely to choose to live in multigenerational arrangements. Pelham and Clark (1987) concluded that the number of children and need on the part of the nonwhite widows dictate their living arrangements. In contrast, Choi (1991) argued that the matrifocal nature of blacks and Mexican American women might lead them to see the stresses of multigenerational family life as more bearable than the stresses of loneliness.

Interestingly, although older persons have often been pictured as being in greater need of care and assistance, recent research suggests that the needs of adult children might be more influential in determining coresidence than the needs of older parents (Ward, Logan, & Spitz, 1992). For example, in a nationally representative sample of recently widowed women age 60+ who lived with someone, in 82.2% of the cases, the *widowed mothers* were the homeowners, suggesting that the living arrangements might have benefited the adult child as much or more than the mother (Cooney, 1988).

THE ESTABLISHMENT OF NEW ROLES IN WIDOWHOOD

At some point, most widowed persons focus less on the past and get on with the task of reorganizing their lives. This can be problematic because, at least in Western societies, there is a lack of norms for appropriate behaviors and roles for widowed persons. Lopata (1979) pointed out that the task of reconstructing a self-identity is most difficult for wives whose various social roles were highly dependent upon their husbands' roles.

In contrast, widowhood might provide the freedom "to discover one's own identity that marriage had obscured" (Adlersberg & Thorne, 1990, p. 8); this is especially true for women who have had abusive and/or alcoholic husbands. Thus, a role shift to that of a single person allows some widows to develop a more assertive, androgynous, and competent self (O'Bryant, in press).

FAMILY INTERACTION AND VARIOUS TYPES OF SUPPORT

Researchers interested in the impact of widowhood on family interaction have found mixed results. For example, Lopata (1973, 1979) studied Chicago women who had been widowed for varying lengths of time. These widows retrospectively reported slight increases in interactions with their children during the first year of widowhood; after that, interactions returned to the prewidowhood level and, in some instances, fell even lower. In considering kin interactions of all types, early studies tended to find long-term decreases for both widows and widowers. Morgan (1984), using longitudinal data, also found a decrease in total amount of interaction with kin for widowed persons; importantly, however, when the *size* of the family network at both measurement times was statistically controlled, there was actually an increase in interaction—at least for older widows. For widowers, there was no change.

Researchers who have compared married persons and widowed persons also report conflicting results regarding the frequency of family interactions. Some report a decrease in family interactions after widowhood; others have found no differences in family interaction levels after a person is widowed; still others have found that interaction with kin is more frequent for widowed persons than for married persons. For low-income widows, frequency of family contact has been found to vary, with Hispanics and blacks having more frequent contact than Asians and whites (Pelham & Clark, 1987). A number of important, potentially confounding factors remain to be examined in relation to this issue. For example, if family members were involved with care of the deceased before his or her death, then family involvement with the remaining spouse is likely to decrease after the death. In contrast, if a spousal caregiver dies suddenly, family involvement with the widowed spouse might quickly increase to replace the caregiver.

Family support for widowed persons is probably best understood when it is broken down into various types of support: (1) daily, instrumental needs; (2) needs related to health care; and (3) affective needs.

The Tasks of Daily Life and Family Assistance

For older couples in good health, the division of household labor is traditionally gender-specific. Husbands maintain the car and yard, make household repairs, and handle financial matters; wives cook, launder, and clean. There is some evidence, too, that women might serve as "health brokers" to their husbands, preparing healthful diets and monitoring prescriptions (Umberson, 1987). After the husband retires, he might help the wife with "her" jobs around the house, or she might help him with "his," but their skills are honed only with respect to the tasks stereotypically assigned to their own gender. Thus, widowhood for either spouse often results in the loss of a relatively specialized household laborer. Widows' highest unmet need is generally in the areas of home repairs and car care, whereas widowers' needs are in the areas of meal preparation, laundry, and housecleaning (Lund, Caserta, Dimond, & Shaffer, 1989). In many cases, the deceased's tasks are assumed by the surviving spouse—whether or not he or she feels well prepared to do them. O'Bryant and Morgan (1990) reported that it is not widowhood per se, but rather widowhood in tandem with poor health and age, that creates a need for family assistance with routine, daily tasks.

Overall, widowed persons receive more types of assistance from children than do married persons. For widowed women, help with household tasks is primarily, although infrequently, provided by their adult children. Other kin are conspicuously absent from the provision of household support to widows. Exceptions to this pattern are childless widows, who sometimes rely on siblings (Anderson, 1987; O'Bryant, 1987). Comparing three different low-income groups, Pelham and Clark (1987) found that Hispanic widows received the most support from children, black widows were midway, and white widows received the least support. Beyond these findings, having a larger family and the widow's perceptions that her children were willing to help are related, not surprisingly, to adult children's providing greater amounts of assistance (O'Bryant & Morgan, 1990).

For widowed men, the performance of daily household tasks appears to be considerably less positive. Widowers are more likely to complain about the difficulty of housework and cooking (Vinick, 1978) and, if they lack experience with household tasks, are more likely to feel useless and lonely (Hogstel, 1985). They also have less orderly lifestyles and have more difficulty carrying out their daily routines (Umberson, 1987); are more likely to learn how to perform household tasks by trial and error rather than receiving instruction (Lund et al., 1989); and are more likely to hire outside helpers (Lovingood, Blieszner, & Hill, 1988). Widowers might feel little reward for assuming the traditionally female household tasks because the wife's role is not as prestigious as that of the husband (Gove & Shin, 1989). In support of this notion, investigators have found that older husbands' involvement in female tasks has little effect on their self-esteem (Keith, Dobson, Goudy, & Powers, 1981).

How might families better assist their widowed relatives with the tasks of daily life? Hansson and Remondet (1988) argued that families must learn to make the necessary support available but at the same time must encourage their older members to develop the necessary skills to cope independently. This might, indeed, be a good plan for the widowed woman, provided her health and resources are adequate. For the widowed man, however, the issues that are involved appear to be more complex.

Family Provision of Other Practical Types of Assistance

Adult children commonly help with decision making, especially with decisions involving large commitments of financial resources—for example, estate settlements, car purchases, or home repairs (O'Bryant, 1987). Interestingly, Lopata's Chicago widows (1979) reported that help with decision making was only rarely needed. When it did occur, daughters more frequently helped their widowed mothers with decision making than did sons. Siblings and other relatives provided 15% of the assistance with decision making that widows received. Family intervention in decision making is not without its problems, however. Lopata (1973) reported that one very important cause of strain in the relations between widows and their families was that the latter provided too much of the wrong kind of advice. In this connection, Hansson and Remondet (1988) suggested that effective coping efforts might be thwarted by well-intentioned advice of various types from family members.

Widowed persons might also need financial support from family members. Analyses of national data sets repeatedly demonstrate that widowed persons—both males and females—have fewer economic resources than do married persons. Financial insecurity is among the most frequently identified problems for widows (Lopata, 1979; Martin Matthews, 1991), and, unfortunately, employment does not appear to be a viable option for most of them. Also, some older widows' inexperience with handling money might create additional problems for them and their families (O'Bryant & Morgan, 1989).

Data from the National Survey of Families and Households indicate that only 3% of parents over age 55 received monetary assistance from their adult children (Eggebeen, 1992). Widowhood apparently increases provision of such support. In Lopata's study (1979) of urban widows, 8% to 9% received financial assistance from kin; when they did, it was almost always an adult child who provided it. Slightly more help (11%) has been reported by rural black widowed persons (Scott & Kivett, 1980). Such modest provision of financial assistance to widowed family members, however, might, in part, reflect low income status, with many families unable, rather than unwilling, to help.

Interestingly, some monetary support goes from the young-old offspring to old-old parents. Seccombe (1988) found that 13% of males age 65 and over contributed financially to the support of an aging parent. Fewer daughters than sons provide direct economic assistance to their parents; however, some reduce their work hours or quit their jobs entirely in order to provide care (Brody, Kleban, Johnsen, Hoffman, & Schoonover, 1987).

Family Provision of Health Care to Widowed Family Members

Recently widowed persons are at more than twice the risk of being placed in a nursing home than are other older persons (Wolinsky & Johnson, 1992). Some widowed persons have no close family; however, many more have families who are unable or unwilling to provide health care assistance (see Dwyer, this volume).

The norm of filial responsibility or filial obligation mandates that adult children take care of their parents; almost half of the states in the United States have laws to this effect. The issues related to their enforcement, however, are exceedingly complex, and, thus, these laws are subject to capricious enforcement (Borgatta, 1987). Many parents and children see such obligations as having definite limits (Finch & Mason, 1990).

It is possible, however, that after being widowed, parents' filial expectations of the types and amounts of children's support change. Seelbach (1978) reported that older people who were widowed or divorced were more apt to express greater expectations of family assistance than were married respondents. With respect to *actual* assistance, however, research results have been equivocal. Pelham and Clark (1987) reported that widowed persons in their California sample received more support from their adult children than married persons, whereas Anderson (1987) did not find any differences in the extent to which widows and married women depended on children for assistance in times of need.

There are certain situations in which family members other than children provide care. For example, Anderson (1987) reported that, with respect to occasional sick care, widowed siblings, not children, replaced the widow's deceased husband as a support resource. Cicirelli, Coward, and Dwyer (1992) found that sibling assistance is given when the widowed person has a functional impairment and few living children. Such care is problematic, however, because the health of the sibling might put limits on his or her ability to provide care.

Long-term caregiving to a widowed person usually falls to an adult child, if there is one, and to a nursing home otherwise. The most common dyad is that of an adult daughter caring for a widowed mother. A number of researchers have found considerable strain for daughters in this role. One study provides some interesting insights. Brody and colleagues (1987) reported that a daughter's employment provides some beneficial respite from the widowed mother's care, although the nonworking daughters with traditional attitudes also fared well. The most strain was reported by daughters who had already quit or were considering quitting their jobs.

Sons who provide care to their elderly widowed parents typically do so only by default; either they are only children, have brothers only, or are the only proximal child. Horowitz (1985) compared sons' and daughters' role performance as the primary caregiver to an elderly parent (80% of whom were widowed). She reported that sons take on the role "only in the absence of an available female sibling, and, when they do . . . they tend to provide less extensive support to their older parent as compared to adult daughters and to have less stressful caregiving experiences" (p. 616). Schoonover, Brody, Hoffman, and Kleban (1988) found that female siblings of primary caregivers of their widowed mothers expressed "more guilt, strain, and other negative emotional effects deriving from their mothers' situation" than did male siblings (p. 400).

Family Support for Affective Needs

Results of classic studies (e.g., Lopata, 1973) and recent studies (e.g., Lund et al., 1993) verify that loneliness is a major problem in widowhood. Family members, however, appear to have little effect on relief from loneliness or on the general psychological well-being of their widowed members. Recent qualitative research suggests that there are often as many negative aspects in family interactions as positive ones (Morgan, 1989). The only kin relationship that reliably provides positive emotional support might be that of widows and their female siblings (Anderson, 1987; O'Bryant, 1988b).

With respect to gender differences, it has been argued by many that widowers are at more of a disadvantage than widows when it comes to affective support from families. Because wives are generally the "kinkeepers," after being widowed, men often do not have the skills to maintain family contacts. In an analysis of longitudinal data, Wan and Odell (1983) found that recently remarried older widowers had higher levels of interaction than married men or widowed men, apparently because their new wives had brought kinkeeping skills and additional family members and friends to the relationship.

DATING AND REMARRIAGE AFTER WIDOWHOOD

Single older women vastly outnumber single older men. Consequently, it is not surprising that older men report having more dating partners as well as dating more often than do older women. Older men and older women also date for different reasons: men are more likely to mention emotional reasons, such as the need for their partner to act as a friend and confidant, whereas women are more likely to mention the prestige and status they attain among their friends as a result of being courted (Bulcroft & O'Connor, 1986). Arguing from the prospective of gender-role theory, Gove and Shin (1989) have proposed that widowers remarry because of their need to resume the more prestigious role of husband. Unfortunately, little research has addressed the patterns and experience of remarriage within various racial or ethnic groups.

Investigators have noted a variety of reasons for older widowed persons' reluctance to contemplate remarriage (McKain, 1972; Moss & Moss, 1980; Vinick, 1978). For example, they might fear social disapproval of their lack of reverence for the deceased spouse or the admission of sexual needs. Also, there might be financial considerations, family oppositions, or simply a fear of change. Researchers list numerous additional reasons why older widowed women do not wish to remarry, including the idealization of the former spouse or, conversely, unhappiness in their prior marriage; not wanting to relinquish their newfound independence; feeling too old to remarry; fear of financial loss or fortune hunters; and not wanting to care for another ill husband (e.g., Lopata, 1980).

There are also some perceived benefits of remarriage, such as companionship, financial security, sexual intimacy, or a wish to provide care to someone (Moss & Moss, 1980). Being married appears to be related to men's well-being, because both married and remarried men have been shown to have higher life satisfaction than widowers (Mouser, Powers, Keith, & Goudy, 1985).

Older widowed persons' satisfaction with remarriage has been examined in three studies. McKain (1972) interviewed 100 couples regarding the success of their new marriages. Five contributing factors were (1) having known each other before they were widowed (e.g., friends or neighbors), (2) receiving approval of the marriage from friends and family, (3) successfully adjusting to other types of role change, such as retirement, (4) moving to a different residence than that of the former marriage, and (5) having sufficient income. Vinick (1978) reported that differences existed in the perceived marital satisfaction of some of the 24 elderly remarried couples she interviewed. For men, happiness appeared to be associated with internal states, such as mental and physical health. For women, marital happiness was related to external states, such as living conditions. One more recent study (Burks, Lund, Gregg, & Bluhm, 1988) followed 109 widows and 40 widowers for four to five years. The sample was white and comprised largely of Mormons. Only 3% of the widows remarried, whereas 30% of the widowers remarried. When compared with a matched sample of those who had not remarried, remarried respondents displayed significantly less stress, greater self-esteem, higher life satisfaction, and higher levels of grief resolution.

With remarriage, a new family is created. The position of these older couples within their mutual extended families is undoubtedly multifaceted and complex. The reactions of their adult children and grandchildren are only a matter of speculation at this time, but are, undoubtedly, an interesting topic for future research.

CONCLUSIONS

Applied Concerns

During the last two decades researchers have made a concerted effort to describe the circumstances—demographic, economic, and social—of older widowed persons. With respect to methodology, research on widowhood has suffered from many of the same limitations encountered in other areas of gerontological research. For example, studies have often relied on small nonprobability samples, limiting the generalizability of findings. Also, women, relatively healthy persons, and volunteers have been overrepresented in these studies. In addition, researchers' questions have often required respondents to provide retrospective answers, which are of questionable reliability. Some researchers have used extant data from nationally based studies of older respondents, including a representative number of widowed persons. Unfortunately, the measures utilized in such studies are generally not constructed with widowed persons' particular circumstances in mind, and widowed respondents are often grouped for analysis with other unmarried persons, obscuring the special circumstances of widowhood.

Many studies have been conducted with widowed women; far less is known about widowed men. On one hand, it can be argued that the problems of widowhood are largely a woman's issue because of their greater likelihood of being widowed and their greater numbers in the older population. On the other hand, in terms of health and familial/social relationships, the literature indicates that widowers might have special problems (Gove & Shin, 1989; Martin Matthews, 1991: Stroebe & Stroebe, 1987). Thus, continued study—but not inappropriate comparisons—of both genders is warranted.

Widowed persons' families might be one of the most salient and stable aspects of their lives, but families are complex. One major shortcoming of research to date is that almost all of our knowledge is based on the responses of widowed individuals about their families, rather than responses of the families about their widowed members. Only a small amount of seminal research with widowed mother-adult child pairs had been reported to date (e.g., Baugher & Berrill, 1991). Families probably vary a great deal with respect to what they are able—or willing—to do for their widowed member and also with respect to their expectations of what the widowed family member is able to do for himself or herself. Theory in the general area of social support (e.g., Heller & Lakey, 1985) could be very applicable and useful to researchers particularly interested in widowhood.

Need for Further Theoretical Development

We noted at the outset that adjustment to the life circumstances of widowhood can present a tremendous adaptive challenge for both the widow(er) and the family system. The research reviewed in this chapter, primarily descriptive and policy-oriented, suggests many potential influences on such variables. Little attention, however, has been paid to theoretical development specific to the area of widowhood or to integrating data from widowhood research into broader theoretical perspectives. An important exception has been the work of Helena Lopata (1973, 1979, 1988), who examined the influence of cultural and historic development (e.g., urbanization, modernization, industrialization) on natural support systems for widows.

There is an obvious shortage of theory for conceptualizing and understanding widowhood in the context of the family. Many researchers have viewed widowhood as a life course event for the individual. Future research should be directed toward investigating widowhood as a new family stage that affects many family members (cf. Aldous, 1990). Common sense suggests that families reorganize in some manner following the death of an older member, although the parameters of that reorganization are unknown. For example, Vess, Moreland, and Schwebel (1985–86) theorized that "person-oriented families characterized by achieved roles, open communication, and flexible power structures, will more effectively reallocate family roles following the death of spouse/parent," than will "position-oriented families characterized by ascribed roles, closed communication and relatively inflexible power structures" (p. 115). To date, however, this theory has not been tested with respect to the death of an older parent (personal communication, J. Vess, May 5, 1993).

Similarly, little theory has been developed regarding the impact of bereavement on the family system, its structure, functions, stability, or capacity to rise to the aid of its most immediately bereaved member (e.g., Rosenblatt, 1988; Walsh & McGoldrick, 1991). In this connection, Hansson and colleagues (1992) recently developed a reliable instrument for assessing the impact of bereavement on the family and for identifying those families likely to be at greater risk for poor bereavement outcome. The Family Bereavement Inventory assesses four dimensions: family disintegration/disruption, family self-esteem, depressive symptoms, and experienced stress. The instrument appears to discriminate reliably between criterion groups based on who in the family died (e.g., child, spouse, parent), and scores indicating greater bereavement are associated with a greater incidence of marital conflict and separation. Early results also suggest that greater bereavement impact is experienced by families reporting preexisting family stress and by families who, prior to the death, were less cohesive or less likely to share core values, interests, and activities.

Similarly, our views regarding the implications of widowhood might be informed by changing views of the social meanings of aging more generally. For example, Neugarten & Neugarten (1986) have shown how traditional meanings of age have blurred over recent decades. With significant extensions in the life span, older adults remain healthy, active, and competent until much later in life. Moreover, individual responses to aging appear to reflect increasing heterogeneity, as many older adults do not identify as being old, do not feel compelled to act in accordance with the demands of the "social clock," and enjoy continuing prospects for social and occupational involvement. It follows, then, that the symbolic and practical implications of an age-related event like widowhood might also become less predictable.

It might also be useful at this point to try to view widowhood within the larger developmental context of later life. The experience of widowhood varies across individuals, across families, and across cultures and is only one of many factors in determining function, competence, and adaptive potential in one's later years. Widowed women, for example, live some 15 years post-loss, leaving considerable time for further development and differentiation. Most are unlikely simply to begin some predictable trajectory of decline.

The life span developmental orientation (Baltes, 1987) might provide a useful model for understanding adaptation among widowed persons. This orientation assumes that development is a lifelong, anormative process, and the specific developmental changes are highly variable with respect to timing, magnitude, and directionality of the change. It also takes a pluralistic view of the potential determinants of individual development in later life. Three general domains of potential influence are tentatively proposed. The first of these is "normative age-graded" influences, those biological and environmental factors generally associated with age, including physical and cognitive maturation, and family and occupational role involvements usually associated with the life cycle. The second type of influences is "normative history-graded." These are the influences associated with a given cohort (generation) of adults. They include the social and economic events that can affect the unfolding of the lives of an entire generation (e.g., the Great Depression or a world war). Finally, and perhaps most important in later life, are the "nonnormative influences." These include any critical life events unique to an individual (e.g., loss of employment, trouble with the law) or that might have been unique in their timing in a person's life (e.g., an early bereavement or an early onset of physical disability). It is assumed that individuals will accumulate a unique history of internal, external, and historical influences, resulting in a rich diversity of developmental possibilities.

It might also be time to address systematically the issue of individual differences in adaptation to widowhood. Researchers have widely assessed the roles of social and economic coping resources. However, little theoretical work has focused on the dispositional factors or coping styles likely to foster premature dependency or decline among older widowed adults. Important theoretical leads have begun to emerge regarding the coping strategies used by older adults in dealing with stressful life events generally (e.g., Aldwin, 1990), and spousal loss has traditionally been an important focus of such analyses. However, widowhood researchers have seldom incorporated these ideas into their thinking.

Another important individual difference is suggested by the interpersonal nature of many of the stressors and situations encountered in widowhood. It is clear from the research reviewed in this paper that family and social support play an important role in the well-being of older widowed persons. It was also evident that the relationships underlying such support can sometimes be interpersonally problematic, reflecting caregiver strain, preexisting difficulties in kin relationship, insufficient financial resources, inadequate housing, and so on. However, the relational competencies an older person brings to the situation can make a difference (Hansson & Carpenter, 1990). Particularly critical competencies are the ability to initiate potentially supportive relationships or to access existing, but heavily burdened, support networks and the ability to enhance, nurture, and maintain such relationships over the long term. For many old persons, the experience of widowhood results in an increased dependency on social or caregiving relationships. Research and theory on widowhood would be enhanced by a more systematic understanding of those individual characteristics likely to facilitate the acquisition, development, and maintenance of such relationships.

Finally, theoretical development regarding the circumstances of widowhood would be considerably enhanced by a greater representation of widowed men and ethnic and cultural minority groups. The research reviewed in this chapter suggests a number of ways in which gender and cultural variables might influence individual adaptation. For example, minority populations tend to experience the death of a spouse at an earlier age. Moreover, such fundamental assumptions as to what constitutes a widowed person's natural family support network can differ widely across cultures. Blacks, for example, are more likely to include in their networks members of their extended family and nonbiological "kin" to whom they have developed deep emotional attachments (Johnson & Barer, 1990). Clearly, the future study of widowhood in the context of the family will require more original thought on the part of investigators.

REFERENCES

Adams, B. (1968). The middle-class adult and his widowed or still-married mother. *Social Problems, 16,* 50–59.

Adlersberg, M., & Thorne, S. (1990). Emerging from the chrysalis: Older widows in transition. *Journal of Gerontological Nursing, 16,* 4–8.

Aldous, J. (1990). Family development and the life course: Two perspectives on family change. *Journal of Marriage and the Family, 52,* 571–583.

Aldwin, C. M. (1990). The elders life stress inventory: Egocentric and nonegocentric stress. In M.A.P. Stephens, J. H. Crowther, S. E. Hobfoll, & D. G. Tennenbaum (Eds.), *Stress and coping in later-life families* (pp. 49–69). New York: Hemisphere.

Alwin, D. F., Converse, P. E., & Martin, S. S. (1985). Living arrangements and social integration. *Journal of Marriage and the Family, 47,* 319–334.

Anderson, T. B. (1987). Widows in urban Nebraska: Their informal support systems. In H. Z. Lopata (Ed.), *Widows: North America* (Vol. 2, pp. 109–135). Durham, NC: Duke University Press.

Baltes, P. B. (1987). Theoretical propositions of life-span developmental psychology: On the dynamics between growth and decline. *Developmental Psychology, 23,* 611–626.

Baugher, R. J., & Berrill, N. G. (1991). Perceptions of the widow's bereavement process by her adult child. *Journal of Women & Aging, 3* (3), 21–38.

Borgatta, E. F. (1987). Filial responsibility. In G. L. Maddox (Ed.), *Encyclopedia of aging.* New York: Spanier.

Brody, E. M., Kleban, M. H., Johnsen, P. T., Hoffman, C., & Schoonover, C. B. (1987). Work status and parent care: A comparison of four groups of women. *Gerontologist, 27,* 201–208.

Bulcroft, K., & O'Connor, M. (1986). The importance of dating relationships on quality of life for older persons. *Family Relations, 35,* 397–401.

Burks, V. K., Lund, D. A., Gregg, C. H., & Bluhm, H. P. (1988). Bereavement and remarriage for older adults. *Death Studies, 12,* 51–60.

Chevan, A. (1987). Home ownership in the older population. *Research on Aging, 9,* 226–255.

Choi, N. G. (1991). Racial differences in the determination of living arrangements of widowed and divorced elderly women. *Gerontologist, 31,* 496–504.

Cicirelli, V. G., Coward, R. T., & Dwyer, J. W. (1992). Siblings as caregivers for impaired elders. *Research on Aging, 14,* 331–350.

Cohen, M. A., Tell, E. J., & Wallack, S. S. (1986). Client-related risk factors of nursing home entry among elderly adults. *Journal of Gerontology, 41,* 785–792.

Cooney, T. M. (1988, November). *Coresidence with adult children: A comparison of divorced and widowed women.* Paper presented at the annual meeting of the Gerontological Society of America, San Francisco.

Crimmins, E. M., & Ingegneri, D. G. (1990). Interaction and living arrangements of older parents and their children. *Research on Aging, 12,* 3–35.

Eggebeen, D. J. (1992). From generation unto generation: Parent-child support in aging American families. *Generations, 17,* 45–50.

Fengler, A. P., Danigelis, N., & Little, V. C. (1983). Late life satisfaction and household structure: Living with others and living alone. *Ageing and Society, 3,* 357–377.

Finch, J., & Mason, J. (1990). Filial obligations and kin support for elderly people. *Ageing and Society, 10,* 151–175.

Gallagher-Thompson, D., Futterman, A., Farberow, N., Thompson, L. W., & Peterson, J. (1993). The impact of spousal bereavement on older widows and widowers. In M. S. Stroebe, W. Stroebe, & R. O. Hansson (Eds.), *Handbook of bereavement* (pp. 227–239). New York: Cambridge University Press.

Gove, W. R., & Shin, H. C. (1989). The psychological well-being of divorced and widowed men and women. *Journal of Family Issues, 10,* 122–144.

Hansson, R. O., & Carpenter, B. N. (1990). Relational competence and adjustment in older adults: Implications for the demands of aging. In M.A.P. Stephens, J. H. Crowther, S. E. Hobfoll, & D. L. Tennenbaum (Eds.), *Stress and coping in later-life families* (pp. 49–69). New York: Hemisphere.

Hansson, R. O., Fairchild, S., Vanzetti, N., & Harris, G. (1992, July). *The nature of family bereavement.* Paper presented at the Sixth International Conference on Personal Relationships, Orono, ME.

Hansson, R. O., & Remondet, J. H. (1988). Old age and widowhood: Issues of personal control and independence. *Journal of Social Issues, 44,* 159–174.

Heller, K., & Lakey, B. (1985). Perceived support and social interaction among friends and confidants. In. I. G. Sarason & B. R. Sarason (Eds.), *Social support: Theory, research, and applications.* The Hague, Netherlands: Martinus Nijhoff.

Hogstel, M. O. (1985). Older widowers: A small group with special needs. *Geriatric Nursing, 1,* 24–26.

Horowitz, A. (1985). Sons and daughters as caregivers to older parents: Differences in role performance and consequences. *Gerontologist, 25,* 612–617.

Johnson, C. L., & Barer, B. M. (1990). Families and networks among older inner-city blacks. *Gerontologist, 30,* 726–733.

Keith, P. M., Dobson, C. D., Goudy, W. J., & Powers, E. A. (1981). Older men: Occupation, employment status, household involvement, and well-being. *Journal of Family Issues, 2,* 336–349.

Kemp, B. (1985). Rehabilitation and the older adult. In J. E. Birren & K. W. Schaie (Eds.), *Handbook of the psychology of aging* (2nd ed., pp. 647–663). New York: Van Nostrand Reinhold.

Lee, G. R., & Ihinger-Tallman, M. (1980). Sibling interaction and morale: The effects of family relations on older persons. *Research on Aging, 2,* 367–391.

Lopata, H. Z. (1973). *Widowhood in an American city.* Cambridge, MA: Schenkman.

Lopata, H. Z. (1979). *Women as widows: Support systems.* New York: Elsevier.

Lopata, H. Z. (1980). The widowed family member. In N. Datan & N. Lohman (Eds.), *Transitions of aging* (pp. 93–118). New York: Academic Press.

Lopata, H. Z. (1988). Support systems of American urban widowhood. *Journal of Social Issues, 44,* 113–128.

Lovingood, R. P., Blieszner, R., & Hill, P. P. (1988). *Coping with widowhood and bereavement: Resource list for human services professionals.* Blacksburg: Virginia Polytechnic Institute and State University, Center for Gerontology.

Lund, D. A. (Ed.). (1989). *Older bereaved spouses: Research with practical applications.* New York: Taylor & Francis/Hemisphere.

Lund, D. A., Caserta, M. S., & Dimond, M. F. (1993). The course of spousal bereavement in later life. In M. S. Stroebe, W. Stroebe, & R. O. Hansson

(Eds.), *Handbook of bereavement* (pp. 240–254). New York: Cambridge University Press.

Lund, D. A., Caserta, M. S., Dimond, M. F., & Shaffer, S. K. (1989). Competencies, tasks of daily living, and adjustments to spousal bereavement in later life. In D. A. Lund (Ed.), *Older bereaved spouses* (pp. 135–152). New York: Hemisphere.

Martin Matthews, A. (1991). *Widowhood in later life*. Toronto: Butterworths.

McCrae, R. R., & Costa, P. T. (1988). Psychological resilience among widowed men and women: A 10-year follow-up of a national sample. *Journal of Social Issues, 44,* 129–142.

McKain, W. C. (1972). A new look at older marriages. *Family Coordinator, 21,* 61–69.

Morgan, D. L. (1989). Adjusting to widowhood: Do social networks really make it easier? *Gerontologist, 29,* 101–107.

Morgan, L. A. (1984). Changes in family interaction following widowhood. *Journal of Marriage and the Family, 46,* 323–333.

Moss, M. S., & Moss, S. Z. (1980). Image of the deceased spouse in remarriage of elderly widow(er)s. *Journal of Gerontological Social Work, 3,* 59–70.

Mouser, N. F., Powers, E. A., Keith, P. M., & Goudy, W. J. (1985). Marital and life satisfaction: A study of older men. In W. A. Peterson & J. Quadagno (Eds.), *Social bonds in later life* (pp. 71–90). Beverly Hills, CA: Sage.

Neugarten, B. L., & Neugarten, D. A. (1986). Age in the aging society. *Daedalus, 115,* 31–49.

O'Bryant, S. L. (1985). Neighbors' support of older widows who live alone in their own homes. *Gerontologist, 25,* 305–310.

O'Bryant, S. L. (1987). Attachment to home and support systems of older widows in Columbus, Ohio. In H. Z. Lopata (Ed.), *Widows: North America* (Vol. 2, pp. 48–70). Durham, NC: Duke University Press.

O'Bryant, S. L. (1988a). Sex-differentiated assistance in older widows' support networks. *Sex Roles, 19,* 91–106.

O'Bryant, S. L. (1988b). Sibling support and older widows' well-being. *Journal of Marriage and the Family, 50,* 173–183.

O'Bryant, S. L. (in press). Widowhood in later life: An opportunity to become androgynous. In M. R. Stevens et al. (Eds.), *Gender-roles through the life-span*. Madison: University of Wisconsin Press.

O'Bryant, S. L., & Morgan, L. A. (1989). Financial experience and well-being among mature widowed women. *Gerontologist, 29,* 245–251.

O'Bryant, S. L., & Morgan, L. A. (1990). Recent widows' kin support and orientations to self-sufficiency. *Gerontologist, 29,* 391–398.

O'Bryant, S. L., & Murray, C. I. (1986). Attachment to home and other factors related to widows' relocation decisions. *Journal of Housing for the Elderly, 4,* 53–72.

Pelham, A. O., & Clark, W. F. (1987). Widowhood among low-income racial and ethnic groups in California. In H. Z. Lopata (Ed.), *Widows: North America* (Vol. 2, pp. 191–222). Durham, NC: Duke University Press.

Rosenblatt, P. C. (1988). Grief: The social context of private feelings. *Journal of Social Issues, 44,* 67–78.

Schoonover, C. B., Brody, E. M., Hoffman, C., & Kleban, M. H. (1988). Parent care and geographically distant children. *Research on Aging, 10*, 472–492.

Scott, J. P., & Kivett, V. R. (1980). The widowed, black, older adult in the rural south: Implications for policy. *Family Relations, 29*, 83–90.

Seccombe, K. (1988). Financial assistance from elderly retirement age sons to their aging parents. *Research on Aging, 10*, 102–118.

Seelbach, W. C. (1978). Correlates of aged parents' filial responsibility expectations and realizations. *Family Coordinator, 27*, 341–350.

Stroebe, W., & Stroebe, M. S. (1987). *Bereavement and health: The psychological and physical consequences of partner loss*. London: Cambridge University Press.

Stroebe, W., & Stroebe, M. S. (1993). Determinants of adjustment to bereavement in younger widows and widowers. In M. S. Stroebe, W. Stroebe, & R. O. Hansson (Eds.), *Handbook of bereavement* (pp. 208–226). New York: Cambridge University Press.

Stroebe, M. S., Stroebe, W., & Hansson, R. O. (1993). *Handbook of bereavement: Theory, research and intervention*. New York: Cambridge University Press.

Thompson, L. W., Gallagher-Thompson, D., Futterman, A., Gilewski, M. J., & Peterson, J. (1991). The effects of late-life spousal bereavement over a 30-month interval. *Psychology and Aging, 6*, 434–441.

Umberson, D. (1987). Family status and health behaviors: Social control as a dimension of social integration. *Journal of Health and Social Behavior, 28*, 306–319.

U.S. Bureau of the Census. (1984). *Demographic and socioeconomic aspects of aging in the United States*. (Current population reports, Series P-23, No. 138). Washington, DC: U.S. Government Printing Office.

Vess, J., Moreland, J., & Schwebel, A. I. (1985–86). Understanding family role reallocation following a death: A theoretical framework. *Omega, 16*, 115–128.

Vinick, B. H. (1978). Remarriage in old age. *Family Coordinator, 27*, 359–363.

Walsh, F., & McGoldrick, M. (1991). *Living beyond loss: Death in the family*. New York: Norton.

Wan, T.T.H., & Odell, B. G. (1983). Major role losses and social participation of older males. *Research on Aging, 5*, 173–196.

Ward, R., Logan, J., & Spitz, G. (1992). The influence of parent and child needs on co-residence in middle and later life. *Journal of Marriage and the Family, 54*, 209–221.

Wolinsky, F. D., & Johnson, R. J. (1992). Widowhood, health status, and the use of health services by older adults: A cross-sectional and prospective approach. *Journal of Gerontology: Social Sciences, 47*, S8–S16.

22

Families and Formal Networks

Shirley S. Travis

INTRODUCTION

Shifts in population demographics combined with changes in the configuration of American families have drastically altered the ways in which families think about, and arrange for care of, dependent members (see Kinsella, this volume). Consequently, during the last decade, a proliferation of information about the nature and scope of formal services for older adults has occurred (e.g., Chappell, 1990; Krout, 1985). Until very recently, however, few researchers attempted to understand the linkages and relationships between formal networks and the families who manage the vast majority of care for frail or impaired older adults.

Given the scarcity of research specifically addressing families and formal networks, the process of reviewing the literature for this chapter necessitated casting a wide net into the pool of aging and long-term care publications. Based on the relevant literature, the chapter is divided into four parts. Part one defines and explains social care and includes descriptions of formal and informal networks of care and functional versus affective forms of assistance. This discussion is followed by two parts that examine theoretical approaches for explaining families' initiation or termination of care arrangements, and conceptual models for studying the coexistence of formal and informal networks. The chapter concludes with recommendations for further study and theory development.

SOCIAL CARE

First described by Cantor (1979, 1989, 1991), *social care* has come to mean both formal and informal caregiving networks existing side by side and providing support for activities required as part of daily living. Unlike health-related care, the language of social care describes functional (task-oriented) and affective (emotional support) assistance in daily living, both of which constitute the predominant long-term care needs of dependent elders.

Functional and Affective Assistance

For the most part, the need for *functional assistance* is determined by the care recipient's ability to perform various tasks of daily existence, which are categorized as either instrumental or basic activities of daily living. *Instrumental activities of daily living* (IADLs) are simply the functions a person might perform in the process of everyday life, including cooking, cleaning, buying groceries, home repair, yard work, and paying bills. Basic *activities of daily living* (ADLs), on the other hand, are the tasks required for personal care and basic survival. These include eating, bathing, dressing, going to the bathroom, maintaining personal hygiene, and getting around (mobility) (see Kane & Kane, 1989, for more detail).

Affective assistance consists of behaviors that convey messages of caring and concern to the care recipient. Typically called emotional support, affective assistance might be directed toward enhancing feelings of self-esteem, contentment, life satisfaction, hope of recovery, dignity, and general well-being (e.g., Brody & Schoonover, 1986; Horowitz, 1985).

As discussed in the next sections, functional assistance is often available from both formal and informal networks. Affective assistance and monitoring the care of formal providers (quality of care, supervision of formal caregivers), however, are traditionally ascribed to the informal network (Bowers, 1987, 1988; Hasselkus, 1988; Kaye, 1985, 1989; Patrick, 1987).

Informal Networks

Informal networks, also called primary groups, include family, friends, and neighbors (see Johnson, this volume). Typically, care provided by informal networks is delivered free of charge, has both emotional and functional components, is ethnically and culturally relevant, and involves tasks that require a low level of specialized knowledge or training, such as assisting with personal care needs (Hinrichsen & Ramirez, 1992; Lipman & Longino, 1982; Litwak & Messeri, 1989; Mayers & Souflee, 1991; Sakaoye, 1989).

A key feature of informal caregiving is a long-term, sometimes lifelong, commitment to the care recipient (Litwak & Messeri, 1989). Family caregiving, in particular, is characteristically motivated by one or more of the following factors: love and affection, a need to reciprocate for past caring (stemming from gratitude or obligation), commitment to the care recipient, a societal norm for filial responsibility, or a desire to avoid feelings of guilt

(Blieszner & Shifflett, 1989; Doty, 1986; Lewis & Meredith, 1988). As Jarrett (1985) pointed out, however, most personal motivations for caregiving are not static. For example, caregiving that is initially driven by affection may evolve into duty and responsibility for the impaired family member. Although very little is currently known about phases of caregiving, Jarrett (1985) warned that, in order to truly understand the dynamics of caregiving, the myth that affection alone drives involvement must be dispelled.

Though actual service use depends on both caregivers' and care recipients' characteristics, in general, older adults seem to prefer the informal assistance of individuals who are closest to, and most involved in, their daily lives. Research on the assistance-seeking behavior of older adults has consistently documented a hierarchical preference for help from kin, usually spouses and children, followed by friends and neighbors, and finally, formal care (Cantor, 1979; Palley & Oktay, 1983).

This kinship preference is problematic because the gendered nature of family care (see Dwyer & Coward, 1992) places harsh expectations on wives or daughters to respond when older adults' informal networks are called on to provide assistance (Brody, 1981, 1985; Finley, 1989; Horowitz, 1985; Stoller, 1990). In the case of caregiving daughters with families of their own, the literature is quite clear about the disruptive effects of parent care on the entire family (e.g., Kleban, Brody, Schoonover & Hoffman, 1989). Many of these women report working the equivalent of two full-time jobs in order to satisfy the household and personal care needs of older family members, along with fulfilling their own employment and family obligations (Brody & Schoonover, 1986; Scharlach, 1987; Stone, Cafferata, & Sangl, 1987). Moreover, women are more apt than men to stay engaged in caregiving for extended periods of time throughout the length of an elder's dependency (Montgomery & Kamo, 1989; Stone et al., 1987).

Formal Networks

Formal service and nonservice networks generally consist of caregivers who have neither filial nor significant prior emotional or social connections with a care recipient. In sharp contrast to informal networks, formal helpers operate within the context of a bureaucratic structure and deliver services in a more or less predictable and organized fashion (Lipman & Longino, 1982; Litwak & Messeri, 1989). Formal care is characterized as being task-oriented and goal-directed, provided for a specified period of time, focused and/or highly specialized, and usually provided for a fee.

Formal networks for dependent older adults typically include individuals who provide an array of home- and community-based care services (e.g., personal care, adult day care, respite care, companion and homemaker services), as well as individuals working with basic entitlement programs (e.g., Medicare and Social Security). In addition, formal networks can also be nonservice in nature. That is, their involvement in caregiving arrangements might occur without prescribed services or predetermined objectives.

Nonservice formal networks include religious organizations; racial/cultural, social, neighborhood, and block groups; and other individuals who originate from formal structures, even though they might personally provide only informal assistance (e.g., mail carriers, shopkeepers, and building superintendents). As purveyors of traditional types of formal services experience service delivery restrictions and resource reductions, many researchers and public policy analysts believe that the nonservice network will play an increasingly important role in the well-being of certain older adult populations (see Harrington Meyer & Bellas, this volume).

THE INITIATION AND TERMINATION OF INFORMAL AND FORMAL CARE ARRANGEMENTS

Neither empirical nor anecdotal information supports the myth that the vast majority of families abandon or ignore the needs of their dependent older members (Coward, 1987; Johnson & Catalano, 1986; McAuley & Arling, 1984). Shifts from a total reliance on informal networks to the utilization of formal care and services do occur, however, for most families providing extended care. For some, these care arrangements involve episodic reliance on in-home or community-based respite services to give the family temporary relief from caregiving responsibilities (e.g., Berry, Zarit, & Rabatin, 1991; Lawton, Brody, & Saperstein, 1989; Lawton, Brody, Saperstein, & Grimes, 1989). For others, formal care might mean a more permanent arrangement in a nursing home or other sheltered care environment, accompanied by a significant reduction in primary caregiving responsibility (e.g., McFall & Miller, 1992).

One thing is very clear: families are not homogeneous with respect to the meaning they place on family caregiving, the formal caregiving arrangements they seek (Brubaker & Brubaker, 1989), or the degree of involvement they want and expect from formal providers (Collins, Stommel, King, & Given, 1991). The challenge for researchers is to overcome methodological and conceptual shortcomings to explain families' choices of care arrangements.

The following discussion of applicable theoretical approaches to explain families' initiations and terminations of care arrangements is divided into two parts. This was necessary because the relevant research tended to emphasize either the personal meaning of caregiving or constructs to describe service utilization patterns.

Note that the caregiver stress, strain, burden, and burnout literature also makes numerous important contributions to the topic. Because several recent sources provide in-depth reviews and analyses of these issues (e.g.,

Barber, 1989; Barer & Johnson, 1990; Hanks & Settles, 1990; Matthews, 1988), and other chapters in this handbook deal tangentially with family caregiving issues (see Dwyer, Harrington Meyer & Bellas, and Johnson, this volume), this literature is not included here.

Theoretical Approaches Emphasizing the Social Psychology of Caregiving

One of the more invisible aspects of informal caregiving arrangements is that, even when the total informal network is quite large, only one person at a time usually functions as the primary source of support, care, and decision making (Cantor, 1989; Johnson & Catalano, 1986; Tennstedt, McKinlay, & Sullivan, 1989). As a result, extraordinary amounts of time and energy are steadily siphoned from the primary caregiver, ultimately having a negative impact on his or her coping ability, sense of well-being, and capacity to provide effective assistance over the long term.

Naturally, many researchers are interested in the meaning caregivers and care recipients assign to these experiences and the ways in which the social psychology of caregiving affects decisions about caregiving arrangements. Through the early 1990s, attachment theory, social exchange theory, and symbolic interactionism were widely used theoretical approaches in the relevant literature.

Attachment theory views caregiving as a developmental phenomenon that not only is desirable but also necessary for optimum adult development and aging (Cicirelli, 1991). This is an important perspective, particularly for long-term caregiving, because it recognizes that even unpleasant and distasteful impairments and disabilities do not sever the lifelong relationship that exists in families. When families decide to seek assistance from formal networks, it is not for the purpose of terminating attachments with dependent family members.

Social exchange theory weighs the rewards or benefits of social interaction against relative costs (Nye, 1979; Thibaut & Kelley, 1959). This model of interdependent relationships has been particularly useful in the family caregiving literature. It provides a venue for understanding why individuals chose to sustain long-term burdensome or stressful caregiving situations with minimal formal assistance, or why some families elect to involve formal networks early in the caregiving experience. In both cases, this approach highlights the important role that relationship benefits play in moderating the perceived costs and benefits of caregiving (e.g., Mutran & Reitzes, 1984; Walker, Martin, & Jones, 1992).

Finally, *symbolic interactionism* is a useful framework for constructing the personal meaning of family care (Burr, Leigh, Day, & Constantine, 1979). One benefit of this approach is that it stresses the need to explore how an individual's interpretations, perceptions, motivations, and expectations are influenced by involvement with others (Dressel & Clark, 1990). Studies of intergenerational caregiving that examine cohort effects on the caregiver-care receiver relationship (e.g., Brody, 1981) are particularly well suited to a symbolic interactionism framework, as are studies that address ways in which the competing demands (roles) on family caregivers affect caregiving decisions (e.g., Brody, Kleban, Johnson, Hoffman, & Schoonover, 1987).

Theoretical Approaches Emphasizing Service Utilization Patterns

Brubaker and Brubaker (1989) proposed an innovative model for conceptualizing ways in which the unique features of families affect their eldercare decisions. The model includes four components: types of dependencies, perception of responsibility to provide assistance, individual and family ethos, and use of services. By far the most interesting feature of the model is the provision for individual and family ethos. According to the model's architects, *ethos* includes political orientation, religious orientation, and past experiences with formal networks. Although untested, the model provides a method to explore questions that are not easily handled with other existing utilization models. For example, does one's political orientation discourage the use of certain government programs? Do religious values affect long-term care placement decisions (e.g., home care versus institutional care)?

The conceptual framework developed by Andersen and Newman (1973) or derivations of their model are by far the most frequently utilized approaches for studying formal service utilization. The model emphasizes the relationship between service use and predisposing factors (background characteristics), enabling factors (accessibility and availability issues), and illness factors (type of problem, duration, intensity, and so on). This framework is particularly valuable in organizing the multitude of variables influencing decisions to engage formal networks.

The major problem with using the Andersen and Newman model has been the model's inability to accommodate the influence of informal caregivers on formal service use or the relationship between coexisting formal and informal networks. Recent conceptual modifications of the model to include characteristics of both caregivers and care receivers (e.g., Bass & Noelker, 1987; Teresi, Toner, Bennett, & Wilder, 1988–89) have greatly enhanced the utility of the model for use with long-term caregiving research.

The revision of the Andersen and Newman model by Teresi et al., (1988–89) is particularly important because it allows researchers to examine determinants of the decision to seek long-term placement and treatment in institutional settings. Insight into this aspect of families' formal service utilization has been sorely lacking in the past. According to the revised model,

informal caregivers decide on institutionalization based on the characteristics of the older person (physical, cognitive, and functional status), characteristics of the informal support system (availability and willingness of
unpaid helpers), and characteristics of the formal system (availability and
eligibility requirements).

THE COEXISTENCE OF FORMAL
AND INFORMAL NETWORKS

The information available on linking formal and informal caregiving networks suggests that the process is analogous to mixing oil and water. In
the following sections I discuss some approaches for conceptualizing the
coexistence of formal and informal networks and summarize the outcomes
most frequently reported when the two caregiving networks converge.

Conceptual Approaches Linking Formal
and Informal Networks

Understanding how families accept and work with formal networks to
meet their elder-care needs continues to present numerous conceptual challenges for researchers. Despite the previously cited literature that compared
and contrasted the two networks, disagreement exists about whether formal care is fundamentally different from informal care, and, if so, how they
differ. Consequently, several diverse conceptual approaches have been used
to explain the coexistence of formal and informal networks (see McAuley,
Travis, & Safewright, 1990, and Noelker & Bass, 1989, for more details).
Brief summaries of the four most commonly used models follow.

The *dual specialization* or *complementary model* (Litwak, 1985) is based
on the notion that formal and informal networks have certain kinds of
caregiving responsibilities and abilities that are best suited to each particular network structure. According to this model, the highly specialized nature of the networks (e.g., functional assistance for formal networks and
affective assistance for informal networks) has the potential to cause fric-
tion and precipitate conflict. Therefore, formal and informal networks
work best when the amount of contact or level of involvement between
them is minimized, and the groups perform only those tasks for which they
are best suited.

Although this separation might have been possible a decade ago, a criticism of this approach is that it is increasingly difficult to differentiate between formal and informal responsibilities in contemporary caregiving
situations (Soldo, Agree, & Wolf, 1989). Informal network members assume responsibility for many of the technical aspects of in-home care (injections, dressing changes, lifting, and mobility) that in the not-too-distant
past were restricted to formal providers. Furthermore, a new generation of

service delivery initiatives, such as case management and adult day care, is designed to provide affective support and empower, rather than supplant, informal contributions (e.g., MaloneBeach, Zarit, & Spore, 1992; Seltzer, Ivry, & Litchfield, 1987).

Thus, the *supplemental model* emerged as an alternative approach for differentiating among caregivers. The model emphasizes the primacy of informal networks and relegates formal care to adjunctive status, to be used when informal resources are unable to meet the older person's needs (Stoller, 1989; Stoller & Pugliesi, 1988). Consistent with this approach, decisions to link with formal services are not accompanied by significant decreases in the amount of assistance provided by informal caregivers (Edelman & Hughes, 1990). Proponents of this caregiving orientation strongly encourage the expansion of home- and community-based services to support family caregiving efforts.

In sharp contrast to the supplemental model is the *substitution model.* This model is based on the assumption that formal services substitute for care that informal networks could and would have provided if formal care were not available (Greene, 1983). In other words, when families with elder-care responsibilities have access to formal care, they tend to allow the formal network to substitute for them. Critics of the expansion of home- and community-based long-term care services use the service substitution argument in public policy debates to criticize and defeat new program initiatives. Fortunately, research results have fairly consistently debunked the service substitution myth and shown that most families sustain caregiving over the long term (Brody & Schoonover, 1986; Hooyman, Gonyea, & Montgomery, 1985).

The *hierarchical* or *kin dependent model* details older adults' hierarchical preference for assistance. According to the model, frail older adults are most likely to look first to spouses, next to adult children, then to other relatives and friends, and finally to formal service providers for care (Cantor, 1979, 1989; Noelker & Bass, 1989; Palley & Oktay, 1983). Much of the family caregiving literature supports this model (e.g., Stone et al., 1987), as do studies documenting formal service use in the United States (e.g., McAuley & Arling, 1984) and Canada (e.g., Penning, 1990).

Unlike the previous three models, which tend to ignore the preferences and influence of the care recipient in determining care arrangements, this model places the older adult in a central decision-making role. The major problem is that the model has limited application for individuals in the oldest age groups. At advanced ages, members of one's kinship network might be unable to provide help because of frailty or death of key members or the fading of friendships (Johnson & Troll, 1992). The sources of support available to these individuals, which directly affect the composition of their caregiving networks, are not necessarily based on personal preferences (e.g., McAuley, Travis, & Taylor, 1987).

Regardless of which of these models a researcher might select, it is clear that the coexistence of formal and informal caregiving networks is complex and has the potential for conflict and disagreement as well as cooperation, harmony, and efficiency among the involved parties. As discussed in the next section, however, most of the existing research has tended to focus on the points of stress and tension in caregiving arrangements that include formal and informal helpers.

Conflict Between the Informal and Formal Networks

In most cases, conflict stems from invisible meanings of caregiving rather than complaints about specific actions (e.g., Hasselkus, 1988). Disagreement over quality of care is the most frequently cited source of conflict. Family members, who feel they know the personal preferences of the dependent family member and have the responsibility to protect their loved one, are apt to question the behavior of formal providers (Bowers, 1988; Hasselkus, 1988; Kaye, 1985, 1989; MaloneBeach et al., 1992; Patrick, 1987). As might be expected, formal caregivers react defensively to concerns about the quality of the care they provide and interpret the questioning behavior as interfering with their work (Kaye, 1985). Evidence also shows that some formal helpers assume that family members complain about care in order to relieve their guilty feelings about the service arrangement (Wells & Singer, 1985).

Because quality of care is a significant point of contention in this small but important body of literature, further research is needed. According to Eustis and Fischer (1991), the first step is to find a rational, quantifiable definition of quality of care that suits both family members and professionals. This will be difficult because very little research exists on the ways in which existing quality assurance regulations, monitoring procedures, and definitions of care can be adapted or modified for the coexistence of formal and informal networks of care (Eustis & Fischer, 1991). Having a good definition of quality of care would lead to subsequent research endeavors that could (1) develop methods to evaluate formal and informal quality of care, (2) link caregiving processes to quality of care, and (3) educate families and professionals to consistently give and recognize quality care.

SUGGESTIONS FOR FUTURE RESEARCH AND THEORY DEVELOPMENT

Although the research specifically addressing families and formal networks is somewhat sparse, the existing literature contains an abundance of suggestions and ideas for future research and theory development. The following discussion highlights a few of the most pressing methodological and conceptual challenges.

A persistent problem is that only a handful of researchers are studying ethnically and culturally diverse populations (Dwyer & Coward, 1992). Studies on small convenience samples of white, middle-class individuals perpetuate certain myths about caregiving arrangements. Take, for example, the myth that most blacks and rural elders prefer and have greater access to informal supports than do their white and urban counterparts. As researchers on black populations point out, there is currently an entire cohort of aging black individuals who, prior to civil rights legislation, were denied access to formal care. The current reliance on informal networks for long-term care may be nothing more than a reflection of the ways in which aging black individuals perceive their need for, choices of, and access to formal health and social services (Hinrichsen & Ramirez, 1992). Similarly, it might be the case that rural elders rely on informal networks for no reason other than the fact that they have few and poorly accessible formal service options in rural areas (Coward & Cutler, 1989; McCulloch, this volume).

The tendency to conceptualize caregiving as a simple linear progression from informal to formal care is a significant conceptual shortcoming (Gubrium, 1991). Overreliance on cross-sectional data has contributed to this misrepresentation of the caregiving experience by masking the ways in which formal and informal caregiving naturally shifts over time (Stoller, 1989; Gubrium, 1991). Researchers who use longitudinal data find complex caregiving histories of dependent elders accompanied by the potential for transitions among a variety of caregiving arrangements (e.g., Travis & McAuley, 1992). Therefore, a fundamental assumption that must undergrid all research on caregiving arrangements is that interactions among care recipients, their families, and formal networks are fluid and dynamic.

Conceptual models and research designs must permit study of change in caregiving relationships and dependent care needs over time. Extant databases and cross-sectional samples are often inadequate to answer questions about when and why families and dependent elders initiate and terminate formal assistance, the types of services they select, and what pathways families select to navigate the long-term care system (Kane & Kane, 1989; McAuley et al., 1990).

Besides acknowledging the dynamic nature of the caregiving system, researchers must give more attention to elements of the caregiving triad (care recipient, formal helper(s), informal helper(s)) as unique individuals. This implies the need to study each individual's interpersonal skills, coping styles, personal competencies and inadequacies, and interpretation of caregiving and care receiving. Such an approach would lead to a better understanding of why some caregiving arrangements work well and others do not.

There is also a need to understand whether preferences for caregiving arrangements during short-term crises differ from the caregiving histories and experiences of individuals in dependent situations over the long term (Gubrium, 1991). As human service planners prepare for the onslaught of aging baby boomers and their associated acute and chronic care needs, they are experiencing a growing sense of urgency to plan a menu of services that will include multiple acceptable social care options.

Similarly, service planners need research-based information that will enable them to quantify the differential effects that formal and informal provision of the same service type have on the caregiving arrangement. For example, practitioners believe that family respite is an important factor for sustaining family caregiving over the long term. Yet, very little research is available to describe the ways, if any, in which respite provided by friends and family differs from respite provided by formal services, such as adult day care or paid sitters in the home (Edelman & Hughes, 1990; Eustis & Fischer, 1991; Soldo et al., 1989). Identification of any such differences will help to clarify who uses which types of respite services, what they expect from the service, and the outcomes of the experience.

CONCLUSIONS

Complex methodological and conceptual hurdles await researchers who wish to understand the ways in which formal and informal caring networks converge and coexist over the long term. The theoretical models and conceptual approaches discussed in this chapter can, for the most part, continue to guide the research initiatives previously described. It is noted, of course, that some of these approaches tend to be better suited than others for addressing certain research questions.

Symbolic interactionism, for example, is easily adapted to studies of caregiving triads and the ways in which the expectations of formal and informal helpers converge or differ over time (McAuley et al., 1990). Other approaches, such as social exchange theory, might be better choices for guiding inquiries about short-term versus long-term service preferences. In every case, conceptual or theoretical advances in research on families and formal networks must enable investigators and practitioners to accommodate changes in family dynamics and family configurations over extended periods of time and across a variety of contemporary care arrangements.

REFERENCES

Andersen, R. M., & Newman, J. F. (1973). Societal and individual determinants of medical care utilization in the United States. *Milbank Quarterly, 51,* 95–124.

Barber, C. E. (1989). Burden and family care of the elderly. In S. J. Bahr & E. T. Peterson (Eds.), *Aging and the family* (pp. 243–259). Lexington, MA.: D.C. Heath.

Barer, B. M., & Johnson, C. L. (1990). A critique of the caregiving literature. *Gerontologist, 30,* 26–29.

Bass, D. M., & Noelker, L. S. (1987). The influence of family caregivers on elder's use of in-home services: An expanded conceptual framework. *Journal of Health and Social Behavior, 28,* 184–196.

Berry, G. L., Zarit, S. H., & Rabatin, V. X. (1991). Caregiver activity on respite and nonrespite days: A comparison of two service approaches. *Gerontologist, 31,* 830–835.

Blieszner, R., & Shifflett, P. A. (1989). Affection, communication, and commitment in adult child caregiving for parents with Alzheimer's disease. In J. A. Mancini (Ed.), *Aging parents and adult children* (pp. 230–242). Lexington, MA: Lexington Books.

Bowers, B. J. (1987). Intergenerational caregiving: Adult caregivers and their aging parents. *Advances in Nursing Science, 9,* 20–31.

Bowers, B. J. (1988). Family perceptions of care in a nursing home. *Gerontologist, 28,* 361–368.

Brody, E. M. (1981). Women in the middle and family help to older people. *Gerontologist, 21,* 471–480.

Brody, E. M. (1985). Parent care as a normative family stress. *Gerontologist, 25,* 19–29.

Brody, E. M., Kleban, M. H., Johnson, P. T., Hoffman, C., & Schoonover, C. B. (1987). Work status and parent care: A comparison of four groups of women. *Gerontologist, 27,* 201–208.

Brody, E. M., & Schoonover, C. B. (1986). Patterns of parent-care when adult daughters work and when they do not. *Gerontologist, 26,* 372–381.

Brubaker, T. H., & Brubaker, E. (1989). Toward a theory of family caregiving: Dependencies, responsibility, and use of services. In J. A. Mancini (Ed.), *Aging parents and adult children* (pp. 245–257). Lexington, MA.: Lexington Books.

Burr, W. R., Leigh, G. K., Day, R. D., & Constantine, J. (1979). Symbolic interaction and the family. In W. R. Burr, R. Hill, F. I. Nye, & I. L. Reiss (Eds.), *Contemporary theories about the family* (pp. 42–111). New York: Free Press.

Cantor, M. H. (1979). Neighbors and friends: An overlooked resource in the informal support system. *Research on Aging, 1,* 434–463.

Cantor, M. H. (1989). Social care: Family and community support systems. *Annals of the American Academy of Political and Social Sciences, 503,* 99–112.

Cantor, M. H. (1991). Family and community: Changing roles in an aging society. *Gerontologist, 31,* 337–346.

Chappell, N. L. (1990). Aging and social care. In R. H. Binstock & L. K. George (Eds.), *Handbook of aging and social sciences* (3rd ed., pp. 438–454). San Diego: Academic Press.

Cicirelli, V. G. (1991). Attachment theory in old age: Protection of the attached figure. In K. Pillemer & K. McCartney (Eds.), *Parent-child relations throughout life* (pp. 25–42). Hillsdale, NJ.: Erlbaum.

Collins, C., Stommel, M., King, S., & Given, C. W. (1991). Assessment of the attitudes of family caregivers toward community services. *Gerontologist, 31,* 756–761.

Coward, R. T. (1987). Factors associated with the configuration of the helping networks of noninstitutionalized elders. *Journal of Gerontological Social Work, 10,* 113–132.

Coward, R. T., & Cutler, S. J. (1989). Informal and formal health care systems for the rural elderly. *Health Services Research, 23,* 785–806.

Doty, P. (1986). Family care of the elderly: The role of public policy. *Milbank Quarterly, 64,* 34–75.

Dressel, P. L., & Clark, A. (1990). A critical look at family care. *Journal of Marriage and the Family, 52,* 769–782.

Dwyer, J., & Coward, R. T. (Eds.). (1992). *Gender, families, and elder care.* Newbury Park, CA: Sage.

Edelman, P., & Hughes, S. (1990). The impact of community care on provision of informal care to homebound elderly persons. *Journal of Gerontology: Social Sciences, 45,* S74–84.

Eustis, N. N., & Fischer, L. R. (1991). Relationships between home care clients and their workers: Implications for quality of care. *Gerontologist, 31,* 447–456.

Finley, N. J. (1989). Theories of family labor as applied to gender differences in caregiving for elderly parents. *Journal of Marriage and the Family, 51,* 79–86.

Greene, V. L. (1983). Substitution between formally and informally provided care for the impaired elderly in the community. *Medical Care, 21,* 609–619.

Gubrium, J. F. (1991). *The mosaic of care: Frail elderly and their families in the real world.* New York: Springer Publishing Co.

Hanks, R. S., & Settles, B. H. (1990). Theoretical questions and ethical issues in a family caregiving relationship. In D. E. Biegel & A. Blum (Eds.), *Aging and caregiving: Theory, research, and policy* (pp. 98–118). Newbury Park, CA: Sage.

Hasselkus, B. R. (1988). Meaning in family caregiving: Perspectives on caregiver/professional relationships. *Gerontologist, 28,* 686–691.

Hinrichsen, G. A., & Ramirez, M. (1992). Black and white dementia caregivers: A comparison of their adaptation, adjustment, and service utilization. *Gerontologist, 32,* 375–381.

Hooyman, N., Gonyea, J., & Montgomery, R. (1985). The impact of inhome services termination on family caregivers. *Gerontologist, 25,* 141–145.

Horowitz, A. (1985). Sons and daughters as caregivers to older parents: Differences in role performance and consequences. *Gerontologist, 25,* 612–617.

Jarrett, W. H. (1985). Caregiving within kinship systems: Is affection really necessary? *Gerontologist, 25,* 5–10.

Johnson, C. L., & Catalano, D. J. (1986). A longitudinal study of family supports to impaired elderly. In L. E. Troll (Ed.), *Family issues in current gerontology* (pp. 32–48). New York: Springer Publishing Co.

Johnson, C. L., & Troll, L. (1992). Family functioning in late late life. *Journal of Gerontology: Social Sciences, 47,* S66–72.

Kane, R. L., & Kane, R. A. (1989). Transitions in long-term care. In M. A. Ory & K. Bond (Eds.), *Aging and health care* (pp. 217–243). New York: Routledge.

Kaye, L. W. (1985). Home care for the aged: A fragile partnership. *Social Work, 30,* 312–317.

Kaye, L. W. (1989). Role divergence and complexity in gerontological home care. *Home Health Services Quarterly, 10,* 177–191.

Kleban, M., Brody, E. M., Schoonover, C. B., & Hoffman, C. (1989). Family help to the elderly: Perceptions of sons-in-law regarding parent care. *Journal of Marriage and the Family, 51,* 303–312.

Krout, J. A. (1985). Relationships between informal and formal organizational networks. In W. J. Sauer & R. T. Coward (Eds.), *Social support networks and the care of the elderly* (pp. 178–195). New York: Springer Publishing Company.

Lawton, M., Brody, E., & Saperstein, A. (1989). A controlled study of respite service for caregivers of Alzheimer's patients. *Gerontologist, 29,* 8–16.

Lawton, M. P., Brody, E. M., Saperstein, A., & Grimes, M. (1989). Respite services for caregivers: Research findings for service planning. *Home Health Care Services Quarterly, 10,* 5–32.

Lewis, J., & Meredith, B. (1988). Daughters caring for mothers: The experience of caring and its implications for professional helpers. *Ageing and Society, 8,* 1–21.

Lipman, A., & Longino, C. F. (1982). Formal and informal support: A conceptual clarification. *Journal of Applied Gerontology, 1,* 141–146.

Litwak, E. (1985). *Helping the elderly: The complementary roles of informal networks and formal systems.* New York: Guilford Press.

Litwak, E., & Messeri, P. (1989). Organizational theory, social supports, and mortality rates: A theoretical convergence. *American Sociological Review, 54,* 49–66.

MaloneBeach, E. E., Zarit, S. H. & Spore, D. L. (1992). Caregivers' perceptions of case management and community-based services: Barriers to service use. *Journal of Applied Gerontology, 11,* 146–159.

Matthews, S. H. (1988). The burdens of parent care: A critical evaluation of recent findings. *Journal of Aging Studies, 2,* 157–165.

Mayers, R. S., & Souflee, F. (1991). Utilizing social support systems in the delivery of social services to the Mexican-American elderly. *Journal of Applied Social Sciences, 15,* 1–50.

McAuley, W. J., & Arling, G. (1984). Use of in-home care by very old people. *Journal of Health and Social Behavior, 25,* 54–65.

McAuley, W. J., Travis, S. S., & Safewright, M. (1990). The relationship between formal and informal health care services for the elderly. In S. Stahl (Ed.), *The legacy of longevity* (pp. 201–216). Newbury Park, CA: Sage.

McAuley, W. J., Travis, S. S. & Taylor, C. A. (1987). Long-term care patients in acute care facilities: Determining discharge arrangements. *Journal of Applied Gerontology, 6,* 67–77.

McFall, S., & Miller, B. H. (1992). Caregiver burden and nursing home admission of frail elderly persons. *Journal of Gerontology: Social Sciences, 47,* S73–79.

Montgomery, R. J., & Kamo, Y. (1989). Parent care by sons and daughters. In J. A. Mancini (Ed.), *Aging parents and adult children* (pp. 213–228). Lexington, MA.: Lexington Books.

Mutran, E., & Reitzes, D. C. (1984). Intergenerational support activities and well-being among the elderly: A convergence of exchange and symbolic interaction perspectives. *American Sociological Review, 49,* 117–130.

Noelker, L. S., & Bass, D. M. (1989). Home care for elderly persons: Linkages between formal and informal caregivers. *Journal of Gerontology: Social Sciences, 44,* S63–70.

Nye, F. (1979). Choice, exchange, and the family. In W. Burr, R. Hill, F. Nye, & I. Reiss (Eds.), *Contemporary theories about the family* (pp. 1–41). New York: Free Press.

Palley, H. A., & Oktay, J. S. (1983). *The chronically limited elderly: The case for a national policy for in-home and supportive community-based services.* New York: Haworth Press.

Patrick, P. K. (1987). Hospice caregiving: Strategies to avoid burnout and maintain self-preservation. *Hospice Journal, 3,* 223–253.

Penning, M. J. (1990). Receipt of assistance by elderly people: Hierarchical selection and task specificity. *Gerontologist, 30,* 220–227.

Sakaoye, K. M. (1989). *Family involvement in treatment of the frail elderly.* Washington, DC: American Psychiatric Press.

Scharlach, A. E. (1987). Role strain in mother-daughter relationships in later life. *Gerontologist, 27,* 627–631.

Seltzer, M. M., Ivry, J., & Litchfield, L. C. (1987). Family members as case managers: Partnership between the formal and informal support networks. *Gerontologist, 27,* 722–728.

Soldo, B. J., Agree, E. M., & Wolf, D. A. (1989). The balance between formal and informal care. In M. G. Ory & K. Bond (Eds.), *Aging and health care* (pp. 193–216). New York: Routledge.

Stoller, E. P. (1989). Formal services and informal helping: The myth of service substitution. *Journal of Applied Gerontology 8,* 37–52.

Stoller, E. P. (1990). Males as helpers: The role of sons, relatives, and friends. *Gerontologist, 30,* 228–235.

Stoller, E. P., & Pugliesi, K. (1988). Informal networks of community-based elderly: Changes in composition over time. *Research on Aging, 10,* 499–516.

Stone, R. S., Cafferata, G. L., & Sangl, J. (1987). Caregivers of the frail elderly: A national profile. *Gerontologist, 27,* 616–626.

Tennstedt, S. L., McKinlay, J. B., & Sullivan, L. M. (1989). Informal care for frail elders: The role of secondary caregivers. *Gerontologist, 29,* 677–683.

Teresi, J., Toner, J., Bennett, R., & Wilder, D. (1988–89). Caregiver burden and long-term care planning. *Journal of Applied Social Sciences, 13,* 192–214.

Thibaut, J. W., & Kelley, H. H. (1959). *The social psychology of groups.* New York: Wiley.

Travis, S. S., & McAuley, W. J. (1992). Hospitalization experiences in the long-term care trajectories of a Medicaid cohort. *Applied Nursing Research, 5,* 20–25.

Walker, A. J., Martin, S. K., & Jones, L. L. (1992). The benefits and costs of caregiving and care receiving for daughters and mothers. *Journal of Gerontology: Social Sciences, 47,* S130–139.

Wells, L. M., & Singer, C. (1985). A model for linking networks in social work practice with the institutionalized elderly. *Social Work, 30,* 318–322.

23

Clinical Interventions with Later-Life Families

Sara Honn Qualls

Theories and techniques of family therapy offer rich concepts to scholars studying families from developmental or sociological perspectives. In this chapter I describe three family problems for which interventions have been designed, drawing primarily from social-psychological and developmental approaches to families. Then I describe four major theoretical approaches used by family therapists. Each approach is illustrated with descriptive and intervention research that demonstrates the value of the clinical models. I conclude with a summary of key concepts used by family therapists that can expand the focus of family research.

DEFINITIONS

Clinical Interventions

What constitutes a clinical intervention? The term *clinical* derives from the medical model of illness and well-being and is generally applied to interventions that alleviate symptoms or dysfunction. In this chapter, the term *clinical intervention* is reserved for interventions designed to relieve distress or dysfunction in any population, regardless of the provider's professional identity or the client-family's help-seeking status. *Clinicians* refers to professionals from a variety of disciplines whose expertise is intervention in behavioral and mental health problems.

Later-Life Families

What families fit the category of *later-life family?* Many criteria for defining this family life stage are possible (e.g., age, family life stage). For the purpose of this chapter, I define later-life families as clinicians do, by the focus of the concern rather than by the structure of the family. Hence, I consider the needs of families in which the key concerns center around the well-being of elderly members of the family. A family may include primarily the nuclear family of an older person, several generations of extended family, or only siblings within the same generation.

Family Interventions

The dominant family therapy paradigm, family systems, assumes that any intervention with an individual that generates behavior change in that person will reverberate throughout the family (Jackson, 1965). Family approaches are marked more by their conceptual framework than by specific techniques used with a certain number of family members. Thus, I include in this chapter studies of *family interventions* with one or more persons who belong to one or many generations. The focus is on interventions that alter the familial experience of aging by offering assistance to at least one family member or to one elderly person with the intent of relieving the stress placed on the family system.

INTERVENTIONS WITH AGING FAMILIES

The needs of later-life families experiencing specific problems have spawned developmental, intervention, and prevention work to describe, explain, and modify those problems. Three of the problems faced by later-life families are examined here. The most visible intervention literature involves family caregivers. Other research focuses on abusive families and families coping with major chronic illness.

Caregiving Families

Since the early 1980s the literature describing family caregivers has grown rapidly, although it generally fails to address the effects of caregiving on the structure or function of families (Gatz, Bengtson, & Blum, 1990). Despite the obvious fact that most caregivers are family members, researchers have not described or explained the dynamics, or inner workings, of later-life families providing care to elders. The family variables that have received the most attention are descriptions of the kinds of care provided by different family members, the community resources used by different family caregivers, the ways in which caregivers maintain contact, the degree of support older people perceive from the caregivers, and the familial and contextual factors that predict negative outcomes for caregivers. Process variables, as clinicians refer to them, are notably sparse in this literature (i.e., *how* families function). For example, conflict in the relationship dynamics in caregiving families affects caregiver well-being (Strawbridge &

Wallhagen, 1991), but little is known about how that conflict emerges, how it proceeds and is resolved, and how it relates to past family history. How do caregiver-care recipient relationships change over the course of a caregiving career? What types of intervention might alleviate conflict among caregivers or increase their capacity to maintain the caregiving role? Are there familial factors that explain the risk to caregivers?

Family caregiver interventions have been targeted at decreasing the primary caregiver's distress (measured variously as burden, depression, or total psychiatric symptoms) by increasing knowledge, teaching problem-solving skills, offering strategies for managing emotions, and increasing feelings of being supported (Zarit, 1990; Zarit & Teri, 1991). Interventions are offered in group or individual format but typically involve only one individual within each caregiving family. The interventions would be appropriate for any person providing care for an older person; it just so happens that most of the caregivers are family members.

Two research programs serve as exceptions because they include families in the intervention. Zarit, Anthony, and Boutselis (1987) evaluated the impact of an eight-session counseling intervention that included one family session to help the caregiver increase support and assistance from family members (the effects of the family session were not examined separately). The caregivers who received the intervention benefited only minimally (Whitlatch, Zarit, & Von Eye, 1991; Zarit et al., 1987).

Mittelman and colleagues (Mittelman, Ferris, Shulman, Steinberg, Mackell, & Ambinder, 1994) evaluated the long-term effectiveness of a multistage intervention for caregiving families that included two individual and four family counseling sessions, with follow-up and support group participation. Their research design allowed flexibility in the amount of contact with counselors in order to meet the need of each family, a design strategy that simulates clinical work but precludes clarity in interpreting the impact of the family counseling specifically. Over a one-year period, however, the intervention increased the amount of contact between family members and the primary caregiver (e.g., number of phone calls) and the amount of unpaid help (e.g., respite care) provided by family members to the primary caregivers. It also improved the caregivers' satisfaction with their social network and family cohesion. Caregivers in the intervention condition reported less physical and mental health decline than caregivers in the control condition, and the number of nursing home admissions was lower in the intervention than in the control group (Mittelman, Ferris, Steinberg, Shulman, Mackell, Ambinder, & Cohen, 1993).

Families Abusing Elders

Elder abuse occurs primarily within the intimate, caregiving context where families, the primary caregivers to most elderly, are also the primary abuse perpetrators (Homer & Gilleard, 1990; Pillemer & Finkelhor, 1989). To date, researchers have identified characteristics of individuals and families who have abused elders but have not conducted controlled outcome studies of intervention with families in which elders are abused.

Descriptions of abusive families focus on family history, personality, and caregiving stress on family members. Abusive and neglectful family caregivers tend to have had a poor premorbid relationship with the abused (Cicirelli, 1986; Homer & Gilleard, 1990). The family tends to have a history of abuse over a period of several years, which includes reciprocal past and present abuse (Homer & Gilleard, 1990; Kurrle, Sadler, & Cameron, 1991). Caregivers' substance abuse often further complicates the picture (Hickey & Douglass, 1981; Homer & Gilleard, 1990).

Does caregiver stress precipitate abuse? Personality problems in the caregiver are more predictive of abuse than is stress on the caregiver (Pillemer & Finkelhor, 1989; Kurrle et al., 1991). Although abused elders tend to be physically or financially dependent, they are no more so than control samples of nonabused elderly (Homer & Gilleard, 1990; Pillemer & Finkelhor, 1989). In fact, the emerging profile of abusive families suggests that physical and psychological abusers are likely to be quite dependent on the abuse victims, leading some researchers to postulate that abuse reflects the perceived helplessness of the dependent caregiver (Pillemer & Finkelhor, 1989). These families with multiple dependent members may be at risk due to their limited resources, including a lack of effective interaction strategies to cope with all members' needs. The family abuse and conflict often preceded the elder-care context. Thus, family-level research on assessment and interventions is critically needed.

Families with Chronic Illness

Interventions with families have emerged in the health psychology literature also. Health psychologists design interventions to offset the negative impact of illnesses on families (as described earlier) and to involve families in enhancing the health of members by changing health behaviors. Because chronic illness is normative in the experience of aging, most older families experience the illness-related changes.

The effect of illness on family members' physical and mental well-being and lifestyle is well documented for several different illnesses (e.g., Croog & Fitzgerald, 1978; Manne & Zautra, 1990; Mayou, Foster, & Williamson, 1978). As noted before, however, little work has been done on the impact of illness on the overall structure or functioning of families. Family-level variables are notably missing from this research, as are conceptualizations of the process by which entire families adapt to illnesses.

Another focus of family health psychology research is the examination of how families influence health and of adjustment to illness. The overall quality of health and the development of specific health problems are associated with several familial variables: marital satisfaction (Weiss & Aved, 1978), family problems (Medalie, Snyder, Groen, Neufeld, Goldbourt, & Riss, 1973), perceptions of family closeness (Shaffer, Duszynski, & Thomas, 1982), and deprivation of key family relationships (e.g., spouse absence; Snyder, 1978). The mechanisms for the impact of family on health might affect basic physiological processes such as arousal (Ewart, Burnett, & Taylor, 1983; Minuchin, Rosman, & Baker, 1978). Families also influence patients' adjustment to chronic illness. For example, perceived spouse criticism and lack of support adversely affected women's adjustment to severe arthritis (Manne & Zautra, 1989).

Intervention studies are sparse and preliminary, but promising. The inclusion of families in medical interventions with chronic illness patients increased the rate of positive change in health behaviors (Hoebel, 1976; Hudgens, 1979). Direct intervention to improve marital communication positively influenced blood pressure control (Ewart, Taylor, Kraemer, & Agras, 1984). These studies are particularly relevant to aging families in which chronic illness is often the factor that initiates a family transition.

Summary

Research on aging families has been primarily descriptive of a few roles family members play in the care of elderly persons, with minimal effort to study the dynamics of later-life families or family interventions. The concepts and methods used to guide the research have relied heavily on individual-level factors such as mental health or distress rather than family processes or structures. Certainly, the approaches of researchers who focus on transitions in the family life cycle and structures and roles of families lay important groundwork for studying family dynamics and interventions. As discussed later, clinicians who design interventions for later-life families offer other frameworks for examining the adaptive and maladaptive ways in which later-life families function while coping with the challenges of aging.

MODELS OF FAMILY THERAPY APPLIED TO LATER-LIFE FAMILIES

Family therapy theories offer rich frameworks for viewing and studying later-life families. In the next section, I describe four family therapy theories, which I illustrate with examples of empirical research that draw from the clinical theory.

Systems Theory

Many family therapists view the family as a system (Jackson, 1965; Watzlawick, Beavin, & Jackson, 1967). The systems approach emphasizes the importance of here-and-now communication patterns between members of the system as the factors that define the system. Regular interaction patterns are circular rather than linear, creating complex feedback loops that provoke and respond to members' behaviors. Interactions tend to be repeated, leading to behavior sequences that are highly predictable to family members. Predictability is an advantage in routine interactions but can hinder adaptability during family transitions (e.g., retirement, onset of illness). Distressed families are likely to attempt repeatedly to use familiar, albeit ineffective, solutions to their problems (Herr & Weakland, 1979). Their poor adaptation is visible in the dysfunction or distress of an individual (the identified patient) or in a set of relationships within the family.

Many systems theorists believe the symptom serves a function in the family by distracting the family from a more fundamental relationship deficiency. The distress might take the form of a behavior problem, a depression, a physical illness, or a severe relationship conflict. In the case of later-life families, the identified patient is frequently either a frail elder or a caregiver (although adult children may also display the symptoms of family dysfunction, creating distress for the older members). For example, an elderly man's excessive disability (the symptom) requires his wife to care for him, thus creating a way for him to be nurtured and precluding her withdrawal from him.

The development of a symptom is not a conscious plan to divert attention from fundamental problems but evolves unknowingly to fulfill that purpose. Symptoms might be resistant to change because of the threat that their resolution would place on other relationships within the family. Therapists use interventions to draw the family into resolution strategies that increase flexibility in meeting members' needs while reducing the focus on the symptomatic elder or caregiver.

Therapists view problems in the context of the broader systems in which they are embedded, including the family, perhaps the medical or social service systems, and broader cultural systems (e.g., based on experiences unique to social class, race, ethnicity, or religion). Examination of one person, or even one dyadic relationship, out of context leads to confusion when attempting to understand specific behaviors, stresses, and responses to interventions.

One directly systemic approach used with elderly families is brief, problem-focused family therapy as described by Herr and Weakland (1979). These authors assumed that persistent problem behaviors are provoked and maintained by the system of interaction within the family, usually inadvertently. The therapist's task is to assist the family in identifying the patterns of interaction that members have used to attempt to solve the problem and to change those patterns so they can generate new solutions that reduce the distress or alter the behavior. The authors use case examples to provide an exceptionally clear, practical description of this approach to therapy with older families.

Murray Bowen's (1978) systemic model of family therapy is multigenerational and easily applicable to later-life families (Hall, 1981). His model emphasizes the intense emotional bonds called *emotional systems* that link family members. Emotional connections become problematic when people do not maintain basic boundaries. For example, a relationship in which emotional intensity in one person is automatically met with similar intensity of feelings in another risks the autonomy of both persons. Family members might engage in aversive or inappropriate behavior to reduce the risk of lost autonomy (e.g., a fight keeps sufficient distance to reduce the risk that a dependent daughter is fully controlled by her powerful father). Maturity produces a differentiation of self in which individual members create a clear boundary between themselves and others and internally distinguish emotional reactivity from beliefs, values, and thoughts. Families that constrain this differentiation (i.e., the creation of separate but linked selves) experience dysfunction in the form of symptomatic individuals or distressing interpersonal conflicts that may lead to cutoff relationships. Cutoffs are dangerous to the well-being of elderly family members and impede the differentiation process of all adults (Quinn & Keller, 1981).

Rooted in the systems approach, Shields (1992) studied problem-solving conversations among 30 depressed caregivers and their other family members. Conversations were videotaped in homes while families discussed a problem chosen for its salience to each individual family. The coding scheme applied to each speech unit recorded negative (sad or angry) or positive (empathic or pleasant) affect. Sequential lag analysis of the affect sequences identified the speech codes most likely to follow each type of affective communication.

Families of the most depressed caregivers responded with more sadness when caregivers expressed negative feelings and with more anger when caregivers expressed positive feelings compared with families of less depressed caregivers. Depressed caregivers showed higher rates of empathic responses to family members compared with less depressed caregivers, and those empathic responses were usually followed by family members' angry responses. The depression level of the caregiver was directly related to the negative affect patterns of family members, but not to the caregivers' negative affect. The caregivers' positive affect (empathy) communications correlated with their depression levels. These data suggest that depressed caregivers attempt to support family members but that their efforts are met with anger.

Behavior Therapy

Behavioral approaches share with systems theories the assumption that interlocking patterns of behavior are involved in maintaining and altering problem behaviors but postulate that behavior is determined primarily by immediate reinforcement contingencies. Behavioral family therapists identify the contingency patterns within the family that maintain problem behaviors and teach families to alter the contingencies.

Clinical researchers have applied the behavioral approach to later-life families. Pinkston and Linsk (1984) offered a behavioral intervention model to use with family caregivers to decrease the frequency of problem behaviors of ill elderly persons. Zarit, Orr, and Zarit (1985) described an intervention program for families of demented persons that offers information, problem-solving skills, and family support. Teri, Logsdon, Wagner, and Uomoto (in press) taught caregivers to be cotherapists who modified their own interactions with depressed demented elders. Both caregivers and the demented care receivers showed reductions in depression and the frequency and impact of problem behaviors.

Structural Family Therapy

Structural approaches to family therapy initially developed by Minuchin (1974) emphasize the definition of family roles and rules that create the structure of the family. For example, the parental dyad in a child-rearing family keeps certain boundaries around the intimacy and decision-making roles of the dyad in which children typically are not involved. Roles and rules shift as children mature. Unclear or excessively rigid boundaries complicate the renegotiation of roles and rules so necessary during transitions in the family life cycle.

Few investigators have examined the views of family members about the various roles assigned in later-life families or the rules by which families function during stable or transitional times. How do families initiate shifts in roles when elderly family members need increasing assistance? How do families adapt to new roles? When an elderly family member becomes cognitively impaired, what are the family rules for changing the decision-making subsystem? How do families renegotiate those rules?

Research conducted by Boss and her colleagues illustrates one aspect of family structure: how families cope with a member whose membership in the family is ambiguous (Boss & Greenberg, 1984). The overarching construct, *boundary ambiguity,* describes a family's perception of when a person is inside or outside the family. Boss and associates found that primary caregivers who saw greater ambiguity in whether the person with Alzheimer's disease was inside or outside the family were more likely to report a low sense of mastery and more depression, regardless of the patient's actual level of functioning (Boss, Caron, Horbal, & Mortimer, 1990).

Role definitions are another aspect of family structure. Scharlach (1987) examined the effectiveness of two brief interventions with middle-aged daughters of elderly mothers: (1) a cognitive-behavioral presentation designed to lower daughters' expectations about their personal responsibility for their mothers and (2) a supportive-educational presentation designed to increase the daughters' knowledge of their mothers' needs. Compared with the supportive-educational intervention, the intervention designed to decrease daughters' sense of personal responsibility was more effective in decreasing the daughters' burden and the mothers' loneliness, as well as in improving both persons' perceptions of the mother-daughter relationship. Implicitly, Scharlach helped these mothers and daughters establish relationship definitions and boundaries. His intervention that encouraged limit setting can be contrasted with almost all other caregiving studies that attempt to increase family members' understanding and their skills and strategies.

Psychoanalytic Models

Family therapy models developed by Ackerman (1958), Framo (1992), and Boszormenyi-Nagy (Boszormenyi-Nagy & Krasner, 1986) share assumptions rooted in psychoanalytic theory. They theorize that family conflicts occur when individuals project onto each other psychological needs and experiences drawn from their families of origin. Family interactions are determined by the developmental histories of each individual. Families are the primary context in which needs are met, typically in a complementary, reciprocal fashion across the span of a lifetime. Needy infants grow into mature adults who meet the needs of their children and, ultimately, their dependent parents. Each individual can meet others' needs only out of his or her own maturity, however. Psychological needs not met in childhood are unconsciously sought in other relationships (e.g., from one's young children), usually in relationships in which one should be giving rather than receiving. Invisible loyalties, based on shared family values built up over generations of perceived or real receiving, dictate obligations to give in return. In later-life families, the obligations to care for a frail parent are powerful motivators regardless of the challenge of having a particular person in the giving role (e.g., a sexually abused daughter caring for the perpetrator, her chronically alcoholic father with Korsakoff's syndrome) (Hargrave & Anderson, 1992). Families that have separated geographically or withdrawn emotionally in order to minimize the conflict caused by their mutually unsuccessful efforts to get individual needs met might be drawn together again in parent- or sibling-care situations that reactivate chronic conflicts or pain into overt interpersonal conflict. These theories offer rich conceptual frameworks for family interventions with later-life families who are faced with complex interpersonal relationships centering on the dependency of an adult family member (parent or child).

SUMMARY AND DIRECTIONS FOR FAMILY INTERVENTION RESEARCH

Most family therapists share the bias that interventions designed to assist one individual need to consider how the broader family structure operates to meet the needs of its members and likely need to involve more than just the target individual. Although traditional designs, measurements, and analytic strategies cannot easily handle these complex data sets (Copeland & White, 1991), the concepts offered in the family therapy literature warrant the attention of researchers. I believe the following key concepts, drawn from the clinical approaches previously described, warrant the attention of family researchers.

1. Focus on interaction between persons rather than one individual's behavior. Factors that influence interaction patterns and the effects of patterns on specific behaviors are the foci of interventions. Internal processes (e.g., physiological responses, affect, beliefs, thoughts) are studied primarily to evaluate their effects on interpersonal behavior.

2. Observational methods are critical supplements to self-description data in order to track patterns of behavior in interactions. Relying on one member's description of reality is too limited; self-descriptions are most informative when they are compared across family members. Observations add a particularly useful set of information about pattern and can be interpreted by family members themselves or by researchers.

3. Macrolevel variables (e.g., gender, age, race) set the stage for interpreting the specific behaviors that reflect the dynamics of the family. Assumptions about culturally shared experiences based on gender or ethnicity, for example, do not specify how particular family events will unfold. Macrolevel variables might predict some general patterns of family interaction processes, however. Researchers need to grapple with the ways in which macrolevel variables organize microlevel processes.

4. Family therapists encourage researchers not to lock onto a priori prescriptions for family roles (e.g., daughter, wife) but to investigate how each person actually functions within the family. Descriptions of what groups of daughters do (using a mean score) are less likely to predict dysfunction or to identify useful interventions than are analyses of the behaviors and experiences of a daughter in a particular family. Furthermore, interactions vary tremendously over time such that a summary variable (e.g., perceived support) offers only an extremely gross measure of a fluid and dynamic process.

5. Change is the variable of interest. Developmental transitions in families necessarily require investigation into change. What provokes change? What strategies do family members use to adapt to a transition? Under what conditions do

families create new adaptational strategies? Under what conditions do they become stuck in familiar patterns of behavior that no longer meet needs? What interventions will promote change? Family therapists seek information about inconsistency in behavior in order to identify conditions under which the problem behavior changes in frequency or intensity. Variability in interactional patterns over time is of greater importance than behavior at one time.

6. The very purpose of families to support individual development makes evident a significant dialectic between individual autonomy and familial interdependence. How can families support individuals without stretching the family bond to the breaking point? Are shifts in this dialectic the main stimulators of dysfunction or distress in families? Some of the theories previously described emphasize the reciprocal influence of individual maturity and family functioning. Family development models mark transitions in families according to maturation of individuals. What happens in families when maturation does not occur (e.g., an adult child does not launch?)

7. Family therapists attend to issues of power and nurturance in families. How are influence and control exercised in later-life families? When is assistance supportive, and when is it intrusive? How are power and support balanced in relationships? Do they shift over time?

In summary, family therapy models focus on the dynamics of interaction in later-life families. They offer constructs for examining interactive behavior as well as the personal meanings of family across the life span. Research on family development can benefit from borrowing constructs and methods from the therapy literature. Similarly, the family therapy literature can build on the descriptive research on families that is already available and can proceed to focus on how to design and evaluate interventions with later-life families. Although the family therapy field is only just approaching the specific issues of aging families (Flori, 1989), theories of family therapy have much to contribute to an understanding of the functioning of later-life families.

REFERENCES

Ackerman, N. W. (1958). *The psychodynamics of family life*. New York: Basic Books.

Boss, P., Caron, W., Horbal, J., & Mortimer, J. (1990). Predictors of depression in caregivers of dementia patients: Boundary ambiguity and mastery. *Family Process, 29*, 245–254.

Boss, P., & Greenberg, J. (1984). Family boundary ambiguity: A new variable in family stress theory. *Family Process, 23*, 535–546.

Boszormenyi-Nagy, I., & Krasner, B. R. (1986). *Between give and take: A clinical guide to contextual therapy*. New York: Brunner/Mazel.

Bowen, M. (1978). *Family therapy in clinical practice*. New York: Aronson.

Brody, E. M. (1985). Parent care as a normative family stress. *Gerontologist, 25*, 19–29.

Cicirelli, V. G. (1986). The helping relationship and family neglect in later life. In K. A. Pillemer & R. S. Wolf (Eds.), *Elder abuse: Conflict in the family* (pp. 49–66). Dover, MA: Auburn House.

Copeland, A. P., & White, K. M. (1991). *Studying families.* Newbury Park, CA: Sage.

Croog, S. H., & Fitzgerald, E. F. (1978). Subjective stress and serious illness of a spouse: Wives of heart patients. *Journal of Health and Social Behavior, 19,* 166–178.

Ewart, C. K., Burnett, K. F., & Taylor, C. B. (1983). Communication behaviors that affect blood pressure: An A-B-A-B analysis of marital interaction. *Behavior Modification, 7,* 331–344.

Ewart, C. K., Taylor, C. B., Kraemer, H. C., & Agras, W. S. (1984). Reducing blood pressure reactivity during interpersonal conflict: Effects of marital communication training. *Behavior Therapy, 15,* 473–484.

Flori, D. (1989). The prevalence of later life family concerns in the marriage and family therapy journal literature (1976–85): A content analysis. *Journal of Marital and Family Therapy, 15,* 289–297.

Framo, J. (1992). *Family-of-origin therapy.* New York: Brunner/Mazel.

Gatz, M., Bengtson, V. L., & Blum, M. J. (1990). Caregiving families. In J. W. Birren & K. W. Schaie (Eds.), *Handbook of the psychology of aging* (3rd ed., pp. 405–426). San Diego: Academic Press.

Haley, J. (1976). *Problem solving therapy.* San Francisco: Jossey-Bass.

Hall, C. M. (1981). *The Bowen family theory and its uses.* New York: Aronson.

Hargrave, T. D., & Anderson, W. T. (1992). *Finishing well: Aging and reparation in the intergenerational family.* New York: Brunner/Mazel.

Herr, J. J., & Weakland, J. H. (1979). *Counseling elders and their families.* New York: Springer Publishing Co.

Hickey, T., & Douglass, R. (1981). Neglect and abuse of older family members: Professionals' perspectives and case experiences. *Gerontologist, 21,* 171–176.

Hoebel, F. C. (1976). Brief family-interactional therapy in the management of cardiac-related high-risk behaviors. *Journal of Family Practice, 3,* 613–618.

Homer, A. C., & Gilleard, C. (1990). Abuse of elderly people by their carers. *British Medical Journal, 301,* 1359–1362.

Hudgens, A. J. (1979). Family-oriented treatment of chronic pain. *Journal of Marital and Family Therapy, 10,* 67–78.

Jackson, D. D. (1965). The study of the family. *Family Process, 4,* 1–20.

Kurrle, S. E., Sadler, P. M., & Cameron, I. D. (1991). Elder abuse—An Australian case series. *Medical Journal of Australia, 155,* 150–153.

Manne, S. L., & Zautra, A. J. (1989). Spouse criticism and support: Their association with coping and psychological adjustment among women with rheumatoid arthritis. *Journal of Personality and Social Psychology, 56,* 608–617.

Manne, S. L., & Zautra, A. J. (1990). Couples coping with chronic illness: Women with rheumatoid arthritis and their healthy husbands. *Journal of Behavioral Medicine, 13,* 327–342.

Mayou, R., Foster, A., & Williamson, B. (1978). The psychological and social effects of myocardial infarction on wives. *British Medical Journal, 1,* 699–701.

Medalie, J., Snyder, M., Groen, J., Neufeld, H., Goldbourt, U., & Riss E., (1973). Angina pectoris among 10,000 men: 5-year incidence and univariate analysis. *American Journal of Medicine, 55,* 583–594.

Minuchin, S. (1974). *Families and family therapy.* Cambridge: Harvard University Press.

Minuchin, S., Rosman, B. L. & Baker, L. (1978). *Psychosomatic families: Anorexia nervosa in context.* Cambridge, MA: Harvard University Press.

Mittelman, M., Ferris, S., Shulman, E., Steinberg, G., Mackell, J., & Ambinder, A. (1994). Efficacy of multicomponent individualized treatment to improve the well-being of Alzheimer disease caregivers. In E. Light, G. Niederehe, & B. D. Lebowitz (Eds.), *Stress effects on family caregivers of Alzheimer's patients* (pp. 156–184). New York: Springer Publishing Co.

Mittelman, M. S., Ferris, S. H., Steinberg, G., Shulman, E., Mackell, J. A., Ambinder, A., & Cohen, J. (1993). An intervention that delays institutionalization of Alzheimer's disease patients. *Gerontologist, 33,* 730–740.

Pillemer, K., & Finkelhor, D. (1989). Causes of elder abuse: Caregiver stress versus problem relatives. *American Journal of Orthopsychiatry, 59,* 179–187.

Pinkston, E. M., & Linsk, N. L. (1984). *Caring for the elderly: A family approach.* New York: Pergamon.

Quinn, W. H., & Keller, J. F. (1981). A family therapy model for preserving independence in older persons: Utilization of the family of procreation. *American Journal of Family Therapy, 9,* 79–84.

Scharlach, A. E. (1987). Relieving feelings of strain among women with elderly mothers. *Psychology and Aging, 2,* 9–13.

Shaffer, J. W., Duszynski, K. R., & Thomas, C. B. (1982). Family attitudes in youth as a possible precursor of cancer among physicians: A search for explanatory mechanisms. *Journal of Behavioral Medicine, 5,* 143–163.

Shields, C. G. (1992). Family interaction and caregivers of Alzheimer's disease patients: Correlates of depression. *Family Process, 31,* 19–33.

Snyder, A. I. (1978). Periodic marital separation and physical illness. *American Journal of Orthopsychiatry, 48,* 637–643.

Strawbridge, W. J., & Wallhagen, M. I. (1991). Impact of family conflict on adult child caregivers. *Gerontologist, 31,* 770–777.

Teri, L., Logsdon, R., Wagner, A., & Uomoto, J. (in press). The caregiving role in behavioral treatment of depression in dementia patients. In E. Light, G. Niederehe, & B. D. Lebowitz (Eds.), *Stress effects on family caregivers of Alzheimer's patients.* New York: Springer Publishing Co.

Watzlawick, P., Beavin, J. H., & Jackson, D. D. (1967). *Pragmatics of human communication.* New York: Norton.

Weiss, R. L., & Aved, B. M. (1978). Marital satisfaction and depression as predictors of physical health status. *Journal of Consulting and Clinical Psychology, 46,* 1379–1384.

Whitlach, C., Zarit, S. H., & Von Eye, A. (1991). Efficacy of interventions with caregivers. *Gerontologist, 31,* 9–14.

Zarit, S. H. (1990). Interventions with frail elders and their families: Are they effective and why? In M.A.P. Stephens, J. H. Crowther, S. E. Hobfoll, & D. L. Tennenbaum (Eds.), *Stress and coping in later-life families* (pp. 241–265). New York: Hemisphere.

Zarit, S. H., Anthony, C. R., & Boutselis, M. (1987). Interventions with care givers of dementia patients: Comparison of two approaches. *Psychology and Aging, 2,* 225–232.

Zarit, S. H., Orr, N. K., & Zarit, J. M. (1985). *The hidden victims of Alzheimer's disease: Families under stress.* New York: New York University Press.

Zarit, S. H., & Teri, L. (1991). Interventions and services for family caregivers. *Annual Review of Gerontology and Geriatrics, 11,* 287–310.

Bibliography

Adams, K., Meiners, M., & Burwell, B. (1992). *A synthesis and critique of studies on Medicaid asset spenddown.* Report by the Office of Family, Community and Long Term Care Policy. Office of the Assistant Secretary for Planning and Evaluation. Washington, DC: Department of Health and Human Services.

Andrews, G., Esterman, A. J., Braunack-Mayer, A. J., & Rungie, C. M. (1986). *Aging in the Western Pacific: A four-country study.* Western Pacific Reports and Studies No. 1. Manila: World Health Organization Regional Office for the Western Pacific.

Antonucci, T. C. (1990). Social supports and social relationships. In R. H. Binstock & L. K. George (Eds.), *Handbook of aging and the social sciences* (3rd ed., pp. 205–227). San Diego: Academic Press.

Bass, D. M., & Bowman, K. (1990). The impact of an aged relative's death on the family. In K. F. Ferraro (Ed.), *Gerontology: Perspectives and issues* (pp. 333–356). New York: Springer Publishing Co.

Bedford, V. H. (1989). A comparison of thematic apperceptions of sibling affiliation, conflict, and separation at two periods of adulthood. *International Journal of Aging and Human Development, 28,* 53–66.

Bedford, V. H., & Gold, D. T. (Eds.). (1989). Siblings in later life: A neglected family relationship [Special issue]. *American Behavioral Scientist, 33*(1), 81–93.

Bengtson, V. L., & Robertson, J. F. (Eds.). (1985). *Grandparenthood.* Beverly Hills, CA: Sage.

Bengtson, V., Rosenthal, C., & Burton, L. (1990). Families and aging: Diversity and heterogeneity. In R. H. Binstock & L. K. George (Eds.), *Handbook of aging and the social sciences* (3rd ed., pp. 263–287). San Diego: Academic Press.

Binstock, R. H., & George, L. K. (Eds.). (1990). *Handbook of aging and the social sciences* (3rd ed.). San Diego: Academic Press.

Bleier, R. (1986). *Feminist approaches to science.* New York: Pergamon Press.

Blieszner, R., & Adams, R. G. (1992). *Adult friendship.* Newbury Park, CA: Sage.
Blumstein, P., & Schwartz, P. (1983). *American couples: Money, work, sex.* New York: William Morrow.
Bott, E. (1971). *Family and social network.* New York: Free Press.
Brown, R. (1984). Medicare and Medicaid: The process, value and limits of health care reform. In M. Minkler & C. Estes (Eds.), *Readings in the political economy of aging* (pp. 117–143). New York: Baywood.
Cantor, M. H. (1991). Family and community: Changing roles in an aging society. *Gerontologist, 31,* 337–346.
Chappell, N. L. (1990). Aging and social care. In R. H. Binstock & L. K. George (Eds.), *Handbook of aging and social sciences* (3rd ed., pp. 438–454). San Diego: Academic Press.
Cherlin, A. J., & Furstenberg, F. F. (1986). *The new American grandparent.* New York: Basic Books.
Cicirelli, V. G. (1992). Siblings as caregivers in middle and old age. In J. W. Dwyer & R. T. Coward (Eds.), *Gender, families, and elder care* (pp. 84–101). Newbury Park, CA: Sage.
Cohen, E. S. (1978). Editorial: Law and aging, lawyers and gerontologist. *Gerontologist, 18,* 229.
Connidis, I. A. (1989). *Family ties and aging.* Toronto: Butterworths.
Connidis, I. A. (1992). Life transitions and the adult sibling tie: A qualitative study. *Journal of Marriage and the Family, 54,* 972–982.
Cook, J. A., & Cohler, B. J. (1986). Reciprocal socialization and the care of offspring with cancer and with schizophrenia. In N. Datan, A. L. Greene, & H. W. Reese (Eds.), *Life-span developmental psychology: Intergenerational relations* (pp. 223–243). Hillsdale, NJ: Erlbaum.
Coward, R. T., Kukulka, G., Bull, C. N., & Galliher, J. M. (Eds.). (in press). *Health services for rural elders.* New York: Springer Publishing Co.
Coward, R. T., & Lee, G. R. (Eds.). (1985). *The elderly in rural society: Every fourth elder.* New York: Springer Publishing Co.
Doka, K. J. (1989). Disenfranchised grief. In K. J. Doka (Ed.), *Disenfranchised grief* (pp. 3–11). Lexington, MA: Lexington Books.
Dwyer, J. W., & Coward, R. T. (1992). *Gender, families, and elder care.* Newbury Park, CA: Sage.
Elder, G. H. (1978). Family history and the life course. In T. K. Hareven (Ed.), *Transitions: The family and the life course in historical perspective* (pp. 17–64). New York: Academic Press.
Elder, G. H. (1982). Historical experiences in the later years. In T. K. Hareven & K. Adams (Eds.), *Aging and life course transitions: An interdisciplinary and cross-cultural perspective* (pp. 75–107). New York: Guilford Press.
Elder, G. H. (1987). Families and lives: Some developments in life-course studies. *Journal of Family History, 12,* 179–199.
Erikson, E. (1959). Growth and crises of the healthy personality. In Identity and the life cycle. *Psychological Issues, 1,* Monograph No. 1, 50–100.
Eustis, N., Greenberg, J., & Patten, S. (1985). *Long term care for older persons: A policy perspective.* Monterey, CA: Brooks, Cole.
Fischer, L. R. (1986). *Linked lives: Adult daughters and their mothers.* New York: Harper & Row.

Gamble, E. R., McDonald, P. J., & Lichstein, P. R. (1991). Knowledge, attitudes, and behavior of elderly persons regarding living wills. *Archives of Internal Medicine, 151,* 277–280.

Gold, D. T. (1990). Late-life sibling relationships: Does race affect typological distribution? *Gerontologist, 30,* 741–748.

Gubrium, J. F. (1991). *The mosaic of care: Frail elderly and their families in the real world.* New York: Springer Publishing Co.

Hagestad, G.O. (1987). Parent-child relations in later life: Trends and gaps in past research. In J. B. Lancaster, J. Altmann, A. S. Rossi, & L. R. Sherrod (Eds.), *Parenting across the life span: Biosocial dimensions* (pp. 405–433). New York: Aldine de Gruyter.

Hagestad, G.O. (1988). Demographic change and the life course: Some emerging trends in the family realm. *Family Relations, 37,* 405–410.

Hareven, T. K. (1978). Historical changes in the life course and the family. In J. Yinger & S. J. Cutler (Eds.), *Major social issues: Multidisciplinary view* (pp. 338–345). New York: Free Press.

Hareven, T. K. (1981). Historical changes in the timing of family transitions: Their impact on generational relations. In J.G. March, R. W. Fogel, E. Hatfield, S. B. Kiesler & E. Shanas (Eds.), *Aging: Stability and change in the family* (pp. 143–165). New York: Academic Press.

Hareven, T. K. (1982). *Family time and industrial time.* Cambridge, England: Cambridge University Press. Reprinted 1993, Lanham, New York, London: University Press of America.

Hareven, T. K. (1991). Synchronizing individual time, family time and historical time. In J. Bender & D. E. Wellbery (Eds.), *Chronotypes: The construction of time* (pp. 167–182). Stanford, CA: Stanford University Press.

Hargrave, T. D., & Anderson, W. T. (1992). *Finishing well: Aging and reparation in the intergenerational family.* New York: Brunner/Mazel.

Harrington Meyer, M. (1990). Family status and poverty among older women: The gendered distribution of retirement income in the United States. *Social Problems, 37,* 551–563.

Herr, J. J., & Weakland, J. H. (1979). *Counseling elders and their families.* New York: Springer Publishing Co.

Himes, C. L. (1992). Future caregivers: Projected family structures of older persons. *Journal of Gerontology: Social Sciences, 47,* S17–26.

Horowitz, A. (1985). Family caregiving to the elderly. *Annual Review of Gerontology and Geriatrics, 5,* 194–246.

Huyck, M. H., & Gutmann, D. L. (1992). Thirtysomething years of marriage: Understanding experiences of women and men in enduring family relationships. *Family Perspective, 26,* 249–265.

Jackson, J. (Ed.). (1988). *The black American elderly.* New York: Springer Publishing Co.

Kahn, R. L., & Antonucci, T. C. (1980). Convoys over the life course: Attachment, roles, and social support. In P. B. Baltes & O. Brim (Eds.), *Life-span development and behavior* (Vol. 3, pp. 253–286). New York: Academic Press.

Kalish, R. A. (1985). The social context of death and dying. In R. H. Binstock & E. Shanas (Eds.), *Handbook of aging and the social sciences* (2nd ed., pp. 149–170). New York: Van Nostrand Reinhold.

Kastenbaum, R. (1987–88). Theory, research and application: Some critical issues for thanatology. *Omega, 18,* 397–410.

Keith, P. M., & Wacker, R. R. (in press). *Older wards and their guardians.* New York: Praeger.

Kelly, E., & Conley, J. (1987). Personality and compatibility: A prospective analysis of marital stability and satisfaction. *Journal of Personality and Social Psychology, 52,* 27–40.

Kendig, H. L., Hashimoto, A., & Coppard, L. (Eds.). (1992). *Family support for the elderly: The international experience.* Oxford: Oxford University Press.

Kingson, E. R., Hirshorn, B. A., & Cornman, J. M. (1986). *Ties that bind: The interdependence of generations.* Washington, DC: Seven Locks Press.

Krout, J. A. (1985). Relationships between informal and formal organizational networks. In W. J. Sauer & R. T. Coward (Eds.), *Social support networks and the care of the elderly* (pp. 178–195). New York: Springer Publishing Co.

Lopata, H. Z. (1979). *Women as widows: Support systems.* New York: Elsevier.

Lopata, H. Z. (Ed.). (1987). *Widows: The Middle East, Asia, and the Pacific* (Vol. 1) and *Widows: North America* (Vol. 2). Durham, NC: Duke University Press.

Lopata, H. Z. (1994). *Circles and settings: Role changes of American women.* Albany: State University of New York Press.

Lopata, H. Z., Miller, C. A., & Barnewolt, D. (1986). *City women in America: Work, jobs, occupations, careers.* New York: Praeger.

Lund, D. A. (Ed.). (1989). *Older bereaved spouses: Research with practical applications.* New York: Hemisphere.

Markides, K. S., & Mindel, C. H. (1990). *Ethnicity and aging.* Newbury Park, CA: Sage.

Marotz-Baden, R., Hennon, C. B., & Brubaker, T. H. (Eds.). (1988). *Families in rural America: Stress, adaptation and revitalization.* St. Paul, MN: National Council on Family Relations.

Marshall, V. W., & Levy, J. A. (1990). Aging and dying. In R. H. Binstock & L. K. George (Eds.), *Handbook of aging and the social sciences* (3rd ed., pp. 245–260). San Diego: Academic Press.

Martin Matthews, A. (1991). *Widowhood in later life.* Toronto: Butterworths.

Mattessich, P., & Hill, R. (1987). Life-cycle and family development. In M. B. Sussman & S. Steinmetz (Eds.), *Handbook of marriage and the family* (pp. 437–469). New York: Plenum Press.

McCrimmon, C. A., & Howell, R. J. (1989). Grandparents' legal rights to visitation in the fifty states and the District of Columbia. *Bulletin Academy Psychiatry law, 17,* 355–366.

Mindel, C. H., Haberstein, R. W., & Roosevelt, W., Jr. (Eds.). (1988). *Ethnic families in America* (3rd ed.). New York: Elsevier.

Minkler, M., Rose, K., & Price, M. (1992). The physical and emotional health of grandmothers raising grandchildren in the crack cocaine epidemic. *Gerontologist, 32,* 752–760.

Mutran, E., Reitzes, D. C. (1984). Intergenerational support activities and well-being among the elderly: A convergence of exchange and symbolic interaction perspectives. *American Sociological Review, 49,* 117–130.

Neugarten, B. (1976). Time, age, and the life-cycle. *American Journal of Psychiatry, 136,* 887–894.
Noelker, L. S., & Bass, D. M. (1989). Home care for elderly persons: Linkages between formal and informal caregivers. *Journal of Gerontology: Social Sciences, 44,* S63–70.
Older Womens League. (1989). *Failing America's caregivers.* Washington, DC: Author.
O'Rand, A. M. (1988). Convergence, institutionalization, and bifurcation: Gender and the pension acquisition process. *Annual Review of Gerontology and Geriatrics, 8,* 132–155.
Pillemer, K., & Suitor, J. J. (1992). Intergenerational relations. In E. F. Borgatta & M. F. Borgatta (Eds.), *Encyclopedia of sociology* (pp. 949–955). New York: Macmillan.
Pinkston, E. M., & Linsk, N. L. (1984). *Caring for the elderly: A family approach.* New York: Pergamon.
Pruchno, R., Blow, F., & Smyer, M. (1984). Life-events and interdependent lives. *Gerontologist, 27,* 31–41.
Quadagno, J. (1984). Welfare capitalism and the social security act of 1935. *American Sociological Review, 49,* 632–647.
Rossi, A. S., & Rossi, P. H. (1990). *Of human bonding: Parent-child relations across the life course.* New York: Aldine de Gruyter.
Rural Sociological Society Task Force on Persistent Rural Poverty. (1993). *Persistent poverty in rural America.* Boulder, CO: Westview Press.
Ryff, C. D., & Seltzer, M. M. (Eds.). (in press). *The parental experience in midlife.* Chicago: University of Chicago Press.
Seltzer, M. M., & Ryff, C. D. (in press). Parenting across the life-span: The normative and nonnormative cases. In D. L. Featherman, R. M. Lerner, & M. Perlmutter (Eds.), *Life-span development and behavior* (Vol. 12). Hillsdale, NJ: Erlbaum.
Shields, C. G. (1992). Family interaction and caregivers of Alzheimer's disease patients: Correlates of depression. *Family Process, 31,* 19–33.
Skolnick, A. (1981). Married lives: Longitudinal perspectives on marriage. In D. H. Eichorn, J. A. Clausen, N. Haan, M. P. Honzik, & P. H. Mussen (Eds.), *Present and past in middle life* (pp. 269–298). New York: Academic Press.
Strauss, P. J., Wolf, R., & Shilling, D. (1990). *Aging and the law.* Chicago: Commerce Clearing House.
Stroebe, M. S., Stroebe, W., & Hansson, R. O. (1993). *Handbook of bereavement: Theory, research and intervention.* New York: Cambridge University Press.
Suitor, J. J., & Pillemer, K. (1988). Explaining conflict when adult children and their elderly parents live together. *Journal of Marriage and the Family, 50,* 1037–1047.
Suitor, J. J., & Pillemer, K. (1993). Support and interpersonal stress in the social networks of married daughters caring for parents with dementia. *Journal of Gerontology: Social Sciences, 48,* S1–8.
Szinovacz, M. (1982). *Women's retirement: Policy implications of recent research.* Beverly Hills, CA: Sage.
Szinovacz, M. (1989). Decision-making on retirement timing. In D. Brinberg & J.

Jaccard (Eds.), *Dyadic decision making* (pp. 286–310). New York: Springer-Verlag.

Szinovacz, M., Ekerdt, D. J., & Vinick, B. H. (Eds.). (1992). *Families and retirement.* Newbury Park, CA: Sage.

United Nations Department of International Economic and Social Affairs (UN-DIESA). (1990, October). *Overview of recent research findings on population aging and the family.* United Nations International Conference on Aging Populations in the Context of the Family, Kitakyushu. IESA/P/AC.33/6.

U. S. Senate, Special Committee on Aging. (1992). *Common beliefs about the rural elderly: Myth or fact? (Serial No. 102-N).* Washington, DC.: U.S. Government Printing Office.

University of Michigan Population Studies Center. (1989–92 & forthcoming). *Comparative study of the elderly in Asia.* Research Report Series (ongoing). Ann Arbor: Author.

Vinick, B. H., & Ekerdt, D. J. (1991). The transition to retirement: Responses of husbands and wives. In B. B. Hess & E. Markson (Eds.), *Growing old in America* (4th ed., pp. 305–317). New Brunswick, NJ: Transaction Books.

Weishaus, S., & Field, D. (1988). A half century of marriage: Continuity or change? *Journal of Marriage and the Family, 50,* 763–774.

Wellman, B. (1990). The place of kinfolk in personal community networks. *Marriage and Family Review, 15,* 195–228.

White, J. M. (1991). *Dynamics of family development: A theoretical perspective.* New York: Guilford Press.

Wilhite, M. (1987). Children, parents and grandparents: Balancing the rights of association and control. *American Journal of Family Law, 1,* 473–489.

Woehrer, C. E. (1978). Cultural pluralism in American families: The influence of ethnicity on social aspects of aging. *Family Coordinator, 27,* 329–339.

Zarit, S. H., & Teri, L. (1991). Interventions and services for family caregivers. *Annual Review of Gerontology and Geriatrics, 11,* 287–310.

Index

About the Contributors

HIROKO AKIYAMA is Assistant Research Scientist in the Life Course Development program in the Institute for Social Research at the University of Michigan, and was a Research Associate at the University of Oklahoma Gerontology Center before joining the University of Michigan. Dr. Akiyama's research interests have focused on gender, culture, and social relations. She has contributed to such journals as the *International Journal of Aging and Human Development,* the *Journal of Gerontology,* the *Journal of Aging and Health,* and the *Journal of Social Science and Medicine* and to the *Encyclopedia of Adult Development.*

KAREN ALTERGOTT is Associate Professor of Family Studies at Purdue University. She was Associate Director of a multiuniversity National Institute on Aging–sponsored training Program in Adult Development and Aging while on the faculty of the University of Missouri and Purdue University. Her publications are in the area of comparative family and aging and family relationships across the course of life. Her current research is on mental health, family, and aging.

TONI C. ANTONUCCI is Program Director in the Life Course Development Program in the Institute for Social Research and Professor of Psychology, both at the University of Michigan. While writing this chapter, she held a Fogarty International Senior Fellowship and was a Chercheur Etrangere at the Institut National de la Santé et Recherche Medicale in Paris, France. Her research interests have focused, for more than 20 years, on social relationships across the life span. This work has ranged from mother-infant attachment research to multigenerational studies of the elderly and, most recently, to comparative life span studies of social relations among a representative sample of people from eight years of age through old age in the United States and Japan. In addition to her contributions to the *Handbook on the Psychology of Aging*, the *Handbook on Aging and the Social Sciences*, the *Handbook of Clinical Gerontology*, and the *Encyclopedia of Adolescence and Adulthood*, she has published in a wide variety of journals.

VICTORIA HILKEVITCH BEDFORD is Assistant Professor of Psychology in the Department of Psychology at the University of Indianapolis. Her research interests and publications are in family relationships of middle and old adults, family relations in a social network context, and life span development.

MARCIA L. BELLAS is Assistant Professor of Sociology at the University of Cincinnati. Her research centers on gender stratification in households and labor markets, and her recent studies examine sources of sex bias in faculty salaries.

ROSEMARY BLIESZNER is Professor in the Department of Family and Child Development and Associate Director of the Center for Gerontology at Virginia Polytechnic Institute and State University. Her research focuses on family and friend relationships and psychological well-being in adulthood and old age. She is coauthor (with Rebecca G. Adams) of *Older Adult Friendship: Structure and Process* (1989) and *Adult Friendship* (1992).

BERTRAM J. COHLER is William Rainey Harper Professor of Social Sciences, the College, Department of Psychology (the Committee on Human Development), Education, and Psychiatry, the University of Chicago. He has been on the faculty of the University of Chicago since 1969. His publications and present research interests concern family, life course, personality, and mental health.

JEFFREY W. DWYER is Director of the Institute of Gerontology and Associate Professor in the Department of Sociology at Wayne State University. His research interests include family caregiving, aging and health policy, the impact of changing social structure on health outcomes, and vulnerable segments of the older population (i.e., women, nonwhites, poor). In 1992 Dr. Dwyer was selected as a Brookdale National Fellow. He is also co-principal investigator of a five-year project to implement and evaluate a behavioral management intervention for severe urinary incontinence among a community-based sample of older women.

DAVID J. EKERDT is Associate Director of the Center on Aging and Associate Professor of Family Practice at the University of Kansas Medical Center. His funded research studies on work and retirement (with colleagues from the Boston Veterans Administration Normative Aging Study) have examined the retirement process and its effects on health, well-being, and marital quality, as well as behavioral expectations in later life. He is currently analyzing panel data in an attempt to specify the long-term processes of anticipation and adaptation that precede and follow the event of men's retirement.

ROBERT O. HANSSON is Professor of Psychology at the University of Tulsa. His research interests involve older adults coping with stressful life transitions. He recently coedited (with Margaret Stroebe and Wolfgana Stroebe) *The Handbook of Bereavement* (1993).

TAMARA K. HAREVEN is Unidel Professor of Family Studies and History at the University of Delaware; Adjunct Professor of Population Sciences and Member, Center for Population Studies, Harvard University; and founder and editor of the *Journal of Family History*. She is author of several books and numerous articles on the history of the family, family and work and the life course, and aging. Her best-known books are *Family Time and Industrial Time* (1982, reprinted 1993); *Amoskeag: Life and Work in an American Factory City* (1978); *Transitions: The Family and the Life Course in Historical Perspective* (1978, ed.); and *Aging and the Life Course in Interdisciplinary and Cross-Cultural Perspective* (1982, coed. with Kathleen Adams). She is currently completing *Generations in Historical Time*, which is based on a cohort comparison of life transitions and generational relations in the later years of life.

MADONNA HARRINGTON MEYER is Assistant Professor of Sociology at the University of Illinois. Her research focuses on gender, race, and class biases within the old-age welfare state. Recent works examine poverty among older women, Medicaid use among the frail elderly, and the Social Security spousal benefit.

MARGARET HELLIE HUYCK is Professor in the Department of Psychology at Illinois Institute of Technology and a Fellow of the Gerontological Society of America. She is the author of *Growing Older* (1974) and (with W. Hoyer) *Adult Development and Aging* (1982), as well as chapters on gender and family relations during the middle years. Her major research has focused on young adult children and their parents in Parkville, a study funded by the National Institute of Mental Health.

COLLEEN L. JOHNSON has studied Italian American families in the Northeast. She has published numerous articles on American families and aging and three books, *Growing Up and Growing Old in Italian American Families, The Nursing Home in American Society*, and *Ex-Familia: Grand-*

parents, Parents and Grandchildren Adjust to Divorce. Dr. Johnson is currently Professor of Medical Anthropology at the University of California, San Francisco, and has a MERIT Award from the National Institute on Aging to study the oldest-old.

SHIRLEY KEETON is a doctoral student in the Department of Sociology at Louisiana State University. Her current work examines changes in women's social networks following status transitions in midlife.

KEVIN KINSELLA is Chief of the Aging Studies Branch of the Center for International Research, U.S. Bureau of the Census, where he has been employed since 1979. His professional activities have focused on the role of women in development, population projections for developing countries (particularly in Latin America), and the demography of aging internationally. Current research interests encompass issues of pension coverage, adult health, and the nature of epidemiologic transition in the Third World.

HELENA ZNANIECKA LOPATA is currently Professor of Sociology and Director of the Center for the Comparative Study of Social Roles at Loyola University of Chicago. Her most recent books include *Circles and Settings: Role Changes of American Women* and *Polish Americans.* Forthcoming is *Widowhood: Myths and Realities.*

JAY A. MANCINI is Professor and Head of the Department of Family and Child Development at Virginia Polytechnic Institute and State University, Blacksburg, Virginia. He is a human development consultant to the National Park Service and the United States Air Force (MWRS). His research has appeared in the *Journal of Marriage and the Family, Journal of Gerontology: Psychological Sciences, Journal of Leisure Research, Family Relations, Research on Aging,* and in many other social and behavioral science periodicals. He is the author/editor of *Aging Parents and Adult Children* (1989).

DAVID J. MANGEN is President of Mangen Research Associates, Inc., a Minneapolis-based firm specializing in the research design and multivariate analysis services for companies throughout the United States. He is the editor (with Warren Peterson) of the *Research Instruments in Social Gerontology* series and *Measurement of Intergenerational Relations* (with Vern Bengtson and Pierre Landry) and was a contributor to the second edition of *Handbook of Aging and the Social Sciences.*

B. JAN McCULLOCH is Assistant Professor with a joint appointment in the Department of Family Studies and Sanders-Brown Center on Aging, University of Kentucky. Her research interests include longitudinal investigations of well-being among older rural adults and older women, rural aging, and methodological issues in aging research. She is currently conducting research examining the effects of social risks and resources on older rural adults' mental and physical health.

MIRIAM S. MOSS has been a Senior Research Sociologist at the Philadelphia Geriatric Center since 1970. Her current research interests are in the area of elderly parent-adult child relationships and the impact of parental death on surviving middle-aged children. She has published widely on gerontology and bereavement.

SIDNEY Z. MOSS is a researcher at Philadelphia Geriatric Center, primarily focusing on study of the impact of the death of an elderly parent. He is on the faculty of the Hahnemann University Master of Family Therapy Program and has an active practice in family therapy. He has published widely on separation and loss over the life course.

SHIRLEY L. O'BRYANT is Professor of Family Relations and Human Development at Ohio State University. For the last decade her research interests have centered on the family-related aspects of widowhood. Much of her research has been funded by the American Association of Retired Persons (AARP) Andrus Foundation. Her research findings have been published in many major journals, including *The Gerontologist* and the *Journal of Marriage and the Family,* as well as in various book chapters. She is a Fellow of the Gerontological Society of American and was named Ohio's Outstanding Gerontology Educator in 1993.

KARL PILLEMER is Associate Professor of Human Development and Family Studies at Cornell University and Director of the Cornell Center for Research on Applied Gerontology. His research focuses on families in later life, with a particular emphasis on troubled parent-child relationships and their impact on psychological well-being.

SARA HONN QUALLS is Associate Professor of Psychology at the University of Colorado at Colorado Springs, where she serves as Director of Clinical Training and Director of the Center on Aging. She also serves as Associate Director for Psychology of the Colorado Geriatric Education Center. Her research focuses on marital development across the life span and family therapy with later-life families. A licensed psychologist, she maintains a private practice working with older individuals and families.

JOAN F. ROBERTSON is Professor, Gerontologist, and Social Worker in the School of Social Work at the University of Wisconsin-Madison. She has been involved in teaching, research, and community service in the area of intergenerational phenomena for many years. She teaches courses at the graduate and undergraduate levels in aging, family problems, and research. She has been doing grandparent research for a number of years and has a variety of publications on grandparenting and other aspects of family life in gerontological, family, and social work journals. She was coeditor of the first volume on *Grandparenthood* with Vern Bengtson. Currently, Dr. Robertson is doing research on the physical and mental health well-being of grandparent caregivers of dependent children.

JULIE ROBISON is a doctoral student in the Department of Human Development and Family Studies at Cornell University. Her research interests lie in intergenerational relationships and family caregiving and elderly housing issues.

CAROL D. RYFF is Professor of Psychology and Associate Director of the Institute on Aging at the University of Wisconsin-Madison. She has been a Fellow at the Center for Advanced Study in the Behavioral Sciences and is currently a member of the MacArthur Research Network on MidLife Development. Her research addresses the topic of psychological well-being across the adult life course—what it means, how it is measured, the factors that influence it. Current studies focus on the effects of particular life experiences and how they are interpreted on multiple dimensions of psychological well-being. She is coeditor (with Marsha Mailick Seltzer) of *The Parental Experience in Midlife*.

DAN M. SANDIFER is Associate Professor of Marital and Family Therapy at Northwest Christian College in Eugene, Oregon. His research concerns intergenerational family relationships and adolescent career development. He has presented his research at the annual meetings of the National Council on Family Relations and the American Association for Marital and Family Therapy.

MARSHA MAILICK SELTZER is Professor, School of Social Work at the University of Wisconsin-Madison and Coordinator of the Applied Research and Technology Unit at the Waisman Center on Mental Retardation and Human Development. Her primary area of research is family caregiving, with special attention focused on aging parents who provide lifelong care to a son or daughter with mental retardation. She is coeditor (with Carol Ryff) of *The Parental Experience at Midlife*.

J. JILL SUITOR is Associate Professor of Sociology at Louisiana State University. Her current work focuses on the effects of status transitions on the structure and function of interpersonal networks and on marital relations in middle and later life. She is conducting (with Karl Pillemer) a longitudinal study of the social relationships of caregivers to family members with Alzheimer's disease.

MAXIMILIANE SZINOVACZ is Assistant Professor of Sociology at Old Dominion University. She coauthored *Family Decision-Making* (with John Scanzoni) and edited *Women's Retirement: Policy Implications of Recent Research*, as well as *Families and Retirement* (with David Ekerdt and Barbara Vinick). She is currently completing research funded by the American Association of Retired Persons (AARP) Andrus Foundation on the effect of couples' employment/retirement status on marital relationships.

SHIRLEY S. TRAVIS is Professor and Parry Chair in Gerontological Nursing in the College of Nursing at the University of Oklahoma Health Sciences Center, Oklahoma City. Her research focuses on a variety of long-term care service delivery issues, including care of mentally impaired older adults, mortality rates across long-term care settings, functional assessment techniques, and the integration of acute and long-term services. Her recent publications appear in such journals as *Applied Nursing Research, Educational Gerontology, Journal of Gerontological Social Work, The Gerontologist,* and *Journal of Health and Human Resources Administration.*

LILLIAN E. TROLL is Professor Emeritus, Rutgers University and Adjunct Professor, University of California, San Francisco. She is author or editor of nine books, the most recent being *Women Growing Older: Psychological Implications* (with Barbara Turner, 1994), as well as many articles, including "Family Embedded vs. Family-Deprived Oldest-Old: A Study of Contrasts" (*International Journal of Aging and Human Development,* special issue edited by Colleen Johnson, 1994). Her primary research interest is life-span developmental psychology with a focus on family and women's issues.

ROBBYN R. WACKER is Associate Professor in the Gerontology Program at the University of Northern Colorado. Her research interests are in the area of later-life families, legal issues, ethnicity, and health behaviors. She is coauthor (with Pat M. Keith) of *Older Wards and Their Guardians.*